Teenagers' Perspectives on th
in their Lives, Schools a
A European Quantitat

Religious Diversity and Education in Europe

edited by

Cok Bakker, Hans-Günter Heimbrock,
Robert Jackson, Geir Skeie, Wolfram Weisse

Volume 7

Globalisation and plurality are influencing all areas of education, including religious education. The inter-cultural and multi-religious situation in Europe demands a re-evaluation of the existing educational systems in particular countries as well as new thinking at the broader European level. This new book series is committed to the investigation and reflection on the changing role of religion and education in Europe. Contributions will evaluate the situation, reflect on fundamental issues and develop perspectives for better policy making and pedagogy, especially in relation to practice in the classroom.

The publishing policy of the series is to focus on the importance of strengthening pluralist democracies through stimulating the development of active citizenship and fostering greater mutual understanding through intercultural education. It pays special attention to the educational challenges of religious diversity and conflicting value systems in schools and in society in general.

Religious Diversity and Education in Europe is produced by two European research groups, in which scholars are engaged in empirical and theoretical research on aspects of religion and education in relation to intercultural issues:
* **ENRECA: The European Network for Religious Education in Europe through Contextual Approaches**
* **REDCo: Religion in Education. A contribution to Dialogue or a factor of Conflict in transforming societies of European Countries**

The series is aimed at teachers, researchers and policy makers. The series is committed to involving practitioners in the research process and includes books by teachers and teacher educators who are engaged in research as well as academics from various relevant fields, professional researchers and PhD students. It is open to authors committed to these issues, and it includes English and German speaking monographs as well as edited collections of papers.

Book proposals should be directed to one of the editors or to the publisher.

Pille Valk, Gerdien Bertram-Troost,
Markus Friederici, Céline Béraud (Eds.)

Teenagers' Perspectives on the Role of Religion in their Lives, Schools and Societies

A European Quantitative Study

Waxmann 2009
Münster / New York / München / Berlin

Bibliographic information published by die Deutsche Nationalbibliothek
Die Deutsche Nationalbibliothek lists this publication in the
Deutsche Nationalbibliografie; detailed bibliographic data
are available in the internet at http://dnb.d-nb.de.

Religious Diversity and Education in Europe, volume 7

ISSN 1862-9547
ISBN 978-3-8309-2118-9

© Waxmann Verlag GmbH, 2009
Postfach 8603, D-48046 Münster

www.waxmann.com
info@waxmann.com

Book cover: Pleßmann Kommunikationsdesign, Ascheberg
Print: Hubert & Co., Göttingen

Printed on age-resistant paper,
acid-free according to ISO 9706

Contents

Part III: European comparison

Wolfram Weisse

Quantitative Study in the Context of the REDCo Project – a Foreword

Introduction

Religion is on the European agenda again. After decades of neglect in academic as well as public discourse, we are entering a new, as yet uncertain phase of addressing religion. The secularisation paradigm has lost its explanatory power and a newly coined term 'post-secularism' is used to describe the realisation that in the current social transformation, religion cannot be ignored any longer. However, we do not yet fully understand its concrete implications for future individual and societal developments in Europe and throughout the world.

Three things above all show the growing relevance religion is accorded today. First of all, a new interest in religion is exhibited by internationally reputed scholars from different backgrounds, among them the philosopher Jürgen Habermas. After decades of concentrating on philosophy and its implications for public responsibility, he started to address religion in 2001 and has since postulated the importance of the great religions in the history of reason and the articulation of contemporary consciousness (Habermas, 2005 p. 12).[1] He hints at the problems of a nonreligious self-definition of western modernity[2] and emphasises the importance of religious tolerance as a "pacemaker" for a correct understanding of multiculturalism and the peaceful coexistence of different cultures in equality.[3]

Secondly, we can observe a growing institutional effort in universities and at the European level to develop new centres of excellence in research on religion and found new institutes such as the Wergeland centre in Oslo – a joint effort by the Council of Europe and the Norwegian government – to strengthen the thematic correlation between intercultural and interreligious education.

Thirdly, religion and interreligious dialogue are referred to more than ever in international declarations. For example: The governments of the 47 member states of the Council of Europe emphasised the great importance and relevance of interreligious dialogue in a "White Paper on Intercultural Dialogue" in May 2008, which contains the statement: "Interreligious dialogue can also contribute to a stronger consensus within society regarding the solutions to social problems" (Council of Europe, 2008, p. 24).

---

1   The orignial wording is: "Ich verteidige in diesem Streit Hegels These, dass die großen Religionen zur Geschichte der Vernunft selbst gehören. […] Religiöse Überlieferungen leisten bis heute die Artikulation eines Bewusstseins von dem, was fehlt. Sie halten eine Sensibilität für Versagtes wach" (Habermas, 2005, p. 12).

2   The original wording is: "Für die Philosophie verbindet sich mit der Wiederbelebung religiöser Kräfte, von der nur Europa ausgenommen zu sein scheint, die Herausforderung einer grundsätzlichen Kritik am nachmetaphysischen und nichtreligiösen Selbstverständnis der westlichen Moderne." (Habermas 2005, p. 7).

3   The original wording is: "Bevor ich auf religiöse Toleranz als Schrittmacher für einen richtig verstandenen Multikulturalismus und die gleichberechtigte Koexistenz verschiedener kultureller Lebensformen innerhalb eines demokratisch verfassten Gemeinwesens eingehe (3), will ich den Begriff der Toleranz schärfer fassen und erklären, worin die Bürde von wechselseitiger Toleranzzumutungen besteht (2)" (Habermas, 2005, p. 263).

The origin of this book: the REDCo project

The quantitative study presented in this book is part of the research effort by the REDCo project. REDCo is the abbreviation for "Religion in Education. A contribution to Dialogue or a Factor of Conflict in Transforming Societies of European Countries." It is part of the section "Values and Religions in Europe" of the European FP6-programme "Citizens and Governance in a Knowledge-Based Society". This project is funded by the research department of the European Commission over a period of three years from March 2006 onwards with a total sum of EUR 1,188,000.

The project includes nine projects from the following institutions in eight different European countries: University of Hamburg (Germany), University of Warwick (England), Ecole Pratique des Hautes Etudes (Sorbonne/France), Free University Amsterdam (The Netherland), University of Stavanger (Norway), University of Tartu (Estonia), University of Muenster (Germany), Russian Christian Academy for Humanities in St. Petersburg (Russia), and University of Granada (Spain). All members of the research group (consortium) have previously co-operated fruitfully. Their respective disciplines (theology, Islamic studies, education, religious education, sociology, political science and ethnology) complement each other in this effort.

In spite of a wide range of societal and pedagogical backgrounds, the research group holds one common conviction: religion must be addressed in schools, as it is too important a factor in social life and for the coexistence of people from different cultural and religious backgrounds throughout Europe to be ignored.

The project's main aim is to establish and compare the potentials and limitations of religion in schools in the educational systems of selected European countries. Our research team has addressed approaches and constellations that can contribute to making religion in education a factor promoting dialogue in the context of European development through historical and contemporary studies. As a result of this work, we have already been able to publish a book titled "Religion and Education in Europe: Developments, Contexts and Debates" (Jackson, Miedema, Weisse & Willaime 2007).

For our research, we adopted an inclusive definition of *religious education*. It covers academic teacher training as well as both philosophical and practical aspects of religious and value education at school. Our main focus with regard to schools is Religious Education (RE) as a formal subject, but we also look at the treatment of religion and religiosity in the context of other subjects.

When studying religion, we do not restrictively focus on abstract belief systems or 'world-religions', but rather concentrate on the various forms of religions and world-views as they are represented by the adherents themselves. With reference to E. Levinas, we are directing our attention to "neighbour-religions" (Weisse, 2003), the views of neighbours in classrooms, in the region, in the state, and the whole of Europe. The world religions are present in the "neighbour-religions", and thus our approach permits us to study them in their current, relevant shapes and their present concrete potential for dialogue and conflict. Our main theoretical stimulus with regard to RE is the interpretive approach to the study of religious diversity (Jackson, 1997).

Our projects look at religious education together with the inclusion of religious issues in other school subjects for school students in the 14–16 year age group in various countries. We combine analyses of the pedagogical concepts informing these approaches to religious education with a study of the concrete views of the pupils themselves.

All REDCo members use the same repertoire of methods. For text analysis, we mainly refer to hermeneutical methods. As our empirical methods, we use participant observation, semi-structured interviews, questionnaires (qualitative and quantitative), and the videotaping of RE-lessons for interaction analysis. All our projects look at classroom interaction in our various countries. On the basis of participant observation and the videotaping of RE-lessons, an analysis of interaction patterns in the classroom is possible.

In a qualitative study, we surveyed pupils' views on the societal function of religion, on their experience with religion in education, and their wishes to include or exclude religion from education (Knauth, Jozsa, Bertram-Troost, Ipgrave, 2008). All questions focus on the possibilities of dialogue and/or conflict. On the basis of the results of the qualitative analysis, we worked out questions for a quantitative survey, which was carried out in February and March 2008. The results are now published in this book.

The impact of the quantitative study for REDCo

The quantitative analyses in this publication form part of the overall research of the REDCo project. This part of our effort admittedly was much more modest in the original design. In our application to the European Commission, we had outlined a plan to test the qualitative findings on the views of the 14–16 years old students surveyed through a quantitative counter-check: "On the basis of the results of the qualitative analysis, questions will be worked out for a quantitative questionnaire. This will be answered by 200 pupils in each country (in Germany 200 in Hamburg and 200 in the region of Muenster)" (Weisse, 2007, p. 19). As is apparent from this publication, the plan has expanded considerably over time. As a result, we are now able to publish a survey, the significance of which for the current debate is difficult to overstate:

–   it is one of the few comparative surveys to address more than half a dozen European countries,
–   it was designed bottom-up: We based our questions on the findings of our previous qualitative study,
–   although it is not statistically representative for the teenagers in our different countries (a trait it shares most prominently with Ziebertz & Kay (2006) along with other prominent efforts), we surveyed a sample of high explanatory significance, according to the composition of pupils in each country,
–   it is the only quantitative study focussing on such vital issues as dialogue and conflict between religions as perceived by the students themselves.

At the same time, we remain acutely aware of its limits: Most prominently, it does not provide enough data for the analysis of questions regarding issues such as tolerance. That is why we are pleading for continuing empirical research efforts, both qualitative and quantitative, in this direction.

The contributions in the first part of this book offer an insight into the research process, its theoretical and methodological background, the sampling process, terminology and organisation. The second part contains national and regional analyses, all structured according to the same pattern and based on interpretations of the same selection of items from the questionnaire. Thus, this book enters the field of comparative studies from two directions. Firstly, each national analysis is commented on by researchers from two other countries of our REDCo consortium to establish an outside perspective. Those comments, found in the second part of the book, are not intended to cover all possible aspects of our survey, but focus on the most striking and interesting points in the analysis of the respective countries. This approach is the first step towards a genuinely international discussion and interpretation of the national analyses, to which we would encourage our readers to add many more. In addition, there are three articles at the end of the book that offer a comparative analysis of all the survey data. These analyses are, of course, written in full awareness of the limitations of any such effort (which is why, for one thing, they do not refer to other international surveys). Nonetheless, they offer valuable interpretations and impulses on the question how teenagers in Europe see the (ir)relevance of religions for dialogue and conflict in their daily lives, in the school environment, and in society as a whole.

Last but not least, I would like to thank all members of the REDCo team who contributed to this research, especially the editors of this book: Pille Valk, Gerdien Bertram-Troost, Markus Friederici and Céline Béraud. Thanks go as well to the colleagues in the Institute of Sociology at the University of Tartu – Liina-Mai Tooding, Rein Murakas, Lauri Veski and Andu Rämmer for their consultations and running the data analysis. Thanks also go to our colleague Sean Neill, who did the language check, to Volker Bach for translations and language check, to Christian Rudelt, who helped in the organisation and the layout of the manuscript, and to Anna Körs for her most valuable comments.

The investment of time and energy for this study has been extremely high, and at times we were not sure whether we would be able to finish the daunting task. With this publication, we are delivering one of the milestones of our research. It marks the completion of yet another stage of our effort, which needs to be continued further. I sincerely hope that members of our REDCo consortium and colleagues throughout Europe and around the world will continue to contribute to the ongoing research in a vibrant field that is gaining ever greater prominence in both the academic and public arena.

Hamburg, 12 January 2009   Wolfram Weisse
                                                             (Coordinator of REDCo)

References

Council of Europe (2008). *White Paper on Intercultural Dialogue "Living Together as Equals in Dignity"*, launched by the Council of Europe Ministers of Foreign Affairs at their 118th Ministerial Session, Strasbourg, 7 May 2008. Strasbourg: Council of Europe. http://www.coe.int/t/dg4/intercultural/Source/White%20Paper_final_revised_EN.pdf, last access 13 January 2009.

Habermas, J. (2005). *Zwischen Naturalismus und Religion. Philosophische Aufsätze*. Frankfurt am Main: Suhrkamp.

Jackson, R. (1997). *Religious Education: An Interpretive Approach*. London: Hodder and Stoughton.

Jackson, R., Miedema, S., Weisse, W. & Willlaime, J.-P. (Eds.) (2007). *Religion and Education in Europe: Developments, Contexts and Debates*. Muenster: Waxmann.

Knauth, T., Jozsa, D.-P., Bertram-Troost, G. & Ipgrave, J. (Eds.) (2008). *Encountering Religious Pluralism in School and Society – A Qualitative Study of Teenage Perspectives in Europe*. Muenster: Waxmann.

Weisse, W. (2003). Difference without discrimination: religious Education as a field of learning for social understanding?, in: R. Jackson (Ed.), *International Perspectives on Citizenship, Education and Religious Diversity*. London, pp. 191–208.

Weisse, W. (2007). The European Research Project on Religion and Education 'REDCo'. An Introduction, in: R. Jackson, S. Miedema, W. Weisse, & J.-P. Willlaime (Eds.), *Religion and Education in Europe: Developments, Contexts and Debates*. Muenster: Waxmann, pp. 9–25.

Ziebertz, H.-G., Kay, W. K. (2006). *Youth in Europe II. An international empirical Study about Religiosity*. Muenster: Lit Verlag.

Markus Friederici

From the Research Question to the Sampling

The article aims to explain the quantitative survey and how the procedure of the data analysis has been developed. This first chapter shows the different steps in a research process from the first look at and contact with the research field to the construction of a complex questionnaire that generates all the relevant information the researcher needs to answer the research question. This process is accompanied by a lot of discussion of problems and different ways to solve them. For the purpose of traceability this research process needs to be explained in more detail.

The starting point of a research project is always a question. On the basis of a perception of a social phenonemon or a social problem you start to ask: Why is it like it is – and not differently? What are the causes of what we see, how could the phenomenon be described, and how will it develop? Which variables influence what we see? And what information do we need to describe, explain and – if we want to – evaluate what we see? Have some questions already been answered elsewhere, at least in part? This is of course speaking very generally and needs to be concretized in terms of the REDCo project and the quantitative youth survey as an essential part of it, which will be addressed in this chapter.

1.   Theoretical and methodological background

Given the process of European unification and the growing religious-cultural plurality of European societies, intercultural and interreligious education are to be considered as key issues for preventing conflict and supporting peaceful coexistence, on both an intranational as well as an international level. In this process, "the question of dialogue between religions and of a dialogical approach to Religious Education is gaining more and more prominence all over the world" (Weisse, 2008, p. 5). The REDCo project is therefore dedicated to the role of religion in education in multireligious societies. Looking at the developments regarding the topic of 'religion in education' in general and of 'religious education' in particular, one becomes aware that the question of dialogue between religions and of a dialogical approach to religious education has gained more and more importance in Europe. There is a rising public awareness of the necessity to see dialogue between religions and worldviews as a tool to prevent conflict and to support a peaceful coexistence in a pluralistic and heterogeneous society. Recent events across the world have remade religion a topic of high public interest, among them the migratory processes bringing to Europe increasing numbers of people from ethnic and cultural groups for whom religion plays an important role in their lives, the collapse of the Soviet system and the revival of religion in many post-socialist countries, and the fear of religious fanaticism in western societies (Knauth, Josza, Bertram-Troost & Ipgrave, 2008, p. 11). It is becoming increasingly clear that we need a deeper understanding of religion in order to deal with religious diversity in a way that prevents discrimination, antagonism or even violence but fosters respectful interaction and peaceful coexistence. To achieve such societal purposes the inclusion of religion in education plays a decisive role. This is also expressed by the great efforts that have recently been made by inter-governmental organisations developing practical guidance and policy recommendations for teaching about religions and beliefs, e.g. the "Draft Recommendation of the Committee of Ministers to member states on the religious dimension of intercultural education: principles, objectives and teaching approaches" by the Council of Europe (2007) and the "Toledo Guiding Principles on Teaching about Religions and Beliefs in Public Schools" by the Office for Democratic Institutions and Human Rights (ODIHR) of the Organisation for Security and Co-operation in Europe (OSCE, 2007).

However the degree to which differences in religion, religious convictions and worldviews bear potential for conflict and lead to exclusion and separation in the lifeworld of young people, and especially in their everyday school life, needs further investigation. Moreover, there is a need for further research to clarify the degree to which interpersonal dialogue, implemented or promoted through the educational system between students with different worldviews or religious backgrounds, can encourage a peaceful coexistence and lead to a decrease in conflict (Weisse, 2008). Rather than dealing with a cross section of society, we turned our attention to the specific teenage perspectives on these questions.

The REDCo project in general, and its quantitative research in particular, are a pioneering comparative research project to investigate how 14 – 16 year old students in different European countries think about religion in education – and about dialogue and conflict in a background of religious diversity. It is this specific focus on education that makes our research special and – in the variety of thematic perspectives – unique.

To find out something about the causes of students' attitudes and opinions we asked about the role of religion in their everyday lives, the meaning of religion in school and society, and the way in which it could be possible for people with different religious beliefs to live together peacefully. The quantitative study is particularly based on the research work that was done in the REDCo project beforehand, that is firstly the analysis of the developments, contexts and debates in the eight participating countries concerning "Religion and Education in Europe" (Jackson, Miedema, Weisse & Willaime, 2007). This initial outcome of the REDCo project addressed the topic of religious education and its potentials for dialogue or conflict in a broad and fundamental perspective. Through this was built the foundation for the process of empirical research work in the REDCo project, starting with a qualitative study that was conducted before the quantitative survey and formed its second basis. For the first time large-scale qualitative findings were presented on the importance of religion and attitudes towards religious diversity and religious education among European school students, entitled "Encountering Religious Pluralism in School and Society. A Qualitative Study of Teenage Perspectives in Europe" (Knauth et al., 2008). Having hereby gained deep knowledge of the young people's attitudes towards other people from different religious or non-religious backgrounds, the quantitative study was aimed at generalizing the qualitative findings by addressing them to a much larger sample size in each of the eight countries. Accordingly, the quantitative youth survey is very closely interwoven with the qualitative study. As predicted outcomes, on the one hand, profound knowledge of young people's perspectives on religion will be acquired for each country; that is necessary in order to deal with practical issues such as appropriate forms and contents of religious education. On the other hand, the data will allow the project to make cross-national and European comparisons in order to find out about the influence of the different (religious-cultural) contexts which are regarded as being (one of) the main factors with effects on the young people's attitudes and perspectives (besides individual factors such as religion, gender etc.).

The benefit of the sequential triangulation of methods chosen here is obvious: The qualitative material firstly provides an informative basis for developing a grounded and systematic set of hypotheses which will then be tested and lead to generalised findings. Combining qualitative and quantitative methods is the attempt to balance the common 'breadth versus depth' trade-off and to reach both; knowledge of education for tolerance in depth and breadth. This procedure also assures that the research is very closely related to the young people's everyday lives, and that, vice versa, the results can be connected especially to the educational issues relating to tolerance. By investigating young people's perspectives on religion and religious education respectively, the research integrates individual attitudes (micro-level) and educational opportunities and constraints (macro-level).

However, the REDCo team of course did not reinvent the wheel, but also built on theoretical and empirical research that has been done by others in the field before and helped us: (1.) to understand the religious and educational situation in different European countries; and (2.) to explore the field on religion in education from the viewpoints of students; to (3.) document how students deal with dialogue and conflict. As a matter of comparison, other quantitative surveys relating to the topic were, however, of particular interest. As mentioned above, our quantitative survey about Religion in School is a pioneering comparative research among students in Europe. Nevertheless there are some European studies that we used to reflect the status quo of the discussion on this specific field of research. Three of them especially gave us helpful information to organize our research design:

–   Ziebertz and Kay (2006) did a comparative investigation in 12 countries with approximately 10,000 respondents aged 17 and 18. The study presents the life perspectives of young people and deals with religious perspectives and the integration of religions and life perspectives.
–   The European Values Study has been carried out since the late 1970s and is a large-scale, cross-national and longitudinal survey research programme. The results document the relation between religion and morality, work and leisure, politics and primary relations. Materials from the third wave of the study, which was conducted in the years 1999 and 2000, served as one of the means for comparison in our data analysis.
–   The Eurobarometer is a series of surveys performed on behalf of the European Commission since 1973. It produces reports of public opinion on certain issues relating to the European Union across the member states. The "Eurobarometer 225" survey "Social Values, Science and Technology" (European Commission, 2005) also had a section on religious issues.

Besides, there are other surveys such as the "International Social Survey Programme" (ISSR) which is a continuous programme of cross-national collaboration running annual surveys on topics important for the social sciences. In 1991 and 1998 the survey included the ISSP Religion module which mainly deals with religious beliefs, religious socialisation, past and current religious practices, religion and governmental connections, religion in comparison to other aspects, and secular aspects. The upcoming 2008 survey will again contain the ISSP Religion module as a partial replication of the 1998 study.

Those were not directly comparable with the REDCo survey, but were used as reference points. The aim of the REDCo quantitative survey was to construct an opinion poll relating to the specific topic of the REDCo project and building on the results of the qualitative study. The quantitative survey therefore provided data material of a different kind which then allowed us to answer our research questions from another additional perspective. While the qualitative study was the first exploration of the field, the quantitative study can be understood as a further exploration.

This refers to to a general limit of the (quantitative) findings due to the underlying data from the selected samples, which were not representative in a statistical sense (see the chapter on sampling in this book). The research study of the REDCo project presented here provides unique data material and empirical findings in terms of the perspectives young people have on religion in education. It will be a future task to carry out studies at a representative level and to test our results and hypotheses by verification or falsification which will lead to general statements. So one might say that the quantitative research is one piece in the complex jigsaw of the REDCo research project; the REDCo project is more than a pure testing of hypotheses but is an attempt at the complex process of comprehending and laying open students' attitudes towards the role of religion in education. The complexity of the field of religions, the different value systems and orientations for personal development, and the strong challenges associated with efforts to organize dialogue and to handle conflict, make it mandatory to gain knowledge about students of different countries, different religious or non-religious orientation, different educational backgrounds and from different social living worlds. This requires us to reflect different perspectives on the topic but also to use varied methods in order to triangulate the outcomes from several researches (Flick, 2004). The aim is (always) to find methods and approaches to come as close as possible to the social reality. In summary, one might say that our quantitative research is one of the cornerstones of the complex investigation of the chances and possibilities, but also the constraints and problems, of religion in education.

2.   The research design – from the problem to the sampling

To say that we would describe the research design from the beginning to the sampling is only half of the truth; as we mentioned before, the starting point of our quantitative research was not the description of problems and phenomena – we had already started with this work before the qualitative research. But one might say that the starting point of the quantitative research was the discussion of the problems and phenomena after the documentation and interpretation of the empirical data of the qualitative research: in which direction does the material that we generated on the qualitative level lead us? Do we have to think again about the problems and phenomena which we have talked about at the very beginning of the project? Do the qualitative results indicate other problems or other weightings of the theoretical problems that we have identified and assumed before? Do we have to change (maybe only slightly) our research question?

Empirical research is always a process – starting with a problem or a phenomenon and ending with the reflection on the data which should give hints to describe, explain or even evaluate the focused problem or phenomena in more detail (and at least to answers the research question). Following this logic, our starting point was the theoretical and empirical basis derived from the qualitative research. This first part of our empirical work showed the directions of thinking for students, the topics which are interesting to them (and which are not) concerning religion in school and outside school, and documented their different reconstructions of social reality. This was one of the most important results of the qualitative research – that there is not one opinion, one pattern and one attitude concerning religious diversity, the possibility of living peacefully together and the options of religious dialogue and conflict, but a broad range of views including also extreme positions. Against this background the general intention behind the quantitative study was to search for statistically strong(er) evidence on the basis of a large number of participants. The aim was to become more certain about the findings from the qualitative survey and to turn presumptions and suggestions into more general statements about strong tendencies concerning the issues identified.

So what we had at the very beginning of the quantitative part of our project was the theoretical background published in the first book of our project "Religion and Education in Europe. Developments, Contexts and Debates", which aimed to present institutional aspects and raise the main issues different European countries have to face in this field (Jackson et al., 2007), the results of the qualitative research (Knauth et al., 2008), and the interpretation of the data by using some principles of grounded theory (which is a systematic research methodology in the social sciences to generate theory from data) but also using other methods like qualitative content analysis (Mayring, 2008). Thus we did not start with a blank slate but already received preliminary answers to our questions from these works. Rather than being representative, our empirical basis for the quantitative survey covered a specific group – students from different European countries who were selected very carefully as is described in the chapter on "Sampling" in this volume. This procedure was appropriate because our quantitative research was planned as testing the qualitative results to describe our research topic with more certainty and to (re-)formulate the research question(s) more precisely. The research design helped us to formulate the main steps of the research process from defining the problem to developing the questionnaire. It covers the following steps which will be explained below.

➡ step 1: **description of problems and phenomena**

➡ step 2: **formulation of research questions**

➡ step 3: **discussion of the qualitative data**

➡ step 4: **selection and operationalisation of the hypotheses**

➡ step 5: **construction of the questionnaire**

Step 1: description of problems and phenomena

As Wolfram Weisse (2007) wrote in his introduction for the book *Religion and Education. Developments, Contexts and Debates* (Jackson et al., 2007) we can state that an increasing secularisation led to a gradual retreat of religion from the public sphere in most European countries. This tendency has reversed itself in the course of the past decade as religion returned to public discourse. So it seems more and more important to reflect the increasing factor of "religion and religiosity" and its ambivalent potential for dialogue on the one hand and conflict and tension on the other hand.

Consequently, the first step of our research was the clarification of the problems and phenomena related to the topic, e.g. religious dialogue and conflict in school, different teaching models concerning religious education, religious diversity in school, and the (im-)possibility of peaceful living together and religious coexistence. The discussions about these topics were helpful and necessary to shape the research focus and the main research question(s) that we had already formulated at the beginning of the REDCo project, as described in the foreword of this book.

One of the problems we faced was the issue of organizing a comparative survey of European youngsters from very diverse contexts. Various cultural and religious backgrounds made it rather complicated to develop an instrument for data collection, suitable for all countries. This issue of diversity raised also questions of translation, and in the semantic field, of terms like dialogue, tolerance and respect. We decided not to predefine these terms at the beginning of the questionnaire but to find items which indicate how the students themselves interpret the intention of these words.

Following this logic, we also abandoned working with a predefined and fixed concept of religion and religiosity in our research – we decided to let the students identify their 'religious background' and the importance of religion in their lives, in order to get the definition not from theoretical discussions but from social reality (see the chapter on semantic differences in this book).

Step 2: formulation of research questions

The discussion about the research questions was the second step of our work: should we stick to the main research question we used already in the qualitative study, or should the research question be reformulated because of a new or modified perspective on the object of investigation? Besides using quotations from the qualitative study to get information concerning specific aspects from a wider range of students, we also made use of triangulation for a better understanding of the object of research.

So one of the main decisions at the beginning of our work was to keep the same research questions. Although there are some differences (concerning the number of questions, the participating schools, the number of students, the role of the teacher etc.) both the qualitative and quantitative questionnaires deal with the following leading question and sub-questions:

What role can religion in education play concerning the way pupils perceive religious diversity? The sub-questions are:

1.   What role has religion in pupils' life and in their surroundings (important others, peers, family)?
2.   How do pupils see religion in school and the impact of religion in education?
3.   How do pupils consider the impact of religions: do they contribute more to dialogue or more to conflict?
4.   Which are the (similarities and) differences between the countries participating in the REDCo project concerning the main research question?

Step 3: discussion of the qualitative data

The main task in the third step of the research process was to figure out how empirical data helps us to formulate our main research hypotheses and to consider our research question(s) from as many perspectives as possible. An important source was the outcome of the qualitative research about religious pluralism in school and society that is presented in the book publication of the same title (Knauth et al., 2008). The results of this research reflect a wide range of perspectives on religion and religious education from the viewpoints of students who described the conflict potential of religion as well as the difficulties people have with religious plurality. The results were not representative but made clear that the opinions of many students are (still) based on stereotypes, prejudices and even racism. On the other hand the findings revealed that students had positive encounters with people of other religions – inside and outside of school. This gives not only hope and trust to establish ways of peaceful living together. It also makes clear that we need information about the question whether specific opinions and attitudes, prejudices and stereotypes, wishes and desires could be generalized and assumed for all of the European countries that participated in our project – and about the role of religious education in school.

While the qualitative study is important in itself to document the diversity of (re)constructions of social reality, it was also necessary and fruitful for the preparation of the quantitative questionnaire. The questionnaire, which is mainly based on closed questions (with Likert scaled items) used items derived from the qualitative research, to be sure that we focused on the relevant aspects of the life world of the students. On the basis of the reactions of students to the qualitative questionnaire and its open questions, we chose quotations from their answers for formulating statements which we placed as items in the quantitative study. In other words: The students in the quantitative survey had to fill in to what degree they agreed or disagreed with the quoted views of their (European) peers.

In this context special attention was given to the aspect of dialogue and conflict. We were particularly interested in the significance of religion for the communication between students and whether religion is a topic that gives rise to conflicts of any kind. To this end, we used the terms "dialogue and conflict" in a rather open way instead of predefining and relating them to particular concepts.

Step 4: selection and operationalisation of the hypotheses

The fourth step was the discussion of the hypotheses which (1.) have to give orientation for the construction of the questionnaire and (2.) are the starting point of the development of the tree of variables and (3.) serve as statements the generated data material has to reflect on.

The ex-post analysis of the qualitative questionnaires showed that we received much more information about religious education and opinions about and attitudes towards religious topics, than we had intended – which is the case in nearly every research study which is working with open questions to which the respondents normally react in manifold ways linking to very different things. So it was quite important (1.) to reflect if we should modify our basic research hypotheses; (2.) to develop some sub-hypotheses to define the frame of the quantitative research; and as a consequence of the variety of empirical results of the qualitative research, (3.) to decide what questions or items should be used and what left out.

Regarding our research questions, we decided to use the following hypotheses to find out more about the meaning of religion and religious diversity in relation to its potential for dialogue and conflict.

1a) Religious students are less tolerant than non-religious students.
1b) Religious students are less open to dialogue on religious issues than non-religious students.

2a) Students who have encountered religious diversity in education are more tolerant.
2b) Students who have encountered religious diversity in education are more open to dialogue on religious issues.

3a) Students who have personally encountered religious diversity are more tolerant.
3b) Students who have personally encountered religious diversity are more open to dialogue on religious issues.

Starting from this point we constructed a tree of variables to operationalise the hypotheses. This scheme should avoid any possibility of omitting relevant variables which have to be included to answer the research questions; the tree of variables would guarantee that all dimensions that are part of the hypotheses are integrated in the questionnaire. So the leading question was to find dependent and independent variables which describe in total the hypotheses.

Thus we got information about dialogue and conflict by using questions about students' personal religious background (questions 37, 38, 126, 127), religion in school (questions 1–5) and the social network (questions 68–75) which can be described as independent variables. Additionally, we generated data material concerning tolerance (questions 55, 76, 77, 83, 103–106) and readiness for dialogue (questions 34, 78, 87–97, 98–102) which can be regarded as the dependent variables.

In most cases it is not suitable to confront people in a questionnaire with abstract variables like "Do you think that peaceful living together is possible?" As an example, tolerance is first of all a theoretical construct that cannot be directly experienced in social reality; there is a need for indicators. Indicators are substitutes which build a connection between the notional construct and social reality by providing information about their existence and quality. An item about readiness for discussions with people of different beliefs or the disposition to accept different opinions, for example, "indicates" the degree of tolerance and the attitudes concerning the possibility of peaceful living together.

Students have the alternative to say (in the case of closed questions) "yes" or "no", or by using Likert-scales to express e.g. their agreement or disagreement in terms of ranges between 1 and 4 (or 5, 6, 7). The value of the answers to such a question is to gain knowledge whether the students think that peaceful living together between students of different religious beliefs is possible or not – and in case of Likert-scales, to what degree students approve or disapprove.

Step 5: construction of the questionnaire

In order to make data triangulation possible the structure of the quantitative questionnaire is quite similar to that of the qualitative study. There is also a direct link from each research question to one of the main blocks in the questionnaire – the first block represents the personal level, the second one the school level and the third one the societal level. All of them are also connected with our main research topic, which is represented by the hypotheses and operationalised by the independent and dependent variables which have been the basis of the questions, and (together with the results of the qualitative research) for the items. From a theoretical point of view one might say that the research questions and hypotheses document the different levels of reflection: the micro-level (focus on the individual), the meso-level (focus on organization, in this case educational institution) and the macro-level (focus on societal structure). The role that religion has in pupils' life is implemented in questions about the personal relevance of religion, the family background, peer relations etc. (questions 37–79, 86, 92, 95, 96, 122–127). How pupils see religion in school is mainly located in the first part of the questionnaire (questions 1–19, 26–36, 80, 81). Finally, the attitudes of the pupils concerning the impact of religion – and the question if religion contributes more to dialogue or more to conflict – is a topic in several parts of the questionnaire (questions 20–25, 82–85, 87–112).

3.   Conclusions

One of the most discussed questions in the REDCo project was about the way in which data could be generated. Empirical social research offers many methods and some of them were already used in the field in which we worked. Following one of the guidelines of social research that not the researcher but the field of research should "decide" which method seems to be suitable to get the relevant information, we developed in the first empirical part of the research a qualitative instrument. The main target was to get deeper information about the wishes, motives, attitudes and opinions of the researched pupils. The results of this research were not only used for regional reports and comparative studies but also for the construction of the quantitative questionnaire in the second phase of our empirical work. Here the intention was to find general patterns and regularities in the attitudes of young people in Europe. Therefore we had to use the data material of the qualitative research to construct items that could be tested in the field. This specific sequence of methods was helpful to analyse the research topic from different perspectives and to get a deeper appreciation of the problems and possibilities of religious diversity.

So we derived our sampling methodology from the focus of the survey – to research what role can religion in education play concerning the way students perceive religious diversity. Thus, our intention is to investigate different schools with concrete forms of religion in education, and students, nested into classes in these particular schools. Because of the limited resources we have to turn to non-probability sampling methods, using purposive or judgemental sampling with certain criteria (Babbie, 2008, p. 204). So our survey was not aimed to "test" some specific hypotheses but has a more exploratory aim – to learn more about this particular field and to look at the outcomes of the qualitative study in the broader context.

The interpretation of the data on an univariate level was the first step of data analysis and leads to more or less interesting results depending on the current research status. The next step of quantitative data interpretation were the bi- and multivariate analyses which allowed us to generate much more detailed information. These more significant methods were used to analyse correlations between two or more variables and show for example what influence students' religious affiliation has on their degree of respecting other positions.

As such procedures are based on a large sample size, patterns and regularities become visible and structures can be identified which is not possible by using qualitative research methods. To focus on the field of dialogue and conflict concerning religious diversity we used an unusual but – as we can say retrospectively – very fruitful way to answer our research question(s). We did not only work with triangulation, which means reconstructing social reality from various points of view and different methods, but also with an innovative research design. So we did not start the research with a deductive-nomological questionnaire to create representative statements – and to look afterwards for deeper interpretations by using a qualitative research instrument. By using the qualitative instrument first we let the "field" define the whole range of issues that are important concerning dialogue and conflict. In the second step we used the quantitative instrument to find out if the attitudes and opinions expressed in the qualitative study are more or less strong tendencies which could be generalised. The results of the research show that this way was not only a good one but also the only alternative to document the complex field of religion and religion in education and society through the eyes of European students.

References

Babbie, E. (2008). *The basics of social research.* Thomson Wadsworth.

Council of Europe (2007). *Draft Recommendation of the Committee of Ministers to member states on the religious dimension of intercultural education: principles, objectives and teaching approaches.*, in: https://wcd.coe.int.

European Commission (2005). *Special Eurobarometer 225. Social Values, Science and Technology.* http://ec.europa.eu/public_opinion/archives/ebs/ebs_225_report_en.pdf (first access 18.12.2005)

Flick, U. (2004). *Triangulation: Eine Einführung.* Wiesbaden: VS Verlag für Sozialwissenschaften.

Jackson, R., Miedema, S., Weisse, W., & Willaime, J.-P. (Eds.) (2007). *Religion and Education in Europe. Developments, Contexts and Debates.* Münster: Waxmann.

Knauth, T., Josza, D.-P., Bertram-Troost, G., & Ipgrave, J. (Eds.) (2008). *Encountering Religious Pluralism in School and Society. A Qualitative Study of teenage Perspectives in Europe.* Münster: Waxmann.

Mayring, P. (2008). *Qualitative Inhaltsanalyse. Grundlagen und Techniken.* Weinheim: Beltz.

OSCE Office for Democratic Institutions and Human Rights (ODIHR) (2007). *Toledo Guiding Principles on Teaching about Religions and Beliefs in Public Schools.* Prepared by the ODIHR Advisory Council of Experts on Freedom of Religion or Belief. http://www.osce.org/publications/odihr/2007/11/28314_993_en.pdf

Weisse, W. (2007). The European Research Project on Religion and Education "REDCo". An introduction, in: R. Jackson, S. Miedema, W. Weisse & J.-P. Willaime (Eds.), *Religion and Education in Europe. Developments, Contexts and Debates.* Münster: Waxmann, pp. 9–25.

Weisse, W. (2008). Foreword, in: T. Knauth, D.-P. Josza, G-D. Bertram-Troost, J. Ipgrave (Eds.), *Encountering Religious Pluralism in School and Society. A Qualitative Study of teenage Perspectives in Europe.* Münster: Waxmann, pp. 5–7.

Ziebertz, H.-G., Kay, W. K. (Eds.) (2006). *Youth in Europe. Vol. 2: An international empirical Study about Religiosity.* Münster: LIT.

Céline Béraud

Who to Survey? Considerations on Sampling[1]

One of the steps in the strategy required for any research by questionnaire is deciding who to survey. The choice of sampling method is subjected to the "constraints of statistics" but also to the "objectives of knowledge" (Singly, 2005, p. 44). This is not, then, a purely technical issue that can be isolated from the rest of the research: from the phases that preceded it (determination of the matter to be studied and construction of hypotheses), or those that follow it (interpretation of data, creation of generalisations and comparisons). The aim of this chapter is to give a fully transparent presentation of the methodology that the REDCo project adopted for its sampling, to comment on the samples finally obtained by the various national teams, and to come to some conclusions on the use of this data, particularly for a comparative perspective.

1.   From general principles to specific choices made in the REDCo project

After a few very general comments on the sampling method, which we hope will be useful to readers unfamiliar with quantitative surveys, we shall present the method that the teams in the REDCo project decided on.

Usually, it is not possible to give a questionnaire to all of the population studied in a given research project. The researcher either has to have considerable resources at his or her disposal (census data for example), or the research must be limited to small groups. We should add that even if an exhaustive survey can be carried out, it will have flaws: as the size of the sample increases, the errors accumulate and the difficulties multiply (omissions, double-counted samples, incorrect answers, etc.) (Martin, 2005, p. 15). In most cases, surveys are not exhaustive; they only study a portion of the population. Working with sample groups relies upon the statistical principle that knowledge of an entire group can be derived from a part of it. Following the example of Jacqueline Freyssinet-Dominjon (1997), we can use the analogy of the soup and the spoon. We do not have to consume a whole pot of soup to know how it tastes. A spoonful is enough.

To make sure that the results obtained from the study of a fraction of the general population can be applied to the population as a whole, an effort is often made to constitute representative samples. In such a case, one must select a group from a given population where the characteristic to be examined, whose frequency is known in the general population, is represented in exactly the same proportions. For this, two methods are typically used: the probability method and the quota method (Freyssinet-Dominjon, 1997). Probability or random sampling is the method preferred by the major public research institutions. It is often seen as "the ideal statistic" (Singly, 2005, p. 41). It requires a *sampling frame*, documents that individually and exhaustively classify the sampling units (for example: electoral registers, telephone directories, membership lists of an association, etc.). Private polling organisations typically use empirical polling, otherwise known as quota sampling. This method is called "empirical"

---

1   I would particularly like to thank Jacqueline Freyssinet-Dominjon, who is a political scientist, for her advice.

because it relies upon experience and practice. It is an example of non-probability sampling. The purpose of the quota method is to respect the profile of the parent population when constituting the sample group through the use of a particular set of criteria, keeping some proportions or quotas constant. In a way, the sample group is a scale model of the total population being studied. To create this sample, there must be statistical data available on the reference population.

Nevertheless, we should point out that representativeness is not always necessary nor possible to reach, especially in an explorative survey; sociologists (like other scientists, biologists in particular) frequently work with non-representative samples. It is in fact "often an illusion to try and respect" the principle of representativeness; researchers do not systematically have exhaustive, precise lists (which makes it difficult to generate a random selection of those to be surveyed) and the characteristics of the reference population are not always known (in this case, the quota method cannot be applied) (Martin, 2005, p. 27).

Given the means available to the national REDCo groups, the choice was made to constitute sample groups that, although they cannot be considered representative samples in the strict sense of the term, have nonetheless been carefully selected. This type of sample, which is known as a "purposive" or "judgmental" sample, uses a non-probability sampling technique that relies upon the knowledge the researcher has of the population in question. The researcher selects the statistical units that possess, in his or her opinion, the typical characteristics of the overall population. In our survey, we did not directly select specific adolescents (considered as statistical units or units of analysis); rather, we selected whole schools (considered as sampling units[2]) and classes within them. The survey took place in several classes in one school, in other words on the group level, which allowed us to limit the expenses associated with supervision of the research and travel. Apart from these practical considerations, working at the level of individual schools was meaningful in relationship to the previous phases of the research: interviews and observations could be carried out at the same level.

A set of criteria was established in order to choose the schools where the questionnaires would be handed out: gender, religious background, national origin, socio-economic background (for the pupils); type of school, method of handling religious education, and whether it is in an urban or rural environment (for the schools). This set of criteria was developed taking the results of the qualitative survey into consideration. It also seemed to be relevant to our research questions and the hypotheses that we developed to answer them. In particular, they seemed to be the appropriate variables for judging each student's openness to dialogue. We can therefore see how the sampling method is never an independent phase of the research as a whole: "The question of the population and the sample is inseparable from the theoretical construction of the object" (Singly, 2005, p. 46).

Using these criteria, the goal was then to construct a sample group that best reflected the regional or national conditions that we hoped to examine. The reliability of a non-probability sample cannot be measured statistically: the variability of the sampling method cannot be estimated, nor can its possible bias be identified. However, the group can be evaluated by comparing some of the results of the survey with information available on the population as a whole. Each national team was asked to comment on the sample group in comparison with the main characteristics of the overall population using the set of criteria as a guideline.

As for the size of the sample, the minimum number of questionnaires to be filled and included in the analysis was set at 400 per country. A sample any smaller would make the

---

2   The advantage of a sampling unit is that it brings together groups of statistical units.

composition of sub-groups complicated. The number of questionnaires was also influenced by subjective factors: it was one that was within our means to deliver.

This sampling technique has undeniable limitations that we will discuss later on. Although it is a widely used technique, its reliability is subject to debate. However, it has the advantage of being relatively fast and easy to implement, as well as being less expensive than other more sophisticated techniques. In conclusion, one must keep in mind that:

> *"(...) there is no absolute criterion that makes it possible to know if a sample is 'good' or 'bad'. There are only general principles of construction that are more or less easy to implement and that guarantee a more or less substantial level of 'representativeness'. Most of all, there is a principle which states that a sample is never absolutely 'good' or 'bad': it is impossible to judge how interesting a sample is intrinsically, taking only its statistical properties into account; one must consider its correspondence to the context of a particular problem or to a series of precise questions. Even the criterion of representativeness is not necessarily an absolute."* (Martin, 2005, p. 25–26)

2.   Comments on the samples obtained by the various teams

Once we received the results, we noted wide variations between the samples each country obtained. This is not at all surprising; ultimately "the sample in question always presents distortions [...] when compared to the sample desired"[3] (Lebaron, 2006, p. 57).

Each team distributed more than 400 questionnaires. However, the size of each sample group varies greatly from one country to the next: less than 500 (Russia and England); between 500 and 1000 (the Netherlands, Spain, Norway and France); more than 1000 (Estonia and Germany). If we look at the number of schools that participated in the survey, we again observe wide differences in the results: less than 10 schools (Norway, Netherlands, Russia), between 10 and 15 (Estonia and Spain), more than 15 (England, France, Germany). The total number of questionnaires handed out and the number of schools in the study may have an impact on the heterogeneity of the sample.

Some of the samples were of a regional or local nature. The Spanish team concentrated on three autonomous regions: Andalusia, Murcia and the enclave of Melilla located in North Africa. The Russian team limited itself to the city of St. Petersburg. The Germans focused on the comparison of two *Länder* (states), Hamburg and North-Rhine-Westphalia, representing two distinct models of instruction dealing with religion. The British study only covered England, as the legal status of RE differs in other countries of the United Kingdom. The Estonians, the French, the Dutch and the Norwegians worked on a (more or less) national level. Of course, it was easier to cover the entire national territory of a country the size of Estonia than one like Russia.

For obvious reasons of convenience, the choice of schools was made in many cases on the basis of interpersonal contacts that already existed between researchers and certain teachers or headmasters.

As for the criteria upon which the samples were constituted, the results that were obtained were equally diverse.

There is a good balance in the samples between the sexes.

---

3   This is true even when probability sampling or quota sampling is used.

All the teams made a point of selecting schools with diverse socio-economic profiles. Information on parents' professions was intended to enable greater accuracy in the sample; unfortunately this information was not as usable as had been hoped, due to numerous omissions or clearly erroneous responses given by the students.

As for the students' "religious background," some samples put great emphasis on those students who state a religious affiliation. In the Dutch sample, special attention was given to "segregated religious schools" (which are clearly overrepresented in the sample in comparison to the national average); this was an inevitable factor in the high level of religious belief observed in the students surveyed, which is not representative of the situation regarding religion in the Netherlands. Incidentally, we should note that information on the religion or worldview of the students' parents, especially the father, is often limited. Some students do not seem to know anything about it (in particular, a large proportion of the English sample) or think that it is a private matter that they shouldn't discuss (which is how some French students reacted for example). Ultimately, most of the samples indicated a great variety of religions and worldviews. However, from a statistical point of view, the percentages of some religious groups were too small for reliable analyses.

The attention given to the type of school revealed itself to be quite necessary in the case of school systems with a tremendous amount of diversity and complexity; here one of the best examples is clearly the English system.

The criterion concerning the form of religious education only seems to be relevant for countries where many different systems of religious education coexist on an institutional level. The German example and the Dutch one are especially interesting in this area.

Most of the teams paid special attention to geographical factors, due to the diverse nature of the regions covered in comparison with other criteria (such as "migration background", religion, socio-economic characteristics, forms of religious education, etc.), as well as the possible contrasts between rural and urban areas. However, in many cases we noticed a particular focus on cities, probably because they are the most common location for secondary schools. It also corresponds with the research topic: religious plurality (and as a matter of fact the need for tolerance and dialogue) is a main characteristic of urbanity.

The concern for diversity in constituting the samples led to skewed representations of some minorities (particular attention was given to students with immigrant backgrounds, certain religious schools, etc.). As a result, the survey overestimates the significance of these groups in comparison with the regional or national situation. This is true for the percentages of Muslim students in many of the samples.

Finally, we note that each team examined the criteria mentioned in the general principles underlying the sample, and gave priority to those that seemed the most relevant to the national and local context that they wished to investigate. Of course, this does not mean that they merely took the other criteria for granted. Such flexibility was ultimately necessary in the context of a Europe-wide survey on a subject – schools and religion – that is profoundly marked by the social and historical realities of each country.

3.   Methodological consequences

The attention given by each team to the sampling method makes it possible to indicate the main trends regarding the relationships that adolescents have to religion and school in the regions examined. Moreover being able to formulate generalisations is a target of any sociological survey, whatever the kind of methodology: "In the same way as surveys that call upon qualitative information (interviews, life stories) [...] the quantitative survey of a non-representative sample allows for [...] the identification of phenomena, mechanisms, processes and typical traits ..." (Martin, 2005, p. 28). However, caution must be exercised when making generalisations based on these observations. The ability to do so is strictly dependent upon the nature of the sample in relation to the national (or regional) situation under consideration. Comparisons between countries must also be carried out with equal caution. It may be possible to identify some of the main trends that countries share, and to observe the lines of tension between different national or regional configurations (this is what the commenting chapters and the conclusion of the work will cover), but a direct comparison between figures considered as necessarily representative of whole countries, and their addition to yield overall data, would be meaningless due to the variations between samples. In this document, we have strived to give a transparent view of the method used and its limits, and to encourage reflection on that method. Under these conditions, being cautious does not mean refusing certain forms of comparison.

We should add that the interpretation of the data from this quantitative survey is also made in the light of the results of the qualitative survey that preceded it. It confirms some of the results obtained during the first phase of the REDCo programme, while modifying other assertions made previously. The results of the quantitative survey are placed in the perspective of the research as a whole, which cannot be reduced to the results of this survey alone. It takes its place as a useful phase of the overall study.

References

Freyssinet-Dominjon, J. (1997). *Méthodes de recherche en sciences sociales*. Paris: Montchrestien, "DEUG AES".

Lebaron, F. (2006). *L'enquête quantitative en sciences sociales. Recueil et analyse des données*. Paris: Dunod, "Psycho sup".

Martin, O. (2005). *L'enquête et ses méthodes. L'analyse de données quantitatives*. Paris: Armand Colin, "sociologie 128".

Singly, F. de (2005). *L'enquête et ses méthodes. Le questionnaire*. Paris: Armand Colin, "sociologie 128".

Gerdien Bertram-Troost & Siebren Miedema

Semantic Differences in European Research Cooperation from a Methodological and Theoretical Perspective – Translation and Terminology[1]

Introduction

One of the important theoretical and methodological issues in a European comparative study is the procedure followed with regard to language issues. We had to face the fact that the participants of the REDCo research group and the respondents we wanted to include in our research have different mother tongues. Next to that we were aware as well – and that aware-ness was even growing during the research project – that it might look very easy to translate a certain term into different languages, but when taking a closer look it is evident that there are in fact different connotations of this term in different languages. But next to these *inter-language differences* in connotation it was even more complicated due to sometimes existing *intra-language differences* as well. We then deal theoretically speaking with the connotation and denotation of the different notions at stake, and from a methodological perspective the objectivity, reliability and validity of the research instruments are issues that urgently need to be addressed. With regard to the *intersubjective accountability* (Van IJzendoorn & Miedema, 1986), thus including the application of the same research instruments in the different coun-tries and the comparability of the findings across countries, it was necessary to develop a transparent procedure for preparing the translation of the questionnaire and for dealing with certain terms which appeared to be difficult to translate. In this chapter we will further elabo-rate on these semantic issues, thus on the translation procedure. In the second part of the chapter we will deal with some issues related to terminology. As it turned out that the term 'religion' (which is a core term in our research) had different connotations in different coun-tries, special attention is given to that term here.

Translation

The working group had prepared an English version of the questionnaire. As the pupils of the different participating countries would not be able to fill in the questionnaire in English, a translation in each country's language was needed. From a very early stage we were aware of this and even before the pre-test was done a translation guide was already composed in Au-gust 2007 to be sure that in every country the translation was done via the same translation rationale. Before that the translation of the pre-test version, the English version of the pre-test (as 'source questionnaire') was prepared. After this source questionnaire was finished, every country was asked to prepare a translation on the basis of the Ask-the-Same-Question model (ASQ, see Harkness, Van de Vijver & Johnson, 2003). The aim of this translation model is to translate the questionnaire in a way such that the intended meaning we had for the questions remained the same. Following the ASQ model, translators were not expected to adapt the

---

1   In this chapter, use has been made of the national reports on the pre-test as national teams elaborated there on translation issues and terminology. We gratefully acknowledge the indirect contribution of many REDCo members to this chapter.

content of the questions. The translators were, however, encouraged to produce questions that did not sound like translations and to use vocabulary that could be understood by pupils of different educational levels too.

As it was very important that the intentions of the questions would remain the same after translation, the working group provided additional information to explain the purposes of the questions to the researchers who were preparing the translations. These explanations were meant for the translators and could, if necessary, also be used in order to give additional explanations to pupils during the filling in of the questionnaire.

In order to reach the best translation results possible, we made use of a translation procedure which was also used in the European Social Survey (ESS): TRAPD[2]. TRAPD is an acronym for Translation, Review, Adjudication, Pre-testing and Documentation. TRAPD is a committee-based combined approach that helps to counteract the subjective nature of translation and text-based translation assessment. It includes documentation steps which make adjudication decisions easier and provides information needed for secondary analysis. Translation is done in teams as this gives the option to choose from different translation proposals. The steps of the TRAPD procedure will be briefly explained:

Translation: Preliminary translation of the questionnaire will be prepared independently by at least two translators. After the translators have prepared their versions, they discuss the different versions and develop an agreed version. The national coordinator is involved in this step of the translation process.

Review: The aim of reviewing is to ensure that translated questionnaires correspond to the basic questionnaire and are mutually comparable. The 'agreed version' is reviewed by members of the REDCo team who are able to understand the respective languages.

Adjudication: the agreed and reviewed translation of the questionnaire will be adjudicated by the national coordinator.

Pre-testing: Pre-testing of the questionnaire was conducted with approximately 50 pupils per country. National teams were asked to give feedback, in pre-test reports, on for instance the way pupils interpreted the questions and if there were any questions which caused problems such as confusion, misunderstandings et cetera.

Documentation: Translations and review decisions were documented so that those reviewing and adjudicating the questionnaire could use the notes in order to make a better decision on the agreed version. The notes on translation could also be used for the analyses. The national teams were asked to prepare documentation with the following information: information on the translation team, information on the translation schedule, files with draft translations, agreed version of the questionnaire and documentation of national translation discussions, including any remaining difficulties.

On the basis of the reports on the pre-tests and the documentation on translation, wordings were changed and additional explanations to certain questions were written in order to avoid any misunderstandings and to create an optimal 'source questionnaire'. The source questionnaire of the main survey was ready in January 2008. Most questions remained the same as in the pre-test version, and due to the comments of the national teams, easier formulations were chosen for certain questions. Thus, following the TRAPD-method, translation of the main survey did not cause many problems because most of the eventual problems which arose

---

2   See for more information on ESS on the internet: http://www.europeansocialsurvey.org/. On this
    website also more elaborated information can be found on the used translation procedure (TRAPD).

during the translation of the pre-test version had been solved by that time. We have above described the process and product lines which warranted and guaranteed the intersubjective accountability of the quantitative research.

Terminology: 'religion' as an important exemplar

During the REDCo meeting in September 2007 in St. Petersburg a plenary was held on the quantitative questionnaire. The translation procedure was explained and the national teams were invited to comment on any foreseeable problem with regard to the translation. During this plenary it became clear that in some countries there were some conceptual problems with the translation: It appeared that for some national teams it was not so easy to decide which word to choose for translating the concept 'religion', actually one of the core concepts in the research. As a result of this plenary it was decided that an open question would be added to the pre-test in order to get a better understanding of what pupils understand by 'religion'. The formulation of this added question was: 'Please explain what the word 'religion' means to you, in your own words'. National teams could add, if needed, more questions in order to be able to make better decisions on which term to choose as translation for 'religion'. For instance, in the Netherlands pupils were asked which word out of three, respectively 'religie', 'godsdienst' or 'levensbeschouwing', was most common to them, which one they used as a kind of synonym for 'religion' but with different connotations, and what they would characterize as the differences between these three terms.

Although the reactions of European pupils to the question 'What does the word 'religion' mean to you?' were very diverse, certain categories which can be distinguished in almost every national setting can be described. From these categories we learn that pupils have different associations with the term 'religion'. When interpreting the research data, it is helpful to have this in mind as it means that, at a certain point, we cannot be too sure about what pupils exactly mean when giving certain answers. As this is always the case when doing quantitative research, and while we created time and space to focus on these different interpretations, there is still, however, a quite strong basis for using a quantitative questionnaire to get more insight into how European pupils look upon religion in school[3].

We will now describe the categories distinguished from the answers to the open-ended question and will include some examples from different national settings (translated into Standard English):

Belief in God:

[religion is …] believing in a God, worshipping a God (England)

[religion is …] Well, it is to know God. All his life and everything he did during his life. Not only believe in him, also to believe in his word (Spain)

[religion is …] Religion for me is a belief. There are many different beliefs. I do not know about them anything, but I know that there are Christians, Jehovah's Witnesses and others. I do not believe in God or Buddha etc. That is why I do not know anything in particular about religion. (Estonia)

---

3   This basis and the theoretical background of the research is further described in this volume in the introductory chapter on theoretical issues.

Belief in something:

[religion is …] the way you believe in something that is important to you (Netherlands)

[religion is …] belief in something, worshipping something (England)

Guidance in life:

[religion is …] Something you believe in. Adapting to rules. Taking it seriously, doing good things and no bad things. It's an important topic in life, at least that's what I think (Netherlands)

[religion is …] to me it is something you believe in. It is some kind of guide in life. It is something one chooses to believe in, and there are differences in how important religion is to different persons. (Norway)

[religion is …] To me it is a thing that can help you much. It also serves to help you in your life when you feel lonely. (Spain)

Elements/forms of religion

[religion is …] The worship of a god, goddess or Deity and the rituals and practices of a group of people (England)

[religion is …] To me religion is thoughts and costumes by which different religions are divided (Spain)

[religion is …] It is about what God they pray to. How you live compared with others. Where they live. (Norway)

Group identities / culture

[religion is …] I think that religion is belief, tradition etc. for example every nation has its own belief. (Estonia)

[religion is …] To me it means the culture all persons have and if we are Catholics or not. The highest leader in religion is the church. (Spain)

[religion is …] being part of a religious group (England)

Conflict potential

[religion is …] The word religion doesn't mean much to me. I think the word religion mostly appears in the media related to fights and wars (Norway)

[religion is …] a cause of unnecessary feuds and debates, creates war and poverty, divides countries (England)

[religion is …] Church always was an institution for keeping people in obedience. Take religion away as far as possible! If your money is already ripped off and you have no more to lose, it does not mean you have the right to do it to others! (Russia)

Religious education

[religion is ...] Religion means for me Religious Education and at the same time it means nothing, as religion unfortunately is not very important for me. (Estonia)

[religion is ...] A subject which is taught in the secondary school that teaches you the characteristics of religion etc. (Spain)

Although for each category examples can be found in every country, it is clear that in some countries pupils' reactions mainly point in a certain direction. From the material it became clear, for instance, that Spanish pupils are inclined to stress the 'cultural function' of religion. One Spanish pupil even states: 'To me the word Religion means Culture'. Another pupil explains it as follows: 'Religion to me is a belief of a human being, carried out through centuries and transmitted by our ancestors, according to personal characteristics, and we should respect what someone believes in'. And another: 'It's a belief that the persons have according to the place and environment they were born in, it's the culture of a place and every person is free to choose it'. In the Norwegian setting it seems that many students, regardless of their religious affiliation, understand the word 'religion' in an almost academic way and they describe different religious dimensions like belief, religious concepts, culture and traditions, rituals and festivals et cetera. In general, the pupils' ideas about and associations with the concept 'religion' seem to be based on knowledge *about* religion, more than on personal experience *with* religion (see Miedema, 2007, p. 281). German pupils are inclined to associate 'religion' with more or less institutionalized religions. They tend to make a difference between 'religion' and 'faith, belief' (Glaube). Some German pupils stated that they are 'not a religious person' but that they are, however, 'believing'. Many Dutch students have the term 'godsdienst' in mind when confronted with the term 'religie' (Dutch equivalent of 'religion'). There are also quite many students who state that they do not know what 'religie' means. This seems to be a matter of the use of terms. We will come back to this in the remainder of this section. In Estonia there are also quite many students who answer that 'religioon' (religion) means 'usk' (belief)'. 'Religioon' is a more academically used term, and in a way also a more neutral term, used for several religions, while 'usk' is usually used for Christianity and has several negative connotations for many Estonians. Out of the 62 Estonian students who participated in the pre-test, there was only one student who answered the question on the meaning of religion with 'I don't know, some kind of god's topic'. So, although several Estonian pupils are more familiar with the term 'usk', in general, they do know the term 'religioon'. They interpret it in both a personal and an 'institutional' way. It is because of the fact that 'religioon' is a more general, neutral term and pupils are familiar with it, that the Estonian researchers decided to use this term in the quantitative questionnaire.

Although it is very important to learn how different European pupils interpret the term 'religion', it is necessary to realize that the reactions of pupils on this open question are not necessarily representative for the countries they live in. The first reason is that only about 50 pupils per country participated in the pre-test (of which this open question was part), and the second reason is that in some countries only one school was involved.

In order not to be too dependent on pupils' reactions, we also asked the national teams to reflect on the meaning of and associations with the term 'religion' in their countries. With regard to the translation of the questionnaire, we were especially interested to learn whether there are alternative terms for 'religion' in the respective countries and, if so, what the relations are between these terms and 'religion'. Some national teams responded only very briefly on the request to reflect on the meaning of and associations with the term 'religion' in their country. Others, however, provided quite lengthy descriptions. In general, the length of the team reports seems to reflect the perceived complexity or clarity with regard to semantic issues in the national language. The following description also mirrors this.

As already made clear, in the *German context* there is a tendency to relate 'religion' to institutionalized religions. 'Faith' or 'belief' (in German 'Glaube') is more often used to describe the personal aspects, such as thoughts and feelings. As we saw earlier, also in the *Estonian* language there are two terms connected to religion ('religioon' and 'usk').

In the *Dutch context*, terminology seems to be even more complex. There are three terms at stake which all relate to 'religion': 'godsdienst', 'religie' and 'levensbeschouwing'. In their report on the pre-test, the Dutch research team makes clear that according to the Van Dale translation dictionary from Dutch into English (Martin & Tops, 1986), 'godsdienst' could be translated as 'religion', meaning the doctrinal side of it as well as the ritual side, but can also be translated as 'faith', that is bound to the personal convictions of a person. 'Religie' could be translated as 'religion' and as 'faith' or 'belief' (Dutch: 'geloof'). So, one could conclude from the dictionary that 'godsdienst' and 'religie' are terms that more or less cover the same object. It is anecdotal that teaching books with chapters on 'difficult Dutch words' present 'religie' as a synonym for 'godsdienst'. 'Levensbeschouwing', the third term at stake here, is translated in this same dictionary as 'philosophy of life' and as 'ideology'.

In the qualitative REDCo study (see Ter Avest et al., 2008, pp. 86–87), the Dutch team decided to use the word 'world view' ('levensbeschouwing'), meaning that everybody in some way or another reflects upon his or her life instead of 'religion' ('godsdienst') and clarified, in an additional comment, to the students that every person has a world view. The decision for this broader term was made to include as many pupils as possible and to avoid reactions like 'I can not participate in the research, because I do not have a religion'. Surprisingly, however, most of the Dutch pupils who participated in the qualitative research seemed to equate 'world view' with 'godsdienst' (religion') or 'godsdienstige levensbeschouwing' (religious world view) and answered the questions as if they were about 'godsdienst' (religion). It is striking that whereas the Dutch research team made the choice to use the word 'world view' ('levensbeschouwing') instead of 'religion' ('godsdienst') in the questionnaire, to make clear that everyone has a way of looking at life, either with or without God/gods, and also to include pupils who do not see themselves as belonging to a particular religion, the pupils still conceptualized and associated the word 'world view' with religion. With regard to the quantitative research (having seen the discussion in the whole research group and the strong wish to use terms in different countries which are as close to each other as possible) the Dutch team decided to use, in the Dutch pre-test, the term 'religie' (English: religion). However, the Dutch team already foresaw problems with the use of this term as 'religie' is more a term used by academics working in theology, religious studies and religious education and not so much part of the pupils' vocabulary. In order to get insight information from the pupils themselves, which might help to make decisions about translation with regard to the final version of the questionnaire, two additional open questions were added at the end of the pre-test version of the questionnaire. Apart from the question 'what does the term 'religion' mean to you?' pupils were asked which of the three words 'levensbeschouwing', 'godsdienst', or 'religie' are most common to them and whether they think these terms mean the same or are different. From the reactions it becomes clear that the word 'godsdienst' is, by far, the most common for the Dutch pupils. Many pupils have the contention that the three terms are more or less the same. In one of the two schools, however, some pupils make a distinction between 'religie' and 'godsdienst' on the one hand and 'levensbeschouwing' on the other hand. Some reactions of pupils, as examples: 'To 'godsdienst' belongs Islam, Christianity, Buddhism and Hinduism. To 'levensbeschouwing' belongs none of the above mentioned things but Humanism, Atheism et cetera. So I think there are differences.', 'I think 'religie' and 'godsdienst' are quite similar. 'Levensbeschouwing' is more how you look upon life'. In fact, pupils' reactions are quite close to what was found in the English-Dutch dictionary as we explained earlier.

On the basis of the study of terminology and the outcomes of the pre-test, the Dutch team decided to translate 'religion' as 'godsdienst' to stay close to pupils' perceptions. Seen from the Dutch perspective it is interesting to mention that some Norwegian pupils expressed that they would prefer the term 'world view' instead of 'religion': "I think you should have written world view instead of religion. Most people have a world view, but not everyone has a religion." The Norwegian research team, however, adds that, on the other hand, many students are not very familiar with the term 'world view' and that this term had to be explained to the students several times. Also in the English context 'world view' is not a very common term. It is used for a set of beliefs or assumptions (often unconscious) that influence our way of living in the world. When used in relation to religion it is often employed as a way of giving equal status to non-religious interpretations of the world and of human life. Sometimes a secular world view is contrasted with a religious world view. Sometimes each religion is treated as a distinct world view and atheist or secular humanist positions are included in this list of world views.

In the *Russian context* there are, in general, three different meanings of the word 'religion'. These meanings are similar to the meanings W.C. Smith identified (1964). Religion can be understood as 'religious piety' or 'religiosity' (религиозность). The Russian term for religiosity is a proper word to describe the essence of a state of mind and a sense of personal devotion. The object of devotion may be different and not necessary 'religious'. The general connotation of this term is positive. Even during the decades of state atheism, the term religion in this sense kept its positive meaning and connotation. In Soviet Russia the term религиозность was not used widely, but if it was used, it was used to describe a commitment to something sacred (for instance Motherland or the memory of the victims of the World War.) The second meaning of religion is 'religion as a system' of beliefs, values and practices shared by a particular community. Originally, there are two words that are used in Russian to describe 'religion as a system'. They are *вера* (faith, belief) and *вероисповедание* (confession, creed). Nowadays these two terms are often replaced by a Russian version of the English word 'confession' (*конфессия*). Until recently no clear distinction has been made, in the Russian use of terms, between 'religious' and 'confessional'. Both concepts are used as synonyms. However, there are some 'stylistic' limitations in the sense that one can not say in Russian that one 'belongs to a (certain) religion', though it is possible to say 'I belong to a (certain) creed'. The third meaning of religion is religion as a phenomenon of human life (*религия*). It is common in Russian culture to look at religion as at the subcategory under the bigger category of 'spirituality'. For instance, a popular textbook on Religious Studies for higher education students defines religion as "one of the spheres of spiritual life, a way of practical and spiritual assimilation of the world" (Yablokov, 1998, p. 461). A consequence for education of this tradition of using terms, is that it is most common to talk about 'spiritual-moral upbringing' (духовно-нравственное воспитание). Usually education in values is meant by this. For those who advocate a system of laïcité the term 'religious education' sounds too confessional, whereas this term sounds too non-confessional for church leaders and advocates of state religion. They would therefore prefer to use the term духовно-нравственное воспитание 'spiritual-moral upbringing' There is a tendency among Russian Christians (not only Orthodox) to avoid the use of 'religion as phenomenon' (религия), as it is associated with the objective scientific discourse and political issues which seem threatening to them. These objections are also present among youngsters. In a Russian survey on the religious and moral beliefs of St. Petersburg students (Kozyrev, 2003) the researchers registered negative attitudes towards the word 'religion' among students of two confessional Christian schools (one Protestant and one Orthodox). They preferred to talk about faith and/or Church, and opposed these two to religion. With regard to the REDCo quantitative questionnaire it has been decided to translate 'religion' as религия and to use the term религиозное образование for Religious Education.

In *Spain*, the semantic field of the word *religion* possesses two dimensions. On the one hand religion is automatically associated with Catholicism and in particular with the Catholic Church. For those who identify themselves with this conception of religion, it is equivalent to values and tradition (just as the pupils' reactions show). On the other hand there is the association with religion as something from the past, which invokes the times of Franco. People who stress this aspect of religion advocate more a system of laïcité. They do not attach much value to religion in public life in a modern society.

In the *Norwegian context*, the conceptualisation of 'religion' is rather complex and the following must therefore be regarded as a simplification. Like in the Netherlands, the term 'religion' is related to other concepts such as 'belief' ('tro'), 'religious belief' ('religiøs tro') and 'God-belief' ('gudstro'). Although these concepts are sometimes used as synonyms of 'religion', none of them can fully replace the term. Other words overlapping with 'religion' may be 'world view' ('livssyn') and 'conviction' ('overbevisning'). Originally, in Norway religion was more or less synonymous with 'Christianity'. Even today this is often the case as quite many teachers and students speak about 'Christianity' when they talk about the school subject KRL (Knowledge about Religions, Worldviews and Ethics, see Skeie, 2007, pp. 230–231). However, because of the increasing number of Muslims in Norway and the exposure of Islam in the media, there is nowadays also a tendency that people associate religion with Islam. In the Norwegian vocabulary it is common to distinguish between 'religion' and 'religiosity'. Religion is more related to a whole system of traditions and ideas, whereas the term 'religiosity' first and foremost refers to personal belief and piety. However, in some regions of the country the two terms are used differently: there to be a 'Christian' means to be devoted, while to be 'religious' means a rather loose affiliation with a belief tradition or certain practices.

The *French context* is also a specific one, and – as we experienced that ourselves in the REDCo research group – not always easy to understand adequately for outsiders. Taking about 'religion' in French schools is taking about 'fait religieux' and the way both teachers and pupils are supposed to deal with such facts. Literally translated 'fait religieux' mean 'religious facts', but precisely that translation is an important reason for a lot of misunderstandings. In order to fully understand that the best translation should be 'religious phenomena' or 'religious issues' we will give a brief description on the basis of the information given by our French colleagues.

It was particularly the highly influential Debray Report (Debray, 2002) that popularised the expression 'teaching of religious facts' in France (see Willaime, 2007). The term 'fait religieux' refers to an approach with its roots in the work of Emile Durkheim involving the treatment of religious facts through explanation rather than comprehensive study, through a distantiated and scientific stance, that is an outsider's view, rather than an 'insider's view'. The purpose of the expression 'fait religieux' is to clearly draw the line between a confessional way of coping with religious issues and a neutral, pluralistic and scholarly rooted way of dealing with them. It is a response to those who feared that teaching about religion in the public educational system would end up with a coming back of catechism and the intrusion of clerics in public schools. Religion is conceptualised as a 'total social fact' covering all possible areas of human experience. This implies a broad way of teaching about religions using various points of view: historical, cultural, symbolic et cetera. All aspects of religious experience are allowed to be taught. This is why the teaching of religious phenomena could be brought into the whole curriculum of public secondary schools, and thus not only in history lessons which was already the major focus since 1989. In conclusion, the term 'facts', seems, from a non-French point of view, to limit the scope of teaching about religions whereas it is precisely the reverse.

The English version of the questionnaire asked the following question: 'Do you have a religion or a worldview?'. The French team decided just to put 'Do you have a religion?'. In fact, the term word 'world view' is difficult to understand for a French pupil. In France, laïcité is the common rule for all religions and groups, more than representing a specific philosophical position as in Belgium, the Netherlands or the UK.

When it comes to religion (just like to politics), teachers are legally obliged to be neutral towards their pupils. It is part of the status of every civil servant including the teachers in public school. Pupils do not have the same constraints: they can openly display their religious beliefs in class within certain limits concerning the wearing of religious visible signs or the expression of racist or fundamentalist ideas. Therefore religion can be an issue in the classroom, and with the teacher being an arbiter in such debates. The religious knowledge of the pupils can be a starting point for the lessons but it should get elaborated and developed in a more balanced and distanced way by the teacher through the use of the different tools of each subject matter in the curriculum (historians use documents, French literature teachers emphasise the symbolic and poetic dimension of sacred texts et cetera).

Finally, it is important to see that also in the *English context* different connotations and terms are used. The term 'religion' is understood variously and its meaning is dependent on the context in which the term is used. Common usages include the following: belief in a transcendent power or powers, religious practice, a particular way of organizing one's life closely linked to a system of morality, a body of sacred truths revered and believed by its adherents around which a structured community of believers and distinctive patterns or practice have developed, (occasionally) used for a cause, principle or activity pursued with great passion, devotion and ritual (from this perspective for instance Marxism or cricket could be described as a 'religion').

In ordinary English language use the terms 'religion' and 'religions' refer primarily to organized religions (the major world religions) or to denominations, especially within Christianity. Many people would understand a question as 'what is your religion?' in a 'cultural' way. People might answer that their religion is 'Church of England' or 'Christian', but that they are not fully practicing or believing members of that group or organization. Members of some 'minority' religious movements might also use the term 'religion' for their belief system – for example Jehovah Witnesses or Mormons. In ordinary language the term 'religion' would not be equivalent to 'spirituality'. There would be many who have a spiritual outlook of some kind who would not relate this to having a religion or being a member of a religion. Spirituality is often associated with a person's inner dimension (their 'spirit') or deepest centre, the point at which, for those with a religious outlook, a person is open to the transcendent and to the experience of ultimate reality.

Finally, 'religion' is, in English, also different from 'belief': 'Belief' is usually used for something that is known as true without necessarily having objective, evidential proof of its truth. Its primary use is for religious belief and here it could be individual, that is personalized, belief, or beliefs that are accepted on the authority of religious leaders, or religious scriptures and religious traditions that are accepted as presenting the authoritative truth. Belief is also used for non-religious contexts. So, someone might believe in the essential goodness of humanity or the equality of all humankind without making a link between these beliefs and any belief in a supreme being or without identifying this with a religious tradition.

Tentative conclusions

All in all we can conclude that 'religion' is a very broad term with different meanings in different contexts. This has to be kept in mind when interpreting the quantitative data. For instance, from the reactions of the Norwegian pupils it became apparent that they are inclined to understand 'religion' in an almost academic and neutral way, and that they focus more on institutionalized forms of religion than on personal religiosity. Many of the Norwegian students in the REDCo study seem to show indifference towards religion, but taking into account the way pupils interpreted the term 'religion' it can also be that Norwegian pupils just distance themselves from institutionalized forms of religion, but not so much from religiosity or spirituality. Thus, it is our contention that when interpreting and comparing data findings, it is important to be aware of the different interpretations both from an inter-language and an intra-language perspective of the term 'religion'.

We further need to conclude in respect with the term 'religion', that, although most frequently used in research, there is no universally accepted and standardized version of the term (see Smaling & Hijmans, 1997, pp. 15–25). In philosophy such terms are characterized as 'essentially contested concepts' (see Gallie, 1956). Crucial for such concepts is that there is continually debate about the connotation and denotation of these concepts. Besides, the different and differing varieties of connation can not be reduced to one single, exclusive or essential meaning. Religious, spiritual and world view education are precisely examples of such essentially contested concepts, which makes the use of these concepts both theoretically and methodologically a rather complicated adventure.

In this chapter we have substantiated this particularly for the term 'religion', on the basis of the processes and outcomes of the quantitative REDCo research project, as an exemplary case study. By focusing on the meaning-in-use (Wittgenstein, 1971) of the concept 'religion' – and to a lesser extent also of the notion 'world view' – and taking into account an inter-language and an intra-language perspective, we were able to articulate our *warranted presupposition* that only in such a way an interpretative framework can be built up for the particular uses of the term 'religion' in the research of an inter-European research group. Only by taking the different and differing contexts into account, thus through contextualisation of the data gathering process as well as the data interpretation procedure, can intersubjective accountable outcomes be supplied.

References

Debray, R. (2002). *L'Enseignement du fait religieux dans l'école laïque*. Paris: Odile Jacob.

Gallie, W.B. (1956). Essentially Contested Concepts. *Proceedings of the Aristotelian Society*, 56, pp. 167–198.

Harkness, J.A. (2003). Questionnaire Translation, in: J.A. Harkness, van de F. Vijver & P.Ph. Mohler (Eds.), *Cross-cultural Survey Methods*, New York: John Wiley and Sons, pp. 35–56.

Harkness, J.A., van de Vijver, F. & Johnson (2003). Questionnaire Design in Comparative Research, in: J.A. Harkness, van de F. Vijver & P. Ph. Mohler (Eds.), *Cross-cultural Survey Methods,* New York: John Wiley and Sons, pp. 19–34.

Kozyrev, F.N. (2003). The Religious and Moral Beliefs of Adolescents in St. Petersburg. *Journal of Education and Christian Belief,* 2003, 7(1), pp. 69–91.

Martin, W. & Tops, G.A.J. (1986). *Van Dale: Groot woordenboek Nederlands-Engels/ Engels-Nederlands, 2 delen.* Utrecht/Antwerpen: Van Dale Lexicografie.

Miedema, S. (2007). Contexts, Debates and Perspectives of Religion in Education in Europe. A Comparative Analysis, in: R. Jackson, S. Miedema, W. Weisse & J.P. Willaime (Eds.). *Religion and Education. Developments, Contexts and Debates.* Muenster: Waxmann, pp. 267–283.

Skeie, G. (2007). Religion and Education in Norway, in: R. Jackson, S. Miedema, W. Weisse & J.P. Willaime (Eds.). *Religion and Education. Developments, Contexts and Debates.* Muenster: Waxmann, pp. 221–241.

Smaling, A. & Hijmans, E. (1997) (Eds.). *Kwalitatief onderzoek en levensbeschouwing* [Qualitative research and world view]. Amsterdam: Boom.

Smith, W.C. (1964). *The meaning and End of religion. A new approach to the religions of mankind.* New York: Mentor.

Ter Avest, I., Bertram-Troost, G.D., Van Laar, A., Miedema, S. & Bakker, C. (2008). Religion in the Educational Lifeworld of Students: Results of a Dutch Qualitative Study, in: Th. Knauth, D-P. Josza, G.D. Bertram-Troost & J. Ipgrave (Eds.). *Encountering Religious Pluralism in School and Society. A Qualitative Study of Teenage Perspectives in Europe.* Muenster: Waxmann, pp. 81–111.

Van IJzendoorn, M.H. & Miedema, S. (1986). De kwaliteit van kwalitatief onderzoek [The quality of qualitative research], *Pedagogische Studiën*, 63, pp. 498–505.

Willaime, J.P. (2007). Qu'est-ce qu'un fait religieux?, in: D. Borne & J.P. Willaime (Eds.) *Enseigner les faits religieux. Quels enjeux?* Paris: A. Colin, pp. 37–57.

Wittgenstein, L. (1971). Philosophische Untersuchungen. Frankfurt am Main: Suhrkamp.

Yablokov, I.N. (1998) (Ed.). *Religious studies: Textbook and Dictionary.* – Moscow: Gardarica. [Религиоведение: Уч. пособие и уч. словарь-минимум по религиоведению / под.ред. И.Н. Яблокова. – М.: Гардарика, 1998.]

Pille Valk

The Process of the Quantitative Study[1]

The following chapter has in a sense a double aim – to give an overview about our quantitative survey procedure, and to offer some advice to those who want to learn from our experiences in setting up something similar.

The management of the research is described through the three main phases of the work – preparation, conducting the main data collection, and data processing. Before I can move forward I would like to point on some important issues we faced in our research design. First of all, the team acknowledged the real complexity of the challenging task – to conduct the survey in eight different countries in eight different languages, having national teams with differing experiences in the field of quantitative research. It also has to be mentioned that REDCo national teams had different scientific backgrounds as well – educational sciences, sociology, theology and religious studies, history, and psychology. On one hand it was enriching and interesting experience to work together, but on the other hand, such variety in backgrounds and 'professional languages' brought along also some difficulties which we had to overcome.

1. Nine months of preparation

The first brainstorming on the REDCo quantitative survey had taken place in February 2007 during the working conference in Melilla. The focused work on the quantitative study and its instrument design began in April 2007 in Hamburg where the quantitative study working group of eight people of the REDCo team, selected in Melilla, had a first working seminar. The meeting aimed to:
  1) set up the theoretical foundations of the survey,
  2) develop the very first draft of the questionnaire,
  3) design the procedure for the planned survey,
  4) find the most suitable *modus operandi* for the quantitative study working group.
The practical questions of questionnaire design are followed through a description of the research preparation procedure.

1.1 Three step procedure

The main target of the quantitative survey working group was to prepare our survey and to benefit from the REDCo framework as much as possible. Regarding conducting the study, we decided to go for the three step scheme: pre-pre-test, pre-test and main survey; the term 'pre-pre-test' was born quite spontaneously in the working process. This scheme took into consideration the complexity of the task we faced and was chosen to provide two feedback phases for reflection and space to make corrections.

The questionnaire for the pre-pre-test was worked out by the quantitative survey working group and it contained 102 items divided into three main groups – students' personal backgrounds and the relevance of religion; students' positions regarding religion and its role in

1   This article was supported by the European Union through the European Regional Development Fund (Center of Excellence CECT).

their relationships, and thirdly, students' view about religion in education. One of the conceptual discussions we had in the instrument design process was about including different scales (e.g. Eysenck Personality Questionnaire, Index of Paranormal Beliefs, Astley Scale of Theistic Belief, Indices of Alternative Spirituality, etc.) in our instrument. These suggestions were finally rejected for the following reasons: the REDCo quantitative research was not aimed to collect data comparable to all possible other surveys, but it had to keep its focus on our own study's research questions, and retain the links to the REDCo qualitative survey. The last issue was important because we were interested in triangulation of the outcomes of both survey outcomes, and our quantitative research was also aimed to test the findings of the qualitative study in a broader context (Cohen et al., 2007, p 142–144). We can point here also to the exploratory characteristic of the REDCo research – it was not aimed to test any particular theory, but to learn about the field, and to collect data to lay foundations for future theoretical developments. (Babbie, 2008, pp. 21–22; 97–99).

The pre-pre-test of the survey was carried out from the end of May until the beginning of June 2007, before the pupils left for the summer holidays in 5 countries (Estonia, Netherlands, Germany, France, and Spain). The pre-pre-test was carried out by at least 5 students, and was aimed to check:
–   how time consuming was the completion of the questionnaire,
–   how understandable were the questions in the instrument,
–   what questions would be criticized,
–   what parts could be de-motivating or interpreted as redundant,
–   which layout worked best?

All national teams where the pre-pre-test was conducted worked on the bases of similar guidelines prepared by the quantitative survey working group, and reported back about the results. On the bases of these reports, the coordinator of the quantitative study prepared a synopsis that served as a base for the future discussions and decision making in the ongoing work with the questionnaire. The pre-pre-test gave also some information about the translation issues we had to take into consideration and provided first feedback from students. It became clear that we need a specific tool to support the translation of the instrument and ensure that all the questionnaires in different languages will still be similar despite the difficulties of translation and allowing for differences between the languages[2]. So the work with a translation guide started. The second important outcome from the pre-pre-test feedback analysis was that the questionnaire could be somehow longer – according to the reports all 102 questions were answered mostly in 15–20 minutes. The pre-pre-test helped to identify which questions to skip or replace, because of their wording being hard to understand for pupils. We tested also different lay outs of the questionnaire – one was more 'uniform', the other with more variety. The preferences of the pupils were for the second one.

Further work with the instrument made it much longer. Being encouraged by the feedback from the pre-pre-test we added several items to the questionnaire, especially the statements from the qualitative survey to ask students' positions regarding the views of their European peers. Finally the pre-test instrument had 183 questions and its lay-out followed the pattern with variety preferred by the students in the pre-pre-test. The main structure of the questionnaire remained the same. The pre-test had also an open question to collect material on how students understand the term 'Religion'.

---

2   For more concrete elaboration on translation issues and terminology, have a look at chapter 1.2.

The pre-test questionnaire and additional tools – translation guide and field guide – were introduced to the national teams during the REDCo working conference in September 2007 in St. Petersburg.

The pre-test was conducted before the end of October and got 422 responses from seven countries. According to the field guide the minimum number of respondents per country was set as 50. Pre-test reports were composed according to the common guidelines. This phase of the work provided also a possibility to practice the data processing technique. To ensure that all data files will 'play together' the basic file for data insertion was prepared by a member of the working group. Data files were sent to Tartu for the analysis. This decision was made by the working group and originated from the idea that the easiest way is to process all data in one place – in Tartu University. One of the reasons behind this decision was also the fact that not all national teams could organize data processing by themselves. This way was considered also as less time consuming and easier to manage.

On the bases of the pre-test national reports and preliminary data analysis the compendium was composed, where all the items in the questionnaire were commented and reflected upon. The main problem the team had to struggle with was, as expected, the length of the instrument. Choosing between the questions also highlighted the different contexts in the different countries participating in our project – several questions had their own defenders, sometimes looking at the instrument from the perspective of different research fields. In this situation it became clear that distance working with 8 people on the final version of the questionnaire was too complicated. So the 'inner group' of four people was elected to finalize the work on the instrument, to calculate all pro et contra arguments and give the instrument its final shape. Although we had to cut out several interesting items, in the other hand, it helped to make the instrument more focused. After language editing and preparation of the toolkit for the main survey we were ready to start with the main test at the end of January 2008.

1.2 Modus operandi

Communication issues have a crucial position in the organization of international comparative research. In our project we dealt with these issues mostly in two levels – organizing the work of the quantitative study working group, and communicating the ideas and guidelines prepared by the working group to the national teams.

Most of the work in the preparation of the instrument and survey process management was done *via* e-mail discussions and especially Skype (internet) conferences[3]. The latter provides the opportunity for a 'virtual' meeting room, where all members could participate.

It is important to ensure that ideas and guidelines prepared in the working group will be communicated to all national teams who do the field work. In our case we used the venues of REDCo regular working conferences to provide information and explanations about the survey issues. Such a format gave also the possibility to get feedback and questions from colleagues, who sometimes pointed out the issues that needed more attention and elaboration.

2. Conducting the main data collection

First I would like to introduce the reader to the set of document tools related to the study and then I will present some outlines about the data collection process itself.

---

3   For more information about Skype and possibilities it provides, visit: http://www.skype.com/intl/et/

2.1   The toolkit of the survey

The inner group responsible for the preparation of the study – the editors of this book – worked out a set of documents, aimed to coordinate and support the survey process. On several practical issues we relied upon the experiences and ideas of the European Social Survey[4]. The European Social Survey is an academically-driven social survey designed to figure and explain the interaction between Europe's changing institutions and the attitudes, beliefs and behavior patterns of its diverse populations.

The REDCo survey toolkit contained the following documents:

a) Materials related to the instrument. The basic questionnaire for the survey was prepared in English, and it was circulated after language editing as a base for translations into national languages. It was agreed that all the national teams would use the same lay-out, and if they want to add some extra questions related to the particular national context they can do so, but the length of this section can not exceed one page. To ensure that all national teams will follow the same principles in translating the instrument, we prepared the translation guide.

b) How to guarantee that the survey will be presented to all students in a similar way in all countries? Foreseeing the possible hermeneutical problems in the classroom in the process of data collection, we prepared the annotation to the questionnaire that aimed to serve as a manual for teacher or researcher explanations, if students need some clarifications regarding the questionnaire and its items.

c) The sampling guide was worked out to ensure the necessary coherence of samples in all countries. This document was aimed to provide possibilities for both comparison between the particular countries as well for the cross-European comparisons. In the case of exploratory research such as this, representativity of the sample is not a crucial point (Babbie, 2008, p. 98).

d) The field guide provided outlines for the survey procedure, reports and documentation of the work. There were cases when the letter of permission from the national team was not enough for the schools. For such cases we prepared a document in which permission for conducting the survey was requested by the coordinator of the whole survey. In their fieldwork reports researchers were asked to describe the general atmosphere of the survey and to point out the circumstances that may influence the students' answers. Concrete examples about these cases are described in the national chapters of this book.

2.2   Main fieldwork

The REDCo quantitative survey was conducted from the end of January until the end of March 2008. All schools where the survey took place were contacted by national team researchers who also agreed upon the concrete procedure. There were countries where all questioning was conducted by our researchers, but there were also countries where out of pragmatic reasons researchers and teachers did the job of collecting data in cooperation.

Although the members of the 'inner group' were 'on-line' during the fieldwork period if the national teams needed advice, it was very important also to meet face to face. This opportunity came with the REDCo working conference in Soesterberg at the beginning of March 2008. The Soesterberg venue gave the opportunity to get an overview about the ongoing process of fieldwork, to find together solutions for the questions raised, provide clarifications regarding data processing procedures and other issues.

---

4   European Social Survey. URL: http://www.europeansocialsurvey.org/ (last accessed 08.12.2008).

3. Data processing and analysis

3.1 From questionnaires into data files

The quantitative survey working procedure prescribed that national teams take care of the data entry procedure. The general procedure was worked out on the bases of the pre-test materials. To ensure the uniformity of national data sets a member of the 'inner group' prepared a basic SPSS data file, which was circulated to all national teams. This system generally justified itself in that data entry was conducted uniformly and on schedule. To ensure that all the different problems would be solved in a way that will not make confusion for data analysis, people who did data entry in different countries had a 'hot-line' for consultation.

Coding of two items created more serious discussions.
a) Model of Religious Education.
   It was pointed on that in several cases the 'official' model of RE can take a very different form to the real class situation. E.g.: if there is a classical model of confessional RE in the country, some schools may concentrate strictly on the learning content related to the particular confession, while others introduce also several other confessions and religions. After discussion in the working group, the decision was made to stick to the official model in the coding of this item but when the schools in the sample are described in the National reports, these varieties may be recorded and analyzed.
b) Much more complicated problems arose about the coding of the professions of pupils' parents. We choose to use the coding system of professions presented by the ESeC project[5]. The project has a comprehensive web site with guidelines and explanations to support data processing. The variable of parents' professions has to be analyzed very carefully, keeping in mind that the validity of this data is not very high. It was decided to leave it to the national teams whether they used this variable in the analysis or not. Thus, we confined ourselves to the usage of information we have about the socio-economical background of particular schools and classes as it was presented by teachers and researchers.
c) Similar problems appeared also with the religious background of parents, especially with fathers' religious affiliation. In some countries (e.g. France) students complained about these questions being too personal. As a consequence, here we faced lots of missing data regarding these variables. And also here it was left for the national teams to make a decision about the usage of this data.

After overcoming most of these problems and difficulties the data files with the REDCo quantitative survey answers were sent to Tartu, Estonia for the analysis.

3.2 Data analysis

The general analysis scheme for our research was developed with the help of colleagues from the Institute of Sociology of the University of Tartu. For this reason the 'inner group' and

5   Funded under the EU's Sixth Framework Program Priority 7 (Citizens and Governance in a Knowledge Based Society), this project was designed to produce a European socio-economic Classification (ESEC) for use in comparative social science research across the EU. The strategic objectives addressed by the proposal were the integration and promotion of socio-economic research across the European Research Area. The project was undertaken between October 2004 and September 2006 by a consortium of nine institutions, lead by the Office of National Statistics in the United Kingdom. For more information, visit: http://www.iser.essex.ac.uk/esec/ and http://www.iser.essex.ac.uk/esec/guide/table1.php.

Tartu team met for a special three day meeting in Tallinn. It was decided to take two princi-ples as starting points for data analysis:
1. simplicity, and
2. closeness to the data.
This approach was chosen because of the following reasons:
-   Great contextual variety among the countries participating in the REDCo project, espe-cially regarding the role of religion in their societies. Also the position of Religion in Education differs from country to country. There are states where Religious Education is a compulsory subject for every pupil, and there are countries where this subject has a marginal place in the educational landscape. More concrete information about these is-sues is presented in the first REDCo project book "Religion and Education in Europe" (Jackson et al., 2007).
-   We did not have opportunities to build up representative samples on the basis of random sampling. Thus we have to be very careful in doing cross country comparison.
-   The data collected in our research is very rich. It is easy to be lost in this 'ocean of infor-mation'. We are quite aware that our data enables elaborated and complicated analysis schemes, especially in particular countries, but in doing an international study we have to keep in mind that 'portraits' of all countries have to be drawn according to more or less similar principles to give a reader the opportunity for comparison.
-   We wanted to develop a transparent scheme of analysis where the rate of subjectivity in data interpretation is as low as possible.
-   Last but not least – our national teams had differing experiences in using quantitative data analysis methods. If we add to this the issue that there are also several controversies among the different schools and traditions in doing quantitative research in different countries (e.g. different positions regarding the Likert scale we use in our questionnaire and its interpretation) the issue of developing the comparative survey acquires an even more challenging look.

The book is focused on the specific research questions, and our choice to approach the data took here the following path – if we could not find the answers to the questions by using simple methods of analysis, we would use the more complicated and complex analysis meth-ods.

Thus, we use mostly the outcomes from the uni- and bi-variate analyses, and different tests (chi-square, ANOVA, U-test) to identify statistically significant differences between the groups in the sample.
    1. The first level is the **uni-variate analysis:** to describe the main tendencies in data through the means[6] (and standard deviations), and frequencies.
    2. The second level is the **bi-variate analysis** (cross-tabulation) by independent variables such as gender, type of Religious Education, type of school, religious background, and migra-tion background (in countries where it makes a difference). The list of criteria was not closed, and national chapters have some variations here. These variations also reflect particular dif-ferences between the different 'schools' and traditions of doing quantitative research, as well the differing expertise our teams had in this field.

---

6   We choose the interpretation of the Likert scale where the responses "neither nor" in the calculation of the mean value were included with the value of 3. Thus, we interpret the "neither nor" position in our case as a "middle-position".

The main analysis of the data was conducted in Tartu using the SPSS program, and the outputs were sent back to the national teams together with the guidelines for writing the national reports. These materials served as foundations for the national chapters in this book. Some teams were able to conduct some additional analysis by themselves, and these results are seen also on the pages of the national chapters.

Conclusion

There are several issues we have learned from the process of conducting our comparative survey. One of the serious issues we faced during the work on the quantitative survey was time pressure. It appeared to be much more complicated than calculated beforehand. Different issues like unpredictable problems (e.g. of access) with some schools, differences in school holidays in different countries etc. slowed our work down. More time was also needed for data processing.

Thus, what role has religion in the lives of youngsters in Estonia, England, France, Germany, Netherlands, Norway, Russia, and Spain? How do they see religion in school and how do they look upon the impact of religion in their society? The following pages offer you the possibility to have a closer look at European students' positions on these issues. I really hope that our book can inspire new research to increase our knowledge about the impact of religions in the pluralistic society.

References

Babbie, E. (2008). *The Basics of Social Research*. Boston: Thomson Wadsworth.

Jackson, R., Miedema, S., Weisse, W. & Willaime J.-P. (2007). *Religon and Education in Europe. Developments, Contexts and Debates*. Muenster: Waxmann.

Cohen, L., Manion, L. & Morrison, K. (2007). *Research Methods in Education*. London: Routledge.

Ursula McKenna, Sean Neill & Robert Jackson

Personal Worldviews, Dialogue and Tolerance – Students' Views on Religious Education in England

1.   Introduction

1.1   Setting the scene

In order to understand the context from which our sample was taken, some brief explanation of religious education (RE) and the educational system in England is necessary. When state education was introduced in England in 1870, state 'board' schools were provided to supplement education already provided voluntarily by Christian religious bodies. Thus there has always been a partnership of state and Church in English public education. In the 1944 Education Act, publicly funded schools were divided into fully state funded 'county' schools and mainly state funded 'voluntary' schools (the religious bodies paid a modest contribution towards buildings and maintenance in voluntary *aided* schools – schools aided by the state).[1] In 1944 voluntary aided schools were mainly Church of England and Roman Catholic, plus some others including Jewish schools. Leaving aside a description of a complex history since 1988, we can say that today what were called 'county' schools are now 'community' schools – schools with no religious affiliation and taking students from the local neighbourhood. The category of voluntary aided has been extended to include more religions – mainly Muslim, but with a few Sikh schools and one Hindu school, more Jewish schools, and other categories of Christian school.[2] RE in community schools is taught according to a local syllabus, written by a local conference consisting of 4 committees (Church of England, other denominations and religions, local politicians and teachers) which has to agree the syllabus content. This enables some adaptation to local religious demography. All such syllabuses must conform to the law (of 1988) which requires that all should include material from Christianity and the other principal religions represented in Great Britain. Various non-statutory documents and examination syllabuses have identified these 'other religions' as Buddhism, Hinduism, Islam, Judaism and Sikhism. There is a withdrawal or 'opt out' clause so that parents can withdraw their children from RE if they wish to do so. RE in voluntary aided schools can be 'denominational', having nurturing aims. Whereas religious instruction was regarded as a form of nurture into a Christian way of life, RE in community schools post the 1988 legislation (and reflecting general practice since the mid 1970s) recognises that RE is concerned with developing pupils' knowledge and understanding ('learning about religion' or a 'non-confessional approach', not aiming to nurture faith), and providing opportunities for young people to re-

1   There is a further category of voluntary controlled schools from the 1944 settlement. These are Church of England schools that pay nothing towards costs. They retain a Christian ethos, but their religious education is the same as for community schools.

2   One further category of school should be mentioned (since we have one in our sample), namely Academies. In March 2000, the Government announced its intention to develop Inner City Academies (later called 'Academies'). Academies are 'all-ability, state-funded schools established and managed by sponsors from a wide range of backgrounds, including high performing schools and colleges, universities, individual philanthropists, businesses, the voluntary sector, and the faith communities', in: http://www.standards.dfes.gov.uk/academies/what_are_academies/?version=1 accessed 15 October 2008). Some of these are sponsored by Church related bodies.

flect on and discuss what they have learned ('learning from' religion). In 2004, a non-statutory national framework for the subject was published for use by agreed syllabus conferences (QCA, 2004). This document is being widely used and is the focus of a debate about whether RE should become centrally organised. In recent years, RE has been regarded officially as a subject that can contribute to citizenship education and to community cohesion.[3]

1.2   Description of sample

1.2.1   The schools

The sample for the English study was taken from a variety of school types mentioned above. In total 421 students (52% males and 47% females) attending years ten and eleven (14–16 year-olds) across sixteen secondary schools in England completed questions concerned with their experience of religion in school, their personal relationship with religion and, the role of religion in their relationships with others. The only school in the sample not following the locally agreed syllabus for RE was school 16 which used a Roman Catholic syllabus. Fourteen of the schools were co-educational and two schools (schools 5 and 6) were boys only. Likewise, fourteen of the schools were 'all ability' and two schools (schools 1 and 5) were grammar schools selecting students on the basis of their ability. Schools were drawn from a wide geographical area covering the North East and North West, South East and South West, Inner and Outer London, East Midlands, West Midlands and South Midlands.

1.2.2   Characteristics of the sample

Slightly over half (55%) of the students were 15 years of age, with more (28%) 14 than 16 (16%); slightly over half (52%) were male. Almost all (95%) were studying RE in the current year, and national legislation required them to have done so in all years since age 4. Almost all (91%) had been born in the UK and were British citizens (90%), with the remainder having been born, and holding citizenship, in a wide range of countries. This applied to an even greater extent to their mothers, of whom only 73% had been born in the UK, and to their fathers, for whom the corresponding figure was 68%. In all three cases, the largest foreign-born groups came from South Asia. A similar pattern applied to the main language/s spoken at home, which was English for 72% of students. A high proportion of students did not know their mother's (20%) and father's (33%) profession; of the remainder, European Socio-economic Classification (ESEC) category 3 was most common for mothers and categories 1, 2 and 8 for fathers. However, these categories do not match the British employment situation precisely. Only a minority of students knew what their father's religion / worldview was (41%); for mothers the figure was somewhat higher (48%), and the same figure applied to the students themselves, perhaps because they had a closer link to their mothers. For all three groups (fathers, mothers and children) a wide variety of religions / worldviews was quoted, but Islam was the commonest after the various varieties of Christianity. The following religious groups were mentioned by those students who claimed they did hold a religion / worldview: Christian (82), Muslim (49), Sikh (18), Hindu (15), Atheist (9), Agnostic (3), Jehovah's Witness (1), Jewish (1), Buddhist (1), Wiccan (1), Spiritualist (1), Deist (1), Pantheist (1). Only the first four groups were included in the comparison between adherents of different religions.

---

3   For more detailed accounts of the history of RE in England see Jackson and O'Grady, 2007 and Jackson, 2008. On the relationship between RE and citizenship education, see Jackson, 2003a.

1.2.3 Reflection on the sample

As the survey questionnaire was being administered in all eight countries within the REDCo Project, and because of limited resources, non-probability sampling methods, using purposive or judgmental sampling with certain criteria (gender, religious background, type of school, socio-economic background, RE model, urban and rural schools and migration background), were used. This sampling methodology was derived from the focus of the survey – to research the role that religion in education can play in the way students perceive religious diversity. The sample was constructed to reflect the diversity of young people in the 14–16 year old age group being educated within the state-maintained schools sector. Without information on the statistical population of 14–16 year olds in England we did not use 'quota sampling' that mirrored the English national situation. However, all of the above criteria were considered when selecting the schools to take part. The majority of secondary schools in England are co-educational, non-denominational community schools that by law have to provide non-confessional RE for all pupils throughout their schooling. England also, in certain parts of the country, has both co-educational and single sex selective grammar schools (with or without a religious foundation). There are also significant numbers of Church of England Voluntary Aided and Voluntary Controlled schools and Roman Catholic Voluntary Aided schools, plus some Academies (see 1.1 for an explanation of these categories). The sample incorporated students from most of these school types and sampling was sensitive to the relative numbers to be found in each category. The aim was to reflect the diversity and heterogeneity of the national population.

1.3   Description of the general procedure

1.3.1 Data collection

Participating schools were asked to follow a standard procedure. The questionnaires were administered in normal class groups to one class of students in each school. Teachers were told they could select any mixed ability class from years nine, ten or eleven. It transpired that no year nine classes were chosen; however each age in the 14–16 age range was represented. When returning the questionnaires, teachers were asked to relay to the research team any general comments or information on any circumstances in their school that might have influenced students' answers. Two teachers provided such feedback.

> *You will be interested to note that generally they found the exercise interesting and rewarding, and some useful conversation resulted. We are indeed a multi faith school of some 1600 students: nobody is withdrawn from RE and we even have a Jehovah's Witness electing first to do GCSE and now A level.*[4] (school 3)

> *The pupils did them well, until the end – they objected to the personal details bit, and so some are less than accurate.* (school 8)

The majority of students were receiving some form of RE in their current year of schooling. Students were given some background to the questionnaire, in particular its relationship to the wider European REDCo project and its aim of finding out the views of 14–16 year olds on the role religion plays or can play in Europe. Students were told they could ask for clarification if any question was unclear. Although students were given the choice not to participate, none decided not to take part in the survey. They were assured of confidentiality and anonymity.

---

4   GCSE and A Level are national exams normally taken at age 16 and 18 respectively.

When answering the open question twenty students made reference to the nature and value of the questionnaire itself. Most students were positive in their feedback, and their comments are illustrated in the following responses:

> *This is a good questionnaire and it has given me more understanding about different religious views. I now know what I believe about religion even though I don't believe in god.* (female, school 3)

Occasionally students objected to some of the information requested in the questionnaire:

> *There are some questions that my answers are not there and are kind of personal.* (female, school 13)

Other comments were directed towards improving the questionnaire:

> *Questions 76 & 77 should have had an answer box that said you don't mind who you walk around with.* (male, school 13)

Only two students protested that the questionnaire was a waste of their time or that they had not enjoyed completing it.

1.3.2 Data analysis

Percentages for each category are given in the text,[5] as means could be misleading where responses fell into two separate groups. As explained in the footnote, chi-square was used to assess differences between groups; differences are marked according to normal practice, (*) to indicate 'significant' ($p<.05$), (**) to indicate 'highly significant' ($p<.01$) and (***) to indicate 'very highly significant ($p<.001$). As there were a large number of questions, it was considered helpful to start by carrying out a factor analysis as this reduces them into a smaller number of factors, which represent questions that were answered in a similar way by the same students. The factor analysis is not presented here, but is used to structure the report, as it provided an overarching view of the underlying conceptual structure that guided students' responses. The second factor represented religious commitment and it is clear, especially for Muslim students, that the degree of religious commitment was the main influence on how students answered the questions.

---

5   Analysis was carried out using SPSS to produce descriptive statistics and cross tabulations. Where percentages are given these relate, unless otherwise stated, to students who answered the question; there was a small percentage (1–3%, varying between questions) of missing responses, and if these were included, some percentages would be slightly lower. Cross tabulations were analysed using chi-square as data from the Likert scales were ordinal and inspection showed that many distributions diverged from normality, for examples, the differences in religious observance, related to belief. Adjusted standardized residuals were calculated to identify the groups which were 'out of line', reflecting divergent attitudes or beliefs.

2. Presentation of results

2.1 What role has religion in the students' lives and their environment?

2.1.1. Data description

Religious observance

If we look first at how often students carried out religious activities, the means give a somewhat misleading impression since the distribution varied between questions. For the two questions which got the most positive responses, about thinking about religion and about the meaning of life, there was a fairly flat distribution, with the mean reflecting the fact that many students thought about these issues daily (29% for thinking about religion and 21% for the meaning of life) or weekly (30% and 21% respectively). Muslim students[6] were very highly significantly (***) more likely to think about religion daily than affiliates of other religions and, with Hindu students, significantly (*) more likely to think about the meaning of life on a daily basis. However, for praying and attending religious events, the distribution was strongly bimodal[7] with about half the students never participating (44% never prayed and 52% never attended religious events), but those who did participate doing so on a daily (24% for praying, 5% for religious events) or weekly (11% and 17% respectively) basis. Muslim and Hindu students were very highly significantly (***) more likely to pray daily than adherents of other religions (Figure 1) and Muslim students were very highly significantly (***) more likely to attend religious events daily. 'Sacred texts' showed a similar bimodal pattern with 10% reading daily and 12% weekly but 61% never reading sacred texts, while internet use showed a unimodal pattern with few using the internet frequently (3% daily, 6% weekly) and most

Figure 1:   How often do you pray? (Non-religious are those students who claim not have a religion/worldview)

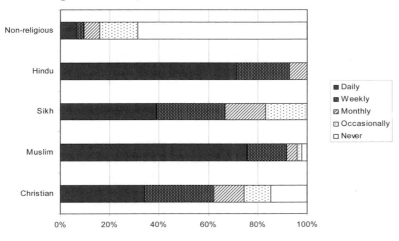

---

6   Throughout students are categorised according to their answer to question 127 on the questionnaire which asked them to write down their religion or worldview.
7   'Bimodal' implies a situation where most students fell into two separated groups, with few holding intermediate opinions, 'unimodal' where most students held similar opinions (which might be in the middle of the scale or at either end).

(59%) not using it at all. Muslim students were very highly significantly (***) more likely to read sacred texts daily than adherents of other religions and they were also very highly significantly (***) more likely to use the internet weekly or daily. However, students who identified with a religion/worldview participated in all these *'religiously committed'* activities highly significantly (**) more often than those who did not.

Importance of religion

When answering questions about religion in relation to themselves Muslim students gave the highest ratings (a mean of 3.79 on an 0-4 scale) but Hindu students (3.43) and Sikh students (2.95) also scored above the average (2.94) for all students who held a religion or worldview: Christian students scored below (2.79). For those who did not hold a religion or worldview, the mean was 1.11. Muslim students were also significantly (*) more likely to express belief in a God (98%: overall 39% held this view, whereas 34% thought there was some sort of spirit or life force and 27% thought there was none: 4% did not answer this question – Figure 2).

Figure 2:   Which of these statements comes closest to your position?

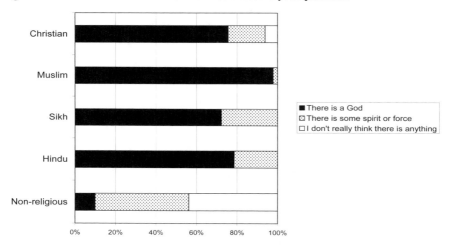

Muslim students very highly significantly (***) disagreed with both the statement expressing doubts about the existence of God (Hindus likewise disagreed with this position, but overall nearly half had doubts, with 17% strongly agreeing and 33% agreeing) and significantly (*) with the view that their beliefs might be open to change (overall more students strongly agreed [10%] or agreed [29%] that their beliefs might change than disagreed, with 33% uncertain as to whether they would or not). In terms of religious practice there was, as mentioned above, a divergence in practice across the sample.

When explaining their personal position with regard to religion (Questions 52-61) Muslim students were more inclined to agree strongly with some statements supporting the personal and cultural importance of religion: significantly (*) more for 'Religion helps me to be a better person' (overall 18% strongly agreed),and very highly significantly (***) more for 'Religion is important to me because I love God' (overall 21% strongly agreed). Overall only a minority (10%) felt 'Religion determines my whole life' but Muslim students were very highly significantly (***) more likely to do so (47% strongly agreed).

Sources of knowledge about religion

Muslim, Sikh and Hindu students saw family (Figure 3) as a very highly significantly (***)
and friends as a highly significantly (**) important source of information about different religions, compared to the other religions. Overall, family was the more important; 35% of students thought family very important, as opposed to 16% respectively for friends. The school
and faith community were also major sources of information, with 23% considering both very
important, but there was no significant difference between religions for their perceived value.
Muslim students also highly or very highly significantly saw books (***), media (***) and
the internet (**) as very important sources of information. Overall 'very important' scores
were 18% for books, 11% for the media, and 16% for the internet:

Figure 3:   How important are family as a source of information?

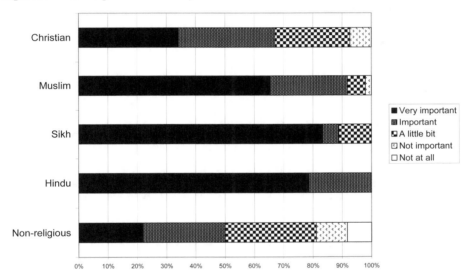

Talking about religion

In the final section of the questionnaire students were asked questions on the role religions
play in different relationships and contexts. Muslim students were very highly significantly
more likely to speak with family (***), friends (***) and religious leaders (***) (Figure 4)
than students from other religions. Overall, 12% of students spoke to family members every
day about religion; 22% did so weekly but 29% never did so: corresponding figures for
friends were 9%, 21% and 32% and for religious leaders 5%, 15% and 56%. There were no
significant differences between the students of different faiths or none with regard to speaking
with classmates, other students in school or teachers. Here the 'daily', 'weekly' and 'never'
figures were 5%, 35% and 24% for classmates (probably reflecting weekly RE lessons), 4%,
14% and 45% for other students in school and 2%, 45% and 26% for teachers (again reflecting weekly RE lessons). Muslim and Hindu students were significantly (*) more likely, at
school, to go around with other young people from different religious backgrounds (overall,
57% did, 24% did not, and 19% did not know their companions' religion).

Figure 4:   How often do you speak with religious leaders about religion?

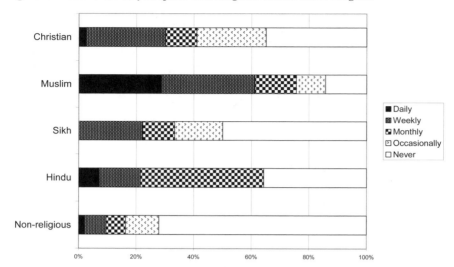

Gender

There was no significant difference between male and female students with regard to how important religion was to them, or whether they believed in God or a life force , or in most forms of religious involvement; but boys were significantly (*) more likely to pray on a weekly basis and were significantly (*) more divergent in how often they thought about religion than girls; boys were more likely to think about religion daily or not at all, girls to think about it on a weekly or monthly basis.

Boys also showed significantly (*) more divergent opinions than girls on whether religion helped them to be better people; boys were more likely to strongly agree and strongly disagree, girls to agree. Girls were highly significantly (**) more likely to doubt whether there was a God or not (Figure 5), and significantly more likely (*) to consider their feelings about religion were liable to change.

Figure 5:   Sometimes I doubt whether there is a God or not

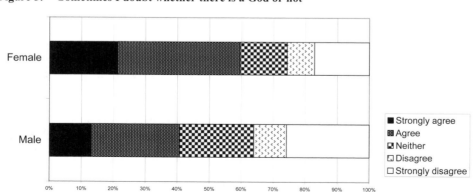

For most sources of information there were no gender differences, except for the faith community as a source, where differences were confined to those who had found it not very important. There were also no significant gender differences for most of the questions about how often students spoke to others about religion, with the exception that girls spoke to other students in school highly significantly (***) more frequently than boys.

Girls were also more likely to go round in school with others of the same religion, whereas boys were significantly (*) more likely to go round with peers of different religions, but there were no other significant gender differences for association with friends or relatives of the same or different religions.

Girls were also significantly (*) more likely to want to know what their best friend felt about religion, but students showed no other significant gender differences about expressing religious identity at school. Boys were significantly (*) more likely to feel that religion was something one inherited from one's family. Where a peer held a different religious view, boys were highly significantly (**) more likely to ignore the other, attempt to convince, or explain that their own opinions were the best, whereas girls were highly significantly (**) more likely to discuss with the other (Figure 6).

Figure 6:   I would try to discuss differing religious opinions with the other

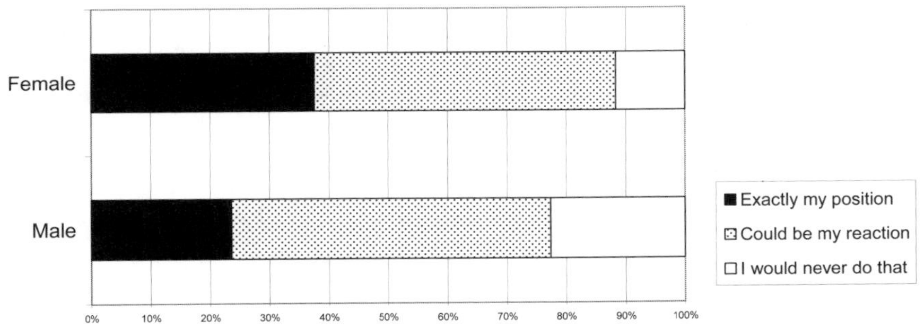

Synopsis of data – role of religion in students' lives
Family and school were easily the most important sources of information about religion. RE in schools and media coverage of current affairs where there is a religious element provide a degree of commonalty in the students' experience of religion, at the same time the diverse backgrounds and upbringings of the students means there is an inequality of experience of religion at a personal and communal level. The most interesting aspects of the data were the bimodal nature of many responses, with a marked dichotomy between those who participated actively in religious practice (participation in religious events, prayer and reading the scriptures) and those who did not, with the degree of participation differing between religions, and the gender differences, with boys tending to be more militant in their attitudes and girls stressing understanding and conformity. Muslim students of South Asian origin and African Christians were more likely to have strong theistic views. Students with commitment to a religion/worldview were more positive towards learning about different religions and were more tolerant in their outlook. The students' current position in relation to religious commitment and belief was strongly influenced by factors relating to their current stage of life and its contingent pressures including school examinations, relationships, youth culture and street culture.

2.1.2   Data interpretation

The fact that Muslim and Hindu students were more likely, at school, to associate with other young people from different religious backgrounds is probably due to Muslim and Sikh students being most likely to have students in their class who belonged to different religions. Again, when asked what would help people from different religions to live together in peace, the only statement that gave rise to differences between those students holding a religion or worldview was 'if they personally know people from different religions'. Differences between girls and boys in the degree to which they associate with people of different religions or speak with friends about religion might reflect their different patterns of socialisation – whether, for example, they spent their break times playing football in larger groups or chatting with a few friends. However, there were no questions in the survey to elicit this kind of information. Differences in religious practice, for example the frequency of prayer, were likely to be influenced by the specific expectations of different religions.

2.2   How students view religion in schools?

2.2.1   Data description

In the first group of questions, the most highly supported responses relate to elements which, when grouped together, correspond to principles and practices that characterise the dominant English inclusive model of approaching religion in school. This includes characteristics such as learning to have respect for everyone, whatever their religion (49% agreed strongly, and 42% agreed), understanding (18% / 52%) and getting knowledge about (34% / 57%) different religions, understanding others and living peacefully with them (20% / 51%), but also developing one's own point of view (30% / 45%) and developing moral values (20% / 46%). Interestingly, there were no significant differences between adherents of different religions on these issues.

The more negative responses had low positive response rates, questions such as there not being a place for religion in school life (40% disagreed strongly and 32% disagreed) and there being no need for the subject of RE (25% disagreed strongly, 35% disagreed). Again there was no difference between adherents of different religions for these questions.

As mentioned above, the feature of this group of questions was that, for almost all the questions, those who professed to having a religion/worldview were highly significantly (**) more positive in their ratings than those who did not. Where a question received a positive response from most students, such as 'At school I have opportunities to discuss religious matters from different perspectives' (overall, 30% agreed strongly) those with a religion /-worldview were highly significantly (**) more likely to agree strongly with the proposition, and those without, to agree or neither agree nor disagree. Where a question received a lower rating, such as 'Learning about religions at school helps me make choices between right and wrong' (35% strongly agreed or agreed, 34% neither agreed nor disagreed and 31% disagreed or strongly disagreed), those with a religion / worldview were very highly significantly (***) more likely to strongly agree or agree. This pattern of very highly significantly (***) stronger support by those who had a religion or worldview applies also to the statement 'Learning about religions at school helps me to learn about myself' where a majority of students overall disagreed strongly (16%), disagreed (25%), or neither agreed nor disagreed (29%). Where a question is negative in respect of the English inclusive approach, such as 'Pupils should study religious education separately in groups according to which religion they belong' (* – overall

35% strongly disagreed and 34% disagreed) and 'There should be no place for religion in school life' (*** – overall 41% strongly disagreed and 32% disagreed) the pattern is reversed, with those with a religion / worldview disagreeing significantly or very highly significantly more strongly than those without.

A large majority of the students, with or without a religion / worldview, favour integrated RE. Similarly, a minority of both groups agreed with the proposition that 'Religious education should be taught sometimes together and sometimes in groups according to which religions students belong to' with no significant difference between them (overall figures were 19% agreeing or strongly agreeing, as opposed to 48% disagreeing or strongly disagreeing).

Overall this pattern applied to almost all questions in this group, and indicates that students with a religion/worldview were committed to inclusive RE; they did not display intolerance towards other religions. The exceptions to the general pattern that this group was more committed to an inclusive approach to religion in schools were that there was no significant difference between the two groups for the statements 'At school I get knowledge about different religions' and 'At school I learn to have respect for everyone, whatever their religion'.

We may also consider differences between religions / worldviews in attitudes to religion in school. When answering questions on the role of religion in school, Muslim students were highly or very highly significantly more likely to agree strongly with those statements which suggested that the outward expressions of faith groups should be accommodated within school. These included the wearing of more visible religious symbols (** – the headscarf was mentioned in the questionnaire: overall 31% of students strongly agreed that such symbols should be allowed), absence for religious festivals (*** – overall, 32% strongly agreed), being excused from some lessons for religious reasons (*** – overall 15% strongly agreed), the provision of prayer facilities (*** – overall 17% strongly agreed but in the UK prayer rooms are increasingly installed in educational establishments such as universities – Figure 7) and voluntary religious services being part of school life (** – overall 12% strongly agreed).

Figure 7:   Schools should provide facilities for pupils to pray in school

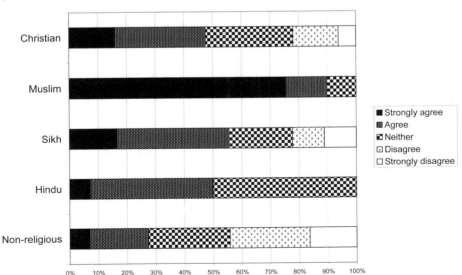

Christian students were mildly in agreement with these statements. Hindu students were significantly (*) more likely to agree that at school students should be able to talk and communicate about religious issues (consistent with majority opinion – overall 24% strong agreement, 50% agreement).

As mentioned in the introduction, most schools in England are non-denominational, community schools, which by law have to provide non-confessional RE for all pupils. As denominational schools in the study, are in the minority it was decided not to divide the schools up by religious background, and a cross tabulation was carried out to compare the schools individually, since, as mentioned in the introduction, the schools varied very markedly in their social and ethnic composition.

School 14 (a rural/monocultural community school) was significantly different from the others, with more students reporting they had not participated in RE this year and fewer reporting classmates of different religions. Correspondingly, students at school 14 had more negative scores for the questions related to inclusive approaches, whereas those at other schools, such as schools 9 and 13 (both inner-city / multicultural schools) had more positive scores. Students at school 14 were significantly less likely to talk to teachers about religion or to socialise with peers with different religious backgrounds after school, compared to students from schools 9 and 13. Together with students at school 16 (the Catholic school, mentioned below) they were significantly more likely to listen to, but not be influenced by, a student from a different religious faith.

There was a different pattern for some categories, but given that all the schools except one (school 16) were following the same model of RE, no overarching significance can be attached to these differences. School 16, a Roman Catholic school, showed few significant differences from the other schools, including on such categories as 'how important is religion to you?' Students at this school were significantly more likely to consider 'There is some sort of spirit or life force' whereas a large majority of those at schools 13 (a school with many African Christian students) and 2 (a school with mainly Muslim students) considered 'There is a God' and were more likely to conform to religious practices, for example to read sacred texts and pray every day. However, students at this Roman Catholic school were significantly less likely to have friends who did not belong to their own religion or whose religion they did not know, and to feel that talking about religion was embarrassing. They were also neutral in their feelings about people from other religions.

Students at schools 2 (with mainly Muslim students) and 13 (with many African Christian students) were also significantly more likely to think about religion every day, to feel religion was important to them because they loved God, to consider religion determined their whole life, and that it made them a better person and to reject the suggestion that religion was nonsense. They also considered religion an important aspect of history and were less likely to doubt whether there was a God. However they considered that talking about religion was interesting because people had different views and felt that talking about religion helped them understand others. Students at school 9 (an inner city school with half its students from ethnic minorities) were less likely to consider religion a source of aggressiveness or that talking about it led to disagreement, and rejected talk of the stupidity of religion or that religion did not interest them at all. They also felt that talking about religion helped them to live peacefully together with people from different religions. They were also less likely to say that they did not know much about religion and therefore could not have an opinion, and to consider that talking about religious topics was boring. Conversely, they felt that talking about religion helped them to understand better what was going on in the world, and were more likely to discuss opinions with a student of a different religious faith, rather than taking a more confrontational view. They also felt that knowing people from different religions personally, or doing something together with them, would help understanding and the ability to live together. However they rejected the idea that confining one's own religion to private life would help those from different religions to live together.

Those at schools 9 (an inner city school with half its students from ethnic minorities) and 13 (a school with many African Christian students) were significantly more likely to take the view that talking about religion helped to shape their own views and felt that respecting the views of others helped to cope with differences. Students at school 13 were significantly more likely to reject the proposition that it did not matter what their friends thought about religion. They also felt knowing about each other's religions would help people from different religions live together, an opinion they shared with the rural school 14 and the Catholic school 16.

Synopsis of data – religion in schools

Students responded to questions of the place of religion in schools, the religion of the teacher and the organisation of teaching (whether in single faith or mixed faith groups) in terms of democracy and citizenship, religious freedom and tolerance. The most striking aspects were the commitment of most students, especially those with a religion / worldview, to an inclusive approach to RE, and that differences between students related primarily to their own belief patterns. Differences between schools reflected the views of their constituent students, since almost all schools followed a similar RE approach. The majority of students were in favour of including religion in school life, holding the view that students should be able to talk and communicate about religious issues, that expressions of faith should be accommodated within school and agreeing with the need for the subject of RE. Students commonly perceived the content of such RE as multi faith and generally favoured RE taught in mixed faith classes; Muslims, Christians and non-religious alike, had assimilated the multi faith and inter faith ethic promoted by the English model of RE. Students who themselves had belief gave stronger support to the idea of an inclusive, integrated RE.

2.2.2 Data interpretation

The preference for an inclusive approach to religion in school is derived from the factor analysis of students' responses and is therefore grounded in students' views rather than being imposed by the researchers, since it draws on answers across different sections of the questionnaire. The analysis indicates that students were perceiving patterns in the questions themselves, rather than following the agenda of the questionnaire. This pattern of response also indicates that students had absorbed the approach which has been widely adopted in English state school RE since the 1970s (Copley, 1997; Jackson, 2007; Jackson & O'Grady, 2007). In this, RE is seen to encompass both 'learning about' religions and 'learning from' religions, including the opportunity for personal reflection as well as some engagement with the impact of religion upon social issues, such as aiming to improve community relations through increased knowledge and understanding. RE is seen to be concerned with the development of understanding of religious traditions, with the development of personal views of participants, and at a social level with what today we might call the promotion of tolerance and social or community cohesion (Jackson, 2005/2006a; Ofsted, 2007; OSCE, 2007). Engagement with the religions, or with particular examples from them, opens up the possibility of learning from them (Grimmitt, 1987) or being edified by them (Jackson, 1997/2004). RE is seen both in terms of gaining knowledge and understanding of different religions, and in developing personally and socially as a result of engaging with that knowledge. What was striking was that students with a religion / worldview were more receptive to this approach, indicating that they were more receptive to teaching about religion (as opposed to teaching of religion) than those without any formulated worldview.

This inclusive religious education attitude also has high loadings for responses which indicate that RE can help deal with the problems in society through better understanding of others and other religions. A majority of students agreed with the statement that at school students should 'learn the importance of religion for dealing with problems in society'. In doing so they support the view proposed in a recent Ofsted report, Making Sense of Religion, which argued that the subject should be more overtly concerned with issues of social cohesion and suggested that, as part of the RE curriculum, students should learn more about the complexities of religion and its role in the modern world (Ofsted, 2007). These students also felt RE would help them communicate better with others and better understand current events. They found RE interesting, and felt it helped them to understand themselves better, develop their own views and make moral choices better. They rejected the propositions that there was no place for religion in school life or that RE should be optional, and felt school was an important source of knowledge about both other religions and to help them learn about their own. They felt respect for those who practised other religions and felt that voluntary religious services could be part of school life, that school meals should take into account religious food requirements, that pupils should be able to wear religious symbols at school, including more visible as well as discreet symbols, and that students could be absent from school at the time of their religious festivals. These students valued personal contact with pupils from other religions and doing things together, and felt what they thought about religions was open to change. In other words, this inclusive attitude sought to understand and tolerate, or even respect, a range of religious views, with the aim of increased social cohesion and harmony. It did so from a perspective where religion was seen as personally valuable, in that students felt religion helped them to be a better person and to cope with difficulties, and these, and the responses related to religious practice mentioned above, showed an overlap between this approach and the religiously committed approach mentioned in the previous section. Those with an inclusive attitude were sympathetic to religion in a diversity of forms and the needs of the religious, while those with religious commitment were not opposed to other religions - but they were opposed to anti-religious views, which their peers were agnostic about.

The other striking aspect of the analysis was that students' attitudes related to their own individual beliefs, rather than their school's approach; this reflects the situation in England, where most schools take an inclusive approach, including those which have a religious character.

2.3   How students view the impact of religion?

2.3.1   Presentation of findings

The group of questions (103-106) on the effect of differences again stressed tolerance, with students agreeing that respect for others' religions helped them to cope with differences, while disagreement on religious issues led to conflict. Students disagreed with the two questions which suggested an intolerant response (105 and 106). Those with a religion / worldview were significantly more likely to agree that 'Respecting the religion of others helps to cope with differences' (overall 21% strongly agreed with this statement and 44% agreed) and to disagree with 'I don't like people from other religions and do not want to live together with them' (overall 51% strongly disagreed and 26% disagreed). There was no significant difference between those with and without a religion / worldview for the other two questions, although those with a religion / worldview were more ready to reject the suggestion that 'People with strong religious views cannot live together' (overall 24% strongly disagreed and 25% disagreed, as opposed to 21% who agreed or strongly agreed).

Figure 8: Religion belongs to private life

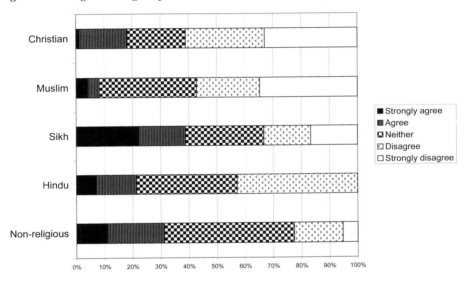

Common interests and understanding were again stressed in the final group of questions, with personal knowledge and joint involvement also seen as important by most students (combining 'very important' and 'important' gave scores of 86% for 'If people share common interests', 85% for 'If they know about each others' religions', 79% for 'If they personally know people from different religions' and 77% for 'If they do something together'). Students with a religion/worldview considered these approaches significantly more important than those without. Strong laws about religion and keeping religion private were rejected by most students, especially those with a religion/worldview in the case of strong laws (overall, 36% thought they were not important and 27% had no view), but there was no difference for keeping religion private (47% thought this was not important and 21% had no view).

A number of questions contained statements linking religion with negative associations, for instance, 'Religion is a source of aggressiveness' (only 4% strongly agreed and 30% strongly disagreed) and 'I and my friends talk about how stupid religion is and what cruelties are carried out in its name' (4% strongly agreed and 36% strongly disagreed).

Muslim students were more likely to strongly disagree with some of these negative statements than other religions; Christian students mildly disagreed. Muslim students were significantly (*) more likely to strongly disagree with views that 'Religious people were less tolerant towards others' (overall 42% were undecided and 15% disagreed strongly; only 5% agreed strongly) and highly significantly (**) more likely to disagree that 'Religion should belong to private life' (Figure 8 – overall 37% were undecided, and 14% disagreed strongly; 10% agreed strongly). Sikh students were significantly (* and ** respectively) more likely to agree strongly with these views. Muslim and Sikh students were significantly (*) more likely to agree with the more positive view that talking about religion helps them to live peacefully with others from different religions (overall 11% agreed strongly, but 34% had no view) and Muslim students were significantly (*) more likely to strongly agree that talking helps them to understand what is going on in the world (overall, 16% agreed strongly and 27% were non-committal).

When asked what would help people from different religions live together in peace the only statement that gave rise to differences between the religious students was 'If they personally know people from different religions'. Muslim students were significantly (*) more likely to feel this was very important, and Christian students to feel that it was not important: overall 33% thought knowing people from other religions was very important, 46% thought it was quite important and 16% that it was not important.

Synopsis of data – impact of religion

The main finding here, consistent with the issues discussed in previous sections, is that those with a religion / worldview were more tolerant towards different religions and worldviews than those without and were prepared to see common experience as a basis for understanding. The ideal of a harmonious multi faith community was very evident in the students' responses overall, though some doubt the possibility of achieving this ideal perceiving there to be conflict potential in religion. The value of inter faith dialogue was generally recognised by students from the different educational contexts. However, there were marked differences between students with different worldviews; contrary to what is often implied by some sections of the British media, Muslim students in this sample were both more committed to the value of religions and to the contribution of those with religious views and to co-existence between those of different religions. The RE lesson was the most likely place for students to engage in discussion between different religious viewpoints. The subject was seen by students as providing a safe forum for dialogue about religious and existential issues. Outside the RE lesson pupils were most likely to discuss religion with those from similar religious backgrounds to themselves. Boys were more likely to associate with friends of different religions and girls to know what their friends think about religion. The discussion of religious issues and personal belief was problematic for the indigenous white students in more rural areas in particular where they faced a climate of youth apathy and negativity towards religion. Religion was more often a topic of conversation in urban areas and among South Asian Muslims and black Christians.

2.3.2   Data interpretation

The results in this section reflect the values propagated in the inclusive approach to RE, discussed in a previous section, where those who had a belief or worldview themselves were more oriented to inter-faith encounters. In other words, those with a religion or worldview saw interpersonal encounters as the most productive way of ensuring harmony and of course school offers an arena for this. It is notable that Muslim students, despite their popular reputation to the contrary, were those most supportive of personal interfaith encounter; for some questions Sikh students were more sceptical.

3.   Comparison with the results of the qualitative survey

Sample comparison

The quantitative questionnaire was designed and used in such a way that the links are very strong between it and the earlier qualitative REDCo study of young people's perspectives on religion in society and school (Knauth et al., 2008; Ipgrave & McKenna, 2008). The statements used in the quantitative questionnaire were taken from findings of the REDCo qualitative study including the English study. The interest in assessing the students' attitudes in relation to qualities of tolerance and open-mindedness reflects the use of such concepts and terminology by the young people themselves in the earlier study and the same themes are revisited (e.g. the accommodation of religious requirements in school, whether or not RE should be taught in separate groups and the degree to which religion is discussed with peers).

The qualitative study included four schools as opposed to the 16 schools which participated in the quantitative study, but these four schools, in location (rural, suburban and inner city) and student population in terms of migration and religious background reflected, within the limitations of the smaller sample, the range of student experience aimed for in the quantitative sample. The two surveys were thus devised so that they could inform each other's analysis, and provide checks, confirmation or extension of each other's findings.

Religion in students' lives

In some cases comparison was straightforward giving the same answers for the larger sample that the smaller sample had offered. Both surveys demonstrated clearly, for example, that family and school were easily the most important sources of information about religions (Ipgrave & McKenna, 2008, p.123). For the analysis and interpretation of the data in both cases, the distinction between those students with belief commitment and those without was found to be useful, often more useful than a distinction between students affiliated to different religions (e.g. Christianity or Islam). Similarities between the outlook of the Muslim students with a South Asian family origin and African Christian students were noted in both studies. The qualitative report recognises the sizeable groups of these students who have been brought up in a religious tradition in their homes, places of worship and instruction, how most have adopted their family and community faith as their own and allowed it to influence their perspectives and practice (Ipgrave & McKenna, 2008, p.125). In the present study it is noted that the Muslim and African Christian students are more likely than their peers to have strong theistic views ('There is a God') and conform to the religious practices of their traditions. The qualitative study suggested an 'inequality' in experience of religion among students according to whether or not they had a background of religious nurture and practice or whether within their school and local context they had opportunities to meet regularly with people of different religions. This inequality or divergence of experience is presented plainly through quantitative methods and the strongly bimodal distribution for students' participation in religious events and prayer and engagement with religious text. In the discourse of the students taking part in the qualitative study, a distinction emerged between 'believer' and 'unbeliever'; it was used by some of the young people themselves as a tool for interpreting certain attitudes and behaviours of their peers (Ipgrave & McKenna, 2008, p.136) and for understanding examples they cited of the lack of mutual comprehension between those who hold theist or atheist positions. The distinction between those with a religion/worldview and those without has also proved pertinent to the analysis of the quantitative survey which has provided more data on the similarities and differences of the viewpoints held by these two categories. The stronger agreement of those with a religion with *'religiously committed'* categories in the quantitative questionnaire was to be expected, but some of the most interesting findings have been the greater degree of agreement with tolerance towards those of other beliefs demonstrated by this group, and the stronger support among them for an inclusive and integrated RE with students taught together whatever their religious background.

Religion in school

Responses from School 14 in the quantitative study confirmed what students from School B in the qualitative study had indicated, that students without religious belief themselves were less likely to know about the religion of their peers (Ipgrave & McKenna, 2008, p. 135). In other areas touched upon there were differences in the kind of information the different approaches were able to uncover. In relation to gender, for example, a few of the girls indicated in an interview that there was a difference in the way girls and boys responded to RE and in their readiness to talk about the 'deeper' themes of religion (Ipgrave & McKenna, 2008, p. 128) but there was insufficient evidence in the rest of the data to draw any conclusions that differentiated between boys' and girls' perspectives. This contrasts with the data produced by the present study which was more definite in finding that the girls gave 'significantly more positive responses' to questions indicating greater understanding of and respect for other religions, and were 'highly significantly more likely' to discuss religion with others, while boys were 'highly significantly' more likely to either ignore the different religious viewpoint of the other or argue that their own view is the right one. In the quantitative data boys were significantly more likely to associate with friends of different religions and girls to know what their best friend thought about religion. This may reflect the different socializing patterns between the boys and girls of this age. There were no significant differences in background variables and whether or not the boys or girls had a religion.

Religion in society

The sensitivity of religion as a topic of conversation gained greater prominence as an issue with qualitative methods. While students in the quantitative survey largely disagreed that religion was embarrassing to talk about or that religion was a source of aggressiveness, students in the qualitative study shared, both in questionnaire answers, and at more length and detail in interviews, their concerns about appearing 'uncool' and being teased if they discussed religious questions out of the RE class, and a sense of a real danger that conflict could arise between different groups at school should religious questions be raised outside lesson time. This may be because the more open format of the qualitative questionnaire and interview enabled students to share and interpret particular instances of tension or discomfort in their school lives (Ipgrave & McKenna, 2008, p. 135, p. 144f.).

Though degrees of support might vary among the students as a whole, whether or not they had a religion/worldview, there were few voices that signalled disagreement with an inclusive and integrated approach to RE. In this, the evidence that the quantitative survey supplies of young people's attitudes towards RE conforms very closely to the findings of the qualitative study. The students in both studies largely answered in favour of a multi faith RE taught with all students together. This preference shows that students, in the 'safe space' of the RE classroom at least, are open to engagement with religious difference and with people of different religions. In the context of English education, the quantitative survey confirms the conclusions of the qualitative report that the students' views about RE were largely conventional and that for the most part 'Muslims, Christians and non-religious alike had assimilated the multi faith and inter faith ethic promoted by the English model of education and accepted the principle that familiarity with the other generates acceptance and respect' (Ipgrave & McKenna 2008, p. 141).

4.   Conclusions

We may consider how the English students responded in relation to the following research hypotheses:

1.a) Religious students are less tolerant than non-religious students.

1.b) Religious students are less open to dialogue on religious issues than non-religious students.

As mentioned above, and further discussed below, these propositions did not apply to the English students. As evidenced in the factor analysis and in the bivariate results, students who answered positively to the belief questions also tended to answer positively to the inclusive learning questions. Intolerant students tended to be those who did not claim a religion/ worldview. This finding is of interest to RE, suggesting that encouraging the affirmation of the faith or worldview of students and providing students with opportunities to explore their own beliefs may be a contributor to the development of positive relations with those of other faiths, at least in the English system. The finding also implies that there is still work to be done to encourage respect for believing positions among those who do not themselves believe. An openness to hearing the views of others and expressing personal views is consistent with an approach to RE that encourages 'learning from' as well as 'learning about' religion(s), an approach which is well established in English RE.

2.a) Students who have encountered religious diversity in education are more tolerant

2.b) Students who have encountered religious diversity in education are more open to dialogue on religious issues.

3.a) Students who have personally encountered religious diversity are more tolerant.

3.b) Students who have personally encountered religious diversity are more open to dialogue on religious issues.

For both 2 and 3, there is relatively limited evidence given that, as discussed above, the RE curriculum followed in most schools stresses religious diversity, and relatively few children in the whole population, and none in this study, learn at schools which have a strong and restrictive ethos. In this respect English schools differ from those in some other countries, (such as Northern Ireland in the United Kingdom) where substantial numbers of schools have a strong religious affiliation. Most students were in urban schools where there are usually representatives of a variety of ethnic groups. As discussed above, the attitude of students in the 'monocultural', rural school does give some support to these four propositions, as these students did appear less open-minded. They contrast with the students in the two multicultural schools (schools 2 and 13). It is also notable that students in the Roman Catholic school, the only one with a specific religious affiliation, shared the attitudes of their peers in the other schools.

In the responses to the questionnaire there was a majority voice and general consensus in favour of the inclusive approach to RE most commonly practised in English schools, with positive messages about the importance of learning together and learning from each other in multi faith RE lessons. Possible reasons for this are:

–   Religious education in English schools is doing a good job in communicating the rationale behind this type of RE and in conveying these positive messages and attitudes.
–   Students tend to be conventional; they find it hard to conceptualise any different model of RE from the one with which they are most familiar (this is also implied by the pan European findings of the qualitative study where students tended to be in favour of the model they were familiar with, even though these models were very different from each other (see Knauth et al., 2008).
–   Religious education reflects the inclusive discourse prominent in society in general and students have picked up the same discourse of tolerance, respect, inclusiveness and listening to others from society (the fact that there is no significant difference between the views of the students who experience Roman Catholic confessional RE and the rest of the sample supports this view).

It is most likely that a combination of these factors influences students. The above three reasons were reflected in responses from students in all schools, with the exception of the Roman Catholic school. The fact that there were variations of degree in students' views points to the influence of other factors, one of which was religious commitment.

As already mentioned, one of the most interesting findings was the greater degree of tolerance towards those with other religions/worldviews and the stronger support for an inclusive RE with students taught together whatever their religious background among 'believers'. What are the implications of this for RE?

The difference in the religious background of young people across the country has led to different suggestions for RE.

a) *Separate RE (understood as religious nurture) for different faith groups*: for example, own faith only RE for different religious groups whether in faith-based schools or separate RE classes (Hargreaves, 1994 [replied to in Jackson, 2003b] and NUT, 2008)
b) *RE with a main emphasis on teaching of children's own faith but also some teaching about other faiths* (as currently found in many church schools)
c) *Inclusive multi-faith RE* (the norm in English community schools)

The findings that those with a religion/worldview showed a high degree of tolerance and that there was support for enquiry based RE suggests that religiously committed students do not want the form of RE exemplified by model a). The findings also show it is very possible to retain firm commitment and integrity of one's own faith while learning about other faiths.

The findings imply that model b) is acceptable, as firm religious commitment of their own appears to have positive impact on the students learning about and respecting others' faith (it is the model of the inter faith movement that promotes dialogue and cooperation between different religious communities across the country). This model seems appropriate in a homogeneous religious context but direct encounter with people of different religions (a more powerful learning experience than anything second hand) would be lacking unless facilitated through strategies such as the use of visitors and visits, school twinning, exchanges and electronic communication, such as email dialogue.

Model c) is positive in promoting the inclusive learning from and about religious differences that the students asked for. However, the findings also show the value of students' own religious viewpoints being affirmed and developed, indicating that those more secure in their own positions are more able to appreciate better the views and commitments of others. The evidence could be used to support approaches that encourage students to articulate, express and exchange their own views and understandings, in addition to 'learning about' religions from teachers who draw on a variety of educational sources.

Trends in the responses from students seem consistent with the open and liberal approach to RE already operating in state community schools in England, and in some religiously based schools. RE is seen by students as potentially an arena for dialogue between those from different religious and secular backgrounds. The move towards including issues related to society, such as community cohesion, as well as issues of personal development, is consistent with this. In developing approaches that capitalise on self expression and student interaction as well as contact with people from the wider community, educators and policy makers might give more attention to recent pedagogical developments, such as those using interpretive strategies (Jackson, 1997; 2004; 2006b; 2008), experiments with young people's dialogue (Ipgrave, 2003; McKenna, Ipgrave & Jackson, 2008) and with critical approaches to the promotion of religious literacy (Wright, 1996).

References

Copley, T. (1997). *Teaching Religion: Fifty Years of Religious Education in England and Wales*. Exeter: University of Exeter Press.

Grimmitt, M. (1987). *Religious Education and Human Development: The Relationship Between Studying Religions and Personal, Social and Moral Education*. Great Wakering: McCrimmons.

Hargreaves, D.H. (1994). *The Mosaic of Learning: Schools and Teachers for the Next Century*. Demos Paper 8, London: Demos.

Ipgrave, J. (2003). Dialogue, citizenship and religious education, in: R. Jackson (Ed.), *International Perspectives on Citizenship, Education and Religious Diversity*. London: RoutledgeFalmer, pp. 147–68.

Ipgrave, J., & McKenna, U. (2008). Diverse experiences and common vision: English students' perspectives on religion and religious education, in: T. Knauth, D-P. Jozsa, G. Bertram-Troost & J. Ipgrave (Eds.), *Encountering Religious Pluralism in School and Society. A Qualitative Study of Teenage Perspectives in Europe Religious Diversity and Education in Europe Series*. Münster: Waxmann, pp. 133-147.

Jackson, R. (1997). *Religious Education: An Interpretive Approach*. London: Hodder and Stoughton.

Jackson, R. (Ed.) (2003a). *International Perspectives on Citizenship, Education and Religious Diversity*. London: RoutledgeFalmer.

Jackson, R. (2003b). Citizenship as a Replacement for Religious Education or RE as a Contributor to Citizenship Education?, in: R. Jackson (Ed.), *International Perspectives on Citizenship, Education and Religious Diversity*. London: RoutledgeFalmer, pp. 67-92.

Jackson, R. (2004). *Rethinking Religious Education and Plurality: Issues in Diversity and Pedagogy*. London: RoutledgeFalmer.

Jackson, R (2005). Intercultural Education, Religious Plurality and Teaching for Tolerance: Interpretive and Dialogical Approaches, in: R. Jackson & U. McKenna (Eds.), *Intercultural Education and Religious Plurality*. University of Oslo: Oslo Coalition on Freedom of Religion or Belief, pp. 5-13.

Jackson, R. (2006a). Promoting Religious Tolerance and Non-discrimination in Schools, in: V. Elsenbast, P. Schreiner & F. Schweitzer (Eds.), *Europa - Bildung - Religion. Demokratische Bildungsverantwortung und die Religionen*. Münster: Waxmann, pp. 211-225.

Jackson, R. (2006b). Understanding religious diversity in a plural world: The interpretive approach, in: M. de Souza, K. Engebretson, G. Durka, R. Jackson & A. McGrady (Eds.), *International Handbook of the Religious, Moral and Spiritual Dimensions of Education*. The Netherlands: Springer Academic Publishers, pp. 399-414.

Jackson, R. (2007). Religion in the Educational system of England and Wales: law, policy and representation, in: John R. Hinnells (Ed.), *Religious Reconstruction in the South Asian Diasporas: From one generation to another*. London: Palgrave Macmillan, pp. 192-219.

Jackson, R. (2008). The Emergence and Development of the Interpretive Approach, in H. Streib, A. Dinter & K. Söderblom (Eds.), *Lived Religion – Conceptual, Empirical and Practical-Theological Approaches: Essays in Honour of Hans-Günter Heimbrock*. Leiden: Brill, pp. 309-322.

Jackson, R. & O'Grady, K. (2007). Religions and education in England: social plurality, civil religion and religious education pedagogy, in R. Jackson, S. Miedema, W. Weisse & J.-P. Willaime (Eds.), *Religion and Education in Europe: Developments, Contexts and Debates*. Münster: Waxmann, pp. 181-202.

Knauth, T., Jozsa, D.–P., Bertram-Troost, G. & Ipgrave, J. (Eds.) (2008). *Encountering Religious Pluralism in School and Society. A Qualitative Study of Teenage Perspectives in Europe Religious Diversity and Education in Europe Series*. Münster: Waxmann.

McKenna, U., Ipgrave, J. & Jackson, R. (2008). *Interfaith Dialogue by Email in Primary Schools: An Evaluation of the Building E-Bridges Project*. Münster: Waxmann.

NUT (National Union of Teachers Conference (2008), see http://news.bbc.co.uk/1/hi/education/7311178.stm (accessed 3 May 2008).

Ofsted (2007). *Making Sense of Religion. A Report on Religious Education in Schools and the Impact of Locally Agreed Syllabuses*. London: Ofsted.

OSCE (2007). *The Toledo Guiding Principles on Teaching about Religion or Belief.* Warsaw: Organisation for Security and Co-operation in Europe/Office for Democratic Institutions and Human Rights.

QCA (2004). Religious Education: *The Non-Statutory National Framework.* London: Qualifications and Curriculum Authority. Available online: http://www.qca.org.uk/libraryAssets/media/9817_re_national_framework_04.pdf (accessed 21 March 2008)

Wright (1996). Language and experience in the hermeneutics of religious understanding, in: *British Journal of Religious Education,* 18 (3): pp. 166-80.

Pille Valk

English Religious Education through Estonian Eyes

Reading the English chapter could make Estonian religious educators somewhat envious (in a good sense of course). For the last twenty years, when Religious Education (RE) has been legally allowed in our schools again after 50 years of atheistic Soviet rule, the development of the subject has been accompanied by constant emotional and fiery debates. RE is blamed for brainwashing, proselytizing, damaging the pupils' capacities for scientific thinking etc. Although practice and research do not confirm these accusations, RE has quite a marginal status in the educational landscape in Estonia. Looking, from this context of constant struggling around RE, at English experiences, one can say that it is first of all encouraging: especially because the current concept of RE for Estonian schools has drawn on the English model in several aspects such as the non-confessional nature of the subject and cooperation with different religious communities in preparing the curriculum and learning resources.

The following comments on the English REDCo team findings deal mostly with the subjectively striking findings. Also some remarks and questions for future research will be presented.

Some striking findings

The very first very impressive matter in the English chapter for an Estonian reader is the fact that 95% of students in the English sample study RE. The situation where almost all students have the possibility to study RE is completely different from the Estonian situation where RE is a privilege, reachable only for 1–2% of students. This thought-provoking issue becomes more eloquent when picking up the items related to the impact and role of RE through the pupils' perspective. It emerges from the survey that RE is an important venue providing possibilities to talk and learn about religious issues. Students have pointed out the importance of such studies in increasing their understanding of current events in the contemporary world, as well as in the development of personal identity. Taking into consideration that students evaluated the knowledge about different religions and joint involvement as the most important prerequisites for peaceful co-existence in the pluralistic world, the potential and possible contribution of RE to social cohesion deserves full attention.

It was interesting to note that religious plurality, differently from Estonia, seems to be a reality in many English schools. I would like to point out some striking findings regarding the possible impact of the context upon students' positions related to religious issues. First there seems to be a pattern in the English sample that experiences with a plurality of worldviews have a positive impact on students' openness and vice versa. As we can read from the chapter: *"The attitude of students in the 'monocultural', rural school did appear less open-minded. They contrast with the students in the two multicultural schools."*

Looking at the possible influence of the school and its ethos upon pupils' opinions and positions, the only Catholic school in the sample caught the eye. According to the findings the percentage of those who agreed that 'there is a sort of spirit or life force' was higher in this school. It was also this school where more students confessed that 'talking about religion is embarrassing'. What lies behind these positions might be an interesting topic for future research.

Moving forward from the school level to the role of religion in pupils' lives, the following issues caught attention. It was remarkable how different are our countries regarding this aspect. When almost every second student in the English sample identified his/her religious or worldview affiliation, in the Estonian sample, only every seventh did so. Whereas two out of five in the English chapter agreed with the statement that there is a God, only one out of five did so in the Estonian sample.

It was striking to see that thinking about religion and the meaning of life attracted quite a lot attention from English youngsters. Almost every third student thinks about religion daily and another third do so on a weekly basis, according to their answers. It was surprising that thinking about the meaning of the life was slightly less popular. What exactly lies behind this 'thinking about religion' deserves further investigation. Time dedicated to thinking about religion is not always related to the religious practices themselves. Almost half of students state that they never pray and never participate in religious events. This 'passive' relation to religion is significantly different from the attitude of Muslim and South-African Christian students. These groups were remarkably similar in several aspects – both had strong theistic views, and practised their religion intensively: e.g. half of Muslim students admit that religion determines their whole life. It was striking how frequently Muslim students talk about religion with their religious leaders. Almost two out of three said they do it at least weekly.

One of the surprising 'red-lines' through the English chapter is the impact of religious affiliation upon students' attitudes towards religious plurality: "Students who answered positively to the belief questions also tended to answer positively to the inclusive learning questions. Intolerant students tended to be those who did not claim a religion or worldview. This finding is of interest to RE, suggesting that encouraging the affirmation of the faith or worldview of students and providing students with opportunities to explore their own beliefs may be a contributor to the development of positive relations with those of other faiths, at least in [the] English system." It is also worth adding that religious affiliation itself seemed to be a more important determinant of pupils' positions than affiliation to some particular religion.

There were also some interesting outcomes related to gender differences. It was striking to read that many boys in the English sample pray weekly and think about religion on a daily bases. The other gender difference pointed out was that girls seem to be more curious to talk about religion. They are more interested what their friends think about religion. Boys instead prefer to go around with friend with different religious backgrounds. Thus – girls like more to talk, boys appreciate action.

Something to think about and over

There are two issues I would like to point out regarding possible different interpretations. The first one is related to Muslim students' responses.

It came forward in relation to several issues that Muslim students tended to give the most positive responses to the questions regarding openness, tolerance and readiness for dialogue. Interestingly the same tendency was traceable also in some other national chapters (e.g. in the German chapter). One of the possible interpretations of these outcomes might simply be that the Muslim students really are more open and tolerant. But it might be worthwhile to investigate these outcomes in a rather wider context: and one of the possible factors to influence such responses might be related also to a certain resistance to and protestation against the image created about the Muslims by media. Probably quantitative research methods are not the best ones to go deeper into these issues. Here some more qualitative and ethnographic research is needed.

The second remark is related to the point made by English colleagues in the section dedicated to the comparison between the qualitative and the quantitative researches. According to this comparison they stated that in the qualitative survey students expressed more about their fears and uncertainties – e.g. that being religious might be not 'cool', and religious students are sometimes afraid of being mocked. One of the possible explanations here could be in the different atmosphere of different surveys. Qualitative research provides more space for personal reflections, especially when the work is done by a good and experienced interviewer. Quantitative research – completing the standardised questionnaire – is more formal, and this formalism might be more conductive more to the 'politically correct' answers obtained.

From these remarks it becomes evident how important it is to explore the complicated research field of religion and education by using different research methods to get a better picture of the field through the triangulation of different research methods.

Last but not least

If in the previous sections I paid attention mostly to the differences between the English and Estonian context; there emerged also some similarities.

First, family had a central role in shaping the knowledge and views about different religions in both countries.

Second, students in both countries were in favour of optional RE. Concerning the different models of RE "*Students tend to be conventional; they find it hard to conceptualise any different model of RE from the one with which they are most familiar. Similar findings and interpretations occur also in the REDCo qualitative survey*".

My final comment takes me back to the pre-Soviet occupation Estonia. Estonian RE went through a very deep reform in the beginning of the 1920s. Instead of the confessional Christianity-based RE a non-confessional model of RE was worked out and World religions were included in its curricula. The reformed RE had to take into consideration pupils' problems and questions, explore the impact of religions in the life of society. The main ideas and objectives of the subject were quite close to those becoming central in English RE after World War II, and this issue brings me back to the beginning of this article. If we read the impressive report about the important role RE has in England in contributing to social cohesion and intercultural dialogue, thoughts inadvertently turn to 'what if'? What if the development of non-confessional RE in Estonia would not been broken down in 1940? What if we did not have to experience strong and wide-ranging militant atheistic propaganda during half a century?

But this thinking is not very helpful and constructive. We have to take into consideration the current context and English experiences can serve here as good and inspiring examples to learn from.

Ina ter Avest & Cok Bakker

Response to the English National Report

Context

Reading the English report on the quantitative questionnaire we observe some (very striking) similarities and (even more) differences between the Dutch and the English groups, especially in a national context. In both countries we find schools with a strongly Christian orientation, and schools that claim to be religiously 'neutral'. Historically, the two countries have arrived at their education system by following totally different paths. Whereas in England the history starts with church-funded Christian schools, in the Netherlands it starts with 'pillarization' in state schools. In recent history, notably in the second half of the 20th century, it was not the church that pioneered the foundation of Christian schools but parents (see Ter Avest et al., 2006); and these were not only parents from a Christian community, but also parents committed to a pedagogic principle (such as those expounded by Maria Montessori). Since the 1990s Muslim parents have also been involved in establishing Islamic schools.

The nature of the relationship between church and state has been different in both countries from the outset. In England it has traditionally been characterized by cooperation, with the local religious communities contributing to the development of the Agreed RE Syllabuses. In the Netherlands, however, church and state are strictly separate. There is no nationwide RE curriculum, nor do religious communities contribute to the process of compiling and agreeing upon an RE curriculum. In the pillarized Dutch educational system[1], Christian schools enjoy a large measure of autonomy when it comes to RE, with a spectrum of approaches ranging from conservative and socializing to liberal and edifying. The curriculum in state schools in the Netherlands includes the subject of *Geestelijke Stromingen* (religious and non-religious worldviews), which is characterized by a 'teaching-about' approach. The teacher is required to adopt a 'neutral' stance when teaching lessons on religious and non-religious worldviews. A similar approach seems to apply to the majority of secondary schools in England, 'co-educational, non-denominational community schools that are required by law to provide non-confessional religious education' (p 3). In the Netherlands as well as in England, the actual content of lessons on religion and religiosity is determined by the teacher after she has closed the classroom door. What really happens once the door is closed is explored in the next paragraph.

In fairness, one could say that initiatives are actually taken from time to time to organize 'a uniform RE'. In the Netherlands organizations at the top of the different pillars occasionally present documents containing ideas, objectives and/or structures for RE; in England, on the other hand, LEAs (Local Educational Authorities, now Local Authorities) produce Agreed RE Syllabuses. Interestingly, the ambition to create a uniform RE appears to be unrealized and unrealizable in both countries. Despite well-intentioned efforts, the curriculum still differs from region to region and slots in with the 'situated knowledge' of religion(s) in England and the 'pillarized' knowledge (with regard to inclusion and exclusion of other religions and traditions) in the Netherlands. In the Netherlands the difference between the Protestant and Roman Catholic pillar on issues such as 'soft' and 'hard' pluralism (Nipkow) is one the rea-

---

1   For a detailed description of the Dutch educational system divided into so-called 'pillars' along religious lines, see the first REDCo book.

sons why it is impossible to introduce one uniform approach to RE in all denominational schools. When it comes to uniformity, the nature and position of RE is in stark contrast with the other subjects!

In this paper we focus on three themes that – when reading the English report – gave us food for thought and prompted some comments. We start with a comment on the differences and similarities between the two countries. Then we reflect on the difference in responses from students who say they feel committed to a religious tradition, and those who do not. Last but not least, since this is one of the spearheads of REDCo, we focus on gender, suggesting an alternative way of reflecting on the differences in the response patterns of girls and boys to the statements in the questionnaire.

Content of RE

In England the Agreed Syllabus, at local level, provides teachers with a guideline for teaching in the classroom. The curriculum clearly demarcates the discussion topics and elaborates on how to focus on the 'situated knowledge' of the students.

In the Netherlands there is no locally Agreed Syllabus or a national curriculum, but nationally defined criteria, which are provided for the above mentioned subject of *Geestelijke Stromingen* (Spiritual and Worldview Movements, since the Primary Education Act of 1985). These criteria demarcate the topics which are to be discussed and studied in class. However, no national criteria or national curriculum has been developed for RE as a subject that aims to edify as well as teach students about phenomena.

The preliminary data from the REDCo research project in both England and the Netherlands point to the primary importance of the family in induction into religion, with religious communities and schools competing for second place. It is clear that, these days, a change has taken place in the role of the religious community in the life of youngsters and created a different kind of responsibility for parents and schools in the religious edification of the students.

In the past, religious edification, in the shape of enculturation into a religious tradition – a process of socialization into the tradition embraced by the parents – was a responsibility shared by parents and religious communities: parents socialized their children and religious communities guided them in the narratives and rituals, the frame of reference, of the community of believers. Since secularization, youngsters have participated significantly less in the activities of religious communities; they meet in school to restore missing links in their knowledge and awareness of religious traditions as horizons against which to position themselves. Muslim students are in a different situation: Muslim students in both England and the Netherlands go to the mosque regularly and participate in praying, fasting and other religious activities.

English as well as Dutch students see school as an important source of information on different religions. Like the absence of regular participation in the activities of religious communities, this seems to be common among European students. Students like to find out more about other religion(s) and agree far less strongly with a statement like 'Religion helps me to learn about myself'. The information about 'the other' might hold connotations of contrasting – sometimes even conflicting – concepts and ideas from different (non-)religious traditions, forcing students to reflect on what they have so far taken for granted and to reconsider their own (religious or secular) commitments – although this aspect of RE might be more of a wished for result of the teacher's pedagogic strategy (Bakker, Van der Want & Ter Avest

2009, in press). In our view, educators should see students' requests for more knowledge about religion(s) as a starting point for religious edification via a 'pedagogic strategy in difference'. Students should be trained in 'faithing' (Slee, 2004), a process which stimulates the capacity to observe and experience the religious dimensions of life. This process should focus on 'conceptual faithing' and stimulate the development of religious literacy in particular.

Religious/non-religious groups emerge from the questionnaire

In both the English and the Dutch sample the responses exposed a clear difference between religious and secularized (or non-religious) students. In the English sample 56% of the students participate regularly in religious activities, such as praying and attending church or the mosque. A smaller group of 39% says that they read religious texts now and then, and the same percentage says that religion is (very) important to them. A similar pattern is discernible in the Dutch sample. Sixty-five percent of the Dutch students say that religion is (very) important to them. This percentage stands at eighty for religious students and only seven for non-religious students. These percentages are related to the (non-)confessional RE that the students receive in their schools. Students who receive confessional RE say more often that they are religious and that they see religion as important in their lives. The two groups differ significantly in their ideas about the characteristics of religion. Students who do not feel committed to a religious tradition are more inclined to agree with the statement 'Religion is nonsense' and are significantly less inclined to respect people who do have a religion. In addition, students without a religion agree to a significantly higher extent with the statement 'You can be a religious person without belonging to a certain religious community' than students with a religion. In the Dutch situation this might point to the revival of a variety of new forms of religiosity in the public domain (Van de Donk et al., 2006).

The answers of the two groups differ not only in character, but also in their degree of agreement or disagreement. Students who say that they are committed to a religious tradition agree or disagree more strongly with particular statements. This pattern is discernible in both the English and the Dutch sample. For example, English religious students show a stronger positive response to inclusive RE, the dominant RE model in the schools participating in the English research. Muslim students are even more outspoken with regard to, for example, the wearing of more visible religious symbols, time-off for religious festivals, being excused from some lessons for religious reasons, and voluntary religious services as a part of school life. Christian students agree more mildly with the statements on these issues. An interesting pattern emerged with regard to the school's task to guide (or not to guide) students towards a religious belief. Although a strenuous response came from religious students on the whole, it turned out that Christian students strongly disagree and Muslim students strongly agree. In the Dutch sample the respondents agree in general that students should be allowed to wear discrete religious symbols, but they agree to a lesser extent on whether they should be allowed to wear more visible religious symbols. Also, they are less in favour of allowing students to miss lessons for religious reasons; 44% strongly disagrees with this statement. The students in the Dutch sample are negative about the (possible) aim of RE with regard to the school as a place for enculturation into a religious tradition. This applied equally to Christians and Muslims, and was an unexpected and surprising revelation for the principal of the Islamic College in the Dutch sample.

Students in England are used to the way RE is organized in their schools. The socialization in the pedagogic strategy of RE seems to be working. In England students are in favour of inclusive RE, which has been implemented there officially since 1988. Students in the Netherlands, although familiar with a pillarized educational system, are of the opinion that RE should be taken by all students as a routine part of the school curriculum, irrespective of their religion.

It emerged in the English as well as the Dutch sample that students' attitudes are more related to their own individual beliefs than to the approach applied by the school. Given the influence that students themselves ascribe to the family in the formation of their religious worldview, further research should include informal religious education when exploring whether religion is a factor in promoting conflict or whether it contributes to dialogue.

It is striking that the more negative the statement ('There is no need for RE'; 'Religion should have no place in school life'), the lower the positive response rates. This might be due to the way the statement is formulated – negativity triggering negativity. More attention should be paid to this in follow-up projects. The same holds for the language. Statements formulated in the male or female gender might, consciously or unconsciously, influence the answers of students of the opposite sex.

Gender and religion

The response from boys and girls differ for some of the statements in the questionnaires. In the Dutch sample the girls' responses are used mainly for comparison with the boys' responses. For example, the Dutch report says: 'Girls seem to value religion in school more than boys'. Girls agree significantly more than boys with the statements: 'I see religion as an important topic at school' and 'I find topics about religion interesting at school'. Moreover, girls are more positive about what they learn at school about religion.

In the English sample sometimes the girls' responses and sometimes the boys' responses are the starting point for a comparison. For example, in the English report we read: 'Where a peer held a different religious view, boys were highly significantly more likely to ignore the other, attempt to convince, or explain that their own opinions were the best, whereas girls were highly significantly more likely to discuss with the other'.

Despite these differences in the presentation of the results, the similarity with the Dutch findings is striking. In general we learn from the quantitative research that girls are more likely than boys to exhibit an open attitude to 'the other' and the other's religion. They seem more willing to talk to 'the other' and to listen to their point of view, whereas boys show a tendency to withdraw or opt out. In other words, boys are more likely than girls to shy away from differences. Boys seem more able than girls to demarcate their own (and hence, the other's) territory within the encounter. Or, as the English report says: 'Boys tend to be more militant in their attitudes and girls stress understanding and conformity'.

In an interesting article, which starts with the different ways little girls and boys throw a ball, Iris Marion Young (1990) elaborates on how children use the body's spatial and lateral potential. She convincingly guides her readers away from the playground perception of 'throwing like a girl' to the striking insight that 'it is the ordinary purposive orientation of the body as a whole toward things and its environment that initially defines the relation of a subject to its world'(Young 1990, p.143). The attitude of boys and girls towards the other's god and religion is likewise defined in different ways. Generally speaking, the girl's attitude is characterized by a certain eagerness to know about her own as well as the other's god and religion; girls use 'talking' as a means of satisfying their need while boys associate with friends by, for example, playing football together. The differences in the responses of the girls and the boys may have been strongly influenced by different gendered socializing patterns in society despite waves of women's liberation and sexual emancipation in both the Netherlands and England.

References

Bakker, C., van der Want, A.C., ter Avest, I. & Everington, J. (2009). *Teacher's pedagogical strategies nested in teacher's personal and professional biography, report of a qualitative study in eight European countries*. Waxmann: Münster (in press).

Slee, Nicola (2004/2008). *Women's Faith Development, Patterns and Processes*. England: Ashgate Publishing Limited.

Ter Avest, I., Bakker, C., Bertram-Troost, G.D. & Miedema, S. (2006). Religion and Education in the Dutch Pillarized and Post-Pillarized Educational System, Historical Backgrounds and Current Debates, in: R. Jackson, S. Miedema, W. Weisse, J.-P. Willaime (Eds.), *Religion and Education in Europe, Developments, Contexts and Debates*. Waxmann: Münster, pp. 203–219.

Van der Donk, W.B.H.J., Jonkers, A.P., Kronjee, G.J. & Plum, R.J.J.M. (Eds.) (2006). *Geloven in het publieke domein, verkenningen van een dubbele transformatie* [Religion in the public domain, explorations of a two ways' transformation]. Amsterdam: Amsterdam University Press.

Young, Iris Marion (1990). *Throwing like a girl and other essays in Feminist Philosophy and Social Theory*. Indiana University Press: Bloomington and Indianapolis.

Olga Schihalejev

Options beside 'and no Religion too' –
Perspectives of Estonian Youth[1]

1.   Introduction

The majority of students in Estonia acquire their knowledge, attitudes and views about religion similarly to the French model, studying about religion in such subjects as History, Civic Education, and Literature. Religious Education (RE) is regulated by the Act of the Basic School and Gymnasium in the national curriculum. The subject occupies an unusual position in comparison to other European education systems. As in some countries (the United Kingdom, Sweden, Norway) the students are not divided into groups according to their religious or confessional background. The subject is inter-religious – it is targeted at developing religious literacy, open identity, and readiness for a dialogue, by introducing different world religions. However, contrary to other countries with non-confessional model of RE, it is not only optional but a voluntary subject. There is no alternative subject to RE; students who have chosen it have an extra lesson at the end of the school day. Although on legislative grounds, it is compulsory for a school to offer RE if there are fifteen interested students. Only a few schools offer RE[2], usually in primary classes or for a year in upper secondary school, according to a letter from the Ministry of Education and Research (Laanoja, 2007). Having 10% of schools with RE and about 10% of classes in each of them having an option to attend RE, we calculate approximately 1–2% of all students in Estonia can attend RE classes, if they wish. As with other optional subjects, the national RE curriculum is only advisory; schools and teachers of RE have the freedom to develop their own curriculum for RE. There is some variety in the terms by which the subject is organised – it can be a voluntary subject after lessons for some interested students or an optional subject for all, in the last case usually under the name of Cultural Studies.

RE in Estonia is shaped by several historical and sociological factors. Let us mention only some of its more important aspects, which can shed some light on the attitudes of the students in our survey. First, 50 years of the Soviet totalitarian occupation and atheistic regime, which forbade RE, has caused a lack of knowledge of religious issues, and many prejudices not only about religions but about any subject dealing with religious issues as well. Second, the secularisation of the indigenous population and the low influx of immigrants, compared to other countries in Europe, has wiped religion from the public sphere.

Some more general attitudes held in Estonia in regards to religion are illustrated well by the fact that the special award in 2008 for advertising Estonia went to a team of young people who presented Estonia as the most a-religious country. The advertisement which was meant to introduce Estonia to foreigners used a verse from John Lennon's song "Imagine" – "Nothing

---

1   This article was supported by the European Union through the European Regional Development Fund (Center of Excellence CECT).
2   It is not regulated how to know if there are some interested persons – the schools do not have obligations to introduce the subject to the pupils and the parents or ask, if anybody would be interested to have RE. As it makes some effort to detect it and to find a teacher of RE, only few head teachers are interested in doing it. See Valk (2007).

to kill or die for and no religion too" (Engelbrecht, 2008), stressing that Estonia is a peaceful secular, country without religion which could cause conflicts.

1.1   Description of the sample

Although the Estonian sample for the REDCo quantitative survey is purposive and not directly representative, it is still designed to be significant and rational. The goal was but to have a bigger sample than the minimum of 400. One thousand, two hundred and eight (1208) students in Estonia between 14 and 16 years of age answered the questionnaire. As a result of our procedure of including all the parallel classes, the gender balance was satisfactory (48% males, 51% females).

There is some statistical data about the 14–16 years old population, so we tried to reflect the diversity and heterogeneity of the Estonian population, with no major groups left out. The main criteria for selecting schools were geographical location, type of school, and model of religious studies. Given the difficulty of obtaining permission to conduct a survey about religion in schools, we had to have a procedure for changing a school if permission was denied. Below are the description of the criteria used and the selection procedure.

Geographical location; urban and rural schools. Although Estonia is small, its regions differ in the composition of people, with diverse migration and national background, religious affiliation, and socio-economic indicators. There are 33% Orthodox and 6% Lutherans in Ida-Viru, but 18% Lutherans and 8% Orthodox in Pärnu[3]. Although most of the Orthodox in Ida-Viru county are Russians, in Tartu, Pärnu and Põlva counties there are many Orthodox Estonians as well. People with a migration background mostly speak Russian as their first language[4]. There are more people with a migration background living in Tallinn and the North-East of Estonia: 69% Russians and 20% Estonians live in Ida-Viru, while 93% Estonians and 4% Russians live in Viljandi county. So the incorporation of different areas increases the likelihood of having a sample with a varied national and religious background.

In order to compare different factors we concentrated on three geographically different regions and added some schools from locations of interest. 1) The *Northern region* of Estonia is an industrial area, and many immigrants live there. We have chosen schools from Tallinn, the wealthiest region in Estonia, and from its surroundings. We added a school from Narva, a town in North-Eastern Estonia, with more Russians and immigrants living there, also a larger percentage of Orthodox, and people having lower economic status. 2) The *Western region* is represented by schools from Pärnu county, with a moderate number of people with a migration background and average income; in addition a school from an island, a remote area with almost no immigrants. 3) The *Southern region* is a rural area, and most of its residents are lower income. We have chosen schools from Viljandi, Põlva and Tartu counties, with an exceptional region of Old Believers[5]. In this region there is also a university town, Tartu. We

---

3   All the statistical data about Estonia is counted according the data on the Web page of the Statistical Office of Estonia. (http://pub.stat.ee/ accessed 16.04.2008)

4   Russian communities, mainly consisting of traders, religious and political dissidents, have lived in Estonia over the last 1000 years of recorded history. Prior to the Second World War, Russian communities in Estonia were small. Soviet russification policies dramatically altered the social and demographic landscape of Estonia. Currently the influence of the pre-war Russian population of Estonia is smaller than that of the later immigrants. Today about one third of Estonian population consists of immigrants from different parts of the former Soviet Union, or their descendants. (Estonian Institute, 1997)

5   The Old Believers (Russian: старове́ры or старообря́дцы) separated from the Russian Orthodox church after 1666-1667 as a protest against introduced church reforms and continue liturgical practices which the Russian Orthodox Church maintained before the implementation of these reforms. The first

tried to find contrasting schools in each region (for example, a school in a city centre, another in the suburbs, and another in a rural area).

Type of school. According to the homepage of the Estonian Ministry of Education and Research every fifth student went to a basic school[6], which is usually smaller in number of students; and four-fifths went to secondary schools last year. The sample reflects the distribution of students according to school type (Table 1).

There are only a few private schools in Estonia and some state schools (usually for students with special needs), while most schools are run by the municipality (Table 1). We included six basic schools and 15 upper secondary schools; 19 municipal and two private schools, including a religious school. We excluded schools for students with special needs, but increased the number of students from private schools to make their number reasonable for the research. One of the private schools is confessional, although only slightly more students with a religious affiliation attend it. Another private school is not religious; the parents pay tuition fees and mostly have higher socio-economic status.

Table 1: Distribution of types of school in Estonia in total and in the sample[7]

	Schools in Estonia	Schools in the sample	Students in Estonia	Students in the sample
Basic	223	6	30 000 (20%)	236 (20%)
Upper secondary	232	15	123 000 (80%)	992 (80%)
Municipal	490	19	147 000 (95%)	1070 (89%)
Private	33	2	4 400 (3%)	138 (11%)
State	32	0	3 600 (2%)	0

The language of instruction was one of the indicators in choosing the schools. In addition to the REDCo qualitative survey about the views of young people on religion (Schihalejev, 2008), many recent studies have revealed differences between schools with Estonian and Russian languages of instruction (e.g. Ruus et al., 2007; Veisson et al., 2007; Toots et al., 2004). Ethnic Estonians make up two thirds of the Estonian population; more than a quarter of the Estonian population consists of Russians (Table 2): the percentage of ethnic Estonians among children of school age (aged 7–16) has increased to 77–78% (Lauristin, 2008, p. 46). Schools in Estonia differ also by the language of instruction – there are 369 Estonian-medium schools, 83 Russian-medium schools[8] (18 of those use both Estonian and Russian languages for studies) and three English-medium schools.[9] For national and migration background we

---

Old Believers arrived in Estonia in the late 17th century, escaping from the persecution of the Russian government. Nowadays, there are almost 15 thousand Old Believers by birth living mostly in eastern Estonia, they comprise an ethnic minority, clearly distinguishable from other Russians in Estonia due to their unique traditions and religion (NGO The Society of Old Believer Culture and Development, http://www.starover.ee/, accessed 18.04.2008).

6   A basic school gives education only until the end of compulsory education, when children are 16–17 of the age. A secondary school have usually classes for children 7–19 years of age.

7   http://www.hm.ee and http://www.ehis.ee/ (accessed 16.04.2008)

8   It is difficult to say how many Estonians and how many Russians are there, as some Russians and students from other countries go to Estonian schools, although most Russians, Ukrainians and Belorussians go to Russian schools.

9   http://www.hm.ee (accessed 16.04.2008)

included schools from areas where there are more recent migrants, as Tallinn and Ida-Viru county. It is difficult to determine the nationality of our sample, as this question was not asked. In our sample, 956 spoke Estonian at home, 230 Russian, four English, one Swedish, one Finnish, one Italian and fifteen did not answer the question. All the students who did not answer the question were from Russian-medium schools. The bigger number of Russian-medium schools would increase also the variety of national background, but it was the most difficult to obtain agreement from Russian-medium schools (of the 36 Russian-medium schools invited to participate, only four agreed), although we used a Russian questionnaire in these schools.

Table 2:   Nationality of the Estonian population and of the sample

	Estonia, nationality	The sample, language spoken at home
Estonians	921 062 (69%)	956 (80%)
Russians	344 280 (26%)	230 (19%)
Others	77 067 (5%)	7

RE and its model. There are no figures on the number of students in Estonia who study RE; probably it is under 1%. It did not make sense to include so few students. In our sample we included schools that have never had RE (8) and those who have RE this year (7) or have RE in the school curriculum, but students 14–16 years of age do not have access to the subject (6). In a school with RE some classes could have RE and others not, some students have chosen the subject, others not. In the year of this study 1078 students in the sample did not study RE and 130 did study it; 162 more have studied RE for least one year during their stud-ies at school. The students differed also by length of RE study. Some schools do not have the subject but religious education is integrated in the school life; students may regularly attend services in different churches or have a chaplain at school. The inclusion of schools, where RE is not taught, where RE is taught only in primary classes, or RE is taught recently or is incorporated into the whole school life, enables the exploration of the views of students with different educational models about living in a pluralistic society.

Religious background of pupils. In regard to religious background we have only the data from a poll of the people 15 years and older in 2000 (Table 3). In order to include most reli-gious groups we looked for Russianspeaking Orthodox students in Tallinn and Narva, Old Believers in Kallaste, Estonian speaking Orthodox students in Värska, and Catholic students and students with other religious backgrounds in two schools with an open Catholic ethos[10].

The number of students who did not define their religious affiliation is higher than ex-pected, while the number of religiously affiliated students is lower. The religiosity of the younger generation is known to be lower than in the overall population, as has been seen in comparison of the overall population to 15–19 year olds[11]. A more important factor was the fact that there were no options added to the question about their religious affiliation; this probably increased the number of those who did not answer the question or did not distin-guish different denominations ('Christian', 'religion').

---

10 There are slightly more students with religious affiliation (19% in schools with catholic ethos, while 15% in other schools). Not only Catholic parents, but with other religious affiliation, choose these schools for their children, as there is no school with their own religious or confessional ethos.

11 http://pub.stat.ee/ accessed 16.04.2008

Table 3:   **Religious affiliation of the Estonian population aged 15 and older, aged 15–19 and of the sample.**

	Total population age 15 and older *Total 1 121 600*	Total number in Estonia age 15–19 *Total 103 772*	Sample *Total 1208*
Not defined[12]	730 845 (65%)	82 019 (79%)	1021 (84%)
Orthodox	143 554 (13%)	8 756 (8%)	52 (4%)
Lutheran	152 237 (14%)	5 278 (5%)	12 (1%)
Atheist	68 547 (6%)	5 978 (6%)	5 (less than 1%)
Other Christians	24 137 (2%)	1 742 (2%)	74 (6%)
Other religions	3 882 (Less than 1%)	235 (Less than 1%)	44 (4%)

The procedure of selection schools and classes for the research

The selection of schools consisted of three steps; each criterion was counter checked. After the primary selection of schools in regard to the first three criteria, the sample was checked to get a better balance of students' religion, socio-economic background, and gender.

In the first step were included schools, where extended fieldwork had been conducted in RE lessons and qualitative research about students' views on religion in the framework of REDCo. Then we found schools without RE, but with similar characteristics in our sample criteria, or the classes from the same school who have no RE. In the second step we listed the schools which have integrated RE in basic school and found their 'twins' as in the first step. In the third step we acquired a balanced sample by adding schools with the criteria missing from the sample list.

According to the research question of REDCo, we surveyed the students who are 14–16 years old; most of them were in grades 8–10. We focused on grade 9, the end of basic and compulsory schooling at the selected schools. In schools where there were fewer than 50 students in grade 9, we asked students from grade 8 to fill out the questionnaires. The grades who studied RE were included in the sample, if students were 14–16 years of age.

Altogether, 71 letters were sent to schools and 21 replied positively. In our sample we have dropped all the responses from students who were younger than 14 (19 students) or older than 16 years old (141), leaving 1208 respondents aged 14–16.

Reflection on the sample. The sample accurately represents the religious, geographical and socio-economic distribution of Estonian students. The higher number of students who have studied RE enables us to compare subgroups but this can influence the reported attitudes of the whole sample. Further evaluation can be made only after presentation and analysis of results.

1.2   General procedure and comments of students

The fieldwork was carried out by three university researchers in seven schools, and by teachers in 14 schools who agreed to collaborate. The field guide with an introductory text was developed for those who conducted the survey in different schools in order to guarantee a

---

12 The respondents who said that they do not have religious affiliation, cannot define it or refused to answer the question.

similar procedure in all schools. The questionnaire was filled out during a school lesson according to the field guide. The questionnaire took 10 to 39 minutes to complete.

Some students (263) wrote comments on the last page of the questionnaire, explaining their choices (74) or evaluating the questionnaire (42 critical or negative and 14 positive). The attitudes to the questionnaire mirrored the range of opinions, from some positive ones who found that it specially helped religious students to feel better, to many negative reactions complaining about the length and irrelevance of the questionnaire. In answering the questions, students without a specific religious background had trouble with many questions. Other students complained that it was impossible to say yes or no, agree or disagree with many statements. To make a decision would require binary thinking, where simple answers could be interpreted in too many ways. Many students (126) wrote about their own belief or disbelief at the end of questionnaire (from very negative *"All believers should be cremated!"* (EST583) to religious ones *"Jesus is my father, my creator and my keeper. I believe in him and you can believe too, then he comes and helps!"* (EST163), also about their attitude to religious education, from a view that it is a waste of time to very positive attitudes that it is an important tool in becoming more tolerant.

2.   General presentation of the results

In the following we look at the responses that the students in Estonia gave on the REDCo questionnaire. The sections are structured to fit the research questions; in all the sections the same order of presentation was used: the groups are compared on their experience of RE, their religious affiliation, their gender and their language.

In the REDCo project we are primarily concerned with the impact of school, so we are interested in how different experiences with religious studies have influenced students' attitudes. Here we distinguish four groups. The first group consists of those who have never studied RE (734 students). The second group are those who do not have a separate subject of RE but the school has integrated it into the curriculum; students may attend religious services, or have a chaplain at school (207 students). The third group are those who studied RE a long time ago, usually as a voluntary subject in primary classes with content oriented to Bible stories and Christian festivals, but dealing also with students' values (83 students). The fourth group consists of those who have studied RE during the previous or current year, with content focused on world religions (159 students). Some of the students studied RE in a school where it was optional and others are in schools where religion is taught as a compulsory subject. From those who studied RE in primary classes, 31 chose to study it themselves and 44 were from classes which had common studies for all. Most of the students who had studied RE recently had it as a subject for all students (150) and only a few (9) chose it according to their own interest. This can affect their motivation but it can also be an important factor in the way they felt when studying.

One may assume that religious affiliation can influence attitudes about religion and religious plurality. It was difficult to decide how to group students according to religion, because there were too few representatives of each religion or denomination. We took the answer to the question 'Do you have a certain religion or worldview?' as the point of departure: does a student constitute himself or herself as belonging to any religious tradition? The students who had a non-religious worldview, such as atheism or agnosticism were grouped with those without any worldview, as the number was too small to group them separately. In the chapter I refer to these different groups accordingly as 'affiliated' and 'non-affiliated', keeping in mind that it does not show their religious beliefs or religious participation. In addition, if questions in the questionnaire are closely related to our research hypothesis, then the dependent variables of tolerance and readiness for dialogue were checked against the independent variables, including religious affiliation, how important they think religion is or what they believe in.

The qualitative survey showed astonishing differences between the religiosity and attitudes towards RE between Russian- and Estonian-speaking students. The groups here were divided by the language of questionnaire that the students used. For brevity, I will refer to the students who filled in the Russian questionnaire as 'Russians' and those who filled in the Estonian questionnaire as 'Estonians', although students who speak at home English, Swedish or Finish, are also included as 'Estonians'.

Data analysis was done with SPSS, using ANOVA and chi-square analyses. Only results with p<.001 are discussed. As there were many results with $0.1 < \Phi < 0.15$, then only $\Phi < 0.15$ are discussed as significant; where there were small differences in the answers of different groups with $0.12 < \Phi < 0.15$, but the small differences are supported by a recurrent pattern of similar statements, these are presented. In the interest of brevity, significant differences are marked as follows: results with differences with significance of $0.15 \leq \Phi < 0.2$ are marked with '*'; results with differences with significance of $0.2 \leq \Phi < 0.3$ are marked with '**'; and with $0.3 \leq \Phi$ with '***'.

Most interesting and telling results are illustrated by figures.

2.1　What role has religion in pupils' life and in their surroundings?

2.1.1　Data description

In this paragraph we will look at the relevance of religion to pupils and the role religion plays in their contacts with peers. As described in paragraph 1.2, almost 85% of respondents did not write about their religious affiliation (q. 126–127). Christians were most numerous among students with a religious affiliation (11%) and few students from other religions were represented (4%).

The number of students who could not specify their religious affiliation was higher among 'Estonians' (88%) than 'Russians' (68%). In addition, Russian-speaking students identified their denomination (usually Orthodox) more than 'Estonians'. Those Estonians who claimed to have a religious affiliation tended to say that they are Christians. Slightly more girls than boys identified their religious or secular worldview (all four agnostics and four of five atheists were girls): 18% and 13%, respectively.

Religious belief and practice

In this section we work with questions 37–44. Low importance of religion, on average, in pupils' life was apparent in almost all questions of this block. Answers to the question about the importance of religion inclined heavily towards a low value of religion for respondents, where a very small importance of religion was declared by more than half of students and only 5% of students claimed that religion was very important for them.

This evaluation is consistent with the content of the beliefs and practices they perform (or do not perform). Every fifth student believes in God, while every third respondent does not believe in God or any kind of spirit or life force. All the graphs of answers for religious activities inclined very heavily towards 'never': three of four students never pray (mean 4.45[13]), almost the same number never read sacred texts (4.56), and over half of respondents never attend religious events (4.39) Thinking about the meaning of life or about religion (3.56) scored higher – only every fifth student never thinks about religion and only every tenth about meaning of life. Thinking about meaning of life was the most practiced from the all activities in the list, with a 'flat' distribution of answers and a mean of 2.9.

Studies of religion. There are no significant differences according to their religious studies in regard to students' or their parents' religious affiliation, what the students believe or how important religion is to them. Distribution of 'affiliated' and 'non-affiliated' among students with different models of RE, was similar. Nevertheless, some answers about how often students participated in religious activities differed significantly. Those who have studied RE think more frequently about religion, even if they studied it long ago (**). The students who have studied RE recently tended to think more frequently about the meaning of life. The students who learned RE 'long ago' used least of all the option 'never' in answers for the frequency of such religious activities as 'visit religious events' (**), 'pray', 'think about meaning of life'.

Religious affiliation. 'Affiliated' students regarded religion as significantly more important (***) and believed in God more than the 'non-affiliated' (***). As it was expected, 'affiliated' students practiced religious activities more than 'non-affiliated'. More surprising was that they were also more likely to think 'about the meaning of life' (***). The smallest difference was using the Internet to obtain information about religion (**), the biggest difference was in frequency of praying (***). A closer look at this in combination with national background is given below.

Gender. There were some differences according to gender in the importance of religion (**). Forty-five percent of females regarded religion as absolutely not important or as not important, while 60% of males did. The option 'very important' is used almost equally by boys and girls, while 'absolutely not important' is more frequently by boys, making religion less important for boys than for girls (Figure 1). In addition there are some differences in regard to what they believe in, but here the differences are slighter. The belief in God is almost the same for both sexes, but girls are more likely than boys to believe in 'some sort of spirit or life force' while boys do not believe in the existence of any of these (Figure 2). In the light of these findings it may be surprising that there were no significant differences between the genders in their answers about any of the practices listed in questions 39–44, with an exception of a minor difference in praying, females praying slightly more frequently (*).

---

13 Scale: 1 – about every day, 2 – about every week, 3 – about once a month, 4 – less than once a month, 5 – never.

Figure 1: **Importance of religion (Q. 37) by gender and language (means)**[14]

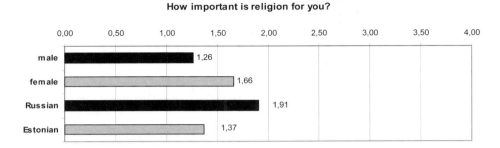

Language. When the two national groups are compared, one must have in mind that there were remarkably more 'religiously affiliated' among 'Russians' than among 'Estonians' (36% and 12% accordingly). Many but not all answers of the 'Russians' are therefore similar to the subgroup of 'Estonian affiliated students'. How has the higher proportion of religious affiliated students among 'Russians' influenced their attitudes? 'Russians' not only belonged to, but also valued religion as more important (**; Figure 1) and believed in God more than 'Estonians' did (***; Figure 2). Significant differences were found in regard to the contents of belief (***): more 'Russians' than 'Estonians' believed in existence of God, while more 'Estonians' than 'Russians' claimed to believe in nothing.

Figure 2: **Statements of belief (Q. 38) by gender and language (%)**

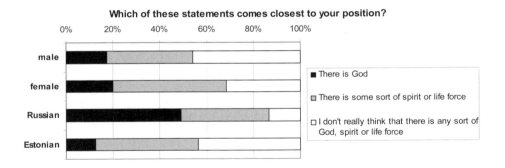

The most interesting distinctions in frequencies of religious practices were found when groups are compared by language and religion. Every fourth Russian-speaking 'non-affiliated' student claimed that religion is important or very important, while only every tenth Estonian 'non-affiliated' student did so. 'Estonian affiliated students' found religion to be very important or important in 61% of cases, 'Russian affiliated students' in 50%. This corresponds well to other statements of the two groups, including believing in God, and participation in different religious activities.

---

14 Means on the scale starting from 0 – absolutely not imortant up to 4 – very important.

Figure 3:   Frequencies of religious practices (Q. 42, 43) by religion and language (%)

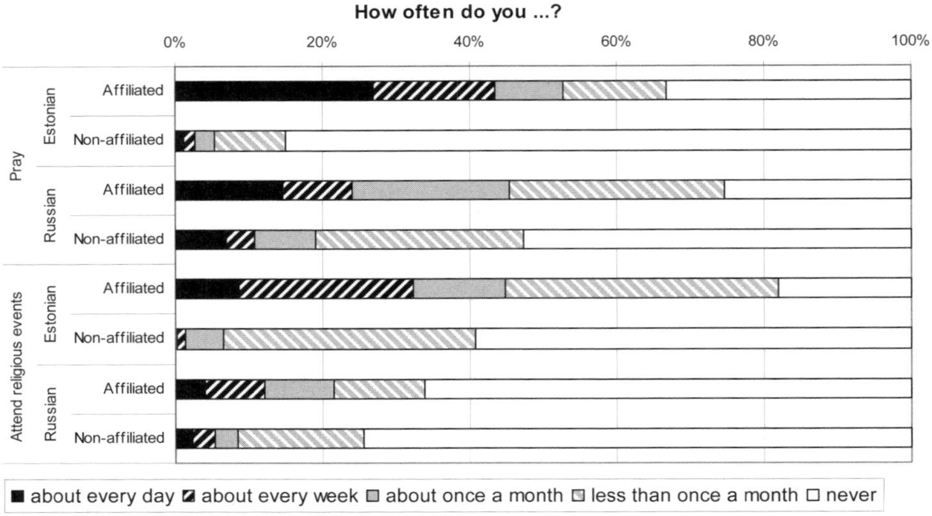

Prayer is practised among 'Russians' more frequently; even some 'Russian 'non-affiliated' pray every day (7%), but 'Estonian religious affiliated students' pray on a regular basis more frequently than 'Russian religious affiliated students' (Figure 3). Religious affiliation for 'Estonian' respondents could be clearly identified by the higher percentage of those praying if they have religious affiliation (63%) or never if they do not have religious affiliation (85%). In contrast, 'Estonians' attended religious services more than 'Russians' (Figure 3): 66% of Russian respondents *with* religious affiliation never attend religious events, while the number of Estonians *without* religious affiliation who do not attend religious services is 59%. If we look at regular attendances (at last once a month, to exclude those who happen to go once a year or have been some years ago to some funerals), we still get similar numbers for 'Estonians' who have religious affiliation (42%); the corresponding number for regular attendance for 'affiliated Russians' is 22%. For those without religious affiliation regular participation in religious events is about the same for both groups. In addition to praying 'Russians' also thought more frequently about the meaning of life (**) and read sacred texts more often (*) than 'Estonians' did.

Sources of information

In this section we work with questions 45–51. For the sample as a whole, family was seen as the most important source of information about religion (2.68)[15] followed by school (3.0). The distribution of positions on the importance of different sources of information followed a normal curve, with a small tendency to 'not important' in all answers except family, where the answers were distributed almost evenly, and 'faith community', where the most frequent answer was 'not important at all'. We may now consider the effect of differences in experience and environment.

---

15 Means on the scale: 1 – very important, 2 – important, 3 – a little bit important, 4 – not important, 5 – not important at all.

Figure 4: Sources of information about religion (Q. 45–51) by model of RE (means)[16]

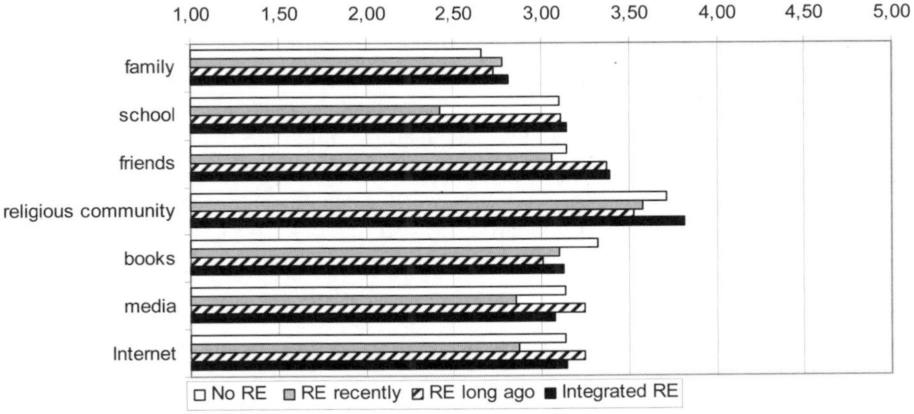

How important is for you as a source of information about religion ...?

Legend: □ No RE   ▨ RE recently   ▨ RE long ago   ■ Integrated RE

Categories (top to bottom): family, school, friends, religious community, books, media, Internet. Scale: 1,00 – 5,00.

Studies of religion. The students who studied RE recently valued school as the most important source of information about religion, where the difference between different groups was the most significant (**). Students who had done RE recently valued school more highly than those who had not, also they used media and Internet more than the others to get information about religion (*; Figure 4).

Religious affiliation. There were significant differences among sources of information between 'affiliated' and 'non-affiliated' students: religious community (***), family (**), books (**) and friends (*) were more important for the 'affiliated' students. Other sources were also more important for the 'affiliated', but without significant differences. The most important informants for the 'affiliated' are family (2.02), books (2.65) and friends (2.76); while family (2.82), school (3.04) and media (3.10) were important for the 'non-affiliated'.

Gender. Girls were more positive about all the sources of information about religion, with significant differences in regard to school (*), books (*) and family (*). Girls, more than boys, chose the options 'very important' and 'important', boys 'not important' and 'not important at all'. The most important source for both groups is family, school having the second place for girls (2.81) and the fourth place for boys (3.2) after Internet (3.11) and media (3.19).

Language. 'Russians' valued all the sources more highly than 'Estonians'. The most significant differences were, family (**) and friends (**). 'Russians' tended to consider family and friends as the most important resources of information about religion, while for 'Estonians' family and school are the most important. In addition differences in opinions about the Internet (*) and media (*) were significant; 'Russians' were more likely to regard the Internet as 'very important' and Estonians more likely to have intermediate opinions about the media. It may be somewhat surprising that faith community did not play any distinctive role for 'Russians' as a source of information, but if we take into account that religious events were rarely attended by 'Russians', this finding makes sense.

---

16 Means on the scale: 1 – very important, 2 – important, 3 – a little bit important, 4 – not important, 5 – not important at all.

Attitudes towards religion

In this section we work with questions 52–61, 86, 92, 95, and 96. More general statements, such as 'religion is important in our history' and 'it is possible to be a religious person without belonging to a particular faith community', but also 'respecting other people' were more agreed with than statements of personal commitment and religion influencing one's life. Although religion is not seen as very important for students, almost half of them disagreed and only every fifth student agreed with the statement that religion is nonsense.

Most of the pupils agreed that religion is a private matter and that religion is inherited from family. For other statements the distribution was flat; respondents did not have an opinion. Every third student (30–40%) used the option 'neither agree nor disagree' for almost all the answers in this group. We may now consider the effect of difference experiences and influences on viewpoints.

Figure 5:   Attitudes towards religion (Q. 55, 56, 58) by gender and model of RE (%)

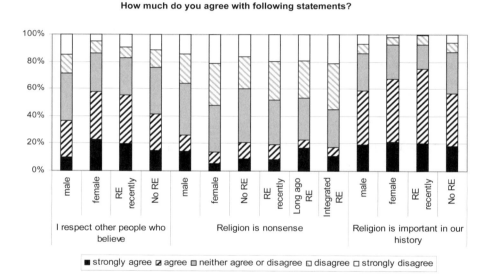

Studies of religion. Four statements in the group on attitudes towards religion had significant differences in responses related to students' experience of religious studies. The students who have studied RE or their school has integrated it into the curriculum, were more likely to agree with the statements 'Religion is important in our history' (*) and 'I respect people who believe' (*) and to disagree that religion is nonsense (*; Figure 5). Interesting is the fact that those who studied RE long ago, agreed more strongly with the last statement than did students of any other group, also they were more likely to think that religion is inherited from family (*).'I respect other people who believe' was disagreed with most by students without any experience of RE (mean 2.79[17], while for others means 2.48–2.5). Those who did not study

---

17 Hence forward if not said otherwise means on the scale: 1 – strongly agree, 2 – agree, 3 – neither agree or disagree, 4 – disagree, 5 – strongly disagree

RE agreed more that they do not know about religion (*); a similar pattern appeared among those who had studied it less, and these were also less interested in talking about religion (*). None of the other answers showed significant differences.

Gender. There are some remarkable differences in attitudes towards religion. Girls agreed more than boys with all the positive statements about religion, while boys agreed with negative ones. Students showed no significant gender differences about more neutral expressions as 'religion is inherited from family' or that it is a private matter. Boys agreed significantly more that religion is a boring topic (*). Slightly more boys agreed also that they are not interested in religion. The biggest differences were for the statement 'I respect other people who believe' (**) and 'religion is nonsense' (**), where girls were more likely to be tolerant and respectful of religious people and of religion as a phenomenon. In both cases negative attitudes among boys were almost twice as widespread as among girls (Figure 5).

Figure 6:   Attitudes towards religion (Q. 55, 56, 54, 59, 60) by religious affiliation (%)

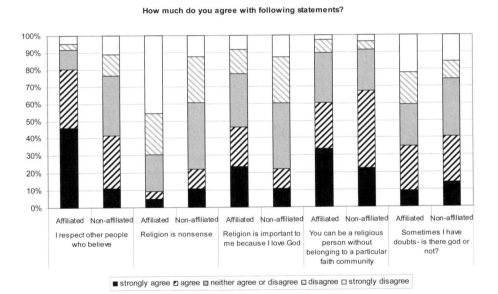

Religious affiliation. The 'affiliated' agreed significantly more strongly with most of the statements in this section, either in regard to their own belief ('Religion is important to me because I love God' (***)) or belief of others ('I respect other people who believe' (***)). When different variables of religiosity are compared, then the statement 'I respect other people who believe' was most agreed by those who valued religion as very important (1.63) and students who declared their religious affiliation (1.87); least agreement was shown by those who found religion as absolutely not important (3.41) and did not believe in god or any spirit (3.11). The 'affiliated' also disagreed more strongly with the negative statement 'Religion is nonsense' (***). There were only three exceptions in this block, where differences were insignificant: readiness to change one's mind, doubts about God (the statement was not applicable to those who do not believe in God) and 'you can be a religious person without belonging to a particular faith community', which were equally supported by both groups (Figure 6).

A strong bipolarity among the 'affiliated', despite no differences of means compared to 'non-affiliated', can be observed in two statements: 'religion is something one inherits from one's family' and 'religion is a private matter', where the 'affiliated' either 'strongly agreed' or 'strongly disagreed' with these statements, while others used more middle options. There were significant differences in answers to statements 'I don't know much about religion and thus I can't have an opinion' (***) and 'Religion does not interest us ...' (**), where the 'affiliated' disagreed more with the statements than the 'non-affiliated'.

Language. 'Russians' agreed significantly more with statements that they love God (**), religion determines their life (*), less significantly with other statements about positive impact of religion on their life, but also in these cases they were remarkably more likely to use the option 'agree strongly'. 'Russians' were more likely to disagree with the statement that religion is open to change (**). The statement of the social impact of religion 'religion is important in our history' was more likely to be disagreed with by 'Russians' than by 'Estonians' (*). 'Estonians' were more likely to accept that a person could be religious without belonging to any religious community (*).

Although more 'Russians' than 'Estonians' agreed that religion belongs to the private sphere (**), 'Estonians' agreed that religion is inherited from family, while 'Russians' were more divergent – likely to strongly agree and even more to disagree with this statement (**). 'Estonians' were more likely to think that they know too little about religion, so cannot have an opinion about it (*).

Talking about religion – with whom?

In this section we work with questions 62–67. Overall, students do not speak about religion hardly with anybody and hardly at all. The most popular option for all the answers of this group was 'never'. It is obvious that students rarely discuss religion – all the means were over 4[18], least spoken with were 'other students at school' and 'religious leaders'. Four students out of five spoke about religion with their family members, friends and classmates less than once a month or never; they were most likely to discuss religion with a teacher, about every fourth spoke with a teacher about religion at least once a month. Again we can look at the effect of different influences on views on these questions.

Studies of religion. There were no differences in some cases, as talking about religion with religious leaders, other students at school and family. There were significant differences for those who have studied RE recently if compared to all other groups in talking more frequently about religion with teachers (***), classmates (***) and some differences in talking with friends (*, Figure 7).

Religious affiliation. Although the 'affiliated' talked more about religion, they rarely talked about it at school. The significant differences occur only outside of school – students talked more often with family (***), friends (**) and religious leaders (***).

Language. Even if 'Russians' valued family and friends as sources of information about religion, the reported frequency in talking about religion with them is almost the same as among 'Estonians'. Significant differences exist in regard to talking with teachers (*) and classmates

---

18 Scale: 1 – about every day, 2 – about every week, 3 – about once a month, 4 – less than once a month,
    5 – never

– 'Estonians' are more likely to talk with them on a regular basis, while the 'Russians' more likely never; instead 'Russians' are a little bit more likely to talk with religious leaders about religion (*).

Figure 7:   **Talking about religion (Q. 62, 64, 66) by model of RE (%)**

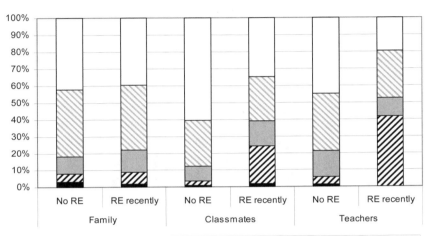

Contacts with different religions

In this section we work with the questions 68–78. Interesting, but perhaps not surprising, is that more than half of the students do not know their friends' or classmates' views of religion, or even if their classmates belong to any religion. Every fourth student believes that there are no students at their class belonging to (another) religion. The data, according to the religious affiliation students stated themselves, shows that 10% of students studied in classes where none of the students had a religious affiliation: 35% of students did not socialise with students of a different religious background outside of school, 28% said that they communicate only with the similarly minded at school. From the comments given in response to the question it seems that religion is not a factor in friendships.

Studies of religion. In two aspects, students who had integrated RE differed from others. They were more likely to believe that their views on religion are different from their parents' (*). They shared views with those who had studied RE long ago, that in school they socialise with students having a different religious background.

Religious affiliation. For the group of questions on how much students associated with people of different religious backgrounds, the biggest differences between the 'affiliated' and 'non-affiliated' was that the 'non-affiliated' were less likely to know about the religion of their friends, classmates or family members and parents, whereas the 'affiliated' tended to mention that they have friends (*), classmates and family members of different religions, and they associate with them in their spare time and at school (Figure 8). However, there was no significant difference between the 'affiliated' and 'non-affiliated' as to whether they *preferred* to socialise with peers of the same religion as themselves at school and in their spare time.

Surprisingly, the less students valued religion, the more they preferred to go with similarly minded people at school and in their spare time. The same was true of students who did not believe in god or any spirit. There were no significant differences on the question about whether friends and classmates share their views according to religious background (Figure 8).

Figure 8:   **Contacts with other religions (Q. 69, 70, 72, 74, 75) by religious affiliation (%)**

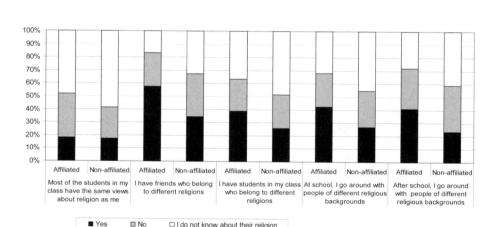

Gender. Although there were no statistically significant differences in the answers to any of the questions, girls had slightly more similar views about religion to their friends and had more friends with different religious backgrounds. Boys used the option 'I do not know about their religion' for all the statements more than girls did.

Language. The most striking difference between 'Russians and 'Estonians' was that 'Russians' were less likely to know about their parents' religion and to have parents of a different religious background (*). In addition they were less likely to know their parents' views of religion and they believed that their parents thought about religion differently from themselves (*). The results contradict the answers given at the end of questionnaire, where students had to report the religion their parents belong to. The differences on religious diversity in the family were not significant in these later questions and 'Estonians' tended to use more frequently the option that they do not know their parents' religion.

Synopsis of data – religion in students' lives
Religion was not considered important by most of the respondents. They saw religion as more important in history than in their own life. Family and school played the most important role in teaching about religion.
There were no differences in terms of belonging or belief in God between the groups who had experienced different models of RE. Students who have studied RE in primary classes believed more in 'some sort of spirit'. Students with experience of RE in primary classes said that they attend religious services and prayed more frequently, and thought more about

the meaning of life or about religion. At the same time they saw religion as nonsense more than others did. More significant differences could be observed in those who had recently studied RE. They used and valued such sources, as school, media and Internet to obtain information about religion and their interest in and readiness to talk about religion with people of different backgrounds was higher than among those who did not have special religious studies. In addition, students who studied RE saw the societal dimension of religion, they valued tolerance more highly, and also they more often saw differences as not only normal but also an interesting part of life.

Students with a religious background were much more positive not only about religion but also about differences in general. They saw religion and all the sources as more important than their peers without religious affiliation. They spoke more frequently about religion, but did so mainly with like-minded groups – family members, friends and religious leaders. Probably more surprising were the findings that the 'affiliated' and 'non-affiliated' have equal doubts about existence of God, are equally ready to change their minds and think that it is possible to be a believer without belonging to any religious community, and without preferring the company of the same religious background in school and in their spare time. The 'affiliated' were more aware of the religious background of their fellows. They spoke more frequently about religion in family and with friends. They did not exchange ideas on religious issues with people of different religious background, such as for example classmates, but neither did the non-affiliated students.

Girls tended to be more positive about religion and its effects than boys for almost all statements, especially for interest in religious topics and respecting people of different religious backgrounds. At the same time, the frequency of different religious practices, as well as talking about religion with different groups, did not differ.

Language proved to be a very important factor in the way religion was understood. 'Russians' believed in the existence of God regardless of their religious affiliation, while for 'Estonians' it was determined by their religious affiliation. 'Russians' valued more 'individual' practice such as prayer; and family and friends to be sources of information about religion. They valued religion more as a moral guide and help in life; they were also less ready to change their mind on religious issues. The opposite was the case for statements about social impacts of religion, taking part in religious events, religion being important in history, valuing school as source of information and a place to talk about religion, which were more valued by 'Estonians'.

2.1.2 Data interpretation

Most of the students in Estonia saw religion as a historical or distant phenomenon, probably relevant for somebody else, but not for them personally. Religion was not a topic to discuss. Most of the students were not hostile to religion but they saw it as a very private matter, not to be shown publicly in any way.

In contrast to some public concerns in Estonia that RE would convert students to Christianity, it was impossible to find any evidence of this. Even those who studied Bible stories in primary classes did not believe in God more than others, although they tended to be less atheistic and to believe more in 'some sort of spirit'. Such a spiritual dimension could be detected in their slightly more frequent attendance at religious services and praying, and more often thinking about the meaning of life or about religion. The students who have studied RE recently used and valued more knowledge-based sources in finding information about religion and showed more readiness to start a conversation with people of different backgrounds. Probably the knowledge they have about different religions, and skills they acquire, lessen their prejudices about religious issues and dread in front of difference. The idea that more tolerant family background may influence the views of students who studied RE seems weak, because the most tolerant views were held by those students who studied RE recently and happened to study at schools where all or almost all students from corresponding classes studied RE. In addition, the students from the same school, but from different classes who have yet not studied RE, showed less tolerant views.

Students' religious background was most influential in the personal dimension of religion, as was expected, but it did not affect doubts about existence of God. Although students with religious affiliation were more aware of their friends' religious background, they did not choose their friends on that basis. They talked about religion and valued people with a similar religious background as theirs, while avoiding topics in segregated groups. This shows their wish to be taken seriously and they achieve it by avoiding topics which could exclude them from their peers.

Although the difference in responses of 'affiliated' and 'non-affiliated' was significant, there was a whole group of statements where distinctions between nationalities proved to be even more significant. The content of belief was based more on nationality than on the religious affiliation of 'Russians'. The beliefs of 'Estonians' seem to be more consistent with their religious affiliation or lack thereof. 'Russians' tended to see religion as a part of their identity, often regardless of their religious affiliation. They saw religion as private and individual, not related to social life. In this respect it can be surprising that 'Estonians' were more likely to accept that a person could be religious without belonging to any religious community. One explanation could be that 'Russians' felt more attached to believing in God, while 'Estonians' believed in some sort of spirit or life force, where religious tradition does not play so important a role. Another surprising tendency was that 'Estonians' were more likely to believe that religion is inherited from family and 'Russians' believed that they do not share beliefs with their parents. Probably it could be explained by confrontation between adolescents and their parents. Among the 'Russians' it is worthwhile to disagree about religion in order to find out one's own, intimate and individual belief, while for 'Estonians' it is just a theoretical question about 'other' people who probably inherited their beliefs from family.

2.2   How do pupils see religion in school?

2.2.1   Data description

It was easier for students to take a stand on questions about religion in school than about religion in general. The number of students who chose the middle option 'neither agree nor disagree' in the questions about religious education was usually about 30%, which is less than in other blocks of questions.

Evaluation of experiences with studies of religion

In this section we work with questions 3–12. The statements of interest and importance of dealing with religion had a distribution with normal curve; almost equal numbers of students agreed and disagreed with the statements. Statements about the good impact of education on religious issues on peaceful and respectful co-existence of representatives of different religions were more agreed upon. The statements about the usefulness of religion in learning about oneself or in making moral decisions were rejected. The statement about possible quarrels because of such studies was strongly rejected. We can now consider the reactions of groups of students.

Studies of religion. The students who have studied RE recently, rated their studies about religious issues much higher in all aspects: they found more than any other group that they gain knowledge about religion (***), they can look at topics from different perspectives (***), RE is interesting (**) and they respect people with different religious backgrounds (**). Together with students who had had RE long ago or had integrated RE they found that it is important to deal with religion at school (*) and it helps to understand contemporary events (*; Figure 9). Only views on making moral decisions and learning about oneself showed no significant differences between groups.

Religious affiliation. The 'affiliated' students were more positive in their ratings than the 'non-affiliated' in this group of questions almost in every case, but the differences were not as significant as the differences between those who learned RE recently and those who had not. The only exception in this respect was for the personal impact of these studies, where the 'affiliated' agreed more with the statement that RE helps them to learn about themselves (**), while there were no significant differences in regard to those who have studied RE or not. The 'affiliated' diverged significantly from the 'non-affiliated' by their strong agreement that they learn at school to respect other religions (*), the religious topics are interesting for them (*) and important to deal with (*).

Gender. Female students gave more positive responses to all the answers in this group except for religion causing problems at school, where there were no significant differences. At a more significant level they agreed that learning about religion is interesting (**), important (**) and it helps people to live in peace (**).

Figure 9:   **Evaluation of religious education (Q. 3–6) by model of RE (%)**

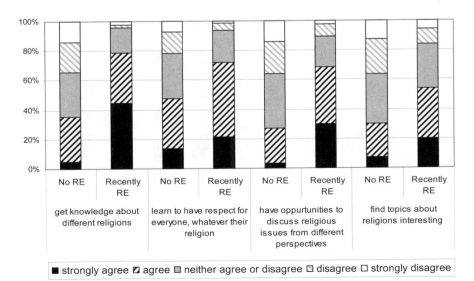

Language. 'Russians' significantly more than 'Estonians' agreed strongly that at school they learn to respect everyone (**). All the other statements in this section were agreed more by 'Estonians'. The statements of societal dimension were significantly more agreed by Estonians: studies on religious issues help to understand current events (**), live together in peace (**), but also that it is important to learn about different religions (**). More personal evaluations, such as 'learning about religion helps to understand oneself' or 'to make moral decisions', did not make significant distinctions.

Manifestation of religion in school

In this section we work with questions 13–19. Only two ways for religion to appear in school were more accepted than rejected – allowing the wearing of discreet religious symbols (mean 1.9[19]) and being absent on religious holidays (2.6). More ritualistic and school-oriented demands, such as a special room for praying (3.8) and voluntary services (3.8) were strongly rejected. Surprisingly, a special menu was not seen as acceptable by many respondents (3.3).

Studies of religion. The students who studied RE long ago or had integrated RE were slightly more likely to be in favour of several ways religion could appear in school, but more for the statement about religious services at school, where they agreed more than disagreed with the statement (**, Figure 10), also they supported the right to be absent from school for religious reasons and to wear more visible religious symbols.

Figure 10:   Manifestation of religion in school (Q. 19, 18, 14) by model of RE, gender and religious affiliation (%)

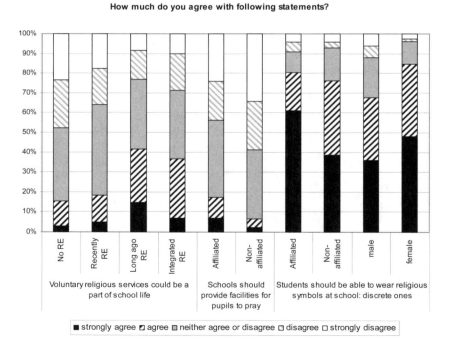

---

19 Statements here and after had to be judged on the scale: 1 – strongly agree, 2 – agree, 3 – neither agree or disagree, 4 – disagree, 5 – strongly disagree.

Religious affiliation. Somewhat surprising was the finding that only two items made significant differences on the basis of religious affiliation: the right to wear discreet religious symbols (*) and that school should provide facilities for pupils to pray (*; Figure 10). In other statements, although 'affiliated' more likely 'strongly agreed', they made no significant differences in their views if agreements and disagreements are compared.

Gender. The only significant difference here was that girls agreed more with the right to wear discreet religious symbols (**; Figure 10). All other differences were insignificant; boys took more extreme positions, while girls were more reserved.

Language. There were no significant differences in this group of questions; several ways for religion to appear were agreed with by 'Estonians' a bit more than by 'Russians'. 'Estonians' agreed significantly more that students should be able to wear visible religious symbols (*; Figure 10).

Aims for RE

In this section we work with questions 32–36. RE, in students' view, should be knowledge-oriented. Students strongly rejected the idea that school should provide religious beliefs for students (mean 3.6). All other aims were more appreciated (2.3–2.5) and 'to get objective knowledge' was the most agreed with.

Figure 11:   Aims for RE (Q. 34, 36, 32, 35) by model of RE, religious affiliation and gender (%)

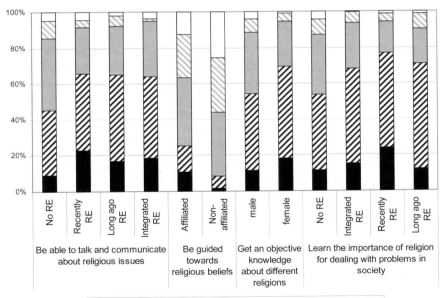

Studies of religion. Only in regard to confessional aims of RE all the students equally disagreed; other statements clearly distinguished students with 'no RE' from other groups. They agreed significantly less that students should be able to talk about religion at school (**; Figure 11) or learn the importance of religion for dealing with problems in society (**). They were less interested in getting knowledge about religion (*) or learn to understand what religions teach.

Religious affiliation. 'Affiliated' agreed more with all the aims, but more significantly with personal aims of RE: to be guided towards religious belief (**; Figure 11), and also what religions teach (*). 'Affiliated' wanted students more to learn to speak about religious issues (*).

The difference is even more remarkable when those who regard religion to be as very important for them are compared to those for whom religion is not important at all (means 1.88 and 3.04). Still, 'be guided towards religious beliefs' was the least valued aim for RE also among 'affiliated' (3.09), while 'learn to understand what religions teach' (2.10) and 'get objective knowledge' (2.14) were the most favoured. The 'non-affiliated' valued objective knowledge (2.38) and importance of religion in society (2.44) more than other aims.

Gender. Girls agreed with all the statements about different aims for RE significantly more than boys (*), except equal disagreement on being guided towards religious belief by both groups.

Language. All aims for RE were valued by 'Estonians' higher, except 'to be guided towards religious belief'. Three answers were significantly different. 'Estonians' valued significantly more that students should learn about impact of religion on society (**) and that students should be able to talk on religious issues (**). Similarly, 'Estonians' agreed that learning about religions should give knowledge about different world religions (*).

Models of RE

In this section we work with questions 26–31. The most agreed statement from the whole questionnaire was that on the voluntary basis of RE (1.9) where more than half of students strongly agreed and about one third agreed with the statement. About half of students agreed strongly or agreed that all they need to know about religion is covered by other subjects. Slightly more students agreed with confessional subject instead of common subject, if the subject should be introduced at school. The statement about no place for religion in school was the most confusing for students – half of respondents could not take a stand.

Studies of religion. Only one statement did not give significant differences between those with different experiences with RE: voluntary participation in RE lessons. Students without RE experience agreed more than the others that there is no place for religion at school (**). The group with recent experience of RE diverged significantly from all others in its opinions about RE. They supported common RE (**; Figure 12), they disagreed with a statement that groups should be separated by religious affiliation (*) and with the statement that RE is not needed as a separate subject (**; Figure 12). Those who studied RE long ago had similar positions regarding RE models to those with no experience of RE, except favouring more the need of religiously segregated groups in studying RE.

Figure 12:   Models of RE (Q. 30, 29, 26) by religious affiliation, model of RE and language (%)

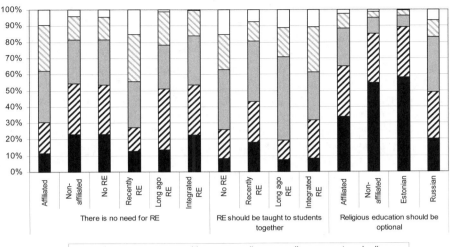

Religious affiliation. 'Affiliated' valued religious studies more highly and rejected the claim that RE as a separate subject is not needed (*; Figure 12) and 'There should be no place for religion in school life' (*). Nevertheless, they opposed more than 'non-affiliated' the forms of RE which could cause their segregation, such as optional studies of RE (**; Figure 12) or studies in confessional groups.

Language. There were no significant differences in opinions about the need for RE. Significantly more 'Estonians' strongly agreed that RE must be optional (***; Figure 12), slightly more also with need to learn it according to own religious background. 'Russians' were more likely to agree with the statement that there should be no place for religion in school (*).

Showing views about religion in school

In this section we work with questions 78, 79, 81 and 82. More students (45%) in Estonia were interested in the way their best friends thinks about religion than were not (23%, mean 2.8)). At the same time, such an interest is often rather passive – 30% of students agreed and 33% disagreed with the statement that it does not bother them what friends think about religion (mean 3.0). Students were more likely to think that a student who openly shows his/her religious belief risks being mocked (2.6) than to think that it is problematic for themselves (3.4).

Studies of religion. The group most interested in the views of their friends were the students who studied RE in primary school (*, mean 2.4) and the most disinterested students were those without any form of RE (2.9). Students showed no significant differences according to religious studies or gender.

Gender. Girls showed more interest in their friends' views about religion than boys did (**, means 2.5 vs 3.1).

Religious affiliation and language. 'Affiliated' were more likely than 'non-affiliated' to agree with personal statements that it is problematic for them to show their religion (**; Figure 13) and they would like to know about the way their best friend thinks about religion (*, means 2.5 vs 2.8), but showed less difference with the general statement that some believers could be teased. For this, more general statement, significant difference was between language-groups, where 'Estonians' agreed more that a student can be teased at school on religious grounds (**; Figure 13). 'Russian' religious affiliated students were most concerned about showing up their religious convictions; they were the only ones who saw their own problems as 'problems of a student', while all other groups believed to be it more a problem for others. Estonians, in spite of their lower religious affiliation than Russians, were more interested in the ways their best friend thinks about religion (2.7 vs 3.1).

Figure 13: Showing views about religion (Q. 81, 82) by language and religious affiliation (%)

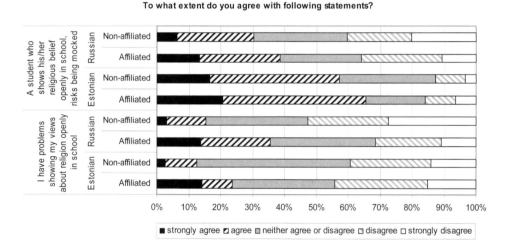

To what extent do you agree with following statements?

■ strongly agree ▨ agree ▤ neither agree or disagree ☐ disagree ☐ strongly disagree

---

Synopsis of data – religion in school

Students surveyed in Estonia did not believe that a school was a good place for religious or personal religious growth, but rather valued the knowledge-based approach and learning to respect each other. The young people, for whom religion seems not to be a part of life, did not see any reason for religion to appear in school or to guarantee rights for students with a religious background; they rather refused these rights, except for wearing discreet religious symbols, as some students do.

Students who had studied RE or had religion integrated in a special way to their school life, valued the subject matter more highly and found it to be helpful in understanding society. The students who had studied the subject recently valued objective knowledge, different perspectives, respect for differences and found it to be more interesting than all other students. They rejected, more than others, being segregated by religiously affiliated groups and wanted all students to learn it together. The students who had studied RE a long time ago were less satisfied with the education on religious issues and believed that RE should be taught according to religious affiliation. In addition students with integrated RE did not see any need for a separate subject, but they were more aware of the religious rights that a person has.

Students with religious affiliation did not ask for special rights or facilities for practicing their faith at school, except more individually exercised rights as wearing discreet religious symbols and a room for individual prayer. Religiously affiliated students valued RE in personal terms, such as making ethical choices and as a point of departure for personal reflection. Although they saw a positive impact of religious studies in personal terms and need for RE, they were more likely to be against studying it in religiously homogenous groups or as an optional subject. Students without religious affiliation do not see a problem in showing their (a-)religious beliefs (although they believe that it can be problematic for some students), while religious students see it as more problematic, both in personal and abstract terms.

Girls were more interested than boys in religious topics and saw learning about religions as valuable for 'peaceful together'. Gender was also an important factor in valuing manifestations of religion in schools; girls were more in favour of several ways that religion may be more visible in school.

'Estonians' were more likely in favour of voluntary RE and about positive impact of religious studies, talking about religion and knowing about its societal dimension, while 'Russians' were against religion at school, including visible religious rights. Especially the similar attitudes to the statement about the right to be excused from school on religious holidays was surprising, as the Orthodox Church of Moscow Patriarchate have different timings for Easter and Christmas from the official holidays which are according to Lutheran and Catholic tradition. Here 'Russians' took more extreme positions than 'Estonians', but 'agreed' with the statement less than 'Estonians', making no difference on total sum of agreements.

2.2.2 Data interpretation

The school was not seen as a place to practice religion, nor for it to be visible. On the one hand this shows awareness of institutional limits, seeing a school as a secular institution where religion should not have any place. On the other hand, the lack of experiences of such a need also plays some role, since religious diversity is not visible in Estonia. Only in schools with integrated RE, where religion and religious diversity are more visible, were religious rights valued more highly. The support for the status quo is seen also in students' general preference for the provision of voluntary RE or confessional RE which would exclude most of them from the obligation to take part in RE. The students were usually satisfied with the form of or lack of religious education they have experienced, whatever it was.

Religious affiliation played the most important role in opinions about religion, and a similar pattern could be found here: students differed most significantly in their opinions about RE, its aims and values, according to their own experience or lack thereof. The students who had studied religion recently valued its impact more highly and appreciated the possibility of learning it. The students with experience of RE in primary school were more sceptical, perhaps due to the Bible-oriented content of RE.

It is difficult to know how religious students feel at school in Estonia, where they cannot practice their faith openly. According to the answers, students with religious affiliation are used to keeping religion private. Although they valued the possible benefits of RE they disagreed with its confessional or optional form. Religiously affiliated students have friends among the 'non-affiliated' and probably do not want to be different from them because of their own religious background or interest on religious issues.

Students without religious affiliation are in a 'majority' position; they do not see it as problematic to show their religious beliefs, while religious students do. 'Non-affiliated' students still can see that it is problematic for some students, although the 'affiliated' saw it as a more urgent problem at the abstract level as well. Probably in this light, religiously affiliated students would like students, themselves as well as the others, to be able to talk about religious issues. One of the influences can be the way religion is dealt in the media and internet forums, where religion and religious people are often severely ridiculed and criticised (Valk, 2006, p. 175).

In regard to language we must remember that there were no Russian schools providing religious studies in our sample, although some students have studied it in some other schools in primary classes and that 'Russians' tended to be more religiously affiliated. Their attitudes towards religion, religious practice and content of belief were consistent, their identity as ethnic Russians overcame the effects of their specific religious affiliation. 'Russian' and 'Estonian' respondents diverged by their attitudes about the personal and societal aspects of religion; their answers to the role of religion in school follow an analogous pattern: 'Estonians' agreed more with religious studies and other societal statements. Maybe surprising was the difference in attitudes to voluntary RE. There could be two explanations – that 'Russians' did not want any form of RE or that the 'Estonian' respondents were more influenced by discussions in the media about the need for voluntary instead of obligatory RE.

2.3   How do pupils see the impact of religion?

2.3.1   Data description

Expected outcomes of religious studies

In this section we work with questions 20–25. Students rejected the idea that school provides or should provide religious beliefs. In addition more personal, although not strictly religious aims, such as developing moral values or one's own point of view were less agreed with than other statements. In students' view religious studies should rather help them to understand the world. The most agreed statement was that knowledge about religion helps to understand history, but not agreed that it should support developing moral values. There were no significant differences according to the experience with RE.

Religious affiliation. 'Affiliated' agreed with all the statements of the block, as with personal outcomes of religious studies: to develop moral values (**; Figure 14), to develop one's point of view (**; Figure 14) or in more interpersonal statement 'to understand others and live peacefully with them' (**) and less diverse in learning about own religion (*).

Gender. Girls agreed more with all the statements about the different effects of religious studies than boys, with more significant differences on item related to 'peaceful together', 'to understand others and learn to live in peace with them' (*; Figure 14).

Language. 'Estonians' agreed slightly more that learning about religions helps to understand history and current events (Figure 14).

Figure 14:   Outcomes of religious studies (Q. 24, 25, 30–32) by religious affiliation, gender and language (%)

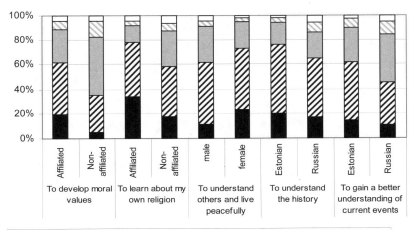

To what extent do you agree that learning about different religions helps:

■ strongly agree ▨ agree ▣ neither agree or disagree ▢ disagree ▢ strongly disagree

Religion in a society

In this section we work with questions 82–85. About half of students did not take a stand on negative or hostile statements about religion or religious people. More students disagreed that 'religion is source of aggression' and that 'without religion the world would be a better place', but many did agree with such statements. The mean was 3.2–3.4.

Studies of religion. The students who studied RE long ago differed most remarkably in all answers of this section. They agreed with those who have integrated RE that religion is a source of aggression (*; Figure 15). Although the other differences are not so significant, but still remarkable as such views occur in some other 'intolerant' statements – those who have studied RE long ago agreed a bit more than the others that the world would be a better place without religion and that religious people are less tolerant. The students who have never studied RE were less than all other groups interested in the views of the best friend about religion (mean 2.89 if compared to those who studied RE long ago 2.44 or recently 2.56).

Religious affiliation. 'Affiliated' disagreed significantly more with hostile statements that religion is a source of aggression (**) and the world would be better without it (**) or religious people are less tolerant (*; Figure 15).

Figure 15:   Religion in a society (Q. 83, 85) by gender, religious affiliation and model of RE (%)

To what extent do you agree with the following statements your peers have made?

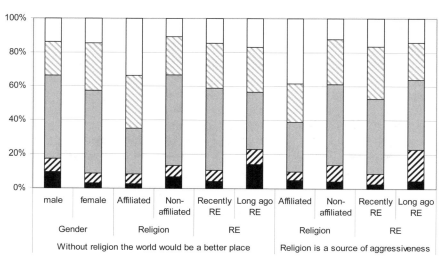

The answers of students were compared also by different independent variables, including religious affiliation, how important they think religion is or what they believe in. The differences are quite remarkable, especially in regard to the importance of religion. 'Without religion the world would be a better place' was less agreed by those for whom religion was very important (mean 4.25), who had religious affiliation (3.91) and who believed in God (3.87), most agreed by those for whom religion was not important at all (2.79) and had no religious affiliation (2.82). The students who valued religion were more likely to be curious about their fellows' views on religion than students for who has no relevance in their lives (means respectively 2.05 and 3.29).

Gender. There were no gender differences as to whether 'religious people are less tolerant towards others'. Boys agreed significantly more with other two more abstract negative statements about religion (*; Figure 15).

Talking about religion – why?

In this section we work with questions 87–97. Despite rarely speaking about religion (see 2.1 "Talking about religion – with whom?") students were not so negative about its effects. Equal distribution characterised most of the answers in this group. Most of all students agreed that talking about religion is interesting because of different opinions (2.5). In addition they agreed slightly more with the statement that they knew too little about religion to be able to talk about it and it does not interest them (2.8). The most disagreed with statements were that it was embarrassing to talk about (3.6) and that they talk about 'how stupid religion' is (3.4).

Studies of religion. Those who did not study RE differed from all other students in many answers of this group. They agreed that they do not know about religion (*) and, with those who have studied RE long ago, that it is embarrassing to talk about religion (*; Figure 16), The same pattern occurred with interest as with knowledge – those who had studied it less, were also less interested in different opinions (*). Although there is a weak significance, it is still remarkable that students, who had studied RE long ago, agreed that they talk about the stupidity and cruelty of religion.

Figure 16:   Reasons to talk about religion (Q. 91, 90, 87) by model of RE, language, religious affiliation and gender (%)

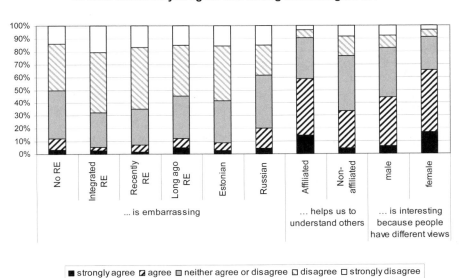

To what extent do you agree that talking about religion ...?

■ strongly agree ▨ agree ▫ neither agree or disagree □ disagree □ strongly disagree

Religious affiliation. All the positive attitudes towards values of talking about religion, are supported significantly more by the 'affiliated' without any exception. The statements 'it helps us to understand others' (**; Figure 16) and 'it helps to shape my own views' (**) were the most distinctive among the positive statements. Some negative statements showed even bigger differences (e.g. 'I do not know about religion …' (***) and 'religion does not interest us …' (**)). There were no significant differences between groups about the statement that it is embarrassing to talk about religion. They very strongly negative statement '… how stupid religion is …' showed only small differences – the percentage of those strongly agreeing with the statement was the same across groups.

More significant differences could be found if the variable of how important religion is taken into account (some examples of means for 'religion is very important' *vs* 'not important at all' are given in brackets): talking about religion is interesting because of different views people held (1.97 *vs* 3.03), it helps to shape one's own views (2.22 *vs* 3.51), it helps to understand others (2.12 *vs* 3.44). All the statements followed the same pattern: the statements were more agreed with the more the person valued the importance of religion for himself/herself.

Gender. Girls were significantly more optimistic about the positive effects of speaking about religious issues, especially positive statements about having different opinions 'To me, talking about religion is interesting because people have different views' (**; Figure 16) and about the effect of mutual understanding 'Talking about religion helps us to understand others' (**). In addition they believed more than boys that talking about religion helps to shape their own views.

Language. Four statements had significant distinctions. 'Russians' were more likely to agree or agreed strongly that it is embarrassing to talk about religion (*; Figure 16). Although 'Estonians' were more likely to think that religion is a boring topic or that they know less about religion, so cannot have an opinion (*), they were more likely to agree that different opinions make talking about religion interesting (*) and helps to build 'a peaceful together' (*).

Meeting a different opinion – how?

In this section we work with questions 98–102. The questions about how students would react to a peer with a different religious view showed that students were likely to listen but not to allow the views of others to influence them, and were least likely to try to convince others of their own views (Figure 17).

Figure 17: Way of reacting to a different view (Q. 100, 99, 102) by gender, religious affiliation and language (%)

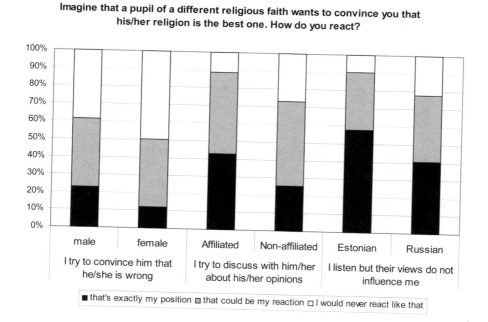

Studies of religion. There were no significant differences in the ways they react to a peer with different religious views between groups according to their experience with RE. Albeit, students without RE tended more to ignore and convince than discuss and find common ground.

Religious affiliation. The only significant difference was in trying to discuss the views (*; Figure 17), where the 'affiliated' said that they would much more likely use the strategy. More significant differences could be found on the bases of importance of religion, the students for whom religion was not important preferred ignoring (1.77 *vs* 'very important' 2.20), while those who valued religion favoured discussing the opinions (1.54 *vs* 'not important at all' 2.77).

Gender. All the questions on the ways to react on different views were significantly different for girls and for boys. Girls were significantly more likely to discuss with (**) and listen to the other (*). Boys were significantly more likely to explain that their own opinions were right (*; Figure 17), to ignore the other (*), or attempt to convince that he is wrong (*).

Language. There were no differences in responses to this block of questions, except 'Estonians' preferred significantly more than 'Russians' to listen to a different view but not to be affected by it (*; Figure 17).

Opinions about people of different worldviews and religions living together

In this section we work with questions 103–106. The statement that representatives of different religions can live together was not answered by almost half of students. The questions on the views about differences revealed that students agreed that respect for others' religions would help to cope with differences and disagreements on religious issues. Students in Estonia more likely disagreed with the statement that they do not like to live with members of other religions.

Studies of religion. In answer to this group of questions, those without RE differed from all other groups. They disagreed strongly that religious differences can lead to conflicts (*). They were almost without exception the only ones who strongly disagreed with it and also with a statement that representatives of strict religions cannot live together (*; Figure 18). In addition they agreed less that respect can help people to live peacefully together (*). In contrast, they were significantly more likely to dislike people from other religions and to want to live separately from them (*).

Religion. Students with religious affiliation tended to have more tolerant attitudes than the 'non-affiliated'. They were significantly more likely to agree that respecting the religion of others helps to cope with differences (Figure 18) and to disagree that 'I don't like people from other religions and do not want to live with them'. There was no significant difference between the 'affiliated' and 'non-affiliated' for the other two questions.

If different variables are compared, there was more respect for living peacefully together by students who valued religion as very important (2.19), respondents who declared their religious affiliation (2.25) and those believing in spirit or life force (2.31). Those who found religion as absolutely not important (2.78) and did not believe in god or any spirit (2.63) showed the least agreement. The very strong statement 'I don't like people from other religions and do not want to live together with them' was most agreed with by those for whom religion was not important at all (3.57) and who did not believe in god or spirit (3.6). It was least of all agreed by students with religious affiliation (4.02) and who found religion to be important for them (4.00).

Gender. Significantly more girls agreed that respect can help people to live peacefully together (*) and disagreed that they do not like representatives of different religions (**; Figure 18).

Language. Striking differences in attitudes towards the possibility to live peacefully together appeared between language groups. 'Estonians' agreed significantly more likely that strict religions cannot live together (**) and disagreements on religious grounds can lead to conflicts (**; Figure 18), but respect can help to peaceful co-existence (**).

Figure 18: Views about people of different worldviews living together (Q. 103–106) by model of RE, religious affiliation and gender (%)

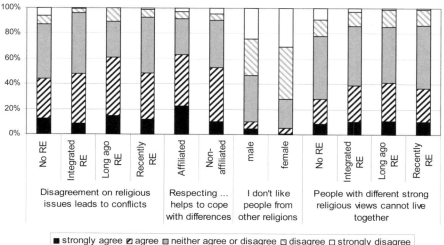

How people of different worldviews and religions could live together?

In this section we work with questions 107–112. Knowledge about different religions was highlighted as the most helpful factor for living 'peaceful together', while keeping religion for oneself and strong regulations by state were not believed to be as effective in building peace.

Studies of religion. Students with 'no RE' believed less than others that knowledge of religions could help to live peacefully together (*; Figure 19) or if they know someone personally (*).

Religious affiliation. For most questions in this group there were no differences between students with and without a religious background, except the effect of strong laws about religion, slightly more agreed with by religiously affiliated students (Figure 19).

Gender. Girls and boys agreed or disagreed with statements in a similar way, with the only exception being that girls valued more highly the influence of knowledge for peaceful co-existence (*; Figure 19).

Language. There were significant differences in this block of questions, 'Estonians' being more positive about all the ways to improve peace among different religions. 'Estonians' valued significantly more highly knowledge about each other (***; Figure 19), but common activities (**; Figure 19), shared interest (**) and personal relations with representatives of a religion (**) were also believed to be more effective. Less agreed upon was keeping religion private, supported especially by 'Russians' (*). 'Russians' believed also slightly less in state regulations.

Figure 19:   Ways for people of different worldviews to live together (Q. 108, 112, 110) by gender, model of RE, language and religious affiliation (%)

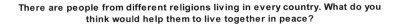

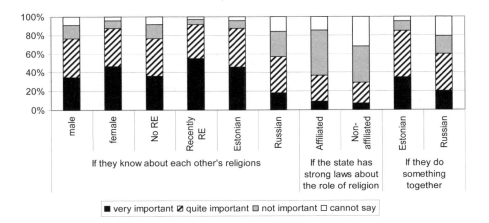

Synopsis of data – impact of religion

Estonian students showed their distant attitude to religion also in this group of question by saying that it does not interest them, they do not know about religion and regarding outcomes of speaking about religion low. Nevertheless, they believed in respect and possibility to live together with people of different religions. They valued the role of knowledge and did not believe that keeping religion private would foster peaceful co-existence.

The students who had learned RE in primary school were more ready to see religion as violent. The students who did not have religious studies at upper grades in school tended to be more negative in their responses to religion and differences on religious grounds than students who have studied RE. They were less likely to believe that religion could cause any troubles but they believed less in possibilities to improve a tense situation if there would be some need for it.

Religiously affiliated students showed more respect and readiness for dialogue with people of different views about religion. They valued more highly respect, knowledge and personal relations to improve peaceful coexistence between different religious groups.

Girls proved to me more looking and finding harmony in their surroundings and between religiously diverse groups; they valued respect and knowledge about religions more than boys. Boys showed themselves to be more militant – they did not like differences and would ignore them or try to convince others of their own views more than girls would.

'Russians' more likely agreed that it is embarrassing to talk about religion. They also believed more that people of strict religions can live together and people do not conflict on religious grounds. At the same time, they were also more sceptical about different means to improve relations, including respect and strong laws.

2.3.2 Data interpretation

The views of students on the role of religion in society contradict their other responses. On the one hand they value knowledge of different religions in fostering peaceful co-existence and did not believe in keeping religion private. At the same time, they say that they do not know about religion and are not interested in religion or in studying about it. Nor did they believe in the good effects of speaking on religious issues. Probably, since religion was not important for them, it was difficult to imagine that it can be important enough for people to fight over, or if the conflict would arise they could not imagine that it could be solved.

Why the students with early RE experience were more hostile to religion? Such a correlation must be checked. It can be that their understanding of religion has not become complex enough and consistent with their development, while the understandings they hold in childhood are rejected. In contrast, students with recent RE experience were more open to religious differences and respectful of religion than were students without such experience.

The more open-minded views on religious diversity of religiously affiliated students could be due to their minority position. As we saw, they were quite well adapted to it and they would only benefit from such an attitude, so they try to create the reality they want by believing in it.

Why did 'Russians', who were less likely to believe that they would be teased on religious grounds think that it was embarrassing to talk about religion? It corresponds to their individual approach to religion discussed earlier. The religion is so private, that is not proper to discuss; religion has primarily an individual, not a societal dimension. That could explain why they believed less in religions' potential to create conflicts and were more sceptical about different means to improve relations, including respect and strong laws. Religion is believed to be a personal matter, not to cause conflicts; for the same reason there is no need for tolerance.

3. Comparison with the results of the qualitative survey

The main criteria for selecting schools in the quantitative and qualitative surveys (see Schihalejev, 2008) were similar. Geographical, demographic, and linguistic factors, religious ethos of the area, and organization of RE were taken into account in both surveys. We wanted to maintain a variety in the qualitative study, as its results would let us identify some patterns in answers of students with different experience of RE and in the language of studies. The number of schools in qualitative study was smaller and was added to by the quantitative study. This enabled us to compare groups with different models of studies about religion and their views on dealing with religious diversity. The qualitative study concentrated only on municipal non-selective schools; in the quantitative study we included selective schools and schools with religious ethos to have a bigger variety of attitudes and backgrounds. Geographical variety was enlarged by adding big schools with presumed religious diversity from Tallinn and Tartu, and smaller schools with presumed homogeneity from different 'border areas' – western islands, southeastern villages, and a northeastern industrial town.

The role of religion in pupils' life. Many students in both surveys found religion to be irrelevant. Few of them saw themselves as associated with a religious tradition and they can think about it only in abstract and impersonal terms, having difficulty defining their own worldview or religious affiliation. However, Russian-speaking students diverged greatly in their attitudes to religion in both surveys. For Russian-speaking students religion was a personal matter, closely related to their identity, in an intimate and personal manner, almost irrespective of their religious affiliation. At the same time, religion has hardly any societal aspect for them; it is not regarded as the means to belong into a group. Although family is important for Russian-speaking respondents, they also rebel against its beliefs and are fighting for their own ways of believing as the quantitative survey shows, more than 'Estonian' students. The qualitative study can shed light on the characteristics of such a search – in this struggle they stay close to the belief in monotheistic God and use many concepts of Orthodox tradition, being hardly aware of other religious traditions.

One of the findings, that school is more important than family as a source of information about religions, for Estonian speaking students, was not confirmed by the quantitative study. Only the students, who studied RE recently, valued school more than family as a source of information. In qualitative survey we noticed that students, who valued school as a source of information about religion, spoke more about different religions and ways of understanding them. It is impossible to say on the basis of the quantitative survey exactly what information students get from family or school, but it is dubious that parents with no education on religious issues can provide their children with balanced or rich information about religion. It can be quite an alarming finding, if the information received from school is valued even less. The understanding of religion must be rather fragmented and unsystematic. In both surveys one can find that students, especially without religious affiliation, confess that they do not know about religion, and they are not interested to look at information about religions in their own initiative.

Both surveys showed that students who have studied RE in the upper grades value religion as a societal force; also they value tolerance and interpersonal competencies more than those students who have learned about religion in different subjects.

The qualitative survey showed that girls were slightly less affiliated with religion, while quantitative survey had slightly more girls with religious affiliation. Although girls showed better attitudes towards religion, the frequency of religious practice did not differ from that of boys. Boys studied in the qualitative survey more 'harsh' expressions; and in the quantitative survey they chose more 'extreme' positions. From the results of both surveys, we can conclude that there are no major gender differences in religiosity, but they differ in frankness on the boys' side and for the choice of peaceful co-existence and respectful attitudes by girls.

The qualitative survey showed that students without special religious studies or personal religious background were hardly aware of the religious background of people around them. The quantitative survey also indicated that students without religious affiliation hardly knew about religious background of people around them. The students who had religious affiliation spoke more about religion, but primarily with people of a similar religious affiliation (family, religious leaders, friends), while those who study RE spoke more with diverse ones (teachers, classmates, but also friends).

Education on religious issues. The most important factor in both studies on students' views about religious studies had been their own experience with RE or lack of it. In both surveys the knowledge-oriented approach in combination with voluntary form of RE was preferred by majority of students, reflecting descriptive views of the *status quo*.

Russian speaking students strongly opposed any form of religion at school. Unfortunately in both studies we did not have enough Russian students with RE to see if the attitude could be changed by experience. Estonian speaking students diverged in their attitudes according to their experience of RE, valuing it much higher if they had had it. The students, who studied RE long ago in their primary years, even if they valued its outcomes, opposed the subject as much as those who had not studied it; only these who had studied the subject recently were in favor and saw it as needed for all students, regardless of their religious affiliation. Most of the students in our sample who had RE as a compulsory part of their school curriculum would not choose it voluntarily, as they feel this option as a factor for segregation and exclusion. Nevertheless, after personal experience of RE they see the positive impacts of religious study. Somehow contradictory to the findings of the qualitative study was the fact that the voluntary basis of RE was the only statement that made no difference among quantitative survey respondents.

In both surveys religious students valued RE more highly and opposed more strongly voluntary religious studies that could cause their segregation. If in the qualitative survey one could find that religious students are in favor of studying more about Christianity, the quantitative survey indicated that they saw more than the others how they could benefit personally from studies, but not in the same way as religious studies given by religious communities. Even if they valued outcomes of RE which help to make personal moral decisions and to build views, they value objective knowledge and learning respect towards others more highly.

In the qualitative survey girls tended to value learning about religions and especially 'learning together', and boys 'learning in groups'; although direction was the same in the quantitative study, the differences were not significant. Still, the girls' interest in being 'peaceful together' by the means of RE could be detected in the quantitative survey.

Attitudes towards religious diversity. Religion was not seen in school or in society as an important factor, so the attitudes towards religious diversity are often not personal. Many positive impacts of RE towards more open attitudes for religious diversity found in the qualitative study, were present also in the quantitative study. Religion was believed by Estonian students without religious affiliation and no experience with RE in both surveys to be so marginal that it is not believed to cause any conflicts. Both surveys identify the same tendencies in assessing different means to improve peaceful co-existence – those without a religious background and without special studies believed less in the different ways to improve peace between different religions and they more likely did not like to live in a multi religious society.

In the qualitative survey girls showed more readiness to talk about religion. The quantitative survey did not show such a trend, but girls believed in positive effects of speaking about religion and preferred using more dialogical approaches in dealing with diversity.

4.   Conclusions

The main conclusions are presented in the last chapter of the article. First, the conclusions in regard to research questions are presented. Second, the tendencies regarding our research hypothesis are discussed.

4.1   Answering the research questions

What role does religion have in pupils' life? The role of religion in pupils' life and in their surrounding is not very visible. Religion belongs more to history and 'others' than to contemporary time and 'oneself' for most students. They do not practice religion or prefer to do so privately. Religion is often regarded as so confidential that they hardly ever speak about it with anybody or know about religion of people around them. Students said that they did not choose their friends according to their religious beliefs, but some of them encounter religious diversity in their everyday life or at school. They get some information about religion primarily from family and from school.

Religiously affiliated students were more positive about religion and religious diversity, and had the same doubts and readiness to change their mind as students without religious affiliation. Religiously affiliated students value friendship and to avoid conflicts they preferred to use mostly a code of conduct to keep their religious convictions private.

How do pupils see religion in school and the impact of religion in Education? Although students in Estonia meet religious diversity at school they did not want to study about it in a systematic way, organized by special RE lessons, or to give special rights to students with religious affiliation. Their attitudes towards the proper format of religious studies mirror their own experience of it, so it is difficult for them to imagine anything beyond their own experience or even more difficult to accept forms of RE which could cause separation from their group. They did not see school as a place to develop personal views on religious issues; rather they would value learning about religion's historical and societal dimensions.

There were no tendencies for the study of religion to make students more religious. However they did value tolerance more and saw differences as not only normal but also as an interesting part of life. Those who studied RE valued school and the media as sources of information about religion. The students who had studied RE showed readiness to talk about religion and interest in talking to people of other religious backgrounds. Students with experience of RE valued studies about religions, the outcomes of such studies for everyday life and showed interest in subject much more than others did. Religiously affiliated students saw RE as a place for self-reflection, not a place to study their own religion in more confessional terms. They did not want to be segregated on religious grounds, not to study RE in confessional groups, not as an optional subject. They would rather renounce the subject than differ from their mates.

How do pupils consider the impact of religions? Although the students valued understanding the social impact of religion as an outcome of studies about religion, the belief in religion's real influence was not as strong, neither in causing conflicts, nor in building peace. They believed most of all in respect as a way to improve harmony. Those who have no experience of religious studies at school were less aware of the societal dimension of religion and believed less that religion could cause troubles. The students with no RE believed more in the risk of being teased on religious grounds. Religiously affiliated students were much more positive not only about religion but also about differences around them.

4.2   Reflections in light of the research hypotheses

1.a) Religious students are less tolerant than non-religious students

It is complicated to tell if religious students are more or less tolerant than non-religious students. First, some indicators for respect were formulated in a way that was easier for religious students to agree with. For example the statements 'I respect other people who believe', 'Without religion the world would be a better place' are probably more acceptable for students who believe or belong to some religion, as they would be giving statements about people like themselves. Some other statements could be regarded as being more neutral. For example 'I don't like people from other religions and do not want to live together with them' or 'Respecting the religion of others helps to cope with differences' means equally to all respondents that the statement is about 'people who have different worldview from mine'.

Second, there are no criteria for a 'religious' student. Can we say that a student who has a religious affiliation is 'religious'? To assess this, dependant variables of tolerance were checked against independent ones, including religious affiliation, how important they think religion is or what they believe in.

The most respectful attitudes were held by those who valued religion as very important for themselves, followed by students with religious affiliation. Nevertheless, we must be cautious not to make too bold statements, as the biggest differences were in statements which were easier to agree with for religious students. Still, the statements about the usefulness of respect and readiness to live together with religiously diverse groups were also significantly more agreed by the students who held religion as important for them. The differences on views about religion's potential for conflict were small, and these statements were least agreed by students for whom religion was very important or who believed in God. Students who valued religion as very important believed most of all in the effectiveness of respect for living peacefully together Those who found religion as absolutely not important and did not believe in god or any spirit showed least agreement.

With some restrictions we can conclude that the survey did not support the hypothesis that religious students are less tolerant. Contrarily, the more they thought that religion is important, the more they were ready to tolerate students with a different religion and also to value tolerance in improving relations between different groups.

2.a) Students who have encountered religious diversity in education are more tolerant

As the students attending different forms of religious studies did not differ by their religious affiliation, it was interesting to see how the students differ in tolerance. A more tolerant family background can be an additional factor in students who studied RE long ago or had integrated religious studies, as sometimes their parents decided their participation in lessons or going to the particular school. In the case of students who studied RE recently it was usually a choice made by their school, so they did not differ in their family background from those without RE. When the answers to questions about tolerance of these groups are compared, the differences are not so big, but a pervasive pattern occurs in the responses.

The students who have never studied RE differed from all other groups for all the statements on respect. The difference was a little bit less significant than in the case of religious affiliation in the case of more 'neutral' statements', while much bigger differences could be found on the ground of religious affiliation for other categories. Students without RE disagreed more that they have respect for believers, they believed also least of all in the effectiveness of respect for living peacefully together, while those with integrated RE or recent RE studies were more optimistic about it. The statement 'I do not like ...' was most agreed by students without RE and least by those with an integrated form of RE.

Somewhat unexpected was the finding that students without RE believed less than the others that religion may cause some conflicts or that people of different religious backgrounds cannot live together; those who studied RE long ago were most ready to believe these statements. It shows that students with no conscious experience of religious diversity at school are less negative or less aware of potentials of religion for conflicts or hardly understand how it could cause conflicts.

It is not unequivocal to say something about the hypothesis. Encountering religious diversity in education can take different forms and have different effects. The trends in our sample let us infer that the schools that have integrated religion in their everyday life, making it more visible and less private, support students' readiness for respect and tolerance. The same can be said about providing special studies of RE, dealing with world religions. The more hostile attitudes of those without any study of religion except for dealing with religion in other subjects can be followed throughout the questionnaire – students without any experience of RE were holding more hostile and haughty attitudes to religion in many questions.

3.a) Students who have personally encountered religious diversity are more tolerant

The answers on religious tolerance of those, who said that they had friends, family members or classmates with a different religious background than themselves, were compared to those who had not, or said that they did not know about religion of the people around them.

The students who encountered religious diversity among their classmates as well as among friends believed significantly more in respect and claimed to respect people with a different religious background, while those who were not aware of their friends' religious background were least in favour of respect. Similarly, students who had religiously diverse companions at school or in their spare time hold less hostile attitudes towards religion in general or religious people in particular. They were also more likely not to prefer to spend time in homogenous groups.

The students who did not know about the religious affiliation of their friends, classmates or family members were less likely to believe that religion can cause some disagreements, while those having diverse friends, believed this more than others.

The students, who have friends or classmates of different religious backgrounds, tended to be more tolerant in their responses than those who did not know about their friends' or family members' religion, or who went to religiously homogenous classes. Even if the results are compared, the causal relationship is ambiguous. For example, if a student has friends of different backgrounds and holds tolerant views, one can ask – is he tolerant because he has such friends or he has such friends because he is tolerant. Similarly, the 'most intolerant group', those who do not know about the religion of their friends or family members, showed their indifference and somewhat arrogant attitudes in all questions. Still, students who said that they have classmates of a different religious background had not chosen this situation but had nevertheless more tolerant views than students from homogenous classes. In our view, if the young people are put into the situation when religious diversity is visible and spoken about, they are forced to develop strategies supporting openness to otherness.

1.b) Religious students are less open to dialogue on religious issues than non-religious students

The findings of the present survey refuted the hypothesis that religious people are less open to dialogue. Not only one, but all the statements about readiness for dialogue, were agreed with significantly more strongly by those who valued the importance of religion for themselves more highly. So, religious students wanted to learn to speak about religious issues at school. They were much more curious about others' views and were interested in shaping their own views by listening to and understanding others and they believed in the good effects of dialogue on religious issues. They chose discussing instead of ignoring a different worldview. The opposite was true for all the statements about showing no readiness for dialogue (preferring ignoring of a person, talking about stupidity of religion, confessing little knowledge and no interest on talking about religion); these were more agreed by persons who regarded religion as not important at all for themselves. Similarly, the less students valued religion, the more they preferred to socialise with like-minded people at school and in their spare time.

The same attitudes showed that when students with and without religious affiliation are compared, the 'affiliated' tended to be more ready for dialogue than the 'non-affiliated'. Students who did not believe in god or any sort of spirit were the least ready for dialogue.

However, before we conclude that non-religious students gave answers less open to dialogue, we must admit that a person who is attached to some topic is always more ready to speak about it than a person who is not. The most significant difference between religious and non-religious students on speaking about religion was interest: non-religious students said that they were not interested in the topic, so all the other statements could be related to their lack of interest.

2.b) Students who have encountered religious diversity in education are more open to dialogue on religious issues

The differences related to diverse models of religious studies were less significant than in the case of religious affiliation. Still, there were some significant differences. There were two possible answers: students with 'No RE' versus 'all the others' and 'RE long ago' (in the elementary school) versus 'RE recently' (in their current secondary school).

Two extreme positions formed with those with no RE on one side and students who have had RE (both, recently or long ago) on the other. The students without RE showed less readiness to have a dialogue on religious issues: they agreed less that 'Students should be able to talk and communicate about religious issues' or 'I like to know what my best friends thinks about religion', that different views would make talking about religion interesting or would help to understand the world.

Not all the statements were agreed equally by students who had RE recently and those who had had it long ago. Those, who had RE long ago believed less than all others that talking about religion could help to understand others, but agreed that talking about religion could lead to disagreement, and were more ready to talk themselves about the cruelties of religion. The most embarrassed to talk were students with no RE or who had it long ago, while the least embarrassed were students with integrated RE. The wish to spend time with like-minded people was least felt by students with integrated form of RE (about every third); and the statement was surprisingly most supported by students who have studied RE in primary school (every second). The more visible role of religion in schools with integrated RE can make students have to encounter people with different views. Why did students with experience of RE long ago feel uneasy talking about religion? It is not possible to answer the question on the basis of this survey. Perhaps they had been teased because of their voluntary studies of RE and the quite hostile attitude in some answers can refer to their protective conduct or embarrassment about the childish views they used to held about religion in primary classes, without having opportunity to have more advanced approaches to religion in their later studies.

A slight, but pervasive tendency emerged, that those who did not have any form of religious studies were less likely to agree with statements about readiness for dialogue and more likely to agree with hostile statements, while the most interested and dialogical group consisted of students who have recently studied RE.

3.b) Students who have personally encountered religious diversity are more open to dialogue on religious issues.

Similarly to 3a, the students having friends of diverse religious backgrounds, especially in their class, not only believed that religion can cause some troubles but also talked how stupid religion is. This did not distract them from entering into dialogue on religious issues. The views of students showed the tendency for those who have personally encountered religious diversity to be more positive about statements about readiness to cooperate. Here, those who encountered religious diversity among their friends usually held the most open views, followed by those who had religious diversity in their family or school. Students who did not know the religion of their family or friends usually held the least dialogical views. Although differences were smaller in a religiously diverse class, some differences were significant here: they were more eager to know about their friends' religious beliefs and found that differences in views made talking about religion interesting. They said that their views could be shaped by such talks and it helps them to understand other people better and what is going on in the world.

Summary

The current study showed that religion is often pushed into a very private sphere in Estonian schools, where the views are often a-religious or anti-religious. Religious people are believed to be less tolerant; conscious contacts with religious people are often limited to meeting with proselytising missionaries. The cultural code in schools where there is no place for religion is an avoidance of religious topics. Such a code in combination with little knowledge of religion is often a contributing factor in a climate where the bigoted attitudes described above stay unchallenged and thus justify the marginalization of religiously affiliated students.

There are more promising models than '*and no religion too*' in creating peace by mutual understanding and respect built upon an open dialogue and religious literacy. Even if students, who explicitly encountered religious diversity at school, had had some negative experiences with members of different religion, they tended to be more open to dialogue on religious issues. Perhaps it works both ways – if there is a need to have dialogue, one can learn the skills needed for it and becomes more ready for it. On the other hand, when a person has the skills needed for peaceful dialogue, he is more ready to enter into dialogue and sees its benefits. From this perspective, schools should offer students an environment for meeting religious diversity, having dialogue and fostering the respective skills. Students could profit from it not only as a point of self-reflection but also seeing a more complex picture about religion and acquiring the skills needed in contemporary pluralistic Europe.

References

Engelbrecht, K. *Noored tutvustavad Eestit paganliku maana* [Young people present Estonia as a heathen country]. Postimees: 12 April 2008.

Estonian Institute. (1997). *Russian Communities in Estonia. A historical overview.* Available online: http://www.einst.ee/factsheets/russians/ (accessed 10 October 2008).

Laanoja, P. (2007). *Answer by e-mail for a request to Olga Schihalejev*, 20.08.2007.

Lauristin, M. (2008). Non-Estonians as part of the population and citizenry of Estonia, in: M. Heidmets (Ed.) *Estonian Human Development Report 2007*. Tallinn: Eesti Ekspress Kirjastus, pp. 46–47.

Ruus, V.-R., Veisson, M., Leino M. (2007). Õpilaste edukus, toimetulek ja heaolu koolis, in: T. Kuurme (Ed.) *Eesti kool 21. sajandi algul: kool kui arengukeskkond ja õpilaste toimetulek*. Tallinn: TLÜ Kirjastus, pp. 59–72.

Schihalejev, Olga (2008) Meeting Diversity – Students' Perspectives in Estonia, in: T. Knauth, D.-P. Jozsa, G.D. Bertram-Troost & J. Ipgrave (Eds.). *Encountering Religious Pluralism in School and Society – A Qualitative Study of Teenage Perspectives in Europe.* Münster: Waxmann, pp. 247–278.

Toots, A., Plakk, M., Idnurm, T. (2004). *Infotehnoloogia Eesti koolides: Trendid ja väljakutsed.* Uuringu "Tiiger luubis" (2000–2004 lõppraport). Tallinn: Tiigrihüppe SA.

Valk, P. (2007) Religious Education in Estonia, in: R. Jackson, S. Miedema, W. Weisse & J.-P. Willaime (Eds.): *Religion and Education in Europe: Developments, Contexts and Debates.* Münster: Waxmann, pp. 159–180.

Valk, P. (2006). Churches and European integration – a challenge for religious education in the postsocialist context, *Die Kirchliche Zeitgeschichte,* 19 (1), pp. 166–186.

Veisson, M., Pallas, L., Ruus, V.R. & Ots, L. (2007). Erinevusi ja sarnasusi Eesti Vabariigi eesti ja vene õppekeelega koolide koolikultuuris, õpilaste edukuses, heaolus, huvides ja toimetulekus, in: T. Kuurme (Ed.): *Eesti kool 21. sajandi algul: kool kui arengukeskkond ja õpilaste toimetulek.* Tallinn: TLÜ Kirjastus, pp. 73–95.

Fedor Kozyrev

How Different after the Shared Past?
Russian and Estonian Youth Views about Religion

The massive and impressive research carried out by our colleagues from Tartu is of tremendous interest for us, at least for three reasons. First, it was conducted in one of the former Soviet republics and so it might be expected to provide valuable empirical material for ongoing reflections on the consequences of state atheism and its impact on the post-Soviet societies. These reflections are of undoubted international importance. Second, the Estonian sample included a considerable proportion of ethnic and cultural Russians. These Russians, living in a very different social and cultural environment, may acquire some distinctive features as 'Russians abroad' and, be it the case, the research would provide material of a certain ethnographic and sociological interest for study of the dynamics of cultures in culturally heterogenous societies. Third, the comparison between Russian and Estonian samples had been made during the previous qualitative research (Kozyrev & Shihalejev, 2008), and the new data could give a basis for another kind of comparison, that between the conclusions of the two surveys. This comparison would have methodological importance. These three points of interest shape the content of the following comments and as the title of this paper indicates, the first point has priority among the three.

Highlighting the Estonian results: differences between
two national samples

The main differences found in the answers of students from Estonian and St. Petersburg schools may be defined in terms of both the level and the quality of religiosity characteristic for the two national samples. They may be described in one sentence. Students in the Russian sample showed themselves definitely more religious than students in Estonia but their religiosity was more private, that is the social dimension of their religious life was of lower concern and importance in their own perceptions. It is much more difficult to write about the similarities between the two samples, for there were really so many of them, located in all the very different segments of data and responsible for the frequency of the almost congenial interpretations and formulation of conclusions that the Russian reader can so easily find when comparing the two national chapters.

To begin with the differences, the level of religiosity among students in the Russian sample can be estimated as at least two times higher than that in the Estonian one. Particularly, St. Petersburg students three times more frequently claimed religion to be very important in their life than the respondents in Estonia: 44% of St. Petersburg respondents declared to have a certain religion or worldview, while only 16% did the same in Estonia; 46% agreed with the statement "there is a God" and 14% denied his existence, while in Estonia these percentages were respectively 18 and 39%. Every tenth student in St. Petersburg and every fifth in Estonia agreed that religion is nonsense.

As regards the main difference in the quality of religious life mentioned above, the most indicative are the reactions in the two samples to the statement "religion belongs to private life". Though in both samples the statement has received a definitely positive reaction and occupied the highest rating position among the other statements in the corresponding block of questions, the level of support in the Russian sample was significantly higher (means 2.14 / 1.48[1]). A sequence of the other results amplifies this observation. For instance, respondents in the Russian sample were found to pay much more attention to praying (means 4.45 / 3.93), thinking about religion (3.53 / 3.21) and about the meaning of life (means 2.90 / 2.18), but at the same time they are slightly more reluctant about attending religious events (4.39 / 4.54). They estimate much more highly the role of the family as a source of information about religion (means 2.69 / 2.02), but they do not differ as much from Estonian students in evaluating the role of religious communities (means 3.69 / 3.59). These figures would come into contradiction with the definitely higher level of religious affiliation among students in the Russian sample, if the more private pattern of their religious life is not taken into consideration. The more cautious attitude of St. Petersburg students to the idea of having RE at school as an optional subject (mean 1.81 / 2.19), and their inclination to agree that there should be no place for religion in school (means 3.31 / 2.93), may be regarded as another sign of this general vision of religion outside public and social life.

Similarities between the two samples

When evaluated against these quite serious differences, numerous similarities found in the two samples look like the marks of a basic unity of the religious perceptions of youngsters, determined by either the shared historical experience and culture, or the leveling effect of globalization. It is hardly possible to decide which of these factors is stronger by means of the bi-national comparison, without referring to the results obtained in other countries that had other historical experiences. Nevertheless one may guess that similar features of the religious life shared in the two countries point to some elements of youth spirituality that are of a more basic and stable nature than views and commitments determined by the current socio-political situation. The fact that the family was identified as the main source of information about religion in the two samples points to one of these 'basic' elements, in our view. The relatively low estimation of religious communities as a source of information about religions in both national samples may be regarded in our view as a sign of the post-atheist situation common to the two countries.

Another element of special importance is the silent style of religious life noticed by both research teams. We have drawn attention in our national chapter to the amazing fact that more than a half of the respondents said they do not know about the religion of their friends. Estonian results correspond to that finding exactly: "Interesting, but perhaps not surprising, is that more than half of the students do not know their friends' or classmates' views of religion". Four students out of five in the Estonian sample spoke about religion with their family members, friends and classmates less than once a month or never. This is very similar to the Russian results where the talk about religion is slightly more frequent in families, less frequent with classmates and is the same as regards friends.

Most interesting are the similarities found in the patterns of influences of the factors regarded as the main determinants of students' perceptions. These factors are religious affiliation, experiences with religion at school and gender. Here are only some examples of these profound and numerous similarities.

---

1   From here on the means are given respectively for Estonian / Russian samples

Both research teams registered the phenomenon of the 'praying atheists', as particularly reflected in the Estonian report: "…even some 'Russian 'non-affiliated' pray every day (7%)".

Russian and Estonian researchers registered many more religious students who strongly agreed with the statement "I respect other people who believe" compared to students without religious affiliation At the same time religious students in the Russian sample "rather unexpectedly supported unbelievers in the idea that one can be a religious person without religious belonging and did not differ much from the non-religious students in openness to change their views on religion". Estonian colleagues identified the same two points as the "exceptions … where differences were insignificant".

Both research teams decisively describe religiously affiliated students as more motivated to know about the religious views of others, more tolerant and more open for inter-religious communication. Both marked as a paradox the fact that religiously affiliated students showed less dislike of people from other religions: "the less students valued religion, the more they preferred to go with similarly minded people at school and in their spare time" (Estonian report).

Regarding differences in the religiosity of boys and girls, both samples showed the very similar patterns with non-significant gender differences in general but with a 1.5–2 times higher percentage of boys who denied the existence of God and claimed religion to be absolutely not important in their lives.

The other gender differences detected in the two samples overlapped considerably and led researchers to come independently to compatible conclusions or observations. As regards religion in personal life: "Girls tended to be more positive about religion and its effects than boys in almost all statements, especially in interest in religious topics and respecting people of different religious backgrounds" (Estonian chapter) –"Girls are more open for communication with others. They are more respectful to the beliefs of other people and are more interested in learning what other people think about religion" (Russian chapter). As regards religion in education: "Girls were more interested than boys in religious topics and saw learning about religions as valuable for 'peaceful [life] together' (Estonian chapter) – "Girls are more motivated to study religions in order to be able to talk and communicate about religious issues, to gain a better understanding of current events and to understand others for peaceful coexistence with them" (Russian chapter). As regards meeting religious proselytisation: "Girls were significantly more likely to discuss with and listen to the other. Boys were significantly more likely to explain that their own opinions were right, to ignore the other, or attempt to convince that he is wrong" (Estonian chapter). "When faced with religious proselytisation girls are much more open for discussion … Accordingly, they are much less inclined to ignore the challenge. At the same time they are also slightly more reluctant to make attempts to convince their opponent [compared to boys]" (Russian chapter).

Results of qualitative and quantitative surveys in bi-national perspective

Four blocks of conclusions were included in the bi-national chapter on qualitative analysis. These were "religion and youth", "gender issues", "phenomena of diaspora" and 'the impact of RE".

The first block of conclusions proved to be in good correspondence with the new findings of the quantitative research. This can be seen from the following quotations: "Religion is seen as something private, even as an intimate relationship with God, and it is often not a subject to be discussed with others […] For many students the privacy of religious matters is supported by the fact that religion is transmitted by the family, not by public institutions like school or the media" (Kozyrev & Shihalejev 2008, p. 322).

The second block stated that "the gender differences are almost nonexistent in Estonia, while there are differences in Russia. In Russia, girls seem to have a more positive attitude towards religion. Only boys had explicitly negative connotations with the word 'religion'" (ibid, 323). It seems that the new findings give grounds to talk more about similarity between the two samples than about differences. This time girls' tendency to avoid 'extreme positions' was registered by Estonian researchers too. A set of distinctive characteristics of male and female religious attitudes was defined in the two samples with amazing levels of correspondence.

The qualitative research showed experience with religious education to affect mostly perceptions of religious education itself, not the religiosity of the students. "In both samples, students who have had religious education as a regular subject in their curricula, showed a more positive attitude towards the subject than those without such experience" (ibid, 324). This observation was supported by the new findings. The Estonian report on the quantitative research states that "there are no significant differences in regard to students' or their parents' religious affiliation, what the students believe or how important religion is to them according to their religious studies. The distribution of 'affiliated' and 'non-affiliated' among students with different models of RE was similar". On the other hand, "the most important factor [...] in students' views about religious studies was their own experience with RE or lack of it". Data obtained in the Russian sample support this conclusion in general, but brings evidence of more complex relations between school experiences and attitudes toward religion in education.

Russians in Estonia and Russians in Russia

The fourth block of conclusions made on the basis of the qualitative research deserves special attention. According to it, Russian-speaking students in Estonia "differ in comparison not only to their peers in Estonia, but also to Russians in Russia. Their positions are almost never 'in between' those of the Estonian and Russian samples, but rather their attitudes form a pole in the range opposite to that of "Estonians in Estonia". They seem to be more religious than their peers in Russia, and their religion is more family-centered. [...] They do not identify their religiosity at a group level, but rather as a personal relation".

The quantitative research did not bring strong additional reasons to talk about the 'phenomenon of diaspora', rather it showed the two groups of Russians to have more similarities than appeared after the qualitative research. Illustrative is the distribution of answers to the three options regarding religious belief ("there is a God", 'there is some sort of spirit or life force", 'I don't think there is a God, spirit or life force"): it was 12:44:44 (%) for 'Estonians' in Estonia, 49:38:13 for 'Russians in Estonia' and 46:40:14 for 'Russians in Russia'. Sometimes 'Russians in Estonia' occupied a median position between the Estonians and representatives of the Russian national sample. For instance the proportion of those who claimed a preference to go around with young people of the same religious background was about 40% among 'Estonians in Estonia', 30% among 'Russians in Estonia' and 20% among St. Petersburg students. In general, differences found between the two language subgroups of the Estonian sample corresponded to differences between the two national samples. 'Russians in Estonia' think more frequently about the meaning of life – and it is the same when Estonian and Russian national samples are compared. 'Russians' agreed more than 'Estonians' that religion belongs to private life – and it is the same with the two national samples again … Most impressive in this respect is the keen observation of our Estonian colleagues concerning the frequency of more social (church attendance) and more intimate (prayers) religious practices among affiliated and non-affiliated students in the two language groups (fig. 3 in the Estonian chapter). The striking lack of correlation between religious affiliation and religious practice in the 'Russian' group led Estonian researchers to claim that "'Russians' believed in the existence of God regardless of their religious affiliation, while for 'Estonians' it was determined by their religious affiliation". We put it in other words, speaking about the religiosity of our respondents being "rather loosely connected with religious communities". But probably we described the same phenomenon.

Yet in some cases 'Russians in Estonia' did differ from 'Russians in Russia'. For instance, the latter occupied the median position between the two language subgroups of the Estonian sample in their attitude toward the optional model of RE. It seems also that the higher level of confrontation between adolescents and their parents reported for 'Russians in Estonia' is not characteristic for St. Petersburg students. These cases, however rare they are, prove the idea of the 'phenomenon of diaspora' to be not without any ground. It requires more detailed study. The high variability found between different schools in our quantitative research explains why the results of the two surveys may differ so much at this point and calls for more caution in tackling this issue.

Differences found: what next?

Those who look for the restoration of religious life in the countries of the post-Soviet space, and need strong arguments to persuade their opponents that this will not be harmful for social cohesion will find good news in the Estonian chapter. Religious young people in Estonia are not less tolerant than non-religious. "Contrarily, the more they thought that religion is important, the more they were ready to tolerate students with a different religion and also to value tolerance in improving relations between different groups". This conclusion is in full agreement with the conclusion of the Russian chapter and it makes the good news even better.

There is a bad news too. Religious education does not seem to make students more religious. May be it is because they do not want it to do. In both samples the perspective to be guided towards religious belief was soundly refused by the students. How will religion in education contribute to mutual understanding and respect in this case? The Estonian chapter give no clear answer to this question and it is hardly possible to have done so, for the quality of RE will be obviously a crucial factor determining the result. The ambiguity of RE influences is also among the convergent conclusions of the two research teams. Differences found in the religious perceptions of respondents in Estonia and Russia stimulate reflections and hypotheses that add to the complexity of the issue.

What if the two main differences observed – that regarding the level of religiosity, and that regarding more a social status of religion among Russians – are not coincidental but interconnected? Indeed, when we think how Russians – who suffered a 20 years' longer period of state atheism and totalitarianism than Estonians, Czechs or Eastern Germans - show today in European polls (EVS) a significantly higher percentage of believers than citizens of the three countries mentioned,[2] one of the answers could be the asocial type of religious life Russians

---

2   The European Values Study: A Third Wave. Source book of the 1999/2000European Values Study Surveys, in: http://spitswww.uvt.nl/web/fsw/evs/documents/Publications/Sourcebook/EVS_Source Book.pdf

used to have. In the situation of persecution it is simply easier to save religion that is family-centered, hidden and silent, and not connected so firmly with attendance at Church or other publicly open practice. A private code of religious life provides a sort of immunity against the intrusion of the state into the depths of human existence.

Paradoxically it is this type of 'privatized religion' which has come as the new wave to Western Europe. What should religious education do about it and how will the purposeful 'socialization' of the private religious life contribute to the tolerant and non-conflictual coexistence of peoples and religions in our plural world? I leave these questions open, hoping that future researches will help us to understand better how should we use the powerful potential of religion in education in order to build a better world.

Robert Jackson & Sean Neill

Commentary on 'Options beside and 'no Religion too' – Perspectives of Estonian Youth'

Most striking points

As pointed out in the introduction, the Estonian religious education system differs sharply from that in much of Europe. Although, to a visitor to the country, the ongoing restoration of Lutheran churches in the major cities of Estonia appears unambiguous evidence of the importance of this religion in the assertion of Estonian identity as independent from Russia, this contrasts with decades of Communist suppression of religion which have, as the introduction points out, left parents and their children sceptical of religious education. This has left a situation where there is great sensitivity in the relations between ethnic Estonians and ethnic Russians. The sensitivity of this issue is apparent from the difficulty the researchers had in getting access to some schools. However, as the chapter points out, the limited number of non-Christians reduces the impact of religious diversity in Estonia.

There is a paradox in the effects of recent (secondary-level) as against earlier (primary-level) experience of religious education, where those who have experienced earlier RE do not differ from those who have never experienced it, but those who are currently experiencing RE are more positive towards the experience. The large proportion of respondents who had no RE experience led to many respondents being unwilling to commit themselves on a number of questions, apparently because they had no knowledge of, and therefore view on, the alternatives.

The analysis shows that exposure to religious education has a marked influence on students' opinion. As a result, the written-in comments indicate that many Estonian students express strong views about religion. However the very diverse experience of religious education by Estonian students who are otherwise similar provides a 'natural experiment' which allows an opportunity to assess the effects of RE, and may help answer some of the issues of encouraging harmony between adherents of different religions in multicultural societies.

The greater intensity of belief of Russian-speakers comes across in most questions, but the Estonian-speakers did – reflecting the churches mentioned above as badges of national identity – regard religion as more important in their national history. However, the Estonian-speakers felt they had gained more from religious education than Russian-speakers. They were also more positive to practical aspects of living together with people of another religion – knowing about the other's religion and doing things together.

New and different ideas and interpretations

The chapter makes a careful analysis and judicious interpretations with which the present authors would agree. What would be interesting would be to speculate about are possible policy recommendations for Estonia based on the research findings. As things stand, in the main, school students are not provided with information about religion in Estonian society and in the wider world. This marginalisation of religion as a subject of study, related to the view that religion is a strictly private matter, contributes to a situation in which religious students and students who are interested in religion feel segregation and exclusion, while all students are, at the very least, deprived of engaging with an important element of human culture. Perhaps more attention to religion as an international and global phenomenon and as a factor in culture – in history and the arts for example – would help to broaden out from a narrow national focus. In this respect, Estonia may be able to learn something from the French re-examination of ways of dealing with religion in public education and also from generic European discussions (from the Council of Europe and the Organisation for Security and Co-operation in Europe, for example) on the role of the study of religions in education for tolerance of difference and respect for the human rights principle of freedom of religion or belief.

Similarities and differences between England and Estonia

One contrast between Estonia and England is in the different perceptions of the role of religion in the public sphere. Not surprisingly, given Estonia's recent history under Communist rule, religion is still largely regarded as a private matter, and for many ethnic Estonians, religion is considered to be a relic of the past. This view is reflected in the research data, where young people often regarded religion as so personal that they hardly discussed it with others, and had a low awareness of the religion of people around them. Students valued families most highly as a source of information about religion, but at the same time mentioned that they rarely discussed religion in the home. Moreover, the influence of religious communities was almost non-existent. In contrast, England has a long tradition of church and state partnership in education, going back to the origins of state education in the nineteenth century. Religious education in England has evolved in such a way that a wider range of religious voices has been introduced over time into educational discourse (see below) and students in community schools are used to discussing issues related to religion in the classroom.

In terms of social setting, the types and degrees of multiculturalism in England and Estonia differ strikingly. In England, migration from former British colonies in South Asia, Africa and the Caribbean (especially since the 1950s and 1960s) created a particular type of multicultural society, with religions such as Islam, Hinduism and Sikhism, as well as Christianity in African, Caribbean and South Asian forms being established in many urban centres, along side long established Christian and Jewish communities. The English education system has adapted to this religious and cultural mix. Religious education in state funded community schools is inclusive of young people from all backgrounds, while the range of voluntary aided schools with a religious character (mainly funded by the state) is gradually being extended to include Muslim, Sikh, Hindu schools as well as some minority Christian schools (such as Greek Orthodox and Seventh Day Adventist), in addition to well established Church of England and Roman Catholic schools, and some Jewish schools. The research data show young people's experience of, and appreciation of, difference where there has been sustained intercultural experience in schools. The data from a relatively mono-cultural rural school present a less positive picture, possibly closer to that given by ethnic Estonian students than by their urban English counterparts.

Estonia's multicultural character is very different from that of England, with a minimal presence of religions other than Christianity. In Estonia two 'national' groups – ethnic Estonians and ethnic Russians – diverge greatly in their understanding of religion and its role in the public sphere. With regard to religious education in school ethnic Estonians showed little interest in or about religion, regarding religion as having little relevance for contemporary people. For ethnic Russians, however, religion is regarded as a personal and private matter. Neither group favoured the introduction of a school subject to cover issues of religion.

Despite their statements of tolerance, Estonian students were less positive towards the actions necessary to express religion than their English counter-parts; for example, prayer rooms and specific religious diets, which are generally supported in England, were rejected by Estonian students. Contrary to what might have been expected, there was no difference between those who had taken religious education and those who had not in their willingness to debate with a peer who held a different viewpoint; those who were religious and girls were more willing to discuss diverging views. This also applied to education about religion, where, similarly to their English counterparts, attitudes were more positive to education *about* religion than education *in* religion.

Alhough the Estonian experience differs from that of students in England, with the existing samples, there remain many similarities between the attitudes of Estonian and English students, both overall (in their preference for education *about* religion) and in the similar differences in attitudes between religious and non-religious subgroups and between girls and boys, the former group being more tolerant in each case in both countries. The majority of Estonian students, reflecting the cultural context, do not profess belief, and in this respect Estonian schoolchildren are even more secular than their English peers, though they have arrived at this point through a different historical route. However there were marked differences related to the intensity of religious belief, similar to those in other countries, and the differences between girls and boys in religious belief were also similar to those in other countries.

Céline Béraud, Bérengère Massignon, Séverine Mathieu & Jean-Paul Willaime

The School – an Appropriate Institution in France for Acquiring Knowledge on Religious Diversity and Experiencing it Firsthand?

1. Introduction

1.1 Context of the research

In Europe, France is the country often seen as the "champion as far as the separation between […] church and state is concerned" (see Bertrand & Muller, 2005), where *laïcité* in schools was instituted even before 1905. Among the participants in the REDCo project, France may seem to be an exception when it comes to a curriculum dealing with religion, as there is no specific course that covers it. The *départements* in the Alsace region (*Haut-Rhin* and *Bas-Rhin*) and the Moselle *département*, for historical reasons[1], are exceptions in the matter. Children and adolescents may take religious classes (Catholic, Protestant or Jewish) in public schools. Attendance in these classes is highest in primary school; there is a noticeable decline in their popularity among students in middle schools, which is even more apparent in high schools. Private institutions, which school 20% of French adolescents, may offer students an hour of religious classes per week. But this situation only affects a small minority of students. However, this does not imply that young French people learn nothing about religion in school. The choice was made to present course material on religion in the national curriculum within pre-existing subjects, mainly History and French; this choice is regularly confirmed by educational authorities. As a result, this material focuses on knowledge and is presented impartially. For about twenty years, there has been growing awareness of the need to reinforce the understanding French students have of the topic of religion; this has led to reforms in the school curriculum (the most notable ones took place in 1996) and it has also led to greater concern for teacher training in this area (following Régis Debray's 2002 report and the creation of the IESR). At first, the main focus of this teaching about religion was to present religion from the point of view of cultural heritage. The idea was to give students information so they could understand monuments and works of art that would be incomprehensible to them without knowledge of religious traditions. Since the year 2000, a period marked by the beginning of the Second Intifada in the Middle East and the September 11 attacks, more emphasis has been placed on the civic dimension of this teaching. Approaching this question through instruction given to young people in school is understood as a possible way to improve intercultural relations and promote mutual respect. In addition, from the point of view of school life, the

---

1 These territories were under German rule during the period when the schools were secularised (the Ferry laws of 1881-1882 and the Goblet law of 1886), and when the law of 1905 was enacted, separating the rest of the State from the Church. Consequently, the relationship between church and state instituted for the Catholic Church by the *Concordat* of 1802 signed by Napoleon, and for three other religions recognised through measures adopted during Napoleon's reign, remained in place there. Neither the German annexation of these territories after the Franco-Prussian War of 1870, nor their return to France after World War I, abolished this system. Since then, there have been various attempts to repeal the exceptions for these territories concerning the role of religion, but they have all failed. The Alsatians and the inhabitants of the Moselle *département* are attached to these legal exceptions, considering them part of their cultural identity. Such exceptions are not limited to religion; they include areas as varied as hunting rights and their social welfare system, to give just two examples.

law of March 15 2004 prohibiting "the wearing of signs or clothes by which the students ostensibly demonstrate a religious affiliation"[2] is often seen as having eased some tensions in schools where there is a great deal of religious diversity. The REDCo project, which is focused on the problems of dialogue and conflict, has given us the means to get the opinions of several hundred adolescents on these questions. This is an innovative kind of research in France, as other surveys have typically only dealt with various difficulties encountered by teachers.

1.2   Description of the sample

1.2.1   Methodology

To construct our sample, we used different methods: some involved stratified sampling, others cluster sampling and still others involved purposive or judgmental sampling. We set ourselves the objective of obtaining 1000 completed questionnaires. In the end, the method used cannot be considered random, even if it comes close. It presents the advantage of being easy and not very expensive to implement.

The sampling base that we have chosen is all of France. The unit of our investigation is the student, knowing that students belong to clusters (classes). The stratification of a universe is the procedure whereby, before building a sample of individuals, it passes through the intermediate stage of homogeneous strata. Our sample is built upon three layers:

–   The five subdivisions of the country, which are based on the first two digits of French telephone numbers – an easier solution to implement than a division based on the twenty *académies* (school districts) of the national educational system – Paris and its region, northeast, southeast, southwest, northwest.

–   Schools (middle and high schools, if possible in the same proportion)

–   Classes of the last year of middle school and/or the first year of high school in these schools.

Classes represent clusters. Schools represent "clusters of clusters" or "mega clusters". The cluster is a group of units. In relation to the subject of the investigation, a unit is attached to one cluster and only one[3]. The choice of mega-clusters and clusters is normally made randomly. Given the difficulty in obtaining the permissions to make a survey about religion in schools, we picked the institutions that we surveyed based on personal contacts that the members of the French team had in those schools (this is not a major methodological problem given that this choice does not have an impact on the characteristics of the studied population). However, the selection had to be reasonable, in accordance with the purposive or judgmental sampling method. We decided to choose the schools in each region according to some criteria: location, presumed religious background, social status and national origins of the students.

To get 1,000 responses to our questionnaire, we decided to survey a total of 40 classes (which meant 8 classes per region). We considered it best to deliver the questionnaire in two classes per school, so we needed to choose 4 schools by region. We decided to include the private sector in our investigation. As this sector is mainly confessional, it appeared interest-

---

2   An official notice from May 18 2005 specifies what is meant by "ostensible religious signs". These are signs "which immediately identify those who wear them as belonging to a religious group, such as the Muslim headscarf, whatever name it may have, the yarmulke, or a clearly oversized cross".

3   A pupil belongs to one class and only one.

ing to compare in our study pupils coming from public schools and pupils belonging to private ones.

1.2.2   Considerations regarding the sample

851 questionnaires were delivered and filled all over the country in 18 schools. We almost reached our quantitative goal.[4] We lacked time to add 2 more schools.

Slightly more girls than boys filled out the questionnaire. This proportion should not be misunderstood. It is obviously linked to the composition of classes. No boy refused to participate in the survey.

Table 1:   Classification by gender

	Frequency	Percent
Gender		
Male	355	41,7
Female	477	56,1
Missing	19	2,2
Total	851	100

As far as the regions are concerned, one can see a slight overrepresentation of Paris and its suburbs.

Table 2:   Geographical classification

	Frequency	Percent
Region		
Paris Region	238	28
Northeast	71	8.3
Southeast	163	19.2
Northwest	220	25.9
Southwest	159	18.7
Total	851	100

One may also notice that private (Catholic only[5]) schools are similarly slightly overrepresented in the sample. In France, around 20% of middle- or high-school students attend private schools. This proportion has remained constant over the past few years. There are some variations along geographical lines: traditionally, the west and the southeast of France and the *Massif Central* (south central France) are regions where there are a large number of private schools. In addition, students who attend such schools are on the average from more privi-

---

4   We would like to thank the other members of the French team, without whom we would not have been able to distribute as many questionnaires throughout France as we did: Anne-Raymonde de Beaudrap, Philippe Gaudin, Claude Proeschel, Sylvie Toscer-Angot and Anna Van den Kerchove. We would also like to thank Sabrina Pastorelli for her technical support since she dealt with SPSS and organized the data. Our thanks also go to Allyn Hardyck for his careful translation.

5   Nearly 200 questionnaires were also handed out in Jewish private schools by one of our colleagues, Joëlle Allouche-Benayoun. They were not included in the current sample (statistically speaking, only a very small percentage of French students attend such schools); however, they will be the subject of a subsequent comparative study.

leged social classes than students in public middle or high schools. But again, these differences are dependent upon geography[6]. The overwhelming majority of private schools under contract with the State are Catholic. Only a small minority of students, less than 50000, attend private schools that do not have such a contract.

Table 3:   Distribution between public / private schools

Type of school	Frequency	Percent
Public schools	653	23,3
Private schools	198	76,7
Total	851	100

One student in two says they have a religion. This seems to be a reasonable figure (comparable with other polls, where young people express a high level of indifference to the question of religious affiliation[7]). Among those who declare membership in a religion, 40% say they are Catholic, 23% Christian (without being more specific) and 4% Protestant. Muslims comprise 24% of the group and Jews 2.5%. Muslim students are noticeably overrepresented in our sample, in comparison with the national average[8]. Such overrepresentation can be associated[9] with an equally higher proportion of students of immigrant origin, which can be derived from two indicators: 13% of adolescents surveyed do not have French nationality (which is twice the proportion in the population as a whole) and 24% speak a foreign language at home.

As far as the income bracket of the students is concerned, two indicators allow us to evaluate the validity of our sample. The first of these is based on the kinds of schools involved in the survey. We carried out our work in Paris high schools that are among the most prestigious institutions in France[10], characterised by a highly selective process of social recruitment, but we also worked in middle schools in the *département* of Seine-Saint-Denis in the Paris suburbs, where some of the students come from very underprivileged backgrounds. We also handed out questionnaires in schools outside of the Paris region, which often have a high level of social diversity. There is therefore a great deal of contrast in the French sample between the locations in the survey. The second indicator is the occupations of the parents of the adolescents in the survey. The European socio-economic nomenclature ESeC used to encode this

---

6   Source: Ministry of National Education, DEP, 2005. The statistical analysis covers the period from 1993 to 2003.

7   It is not that easy to compare surveys. In large international quantitative surveys, such as opinion polls carried out in France, the category of "young people" typically involves people from 18 to 29 years old, in other words older individuals than the adolescents participating in the REDCO research project.

8   It is illegal for the French government and its various departments to generate statistics involving religious categories. The figures given by polling groups constantly cause controversy, especially regarding the percentage of Muslims.

9   This is only a possible connection, not an automatic outcome. The part of the population of immigrant origin cannot be reduced to those from North Africa. Moreover, not all North Africans (and much more importantly, not all of their children) are Muslims. Some of them do not have a religion. On this subject, the demographer Michèle Tribalat has repeatedly criticised the temptation to "naturalise" religious affiliation by assigning people a religion based on their origins or their family backgrounds without explicitly asking them about it.

10   Located in fashionable Paris neighbourhoods, these schools offer preparatory classes for entering the *grandes écoles* [for example the *Ecole Polytechnique* or the *Ecole Normale Supérieure*], which are a typical feature of French republican meritocracy.

information does not correspond exactly with the PCS (*Professions et catégories socioprofessionnelles*) categories used by the INSEE[11]. However, it is possible to match up some of these categories. If only the father's occupation is taken into account, employees and workers (classes 6, 7, 8 and 9) make up at least 25% of the total, intermediate-level occupations (classes 2 and 3) one third, and high-level intellectual occupations (class 1) 16%[12]. Intermediate-level occupations seem to be substantially overrepresented, in comparison with employees and workers. However, one may wonder: do these figures have something to do with the way adolescents answered these questions? Did some of them lie to hide the fact that they come from a working-class background, therefore overstating the importance of their father's occupation in order to give the impression that they belong to the middle class?

1.3   The atmosphere of the survey: reactions and comments

In order to give an idea of the atmosphere in which the survey took place, we will concentrate on the reactions from adults (headteachers and teachers for the most part), then on reactions from adolescents.

Actually, the members of the French team had to face a great variety of reactions about the subject-matter of the survey in public schools. Here are some examples. One headteacher asked for the permission of the regional board of education. She was particularly reluctant because she had had to deal with the case of a teacher who tried to proselytise her students, a few years ago. The permission was granted but some time was lost. Another headmaster reacted in the same way. He was frightened by the possible reactions of the parents. Actually the parents expressed no opposition, and in the end he seemed very proud to be involved in a European research project. Only one headteacher who was quite embarrassed by the questions about religious symbols (the law of February 2004 meant that students may no longer wear anything indicating membership in a particular religion) prevented the study from taking place in her school. In another school, the headmaster was especially accommodating. But one of the teachers refused to participate. She argued that some of the questions went against the principle of *laïcité*. At another school, the questionnaires were delivered without difficulties. One of the teachers, however, seemed somewhat embarrassed. In many schools we did not have to face hostility. Earlier this year (first in a speech given at the Basilica of St. John Lateran in Rome on December 20, 2007, then in a second speech in Riyadh on January 14, 2008), President Sarkozy made some controversial declarations about the role of religion in society. The most questionable of his declarations, which was also the one most criticised, concerned schools. "The teacher can never replace the pastor or the priest – although he or she should strive towards that – because he or she will always lack that radical quality which comes from sacrificing his or her life, and the charisma of a calling that is based on hope."[13]

---

11 The national statistical agency.

12 There are also 9% who are self-employed (classes 4 and 5), 3.5% who do not work or have been unemployed for some time (class 10), and 11% who gave no response or one that could not be used.

13 Here, two errors that President Sarkozy made become apparent. "Firstly, he seemed to forget that the replacement of the priest by the teacher, in other words *laïcité* in schools, was one of the Republic's key victories, and that teachers in public schools, with a great deal of dedication, still play an essential role in education by teaching their students to be free, responsible citizens through transmission of knowledge and training in critical thinking. Secondly, he did not realise that after this irreversible advance, the old rivalry between the priest, the pastor and the teacher is no longer relevant. What matters now is the possibility that they may complement each other in their educational roles, while maintaining complete autonomy in their respective missions, so as to avoid the moral relativism associated with the commodification of the world." (Willaime, 2008, pp. 80-81)

As a result, the French passion for issues involving *laïcité* was reawakened.[14] This was not helpful for our project because some teachers and headteachers considered Nicolas Sarkozy declarations as a threat to *laïcité*. As a matter of fact, they refused to take what they consider as a risk and to give us the permission to distribute the questionnaire which according to them dealt with such a "hot" topic. The role of religion in education remains a sensitive topic among some headteachers and some teachers. They needed to be reassured. The fact that a scientific laboratory was conducting the survey helped give them more confidence about it. In private schools (Catholic schools under contract with the State only), the subject was not likely to be considered as sensitive. In some Catholic schools, the headmaster and teachers seemed to be interested in the goals of the survey. But this was not always true. Some teachers argued they are very busy and stated that they did not want to waste time on it.

Students did not seem that concerned about participating. The written comments made on the last page of the questionnaire reveal the point of view of the adolescents surveyed. These statements, whose length varied considerably between questionnaires, were sometimes positive about the project, sometimes very critical. The profile of those who left comments is not significantly different from that of the sample as a whole. Generally, students' remarks on the questionnaire are positive. They often express their interest in the questions, saying that the questionnaire made them think about issues rarely debated in the classroom. Among the topics that they bring up, the following appear repeatedly: the importance and the usefulness of religion in personal life; the fact that it can contribute to respecting others and to peace in the world; the role of Islam in society and the issue of the headscarf; *laïcité* and the right to not have a religion; and the influence that parents may have in the matter. They also criticise the structure of the questionnaire, observing that even if questions are asked well, they are very often repetitive and similar. Some of them remarked that Europe should spend money in other fields of research, rather than on religious issues. They sometimes ask questions about "who" created the questionnaire, expressing the belief that the opinions of non-religious people are very often not taken into account and hypothesising that religious researchers were mainly responsible for the questionnaire. In addition, French students' lack of knowledge about the school systems in other European countries, and the role given elsewhere to religion in the school curriculum, makes it hard for them to understand the relevance of some questions which do not make sense in the French context, particularly those dealing with the debate on having courses on religion open to everyone vs. having separate courses based on the students' religions. The answers given for these questions are therefore neither very meaningful, nor directly usable.

In conclusion, we can make the following points on how the survey was carried out. In the end, getting the necessary authorisations for distributing the questionnaire was less difficult than we had feared. The high level of scientific prestige associated with the institutions to which we belong certainly made our work easier. The rejections we received from headmasters and teachers, or the fears they had, came in two forms. Some saw the project as a threat to the principle of *laïcité*; more specifically, they were afraid that the heated debate on this topic would return, years after the enactment of the 2004 law banning the headscarf in schools. Another reason, not directly related to religion and *laïcité*, was probably that teachers did not wish to spend hours in class doing something that was not a direct part of the school curriculum. We may conclude that the demand for efficiency, fed by a consumerist attitude, has an influence on the French school system (which is probably much greater in private schools).

---

14 To get a better idea of the debate in this area, see Baubérot, 2008 and Willaime, 2008.

As for the students, they did not as a whole express either enthusiasm about the project or rejection of it. They answered the questions seriously, ultimately respecting the instructions quite studiously.

2.   Presentation of the results

2.1   What role does religion have in students' lives?

2.1.1   Data description

We should first say that religion is not one of the main concerns of French students: it is unimportant or completely unimportant for 45% of them, and important for 32% of them. For 34%, God exists[15], for 33% He does not, while 28% think there is some sort of life force. 24% of students never think about religion whereas 39% of them think about it every day. Religion does not play an important part in their everyday lives, according to them: 43% of them "disagree" or "strongly disagree" with the statement "Religion helps me to cope with difficulties", whereas 31% "agree" or "strongly agree". The same feelings predominate when asked whether religion helps them "to be a better person": 45% "disagree" or "strongly disagree" and 29% "agree" or "strongly agree". It is interesting to note that on these statements, more than 25% of students have no opinion. This percentage rises to 37% for the following statement: "You can be a religious person without belonging to a particular faith community" and 32% for this statement: "What I think about religion is open to change" (39% of students "agree" or "strongly agree" with this). This could probably explain why there are still 43% of students who agree or strongly agree with the following sentence: "Sometimes I have doubts – is there a god or not?" At this time in their lives, the adolescents we met are still not sure yet about religion: it is not the main focus of their attention. So they say that they may change their minds, but the questionnaire is not in a position to indicate the direction they may go (toward more religious practice? More intolerance? Increased indifference?)

Besides the fact that they do not have the same opinions about religion, it appears as though these students spend time together without discussing the subject. But the percentage of those who consider the topic uninteresting is slightly less (35%)[16] than those who disagree with that (37%). For 41% of the students we encountered, religion is not a "boring" topic. 47% feel that just because they do not know much about it does not mean that they cannot have an opinion on it. In this context, the overwhelming majority of the young people we met think about the meaning of life, which is normal for adolescents: 51% of French students say that they think about it fairly often.

62% of students disagree with the statement "Religion is nonsense"; along the same lines, 59% think that "talking about religion helps me to understand better what is going on in the world". So even though religion does not play a major role in their lives as adolescents, they are not at all against it, nor are they unwilling to ask questions about it.

When studying the role religion plays in the lives of the students surveyed, some cross-tabulations were found to be very useful, involving the distinction between public and private schools, the social status of the family, gender, and religious affiliation.

---

15 In comparison, in an IFOP poll in April 2004, 55% of French people said they believed in God.

16 According to the context, The percentages combine the answers "strongly agree" and "agree" or "strongly disagree" and "disagree".

As a result of these cross-tabulations, we see differences in beliefs between private and public school students. For example, when considering the importance of religion, in what seems like a paradox, more public school students than students in religious private schools think that religion is important (32% vs. 27%). But thinking that religion is something important does not necessarily mean being religious: it could just mean recognising its role in modern society.

Whereas more students from public schools do not believe in God than those from private schools (37% vs. 28%), they believe in God in the same proportions (36% vs. 34%). Unsurprisingly, students in private schools (which are all Catholic schools in our survey) think about religion more often (51%)[17] than their fellow students in public schools (37%), but if we take both systems into account, the majority of students never read sacred texts (68%) and 28% of them think that there is "a sort of spirit or life force".

Between private and public schools, there is a difference in what students report as their parents' religion. In private schools, there are more Catholics, which is not surprising given the status of private schools in France. Consequently, there are only a few Muslims in these schools (concerning religious affiliation of the pupils' parents, the figures are almost the same whether one considers the father's religion or the mother's). In private schools, 68% of the students have a father who is Catholic and 4% a Muslim father. In public schools, those figures are respectively 32% and 35%.

The social status of the students is another interesting variable to observe. Among those who think that God does not exist, 35% of them are upper-class[18] students and 24% working class students. Among those who believe in God, 33% are upper-class students and 49% working-class students.

As for the variable of gender, more girls believe in God than boys (38% vs. 32%), a slight difference which nevertheless confirms the traditional statement that women are more fervent about religion[19]. For those without a religion, not surprisingly, only 6% believe in God but 32% of them believe "there is some sort of spirit or life force".

Students' beliefs are also connected with their religious background. Whereas 97% of the students who declared themselves as Muslims believe in God, 53% of students of Catholic origin say so (and 34% of all students). Students of Muslim origin are more religious than others: for 57% of them, "religion determines my whole life" (15% of the total), while only 17% of Catholic students agree with this statement.

Levels of religious involvement

For these adolescents, who live in a secularised society and public sphere, religion is not an important part of their lives, as we already mentioned. When it comes to religious practices, 57% of them never pray, whereas 14% pray every day. More working-class students pray every day than their upper-class classmates: 25% and 15% respectively. 45% of all students never go to religious services and 32% go less than once a month. For 15%, "religion deter-

---

17   This percentage combines the answers "About every day", "About every week", and "About every month".

18   In order to analyse our results based on occupational variables, we used the European socio-economic nomenclature EseC. Here we will consider class 1 of this system, "large employers higher grade professional", as "upper classes", and class 9, "routine occupations", as "working classes".

19   For a historical view of this tendency, see Claude Langlois, "'Toujours plus pratiquantes'. La permanence du dimorphisme sexuel dans le catholicisme français contemporain", *Clio*, issue entitled *Femmes et Religions*, 2-1995, online.

mines my whole life": this percentage is 26% for working-class students and 13% for upper-class students. We can see that religious students in our sample mostly have working-class backgrounds.

In the REDCO survey, almost half the students have no religion: 45% vs. 52% who say they have one. When parents are religious, it is the mother more often than the father (57% vs. 49%), which demonstrates the traditional tendency for women to be more religious than men. But the small difference between the two figures shows that this tendency is not as important as it used to be. 13% of the students we met do not know their father's religion, but this could be because this answer sometimes comes from students who live with their mother and know almost nothing about their father. 10% of the students do not know their mother's religion. We should also note that when we handed out the questionnaires, some students told us that it was a private matter, so they did not answer that question.

Table 4:   Religion and social status

%	Upper classes (1)	Working classes (9)	Total[20]
Muslim	3.6	49	13%
Catholic	65	32	21%

With these figures in mind, let us first observe that in our sample, the fathers of the students who have a religion are located on either end of the social scale. We can also point out that when working-class students have a religion, it is Islam. These are probably the students we met in the suburbs of Paris and Marseille. Conversely, upper-class students are mainly Catholic.

Examples of socialisation

The family is still the traditional place for religious socialisation. 68% of the students we encountered think that the family remains a very important or important source of information on religion. This percentage drops to 37% when they are asked to evaluate the school's role in the matter. The objectivity of their classmates is also questionable: 31% of students feel that their fellow students can be an important source of information whereas 38% think that they are not or definitely are not. For 60% of students, the best source of information is still the faith community. Is this a sign that it is impossible to be objective in this area? Yet books are also seen as an important source of legitimate information for 54% of students.

As for the media (i.e. the television and the press), in the context of answers given in the questionnaires, 33% of students think that they are an important source of information, but 34% do not think so. We should also note that while most middle- and high-school students use the Internet often, 80% of them do not use it to get information about religious questions. For 48% of them, the Internet is not an important source of information on religion.

---

20 In comparison, in a CSA/Le Monde poll in 2003, 62% of French people surveyed said they were Catholic and 6% Muslim, while 26% said they had no religion.

Discussing religious matters with family, friends, and confidants

To the question "How often do you talk about religion with others?", the family comes first among the answers, followed by friends: 44% and 30% respectivel.[21] A majority of students never bring up religion with their classmates (51%), religious authorities (63%) or other students (69%). The role of teachers here is between the two: 40% of students never talk about religion with their teachers whereas 13% of them do, probably during classes on history where this subject is covered. As a result, when they bring up religion with their teachers, they do not talk about it like they do with their classmates; it has more to do with the school curriculum than with the questions they may personally have on the issue.

As we have said, the two surveys show the great importance of the family in religious socialisation. We should correlate this fact with other answers. Most of the time (for 76% of them), students have the same opinions on religion as their parents. The family is a relatively homogeneous unit when it comes to religion: thus, 63% of students say that all the members of their family belong to the same religion. But they are not as ready to agree that religion is inherited from the family: yes for 39%, no for 39%, and 22% without an opinion. Students in religious private schools are more likely to think that people inherit their religion from their family (54%); these students are also more willing to discuss religion with religious authorities, which can probably be explained by the important role the chaplain plays in these institutions and the importance given to religious instruction there.

The situation of students whose parents are farmers or employees can help to put this influence of the family into perspective. In each of these social categories, hardly more than 1% of students think that the family is an important source of information regarding religion. We should emphasise, however, that most of the children we met from farming families come from Limousin, a secular and "left-leaning" region, which partly explains why children there are not likely to gather knowledge about religion at home, as these families are often anticlerical.

As far as friends are concerned, they can be divided in two groups. First, students have a group of close friends, whose religions they know and are interested in; they then have an extended group of friends whose religions are less important to them. In the first case ("I like to know what my best friend thinks about religion"), 42% of students respond yes vs. 24% no. On the other hand, in the second case ("It doesn't bother me what my friends think about religion"), 68% say yes and 24% no.

Living in a religiously diverse world: shared friendly relations?

On the whole, students live in a pluralistic context involving many religions, at school and after school: 76% of them have friends with different religions (74% of the boys and 77% of the girls). At school, 72% of adolescents spend time with classmates who have other religions, or who have none at all (70% of the boys and 74% of the girls) and 92% refuse to be limited only to friends with the same religion (90% of the boys and 93% of the girls). All things being equal, the same can be said of what goes on outside of school, during the students' spare time. After school, 58% of students have friends who do not share their religion and 95% do not see why they should have to spend their spare time only with people with the same religious background. However, 53% say that most of their friends share their views on religion (51% of the boys and 54% of the girls), whereas only 26% say this about their other

---

21 These percentages combine the answers "About every day", "About every week", and "About every month".

classmates. Do these results indicate a discrepancy between what students say and what they really feel? Not necessarily: when asked whether "most of the students of my class have the same ideas about religion" as they do, most students say either that they do not know their friends' religions (35%) or just say "no" (37%). Similarly, to the statement "I have students in my class who belong to different religions," 22% say that they just do not know their class-mates' religions. These answers are along the same lines as those involving the level of inter-est in their classmates' religions. Here, there are no significant differences between the way girls and boys respond to these statements, which minimizes the importance of gender when analysing the influence of religion in how students interact with others in school and outside of it.

Table 5: **With whom do students talk about religion?**

%	Upper classes (1)	Working classes (9)	Total
Talk about religion with their family	26	35	25
Talk about religion with their friends	12	18	14
Talk about religion with their classmates	9	10	9

Taking the students' social status into account, we see that those who talk about religion in the family are often young people from the suburbs, or at least those coming from disadvan-taged backgrounds – Muslims or evangelical Protestants were those we encountered. It ap-pears as though students from this group are more willing than others to talk about religion with their friends; this can probably be explained by the composition of the student body in middle schools in the French suburbs, where there is both social and religious homogeneity (Muslim families with modest incomes). In our sample, in the two middle schools in suburbs of Paris, nearly two third of students (63%) are Muslims whereas the general average percent-age of Muslim students in our sample is much lower (24%). According to our survey, these students talk about religion with each other. For them, religion is important and plays a major role in their lives, so it is both an everyday and a legitimate topic of conversation. Religion may also be seen as a form of knowledge that is more rewarding than what is learned in school, where these students often have difficulties.

The existence of what some people hastily call "ghettos" casts doubt on the idea that a plu-ralistic, tolerant, and religiously diverse society is possible. But the phenomenon of religious groups isolating themselves from the outside world is not limited to these underprivileged neighbourhoods. Whereas 76% of students in public schools have friends with different reli-gions – as we have said – this figure drops to 42% in private schools, which can be easily explained by the religious nature of the institutions we investigated.

A little more than half of the students have internalised the principle of *laïcité*. Following one of the main ideas of this principle, 52% of them "agree" or "strongly agree" with the state-ment "Religion is something private". And yet they seem to tolerate and accept religious diversity, and this demonstrates their acceptance of one might call a culture of debate. 46% "disagree" or "strongly disagree" with the statement: "I have problems showing my views about religion openly in school". We can also note that 31% have no opinion on this subject. And in accordance with this concern for tolerance, 58% of students "disagree" or "strongly disagree" with the idea that "a student who openly demonstrates his/her belief in school risks being mocked".

So there is a kind of shared space where students from different religions can come in contact with each other and get to know each other, where religion, incidentally, is not the most important thing they talk about; far from it.

Most (86%) students agree with the statement: "I respect other people who believe", which means they subscribe to the fundamental principles of human rights and the rights of the citizen. Students have made the rules of living together in community their own, and the public school system is seen by most of them as the very home of tolerance given that, as a secular institution, it contains students from all kinds of religious and cultural backgrounds. At the same time, 82% of students "agree" or "strongly agree" with the idea that "Religion is important in our history": in a country characterised by the norms of *laïcité*, students know that the past cannot be erased; what is more, they learn about that every day in the secular context of school. Religion is part of their cultural heritage.

Synopsis of data – religion in students' lives

Firstly, religion is a secondary concern for teenage students but they do think about the meaning of life and are not unwilling to talk about religious topics. Girls are slightly more religious than boys. Religion plays a very important part in the life of Muslim students whereas Catholic students are rather close to the average: for them religion is not a central part of their lives. As the European Value Survey (EVS) (Lambert, 2000, 2004) showed, non religious students are not all atheist: one third of them believe "there is some sort of spirit or life force" and even 6% of them believe in God.

Besides, concerning the levels of religious commitment, as other surveys have shown[22], there is in general today a certain amount of indifference towards religion; this is even truer for young people than for adults. Almost half of the students surveyed are non- religious, never pray and never go to religious services, with the exception of students coming from a working-class background who mostly are Muslims.

Then, family and faith communities are the main places to be socialised into religion for three quarters of the students, which means a homogeneous context of socialisation. The media and internet come last. As far as the media are concerned, they are probably suspected of twisting the facts and presenting only a one-sided view of things, mainly concerning the way they represent Islam and Muslims, a result that clearly came out of the quantitative survey

Furthermore, religion is a personal matter which is only discussed with those closest to them (family, close friends). Teachers, religious authorities and classmates come last. Since most students share the same view about religion as their parents, we must conclude once again that religious socialisation is homogenous.

Students from public schools are divided on the issue whether religion is a choice more than something one inherits, whereas half of the students from private schools think religion is inherited. The individualisation of religion, that is choosing one's religion rather than inheriting it, a tendency that sociologists of religion have observed recently, is not readily apparent in our survey. There seem to be two opposing tendencies that are currently

---

22 See in particular Lambert & Michelat, 1992 and Campiche, 1997.

at work. One tendency highlights the lasting importance of traditional religious affiliations; when someone has a religion, it is most often the one their parents had. The other tendency is representative of a line of thinking that adolescents have fully accepted regarding religious individualism, which assumes that someone has to choose the religion they believe in.[23]

Finally, school is the major place where students encounter religious diversity and build up friendly relations with classmates of different religious backgrounds. However, as far as closest friends are concerned, they share the same religion. However, one most stresses the fact that most students do not know about their classmates' religion. This finding emphasises the already mentioned fact that religion is not the main issue discussed among youngsters and does not play a central role in their life, with the exception of Muslim students. Besides, more than half of students have internalized the principle of *laïcité*: "religion is a private matter".

Students in private confessional schools have less experience with religious diversity in school since Catholic private schools are more homogeneous from a religious point of view (see Tables 9 and 10). Besides, students are tolerant towards other's religion, a good basis for living in religiously pluralistic society. Religion is recognized as an important part of their cultural heritage, a fact that is stressed in the school curriculum concerning religious phenomena.

2.1.2 General interpretation of the data

Ultimately, pluralism is a value shared by all the students we met, if their questionnaires are any indication. But sometimes this is a "politically correct" pluralism since their religious socialisation is homogenous: family, faith communities and closest friends (most often from the same religion) are the ones with whom they most often learn and discuss about religion. When we ask them questions, we present ourselves as secular researchers, representatives of a public institution. There may be a discrepancy between what they say and what they really think, demonstrating that a sort of "religious correctness" exists. Nevertheless, within the school context, different groups coexist, and there are tensions between them, obviously, but not insurmountable ones. Unfortunately, the ability of different groups to coexist is also due to the social and territorial segregation of the country, which means that people remain in the region where they feel accepted socially and religiously and where they can accept others: this is the case for both Catholic private schools and public schools in the surroundings of Paris where two third of the students have the same religion, respectively Catholicism and Islam[24].

In any case, the French students we met live in a secularised society, where religion is a secondary concern, open to question; they are free to change their mind about it. However, in this context, religion still has a role to play in the area of cultural heritage, which is legitimised by its presence in the school curriculum (in History, Literature, and Philosophy).

---

23 On this topic, see Hervieu-Léger's analysis of "internal converts" (1999).
24 On this topic, see the analyses of D. Borne, particularly in Borne & Willaime, 2007, pp. 97–119, 197–216 and Michel, 1999.

2.2   How do students see religion in school?

2.2.1 Data description

In the French system, there is no school subject specifically devoted to religious phenomena. To take this absence into consideration, we added a question at the beginning of the French version of the questionnaire asking students in which subjects religion is covered. The results are clear: students hear about religion most often in History classes (67%). The second subject where religious facts are discussed is Civics (33%). Analysis of different school curricula confirms as a matter of fact that History is the main subject where religion is discussed. We must also mention that the approach "toward religious facts in France, Europe and the world, relying in particular on founding texts (especially extracts from the Bible and the Koran) in a spirit of *laïcité* that respects the freedom of conscience and of belief" is part of "all that must be mastered by the end of mandatory schooling"[25] (Decree of July 11 2006 pertaining to the *fundamentals of knowledge and skills*, which modified the educational code). But, in France, only the students in the public school system of the three *départements* in the east of the country (Moselle, Bas-Rhin and Haut-Rhin), and students in some private schools, have the chance to take courses on religion. This is why only 10% of the students in our survey answered "yes" when asked if they take any religious courses during their school year. Only 27% of students in religious private schools say they took religious courses during the year. This shows that these schools do not primarily teach the Christian faith, despite maintaining their identities as religious institutions; they are nearly all under contract with the State and as a result are required to be open to all students regardless of their religious beliefs. Although some bishops attempt to "recatholicise" these schools (90% of which are Catholic), the reasons why parents choose a Catholic school over a public one are not for the most part religious ones. According to empirical surveys[26], by making this choice, families wish above all to avoid the educational, ethnic and religious diversity of public schools by sending their children to what they feel is an institution of higher quality.

Religion at school: the students' experiences

French students clearly emphasise the three following items in their answers to the question: "What are your experiences of religion in school? How much do you agree, that:"

1) "At school, I learn to have respect for everyone, whatever their religion (89% agree)[27]".

2) "Learning about different religions at school helps us to live together" (70% agree).

3) "At school, I get knowledge about different religions" (68% agree).

From the point of view of French students, it is essential to respect everyone regardless of their beliefs. They think so whether they have a religion or not. As a result, learning about

---

25 In France, schooling is mandatory until age 16.
26 According to the poll IFOP-La Vie in 1978, only 21% of parents choose a Catholic private school for religious reasons; 21% choose it because the discipline is stricter, 25% choose it for the quality of the studies. According to Robert Ballion (1982) one third of catholic private schools do not provide a catechetical teaching. For him, Catholic private schools appear as a "teaching made to measure for a selected public". The social reasons of such choice (staying with people from the same social background) are more difficult to confess, but do exist. See *Le Monde de l'éducation* "Juifs, musulmans, catholiques. Ceux qui font école à part", janvier 2008, n°365
27 For the remainder of the text, the percentages that are mentioned combine the percentages of those who answered "Agree" and "Strongly agree".

religion in school seems useful to them in order to live together with others and gain knowledge of other religions. Of course, the students say that they learn to have respect, but we do
not know if they respect others in reality. They just make it clear to us here that they endorse
the school as the place where they learn to respect others. This point of view is expressed
significantly more often by students who have a religion (76% and 74% agree with these two
items) than by those who do not (64% for both). There are many more students in public
schools (67%) than those in private schools (41%) who say that they have learned about
different religions in school.

Table 6:   The school: a space to learn about and experience religious diversity

% of students who approve	Total	Students with a religion	Students without a religion
At school, I learn to have respect for everyone, whatever their religion	89	88	92
Learning about different religions at school helps us to live together	70	76	64
At school, I get knowledge about different religions	68	74	64

On the whole, 57% of students think that "Learning about religions at school helps them to
understand current events". Conversely, only 16% of students think that "Learning about religions at school helps them to learn about themselves" (25% of students who say they have a
religion and 7% of students without a religion). On the other hand, there are no differences
between students with religions and those without when asked whether "Learning about religions at school helps them to make choices between right and wrong" (only 23% of all students think so). Most of the students put less emphasis on their personal experience of religion
at school. However, 53% appreciate the fact that they have a chance at school to "discuss religious issues from different perspectives" and 50% think that "topics about religions [are]
interesting at school". On this point, there is a clear difference between students with religions
and those without: whereas 61% of the first group think it is interesting to discuss religion in
school, only 38% of the second group think so. Notably, only 16% of students feel that
"Learning about religions leads to conflicts in the classroom". Nevertheless, all these results
must be seen in the light of the fact that only 33% of students think that "Religion as a topic is
important in school". Here again, we observe a clear distinction between students with religions and those without: whereas 42% of the first group feel it is important to study religion
in school, only 23% of the second group agree. School is accepted by 89% of students as the
place where they learn to respect others, but this does not mean they think that has to happen
in a course dealing with religion. Again, many students are not particularly interested in religion: whereas 50% acknowledge that it is "interesting" to talk about it in class, only 33%
think it is "important" to do so. There is a significant distinction to be made between the two
positions.

Religion at school: What is its proper place according to the students?

To the question "Religion could appear in the school in many different ways. Imagine you are
a person in authority who can decide on school matters. How far would you agree with the
following positions?", the answers change depending on the choices offered. The answer that

French students give is quite clear when asked if they "should be able to wear religious symbols at school": 78% agree if this means discreet symbols, but 58% are opposed if this means more visible symbols such as a headscarf or a yarmulke (only 17% are in favour, including 21% of students who have a religion and 13% who do not). There is not much difference between the answers that students in public and private schools give to this question. On the question of allowing religious signs that are more visible than is currently permitted in schools, Muslim students are more reluctant to answer than Catholic students. While 36% of Muslim students agree, 32% disagree and 35% have no opinion, these figures are respectively 15%, 63% and 21% for Catholic students. It is obvious that Muslim students are less willing to give answers than Catholic students, and that they are clearly divided on this issue.

Table 7:   Religious symbols: different levels of understanding (%)

	Agree	Disagree	No opinion
Students should be able to wear religious symbols at school: discreet ones	78	10	11
Students should be able to wear religious symbols at school: more visible ones	17	58	22

On the whole, 61% of students say that they agree with the idea that "at school meals, religious food requirements should be taken into account". Here, public and private school students give different answers: 66% of public school students and 47% of private school students agree that school cafeterias should make allowances for the dietary laws of religions. Half (52%) of students think that they "can be absent from school for their religious festivals" (26% do not agree and 22% have no opinion). Concerning absences from school for religious reasons, many more students who have a religion are in favour of them (63%) than students who do not (40%). The great majority of those surveyed (61% of the total, 55% of students with a religion and 70% of those without) do not agree with the statement "Students should be excused from taking some lessons for religious reasons" and 62% do not agree with the statement "Schools should provide facilities for students to pray in school" (53% of students with a religion and 73% of those without, 70% of public school students and only 39% of private school students), even though, for both questions, there is a clear difference between students with and without religions. As for the statement "Voluntary religious services (e.g. school worship, prayers) could be a part of school life", it is interesting to note that only 35% of those surveyed disagree with this and that 27% agree (37% have no opinion). As we could have expected, there are more students with a religion (32%) than those without (22%) who approve of such a possibility, but the fact that those 22% agree is something important to remember, as is the fact that only 41% of private school students are in favour of optional religious services at school.

How should schools handle instruction covering religion?

In accordance with the point of view mentioned in the previous section, it is therefore understandable that most French students (82%) feel that a course dealing specifically with religion must be optional. This attitude is due to the absence of mandatory religious education in French public schools; students are therefore wary of a context where such a course would be required. It was clearly hard for French students to respond to the question "What is your position regarding different models of religious education in school?", due to its strangeness in a French context, where there is no religious instruction in school. It is therefore natural that a majority (59%) do not agree with the statement "Students should study Religious Education separately in groups according to which religion they belong to". But French students are divided on their responses to other statements and it is hard to interpret these wide differences: it seems as though students hesitate in their reactions. For example, 44% agree, 32% have no opinion and 24% disagree with the statement "There is no need for the subject of Religious Education. All the relevant topics are covered by other school subjects (e.g. literature, history etc)". But the answers that students from public schools give to this question are markedly different from those given by students from private schools: whereas 48% of the first group agree, only 33% of the second group do (38% of private school students have no opinion). The reason for this difference is that students from private schools have access to catechetical courses (which are usually optional but required in some cases) among those courses dealing with religion. Here, there is a clear split between students with a religion and those without: while 34% of the first group feel it is necessary to have a specific course, 57% of the second group think so. But even among students with a religion, there is not an overwhelming desire for such a course: only 33% of them want one. As a result, it is easier to understand why only 18% of those surveyed (24% of students with a religion and 11% of those without) agree that "Religious Education should be taught to students together, whatever differences there might be in their religious or denominational background" (54% disagree and 27% have no opinion). Among the 54% who disagree, 65% have no religion and 47% do. It is no surprise then that there seems to be some hesitation in responding to the following statement: "Religious Education should be taught sometimes together and sometimes in groups according to which religions students belong to". The answers do not seem to align themselves in a particular direction: 58% have no opinion, 14% agree and 25% disagree. In reality, this item was only relevant to those students who agree with the idea of a specific school subject covering religion.

Ultimately, it is not obvious to French students that there has to be a place for religion in school. Only 34% (44% of students with a religion and 23% of those without) disagree with the statement "There should be **no** place for religion in school" (28% agree and 38% have no opinion).

What do French students expect from school if religious facts are discussed there?

What do French students expect from their teacher if he or she brings up religion in class? Their priority is quite clear: they expect to "get an objective knowledge about different religions" (63%) and to "be able to talk and communicate about religious issues" (63% of the total, 70% of students with a religion and 57% of those without). They also want to "learn the importance of religion for dealing with problems in society" (58%) and to "learn to understand what religions teach" (56% of the total, 65% of students with a religion and 45% of those without). But in studying religion at school, they do not expect to "be guided towards religious belief": only 9% agree (13% of all students with a religion – 12% of Catholic students and 20% of Muslim students – and 3% of those without religion) and 52% disagree with this statement. In the religiously diverse context of France today, young people live in a culture that encourages debate. It does not bother them to express their own views on religious issues (not embarrassed: 46%; embarrassed: 23%). Most of them do not think that they risk being mocked if they openly demonstrate their religious beliefs in school (58% of the total,

54% of students with a religion and 63% of those without); only 23% think they do. But it is interesting to note that more Catholic students (28%) than Muslim students (18%) are afraid of being mocked if they openly express their religious beliefs.

Synopsis of data – religion in school

First of all, for students, school is the right place to learn to have respect for every religion. Learning about different religions helps them to live together. They, thus, support the civic dimension of the French curriculum in teaching about religious phenomena. On the contrary they refuse a teaching of religion that would have an impact on their personal believes, for they consider them as private matter. However, one must stress the fact that the teaching about religions is not a major concern for students, especially for those who are not religious. It is an interesting topic among others but not an important one. This finding relates to the previous sub-chapter which clearly emphasises that religion is secondary for teenage students. To conclude, learning to live together is of course one major aim of the teaching of religious phenomena but it is a more general aim of the whole school system that can be achieved within any subjects and within school life.

Then, most French students, whenever they come from public or private confessional schools, have internalized the principle of *laïcté* and have accepted the consequences of the law of 2004 forbidding the wearing of ostensible religious symbols. They are in favour of certain accommodations such as the wearing of discreet religious symbols, special meals in the cafeteria according to religious prescription or absences for religious festivals which are not public holidays whereas they disagree with the wearing of visible religious symbols and the refusal to take one lesson for religious reasons, which case is considered as absenteeism in opposition to the principle of school obligation. They do not feel that school is the proper place to pray or have voluntary religious services, except (only) a strong minority of pupils from private confessional schools who have this opportunity. However, one must consider the case of Muslim students. They are divided on the issue of wearing ostensible religious signs; but only a minority (one third) openly disagrees with the law of 2004 while one third agrees and one third has no opinion

Besides, when asked about different school systems in teaching religious phenomena, French students seem slightly hesitant since they do not have the direct experience of different systems from theirs. However, they clearly refuse a mandatory religious education or a teaching of religious issues which separate students according to their religious belonging. They are divided on the issue whether a special course on religious issues is needed. Pupils in private schools are more in favour of it than pupils in public schools because they already have access to catechetical courses among those courses dealing with religion. Only one third of students who say they are religious are willing to have such an opportunity. This does not mean there should be no place for religion in school, either in the curriculum or in school life (only one third states so) but they tend to agree with the French choice of teaching religions within different subjects to students altogether

To conclude, most of the students approve the choice made by the French curriculum: teaching religious phenomena. For them it is knowledge-oriented and not value-oriented. They do not want a religiously-oriented teaching on religion. They expect knowledge on past and present issues as well as the skills to handle these religious issues. They do not express fear of expressing their own point of view on the matter. For them, religious questions are not that sensitive and can be discussed like any other questions.

2.2.2   General interpretation of the data

Public and private school students share the same ideas on the most important objectives and the most necessary content of courses that deal with religion. For both groups, instruction should be based on knowledge rather than on moral principles. The fact that public andprivate schools use the same curriculum and offer the same subjects (History, Geography, Literature …) probably explains the absence of major differences between students from these two categories of schools (according to the survey results). So when it comes to religion at school, French students are most interested in acquiring knowledge and learning how to improve relations between groups in society.

There is a possible explanation for the differences noticed between the answers given by students with a religion and by those without. Students without a religion tend to think that studying religion in school only concerns students interested in the issue. In the area of religion as in others (Mathematics, Biology, Literature …) students could respond on the basis of their personal tastes rather than for other reasons. By the clear distinction students make between wearing discreet and ostentatious religious symbols, this survey shows that French students, including those who say they have a religion, approve of the law enacted in this area. We should remember that according to the law of March 15 2004, "in elementary, middle and high schools, it is prohibited to wear signs or clothing ostensibly indicating a religious affiliation. School regulations stipulate that the application of disciplinary measures must be preceded by a discussion with the student." But the answers students gave to other items shows that just because they are against wearing religious signs at school, this does not mean that they are against the school showing tolerance toward students when it comes to what their religions require them to do or prohibit them from doing. In other words, students are in favour of making allowances for their classmates' religions, but they are against anything that could undermine the school curriculum, and they reject the visible presence of religious practices such as school prayer (however students in religious private schools are in favour of the existence of facilities in school where they may pray if they wish). They show tolerance toward each person's freedom of worship and they respect their classmates' religions, but the public and non-religious nature of school is important to them. However, the quantitative survey could only take note of the students' point of view; it tells us nothing about what happens in reality. We should also remember that 21% of students think that "talking about religion only leads to disagreement" and 27% feel that "without religion the world would be a better place". Nevertheless, we can say that in the minds of French students in general, this does not mean they are hostile toward religion or that they reject it. As to the possibility of optional religious services at school, what is important to them is precisely that such services be optional. Students think that each of them has the right to do what he or she wants, on the one condition that whatever that is should not be required of other students. It is probably because religious services are mandatory for students in some private schools – although this is prohibited by law for private schools under contract with the State – that students in these schools are somewhat reluctant to have religious services in school, even as something optional.

Although 24% of French students consider that the state school system's approach is insufficient, we can still say that, on the whole, a relative majority (44%) of them explicitly approve of the choice made by France to teach religious facts exclusively within existing school subjects. They are on the same wavelength as the choice made by their country: to teach religious facts within existing school subjects instead of creating a special subject dealing with this material. But in order to place this result in perspective, we must note that a large majority of French students are unfamiliar with other ways of dealing with religion in school, and have not experienced other models firsthand. Their opinions are therefore based upon what they know. Moreover, even if French students are interested in learning something about religions in school, this does not mean that there is a great deal of enthusiasm from students concerning religion in school. Our view is that, for them, discussing the role of religion in school is more about the expression of feelings and religious practices than the existence of courses dealing with religion.

Finally, French students, whether they have a religion or not, are mainly interested in an approach to religion in school that provides them with knowledge, skills and the intellectual ability to understand religious phenomena for what they are and the role they play in society. For 52% of them, religion is first and foremost a private matter, but this does not mean that they think schools should avoid discussing it. By insisting upon an educational approach to religious facts based on knowledge and intellectual skills, French students have fully accepted the specific nature of the French secular school environment. In this way of thinking about religion at school, we see that French students do not think that school is the right place to practise religion or to discover one's own spirituality, even if what students learn in school may have some consequences on their own personal choices in this matter.

2.3   How do students see the impact of religion?

2.3.1   Data description

Why discuss religion in class?

The most popular reason French students give when asked why religious facts should be taught in school is "To understand the history of my country and of Europe" (80%). This answer is more prevalent among Catholic students (87%) than Muslim ones (59%). The second most popular response is "To develop my own point of view" (67%), followed by "To gain a better understanding of current events" (62%) "To understand others and live peacefully with them" only comes in fourth place (57%). However, there is a higher percentage of Muslim students who answer "yes" to this choice (79%); in fact, this answer comes in first place for them. The last-place choice is "To learn about my own religion" (55%). On the other hand, this is an important objective for both Catholic students (73%) and Muslim ones (76%). Finally, French students are divided on the normative value of courses that cover religious facts (transmitting values) – no opinion: 38%, yes: 36% (43% of Muslim students); no: 25%.

It seems as though there is something specific to Muslim students regarding their expectations on courses dealing with religious facts: they expect to learn about values, particularly those that encourage living with others as a community. They are less interested in the part of courses on religious facts devoted to cultural heritage, which may mean that they see themselves as being outside of mainstream culture, as some teachers working with Muslim-majority classes in disadvantaged suburbs have told us. The percentage of Muslim and Catholic students who hope to get information on their own religion in the course on the history of religions is much higher than for students on average.

Table 8:   Why discuss religion in school? Differences and commonalities between students in public and private schools (%)[28]

	Public schools	Private religious schools
To understand the history of my country and of Europe	79	83
To gain a better understanding of current events.	61	66
To understand others and live peacefully with them	59	50
To learn about my own religion	52	63
To develop moral values.	35	41

Students going to private schools do not have exactly the same goals as their counterparts in the public system when it comes to courses on religion. Here are the similarities: the purpose of courses on religious facts is to understand history and current events, less for developing moral values – the latter receives a smaller proportion of positive answers from students in both systems. As for the differences, the teaching of religious facts is the way to learn about one's own religion for a large majority of private school students. For private school students, the goal of courses on religion is less to understand other religions and live peacefully with them than it is for public school students. This difference should be put into perspective: for students in both systems, these objectives are secondary; the demand for knowledge comes first.

How can we explain these similarities and differences? Students in public schools and those in private schools under contract to the state take the same classes. It is natural that for students in both systems courses on religious facts are more useful for obtaining information (learning history and interpreting current events) that for learning norms (developing moral values). However, private religious schools add an extra goal, considered part of their "special nature"[29]: passing on the faith. So it is not surprising that students in private schools expect to hear more about their religion than other religions. Their lesser interest for the civic value of teaching religious facts (understanding others and living in peace with them) can be explained by the greater religious homogeneity of private schools as compared to public schools (see Tables 9 and 10), where all religions come in contact with each other and have to learn how to live together.

---

28 These figures combine the answers "strongly agree" + "agree"

29 The "special nature" of religious schools, which was mentioned in the Debré law of December 31 1959 allowing these schools to be under contract to the State, is an all-purpose notion. It acts as a framework for the specificity and the distinctive characteristics of these institutions, which can appear in various ways: "for example in a special teaching method, a particular way of organising the courses of study, or in the way the school is run, the personalities of its founders, its administrators or its teachers. But what constitutes the heart of the notion of a school's special nature is the fact that it is religious". Here, the law specifies that "the school, while maintaining its special nature, must offer instruction while completely respecting freedom of conscience. It must be open to all children regardless of their origins, their opinions or their beliefs." (Messner, Prélot & Woehrling, 2003, p. 1201).

Table 9:   Religious classification: public and private confessional schools (%)[30]

	Catholics	Chris- tians	Protes- tants	Muslims	Jews	Others	No answer
Private school	68	23	0,02	0,04	-	-	9
Public school	29	23	0,06	32%	0,03	0,05	16

Table 10:   Religious classification: public and private confessional schools (%)[31]

	Religious	Without religion
Private school	67	33
Public school	50	50

A culture of debate that promotes dialogue?

A large majority of students state that getting different points of view about religion from other people is interesting (65%). Bringing up the subject does not bother them (66%). They are willing to do so even if they have a limited grasp of the matter (48%).

When students are confronted by a classmate who tries to proselytise them, nearly all say that they are willing to listen to him or her without feeling obliged to change their opinion about anything: 90% say: "I listen but their views do not influence me". A large majority are willing to talk about it: 86% say that they discuss or could discuss their opinions with their classmate. Among the minority of students who hold the opposite view, there are more boys (20%) than girls (8%). A slight majority of the students surveyed are inclined to criticise what appears to be a proselytising attitude: 52% state: "I try or could try to convince him that s/he is wrong". But the point of this discussion is not to convert the other person to his or her point of view – 74% (but only 54% of private school students) reject the following statement: "I try or could try to explain that my own opinions about religion are the best ones".

So a student's proselytising attitude does not lead to counter-proselytising from the person to whom he or she is speaking, which could result in conflict.

However, it must be stressed that the majority of students do not pay any attention to their classmate's religious declarations: 61% say: "I try or could try to ignore him/her"; only 38% say the opposite. Students from upper-class backgrounds (54%) demonstrate less indifference than those from working-class backgrounds (73%).

A positive image of religion?

About half the students do not think that religious people are less tolerant than others (no: 52%) or aggressive (no: 47%). However, these seem to be embarrassing questions: one third of students prefer not to answer them (30% and 31% respectively). It is important to note that students are divided on the question of whether the world would be a better place without religions (yes 27%, no 40%, no opinion 33%). However, half of the students surveyed reject

---

30 Results according to our sample.
31 Results according to our sample.

offensive statements about religion such as associating it with stupidity or cruelty ("no": 49%). The different variables cause significant distinctions to appear. Boys are slightly more critical about religion than girls, especially when considering the most definite answers possible ("Strongly agree" / "Strongly disagree"). The religious students have a more positive view of religion than those without religion, especially Muslim students who share a much better image of religion than young Catholics who are close to the average.

Table 11: **Image of religion: differences according to gender and religion (%)[32]**

	Total	Boys	Girls	Religious	Without religion	Catholics	Muslims
"Religious people are less tolerant towards others."	18	23	14	16	20	18	14
"Religion is a source of aggressiveness."	21	23	19	17	27	18	6
"Without religion the world would be a better place."	27	32	19	20	37	23	5

Why talk about religion?

Students discuss religion among themselves first of all because they think it is interesting to talk with people who have another point of view than they do (65%); then because it helps them understand others (60%); then because it helps them get a better idea of what is going on in the world (58%), and finally because it helps them shape their own views (53%).

It seems as though the main function of dialogue on religious matters is to be receptive to others, more than being interested in general questions or in asserting one's identity or point of view. That is a major point for it favours an *interpersonal* dialogue between students. Students are eager to discuss religious issues on a face to face basis, rather than having general debates on the matter. However, one must not forget that, for a majority of students, religion is a secondary concern and that they do not wish to speak about it. For some of them, the reason is indifference towards religious matters; for some others, religion is a too intimate topic to be shared with other students.

---

32 These figures combine the answers "strongly agree" + "agree"

Table 12:   Positive reasons for talking about religion: differences according to gender and reli-
gion (%)[33]

	Total	Boys	Girls	Catholis	Muslims
"To me talking about religion is interesting because people have different views."	65	55	67	70	78
"Talking about religion helps to shape one's own views."	53	53	54	66	71

In general, boys and girls have the same opinions here, but girls seem more willing to think that discussions help them understand others. For this group of questions, students without religion differ from religious students when it comes to the most definite answers ("Strongly agree" / "Strongly disagree"), while being less interested in discussing religious issues, without however being opposed to doing so Muslim students are more interested in religious discussions than Catholic students and students in general.

Table 13:   Low interest in talking about religion: differences according to gender, religion and
socio-economic background (%)[34]

	Total	Boys	Girls	Religious	Without religion	Catholics	Muslims	Middle class	Upper class	Working class
"Religion doesn't interest me at all – we have more important things to talk about."	35	37	31	19	54	21	5	44	34	35
"For me talking about religious topics is boring."	33	38	33	21	47	19	7	41	29	33

But the results in Table 13 should not be over-interpreted: students are nonetheless divided on whether they agree with the statement "Religion doesn't interest me at all – we have more important things to talk about" ("yes" 35.5%, "no" 37%). The same ambivalence can be seen, to a lesser extent, when students are asked if religion bores them ("yes" 33%, "no" 41%, no opinion 25%). However, the variables of gender, religion and social status affect these results.

The quantitative survey makes it possible to go beyond the simple observation that students are relatively uninterested in religious issues. It also reveals a more consistent interest in the matter from girls than from boys, but the different is slight and those expressing interest are in the minority. On the other hand, a majority of students without religion are not inter-

---

33   These figures combine the answers "strongly agree" + "agree"
34   These figures combine the answers "strongly agree" + "agree"

ested in religious issues; many members of this group come from the middle classes. Conversely Muslim students are the ones most interested in religious matters.

As for the usefulness of discussing religion, in other words if it fosters dialogue or rather conflict, the responses are ambiguous, especially if those students with no opinion are taken into account. Students are divided on whether they agree with the statement "Talking about religion helps me to live peacefully together with people from different religions" (yes 26%, no 35%, no opinion 27%). The opposite position, however, does not yield the same result. A slight majority of students (53%) do not agree with the statement "In my view, talking about religion only leads to disagreement"; 20% agree and 25% have no opinion. There are a slightly larger number of girls who disagree than boys (55% vs. 50%) but boys and girls agree in the same proportions. Students without religion do not differ greatly from religious students on this question. Muslim students give more importance to dialogue on religious matters (yes 43.5%) and are less concerned about the conflict that could result (no 67%).

Living together with our differences

Students categorically deny that they only want to live with people who have the same religion or worldview as they do (84%). Moreover, for a majority of students, even for those without religion (58%), being very religious is not seen as an obstacle to living with others in a community. But students are aware of the difficulties in living with others: a large majority is worried about religious conflict in the event of disagreements (72%), but this proportion decreases, as we have seen, when it comes to discussions between young people in face-to-face relationships (53%). The way the question is worded influences the answers students give. Young people from privileged backgrounds seem more concerned about conflicts caused by religion (79%) than those from disadvantaged backgrounds (54%), but when there is the possibility of a discussion between their peers, they express these fears less often and the percentages even out.

For students the guiding principle for peaceful coexistence among people of different religions is respect (yes: 80%). Sociologists who study the young have found that "respect" is the favourite word of adolescents seeking recognition and authenticity (Dubet, 1991). Students have also suggested other preconditions for living in harmony with people from other religions.

First, it is necessary to know about other people's religions (75%); then, to personally know people from different religions (70%); then, it is best if people do things together and have shared interests (68% of positive answers to both items). The role of the State is a secondary matter, or the question makes no sense to adolescents who most often say they have no opinion (41%) on whether it is desirable that "the country have strict laws about the role of religion in society". A sizable minority of students think that *laïcité* can help people live in peace: 46% agree to the requirement that "everyone keep to themselves about their religion". There is a noticeable difference of opinion on this point between students from public and religious private schools: the latter are less likely to feel that religion should be a private matter ("yes" 40% vs. 48.5% of public school students). Catholic students do not differ greatly from the average ("yes" 42%). Muslim students are divided on the question ("yes" 38%, "no" 27%, no opinion 34%). The more direct statement: "Religion is something private", on the other hand, has a higher percentage of students agreeing with it (53%), while maintaining the distinction between students from private schools ("yes" 43%) and public schools ("yes" 57%). The percentages for Catholics (47%) and Muslims (48%), however, are comparable.

Synopsis of data – impact of religion

Firstly, students have accepted the official objectives of teaching religious facts: to present courses on religion in a comparative, pluralist and neutral manner, not to impart values– in other words "teaching about religion", not "teaching into religion"[35]. This does not prevent Catholic or Muslim students from attempting to gather information about their faiths in courses dealing with religion. The curriculum in France is also intended to develop the students' critical faculties: this is how their desire to develop their own point of view should be interpreted, not as a desire to express their religious beliefs in class, which would be "teaching from religion".

For French students, courses on religious facts encourage them to get to know other people and live in peace with other religions; this is especially important for students in public institutions whose school environment involves students from many religions, unlike private Catholic schools, which are more homogeneous as far as religion is concerned (see Tables 9 and 10); Muslim students expect much in this area. This particularity raises some questions. Are Muslim students more eager to learn things about other religions than non-Muslims? Or do they feel that emphasising peaceful coexistence will help them (which implies that they expect the other students to learn more about Islam)? However, for French students in general, this objective of peaceful coexistence through teaching religious issues is not the main focus of the teaching of religious facts. So it is not possible to interpret these results in way that could clearly lead us to conclude that courses on religious facts in France are explicitly intended, before anything else, to encourage peaceful coexistence between religions, even if course material dealing with all religions obviously helps attain this goal.

Secondly, French pupils share a culture or debate. In the multicultural context of France today, students have a common interest in fostering debate. However a two-sided attitude is highlighted by the results of our survey (willingness to discuss the issue but indifference to the other's opinion). It may be explained by the results of the European Values Survey (EVS)[36]. A majority of people, especially the young, do not think that there is only one truth – theirs. As is shown above, a majority of the students surveyed do not try to explain that their own opinions about religion are the best ones if facing the proselytising attitude of one of their comrades. The atmosphere encouraging debate that exists among students is accompanied by a relativist point of view regarding religious values, which is apparently less noticeable among upper-class students. So, it is more a matter of passive tolerance than active dialogue. However, girls are more willing to discuss the issue; on the other hand, when boys express a contrary opinion, these are only a minority of boys.

Thirdly, in general, it cannot be said that French students have a negative opinion of religion. Students without religion have a more critical attitude about it than their religious classmates. As the European Values Survey (EVS) indicates, young people are less often atheist than their parents, and more often agnostic or without religion but with a certain openness to spirituality. Our quantitative REDCo survey shows that having no religion is still associated with a certain level of anticlericalism, but this is not a formal anticlerical stance as was the case in previous generations. Moreover, generally speaking, only a minority holds even this informal position. Muslim students defend a more positive view of religion (of their religion?) than Catholics, probably in order to reject the negative stereotypes that are propagated about Islam.

---

35 For the distinction between "teaching into", "teaching about" and "teaching from" religion, see Jackson, 1997.

36 For more details about the results of the EVS, see Lambert, 2000, 2004.

Fourthly, discussions with people of different religions and beliefs may be personally rewarding, but they do not appear to be a clear factor for peace; this does not mean, however, that they are seen as a factor for conflict. Indifference to religious issues predominates among French students, more with boys than girls, and much more with those who have no religion than with religious students. The answers given by students without religion should not be interpreted as an unwillingness to talk about the matter as a school subject, but since religion has no meaning to them, their discussions with classmates must focus on other topics in everyday life. Muslims are the ones who talk about religion the most and are the most interested in it, probably because religion plays a more important role in their lives.

Finally, students mention different prerequisites for living together despite their religious differences. Living in the same community with people from other religions, or having other worldviews, is possible, even desirable, but must be handled delicately. In a situation where young people know each other and can talk to each other, the fear of conflict between different religions is less than if they are asked to see things from a general point of view.

Respect is the cardinal value for young French people. The need to treat religion as a private matter, which in France is the secular, Republican attitude *par excellence*, seems to have been accepted by a majority of students; however they apparently do not all feel attached to this principle the same way. On the whole, it is seen more as an abstract rule that is known and accepted (it is the law) than a value they strongly share.

2.3.2   General interpretation of the data

In the opinion of French students, they participate in a cultural context that is open to discussion, where the values of respect and tolerance and the recognition of diversity predominate. These values could promote dialogue between people from different religions, but there clearly seems to be a certain level of indifference to other worldviews, which are seen relatively to each other. Religion does not seem to be what unites adolescents most often, except the most religious among them, Muslims in particular. The general attitude is therefore one of passive tolerance more than active dialogue. It does not seem as though this attitude is motivated by the fear of conflict that overt expressions of religious ideas could cause, especially when students discuss religion with their peers.

French students live together in a context involving close contact, founded on awareness of their differences, on personal relations and on shared commitments, but religion does not seem to be what unites them the most, except the most religious among them.

French students live in a secularised world where religion is an opinion among others, to be respected like any other worldview. Religion appears as an uncontroversial subject, not that important, except among more religious Muslim students who fight against the negative stereotypes that are propagated about Islam: these students are interested in dialogue mostly to defend a positive image of their faith. Girls are more interested in religious topics and have more faith than boys in the positive value of discussion, but only a minority of boys remain sceptical about discussing religion. Even if students without religion have a more negative view of it than religious students, this still does not encourage them to create conflict in the name of anticlerical ideals; rather, it leads them to be indifferently aloof about the issue.

In short, the dominant point of view among French students is tolerance in the weak sense of the term – somewhere between indifference toward other people and curiosity about them – rather than an active commitment to dialogue with people of other religions. What emerges from our survey is more a sense of peaceful coexistence than a conscious desire to live with others in community. The knowledge of other religions that is offered in school can promote better understanding of both past and present religious phenomena, thus helping to dispel stereotypes. Undertaking dialogue with other religions, however, is something that is entirely up to the students themselves.

3.   Comparison with the results of the qualitative survey

A few words on the samples

The sample chosen for the quantitative survey allowed us to collect data in all of France[37]. More specifically, we chose to include private schools under contract with the State, all of which are Catholic. As a result, we were able to make comparisons between the opinions of two groups of young people: on the one hand, those going to private schools who come from relatively privileged backgrounds and who often have the same kind of religious affiliation, and on the other hand, students in public middle and high schools. The size of the sample allowed for a more in-depth look into differences based on religious affiliation. The most significant distinctions were discovered between students saying they had no religion and those claiming membership in a religious tradition. We could thus highlight the specific aspects of Muslim students; some of these aspects were already noticeable in the results of the qualitative survey, but we can now go into more detail about them.

Role of religion in pupils' lives and their surroundings

The quantitative method does not appear to be the one most adapted for getting a sense of religious experience in all its richness and complexity. This observation, which is not that original, seems especially true for minority religions. However, the questionnaire is useful for evaluating some levels of religious affiliation, beliefs and practices, through the numerical data obtained.

The indifference that French adolescents have toward religion, which was observed during the analysis of the qualitative data, is readily apparent here. Only one out of two adolescents mentions their religious affiliation. This tendency toward indifference does not preclude the existence of a minority of young people who are religious and observant; around one out of ten. Apart from this minority, the quantitative survey confirms that religion is not a very important part of the daily lives of young people or their conversations. However, this lack of importance given to religious affiliation is not associated with a comparable decline in religious belief: six students out of ten believe in God, spirits or life forces. For many of them, these beliefs are associated with some doubts. Finally, the analysis of the quantitative data confirms the marginal nature of anticlerical attitudes, or points of view that are the product of organised atheism.

---

37 The qualitative survey was delivered to 103 students of 14-16 years old coming from different public schools: six in Paris and its surroundings, one in the West part of France and another one in the East part France where Catholic, Protestant and Jewish confessional teaching of religion is offered to the students.

As the previous survey showed (Béraud, Massignon & Mathieu, 2008), the family maintains its role as the traditional source for religious socialisation. It comes first among the places to obtain information regarding religion and is the preferred site for discussions on religious matters. The importance of the media, which adolescents mentioned so regularly during the qualitative phase of the research, seems to be more limited here. It is only fifth on the list of information sources. However, this modest rank could be related to the very critical attitude toward the media that participants exhibited in the first survey: they do not put much trust in it.

Religion in school

The quantitative survey fully confirms one of the main results obtained during the qualitative phase of the research. The majority of French adolescents seem to agree with the French decision to deal with religious facts via existing school subjects. In the two surveys, two thirds of the adolescents we interviewed mention History as the course in which they hear about religion regularly. The role of the other subjects (mainly French and Civics) seems less clear; the order in which they are mentioned varies significantly from one survey to the next. The experience of having a course that concentrates specifically on religion, like that is available to students in the Moselle *département*[38] and those in private schools, appears as a choice available to only a minority of students (one out of ten) as well as a relatively unimportant phenomenon (it is not a model that can be used throughout the entire French school system). Here, we may return to one of the conclusions of the qualitative research: only a minority of students feel the need to create a specific course on religion, as some of our European neighbours have done.

As for the topics that should be discussed in courses covering religion, two stand out in the analysis of the questionnaires: living together in community with others and the role of cultural heritage. However, the differences in importance that students assign these two objectives, from question to question, make it impossible to give one precedence over the other. In any case, these results require the re-evaluation of the role of cultural heritage from what came out of the first survey. As in that survey, only a minority of French students expect that courses dealing with religion will help them develop their own values. Even fewer students hope to learn more about their own religion in school. It is not possible to add anything to the analysis that was carried out in the first survey on the content of course material and the role of the teacher, as there were no questions relating to these topics in the questionnaire. However these were not controversial issues. Only a small minority (16%) think that there is a risk of conflict in class. The few incidents that were mentioned during the unstructured survey, some of which were fairly violent on a symbolic level, end up losing importance at a statistical level.

The analysis of the questionnaires helps specify the role that adolescents wish religion to play in school life; in particular, it clarifies their point of view on the 2004 law on religious signs in school. As a result, the relatively severe criticism that Muslim students made of this law during the qualitative survey is put into perspective through the quantitative analysis. The percentage of young Muslims who say they are in favour of wearing visible religious signs at school is twice as high as all the students surveyed taken as a whole. However, these young people comprise only a minority of all Muslim students, little more than a third.

---

38 Our sample does not include any school in the Alsace region, where religious courses are also offered in public schools.

The impact of religion

The questionnaire puts clear emphasis on a fact that the first survey was not in a position to evaluate: most of the adolescents surveyed live in religiously diverse environments where the people around them, both in school and outside of school, have many different kinds of beliefs or even none at all. For these students, religious affiliation does not appear to be a criterion that influences their choices of friends or acquaintances.

As with the qualitative survey, we see in the quantitative data that adolescents identify with the values of respect and tolerance, and that they respect the right of everyone to speak their mind. Another point highlighted in both surveys is the role of the school as one possible place, perhaps even the best place, to experience diversity firsthand and learn how to live with others. Whereas one adolescent in two thinks that religion is a private matter, this does not mean that the secular nature of school prevents students from being able to discuss religion there. Only a very small number of students have problems speaking their mind on religion in school or are afraid of being mocked; the students involved in the first survey brought up the possibility of this happening, but its importance may have been overestimated as a result. As for teachers, they seem to be people with whom the adolescents surveyed can discuss religion: only 40% of students say they have never talked about religion with their teachers. Students' opinions of religious people may not be generally negative, but they do seem to be somewhat embarrassed by such people.

The qualitative survey is a more efficient tool for understanding the stereotypes students have of religion in general and some religions in particular. From this point of view, the results from the questionnaire are not that useful. They may even understate the tensions on some issues.

4.   Conclusion

The adolescents we met confirm the phenomenon of young people's indifference (see Campiche, 1997; Lambert, 2005) to religious institutions: half of them say they have no religion. Religion is of secondary importance to these young people. A minority of students, comprised principally of two religions (Catholics and Muslims), distinguish themselves from the others by the intensity of their religious beliefs.

In our view, one of the main contributions of the survey is that it appears to indicate French adolescents' acceptance of the school system's specific nature as a social sphere and as an institution. The opinions expressed in the survey seem to demonstrate that young people are flexible and can modify their behaviour depending on their surroundings. Some attitudes that can be fully accepted in the family, among people with the same religion, or even among friends, are recognised as unacceptable in a school environment. As a result, nearly all of the middle- and high-school students we surveyed have completely internalised the French model regarding the role of religion in school. As to the climate within public schools, students seem to be in general agreement with the 2004 law on religious signs in schools and with school regulations in other areas (which accommodate certain special needs, including the food that is served in the cafeterias or the wish to be absent from school on some non-Christian holidays). In the area of instruction, nearly all students demonstrate a commitment to the idea that religion should be discussed impartially within existing subjects, History above all. Results like these make it possible to moderate the concern that schools are undergoing a crisis regarding their role in socialisation[39]. Contrary to some stereotypes associated with the situation in France, we should also note that French adolescents willingly agree that religion has a role to play in school, both in the curriculum and in school life, provided that the school's secular structure is respected.

Concerning the question of tolerance and the ability to talk with others, we must once again stress that there does not seem to be open hostility between young people disinterested in religion and people for whom it plays a major role. Religion is of no concern to a large number of the adolescents surveyed. But only a small minority of them have adopted categorically anticlerical or antireligious attitudes. On the contrary, these adolescents emphasise that respecting other people's beliefs is important. They do not believe that the various religious traditions have a monopoly on absolute truth. This indifference and this tendency to see the situation in relative terms are as important if not more important than the ability to exchange opinions and the knowledge acquired of other people's religions when accounting for the generally relaxed way in which students approach religion. We can thus speak of a kind of passive tolerance.

Now we will reflect on our results in the light of our hypothesis:

1. a)   Religious students are less tolerant than non-religious students.

This first hypothesis could not be verified. Far from it: the adolescents who criticise religion most often are those who say they have no religion. We should note, however, that these students do not express this lack of tolerance toward religious people, but toward religion itself as a social fact.

1.b)   Religious students are less open to dialogue on religious issues than non-religious students.

This second hypothesis seems to be baseless. On the contrary, students who say they have a religion seem to be more interested in these kinds of discussions than non-religious students. There may be a simple reason for this: religion is a part of their lives, so it is something they can easily talk about. Muslim students are a perfect example of this.

2.a)   Students who have encountered religious diversity in education are more tolerant.

Comparing the public and private school systems may yield interesting results in determining the validity of such a hypothesis. Classes in private middle and high schools are more homogeneous on the level of students' religions than those in public schools: students seem to be less open-minded.

2.b)   Students who have encountered religious diversity in education are more open to dialogue on religious issues.

It seems to be easier for students to engage in dialogue with each other if their school environment is characterised by religious diversity. Here again, we may be able to see a pragmatic reason for this. Adolescents who find themselves in such a situation are not necessarily more

---

39 On this issue, see especially Dubet, 2002.

open-minded than others. They just feel the need to discuss the matter. To a certain extent, the school environment may be considered as one that is favourable for such discussions.

3.a)   Students who have personally encountered religious diversity are more tolerant

The great majority of the respondents consider that they have personally encountered religious diversity. They declare they have family members, classmates and/or friends, who have different religious backgrounds. Encountering religious diversity is an experience mostly outside the family, which is still quite homogeneous concerning views about religion. Only 29% of the respondents have family members who belong to different religions. School appears as an appropriate institution for experiencing religious plurality firsthand, since 72% of the respondents declare they there go around with youngsters who have different religious backgrounds and 61% consider that they have students in their class who belong to different religions. Three respondents out of four claim that they have friends who belong to different religions.

The students who declare they have personally encountered religious diversity give some answers that can be considered as a bit more tolerant. The proportion of those who claim they respect other people who believe is higher than the average. On the contrary, they disapprove more of the following statements "Without religion the world would be a better place" and "I do not like people from other religions and do not want to live together with them", but the differences with the others are slight.

3.b)   Students who have personally encountered religious diversity are more open to dialogue on religious issues.

If we consider the ability for dialogue on religious issues, the same kind of analyses can be developed. The students who declare they have personally encountered religious diversity respond in a way that can be considered as more open to dialogue. They approve more than the average of the statement "To me, talking about religion is interesting because people have different views" and disapprove more of the view "talking about religion is embarrassing". But here again the differences with the others are slight.

To conclude, one can make the hypothesis that tolerance and dialogue are shared values among French youngsters, not necessarily linked to personal experiences. But one can also add that according to the responses of the students, to be in relationships with people coming from different religious backgrounds is something banal in their everyday life.

References

Le Monde de l'éducation n°365 (janvier 2008): *"Juifs, musulmans, catholiques. Ceux qui font école à part"*.

Ballion, R. (1982). *Les consommateurs d'écoles*. Paris: Stock.

Baubérot, J. (2008). *La laïcité expliquée à M. Sarkozy [...] et à ceux écrivent ses discours*. Paris: Albin Michel.

Béraud, C., Massignon, B. & Mathieu, S. (2008). French pupils, religion and school: The ideal of laïcité at stake with religious diversity, in: T. Knauth, D.-P. Jozsa, G. Bertram-Troost & J. Ipgrave (Eds.), *Encountering Religious Pluralism in School and Society – A Qualitative Study of Teenage Perspectives in Europe*. Muenster: Waxmann, pp. 51–80.

Bertrand, J-R. & Muller, C. (2005). France. The growth of religious plurality, in: H. Knippenberg (Ed.), *The Changing Religious Landscape of Europe.* Amsterdam: Het Spinhuis, pp. 14–43.

Borne, D. & Willaime, J.-P. (Eds.) (2007). *Enseigner les faits religieux. Quels enjeux?* Paris: Armand Colin, "Débats d'école".

Campiche, R.J. (Ed.) (1997). *Cultures jeunes et religions en Europe.* Paris: Cerf "Sciences humaines et religions".

Debray, R. (2002). *L'enseignement du fait religieux dans l'école laïque. Rapport au ministre de l'Éducation nationale.* Paris: Odile Jacob, Scéren.

Dubet, F. (1991). *Les lycéens.* Paris: Seuil.

Dubet, F. (2002). *Le déclin de l'institution.* Paris: Seuil, "L'épreuve des faits".

Felouzis, G., Liot, F. & Perroton, J. (2005). *L'apartheid scolaire. Enquête sur la ségrégation ethnique dans les collèges.* Paris: Seuil.

Freyssinet-Dominjon, J. (1997). *Méthodes de recherche en sciences sociales.* Paris: Montchrestien.

Hervieu-Léger, D. (1999). *Le pèlerin et le converti. La religion en mouvement.* Paris: Flammarion.

Jackson, R. (1997). *Religious Education: an interpretive approach.* London: Hodder & Stoughton.

Lambert, Y. (2000). Le rôle dévolu à la religion par les européens, *Sociétés contemporaines*, pp. 11–33.

Lambert, Y. (2004). Des changements dans l'évolution religieuse de l'Europe et en Russie, *Revue française de sociologie*, n°45.2, pp. 307–338.

Lambert, Y. (2005). Un regain religieux chez les jeunes d'Europe de l'Ouest et de l'Est, in: O. Galland & B. Roudet (Eds.), *Les jeunes Européens et leurs valeurs.* Paris: La Découverte, "Recherches", pp. 65–91.

Lambert, Y. & Michelat, G. (Eds.) (1992). *Crépuscule des religions chez les jeunes? Jeunes et religions en France.* Paris: L'Harmattan.

Langlois, C. (1995). "Toujours plus pratiquantes". La permanence du dimorphisme sexuel dans le catholicisme français contemporain, *Clio*, numéro Femmes et Religions.

Maurin, E (2004). *Le ghetto français: enquête sur le séparatisme social.* Paris: Seuil.

Messner, F., Prélot, P-H. & Woehrling, J-M. (Eds.) (2003). *Traité de droit français des religions.* Paris: Litec.

Michel, P. (1999). *La religion au musée. Croire dans l'Europe contemporaine.* Paris: L'Harmattan.

Willaime, J.-P. (2008). *Le retour du religieux dans la sphère publique. Vers une laïcité de reconnaissance et de dialogue.* Paris: Olivétan, "Convictions & société".

F. Javier Rosón Lorente

Two Sides of the Coin – French and Spanish Approaches to Religion in the School

From a Spanish perspective perhaps the most surprising feature is the increasing relevance of religion in the school curriculum in France. This phenomenon, preceded by a public debate and the work of philosopher Regis Debaray in the 80s–90s, meant the analysis of religious teaching within a lay education, with the intention of "refocusing" the apparent lack of religious knowledge among French pupils. As the phenomenon grew beyond national borders, it sparked new debates in neighbouring Spain which discussed the effectiveness and efficiency of the new *laïcité* model.

In the French case, religion is taught throughout the entire educational period without requiring a confessional RE lesson aimed at this particular subject. Remarkable in this sense was the pioneer Jules Ferry who introduced the term "instruction civique" in 1882. In any case it is interesting since in Spain we have only come to now the opposite model: in Spain, the Catholic confessional "monopoly" is struggling to maintain its hegemonic role in a context of transformation and religious diversification.

We would also like to draw attention to another characteristic of the French religious scenario: the presence of Catholicism in its history and national culture. If we look at it from a distance (from a Spanish perspective), one gets the impression that historical reforms related to *laïcité* and secularisation have turned France into one of the least religious countries in Europe and, if any, the debate revolves around the role education has played in this non-religiosity. Far from essentialising and/or repeating the existing prejudices around the French case, we have observed that the commitment to *laïcité* is ensuring an interesting way of managing religion and religious diversity within the Republic's bounds. At this point, it is important to bear in mind that school plays an important part in raising awareness of religion, transmitting different "messages" in each country, but in both cases, performing a crucial role in terms of providing information about religions. In Spain a large group of students have only had access to this information through their school centres, as opposed to France where, regardless of their secular nature, it is inside school walls where students have an opportunity to discover religion, the beliefs and the practices of others, etc.; something that it is not detectable in the Spanish context, and should be underlined as a relevant differentiation, given that in Spain students did not communicate a discernable consciousness about religious diversity either inside or outside school.

Lastly, we would like to add the noticeably higher religious diversity in the quantitative sample of the study. In the case of Muslims and other minority religions the respondents show how "students' beliefs are also connected to their religious background".

Public / private debate: old and new phantasm in the religion field

Here we should point out some of the interpretations made in the French case at the comparative level. First of all, the internalisation of the principle of *laïcité*, (i.e. how it has been taken in by the students) which comes in the shape of the following assertion: "religion is something private". In this sense, the French case "a little more than half of the students have internalised the principle of *laïcité*". Likewise, they seem to tolerate and accept religious diversity, but this again just demonstrates their acceptance of *laïcité*. This reflection should be clarified by considering the Spanish case, seeing that in our investigation we have observed that almost half of the students commented on the privacy of religion being "very or quite important" to be able to live together in peace. As a result of this, we think it is necessary to question to what extent religion and the pupils' religiosity, its expression in daily public and/or private life, is related to the principles of *laïcité* or with the non-denominational Spanish state. Does this mean that the concept of tolerance entails the need for a significant development of *laïcité* by which religion should stick to the *private*?

In the second place, almost all of the French students agree that they "respect other people who believe". From this point of view, this means that they subscribe to the fundamental principles of human rights and the rights of the citizen, and accept the law of 1905 which separates Church and State. In the Spanish case, the number of students who agree with this assertion is almost the same. Nonetheless, the national context makes us wonder: what relation is there between respecting the "other" (the Believer) and non-determinism and the "non-separation" of Church and State? From our point of view we should define here the limits of some moral and coexisting aspects that have not been taken into account yet in the French case. Also, these questions cannot leave aside the external context and the tragic events of September 11th 2001 and the Madrid bombing of 11th March 2004, which made some of the social actors involved question religiosity and belief. What is more, we should ponder over the role that religious minorities play and how some of them come from contexts in which the separation between State and Church does not exist.

Students' views: some differences and commonalities between neighbours' countries

From a comparative perspective, if we analyse the Spanish and French context in relation to students' views and experiences with religion, the main difference that emerges is that in the Spanish context the great majority of students tend to identify religion with their own confession. In contrast, in the French context the research indicated that students take a pluralistic point of view that associates the three monotheistic religions. It is relevant to underline the fact that about one French interviewee in every two declares he or she does not belong to a religion at all. In Spain, the proportion of "atheists" and "non believers" is much lower (35.4%).

One of the similarities that appeared from the research is that religious socialisation for believers take place mainly within the family. In the French case, the family is still the traditional place for religious socialisation: 68% of the students we encountered think that the family remains a "very important" or "important" source of information on religion. This percentage drops to 37% when they are asked to evaluate the school's role in the matter. In Spain the figures are very similar with the family the most valued, above school, their peers and other resources. In that sense, for Spanish and French teenagers, religion is not a big issue and students do not talk much about it in their respective groups. Moreover, it was detected that for the young, religion did not appear to be a 'cool' topic to talk or to worry about. It was occasionally associated with 'old fashioned things' (a topic from the past).

Other similarities emerged over the issue of "religion of the people around me"; both national case studies present similar results. On the one hand, it is interesting to observe how, in the French case, students live in a pluralistic context, involving many religions at school and outside school. In both cases the students indicate that they have had friends from different religious backgrounds, maintained relationships with them, regardless of their religion, and were aware of the religious diversity in their school and in their immediate environment. Paradoxically, although students recognised diversity in their classroom and in their immediate environments they did not know their classmates' points of view on religion. In both cases, the answers follow the same lines of indifference as those involving the level of interest in their classmates' religions.

Again in both cases, students confirmed this result (56%), emphasising the need to listen to "others" although this would not necessarily influence their own vision of religion. The lack of proselytism was brought up in both cases, although it was somewhat less common in the Spanish case. We have however come across substantial differences concerning the option "I try or could try to ignore him/her". In the Spanish case, only 28% agreed with this statement whilst in the French case the numbers increased to 38%.

It is interesting to note how in both cases students discuss about religion among themselves first of all because they think it is interesting to talk with people who have another point of view to theirs. Still the following answers do show different priorities. For example, the claim "talking about religion helps us to understand others" is less valued in the Spanish case, as is "talking about religion helps me to understand what is going on in the world better". In our research context, a significant number of pupils think that the second most important affirmation is: "talking about religion helps to shape my own views". This mirrors important differences in the ways of facing cultural and religious diversity in our country, reflecting that the French migratory tradition dates from much earlier than the Spanish one.

Marie von der Lippe

The French Situation from a Norwegian Point of View

Looking at the French study from a Norwegian point of view there are striking similarities between French and Norwegian students in terms of their view on religion in education, even if the school systems have different models for dealing with religion. They also seem to have several perceptions and attitudes about religion and religious diversity in common. This is an interesting result, especially in light of some obvious differences between the two countries regarding religious diversity and the relationship between religion and state. The French society is much more diverse than the Norwegian society both from socio-economic and socio-cultural perspectives, and since 1905 France has a sharp division between state and church. The relationship between the Norwegian state and the Church of Norway is for the time being under revision, but is still formally a state-church ('established church') system. Thirdly, there are distinctive differences between how religion is dealt with in the French and Norwegian school systems. In France religion is not taught in a specific course but taught as 'religious facts' in subjects such as History and French. In Norway a non-confessional multi-faith subject was introduced as mandatory for all students one decade ago. Based on the principle of *laicité*, French students are not allowed to wear visible religious symbols at school, while there are no legislation or restrictions on this in Norway. Despite these differences, the results from the two studies are surprisingly similar, which calls for reflection.

A comparative perspective

The French sample is more diverse than the Norwegian one. Schools from all over the country are included, as well as both public and private (Catholic) schools. In France 20% of the students go to private schools, while this goes only for 2–3% of the Norwegian students. The French study has included students from both privileged and unprivileged areas and schools, and class is an important variable in the analysis. Despite socio-economical differences in Norwegian society, Norway has, contrary to France, very few schools dominated by economically privileged or underprivileged students. Social class has therefore not been an important variable in the Norwegian study. The French sample is also more diverse regarding students' religious and cultural background.

In general religion does not seem to be a subject of interest to the French students. But there are striking differences when the role of religion in students' life is correlated with type of school (public/private), class background, religious affiliation and gender. These differences are sometimes more distinct within the French sample, than they are on a cross-national level compared to the Norwegian students. One in three French students value religion as important in their personal life, while 45% think religion is of no relevance. On issues whether they think there is a 'God or some kind of spirit or life force', one third of the French students believe in God, while one third do not. Another 28% have a more alternative approach to religion, and believe in some kind of spirit or life force. We find almost the same figures in the Norwegian sample, regarding belief and how they value the importance of religion in their personal life. Looking at the public and the private (Catholic) schools in France one would expect that the students at the private schools would be somewhat more religious than students in the public schools. But in France this is actually not the case. More students in the public than in the private school find religion to be of importance. At the same time the French study shows that religious students mainly belong to the working-class, and this may explain why more students in the public than in private schools are religious (more middle- and upper-class students attend private schools). Another interesting result is that students with working-class background, who have a religion, mainly belong to Islam. This may also be one of the reasons why working-class students practice religion more often than upper-class students.

There is a distinct group of religious students in both France and Norway who think religion plays a very important part in their life, and who practice religion more often than their peers. Muslim students tend to belong to this last group. Comparing students with different religious affiliations reveals that almost all the Muslim students believe in God, while this goes only for half of the students with a Christian background in the two countries. If we look at gender in the two studies, more girls than boys believe in God, and more mothers than fathers seem to have religious affiliations. Even if there are only slight differences these tendencies confirm that women still seem to be somewhat more religious than men. Comparing French and Norwegian adolescents there is a general tendency of indifference towards religion, and a main trend is that neither find religion to be of particular interest. In other words religion does not seem to play a major role in the life of the majority of students either in France or Norway, but at the same time they are not being negative or reluctant towards religion or religious believers as such.

In France family is understood to be the most important source for information on religious issues (68%), while faith communities are the second most frequented (60%). School seems not to be understood as an equally important source, and only half as many report school to be a place where they gain information about religion. Also for Norwegian students family and faith communities are important sources, but this goes mainly for the most religiously committed group of students. Among Norwegian students without religion, school is clearly the most central information channel. Family is obviously an important place for religious socialisation and family members are also those the French students prefer to talk to about religious issues. Religion is for a large part of the French students considered as a private matter, and that may be one of the reasons why they discuss religion with close relations (family/ friends) rather than with classmates and teachers. A majority report that they never talk to their classmates about religion, and only 13% talk to the teacher about religious issues. These are interesting results compared to the Norwegian study. While French students seldom talk to their teacher about religion, the teacher is the most often approached among the Norwegian students. They also talk more to classmates about religion than their French peers. It seems that school among French students not is regarded as a forum where they discuss religious matters, but rather a place where they receive knowledge about religion. On the contrary school seems to be an important place for dialogue about religion in Norway.

The French students seem to be acquainted with religious plurality in their surroundings. Most of them report that they have friends who belong to different religions, and more than 90% do not see religious affiliation as a criterion for friendship. They actually refuse to be limited to friends with the same religion, but at the same time half of the students say that most of their friends share their view on religion. On these issues there are more apparent differences between students from public and private schools in France, than between the French and Norwegian samples in general. Half of the students in the French private schools, compared with the public schools, have friends with other religions. Even if religion does not seem to be an important factor for friendship, public schools seem to be an arena where students from different religions meet and where they might have conversations about religion. This may be one reason why French and Norwegian students (who attend public schools) in general have more in common on these issues, than the French students belonging to different school systems.

Both French and Norwegian students are open to religious diversity and they respect other people who believe. Many students consider religion to be of a private character, but at the same time they seem not to have difficulties in showing their own view of religion in school. Again we find very similar patterns between French and Norwegian adolescents. They share also a rather dynamic view on religion in the sense that they acknowledge the right to believe in one's own way and that what they think about religion is open to change. There is a general difference in France and Norway between students with and without religion regarding issues of tolerance, where non-religious students are the more critical ones. This is however not a lack of tolerance towards religious people as such, but more towards religion as a social phenomenon. It is not so much a formal anticlerical stance, which apparently was historically more common in France.

Only one in three French students think religion is an important topic at school. They find religion to be an *interesting* topic at school, but they do not consider it to be an *important* subject. The Norwegian students on the other hand value *interest* and *importance* equally. In both samples, the religious students emphasise respect even more than students without a religion. In general French and Norwegian students expect school to give them objective knowledge about religion and not guide them towards religious belief.

Looking at the more practical aspects of religion in school, almost 60% of French students are negative towards the wearing of religious symbols. Muslim students seem less willing to give answers than Catholic students on these issues, and they are clearly divided in their opinions. Here we find a significant difference compared to Norwegian students, where more than 60% think it should be allowed to wear visible religious symbols in school. The French and Norwegian students are more in line when it comes to other practical aspects related to religion in school. The majority of all students think school should take account of religious food requirements and that students should have some days off during religious festivals, but should not be excused from lessons for religious reasons and school should not provide prayer rooms. Despite the different attitudes between French and Norwegian students about the wearing of religious symbols, religion has obviously a role to play in school, both in curriculum and school life, as long as the secular character of school is preserved.

Comparing French and Norwegian students there is a tendency among them to be in line with the politics of their respective countries. They favour the model for 'religious education' they know, and they want mainly to obtain objective knowledge about religion. This is also the main emphasis in the two curricula. The students approve also of existing legislation about religion in the public sphere including public schools. In other words young people in France and Norway seem to be quite attuned with their countries' politics on issues dealing with plurality and religion in school. This may be interpreted as a tendency towards political conformity, more than specific political positions they hold.

Possible alternative perspectives

Many of the results from the French survey are interpreted from the principle of *laïcité*, and how students relate to this principle in their opinions about religion and religion in school. The students are understood to be in line with French policy on how to deal with religion in school, both in the curriculum and school life in general. The fact that almost half of the French students prefer to learn about religion in already existing subjects, and want to obtain knowledge *about* religion rather than to learn *from* religion, is interpreted as if the students agree with French educational politics. The same is the case with the law of 2004 prohibiting students to wear religious symbols in school. The students' acceptance of this law is also interpreted as if they are in line with French politics and the principle of *laicité*. This seem to be a reasonable interpretation, but as also pointed out in the article, these results might well have additional explanations. Students favour the model they know, and see this as a proper way of dealing with religious topics in school. Their lack of interest in religion in general may also be an explanation of why they do not want a specific course on religion. The fact that the majority of students agree that students should not wear religious symbols in school, including many Muslim students, can be related to the intense debate about this issue in France, and their resistance towards getting into these kinds of discussions. The law is then understood as a regulating practice in a plural society.

A majority of French students want to learn about religion in order to understand the history of their own country and Europe. The Muslim students are not equally interested in the cultural heritage aspect, but more interested to learn to understand others in order to live peacefully together. They would also like to know more about their own religion (this goes also for other students who value religion as important). This is mainly interpreted as lack of integration in the French mainstream/majority culture. Another interpretation may be that the cultural heritage is presented mainly from a 'Christian' historical perspective, or is interpreted to be so because the majority was historically Christian. This may be enforced by a possible imbalance in the curriculum, with considerably less focus on Islam than on Christianity. School is then reinforcing mainstream culture. This issue is also familiar in the Norwegian situation, and there is a hot discussion related to religious education, on how to balance the cultural heritage perspective with recognition of a multicultural society.

Reflections about France and Norway

In short both French and Norwegian students find little interest in religion, and the majority do not consider religion to be an important part of their life. There is however a distinctive group of students who think religion plays an important role in their life. In both France and Norway Muslims belong to this group of students. The students are in general tolerant towards religious plurality, and positive towards peaceful coexistence independent of religion. At the same time both French and Norwegian students spend more time with friends who share their own view on religion. This result has been difficult to interpret in both the French and the Norwegian study. It may seem like the students perform some kind of passive tolerance, not putting them under any obligations, more than an active dialogue. It might be some sort of *toleration* of the right of others to believe, more than *tolerance* towards their religion or what they actually believe in. The discrepancy between what students in both countries say and what they do, indicate that their attitudes are not necessarily put into practice. At the same time religion is not conceived to be a contributor to dialogue or a factor of conflict among the students. However, these issues would need to be further investigated to get a clearer perception of young people and their relation towards religious and cultural diversity.

It is possible that the political ideology of *laicité* is less of a 'French speciality' than it is often considered from a Norwegian point of view. Norwegian politics have since the 1940's been dominated by social-democratic ideas, and the Norwegian social democrats have tradi-

tionally been critical towards church influence, even compared with other Scandinavian countries. Even if it is a long way from the Norwegian 'established' state church to the state-
church relations in France, it could also be argued that the differences may be less in terms of
the role of religion in social life. Norwegian daily life is highly secularised, and there is
clearly a strong privatisation of religion which may have similarities with the French separation of public and private. The attitudes of young people in France and Norway may therefore
reflect secularisation and privatisation more than political ideologies and institutional politics.
Despite the different models of dealing with religion in school in France and Norway, school
seems nevertheless to be an important forum where students learn about different religions
and learn to respect everyone independent of their religious or non-religious background. A
main impression is that French and Norwegian students share a common interest in living
peacefully together in a plural society.

Dan-Paul Jozsa, Thorsten Knauth & Wolfram Weisse

Religion in School – a Comparative Study of Hamburg and North Rhine-Westphalia

1. Introduction

The article highlights the results of the REDCo quantitative study in Hamburg (HH) and North Rhine-Westphalia (NRW). This study is part of a more comprehensive study focusing on the western federal states in Germany with a total number of 3487 student respondents. We nevertheless decided to restrict ourselves to Hamburg and NRW in this article, following the procedure of our previous qualitative study where such a restriction was established (see Knauth et al., 2008). This way a more thorough data triangulation is possible, and we are able to reflect on the results of the quantitative questioning in the light of the qualitative findings. As the different federal states in Germany are independent in their educational policies – including the basic models of religious education –, the concentration on Hamburg and NRW provides a good opportunity to compare two contexts with different religious education models.

NRW has a system of confessional religious education – students are taught separately according to their religious background. Besides Catholic, Protestant, Orthodox and Jewish religious education, a subject called 'Study of Islam' is also available for Muslim students in the context of a 'pilot project' in a number of schools. For students who opt out of religious education '(Practical) Philosophy' was introduced some years ago as an alternative compulsory subject[1].

Hamburg, instead, offers religious education as one subject that is open to all students, irrespective of their religious background. The subject is conceptualized as a place for interreligious learning, where the personal dialogue between students is especially encouraged. However there are also alternative subjects available for the students such as 'Ethics' or 'Philosophy'. In private Catholic or Jewish schools mostly only confessional religious education is offered.[2]

1.1 Sample

1.1.1 Sampling and data collection

In general we tried to include students attending different religious education models as well as students who do not attend religious education in the sample. We tried to reach a balanced, heterogeneous sample with regard to 'school type' and 'socio-economic', migration as well as religious background and gender. To achieve this aim, we made a list of schools of different 'types' located in different 'socio-economic areas' and we used those schools belonging to each of the different categories that consented first to the research. We stopped including further schools, when we thought to have reached a 'balanced' sample and our 'resources' were 'consumed'.

---

1 For further information see Jozsa (2007, 2008).
2 For further information see Knauth (2007, 2008) and Weisse (2008).

Generally the administration of questionnaires was carried out by the schools themselves. We only provided the questionnaires and guidelines. We specifically mentioned that the administration should and could be done in 'general' classes, i.e. not only in religious education classes and not only by religious education teachers. We wanted to assure in this way that not only students who attend religious education were questioned: in the end 43% of the students in the Hamburg sample and 29% in the NRW sample did not attend religious education at the time of the questioning. The teachers who conducted the administration were asked to explain the purpose and the context of the research, to stress the anonymity of the survey and the fact that it is not a 'school test', the interest being to learn the opinion of each pupil. Only in exceptional cases were researchers involved directly in carrying out the questionnaire.

With respect to the difference between urban and rural areas in NRW our sample is 'unbalanced' because we have only schools from cities and towns, which somewhat reflects the situation in Germany, where schools are less frequent in rural areas; students from these areas usually attend schools in the nearest town or city.

With regard to age: we went for the age group 14–16, which generally means grade 9 and 10 in Germany. However in some schools which carried the administration on their own, other grades were included. The consequence was that the age range of the questioned students is 13–20. For this article we restricted ourselves to analyse only the questionnaires of students in the age group 14–16 in Hamburg and NRW.

1.1.1   Details for Hamburg

In Hamburg, in most cases in cooperation with teachers and schools we knew from previous field-work, we distributed the questionnaire in 12 schools: 5 'grammar', 2 'comprehensive' and 5 'lower secondary schools'. Altogether 69 classes were polled. Regarding the distribution of schools, we opted for schools from different areas in terms of the socio-economic background of the population. According to the three-scale European Socio-Economic Classification (ESCE)[3] 31% of the students included in the sample have parents belonging to the 'salariat'[4], 36% to 'intermediate occupations', 10% to the 'working class', 2% state that both parents are 'unemployed' whereas 21% of the students did not indicate the professions of their parents. So in view of the socio-economic background, our sample includes most important layers of German society.

In total, we questioned 1261 students, but only 1099 fall into the age group 14–16 and were included in the analyzed sample. Of these, 44% are male and 56% are female; 17% are 14, 46% are 15 and 37% are 16 years old; 39% have a Christian background, 43% claim to have no religion or worldview, 14% have a Muslim background and 4% are classified in the unspecified but very heterogeneous group of 'other religions' which consists of very small percentages of e.g. Jews, Hindus, Heathens, Jehovah Witnesses, Pagans, Sikhs, Satanists, and 'own religion'[5]; 53% of the students are from grammar schools, 19% from comprehensive

---

3   See http://www.iser.essex.ac.uk. For the socio-economical classification given here resp. 'higher' profession of the two parents was taken into account.

4   This category includes: employers, professionals, administrative (including politicians) and managerial occupations, higher grade technician and supervisory occupations. Since we had no information with respect to the size of the business of the parents, we classified all parents whose profession was described as 'entrepreneur' as belonging to the category 'salariat'. The term 'upper class' might be used in other studies in a broad sense to describe this category, however this term is not employed in the ESCE classification and is used not only very differently in the literature but also often in a vague way without a clear definition.

5   We refer only to the classifications employed by the students themselves here.

schools, and 28% from lower secondary schools; 39% of the students have a migration background.

1.1.2   Details for NRW

In NRW we distributed the questionnaire in 6 schools: 3 'grammar schools' – in Unna, Dortmund and Hamm, and 3 'lower secondary schools' – in Bönnen and Dinslaken. Altogether 32 classes were polled. According to the ESCE socio-economic classification 43% of the students have parents who belong to the "salariat", 28% to "intermediate occupations", 17% to the "working class", 4% state that both parents are "unemployed" whereas 9% of the students did not indicate the professions of their parents.

In total we questioned 672 students, but only 573 fell into the targeted age group and were consequently included in the analysed sample. Of these, 56% are male and 44% are female; 14% are 14, 46% are 15 and 40% are 16 years old; 54% have a Christian background, 33% claim to have no religion or worldview, 11% are Muslims and 2% are summarized to the very heterogeneous group of "other religions" including e.g. Buddhists, 'Christian-Nationalists', Heathen, own religion; 59% of the students are from grammar schools and 41% from lower secondary schools; 31% of the students have a migration background.

1.1.3   Reflection on the sample

The sample is not a 'random sample', it is also not a 'quota sample' since we did not try to achieve fixed quotas for different groups. We only tried to have a 'balanced' distribution with respect to 'school type' and 'socio-economic background'. We also tried to include the most important religious backgrounds in the sample. However due to the relatively large numbers of sampled students we think that the findings point out at least some general tendencies and allow us to make also some general statements[6].

1.2   Comments of the students

Students in Hamburg as well as in NRW made intensive use of the possibility to comment at the end of the questionnaire. More than a third of them wrote comments. Apart from some flippant remarks, there are many content-related answers, offering a most valuable resource of interesting and intelligent comments on dialogue between religions and the importance or 'nonsense' of religion. There are also a range of comments dealing with the questionnaire, showing the same aspects in Hamburg and NRW. We find both positive and many critical comments. The positive comments underline the importance of such a questionnaire and the interest of the students to get a feedback of the results.

> *"I appreciate the questionnaire, being anonymous and yet offering the possibility to know more of the opinions of youngsters."* (NRW 370)

Other positive statements refer at the same time to the limits and dangers of such a questionnaire.

---

6   The percentages of students with a 'migration background' in our samples might appear at first sight to be very high. However these percentages correspond to the percentages found in statistically significant studies. In 2005 c. 44.8% of population in the age group 6–18 had in Hamburg a 'migration background'; see http://www.statistik-nord.de/fileadmin/download/presse/SI06_106_F.pdf (last access 10.11.2008). In NRW c. 33.4% of the population in the age group 1–25 had a 'migration background' – calculated from the data of the 'Mikrozensus 2005', see http://www.mags.nrw.de/sozber/sozialindikatoren_nrw/rahmendaten/demografie/indikator2_3/index.php (last access 10.11.2008).

"I appreciate that you are doing such a questionnaire, but some of the questions are too private." (HH 316)

"Questionnaires of this type are difficult. One can only make a cross, but those who are analysing the questionnaire do not know, why the cross has been made, or what sort of thoughts have been connected to it." (HH1054)

The criticism takes two main directions. To many students it was boring and annoying to answer so many questions that seemed similar or identical to them. Some of the students saw an inherent tendency in the questionnaire, so that questions like *"who is behind it"* (NRW 415) and speculations – is it from Scientology or another cult? – were raised. Some of the questions were understood by some students as too personal and inappropriate. The most emotional and critical comments were voiced – mainly in schools with many students with a lower socio-economic background – with respect to the questions at the end of our question-naire, asking for the professions of parents:

"I consider the questions inappropriate, e.g. 120/121. The questions make to some extent no sense, and are partly very personal." (NRW 624)

It should not bother you if my father is a dustman or a banker. And I really don't know what this has to do with your study." (HH 614)

2.   General presentation of the results

To analyse the data we used SPSS 15. For each of the corresponding groups of items we will present first the results of univariate and multivariate analysis, where we will focus on corre-lation analysis. We explore the differences with respect to 'gender', 'type of school', 'age', 'migration' and 'socio-economic background', 'importance of religion', 'religious education this year or not?' etc. We chose to use correlation analysis in order to have also a measure for the size of differences between groups. When correlation analysis could not be used – this was the case when exploring the differences with respect to worldview – we used the Kruskal-Wallis test ('H-test') and the Man and Whitney test ('U-test')[7]. To explore differ-ences between the answers to different items we used the Wilcox as well as sign tests. In presenting the findings we will not mention the respective tests used, but these should be obvious from the relationships and connections presented.

We will give either the frequencies or the means of the answers to each item and for each federal state in tables. When giving frequencies, we will give only the integral numbers for reasons of readability. For bi-variate correlation tests between the variables we used Spear-man's rank correlation coefficient due to the fact that most of the variables do not follow a normal distribution[8].

Because the number of students belonging to 'other religions' is low in Hamburg and NRW alike and they form very heterogeneous group, we will focus on comparisons between Christian, Muslim and students with 'no religion' with regard to 'worldview'. The variable

---

7   We choose to use non parametric tests because the variables generally do not follow a normal distribu-
      tion (tested with the Kolmogorow-Smirnov-Test).
8   When talking about significance, we will use the wording 'not significant' for $p > 0.05$, 'significant' for
      $0.01 \leq p \leq 0.05$, 'very significant' for $0.01 < p \leq 0.001$ and 'extremely significant' for $p < 0.001$. Referring to
      correlations, we will disregard 'correlations' when the correlation coefficient is 'very small', i.e. be-
      tween 0 and ± 0.1, we will use the wording 'small correlation' for coefficients between ± 0.1 and ± 0.3,
      'medium correlation' for coefficients between ± 0.3 and ± 0.5 and 'large correlation' for coefficients be-
      tween ± 0.5 and ± 1.

'migration background' was generated from the data collected with respect to the country of birth of the respective student and his/her parents as well as the 'main languages' spoken at home: a student was considered to have 'no migration background' if he/she and his/her parents were born in Germany and no other language besides 'German' was stated to be spoken in the family. The 'socio-economic' background was generated on the basis of the information collected with respect to the 'profession' of the parents: the 'socio-economic' background of the student was defined as being the 'highest' of those of his/her parents according to the profession stated.

'*Spurious (cor)relations*'[9]: we will use the term to describe (cor)relations, where a statistically significant relation is identified through bi-variate analysis, which 'disappears' in partial correlation or multivariate analysis. Such a situation arises for our sample sometimes for example with respect to differences between Hamburg and NRW related to a certain variable (item) *x*, when a strong correlation occurs between this variable and gender. But in those cases, when partial correlation analysis, with 'gender' as control variable shows no significant differences between Hamburg and NRW, we argue that the significant difference found between Hamburg and NRW in bi-variate correlation analysis, only reflects the gender distribution in the subsamples for Hamburg and NRW, with 56% girls in Hamburg and only 44% girls in NRW. That is why we refer to such a correlation found between the respective variable *x* and the federal state as being 'spurious'. We argue that the 'real cause' for the difference found is related to 'gender' and not to the 'federal state'.

An analogue situation arises for our sample even more often when taking into consideration the 'importance of religion' for the respective students in relation to 'worldview', to 'migration background' or to 'gender'. Due to the fact that in our sample e.g. students with a migration background consider religion significantly more important than students with no migration background, it occurs, when there is a strong (cor)relation between the 'importance of religion' and another variable (item) *x*, that the analogue relation applies also between the respective variable *x* and the 'migration background', even if in partial correlation analysis, using the 'importance of religion' as a control variable, no significant correlation is found. That is why we refer to such a statistically significant difference as being 'spurious'. We argue that in such a situation, the 'real' cause for the difference is related to the 'importance of religion' and not to the 'migration background'.

2.1   What role has religion in pupil's life?

2.1.1   Data description

13% of the students in Hamburg and NRW stated that religion is 'not important at all', whereas 24% in Hamburg and 21% in NRW stated that religion is 'very important' to them. The rest of the students placed the importance of religion for themselves between these extremes.

No significant differences exist between Hamburg and NRW with regard to the 'importance of religion'. Likewise there are no significant correlations with school type and the

---

9   See Voigt (1993) for an introduction into the concept and Simon (1985) for a debate on the matter. What is criticized in the concept is that taking into consideration that correlation generally does not imply causation, it might be misleading to speak of a 'spurious' correlation, when statistically a correlation arise, and imply thus that some correlations are 'true', i.e. implicitly claiming that they might possibly imply causation, as opposed to those one considers 'spurious', where a causational relationship is excluded.

socio-economic background. The correlation between the 'importance of religion' and gender ($\rho=0.13$, $p<0.001$) as well as 'migration background' ($\rho=0.353$, $p<0.001$) and whether the student is religiously affiliated or not ($\rho=0.642$, $p<0.001$) is extremely significant, with religion being more important for girls and students with a migration background.

There are also significant differences between the beliefs with respect to the 'importance of religion', with Muslim students attributing the highest importance to religion, followed by Christian students. This is in line with the fact that 71% of the Muslim, but only 21% of the Christian students and 9% of the students with 'no religion' claim that religion is 'very important' to them.

When asked about their views with regard to the existence of God, 54% of the students in Hamburg and 46% in NRW asserted that 'there is a God', 38% and 30% respectively stated that there is 'some sort of spirit or life force'; the rest subscribed to the sentence 'I don't really think there is any sort of God, spirit or life force'.

No significant or only spurious correlations exist between these statements and the federal state, the socio-economic background, the school type, the age, gender, and the fact whether the respective student currently attends religious education or not. There are, however, significant correlations between the abovementioned statements and the migration background ($\rho=-0.314$, $p<0.001$), and the 'worldview' ($\rho=-0.427$, $p<0.001$), with students with a migration background and students having a religion tending more towards the statement 'there is a God'. Muslim students tend more towards the statement 'there is a God' than Christian students, who again tend more towards it than the students with 'no religion'. This is in line with the fact that 94% of the Muslim students, but only 59% of the Christian students and 27% of the students with no religion think that 'there is a God', while 1% only of the Muslim students, 6% of the Christian students and 31% of those with no religion think that there is no God, spirit or life force whatsoever.

Table 1 gives the frequencies of 'activities' related to religion; 52% of the students in both states report thinking about religion, 48% in Hamburg and 54% in NRW report thinking 'about the meaning of life', 35% and 47% respectively report praying and 23% and 31% report attending 'religious events' at least 'about every week'. Only 17% and 16% say the same about reading 'sacred texts' for themselves and only 8% and 10% about looking 'on the internet for religious topics'.

Significant differences between Hamburg and NRW occur with respect to 'praying' ($\rho=0.128$, $p<0.001$) and 'attending religious events' ($\rho=0.121$, $p<0.001$), with students in NRW tending to be involved in these activities more often.

There are extremely significant – mostly medium and large – correlations between all these activities and the 'migration background' resp. the 'importance of religion', with students with migration background and those who consider religion more important for them being more often involved in the mentioned 'activities' than the other groups. Relations to gender are much lower, but there are still significant differences between boys and girls with regard to 'praying' ($\rho=-0.108$, $p<0.001$) and 'thinking about the meaning of life' ($\rho=-0.109$, $p<0.001$), with girls being more involved in these 'activities'.

There are also extremely significant differences between Muslims, Christians and students with no religion, with Muslim students being in general more often engaged in the mentioned activities than Christian students followed by the students with 'no religion', e.g.: 47% of the Muslim students in Hamburg and 67% in NRW report 'attending religious events' at least once a week, as opposed to only 31% and 34% of the Christian and only 9% and 15% of the students with 'no religion'.

Table 1:   **Frequency of activities related to religion (percentages)**

How often do you:	about every day		about every week		about once a month		less than once a month		never	
	HH	NRW	HH	NRW	HH	NRW	HH	NRW	HH	NRW
think about religion?	18	17	34	35	22	21	16	17	10	11
read sacred texts for yourself?	5	4	12	12	13	12	23	26	47	47
look at the internet for religious topics?	2	3	6	7	16	16	29	28	46	46
pray?	17	27	18	20	15	13	19	18	31	22
attend religious events?	3	5	20	26	17	21	29	27	31	21
think about the meaning of life?	25	26	23	29	23	24	18	12	11	9

Interestingly enough, there is no significant difference between Muslim and Christian students with regard to how often they pray; e.g.: 28% of the Muslim, 24% of the Christians, and 4% of the students with no religious affiliation report praying 'about every day' in Hamburg while 36%, 38% and 8% report doing so in NRW.

Table 2 gives the means[10] for Hamburg and NRW with regard to the importance of different sources for information about religions. Comparing the means we see that generally 'family' is the most important source of information about religions in Hamburg and NRW alike, followed in both states by 'school'. There are extremely significant differences between 'family' and the other sources of information in Hamburg and NRW alike. The internet is the most 'unimportant' source of information about religions in both states, with significant differences to all other sources.

Table 2:   **Sources to get information about different religions (means of estimates, scale from 1 – strongly agree to 5 – strongly disagree)**

How important as source to get information about different religions is:	no religion		Christian		Muslim		boys		girls		total	
	HH	NRW	HH	NRW	HH	NRW	HH	NRW	HH	NRW	HH	NRW
Family	2,42	2,37	1,93	2,07	1,19	1,13	2,25	2,15	1,88	1,98	2,04	2,08
School	2,82	2,83	2,59	2,41	2,52	2,50	2,84	2,64	2,56	2,56	2,68	2,60
Friends	2,91	2,95	2,63	3,23	2,20	1,85	2,91	3,09	2,53	2,89	2,70	3,00
religious community	3,63	3,32	2,48	2,66	1,95	1,59	3,05	2,85	2,79	2,70	2,90	2,78
Books	3,31	3,32	2,80	2,97	1,95	2,00	3,11	3,13	2,73	2,82	2,89	2,99
Media	2,91	2,97	2,85	2,95	2,76	2,52	2,94	2,95	2,81	2,89	2,87	2,92
Internet	3,17	3,10	3,09	3,29	2,64	2,44	3,08	3,23	3,05	3,05	3,06	3,15

There are extremely significant differences between Muslims, Christians and students with no religion with regard to the importance of 'family' and the 'faith community' in Hamburg and

10 When we refer to 'means', we mean 'arithmetical means'. In order to derive the means in this case, we ascribed the value 1 for the statement 'very important', 2 for 'important', 3 for 'a little bit important', 4 for 'not important' and 5 for 'not important at all'. In this way, the lower the mean in table 2, the more 'important' is the respective 'source of information' for the students.

NRW alike, with Muslim students considering these sources to be more important than Christian students, who again consider them more important then students with 'no religion' do. There are no significant differences between Christian and Muslim students in Hamburg and NRW alike with respect to the importance of 'school' as a source of information, both groups, however, consider it significantly more important than students with 'no religion' do.

Table 3 gives the frequencies with regard to some statements concerning the importance of religion. The low percentage of students in Hamburg and NRW alike who consider religion as 'nonsense' ($\approx$10%) and the high percentage of those who at least agree with the statement: 'I respect other people who believe' ($\approx$90%) are striking. There is an extremely significant difference between the federal states in the positions on the statement 'I respect other people who believe', with students in Hamburg tending more to respect others than their fellows in NRW ($\rho=-0.108$, $p<0.001$).

In Hamburg and NRW alike 37% at least agree that religion helps them 'to cope with difficulties', while 38% in Hamburg and NRW alike at least agree that religion helps them 'to be a better person'. Only 11% in Hamburg and 13% in NRW agree at least that 'religion is important to me because I love God', while 18% in Hamburg and NRW consider religion as a determining factor for their whole life: 42% in Hamburg and 44% in NRW agree at least that one can be a religious person without belonging to a particular faith community, while 32% and 44% report having doubts whether there is God or not sometimes, while 37% and 42% say that what they think about religion is open to change.

Table 3:   **Importance of religion (percentages)**

How far do you agree that:	strongly agree		agree		neither agree or disagree		disagree		strongly disagree	
	HH	NRW	HH	NRW	HH	NRW	HH	NRW	HH	NRW
Religion helps me to cope with difficulties	12	9	25	28	34	33	14	13	15	17
Religion helps me to be a better person	15	17	23	21	29	28	17	17	16	17
Religion is important to me because I love God	3	5	8	8	30	26	23	25	36	36
I respect other people who believe	63	52	27	35	7	8	1	3	1	2
Religion is nonsense	4	7	5	5	17	18	19	21	55	49
Religion determines my whole life	8	8	10	10	20	24	23	19	39	39
Religion is important in our history	17	19	35	39	33	27	9	10	6	5
You can be a religious person without belonging to a particular faith community	17	15	25	29	32	30	11	11	14	15
Sometimes I have doubts – is there a God or not?	12	17	20	27	23	19	13	10	31	26
What I think about religion is open to change	12	11	25	31	31	28	13	12	19	19

The largest correlations with respect to all items of table 3 exist in the 'importance of religion', with students for whom religion is more important tending to agree more that religion helps them 'to cope with difficulties' ($\rho=-0.683$, $p<0.001$) and 'to be a better person ($\rho=-0.694$, $p<0.001$), that religion is important to them because they 'love God' ($\rho=-0.338$, $p<0.001$), that they 'respect other people who believe' ($\rho=-0.227$, $p<0.001$), that religion determines their 'whole life' ($\rho=-0.678$, $p<0.001$), that 'religion is important in our history' ($\rho=-0.412$, $p<0.001$). At the same time they tend to agree less that 'religion is nonsense' ($\rho=0.643$, $p<0.001$), that one can be a 'religious person without belonging to a particular faith community' ($\rho=0.159$, $p<0.001$), that they 'have doubts – is there a God or not?' ($\rho=0.326$, $p<0.001$) and that what they 'think about religion is open to change' ($\rho=-0.225$, $p<0.001$).

Analogous correlations with respect to all items of table 3 also exist with 'migration background', but some of these prove to be spurious and be only caused by cross correlations to the 'importance of religion'. In less technical terms: it is rather the 'importance of religion', than the religious or migration background, that is decisive for the level of approval to the abovementioned items. As an example: significantly more Muslims than Christians or students with 'no religion' strongly agree that they 'respect other students who believe': 72% of the Muslims, 62% of the Christians and 'only' 51% of the students with 'no religion' do so. Does this mean that 'Muslim' students tend to respect 'others who believe' more then the other groups, because they are 'Muslims' or that students with 'no religion' tend to 'respect others who believe' less, because they have 'no religion'? The answer is no: the correlation is 'spurious' and is only caused by the fact that more Muslim students than Christian students than students with 'no religion' consider religion 'very important' to them, while the same time, students who consider religion more important tend to agree less that they 'respect other students who believe'. This might be exemplified by the fact that there is almost no difference between the different worldview groups with respect to those students who consider religion as being 'very important': 76% of the Muslims, 72% of the Christians and 71% of the students with 'no religion' who consider religion 'very important' also 'strongly agree' to the statement that they 'respect other students who believe'.

Students with a 'migration background' tend to agree more that religion helps them 'to be a better person ($\rho=-0.219$, $p<0.001$)[11], that religion determines their 'whole life' ($\rho=-0.275$, $p<0.001$) and, less strongly, that one can be a 'religious person without belonging to a particular faith community' ($\rho=0.162$, $p<0.001$), that they 'have doubts – is there a God or not?' ($\rho=0.234$, $p<0.001$) and that what they 'think about religion is open to change'($\rho=0.211$, $p<0.001$).

Extremely significant correlations with respect to the statement 'religion helps me to cope with difficulties' exist with gender ($\rho=-0.104$, $p<0.001$) with girls being more inclined to agree with it. Likewise, Muslims tend more to this statement than Christian students do, who again are more inclined towards it then students with 'no religion'. The same is true for the statement "I respect other people who believe", "Religion determines my whole life", while the opposite is true with respect to the statements "Religion is nonsense", "Sometimes I have doubts – is there a God or not?" and "What I think about religion is open to change".

Table 4 lists the frequencies of how often students speak about religion. Fewer than 10% of the students in both states talk about religion with the mentioned groups approximately 'every day'. The number of those who 'never' speak about religion ranges between c. 20% and 50%.

---

11 We give only the partial correlation coefficients with the 'importance of religion' as control variable here.

This means on the other side that at least the majority of students do talk about religion with the mentioned groups. However, only c. 10% to 30% of the students speak about religion with the mentioned groups at least 'about every week'.

Table 4:   Frequencies of speaking about religion (percentages)

How often do you speak with others about religion:	about every day		about every week		about once a month		less than once a month		never	
	HH	NRW	HH	NRW	HH	NRW	HH	NRW	HH	NRW
family	9	7	22	26	28	25	24	24	18	18
friends	6	3	18	16	25	21	27	28	25	31
class mates	3	1	22	18	24	20	26	25	24	35
other students	2	1	8	7	17	16	27	27	47	49
teachers	1	2	29	32	18	18	22	18	29	30
religious leaders	3	5	14	14	13	16	20	21	50	43

Significant differences between the Hamburg and NRW samples exist only with respect to discussions with 'classmates' ($\rho=-0.116$, $p<0.001$), with students in Hamburg tending to talk more often about religion with 'classmates'. The only significant correlations between speaking about religions with the mentioned groups and the 'attendance at religious education' occur with regard to speaking with 'teachers' ($\rho=0.405$, $p<0.001$) and 'classmates' ($\rho=0.139$, $p<0.001$), with students who currently attend religious education tending to speak more often with these groups then those who do not. However if one considers that students have religious education at least once a week in both states it is puzzling that only 47% say they speak at least about once a week with teachers and only 28% with 'classmates'. If we look at the frequencies of speaking about religion in the context of school[12], then we find that 4% speak 'about every day', 38% 'about every week', 24% 'about once a month' and only 14% 'never' do so.

There are extremely significant differences in both states with regard to the frequencies of talking about religion with 'family' and all the other groups, 'family' being the category with whom students in Hamburg and NRW alike talk most frequently about religion: 31% in Hamburg and 33% in NRW talk about religion at least about every week with 'family'. However, if we compare speaking about religion with 'family' and 'in the context of school' (see the aggregation of this variable above), we find that students tend to talk more often about religion in the context of school than with 'family', however the difference is smaller then expected, taking again into account that students have religious education at least once a week.

No significant differences exist between the frequency of discussions with 'friends', 'classmates' and 'teachers' in Hamburg (talk to these groups occurs at least about every week for c. a quarter or the students), while in NRW the students talk significantly more rarely with 'friends' and 'classmates' than with 'teachers'. 'Religious leaders' and 'other students at school' are the groups of people with whom discussions occur less then once a month or never for the majority of the students, with significant differences between the frequency of talking about religion with these groups and all other groups mentioned. These findings might be highlighted by considering that c. 60% talk about religion at least 'once a month' with

---

12 For this purpose we looked at how often a student speaks about religion with teachers, classmates or other students at school and we aggregated a new variable from the respective frequencies.

'family', c. 50% with 'friends', 'classmates' and 'teachers' whereas only c. 30% do so with 'religious leaders' or 'other students'.

There are medium to large, extremely significant correlations between the 'importance of religion' and the frequency of talking about religion with all mentioned groups, except with the group of 'other students', where the correlation is low but still extremely significant. This finding might be exemplified by the frequencies of talking with 'family': only 7% of the students who consider religion 'absolutely not important' in Hamburg and 8% in NRW talk about religion with 'family' at least 'about every week', while in the group of students who consider religion 'very important' the corresponding frequencies are 72% and 79%.

The correlations between the frequency of talking about religion and gender are only significant with respect to 'friends' ($\rho=-0.119$, $p<0.001$), with girls talking more often to these groups than boys do.

There are extremely significant differences between Muslims, Christians and students with no religion in NRW and Hamburg alike for the frequencies of talking about religion to all listed groups. Generally Muslims talk significantly more often about religion to others than Christians, who again talk significantly more often to others than students with 'no religion' do; this might be highlighted by the frequencies of talking about religion to 'family': 72% of the Muslim students in Hamburg and 80% in NRW talk at least 'about every week' with 'family', while only 31% and 32% of the Christians and only 14% and 19% of the students with 'no religion' do so.

Table 5: **Religious diversity in the life world of students (percentages)**

With regard to people around you, would you say that:	Yes		no		don't know about their views …	
	HH	NRW	HH	NRW	HH	NRW
most of my friends have the same views about religion as me	56	65	25	18	19	18
most of the students in my class have the same views about religion as me	26	44	39	27	35	29
I have friends who belong to different religions	85	74	9	20	7	6
I have family members who belong to different religions	31	29	54	62	15	10
I have students in my class who belong to different religions	90	65	5	32	5	3
my parents have totally different views about religion from me	15	16	71	71	14	13
at school, I go around with young people who have different religious backgrounds	89	59	6	35	4	6
after school, I go around with young people who have different religious background from me	61	47	27	42	12	11
at school, I prefer to go around with young people who have the same religious background as me.	17	29	83	71		
in my spare time, I prefer to go around with young people who have the same religious background as me.	21	27	79	73		

Table 5 and 6 give the frequencies with regard to items concerning the role religious diversity plays in the life-world of students. In Hamburg as well as in NRW there is a strong tendency towards having friends with the same view about religion – 56% of the students in Hamburg and 65% in NRW affirm that most of their friends have the same views about religion as themselves. But conversely, an even higher percentage of pupils report also having friends belonging to different religions: 85% in Hamburg and 74% in NRW. The multicultural setting in Hamburg is the reason for an extremely high percentage of classmates who belong to different religions: 90% in Hamburg, but even in NRW almost two thirds. Religion in the eyes of the pupils is not a reason for separation after school. Clear majorities do not prefer to be with people who have the same background in their spare time: 79% in Hamburg and 73% in NRW. Nevertheless the figures show that in practice encounters between pupils of different religions are much more frequent during school-time than afterwards.

There are significant differences between Hamburg and NRW for most of the items in both tables, which can be also exemplified by looking at the frequencies: students in Hamburg significantly more often state they have 'friends who belong to another religion', 'students in my class who belong to a different religion', to 'spend time with young people who have a different religious background' at school as well as after school.

Among the Muslim students 93% in Hamburg and 95% in NRW report having friends of a different religion, while only 89% and 70% or the Christians and 77% and 67% of the students with 'no religion' do so. That Muslim students more often have friends of another religion should not be astonishing, since they form small minorities. It can be considered more surprising that Christian students more often have friends of a different religion than students with no religion. However, the difference between these groups is not significant in NRW, while it is extremely significant in Hamburg and remains so even after taking into account partial correlations, e.g. with respect to attending or not religious education classes, with gender, and with migration background.

Table 6:   Others and religion (percentages)

How far do you agree:	strongly agree		agree		neither agree or disagree		disagree		strongly disagree	
	HH	NRW	HH	NRW	HH	NRW	HH	NRW	HH	NRW
I like to know what my best friend thinks about religion.	17	13	32	32	32	33	11	12	9	10
it doesn't bother me what my friends think about religion	11	12	16	23	30	29	28	25	15	11
religion is something one inherits from one's family	15	18	30	35	31	29	13	8	11	9
Religion doesn't interest me at all- we have more important things to talk about.	9	12	11	13	28	27	23	21	30	27
I don't know much about religion and thus I can't have an opinion	3	2	4	5	22	21	34	36	37	36
For me talking about religious topics is boring	6	10	11	16	26	26	30	26	26	22

There are significant differences with respect to preferences for spending time with people of the same religion, during school as well as during spare time, between Muslims and the other groups, who are homogeneous in this respect, with more Muslim students preferring to spend time with young people of the same religious background. This result can be exemplified by the fact that 38% of the Muslim students in Hamburg and 56% NRW prefer to spend time with young people of the same religion in their spare time, while only 15% and 28% of the Christians and only 16% and 25% of the students with 'no religion' do so.

2.1.2   Data interpretation

Personal religious background

One has to emphasize that more than three fourths of the students questioned relate to religion in a positive way, in so far as they consider the existence of a transcendent dimension of being. A remarkable group of about 40% in both samples agree to an understanding of religion which is more related to individual persons than to faith communities and is also open to development and changes. Almost every second considers religion important and more than every third affirms that religion helps them to cope with difficulties. Fully in line with these findings is the fact that about every second practices religion regularly, involving praying and attending religious events at least every week. It also deserves to be mentioned that 18% in Hamburg as well as in NRW claim that religion determines their whole life, while only 13% in both states consider religion as being 'not important at all' for them personally.

Relating these findings to answers concerning the religious affiliation, we see that a remarkable proportion of those students who claim to have 'no religion' are open to religion as a transcendental dimension, be it God, spirit or life force and consider religion as not being 'not important at all' for them. In fact only 8% of the students state that 'religion is not important at all' for them and the same time that they 'don't really think there is any sort of God, spirit or life force'.

There is a striking difference between the Christian and the Muslim students concerning the 'importance of religion' for them: 71% of the Muslim students claim religion to be 'very important'; 56% in Hamburg and even 74% of the Muslim students in NRW affirm that religion is life-determining. The corresponding numbers concerning the Christian students are much lower: only 30% of the Christian students think that religion is 'very important'; only 17% in Hamburg and 10% in NRW state that religion determines their whole life. With regard to the last item it might also be worthwhile to have a look at the negative answers: 56% of the Christian students in the Hamburg sample and 60% in the NRW sample, but 23% and only 7% of the Muslim students in the two states, would at least disagree that religion determines their whole life.

This finding that the percentage of Muslim students who stress the personal importance of religion is higher compared to the Christian students is also mirrored by their positions with regard to the role of religion for coping with problems: nearly twice as many Muslim as Christian students affirm that religion helps them to cope with difficulties (43% versus 73%).

Speaking about religion / peer relations and diversity

Our analysis has so far indicated that religion is important for almost every second pupil of the sample and even life-determining for a significant minority. We can explore similar figures with regard to readiness to speak about religion – for about every second respondent, religion is a regular topic of conversation. We can, however, observe differences with regard to the spheres in which discussions about religion seem to take place. Talking about religion within the sphere of family is more common than talking about religion within the peer group. Nevertheless, religion is not a non-topic among peers. This is rather the case for a majority of students with regard to religious leaders – they do not talk to them much.

Religion is a topic of conversation, but only a minority (below 10%) talks about religion with their family, with friends or classmates almost every day. Although the occasions for talking about religion among peers are not used very frequently, we can see that, after all, almost every second pupil talks at least about once a month about religion with friends; and it is also remarkable that almost every second is interested to know what their best friend thinks about religion. The role of the family for religious communication is comparatively great – with only one fifth of students who state that they never talk about religion in their family. But school also is an important arena for discussing religious topics.

With regard to the perceived plurality in school as well as in the students' life, plurality is on one hand a matter of fact for the majority in both states. Students in Hamburg and in NRW are not only familiar with religious heterogeneity, they are used to relating to students from different backgrounds and they are – generally speaking – also acquainted with different views about religion. Clear majorities state not to prefer to spend time with people who have the same background in school and in their spare time. Nevertheless the encounters between pupils of different religions seem to be more frequent during school-time than afterwards.

2.2   How do pupils see religion in school?

2.2.1   Data description

Table 7 gives the percentages with respect to attendance at religious education. The total ratio of students who had religious education at the time of the survey is significantly higher in NRW than in Hamburg. The percentage of Christians and of students with 'no religion' who attended religious education at the time of the survey was significantly higher in the NRW sample. The percentage of Muslim students who attended religious education was significantly higher in the Hamburg sample.

Table 7:   Religious education this year or not? (percentages)

religious educa-tion this year or not?	total		no religion		Christian		Muslim	
	HH	NRW	HH	NRW	HH	NRW	HH	NRW
Yes	57	71	54	70	63	80	53	34
No	43	29	46	30	37	20	47	66

In Hamburg and NRW alike, Christian students attend religious education significantly more often than the other groups. The difference between Muslims and students with 'no religion' is not significant in Hamburg, while it is extremely significant in NRW.

Regarding the number of years the students attended religious education, the position is similar: the number of years the students surveyed have studied religious education is higher in NRW. The average number of years is 7.75 in NRW, in Hamburg it is 4.79. There are conspicuous differences between the groups: the average number of years for Christian students is 8.70 in NRW and 5.36 in Hamburg, while for students with 'no religion' the numbers are 7.41 and 4.54, and for Muslim students 3.58 and 3.92.

Likewise the Christians and the students with 'no religion' in the NRW sample have studied religious education significantly longer, while the difference between Muslim students is not significant. At the same time, in both states, Christian students have studied religious education significantly longer than all other groups, while students with 'no religion' have studied religious education significantly longer than the Muslim students in both states.

Table 8 gives the frequencies with regard to items concerning experiences with religion in school. The majority of students in Hamburg and NRW at least 'agree' that at school they 'get knowledge about different religions' (73% and 78%), 'learn to have respect for everyone, whatever their religion' (77% and 67%), 'have opportunities to discuss religious issues from different perspectives' (62% and. 57) and that 'learning about different religions at school helps us to live together' (59% and. 55%). A lot of the students also state that 'learning about religions at school helps me to understand current events' (49% and 45%) and that they 'find religions as a topic at school' important (51% and 48%) and, only a few percent less, 'interesting' (45% and 42%). The percentages of students who reject these statements is relatively low.

It is only a minority who at least 'agree' that 'learning about religions at school helps me to make choices between right and wrong' (24% and 29%) or 'helps me to learn about myself' (23% and 27%). On the other hand the majority of students at least disagree that 'learning about religions leads to conflicts in the classroom' (54% and 62%), that they have problems showing their 'views about religion openly in school' (73% and 78%) and at least in Hamburg that 'a student who shows his/her religious belief openly in school, risks being mocked' (55% and 42%). It is, however, puzzling that for most of the items in table 8 there are large groups in both states, who 'neither agree or disagree'.

Table 8:   Experiences with religion in school (percentages)

How much do you agree that:	strongly agree		agree		neither agree or disagree		disagree		strongly disagree	
	HH	NRW	HH	NRW	HH	NRW	HH	NRW	HH	NRW
At school, I get knowledge about different religions	23	17	50	61	17	15	6	5	4	2
At school, I learn to have respect for everyone, whatever their religion	35	29	42	38	18	25	3	5	2	3
At school, I have opportunities to discuss religious issues from different perspectives	18	14	44	43	28	29	7	11	3	4
I find topics about religions interesting at school	14	8	31	33	35	34	13	17	8	9
I find religions as topic important at school	20	19	31	29	29	29	10	13	9	9
Learning about different religions at school helps us to live together	21	16	38	39	29	29	8	10	4	5
Learning about religions at school helps me to make choices between right and wrong	7	8	17	21	37	36	19	20	19	15
Learning about religions at school helps me to understand current events	13	9	36	36	35	36	10	14	6	4
Learning about religions at school helps me to learn about myself.	6	6	17	21	36	32	20	22	21	19
Learning about religions leads to conflicts in the classroom	6	5	12	11	28	23	26	28	28	34
I have problems showing my views about religion openly in school	2	3	6	9	19	20	33	33	40	35
a student who shows his/her religious belief openly in school, risks being mocked	4	8	13	21	27	30	26	23	29	19

There is only one significant correlation between the 'federal state' and the items of table 8: students in NRW tend to agree more that 'a student who shows his/her religious belief openly in school, risks being mocked' ($\rho=-0.155$, $p<0.001$). There are also no significant differences between girls and boys.

As exemplified above, school is widely recognized as an institution which transfers knowledge about different religions, with large majorities of students at least agreeing that at school they 'get knowledge about different religions'. This high level of approval can be further differentiated by highlighting some differences between the different religious sub-groups. In NRW, Christian students tend to agree significantly more with the statement that at school they 'get knowledge about different religions' than Muslims as well as students with 'no religion', but the same time Muslim students agree significantly less than students with 'no religion'. In Hamburg, Christian students also tend to agree significantly more with the statement than Muslims and students with 'no religion' do, while there is no significant difference between the last two groups. There are no significant differences between the two states with respect to Christians as well as students with 'no religion'. However, the difference with respect to Muslim students between the two states is very significant, with Muslim students in Hamburg tending to agree more that they 'learn about different religions in school' than those in NRW.

These results can be highlighted by the fact that 28% of the Muslim students in NRW at least 'disagree' with the statement, while only 11% of the Muslim students in Hamburg do so. Likewise, only 5% of the Christian students in NRW and 8% in Hamburg and only 10% and 11% of the students with 'no religion' do so. On the other hand 84% of the Christian students in NRW and 78% in Hamburg at least agree with the statement, while 78% and 71% of the students with 'no religion' and 51% and 68% of the Muslim students do so.

However, the most substantial difference concerning the statement 'at school, I get knowledge about different religions' arises with respect to whether students are currently attending religious education or not, with students who had religious education at the time of the survey tending more to agree with the statement ($\rho=0.351$, $p<0.001$).

Interestingly enough, no significant correlation occurs between respect to learning 'to have respect for everyone, whatever their religion' and attendance at religious education. The same is true with respect to migration background, school type or socio-economic background. However, some significant differences occur between the religious groups. There is no significant difference between the groups in Hamburg. In NRW there are also no significant differences between Christians and Muslims, however these two groups are significantly different from students with 'no religion', who tend to agree with the statement significantly less. Comparing the different groups between Hamburg and NRW shows that there is no significant difference between the Christian students in the two states and the same is true for Muslim students, while the difference between students with 'no religion' is extremely significant ($\rho=-0.192$, $p<0.001$), with students with 'no religion' agreeing in Hamburg more than those in NRW with the statement[13].

There is still a majority of students in Hamburg and NRW who at least agree with the statement that they have at school 'opportunities to discuss religious issues from different perspectives'. It is, however, conspicuous that the percentages of agreement with this statement are remarkably lower compared to the item 'at school, I get knowledge about different

---

13 Partial correlation analyses show that this correlation is not spurious and especially that it is independent from currently attending religious education or not.

religions', the difference between the levels of approval for the two items being extremely significant.

With regard to the level of agreement with the statement that students have 'opportunities to discuss religious issues from different perspectives' in school, there are no significant correlations to gender, migration background, socio-economic background; low but extremely significant correlations to 'school type' prove to be spurious. The highest correlation with regard to this item occurs with respect to currently having religious education or not – in Hamburg (ρ=0.312, p<0.001) and NRW as well (ρ=0.255, p<0.001), with students who currently attend religious education tending to agree more.

Concerning the statement that 'learning about different religions at school helps us to live together' there are low but extremely significant correlations to 'migration background' (ρ=−0.138, p<0.001) and 'gender' (ρ=−0.154, p=0.014), with girls and students with a migration background tending to agree more with the statement. There are also extremely significant differences between students with 'no religion' and Christian as well as Muslim students in Hamburg and NRW alike, with students with 'no religion' agreeing less with the statement. The difference between Christian and Muslim students in Hamburg is not significant, while it is in NRW, with Muslim students tending to agree more with the statement. Some frequencies can highlight these findings: 68% of the Christian as well as the Muslim students in Hamburg at least 'agree' with the statement, while only 50% of the students with 'no religion' do so. Likewise 12% of Christians, 5% of Muslims and 13% of the students with 'no religion' at least 'disagree'. The corresponding frequencies for NRW are: 60%, 71% and 42% respectively 12%, 5% and 24%.

Concerning the statement 'learning about religions leads to conflicts in the classroom' there are significant correlations in Hamburg to 'migration background' (ρ=−0.109, p<0.001) and 'religious education this year or not' (ρ=−0.160, p<0.001); in NRW to 'migration background' (ρ=−0.258, p<0.001), 'religious education this year or not' (ρ=−0.109, p=0.009) and interestingly enough 'school type' (ρ=−0.284, p<0.001)[14], with students with a migration background, students who currently attend religious education and, only in NRW, also students from schools with a 'lower education level' tending to agree more that 'learning about religions leads to conflicts in the classroom'.

In Hamburg, there are no significant differences between Christians and students with 'no religion' on one hand with regard to their approval of the statement 'learning about religions leads to conflicts in the classroom', but a significant difference between the latter and Muslim students, with Muslim students tending to agree more with the statement. In NRW, on the other hand, there are significant trends in the differences between students with 'no religion', Christian students and Muslim students respectively, with Muslim students tending to agree most, followed by students with 'no religion' and then by the Christian students. These findings can be exemplified by some means and frequencies with regard to the different groups. In Hamburg the means are: 3.34 for Muslims, 3.66 for Christians and 3.64 for students with 'no religion', with 26% of the Muslim students who at least agree, respectively 13% of the Christian students and 17% of the students with 'no religion', while the corresponding percentages of students who at least 'disagree' are: 42%, 67% and 56%. In NRW the means are: 3.10 for Muslims, 3.97 for Christians and 3.62 for students with 'no religion', with 31% of the Muslim students who at least agree, 11% of the Christian and 16% of the students with 'no

---

14 Bivariate analysis also suggests significant correlations to the socio-economic background in Hamburg and NRW and to school type also in Hamburg. Partial correlation analysis proves these however to be spurious.

religion' respectively, while the corresponding percentages of students who at least 'disagree' are: 29%, 71% and 57%.

Table 9 gives the frequencies with regard to some statements concerning religion in school. We can not enter into detail here , however one can generally state that the majority of students in Hamburg and NRW alike at least 'agree' that religious dietary laws should be taken into account in school, that students should be able to wear 'discreet religious symbols' and that they can be absent from school 'for religious festivals'. On the other hand about the half of the students in Hamburg and NRW at least 'disagree' that students 'should be excused from taking some classes for religious reasons'.

Table 9:   Religion in school (percentages)

How far do you agree with the following positions?	strongly agree		agree		neither agree or disagree		disagree		strongly disagree	
	HH	NRW	HH	NRW	HH	NRW	HH	NRW	HH	NRW
at school meals, religious food requirements should be taken into account	30	21	36	33	22	22	6	13	6	12
students should be able to wear religious symbols at school: discreet ones	47	34	31	37	16	16	3	4	3	9
students should be able to wear religious symbols at school: more visible ones	23	16	23	15	27	22	13	20	14	27
Students can be absent from school when it is their religious festivals	26	26	31	27	23	22	10	10	10	15
students should be excused from taking some classes for religious reasons	9	13	11	18	26	22	26	25	28	23
schools should provide facilities for pupils to pray in school	9	13	15	26	39	33	21	13	16	15
voluntary religious services could be a part of school life	11	16	20	31	32	30	17	11	20	12

There are some low but extremely significant correlations e.g. between 'federal state', 'gender', migration background' with students in Hamburg, girls and students with a 'migration background' tending to agree more that religious dietary laws should be taken into account, that students should be allowed to wear 'more visible religious symbols', while on the other hand students in NRW tend to agree more that 'voluntary religious services could be a part of school life'.

There are also some extremely significant differences between the religious groups. e.g. Muslim students tend, in Hamburg and NRW alike, to agree more than Christians and students with 'no religion' do with almost all the statements of table 9, except the statements that 'students should be able to wear discreet religious symbols' and that 'voluntary religious services could be part of school life', with regard to which there are no significant differences.

Table 10 gives the frequencies with regard to statements regarding religious education and religion in school. The majority of the students in Hamburg and NRW alike at least agree that 'religious education should be optional' (61% and 74%) and at least disagree with the statements that 'there should be no place for religion in school' (66% and 71%) and that 'there is no need for the subject of religious education ...' (59% in both states). The differences between Hamburg and NRW with respect to these items are not significant or only spurious. However, extremely significant (though low) relations occur between these items and the 'importance of religion' and 'religious education this year or not', with students to whom religion is more important and who currently attend religious education agreeing less that religious education should be optional, at the same time disagreeing more that religion should not have a place in school and that 'there is no need for the subject of religious education …".

There are also significant differences with regard to the above-mentioned statements between the religious groups in the two states: generally Christian students tend to agree less than the other groups that religious education should be optional[15], while Muslims and Christians agree less than the others that 'there should be no religion in school life'[16], while in both states students with 'no religion' agree more than the others that 'there is no need for the subject of religious education …'.

Table 10:   Positions concerning religious education in school (percentages)

What is your position regarding different models of religious education in school?	strongly agree		agree		neither agree or disagree		disagree		strongly disagree	
	HH	NRW	HH	NRW	HH	NRW	HH	NRW	HH	NRW
Religious education should be optional	37	39	24	25	20	15	12	12	7	9
Pupils should study religious education separately in groups according to which religion they belong	5	34	5	27	15	20	23	10	52	9
There should be no place for religion in school life	7	8	5	3	21	18	23	23	43	48
religious education should be taught to students together, whatever differences there might be in their religious or denominational background	42	9	31	13	18	27	4	22	4	28
There is no need for the subject of religious education. All we need to know about religion is covered by other school subjects	8	7	8	6	25	19	31	31	28	38
religious education should be taught sometimes together and sometimes in groups according to which religions students belong to	6	8	11	24	28	35	26	18	30	16

The difference between Hamburg and NRW is extremely significant when it comes to models of religious education. Correlation analysis confirms the impression one gets by only reading the frequencies: there are extremely significant relations between 'federal state' and 'Pupils should study religious education separately …' ($\rho=0.572$, $p<0.001$), 'religious education should be taught together …' ($\rho=-0.514$, $p<0.001$) and 'religious education should sometimes

---

15 This finding regarding the optionality of religious education can be highlighted by some frequencies. In Hamburg 68% of the students with 'no religion', 65% of the Muslims and 54% of the Christian students at least agree that religious education should be optional; the corresponding numbers in NRW are: 82%, 80% and 51%.

16 Only 17% of the students with 'no religion' in Hamburg and 18% in NRW are in favour of a school with no place for religion, compared to the 7% and 6% of the Christians and 9% and 8% of the Muslim students.

be taught together …' ($\rho=0.221$, $p<0.001$), with students in NRW agreeing more than those in Hamburg with the first and the third model, while the opposite is true for the joint religious education model.

Only 10% of the students in Hamburg at least 'agree' with a confessional religious education model, and 75% disagree, while the corresponding numbers for NRW are: 61% and 19%. On the other hand, 73% of the students in Hamburg at least 'agree' with a joint religious education model and only 8% disagree, while the corresponding numbers for NRW are: 22% and 60%. When it comes to a kind of 'confessional-cooperative' model only 17% of the students in Hamburg at least 'agree', while 56% at least 'disagree'; the corresponding numbers for NRW are: 32% and 34%.

In Hamburg: Christians tend to reject a confessional religious education model[17] significantly more than Muslims ($p=0.071$) and students with 'no religion' ($p=0.005$)[18], while on the other hand students with no religion tend to be more in favour of an interreligious religious education model[19] than Christians ($p<0.001$) and Muslim students ($p<0.001$)[20] There is no difference between these groups with respect to the 'cooperative-confessional' religious education model.

In NRW: Muslim students are more in favour of a confessional religious education model than Christians ($p<0.001$) and than students with 'no religion'[21] ($p=0.007$)[22], while there is no significant difference between the groups with respect to the interreligious model. With respect to the 'cooperative-confessional' model the only significant difference arises between students with 'no religion' and Christian students ($p=0.018$), with the former being more in favour of the 'cooperative-confessional' model.

As mentioned before, the difference between Hamburg and NRW with respect to approval for the 'cooperative-confessional' religious education model is extremely significant: 20% of the Muslims, 17% of the Christians and 15% of the students with 'no religion' in Hamburg are in favour of this model, while the corresponding numbers for NRW are: 28%, 38% and 23%. In Hamburg 51% of the Muslims, 60% of the Christians and 55% of the students with 'no religion' reject this model; in NRW the corresponding numbers are: 33%, 31% and 36%.

There are some extremely significant though low correlations with respect to the preferences regarding the different models, with some interesting differences between Hamburg and NRW. Regarding the confessional religious education model, there are some correlations to 'school type'($\rho=-0.241$, $p<0.001$) and 'religious education this year or not' ($\rho=-0.144$, $p<0.001$)in Hamburg, with students from schools with a 'lower' educational level[23] and students who do not currently attend religious education tending to prefer the confessional

---

17 However, the level of rejection is high for all groups, with 81% of the Christians at least disagreeing with the confessional religious education model, 69% of the Muslims and 73% of the students with 'no religion'.

18 There is no significant difference between Muslims and students with 'no religion' on this issue.

19 However, the level of agreement is high for all groups, with 81% of the Christians at least agreeing with the interreligious religious education model, 77% of the Muslims and 64% of the students with 'no religion'.

20 There is no significant difference between Muslims and Christians students on this issue.

21 There is no significant difference between Christians and students with 'no religion' on this issue.

22 Exemplified by the fact that 77% of the Muslim students at least agree with the confessional religious education model, while only 57% of the Christians and 64% of the students with 'no religion' do so.

23 Consequently run U-tests show that there are significant differences between all 'school types', with students from 'lower secondary' schools tending to prefer the confessional model more then those from 'comprehensive school', who again tend to favour this model more then students from 'grammar schools'.

model; in NRW there are correlations with 'school type' ($\rho=0.213$, $p<0.001$) and 'importance of religion' ($\rho=-0.167$, $p<0.001$), with students from schools with a 'higher' educational level and students to whom religion is more important tending to prefer the confessional model.

Table 11:   What should students learn in school? (percentages)

To what extent do you agree that at school pupils should:	strongly agree		agree		neither agree or disagree		disagree		strongly disagree	
	HH	**NRW**	**HH**	**NRW**	**HH**	**NRW**	**HH**	**NRW**	**HH**	**NRW**
Get an objective knowledge about different religions	38	32	44	48	16	15	2	2	2	3
Learn to understand what religions teach	17	18	40	45	34	30	5	5	3	3
Be able to talk and communicate about religious issues	26	21	46	42	22	28	4	7	2	2
Learn the importance of religion for dealing with problems in society	23	20	46	48	24	26	3	5	2	2
Be guided towards religious beliefs	9	14	11	18	32	30	19	15	30	23

Table 11 gives the frequencies with regard to some statements regarding 'teaching aims' of religious education, or, generally speaking, of dealing with religion in school, since religious education was not mentioned in the questionnaire in this context. However, the probability that students in Germany understood these items as addressing religious education is high. The majority of students in Hamburg and NRW alike are in favour of getting 'objective knowledge about different religions' as well as of learning 'to understand what religions teach', of learning to 'communicate about religious issues' as well as of learning 'the importance of religion for dealing with problems in society'.

Only with respect to being 'guided towards religious belief' are the positions more mixed, with only 21% in Hamburg and 32% in NRW at least agreeing, while 49% and 38% respectively at least disagreeing. This is also the only item where significant differences between Hamburg and NRW arise ($\rho=0.102$, $p<0.001$), with students in NRW tending to agree more with the statement. The highest correlations between all the items of table 11, however, occur with respect to the 'importance of religion', students tending to agree more with all the statements, the more important religion is to them[24].

Looking at the frequencies it seems that there are substantial differences between the religious groups in Hamburg as well as in NRW, especially Muslim students who are remarkably different from all other groups concerning all items. However, multivariate analysis shows that these differences are almost all spurious, being caused by correlations between 'worldview' and 'importance of religion'.[25] Only one significant difference exists between Muslim students and the other groups in Hamburg and only one in NRW: Muslim students in Hamburg tend indeed to agree more that in school students should 'learn to understand what religions teach', while in NRW they tend to agree more that in school they should 'be guided towards religious belief'.

---

24 The correlation coefficient ρ between the 'importance of religion' and the items are, in the order given in table 11: -0.295, -0.421, -0.398, $.0.380$, -0.461, all correlations being extremely significant.
25 See for some explicative remarks footnote 8.

2.2.2 Data interpretation

Students in Hamburg and NRW appreciate school as an institution that transfers knowledge about religions. They also understand that they learn in school to respect others approve regardless their individual background. Wide approval is also found with respect to the possibility of looking at religions from different perspectives. However, the level of approval decreases considerably when it comes to the question whether learning about religion in school helps to learn about oneself and to live together with others. Students seem thus to be more sceptical about existential and societal issues in dealing with religion in school.

This might be the case because the students are aware of the institutional limits of these tasks: religion in school is regarded as religion in an institutional setting which is subject to specific tasks and codes of conduct (see Knauth et al., 2008). These rules can obviously limit the possibilities of religion, but they serve as a general framework which underpins social conduct in the public sphere. The students apparently accept the role school assumes: on the one hand they plead for respecting individual characteristics of religious belonging by allowing them in the public space in school, on the other hand they also see the necessity of subordinating the truth claim of religion to the general rules of teaching. That might be the reason why they do not approve of the possibility to get exemption from classes due to religious reasons.

Anyway, an impressive majority of the students holds positive views about the potentials of learning with regard to religions in school. Talking about religion is highly appreciated especially when the communication is related to the societal aspects of religion. Looking at the effects of religious backgrounds it is conspicuous that there are differences between Muslims and Christians with the Muslims focusing more on the teachings of religions and individual belief.

Likewise, although most of the Muslim and Christian students in Hamburg share the view that learning about different religions helps them to live together, more Muslim than Christian students state that learning about different religions leads to conflict in the classroom. In NRW the share of the students who are sceptical with regard to the potentials of learning about different religions for a peaceful coexistence is lower in the group of Christian students then in the group of Muslim students, while there is no difference between these two groups in Hamburg. On the other hand more Muslim students in NRW are aware of the possibilities of conflicts provoked by learning about different religions than their fellows in Hamburg, whereas in NRW even more Christian students than in Hamburg deny this potential of learning about different religions in school.

There is also an interesting observation in terms of gender difference. Regarding the possibility that learning about different religions helps them to live peacefully together there are noticeably more girls than boys who agree. However, when it comes to the questions of conflict, this difference disappears and boys and girls answer in almost equal numbers in Hamburg and NRW alike.

The students in Hamburg and NRW favour the religious education model they are used to. The level of approval to the existing model in Hamburg is higher than in NRW. The rejection of confessionally separated religious education in Hamburg is most prominent among Christian students – but more than two thirds of Muslim students are also against such a confessional model. In Hamburg and NRW alike, the majority of students with 'no religion' are in favour of religious education and also advocate a place for religion in school. Students in Hamburg and NRW alike do not reject the confessional-cooperative model of religious education as strongly as they reject the confessional compared to the non-confessional model of religious education. It seems, thus, that students in Hamburg and NRW regard the 'cooperative-confessional' religious education model as an intermediate model between the two other two models.

As a general picture one can state that students predominantly are in favour of religious education which focuses on the societal and the communicative dimension of religion. Objectivity with regard to knowledge about religions is also advocated, whereas the students are not so much convinced that religious education should guide them towards religious beliefs. After all a majority thinks that they should understand what the respective religions teach. The preferences of the students in Hamburg are in line with those of the students in NRW. The only difference seem to be that more students in Hamburg than in NRW agree that in religious education it is important to learn to talk and communicate about religious issues, and that more students in NRW than in Hamburg agree that religious education should guide them towards religious belief.

In both states there is a quite strong minority of students (16% in Hamburg and 13% in NRW) who think that religious education is not needed in school, because the topic 'religion' is already sufficiently covered by other subjects. The percentage of those who think that religion should have no place at all in school is only slightly lower in Hamburg and NRW alike, with 12% and 11% agreeing.

We conclude for Hamburg that Muslims as well as Christian students obviously prefer a religious education for all which focuses on the teachings of religions. This can go along with their wish to receive objective knowledge about different religions. But it is surprising that a noticeable part of the Muslims as well as a smaller minority of Christian students would not reject being guided towards a religious belief.

As for NRW, although the majority of the students prefer a confessional model of religious education, it is surprising that the students stress the importance of objective knowledge about different religions and learning what religions teach more than being guided towards religious belief, which is regarded by the majority as not important, although more students in NRW than in Hamburg agree on the importance of being guided towards religious belief through religious education, with Muslim students in NRW being even more in favour of this teaching aim than the other groups.

2.3   How do pupils see the impact of religion?

2.3.1   Data description

Table 12 gives the percentages reflecting the attitudes of the students surveyed with respect to the effects of learning about different religions. Considerable majorities in Hamburg and NRW alike at least 'agree' with almost all the statements listed. Only with regard to the statement that learning about religions helps 'to develop moral values' does the majority not agree in Hamburg. And only small minorities – below 15% – (at least) disagree with the statements in table 12. No significant differences occur with regard to the items of table 12 between Hamburg and NRW.

However there are extremely significant correlations[26] between all the items in table 12 and the 'importance of religion', with students to whom religion is more important tending to

---

26 The correlation coefficient ρ between the 'importance of religion' and the items are in their order in table 12: -0.423, -0.357, -0.316, -0.324, -0.374, -0.467, all correlations being extremely significant.

agree more to all items.[27] Significant differences between girls and boys exist only regarding the first item, with girls tending to agree more that learning about religion helps 'to understand others ...' ($\rho=-0.132$, $p<0.001$).

Table 12:   Learning about different religions (percentages)

To what extent do you agree, that learning about different religions helps:	strongly agree		agree		neither agree or disagree		disagree		strongly disagree	
	HH	NRW	HH	NRW	HH	NRW	HH	NRW	HH	NRW
To understand others and live peacefully with them	20	15	41	46	31	28	5	6	3	4
To understand the history of my country and of Europe	19	16	43	45	27	25	8	10	3	3
To gain a better understanding of current events	15	12	43	39	30	34	8	11	4	4
To develop my own point of view	22	20	38	41	28	26	8	8	4	5
To develop moral values	11	13	36	39	40	36	9	7	4	4
To learn about my own religion	28	31	35	40	23	19	6	6	8	4

Table 13 gives the percentages with regard to some statements on religion and religious people. The majority of the students in Hamburg and NRW alike at least 'disagree' that 'without religion the world would be a better place' (63% and 64%). Likewise about the majority at least agree that 'religion belongs to private life' (50% and 49%). Only 19% in Hamburg and NRW at least 'agree' that 'religious people are less tolerant', while 41% and 40% at least disagree, the share of those who 'neither agree or disagree' being 41% and 42%. The shares with regard to the statement that 'religion is a source of aggressiveness' are quite similar: only 19% and 23% at least agree, while 50% and 45% at least disagree.

Table 13:   Attitude towards religion (percentages)

To what extent do you agree that:	strongly agree		agree		neither agree or disagree		disagree		strongly disagree	
	HH	NRW	HH	NRW	HH	NRW	HH	NRW	HH	NRW
religious people are less tolerant towards others	5	6	14	13	41	42	20	24	21	16
without religion the world would be a better place	4	7	6	7	26	22	25	27	38	37
religion belongs to private life	23	20	27	29	32	33	11	11	8	8
religion is a source of aggressiveness	5	8	14	15	31	32	21	20	29	25

No significant correlations occur to 'federal state'. The highest correlations with respect to all items of table 13 occur with respect to the 'importance of religion', with students to whom religion is more important tending to agree less with all the statements.[28]

---

27 Correlations to 'migration background' prove to be only spurious and caused by cross correlations to the 'importance of religion'. Muslim students tend to agree more than other groups with all the items of table 12. But again multivariate analysis taking into consideration the correlations between the religious groups and the 'importance of religion', show that these differences between the religious groups are also only spurious.

There are also some extremely significant differences with respect to 'gender', 'migration background' and 'worldview'. However, due to existing correlations between all these variables and the 'importance of religion' some but not all prove by multivariate analysis to be spurious. However even taking into account 'the importance of religion', girls as well as students with a 'migration background' tend to agree significantly less that 'religion is a source of aggressiveness';[29] girls also less that 'religious people are less tolerant toward others'.[30]

Taking into account cross-correlations between 'worldview' and the 'importance of religion' many of the differences between the groups concerning the items of table 13 prove to be spurious. However, students with 'no religion' still tend to agree significantly more than Christians and Muslim students that 'religious people are less tolerant towards others', while Muslim students tend to agree significantly less then Christians and students with 'no religion' that 'religion is a source of aggressiveness' and that 'without religion the world would be a better place'.

Table 14 gives the frequencies with regard to some statements concerning religion as a topic of discussion. The majority of the students in Hamburg as in NRW at least 'agree' that for them talking about religion is 'interesting because people have different views', that it 'helps' them to shape their own views and 'to understand others'. Likewise the majority at least disagrees that they talk with friends about 'how stupid religion is and what cruelties are carried out in its name', that 'talking about religion is embarrassing' and that it 'only leads to disagreement'. That religion helps them 'to understand better what is going on in the world' is at least agreed to only by 46% of the students in Hamburg and 44% in NRW, while 35% in Hamburg and NRW alike 'neither agree or disagree', however only 20% and 22% at least 'disagree'. Although on the other hand only 27% in Hamburg and NRW alike at least disagree that 'talking about religion helps me to live peacefully together with people from different religions', only 30% in Hamburg and NRW alike at least agree with the statement, while 42% 'neither agree or disagree'.

No significant correlations occur between the items of table 14 and 'federal state'. There are also no significant correlations to attendance at religious education, though interestingly enough there are some significant correlations to the 'numbers of years' the students studied religious education, but only in NRW. Students in NRW tend to agree more, the longer they had religious education in school, that talking about religion 'is interesting because people have different views' ($\rho=0.192$, $p<0.001$), that it 'helps to shape' their own views ($\rho=0.107$, $p=0.013$), 'to understand others' ($\rho=0.189$, $p<0.001$) and helps them 'to live peacefully together with people from different religions', and less, that they talk with friends 'about how stupid religion is ...' ($\rho=-0.136$, $p<0.001$), that 'talking about religion is embarrassing' ($\rho=-0.103$, $p=0.016$) and that 'religion doesn't interest me ...'.

---

28 The correlation coefficient ρ between the 'importance of religion' and the items are in their order in table 13: 0.166, 0.513, 0.206 and 0.337, all correlations being extremely significant.

29 The partial correlation coefficients with the variable 'how important is religion to you' as 'control variable' are to 'gender' 0.105 and to 'migration background' 0.098. The corresponding bivarite correlation coefficients are to 'gender' 0.142, to 'migration background' 0.193.

30 The partial correlation coefficient with the variable 'how important is religion to you' as 'control variable' is 0.098. The corresponding bivarite correlation coefficient is 0.118.

Table 14:   **Religion as a topic of discussions (percentages)**

To what extent do you agree:	strongly agree		agree		neither agree or disagree		disagree		strongly disagree	
	HH	NRW	HH	NRW	HH	NRW	HH	NRW	HH	NRW
To me, talking about religion is interesting because people have different views	28	18	39	45	22	22	5	8	5	6
Talking about religion helps to shape my own views	13	12	33	34	33	30	13	15	9	9
I and my friends talk about how stupid religion is and what cruelties are carried out in its name	4	5	9	14	25	25	24	24	37	33
Talking about religion helps us to understand others	12	10	39	40	32	32	10	12	7	6
In my view, talking about religion is embarrassing	2	1	2	4	13	18	29	33	55	45
in my view, talking about religion only leads to disagreement	3	5	10	13	30	32	34	31	22	19
talking about religion helps me to live peacefully together with people from different religions	7	7	23	23	42	42	18	18	9	9
Talking about religion helps me to understand better what is going on in the world	11	10	35	34	35	35	12	14	8	8

The largest correlation, with respect to all items of table 14 on the 'importance of religion', occurs with students for whom religion is more important. They tend to agree more that for them talking about religion is 'interesting because people have different views' ($\rho=-0.479$, $p<0.001$), that it helps them to shape their own views ($\rho=-0.430$, $p<0.001$), 'to understand others' ($\rho=-0.384$, $p<0.001$), to 'live peacefully together with people from different religions' ($\rho=-0.414$, $p<0.001$), to 'understand better what is going on in the world' ($\rho=-0.428$, $p<0.001$) and less that they 'talk about how stupid religion is ...', ($\rho=0.330$, $p<0.001$), that 'talking about religion is embarrassing' ($\rho=-0.240$, $p<0.001$) and 'only leads to disagreement' ($\rho=0.290$, $p<0.001$).

With respect to almost all items of table 14 there are extremely significant correlations to gender, and migration background and to differences between the religious groups. However, most of these correlations prove to be spurious and be only caused by cross-correlations to the 'importance of religion'[31]. Nonetheless girls, Muslims and students with a 'migration background' tend to agree less that 'talking about religion is embarrassing', while girls tend also to agree more that 'talking about religion is interesting because people have different views'.

Table 15 gives the frequencies of possible reactions to an attempt at proselytism by another student. There are extremely significant differences between the willingness to adopt all the proposed reactions, except between trying 'to ignore him/her' and trying 'to convince him/her that he is wrong', between which there is no significant difference. The 'reaction' with the 'highest level of approval' is to listen without being influenced: only 9% of the students in Hamburg and 8% in NRW state that they 'would never react like that', while 65% and 64%

---

31 See for some explicative remarks footnote 8.

state that this would be exactly their reaction. The attempt to 'discuss with him/her about his/her opinions" is the reaction with the next highest level of approval: only 12% and 15% 'would never react like that', while 48% and 46% consider it to be exactly their reaction. The reactions with the 'third highest level of approval' are to 'try to ignore him/her' and to 'try to convince him that she/he is wrong': only about 20% of the students consider this to be exactly their reaction, while about 40% 'would never react like that'. The reaction with the 'lowest level of approval' is to try to explain that 'one's own opinions about religion are the best ones': the majority in Hamburg and NRW alike state that they 'would never react like that'.

Table 15:   Dealing with proselytism (percentages)

Imagine that a pupil of a different religious faith wants to convince you that his/her religion is the best one. How do you react?	That's exactly my reaction		That could be my reaction		I would never react like that	
	HH	NRW	HH	NRW	HH	NRW
I try to ignore him/her	21	20	43	41	36	39
I try to discuss with him/her about his/her opinions	48	46	40	39	12	15
I try to convince him/her that s/he is wrong	22	23	37	36	41	41
I try to explain that my own opinions about religion are the best ones.	16	23	28	27	56	50
I listen but their views do not influence me.	65	64	26	28	9	8

Table 16 gives the frequencies of some statements for students in Hamburg and NRW with regard to the 'possibilities of living together'. The vast majority of students in Hamburg and NRW at least 'agree' that 'respecting other religions helps to cope with differences' (68% in both states) and at least disagree that they 'don't like people from other religions …' (82% and 80%). With respect to the other statements there are about 40% of the students who 'neither agree or disagree', however 42% and 48% at least agree that 'disagreement on religious issues leads to conflict', while only 15% and 10% at least disagree. On the other hand 16% and 25% at least 'agree' that 'people with strong religions can not live together', while 43% and 34% at least disagree.

Table 16:   Possibilities of living together (percentages)

When discussing how people of different worldviews and religions can live together, your peers have made following statements. How far do you agree?	strongly agree		agree		neither agree or disagree		disagree		strongly disagree	
	HH	NRW	HH	NRW	HH	NRW	HH	NRW	HH	NRW
"Disagreement on religious issues leads to conflicts."	10	11	32	37	41	41	10	6	5	4
"Respecting the religion of others helps to cope with differences."	29	25	39	43	27	25	2	5	2	2
"I don't like people from other religions and do not want to live together with them."	1	3	4	4	13	13	21	28	61	52
"People with different strong religious views cannot live together."	4	7	12	18	40	41	25	21	18	13

The only significant differences between the federal states occur with respect to the statement 'people with strong ... views ...' with students in NRW tending to agree more to it ($\rho=-0.106$, $p<0.001$). However, students to whom religion is more important tend to agree less that 'disagreement on religious issues leads to conflict' ($\rho=0.121$, $p<0.001$). Students to whom religion is more important ($\rho=-0.212$, $p<0.001$), girls ($\rho=-0.130$, $p<0.001$) and students from schools with a 'lower education level' ($\rho=0.111$, $p<0.001$) tend to agree more that 'respecting the religion of others helps to cope with differences'[32]. Boys ($\rho=0.183$, $p<0.001$) and students from schools with a 'lower education level' ($\rho=-0.120$, $p<0.001$) as well as students with 'no religion' tend to agree more that they 'don't like people from other religions'. Students to whom religion is more important ($\rho=0.207$, $p<0.001$) and Muslim students – in NRW also the students who have studied fewer years of religious education ($\rho=0.152$, $p<0.001$) – tend to agree less to the statement that 'people with different strong religious views cannot live together'.

Table 17:　What helps us to live together in peace? (percentages)

There are people from different religions living in every country. What do you think would help them to live together in peace?	Very important		Quite important		Not important		Cannot say	
	HH	NRW	HH	NRW	HH	NRW	HH	NRW
If people share common interests	25	24	51	56	16	14	8	6
If they know about each other's religions	34	33	49	46	12	15	5	7
If they personally know people from different religions	30	25	44	47	18	18	7	10
If they do something together	28	24	46	50	18	17	8	10
If everyone keeps their own religion in private	17	17	29	29	34	35	19	19
If the state has strong laws about the role of religion in society.	10	12	23	22	39	39	28	27

Table 17 gives the frequencies with regard to some 'strategies' to help people of different religions to live together in peace. The vast majority of students, about 70%, in Hamburg and NRW alike, think that it is at least 'quite important' that 'people share common interests', 'know about each other's religion', 'personally know people from different religions' and 'do something together' in order that they live together in peace; 46% in Hamburg and NRW alike think that it is at least 'quite important' for this issue that 'everyone keeps their own religion in private', while 34% and 35% think that this is 'not important'. Only 33% and 34% think that it is at least 'quite important' that 'the state has strong laws ...', while 39% think that it is 'not important'.

There are no significant correlations to the 'federal state' with regard to the items of table 17. With regard to the last two items in table 17, there are no significant differences between students on basis of 'worldview', 'gender' etc. For the other items the largest correlations occur with respect to the 'importance of religion', with students for whom religion is more important agreeing more that for peaceful coexistence it would be important that 'people share common interests' ($\rho=-0.127$, $p<0.001$), 'know about each other's religion'($\rho=-0.305$, $p<0.001$), 'know personally people from different religions' ($\rho=-0.229$, $p<0.001$) and 'do

---

32　Since there are cross-correlations between the 'importance of religion' and gender and school type, we mention only the partial correlation coefficients with 'importance of religion' as 'control variable'. Correlation to the migration background and differences between the religious groups prove to be spurious, only caused by cross-correlations to 'importance of religion'.

something together' ($\rho=-0.192$, $p<0.001$). Correlations to 'gender', 'migration background' and differences between the worldview groups prove to be generally spurious and only caused by cross correlations between these variables and the 'importance of religion'.

2.3.2 Data interpretation

Students share common views on the preconditions of peaceful coexistence in impressive numbers. It is most remarkable to see for example that 61% in Hamburg and 62% in NRW at least 'agree' with the statement that learning about different religions helps to 'to understand others and live peacefully with them'. Roughly speaking more than 70% in both states would regard the following preconditions as important for a peaceful social cohesion: sharing common interests, knowledge about each other's religion, personal contact and encounters. Students also tend to vote very clearly with regard to aspects of personal respect towards others. On the item: 'I don't like people from other religions and do not want to live together with them' there is a clear tendency of disapproval with 82% in Hamburg and 80% in NRW who at least 'disagree'.

Considerable majorities in Hamburg and NRW alike agree that learning about different religions helps to understand 'others and live peacefully with them', 'to understand the history of one's own country and of Europe', 'to gain a better understanding of current events' and to develop their own point of view. Most of the students in NRW and a considerable minority in Hamburg also agree that learning about religions helps them 'to develop moral values'. The majority of the students in both states disagree that 'without religion the world would be a better place', about the majority agrees that 'religion belongs to private life' and disagrees that 'religion is a source of aggressiveness' and that 'religious people are less tolerant'.

It is also worthwhile to emphasize that students are generally positive about the significance of talking about religion. The majority of the students in both states agree that for them talking about religion is 'interesting because people have different views', that it 'helps' them to shape their own views and 'to understand others'. Likewise the majority disagrees that 'talking about religion is embarrassing' and that it 'only leads to disagreement'. So we can conclude that religion is not a 'non-issue' in conversations among the students.

On other issues a majority position is not that clearly determined. It is conspicuous that regarding items that stress negative aspects of religions such as intolerance on the part of religious people or religion being a source of aggressiveness, there are large numbers of students who would 'neither agree or disagree'.

Although considerable majorities of the students report spending time with people from different religions, and the majority also appreciate the importance of learning about religions in order to live together in peace and discussions about religion 'to understand others', many of the students are more sceptical when it comes to whether talking about religion 'helps to live together with people from different religions' with only 30% of the students agreeing with the last statement and 43% who 'neither agree or disagree'.

There are significant correlations between the personal 'importance of religion' and most of the items regarding the 'role and impact of religion'. This appears to be the most decisive factor for the way the students see the 'role and impact of religion', with students tending to be generally more positive, the more important religion is to them, with respect to the role of religion, the impact of learning and talking about religion for themselves as well as for understanding others and living together in peace, and less critical about religion and religious people etc.

To be more precise, the more important religion is for students, the more they tend to agree that learning about different religions helps 'to understand others and live peacefully with them', 'to understand the history of my country and of Europe', 'to gain a better understanding of current events', to develop their 'own point of view' as well as 'moral values' and to learn about their 'own religion', that talking about religion is 'interesting because people have different views', that it helps them to shape their own views, 'to understand others', to 'live peacefully together with people from different religions' and to 'understand better what is going on in the world'; that 'respecting the religion of others helps them to cope with differences', that for living together in peace it would be important that 'people share common interests', 'know about each other's religion', 'know personally people from different religions' and 'do something together'. The same time they agree less that they 'talk about how stupid religion is ...', that 'talking about religion is embarrassing' and 'only leads to disagreement', that 'religious people are less tolerant towards others', that 'without religion the world would be a better place', that 'religion belongs to private life' and it would be 'a source of aggressiveness'; that 'disagreement on religious issues leads to conflict' and that 'people with different strong religious views cannot live together'.

What is true for the students who consider religion more important is also true for girls compared to boys and Muslim students compared to Christian students compared to students with 'no religion'. However, there are also correlations between gender and 'worldview' and the 'importance of religion', with girls considering religion personally more important than boys and Muslims considering it more important than Christians, who again consider it more important than students with 'no religion'. Partial correlation analyses suggest that most of the respective correlations to gender and to 'worldview' are only spurious.

3. Comparison with the results of the qualitative study

When comparing the results of the quantitative study presented here to those of the qualitative study of the REDCo project (see Knauth et al., 2008), one has to keep in mind on one hand that the quantitative questionnaire was developed on the basis of the results of the qualitative study with the aim to test or verify the main results of the qualitative study on a broader basis, and on the other hand that the qualitative surveys in Hamburg as well as in NRW already included considerable numbers of students (143 and 174).

Speaking in general terms, the first results of the quantitative study in Hamburg and NRW presented here partly complement and partly confirm the findings of the qualitative studies which we conducted in 2006 in the two states (see Knauth, 2008 and Jozsa, 2008). Comparing the two qualitative studies, many similarities between the two states become obvious. The quantitative study confirms this impression: comparing the general tendency of attitudes and views of students in Hamburg and NRW, there are far more similarities than differences. There are some significant differences between Hamburg and NRW, which are sometimes remarkable; however, the general picture of the views of the students is quite similar in both states. They are aware of the relevance of religious plurality, they appreciate the potentials of this plurality and they like to deal with it. The only remarkable difference concerns the preferred religious education model, which was already one of the main differences revealed by the qualitative studies.

Students in Hamburg and NRW are familiar with a pluralistic setting in terms of religious and cultural backgrounds in school; although the plurality of social relations tends to slightlydecrease outside school, it remains at a surprisingly high level. Despite their proclaimed experiences with heterogeneity inside and outside school, students prefer to socialise with friends who have same views about religion. This phenomenon also could be found in the qualitative analysis: even though they are used to heterogeneous settings students tend to prefer commonly shared views and attitudes. Is this an indication that there is a kind of avoidance of difference when it comes to closer relations between students, as we concluded in our qualitative studies?

However, students in Hamburg and NRW tend to appreciate this pluralistic setting; and the majority of them also favour that religion should have a place in it. There is only a small minority of about 10% which would reject religion in general as nonsense. It is, secondly, not too surprising that a considerable majority of students also tend to hold positive views about the potentials of learning with regard to religions in school. Knowledge about religions, but also communication about religion and topics dealing with religion and society, are appreciated. This finding is coherent with a strong acceptance of other people who believe. Tolerance is not a critical issue to students in Hamburg and NRW.

It is likewise a confirmation of the findings of the qualitative analysis that the students in Hamburg and NRW favour the religious education model they are used to: 73% of the students in Hamburg are in favour of a model of religious education where all students are taught together irrespective of their religious background, and only 8% are against such a model. On the other hand this model is only approved by 22% of the students in NRW, whereas 50% of the students are against such a model. However, the approval of the students in Hamburg for the existing model is much higher than the approval of the students in NRW for the existing confessional model there. This result is also underlined by the positions of the students in Hamburg compared to NRW with regard to a confessional-cooperative model of religious education where religious education is taught 'sometimes together and sometimes in groups according to which religions students belong to': only 17% of the students in Hamburg are in favour of such a model while 56% reject it, whereas 32% of the students NRW are in favour of such a model, and only 34% reject it.

If it is true that the students in Hamburg and NRW on the one hand are in favour of the religious education model they are used to while on the other hand they generally share the same views regarding religious plurality in school and society, a new perspective has to be developed in Germany regarding the impact of religious education on peoples' attitudes about religious plurality.

Besides finding remarkably high similarities between the positions of students in Hamburg and NRW, another somewhat surprising result that calls for a deeper analysis, critical reflection and further discussion, needs to be mentioned here. It concerns the conspicuously high percentage of students who claimed to neither agree nor disagree when it comes to questions dealing with conflictive or problematic aspects of religion, such as: religious people are less tolerant towards others; religion is a source of aggressiveness, etc. Between 30% and 40% of the students did not clearly express either approval or disapproval on the question whether religious issues could lead to conflicts. This can be interpreted as an expression of realistic as well as balanced views on the issues discussed. Rather than an indication of indifference it could be concluded that students are quite aware of the ambivalent effects of religion on people's attitudes and social cohesion, which would be in line with findings of the qualitative studies regarding the societal dimension of religion. Students in the qualitative studies in Hamburg and in NRW clearly formulate preconditions for a peaceful coexistence of people with different religions. Their views are far from naive; instead, they indicate the problems but also express the wish to overcome the potential difficulties in order to establish peaceful and harmonious relations between people of different religions.

General reflections

Generally we see a lot of common ground with the findings in surveys such as the Shell Youth Surveys (Deutsche Shell 2000; 2006), the Religionsmonitor (Bertelsmann-Stiftung 2007) or the in-depth study on youth in Europe carried out by a consortium led by Ziebertz & Kay (2006). This is true for the general affirmation of the positive views of youngsters towards religious heterogeneity throughout Europe (Ziebertz & Kay 2006 b, p. 256) and in Germany (Ziebertz 2006, Krech 2007). Our research patterns allows to direct our attention to the three fields of personal appreciation of religious diversity, the possibilities of schools coping with religious heterogeneity and the overall question how religions are seen in their potential for dialogue and conflict.

The general trend with regard to our sample in Hamburg and NRW is quite clear: religious plurality is part of the daily experience of pupils. They have personal encounters with classmates of different backgrounds, more in school than in their free time after school. Many of them speak about religious issues at least once a month, although this topic is not a hot issue in the exchanges of youngsters in their free time. The relevance of the school cannot be overestimated when we look into our results. There are extremely positive answers to items like: "At school, I learn to have respect for everyone, whatever their religion" (see above table 9). Being aware of the fact that religious plurality at school is experienced more strongly in Hamburg and that the models of religious education are quite different in the two federal states of Germany, we see only one truly major difference between the pupils' views in NRW and Hamburg: They are mostly in favour of their own respective models of religious education. In NRW, they favour a separate confessional structure of religious education, and in Hamburg they even more clearly favour an integrated religious education for all. This is evidently due to the power of the structural setting. This poses a challenge for conceptualisation of religious education. In addition, it could be worthwhile to further develop the perspective which is evidently attractive for the pupils in both federal states: the cooperative-confessional model.

An overwhelmingly clear answering pattern is found, with respect to the views of youngsters concerning religious heterogeneity and the role the school is able to play. We refer to the results above, where a clear majority in Hamburg as well as in NRW is of the opinion that "learning about different religions helps to understand others and live peacefully with them" (see above table 13). This is also reflected in the answers to the items on "possibilities of living together". Here we see that, although students are also aware of possible conflicts caused by religions, there is a clear vote in favour of respect for other religions in order to cope with differences (see above table 17). But there are enough reasons for further research, e.g. in view of the above-mentioned high abstention rates on questions about the negative aspects of religions, future models and structures of religious education in German schools, and a possible correlation of religiosity and social background (see above data explication of table 11).

4.   Conclusions

In this last part, we will first try to derive some conclusions from our findings and interpretations with regard to some general questions: 'what role does religion play in students' life?', 'how do students see religion in school and the impact of religion in education?' and 'how do students consider the impact of religions: do they contribute more to dialogue or more to conflict?' in order to answer finally the question: 'what role can religion in education play concerning the way students perceive religious diversity'?

We close this article by considering the hypotheses of our overall REDCo research concerning 'tolerance' and 'dialogue on religious issues':

– "Religious students are less tolerant than non-religious students."
– "Religious students are less open to dialogue on religious issues than non-religious students."
– "Students who have encountered religious diversity in education are more tolerant."
– "Students who have encountered religious diversity in education are more open to dialogue on religious issues."
– "Students who have personally encountered religious diversity are more tolerant."
– "Students who have personally encountered religious diversity are more open to dialogue on religious issues."

Role of religion in students' life

Our findings suggest that for the majority of students in Hamburg and in NRW, religion is a topic they consider worthwhile thinking and talking about. It seems that irrespective of personal religious affiliation and of the role students assign to religion in their personal life, religion is a topic of discussions and regarded as a factor that is taken into account in social relationships: in the family, with friends, and in school.

For the vast majority of students, religion is inseparably related to diversity insofar as they are confronted in school and in their spare time with young people of different religions. Students are familiar with a pluralistic setting in terms of religious backgrounds; although the plurality of social relations tends to slightly decrease outside school, the number of students who claim to 'spend time' with young people of a different religion is surprisingly large. Students are thus not only used to religious diversity but also experience it in personal relations.

However, it has to be taken into consideration that there is a tendency to be with friends who have the same views about religion: the majority of the students state that most of their friends have the same views about religion. There seems thus to be a gap between a more general appreciation of diversity and the actual social contacts that tend to be characterised by a higher level of homogeneity than that represented in their social environment for the majority of the students.

Religion in school and the impact of religion in education

The majority of students in Hamburg and NRW agree that they learn about different religions as well as to have respect for everyone irrespective of their religion at school and that they get the opportunity to discuss religions from different perspectives. Again, the majority believe that learning about different religions at school helps them to live together peacefully. Almost the majority also believes that learning about different religions at school helps them to understand current events, and they consider religions as an important and interesting topic at school. On the other hand, the majority of students disagree that learning about religions would cause conflicts in the classroom and that they have problems showing their views about religion openly in school. Also, the majority in Hamburg and almost the majority in NRW disagree that students risk being mocked if they show their religious belief openly.

Students are also open with respect to considering religious issues in school: the majority of students in both states that agree that religious dietary laws should be taken into account in school, that students can be absent from school 'for religious festivals' and that they should be able to wear 'discreet religious symbols'. With regard to 'more visible' religious symbols, the views are more mixed. Only about a third seems to be inclined to forbid students to wear them outright. However, some suggestions that contradict their views of the role of the school are rejected: only about every fourth respondent would excuse students from taking some classes for religious reasons.

Again, the majority of the students questioned in both states favour an optional religious education and the same time regard school as a place where religion as well as religious education should have a place. For the majority of students, the aim of religious education is providing objective knowledge about different religions as well as helping students to understand what religions teach, learning about the importance of religions for dealing with problems in society and learning to communicate about religious issues. One could say that they are interested in a historical, critical, sociological as well as an ethical 'outsider perspective' as well as in the 'insider perspective' of the 'subjective' believer. However, only a minority would go so far as to regard guiding students towards a religious belief as a task of religious education.

Impact of religions on dialogue and conflict

Considerable majorities in Hamburg and NRW alike agree that learning about different religions helps them to understand others and live peacefully with them, helps them to understand history, to gain a better understanding of current events as well as to develop their own point of view. The majority of the students in both states disagree that without religion, the world would be a better place, about the majority agrees that 'religion belongs to private life' and disagrees that religion is a source of aggressiveness or that religious people are less tolerant.

The majority of the students in both states also agree that for them, talking about religion is 'interesting because people have different views', that it 'helps' them to shape their own views and 'to understand others'. Likewise, the majority disagrees that they talk with friends about 'how stupid religion is and what cruelties are carried out in its name', that 'talking about religion is embarrassing' and that it 'only leads to disagreement'.

The vast majority of students in both states think that respecting other religions helps them to cope with differences and would not say that they do not like people from other religions. They think that it is important for peaceful coexistence that people share common interests, know about each other's religion, personally know people from other religions and do things together.

Students are generally positive about the impact of exchanges about religion. The majority of them do not feel embarrassed to do so and put trust in the positive outcomes of religious conversations: one gets to know different views, one's own view is improved and it helps a better understanding of people. That is why we concluded that religion is not a non-issue in conversations among students. Most of them are, though, sceptical that talks about religion help them to live together in peace with people of different religions.

Role of religion in education

As the overall conclusion of our analysis on the role of religion in students' life we can say that religion seems to be widely considered a positive factor and an essential aspect of diversity. Concerning the role of religion in education we can conclude that school is regarded by the majority of students as a space where religion should have its place. Students should be free to express their opinions with regard to religion and show their religious conviction in their school life and the school should take the religious convictions of their students into consideration.

However, most of the students do no regard school as an appropriate forum for 'religious life': only small minorities think that religious service, i.e. worship, could be a part of school life or that school should provide opportunities for students to pray. School seems to be regarded as a place of learning, of impartial learning one could say. This also applies to religion: the view of the students with regard to religion in school in general and in religious education in particular could be called 'knowledge based': the school should provide knowledge about different religions and help them to develop abilities to communicate about religions, to understand their teachings and the role they play in society. The knowledge they want is first of all an 'objective knowledge' that we can presume to include a critical and historical perspective on religion, but also to provide them with information about what the respective religions themselves teach. Religious education for most of the students is not a place to be introduced to a specific religion, not even in NRW where a confessional model of religious education prevails and is favoured by most of the students there.

It is however puzzling that the attitudes of the students with regard to most items of our questioning seem to be not only independent from the federal state, and consequently from the model of religious education the students attend, but also from their current attendance of religious education as well as from the length of their attendance of religious education[33].

'Tolerance' and 'openness to dialogue on religious issues'

Some of the above mentioned hypotheses regarding 'tolerance' and 'openness to dialogue' can not be answered in a definite way with respect to our sample. The reason is that the hypotheses are formulated in a general way; the proposed concepts of 'tolerance' and 'openness to dialogue on religious issues' are 'open' on the other side, in other words their antitheses are not defined. The editors proposed the items 55, 76, 77, 83, 103–106 as indicators for 'tolerance' and the items 34, 78, 87–102 as indicators for 'openness to dialogue on religious issues'; the items 37, 38, 126 and 127 were regarded as referring to the 'personal religious background'; the items 1–5 as referring to the diversity of experience with regard to religion in education; and items 68–75 as referring to the personal experiences with religious diversity[34]. We will restrict ourselves, with respect to some of the hypotheses, to reflections and comments with regard to the differences between the envisaged groups with regard to items proposed as indicators.

---

33 What is the reason for this generally low impact of religious education respectively of the model of religious education on issues concerning religion in school as well as dialogue and conflict is however difficult to answer in a definite way without further research. It could be that the general attitudes to most of the issues raised in our questionnaire are built 'outside' the religious education classes. It might be that the general teachings and attitudes adopted in school in general or in the society at large, have more impact on the issues raised, then the teaching in religious education. But it could also be that irrespective of the specific model the teaching in religious education concerning most of the issues raised are in line with the attitudes and the general teaching in school and reflect general trends in society in general.

34 For the items corresponding to these numbers see the questionnaire in the annex. Our first attempt when dealing with these hypotheses was to do a confirmatory factor analysis with regard to the items proposed as indicators for 'tolerance' and 'openness to dialogue', restricting the factors to two. However this analysis 'failed', the emerging factors could not be regarded as referring to 'tolerance' respectively 'openness to dialogue' in a coherent way. We decided thus to try to answer the hypotheses simply considering and reflecting upon the results of correlation analyses with regard to the items proposed as indicators for the different issues by the editors.

'Tolerance' and the 'importance of religion'

Students tend to agree significantly more that they 'respect other people who believe' and that 'respecting the religion of others helps to cope with differences', the more important religion is to them. On the other side students tend more to think that 'without religion the world would be a better place', that 'people with different strong religious views cannot live together' and that 'religious people are less tolerant towards others', the less important religion is to them. At the same time students have a greater tendency 'to prefer to go around with young people who have the same religious background' at school as well as in their spare time, the more important religion is to them, and to state that they would 'try to convince him that (s)he is wrong' and 'to explain him/her that my own opinions about religion are the best ones' if a student of a different religious faith wants to convince him/her that his/her religion is the best one, the more important religion is to them. The correlations between the 'importance of religion' and the statement 'I don't like people of other religions ...' are significant but very low, however with people for whom religion is more important tending to disagree more with the statement. However the vast majority of the students – around 80% – at least disagree with the statement, no matter what their position on religion is.

Summing up it seems that students show more 'respect' and consider 'respect' related to religion as more important, the more important religion is to them. Students tend to prefer more to 'socialise' with students with the same views about religion and to be more 'convinced' about their views about religion – being ready to go so far as to try to convince others that the own views about religion are 'the best ones' – the more important religion is to them. At the same time students to whom religion is less important tend to be more 'critical' towards religion and religious people, tending to blame 'religion' as being responsible for problems in the world and considering a strong 'religious belief' an impediment of living together.

'Openness to dialogue on religious issues' and the 'importance of religion'

Students for whom religion is more important can be regarded as more open to 'dialogue on religious issues' in so far as students for whom religion is more important also tend to agree more that: students should learn at school to 'be able to talk and communicate about religious issues'; that they 'like to know what my best fried thinks about religion'; that 'talking about religion is interesting because people have different views'; that 'it helps to shape my own views'; 'to understand others'; 'to live peacefully together with people from different religions'; 'to understand better what is going on in the world'; that they agree more that they 'try to discuss with him/her about his/her opinions', if a students tries to convince them that his/hers views about religion are the best ones.

However 'openness to dialogue' might seem in this context to be a very 'pretentious' term. The findings suggest actually that students also tend more to like to talk and communicate about religion, and appreciate the potentially positive outcomes of 'talking about religion', the more important religion is for them. This should be not so surprising; the same as it is not surprising that students tend to agree more that 'religion doesn't interest me at all – we have more important things to talk', that they 'don't know much about religion and thus I can't have an opinion' and that 'talking about religion is boring', the less important religion is to them.

'Tolerance' and 'religious diversity in education'

Although it might be difficult to conclude that students who have experienced religious diversity in education are more tolerant in a general way, one could at least claim that the data might reveal such a tendency in so for as the following significant correlations apply: the more students agree to the statement that they learn at school to 'respect everyone ...', the more they tend to agree that they 'respect other people who believe', that 'respecting the religion of others helps to cope with differences'' and the less they agree that 'without religion the world would be a better place' and that 'people with strong religions can not live together'. Likewise the more students agree that 'they have opportunities to discuss religious issues from different perspectives', the less they tend to agree that 'without religion the world would be a better place', and that 'respecting the religion of others helps to cope with difficulties'; with respect to the last statement there is also a significant correlation with getting knowledge about different religions – the more students agree that at school they get knowledge about different religions, the more they tend to agree that 'respecting the religion of others helps to cope with difficulties'.

'Openness to dialogue' and 'religious diversity in education'

There are a lot of significant correlations between the items regarded as indicators for 'openness to dialogue' and those regarded as indicators for experience with 'religious diversity in education', with students who agree more that they 'get knowledge about different religions', 'learn to respect everyone ...', and 'get opportunities to discuss religious issues form different perspectives' at school, tending generally to be more 'open' for dialogue on religious issues, so that we conclude, without going into detail, that students who have encountered religious diversity in education are more open to dialogue on religious issues.

'Tolerance' and 'personal encounter with religious diversity'

Students who have 'friends who belong to different religions' and who 'spend time with young people who have a different religions background', especially 'after school', tend to agree significantly more that they 'respect other people who believe', and less that they prefer at school as well as after school 'to go around with young people with the same religious background' as themselves, that 'they do not like people of other religions and do not want to live together with them', and that 'people with strong religious views can not live together'. Summing up, it seems that students who have personally encountered religious diversity tend to be more 'tolerant' with respect to other religions.

'Openness to dialogue' and 'personal encounter with religious diversity'

There are a lot of significant correlations between the items regarded as indicators for 'openness to dialogue', and for having or not having 'friends who belong to different religions', and for the items 'after school' and 'at school I spend time with young people who have a different religions background'; with students who have friends of a different religion, and students who spend time with young people of a different religion in school as well as after school, tending to be more 'open' for dialogue on religious issues, so that we conclude, without going into detail, that students who have personally encountered religious diversity are more open for dialogue on religious issues.

References

Bertelsmann Stiftung (2007): *Religionsmonitor 2008*. Gütersloh: Gütersloher Verlagshaus.

Bertram-Troost, G., Ipgrave, J., Jozsa, D.-P. & Knauth, T. (2008b). European Comparison. Dialogue and conflict, in: T. Knauth, D.-P. Jozsa, G. Bertram-Troost & J. Ipgrave (Eds.), *Encountering Religious Pluralism in School and Society – A Qualitative Study of Teenage Perspectives in Europe.* Muenster: Waxmann, pp. 405–411.

Council of Europe (2008). *White Paper on Intercultural Dialogue "Living Together as Equals in Dignity"*, launched by the Council of European Ministers of Foreign Affairs at their 118 th Ministerial Session (Strasbourg, 7 May 2008). Strasbourg Cedex: Council of Europe.

Deutsche Shell (Ed.) (2000). *Jugend 2000.* 13. Shell Jugendstudie, 2 Vol. Opladen: Leske + Budrich.

Dietz, G. (2008): Konfessionell segregierter Religionsunterricht in einer multikulturellen Gegenwartsgesellschaft? Eine spanische Perspektive, in: W. Weisse (Ed.), *Dialogischer Religionsunterricht in Hamburg. Positionen, Analysen und Perspektiven im Kontext Europas.* Muenster: Waxmann, pp. 167–174.

Europaeische Kommission (2008). Diskriminierung in der Europäischen Union. Wahrnehmungen, Erfahrungen und Haltungen. *Eurobarometer Spezial 296*, available online: http://ec.europa.eu/public_opinion/archives/ebs/ebs_296_de.pdf, first accessed: October 15, 2008.

European Commission (2003). Public opinion in the candidate countries. Youth in new Europe. *Eurobarometer 2003.1.*

European Commission (2007). Intercultural dialogue in Europe. *Flash Eurobarometer 217*, available online: http://ec.europa.eu/public_opinion/flash/fl_217_sum_en.pdf, first accessed: October 15, 2008.

European Monitoring Centre on Racism and Xenophobia (Ed.) (2005). *Majorities' Attitudes Towards Minorities: Key Findings form the Eurobarometer and the European Social Survey.* Vienna: EUMC.

Feige, A., Gennerich, C. (2008). *Lebensorientierungen Jugendlicher. Alltagsethik, Moral und Religion in der Wahnehmung von Berufsschülerinenn und -schülern in Deutschland.* Muenster: Waxmann.

Hasenclever, A. (2003). Geteilte Werte – Gemeinsamer Frieden? Überlegungen zu zivilisierenden Kraft von Religionen und Glaubensgemeinschaften, in: H. Küng & D. Senghaas (Eds.), *Friedenspolitik, Ethische Grundlagen internationaler Beziehungen.* München: Piper, S. 288–318. available online: http://ec.europa.eu/public_opinion/archives/cceb/2003/2003.1_youth_analytical_report_en.pdf, first accessed: October 15, 2008.

Jackson, R. (2008). Internationale Trends und lokale Vorgehensweisen in der Religionspädagogik. Entwicklungen in England und in Hamburg, in: W. Weisse (Ed.), *Dialogischer Religionsunterricht in Hamburg. Positionen, Analysen und Perspektiven im Kontext Europas.* Muenster: Waxmann, pp. 189–199.

Jackson, R., Miedema, S., Weisse, W. & Willlaime, J.-P. (Eds.) (2007). *Religion and Education in Europe: Developments, Contexts and Debates.* Muenster: Waxmann.

Jozsa, D.-P. (2007). Islam and Education in Europe, with special reference to Austria, England, France, Germany and the Netherlands, in: R. Jackson, S. Miedema, W. Weisse & J.-P. Willaime (Eds.), *Religion and Education in Europe.* Muenster: Waxmann, pp. 67–86.

Jozsa, D.-P. (2008). Religious Education in North Rhine-Westphalia: Views and Experiences of Students, in: T. Knauth, D.-P. Jozsa, G. Bertram-Troost & J. Ipgrave (Eds.), *Encountering Religious Pluralism in School and Society, A Qualitative Study of Teenage Perspectives in Europe.* Muenster: Waxmann, pp. 173–206.

Jozsa, D.-P. & Friederici, M. (2008): European Comparison: Social Dimension of Religion, in: T. Knauth, D.-P. Jozsa, G. Bertram-Troost & J. Ipgrave (Eds.), *Encountering Religious Pluralism in School and Society – A Qualitative Study of Teenage Perspectives in Europe Europe.* Muenster: Waxmann, pp. 389–369.

Knauth, T. (2007). Religious Education in Germany – Contribution to Dialogue or Source of Conflict? A Historical and Contextual Analysis of its Development since the 1960s, in: R. Jackson, S. Miedema, W. Weisse & J.-P. Willaime (Eds.), *Religion and Education in Europe.* Muenster: Waxmann, pp. 243–266.

Knauth, T. (2008). "Better together than apart": Religion in School and Lifeworld of Students in Hamburg, in: T. Knauth, D.-P. Jozsa, G. Bertram-Troost & J. Ipgrave (Eds.), *Encountering Religious Pluralism in School and Society – A Qualitative Study of Teenage Perspectives in Europe Europe*. Muenster: Waxmann, pp. 207–245.

Knauth, T., Jozsa, D.-P., Bertram-Troost, G. & Ipgrave, J. (Eds.)(2008). *Encountering Religious Pluralism in School and Society – A Qualitative Study of Teenage Perspectives in Europe.* Muenster: Waxmann.

Kozyrev, F. (2008). Der Hamburger Ansatz des Religionsunterrichts. Eine Betrachtung aus russischer Sicht, in: W. Weisse (Ed.), *Dialogischer Religionsunterricht in Hamburg. Positionen, Analysen und Perspektiven im Kontext Europas*. Muenster: Waxmann, pp. 201–212.

Krech, V. *(2007)*. Exklusivität, Bricolage und Dialogbereitschaft. Wie die Deutschen mit religiöser Vielfalt umgehen, in: Bertelsmann Stiftung (2007)*: Religionsmonitor 2008*. Gütersloh: Gütersloher Verlagshaus, pp. 33–43.

Peukert, H. (2005). Identität, in: P. Eicher (Ed.), *Neues Handbuch theologischer Grundbegriffe (Vol. 2)*. Muenchen: Koesel, pp. 184–192.

Ricoeur, P. (2006). *Wege der Anerkennung. Erkennen, Wiedererkennen, Anerkanntsein*. Frankfurt am Main: Suhrkamp.

Shell Deutschland Holding (Ed.)(2006). *Jugend 2006. Eine pragmatische Generation unter Druck*. 15. Shell Jugendstudie. Frankfurt am Main: Fischer Taschenbuch Verlag.

Simon, H.A. (1985). Spurious Correlation: A Causal Interpretation, in: H.M. Blalock, (Ed.), *Causal Models in the Social Sciences* (Chicago, Aldine), 7–21 [reprinted from the *Journal of the American Statistical Association* 49 (1954): pp. 467–479].

Skeie, G. (2008). Dialog und Identität. Einige Gedanken zum Hamburger Modell aus norwegischer Sicht, in: W. Weisse (Ed.), *Dialogischer Religionsunterricht in Hamburg. Positionen, Analysen und Perspektiven im Kontext Europas*. Muenster: Waxmann, pp. 213–216.

Ter Avest, I., Miedema, S., Bakker, C. (2008). Getrennt und zusammen leben in den Niederlanden, oder: Die Bedeutung des interreligiösen Lernens, in: W. Weisse (Ed.), *Dialogischer Religionsunterricht in Hamburg. Positionen, Analysen und Perspektiven im Kontext Europas*. Muenster: Waxmann, pp. 179–188.

Vogt, W. P. (1993). *Dictionary of Statistics and Methodology: A Nontechnical Guide for the Social Sciences*. Newbury Park: Sage.

Weisse, W. (2007). The European Research Project on Religion and Education 'REDCo'. An Introduction, in: R. Jackson, S. Miedema, W. Weisse & J.-P. Willaime (Eds.), *Religion and Education in Europe: Developments, Contexts and Debates*. Muenster: Waxmann, pp. 9–25.

Weisse, W. (Ed.) (2008). *Dialogischer Religionsunterricht in Hamburg. Positionen, Analysen und Perspektiven im Kontext Europas*. Muenster: Waxmann.

Willaime, J.-P. (2008). Bemerkungen zum "Religionsunterricht für alle" in Hamburg. Eine französische Sicht, in: W. Weisse (Ed.), *Dialogischer Religionsunterricht in Hamburg. Positionen, Analysen und Perspektiven im Kontext Europas*. Muenster: Waxmann, pp. 175–177.

Ziebertz, H.-G. (2006). Germany: belief in the Idea of a higher reality, in: Ziebertz, H.-G., Kay, W.K. (Eds.): *Youth in Europe II. An international empirical study about religiosity*. Berlin: LIT Verlag, pp. 58–80.

Ziebertz, H.-G. (2007). Gibt es einen Tradierungsbruch? Befunde zur Religiosität der jungen Generation, in: Bertelsmann Stiftung: *Religionsmonitor 2008*. Gütersloh: Gütersloher Verlagshaus, pp. 44–53.

Ziebertz, H.-G. & Kay, W.K. (Eds.)(2006a). *Youth in Europe II: An international empirical Study about Religiosity*. Berlin: LIT Verlag.

Ziebertz, H.-G., Kay, W.K. (2006b). Religiosity of Youth in Europe – a comparative Analysis, in: Ziebertz, H.-G., Kay, W.K. (Eds.), *Youth in Europe II. An international empirical study about religiosity*. Berlin: LIT Verlag, pp. 246–265.

Geir Skeie

Religion in School – a Comparative Study of Hamburg and North Rhine-Westphalia. Commenting Chapter from a Norwegian Perspective

Introduction

The two countries of Germany and Norway have many similarities in terms of religion and education, in spite of differences in terms of how religious education is organised. The similarities do provide opportunities for fruitful discussion, as also was done in the comparative article based on the REDCo qualitative study (Skeie and Weisse, 2008). Some of the same issues appear in the following comments on the German quantitative study.

Some striking observations

The fact that the German study is written as a comparison between two different contexts, one being Hamburg and the other North Rhine-Westphalia (NRW), makes it particularly valuable. Seen within the framework of the entire REDCo quantitative study it shows that different local or regional contexts may also give different pictures of religion in young people's lives and in school. This is in itself an important result, because it reminds us that we are not necessarily getting data about national trends, but about certain local settings. The data on religious diversity in the life of students show that the contact and experience with diversity is more prominent in Hamburg than in NRW. When it comes to religion in school, there is a stronger and more widespread support for learning about religion as a positive contribution to living together in Hamburg, than in NRW, where some more pupils are anxious that this may lead to conflict. Also more pupils in NRW than in Hamburg accept religion in school as a way of being guided towards religious belief, and the same goes for developing moral values.

Having said this, there are still more similarities than differences between the two German contexts. In general there is a relatively high degree of general interest and positive attitude towards religion, and the religiously committed seem to be even stronger in their commitment. Only a small minority of the German pupils do not believe in God or some transcendental being, and a considerable minority claim that religion determines their whole life. Also religious practice is quite widespread, such as reading sacred texts, praying, attending

religious events and looking for religion on the internet. In terms of religion in school, the German pupils are quite positive about this and they support the type of religious education they are having. When asked about the content and aims they seem to prefer the teaching to focus on learning about religion, and not to focus too much on existential questions or on the truth-claims of the different religious and world-view traditions.

The similarities between the countries also include the fact that religiously committed pupils are more tolerant towards other religions. This is important in view of the overall research questions.

Beneath the general mean results, there are some striking crosscutting differences in the material, not only related to the different Länder. Muslim students seem to come out with a distinct profile in the study compared with Christian students, but on the other hand this is related to the fact that Muslims find religion to be more important than Christians do. Muslims find family and faith community to be more important to them as information sources about religion, and generally Muslims also talk more about religion with peers, family and religious leaders. They also prefer more to be together with friends from the same religious background. In school they are more in support of liberal rules for carrying religious symbols and towards confessional teaching, but on several issues it turns out that Muslims in Hamburg and NRW do not answer in the same way. This means that the positions of Muslim students should not be generalised.

The last point may also be supported by the fact that occasionally answers from girls differ from boys in the same direction as the answers from Muslims as compared to Christians. Religion is more important to girls than to boys; they use all sources of information about religion more than boys do; and are more liberal towards religious symbols and dietary laws in school. Girls also agree more that learning about religions helps people live peacefully together, even if they are not surer than boys that this will mean avoiding conflicts. When asked about religion in general more boys than girls see the problematic sides, while more girls than boys find it interesting to talk to people with different views on religion.

Possible alternative perspectives

The German study seems to be focused on two main issues in the interpretation of data: the differences between Hamburg and NRW; and the understanding of how Muslim students appear in the material. In both cases differences are shown, while on the other hand these differences are played down in the final analysis. The different Länder are seen as being in the main similar when it comes to attitudes towards religious plurality though their pupils are still supporting different religious education models. This is taken as a sign that 'a new perspective has to be developed in Germany regarding the impact of RE on peoples' attitudes about religious plurality.' It is not clear what this means, but possibly it points in the direction of RE having little influence on pupils' views. This is however may be not so surprising, given the other main issue in interpretation; the understanding of the positions of Muslim students.

Several times through the analysis it is pointed out that statistical analysis is showing the position of Muslims to be not a 'Muslim' position as such, but the position of a differently defined group; those who find religion to be important (or 'very important') in their life. This group is larger among Muslim pupils, than among Christians. In other words, the main difference is not the different positions of Muslims and Christians, but the positions of religiously committed pupils and others. If this is the case, and it is convincingly argued so, this means that positions on religious commitment are mainly developed outside school rather than inside. We should not assume that religious commitment is mainly dependent on religious education, but rather on other, informal or formal ways of socialisation. Based on the German material, it is fair to assume that the main source of influence is the family rather than the religious community. If this line of reasoning holds water, an interesting and challenging problem is to find out more about *why and how* the attitudes towards plurality are influenced through positions on religious commitment. This cannot be done by investigating religious education as such, but by investigating religion through other dimensions of the pupils' lives.

The gender perspective on the material does not point in the direction of strong differences between boys and girls. Still there are issues where they differ, and mainly this means that girls are more positive towards religions, more interested in learning about religion etc. Even if some of these differences are there because girls (like Muslims) find religion to be more important, there are still trends detectable in the material indicating that gender means something. What lies behind these differences we do not know, but one hypothesis could be that gender, as for religion, is socially and culturally constructed mainly in the family and in communication and action together with 'significant others'.

Reflections about Germany and Norway

The main impression when reading the German study is related to the obvious similarities between the two countries as they are appearing in the REDCo quantitative study. This relates to most of the issues mentioned in the first paragraph. Pupils are well acquainted with religious plurality and they want to live together in peace and to avoid conflicts. In both countries the young people are more positive towards this plurality in attitudes than they seem to be in daily life, meaning that they prefer to be together with peers like themselves. Religion in education is mainly seen as learning objective knowledge about religion, and there are some reservations against too high ambitions regarding dialogue and change, as well as against supporting religious belief through RE. With so many similarities it is even easier to point out the differences and the main one has to do with the general attitude towards religion. The German pupils are clearly more interested in religion than the Norwegian ones.

Only a minority of the German pupils do not believe in God or some kind of transcendental being, while this is the position of 40% in Norway. Also the importance of religion is clearly higher in Germany, and the group saying religion is absolutely not important is only half as big in Germany (13%) as it is in Norway (26%). This does not mean that the two samples are all that different in terms of religious pupils. There are about as many pupils declaring their affiliation with Christianity and Islam in the two countries, but 18% claim that religion determines their whole life in the German study, while this is only the position of 7% in Norway. We find the same pattern repeated in religious practice. Almost half of the German students never read sacred texts for themselves, while in Norway this goes for three-quarters. Similar differences are also traceable in questions about praying, attending religious events and also looking for religion on the internet. But if we move from these kinds of religious practice to the more general and open question about whether pupils are thinking about religion or about the meaning of life, responses in the two countries are strikingly similar. The difference between pupils in Norway and Germany therefore concerns their attitudes towards organised religion, not a difference in their preoccupation with existential questions.

In the analysis of the Norwegian questionnaires we have found that the most fruitful background variable seems to be 'importance of religion'. This is also a recurring explanatory variable in the German study. Especially the discussion about Muslim pupils in the German study shows that this can be an important insight. As in Norway, the Muslim pupils in Germany are finding religion more important than Christian pupils. The deeper analysis shows that in several questions where Muslim pupils differ in their answers these differences are not necessarily due to them being Muslims, but rather to the fact that they are in the group finding religion to be important. The same is partly true for the gender dimension, since girls are finding religion more important than boys. It is of particular interest that this features in both countries, because it may point in the direction of insights that may be relevant in several countries. It could indicate that pupils in this age group see themselves as different more in terms of their religious commitment than in terms of commitment to different religions. Since we have little representation of religious groups outside Muslims and Christians in the Norwegian and German sample, we do not know whether this goes for all kinds of religious backgrounds, but it certainly seems to be relevant for Christians, Muslims and non-religious pupils. It also seems that the pupils are not very interested in changing their positions towards religion. In both countries they reject proselytism in a non-confronting way; they listen, but do not want to be influenced. This goes for most of the pupils, whether they are religiously interested or not. In other words, both religious, indifferent and the non-religious pupils have positions they appreciate.

A final common result in Germany and Norway is that on issues related to the impact of religion on society there is a large proportion of the pupils who have difficulties giving a clear answer. Both studies have concluded that this may reflect a very realistic ambivalence which also can be affirmed by other kinds of research; that these are complex questions for all of us.

Reference

Skeie, G. & Weisse, W. (2008). Religion, Education, Dialogue and Conflict: Positions and Perspectives of Students in Germany and Norway, in T. Knauth, D.-P. Jozsa, G. Bertram-Troost & J. Ipgrave (Eds.), *Encountering Religious Pluralism in School and Society. A Qualitative Study of Teenage Perspectives in Europe.* Muenster: Waxmann, pp. 327–338.

Ina ter Avest & Cok Bakker

Response to the German National Report on the REDCo Questionnaire

The REDCo quantitative research project (preceded by qualitative explorative research) focuses on the role of religion in the life of secondary school students aged 14–16 and the possibilities they envisage for living together with people from different ethnic backgrounds and with different (religious or non-religious) worldviews. Barack Obama drew attention to intercultural and interracial background in his keynote speech to the Democratic National Convention in 2004, when he pointed to the importance of international and interreligious heritage in his own upbringing, reminding his listeners that he was born in Honolulu, Hawaii, to a Kenyan father and a white mother from Kansas. He emphasized the influence of education in his personal life as well as in his professional and political career, in which, he said, the power of hope had played a pivotal role. According to Obama, president-elect of the United States (in 2008), hope is 'God's greatest gift'. Obama also spoke of the audacity that, in his eyes, forms an integral part of hope. The title of his address and his book (*The Audacity of Hope, Thoughts on Reclaiming the American Dream*, 2006) highlights an important concept in world religions: the hope that gives people strength in their efforts to live together and to create a human world.

In this paper we elaborate on three aspects of the German report on the quantitative research by the REDCo project. First, we focus on the role of hope, the high positive expectations that the students in the German sample display for the role of knowledge about religion(s). Next, we look at the migration background in the responses. Third, we elaborate on the lack of information on the developmental aspects of identity formation in this REDCo project, paying particular attention to the lack of longitudinal data on religious identity formation. Or in more positive terms: the hints we pick up from the responses with regard to developmental aspects in the reception of religion as either a conflict-promoting factor or a contribution to dialogue. Last but not least, we stress the need to include religious identity formation in the concept of citizenship education in connection with the transformation of European societies.

The German researchers applied correlation analysis to the REDCo data. We will use their findings on 'importance of religion', 'migration' and – since it is a REDCo spearhead – 'gender'.

Importance of religion

As mentioned above, Barack Obama sees hope as God's greatest gift. To Obama, this hope goes hand in hand with audacity. We find no cues for audacity in the responses of the German students in the quantitative research, but we do see a hopeful (!) sign in the (strong) agreement with 'Learning about different religions at school helps us to live together' (HH 59%, NRW 55%). Only 18% and 16% agreed respectively with the contra-statement 'Learning about religions leads to conflicts in the classroom'. According to the students in the German sample, at school they 'get to know about different religions', which, they believe, helps them to live together. Christian students tend to agree more strongly (than Muslim students) with the statement that the school is an institution where knowledge is transmitted about religion(s). It seems that Muslim students feel they do not learn about religion(s) in school. This might be due to the fact that, for Christian students, Islam is a new religion with many new aspects to learn about. Since knowledge about Christianity is possibly not expressed in such explicit terms, Muslim students do not feel that they are gaining new knowledge in RE classes. It is, however, interesting that students in the Hamburg area, who are familiar with the pedagogic strategy of *Religion für Alle* [Religion for All], tend to agree more with the proposition that they learn about different religions in school. As in England, inclusive RE seems to be paying off! Muslim students agree more strongly than the rest that 'Learning about religions leads to conflicts in the classroom'. This may relate to their expectations, an unknown difference that they fear.

In the Dutch sample girls are significantly more in agreement than boys with the statement 'Learning about religion helps us to live together (f = 2.3 versus m = 2.5). Boys and girls both disagree strongly with the contra-statement 'Learning about religions leads to conflicts in the classroom'. A gender difference as well as a difference between religious and non-religious students emerges in the responses to 'Learning about different religions at school helps us to live together' with the strongest agreement from religious students and female students. Learning about religion(s) may indeed help us to live together, but as far as the students are concerned it does not enhance their knowledge about themselves. This is one of the signals we have picked up in connection with the developmental aspects of the reception of religion as a contribution to dialogue or a conflict-promoting factor.

We see another cue for the developmental aspects in the significantly different scores of the German students for the statements about 'gaining knowledge' and 'discussions' in RE classes. It is interesting in relation to the 'learning-about strategy' that a significant difference emerges between agreement with the statement 'At school I get knowledge about different religions' and the statement 'At school we have opportunities to discuss religious issues from different perspectives'. The percentages for the latter statement are remarkably lower than for the former. Students seem to perceive RE classes as places where they gain objective knowledge without actually discussing the topic. These ideas together with the low percentages of students who fear conflict in RE classes highlight the need to explore the interrelatedness of conflict and dialogue in greater depth: conflict being part of dialogue, and dialogue being necessary for coping with conflicts.

Migration

A long footnote is dedicated to the influence of migration on the responses and response patterns of students in the German research population. We quote from the tenth footnote: "It is rather the 'importance of religion' than the religious or migration background, that is decisive for the level of agreement with the above statements" (referring to the items in Table 3). In our view the 'importance of religion' and the 'migrant background' are 'nested variables'. Migrant families – usually with a working class background and sometimes educated young people in the cities – find themselves far from home without the traditional support of their extended families. Building on the cultural and religious traditions of associational life and implicitly encouraged by the negative media coverage in the 'host' countries with regard to 'them' being 'the other', migrants tend to form social support organizations – among which religious communities are not the least influential – and strengthen their ties with their place of origin (see Okafor and Honey, in Honey, 1999, p. 185). To the migrants, cultural organizations and religious communities are 'spaces of dependence' i.e., "those more-or-less localized social relations upon which we depend for the realization of essential interests … for which there are no substitutes elsewhere [and which] define place-specific conditions for our material well-being and our sense of significance" (Howard, 2007, p. 243). For the students in our REDCo research, the family that creates a 'space of dependence' is more meaningful than the religious community, and probably even more a 'space of engagement', i.e., a space in and through which these youngsters construct a network of interlocuted relations with others who have been assigned the same position in the 'host' country and 'situated knowledge' (through the internet) located elsewhere. Together with their peers – 'partners in adversity' – students build new and hybrid identities. For example, in Amsterdam we see young Moroccan Muslim women wearing a headscarf as a sign of their religious commitment when they meet their friends in a bar for a glass of wine (see the article *Halal met een rood wijntje erbij* ['Halal and Red Wine'], Rob Pietersen in the Dutch newspaper *Trouw*, December 4, 2008). The headscarf represents the 'protective wrap', affirming the emotional attachment to (religious) family values and regulations (Kitlyn Tjin A Djie, 2000), the 'red wine' represents the tension between loyalty to the family and solidarity with friends in a changing personal context (Bossormenyi-Nagy and Krasner 1986/2005; Nussbaumm, 2001).

Gender

Gender appears to be a distinctive factor in the importance of religion; the strongest agreement on statements regarding the importance of religion at school and the encounter with the religious 'other' comes from female migrant students. Also, significant correlations are observable between gender and religious activities such as 'praying' and 'thinking about the meaning of life'. The German sample shows extremely significant gender correlations for the statement 'Religion helps me to cope with difficulties'. Remarkably, Muslims tend to agree more with this statement than Christian students. The same applies for the statements 'I respect other people who believe' and 'Religion determines my whole life'. The pattern is similar to the one found in the Dutch sample. Agreement with 'Respecting the religion of others helps to cope with differences' and 'Religion determines my whole life' is significantly stronger among girls than boys (f = 3.2 versus m = 3.4).

There seems to be a shared underlying motive in the significantly different positions taken by girls and Muslim students on some of statements in the quantitative questionnaire. It certainly raises the question of how it is possible that after a third 'wave of female emancipation' girls still exhibit signs of characteristic female behaviour with regard to the importance of religion. What are the societal forces that make girls stick to femininity and seemingly, by consequence, boys stick to masculinity? This point is also made in one of the footnotes in the English report on the quantitative REDCo research: 'Differences between girls and boys in the degree to which they associate with people of different religions or speak with friends about religion might reflect their different patterns of socialization – whether, for example, they spend their break times playing football in larger groups or chatting with a few friends' (English report. P. 13). We will explore the gender differences in each of these countries and comparatively in the eight participating countries in more detail in the D 5.3 report (Ter Avest & Jozsa, 2009).

Gender and identity formation is not only a personal matter; when it come to flexible interaction, it is also is a public matter. Or to put it bluntly: without the encounter with the other in the public domain, there is no personal identity (see Levinas 1969/2003). The encounter between citizens, women and men, in the public domain plays a key role in the development of personal identity. The education of persons as citizens of a multicultural and multi-religious society has been included in the compulsory subject of citizenship in the Dutch curriculum since 2006.

In an interview in the Dutch newspaper *De Volkskrant* (December 6, 2008), the Nigerian expert-curator Okwui Enwezor expresses clear views on living together in the public domain of changing societies. He says that we can no longer speak of a dominant culture hosting migrant cultures. Instead, he sees a multiplicity of *niches*, constructs of relevant (sub-)cultures, instead of one dominant culture, to which newcomers have to adapt. He does not believe that we are on our way to one dominant new European culture in which different elements of the existing sub-cultures are integrated. Enwezor argues that it is impossible to integrate 'the other', to force 'the other' to assimilate Dutch values in his or her life. The question is, in the eyes of this Nigerian 'outsider': 'Are we willing to assimilate in a post-colonial Europe?' The Diaspora is not for 'immigrants' only; we all are in Diaspora, as nomads in, and into, a new world. Research is needed to address the question of how to shape citizenship as a subject in order to educate and prepare young girls and boys to build such a society. The results of the German REDCo research give us hope through the optimistic view expressed by the youngsters on the possibilities of living together with 'the other' (see the clarification and interpretation of Tables 7 and 8), girls and boys each equally with their own unique composition of gendered qualities. As educators, we are expected to help students to gain the courage to 'assimilate in a post-colonial Europe' and to show the audacity of hope.

References

Boszormenyi-Nagy, I. & Krasner, B.R. (1986/2005). *Tussen geven en nemen, Over contextuele therapie* [Between give and take – a Clinical Guide to Contextual Therapy]. Haarlem: Uitgeverij De Toorts.

Enwezor, O. (2008). *Interview with the Nigerian expert-curator Enwezor in the Dutch newspaper De Volkskrant*, December 6, 2008.

Harod, A. (2007). Scale: The Local and the Global, in: S.L. Holloway, S.P. Rice & G. Valentine (Eds.), *Key Concepts in Geography*. Los Angeles: Sage Publications, pp. 229–247.

Honey, R.D. (1999). Nested identities in Nigeria, in: G.H. Herb & D.H. Kaplan (Eds.), *Nested Identities, Nationalism, Territory, and Scale*. Boston: Rowman & Littlefield Publishers.

Levinas, E. (1969/2003). *Het menselijk gelaat (The human face): Essays*. Amsterdam: Ambo.

Murphy, A.B. (1999). Rethinking the concept of European identity, in: G.H. Herb & D.H. Kaplan (Eds.), *Nested Identities, Nationalism, Territory, and Scale*. Boston:Rowman & Littlefield Publishers, pp. 53–73.

Nussbaum, M. (2001). *Oplevingen van het denken, Over de menselijke emoties* [Upheavals of thought, The intelligence of emotions]. Amsterdam: Ambo.

Obama, B. (2006). *The Audacity of Hope, Thoughts on Reclaiming the American Dream*. New York: Crown Publishers.

Pietersen, R. (2008). Halal met een rood wijntje erbij [Halal and Red Wine], in the Dutch newspaper *Trouw*, December 4, 2008.

Ter Avest, I. & Jozsa, D.-P. (2009). *The role of gender in relation to religions' influences in future Europe*, REDCo report, in press.

Tjin a Djie, K. (2003). Protective wraps, A way of counselling by which parents and children from We-systems are embedded into their families and cultures. *Systems Therapy, 15* (1), pp. 17–39.

Gerdien Bertram-Troost, Siebren Miedema, Ina ter Avest & Cok Bakker

Dutch Pupils' Views on Religion in School and Society – Report on a Quantitative Research

1.   Introduction

1.1   Setting the scene

During the second half of the last century Dutch society could be described (more or less) as a mono-cultural, homogeneous and 'pillarized' society, that, however, transformed into a multi-cultural and multi-religious society (see Ter Avest, Bakker, Bertram-Troost & Miedema, 2006). The concept 'pillarized' society points to a society in which almost all societal institutions and groups were fragmented along denominational lines. Different (religious) groups were locked up in their own organizations and institutions (including schools, sporting clubs, political parties, newspapers etc.). Only via the leaders at the top of the pillars, among the elites, there was co-ordinated co-operation between the different groups. While the pillarized character of society as a whole has (almost) disappeared, Dutch educational system is "still characterized by its 'pillarized' nature based on religious diversity" (Ter Avest et al., 2006, p. 208). Only 25% of the schools are state schools. The other schools are denominational private schools, rooted in a specific religious tradition or a specific pedagogical or world view concept, for instance Roman Catholic, Protestant, Islamic, Montessori, Waldorf schools and others. In total about 65% of the schools in the Netherlands are – formally speaking – Christian schools. There is, however, a variety of ways in which these schools give shape to their Christian identity and different goals for religious education can be distinguished.

Most state schools for secondary education do not include religious education in their curriculum. Religious denominational schools differ in the way they specify the content of religious education. At Christian schools religious education can be either confessional or non-confessional. Because of this great diversity, it is not possible to give a general description of what religious education looks like at religiously affiliated schools (see Ter Avest, Bertram-Troost, Van Laar, Miedema & Bakker, 2008).

1.2   Description of the sample

In total 565 pupils with a mean age of 14 years and 11 months took part in the research (240 male (42%) and 325 female (56.9%)).

We involved 8 schools with three or four classes participating in each school (with an average of 25 pupils per class). The educational levels differ from vmbo-kb (which prepares pupils for professional education on a lower level), vmbo-t (which prepares pupils for professional education on a average level), havo (which prepares pupils for professional education on a higher level) to vwo (which prepares pupils for university). Most of the participating schools include all these three levels.

When selecting schools, we took into account the following aspects: in/outside urban agglomeration in western part of the country, denominational/state school, segregated school/denominational schools which are open to all pupils, socio-economic background (low, mean, high), religious background of pupils (homogeneous/heterogeneous, one dominating religion versus diversity).

1.2.1 Description of schools[1]

Grotius College is situated in the urban agglomeration in the western part of the country. 70% of the pupils have a migrant background (many Muslims). Socio-economic status is mainly low. The school is officially a Christian school but no 'exclusivistic truth claims' about any religion are accepted. RE-lessons deal with many themes. Christianity is not getting so much special attention. Topics are also on ethics and philosophy. It is mainly in RE-lessons that pupils deal with religion in school. Two havo classes (fourth year) and one vwo class (third year) participated:[2] in total 68 pupils. (Abbreviation: GC)

Zwingli College is a 'segregated' Christian school situated in the urban agglomeration in the western part of the country, mainly pupils with Dutch nationality. Only pupils and teachers from a specific Christian background ('reformatorisch', which is an orthodox (strict) denomination within Protestantism) are welcome. Socio-economic status is diverse. Lessons are confessional and from a Christian perspective (also 'teaching in religion'). Only little attention is paid to other religions ('teaching about'). One vmbo-t class[3] (third year), one havo class (fourth year) and one vwo class (fourth year) participated. In total 71 pupils. (Abbreviation: ZC)

El Habib is a 'segregated' Islamic school in the urban agglomeration in the western part of the country. Both pupils and teachers must be Muslim (or, for teachers, at least respect Islamic assumptions). Many pupils have a migrant (sometimes refugee) background. Socio-economic background is mainly low. Two vmbo-kb classes (third year)[4], one vmbo-t class (third year) and one vwo class (third year) participated. In total 78 pupils. Abbreviation: EH.

Het Kompas is a state school which is situated in the urban agglomeration in the western part of the country. Many pupils have a migrant background (among others Surinamese). Pupils have very diverse religious backgrounds. All pupils are welcome. There are no RE-lessons and not so much explicit attention is given to religion in school. Socio-economic status is low/average. Three vmbo-t classes (third year) participated. In total 58 pupils. (Abbreviation: HK)

Christian Lyceum is a Christian school situated in a village in the middle of the country (in a rural setting). There are not so many pupils with a migrant background. Many pupils (or at least their parents) and teachers have a Christian background and/or are related to a (protestant) church. Pupils from a non-Christian background are welcome as well. RE-lessons are from a Christian perspective, especially in the lower classes. Socio-economic status is average/high. Two havo classes (fourth year) and one vwo class (fourth year) participated. In total 74 pupils. (Abbreviation: CL)

De Watermolen is a state school which is situated in a rural setting, in the middle of the country. No RE-lessons are provided and not much explicit attention is given to religion in school. Although there are no RE-lessons there is a curriculum module called 'History of Culture and Christianity'. Notice that in the Netherlands it is quite exceptional for a state school to teach such a subject. Socio-economic status is high. One vmbo-t class (third year) and two havo classes (second year) participated. In total 72 pupils. (Abbreviation: DW)

---

1   We used fictive names for the schools.
2   Havo prepares pupils for professional education at a higher level, vwo prepares pupils for university.
3   Vmbo-t prepares pupils for professional education at an average level.
4   Vmbo-kb prepares pupils for professional education at a lower level.

Da Vinci Lyceum is a Catholic school situated in a city in the Southern part of the Netherlands. This part of the country is mainly Catholic. On the school website no explicit attention is paid to Catholicism. It is stressed that everyone is welcome and can develop his/her own religious identity. The researcher notice that many pupils did not relate themselves to a certain religion and were not so much interested in religion at all. All pupils attend a subject called 'Worldview'[5]. In the first classes there is teaching about religion. In the lessons there is also much attention given to values and citizenship education. In the higher classes a lot of attention is paid to ethics and philosophy. (So the subject is very broad.) Socio-economic status is mean/high. Two havo classes (third year) and one vwo class participated. In total 74 pupils. (Abbreviation: DVL)

Franciscus College is a Catholic school which is situated in the middle of the Netherlands. It used to be an explicitly Catholic school, but the school tried to create more openness towards religious diversity. There is no clear vision on what that actually means for the school. Most of the pupils do not count themselves to any religion. Many parents have weak ties to Catholicism. There are some Christian and Islamic pupils. Socio-economic status is high. It is a so called 'white school' which means that there are only few pupils with a migrant background. RE-lessons are to a great extent 'teaching about'. Attention is paid to several world views and also to ethics, philosophy et cetera. Lessons are non-confessional. Three vwo classes participated (one class third year and two classes fourth year). In total 74 pupils. (Abbreviation: FC)

1.2.2 Models of RE

The different models of Religious Education (RE) give an indication of how religious education is given shape in the different schools. The three relevant models for the Dutch situation are: no RE, compulsory non-confessional RE (CNRE) and compulsory confessional RE (CCRE). For some schools it was quite obvious what code to use for the model of RE (respectively ZC, EH, HK). However, for GC and CL for instance it was more difficult to categorize the school. GC is officially a Christian school, but as in the lessons there is no special focus on Christianity (or any other religion) we coded this school as compulsory non-confessional RE (CNRE). For CL we decided to use the coding compulsory confessional RE (CCRE) although, especially in higher classes, attention is paid to other religions and worldviews as well and lessons are not focussed on institutionalized religion. (In fact, the coding 'CCRE' for CL should be interpreted differently from the coding 'CCRE' for ZC and EH as at these two last mentioned schools the focus is really on Christianity or Islam). The question is whether DW should have the CNRE code as well: It is a state school, but pupils attend the subject 'History of Culture and Christianity'. As we had the feeling that this subject is quite different from what is normally understood in the Netherlands by the subject 'RE' or 'Worldview'[6], we decided to code this school as having No RE.

---

5   See Ter Avest et al., 2007, on the use of terms 'religion' and 'worldview' in the Dutch context: The name of the subject 'worldview' shows that the school has chosen a broad conception of religion and does not focus mainly on a particular religion. In the chapter on terminology in this volume an extensive elaboration on these issues can be found.

6   The main aim of the subject 'History of Culture and Christianity' is that pupils learn that culture (including literature, arts, architecture etc.) has been influenced by Christianity and that they learn how to understand this culture. The subjects 'religious education' or 'world view' focus on more aspects than the role of Christianity in culture. To a more or lesser degree these subjects also deal with 'teaching in' and 'teaching into' religion (see also Ter Avest, Bakker, Bertram-Troost & Miedema, 2007) and focus

The most important remark is that the coding system of the models of RE should not be taken too absolutely as national and/or regional differences call for nuances. In this study we coded the schools as follows. No Religious Education (No RE): Het Kompas, De Water-molen, compulsory confessional religious education (CCRE): Zwingli College, El Habib, Christian Lyceum, compulsory non-confessional Religious Education (CNRE): Grotius College, Da Vinci Lyceum, Franciscus College.

The distribution is as follows: 131 pupils do not receive any RE at their current school (22.8%). 223 receive compulsory confessional RE (38.9%) and 217 pupils attend compulsory non-confessional RE classes (37.8%).

1.2.3   Religious backgrounds of pupils

14 pupils (2.4%) did not answer the question on religious background. 372 pupils (65.1%) state that they have a certain religion or worldview. 185 pupils (32.4%) state they do not have a certain religion or worldview. [7]

Of the pupils who indicated that they have a certain religion or worldview, 360 pupils gave a further description (97%). (Ten pupils left the item open and two pupils answered with a question mark.) Three reactions of the pupils were difficult to interpret. Namely: 'all', 'don't know which God' and one reaction could not be read.

As some pupils (especially of ZC) gave very specific information on their religious background, which would make an overall comparison between pupils of different religious background more complicated, we inserted 'Christianity' instead of mentioning the specific (church) denominations some of the pupils wrote down. Anyhow, all the pupils at ZC are Protestant and most of them belong to strict, traditional churches.

Pupils of CL who have a Christian background are mainly Protestant. So here 'Christianity' could also be read as 'Protestant'. If a pupil has filled in that he/she has a Catholic background, we coded this as 'Catholic' (at Christian Lyceum Catholic pupils are a kind of 'religious minority').

As Franciscus College is a Catholic school, the impression is that many of the pupils who answered that they are Christians, have a Catholic background (and maybe this is also the case for pupils at DVL). Nevertheless we only coded 'Catholic' or 'Protestant' here if the pupils used this term themselves.

216 pupils assign themselves to Christianity (this is 58% of the pupils who indicated having a religion or worldview). Out of this group 31 pupils explicitly call themselves Catholic. 134 pupils assign themselves to Islam (this is 36% of the pupils who indicated a religion or worldview). 9 pupils consider themselves as Hindu (2.4%). Next to that, there are some religions/worldviews (or combinations of religions/worldviews) which are only mentioned once (9 pupils, 2,4%): agnostic, atheism, Christianity + Buddhism, hip-hop, Jehovah's Witness, papuaism, Seventh Day Adventist, Sikhism and Wicca.

1.2.4   Socio-economic and migration background

In our research we used two indicators to describe the socio-economic background of the participating students. One indicator is the overall socio-economic background of pupils of

---

(also) on the religious identity formation of pupils (including moral reasoning and citizenship). Besides that, even at confessional schools attention is also paid to other religions than Christianity.

7   In the (bi-variate) analyses described in the next part of this contribution, the distinction between pupils with religion (abbreviation = R, from Religion) and pupils without a religion (abbreviation = NR, from No Religion) is based on this question.

the participating schools. We asked directors and/or teachers to describe the overall socio-economic background of their pupils. Their answers are integrated in the school descriptions in 1.1. Another indicator is the description pupils give of their parents' professions. In general, it turned out to be very difficult to use these descriptions as many pupils gave rather 'vague' descriptions of their parents' professions or simply wrote something down which we knew was not true (like 'queen' or 'oil sheik'). Therefore we decided not to use the questions on parents' profession. As a result, we have only some very general indications on the socio-economic background of the pupils.

Information about migration background can be derived from the birth country of pupils and their parents and the country / countries where pupils hold citizenship. 517 pupils (90.5%) were born in the Netherlands. 10 pupils (1.8%) are born in Morocco, 10 in Surinam and 4 in Turkey. Next to that there are several countries were one or two pupils were born, e.g. Afghanistan, India, Russia, Vietnam, Zimbabwe.

488 pupils (85.5%) do only hold citizenship in the Netherlands. 32 pupils indicated that they hold citizenship in the Netherlands and in another country.[8] In total there are 35 pupils who indicated that they only hold citizenship outside the Netherlands (out of which 7 pupils hold citizenship in Turkey and 10 in Morocco).

1.3   Reflection on the sample

The aim was to find a heterogeneous sample with regard to gender, religious background of pupils, type of school, socio-economic background, RE model, urban versus rural, and migration background. The description of the sample shows that with regard to most aspects, the Dutch sample meets this aim for diversity quite well. However, we need to mention that the focus is more on urban schools than on rural schools. Quite many schools are situated in the urban agglomeration in the western part of the Netherlands or not so far from there.

Another issue is that the percentage of girls is slightly higher in our sample than it is in the whole national population of pupils attending education at the levels we included in our research. For instance, in 2007/2008 53,6% of the pupils who attend the highest classes of 'vwo' were female. For 'havo' this percentage was 51,1%[9]

Next to the facts that the emphasis is more on the urban setting and that the percentage of girls in our sample is a bit higher than in the national population, there are, in general, also relatively few pupils with a migrant background in our sample. This probably relates to the fact that, in general, 'havo' (which prepares pupils for professional education at a higher level) and 'vwo' (which prepares pupils for university) are more strongly represented than the lower educational level 'vmbo' (which prepares for professional education at a lower level).[10] In the Netherlands, migrant pupils are to a significantly lesser degree represented at higher educational levels.

Finally, in comparison to the educational situation in the Netherlands as a whole, the percentage of segregated religious schools is relatively high in the sample (one Christian and one

---

8   Morocco, Turkey and Surinam are most often mentioned: 10 pupils have Dutch + Moroccan citizenship, 12 pupils Dutch + Turkish, 4 pupils Dutch + Surinam citizenship). Other mentioned countries are China, Croatia, Indonesia, Saudi Arabia and Yugoslavia.

9   This information is derived from CBS, Centre for Statistical Information. No separate information for 'vmbo' was available.

10 Within the context of REDCo we pay explicit attention to 'vmbo' in a special pilot project (carried out by Gusta Tavecchio and Ina ter Avest).

Muslim segregated school). This may influence our findings on for instance the religiousness of pupils and the role religion plays in their lives. In our sample we found for instance that 58% of the pupils consider themselves as Christian and 36% see themselves as Muslims. Statistical information for the whole Dutch population (Van de Donk et al., 2006) indicate that 44% of the population is Christian and 5,8% is Muslim. We can clearly state that the pupils in our sample are more religious than the Dutch population in general and that especially the percentage of Muslims is higher in our sample (because of the inclusion of a segregated Islamic school).

However, we have to bear in mind that we did not strive for a representative sample. Instead, we tried to picture the diversity in the Dutch school system. As segregated religious schools are part of that system, we did want to include them in this research. Next to that, elsewhere we explained (Ter Avest, Bakker, Bertram-Troost, Miedema, 2006) that about two thirds of the Dutch schools are denominational. In our sample 75% of the schools are denominational. So there is a stronger focus on denominational education. However, as in most analyses the fact whether pupils attend denominational schools or not is taken into account, we found a way to split the overall data and to avoid drawing general conclusions for the whole sample whereas in fact there might be differences between pupils of denominational and state schools. So we have avoided that the answers of pupils who attend denominational education would undeservedly dominate the overall research findings.

1.3   Description of the general procedure

1.3.1 Information on data collection

Several researchers and student assistants went to the schools to introduce the questionnaires and to be present during the filling in of the questionnaire. At one school, the teacher introduced the questionnaire himself after careful instruction by the researcher. All data have been inserted in SPSS by the researcher of the REDCo team.

In several classes it was difficult to motivate all pupils to work seriously on the questions. Especially the last page of the questionnaire 'triggered' pupils to just make up something (like the country of birth, home language etc.). This relates especially to the professions of the parents. Although most pupils filled in these questions seriously, some pupils did not know the profession of their father/mother, some did not know the (official) Dutch expression and sometimes it is clear that they just made up a profession (like queen, oil sheik et cetera).

It was the experience of most of the researchers who visited the schools that many pupils had problems remembering for how many years they have attended RE-classes. It seems that we should be a bit careful in interpreting and using this data. (Especially as there were also some pupils who were not sure about what we meant by 'RE-classes'.)

During the completion of the questionnaires, it was sometimes rather noisy. In some classes, it was difficult to motivate the pupils and there were a lot of comments and questions by the pupils.

1.3.2 Additional comments of pupils

Although pupils were invited to write down all their comments, further questions et cetera on the last page of the questionnaire, not so many pupils made use of this opportunity. All in all only 47 pupils out of 571 wrote down additional information. Of these 47 reactions, 20 reactions are comments on the questionnaire. There are some very positive comments like: *'Good luck with the research!'* and *'I think your project is quite okay. Go on like this!'*, but there are also quite some reactions in which pupils express their negative feelings towards the questionnaire: *'Some questions are really stupid!'*, *'Next time less questions, please'*, *'Boring test'* and *'The questionnaire is far too long and boring'*.

In the other 27 reactions pupils give explanations for their answers or give additional information which might, in their eyes, be important for a better understanding of their position. Examples of these reactions are: *'I am really glad to be a good Muslim'*, *'I believe in God, but I am not sure if I trust him'*, *'I don't have a belief, but I do not know if there is a god or not. And I respect if others do have a belief'*, *'I am baptised but we are not practising our belief. I don't see that as a belief'* and *'I do not count myself to a specific belief. I believe that all religions make some sense'*.

2. Presentation of the results

2.1 What role has religion in pupils' life and in their surroundings?

In this paragraph we will go further into the relevance of religion to pupils, their family background with regard to religion and the role religion plays in their contacts with peers. The first part of this paragraph follows questions 37 to 79 and 82 to 86 of the questionnaire.

2.1.1 Data description

Importance of religion

Figure 1 clarifies that religion is significantly more important to pupils who attend confessional RE than to pupils who attend non-confessional RE or no RE. Of the pupils who attend CCRE 86.5% indicated they have a religion. Of the pupils who attend CNRE this percentage is 53.5 and 48.1% of the pupils who do not attend RE indicated they have a religion.

Pupils who do not have a religion (further indicated as NR), attach much less importance to it than pupils who have a religion (further indicated as R). Figure 1 clearly shows this.

Figure 1: **Importance of religion by religious background and model of RE, % (Q. 37)**[11]

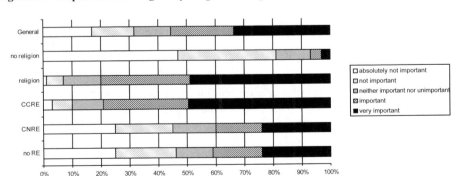

---

11 As boys and girls do not differ significantly on the question 'how important is religion to you?' there are no special bars for gender included in Figure 1.

Content of religion

The differences between the Dutch sample as a whole and the groups separated by religion/no religion and model of RE with regard to the importance attached to religion, is also visible with regard to the pupils' thoughts on the existence of God or life forces. In general, 62% of the pupils chose the statement 'There is a God', 19% chose 'There is some sort of spirit or life force' and another 19% had the feeling that the statement 'I don't really think there is any sort of God, spirit or life force' came closest to their thoughts.

As already shown in Figure 1, pupils who attend CCRE attach more importance to religion. They also more often chose for the option 'There is a God' to describe their own thoughts about religion (90%) than pupils who attend CNRE (49%) or no RE (41%).

Also the fact whether pupils assign themselves to a religion or not, has an impact on the way they answered this question. For instance: Pupils who do not have a religion more often stated that they do not know whether there is a god or life spirit (53%) than pupils who have a religion (4%).

Sources of knowledge about different religions

As we were interested in finding out how pupils get knowledge about different religions and which role people in their surroundings play with regard to religion, we asked them how important certain persons or aspects are to them as source to get information.

For Dutch pupils family is by far most important as source to get information about different religions. 43.8% of the pupils stated that family is very important. For the sample as a whole the following ranking appears when we look at the mean values (the lower the value, the more importance[12]): family (2.1), faith community (2.5), internet (2.6), friends (2.7), books (2.7), school (2.7) and media (3.1). Further analysis shows that this question on sources is strongly related to whether pupils are religious or not. Pupils without a religion ascribed significantly[13] less value to the mentioned sources to get information about religion. Only with regard to media and internet, have no significant differences between pupils with and pupils without a religion been found. For pupils without a religion, the ranking of importance of different sources is: internet (2.7), family (2.8), school (3.1) and friends (3.1), media (3.2), books (3.4), faith community (3.7). For pupils who have a religion faith community and books (probably including holy books like the bible and the Koran) were much more important: family (1.8), faith community (1.9), books (2.4), friends (2.5), school (2.5), internet (2.5), media (3.0).

We can also see differences in how important different persons/aspects are as source to get information about religion with regard to the model of RE. Especially relevant with regard to our research topic is the role of school. Pupils who attend CCRE attached significantly higher importance to school as a source to get information (mean = 2.4) than pupils who attend CNRE (2.9) or pupils who do not have any (official) RE lessons (2.9). Faith community was also significantly more important to pupils who attend CCRE (1.9) than to the pupils who do not (no RE = 2.7 and CNRE = 2.9). However, in all three groups family came at the first place, school at the fifth place and media at the last (seventh) place.

---

12 1 = very important, 2 = important, 3 = neither important nor unimportant, 4 = not important, 5 = not important at all.
13 Every time we speak about 'significant differences', we refer to statistically significant differences (on the basis of ANOVA). See also footnote 15.

Thoughts on (the role of) religion

We confronted pupils with quotations from their (European) peers[14] and asked them to indicate to what degree they agreed with the statements on religion in general. Figure 2 shows some of the quotations and the mean scores for the whole group and (some) subgroups. Means for subgroups are only mentioned if the differences in means are significant[15].

One thing that strikes in Figure 2 is that the mean score for 'religion is nonsense' is quite high (4.2). This means that most Dutch pupils do not agree with this statement[16]. Girls significantly disagreed more strongly with the statement 'religion is nonsense' than boys (f = 4.3 versus m = 3.9). Another striking result is that many of the Dutch pupils stated that they respect other people who believe (mean value is 1.7). More than half of the pupils did not agree with the statement 'religion determines my whole life' (mean value = 3.3). Female pupils significantly agreed more strongly with the statement 'religion determines my whole life' than male pupils (f = 3.2 versus m = 3.4).

Figure 2 also shows that most pupils disagreed with the statements that without religion the world would be a better place and that religion is a source of aggressiveness. With regard to the question whether religion belongs to private life, pupils did not have a very outspoken view (general mean is 2.9).

From the data it becomes clear that girls, pupils who have a religion and pupils who attend confessional RE lessons were more positive towards religion. We will elaborate a bit on this now. Girls agreed significantly more often with the statement on respecting other people who believe (f = 1.5, m = 2.0) and disagreed stronger with statements such as 'religious people are less tolerant towards others', 'without religion the world would be a better place' and 'religion is a source of aggressiveness'. (resp. f = 3.9 versus m = 3.6, f = 4.2 versus m = 3.8, f = 4.3 versus m = 4.0).

Depending on the model of RE pupils have experiences with, they also had different ideas about religion. Pupils who attend CCRE were more positive towards religion. They more strongly agreed with the statement 'religion determines my whole life' and were less inclined to state that religion is nonsense. Apart from that, pupils who attend CCRE disagreed more strongly than other pupils with the statement that one can be a religious person without belonging to a particular faith community (mean values CCRE = 3.0, CNRE = 2.6, no RE = 2.5).

Pupils with and pupils without religion had significantly different ideas about the characteristics of religion. Pupils who do not have a religion (No Religion = NR) were more inclined to agree with the statement 'religion is nonsense' (NR = 3.3 versus R = 4.6) and were significantly less inclined to respect other people who have a religion (R) (NR = 2.0 versus R = 1.6). Next to that, they agreed significantly more often than pupils who indicate that they have a religion, with the statement 'You can be a religious person without belonging to a certain religious community'. (NR = 2.6 versus R = 2.8) and with 'What I think about religion is open to change' (NR = 3.2 versus R = 3.6).

---

14 The quotations are derived from the qualitative REDCo study. See Knauth, Josza, Bertram-Troost and Ipgrave, 2008.

15 Means were compared with the help of ANOVA. *P*-values smaller than .05 are considered to be significant. As ANOVA takes into account the standard deviations of the described means in order to calculate whether differences in means are significant or not, in this report no further attention is paid to standard deviation. If there were no significant differences found between subgroups, the general mean is depicted in a separate bar as this gives a (visual) indication of the fact that no significant differences with regard to this item were found.

16 1 = strongly agree, 2 = agree, 3 = neither agree nor disagree, 4 = disagree, 5 = strongly disagree

Figure 2:   Quotations of European peers on religion by model of RE, religious background and gender, (means of estimates, scale from 1 – strongly agree to 5 – strongly disagree) (Q. 55–61, 82–86)

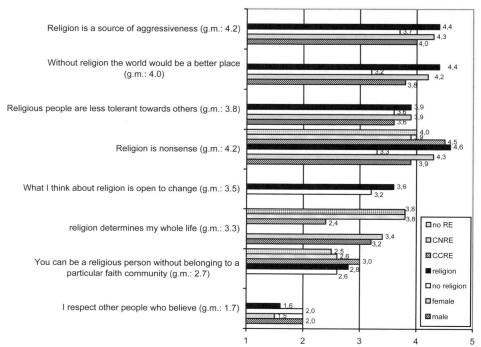

Talking about religion

Now we have gone further into how pupils look upon religion and the role it plays in their life, we can elaborate on the role religion plays in contact with others. In the questionnaire, there was a question on how often pupils talk with others about religion. We will not go into this question here in detail. The most important finding is that, in general, pupils were most likely to talk about religion with their family. Generally speaking, 23% of the pupils talked about religion within the family (about) every day and 28% (about) every week. Friends and classmates came at the (shared) second place. Girls talked significantly more often than boys to friends and classmates about religion.

Pupils who attend CCRE spoke more often about religion with family members, friends, classmates, other students at school, teachers and religious leaders. It is striking that there are also some significant differences between pupils who attend CNRE and pupils who do not follow any RE lessons: the first mentioned pupils spoke significantly more often about religion with classmates and teachers. This can be explained by the fact the RE-lessons as such (whether confessional or not) offer an opportunity to talk about religious issues.

Pupils who do not have a religion spoke significantly less with others (family, friends, teachers etc.) about religion.

Relations with others

It is helpful to take a closer look at the contacts pupils have with family, friends and class-mates and the role religion plays in these contacts. In Figures 3 to 6 percentages which indicate how pupils looked upon the religious backgrounds of people around them, are shown.

Figure 3: **'Most of my friends have the same views about religion as me' (frequency distribution for whole sample and separated by religious background) (Q. 68)**

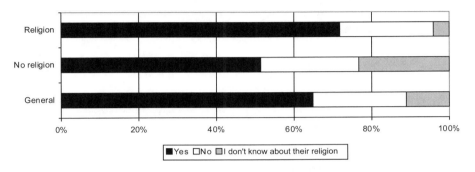

From Figure 3 it becomes manifest that in general 65% of the pupils agreed with the statement that most of their friends have the same views about religion as they themselves. 11% answered that they do not know about the religion of their friends. From this finding we can conclude that the other (about) 90% of the pupils knew about the religion of their friends. Pupils who do not have a religion agreed significantly less with the statement 'most of my friends have the same views about religion as me' (51.4% agreed in comparison to 71.8% of the pupils with a religion) and they were less well informed about the religions of their friends.

Figure 4 makes clear that the reactions on the statement 'At school, I go around with young people who have different religious backgrounds' were very diverse. Pupils who attend CCRE schools agreed less with this statement (CCRE: 19.7%, CNRE: 68.8%, no RE: 77.5%). With regard to the contacts pupils have after school, the differences between the three groups were less big and not significant. Pupils who do not have a religion stated significantly more often than pupils who have a religion that at school they go around with young people who have different religious backgrounds (66.5% versus 43.8%). It is striking that when it comes to going around with people of different religious backgrounds after school no significant differences were found with regard to model of Religious Education and/or religious background. Therefore Figure 5 only shows the general frequency distribution.

Figure 4:   **'At school, I go around with young people who have different religious back-grounds', whole sample and by model of RE and religious background, % (Q. 74)**

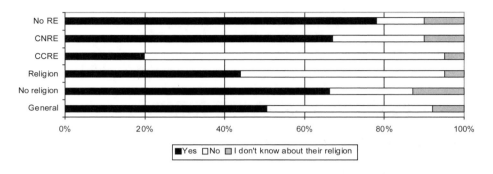

Figure 5:   **'After school, I go around with young people who have different religious back-grounds from me', whole sample, % (Q. 75)**

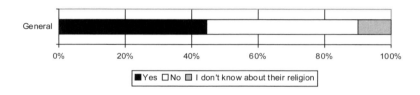

What is striking is that the percentage of pupils who go around with young people from different religious backgrounds at school (51%) (Figure 4) was higher than the percentage who does so after school (45%) (Figure 5). We will elaborate on this later.

Figure 6 clearly shows that there were differences between pupils who have experiences with different 'models of RE' in the relations they have or do not have with people of different religions. Pupils who attend CCRE less often answered with 'yes' the statement 'I have friends who belong to different religions'. (CCRE = 29.6%, NCRE = 52.5% and No RE = 55.7%).

Figure 6:   **'I have friends who belong to different religions', whole sample and by model of RE, % (Q. 70)**

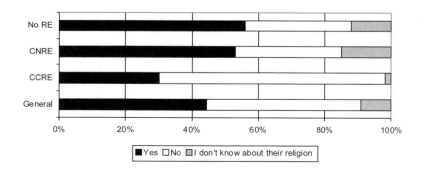

Preferences with regard to religious diversity versus uniformity

Figure 7 and 8 give information on whether pupils preferred religious diversity in their spare time and/or at school or not.

Figure 7:   'At school, I prefer to go around with young people who have the same religious background as me', whole sample and by religious background and model of RE, % (Q. 76)

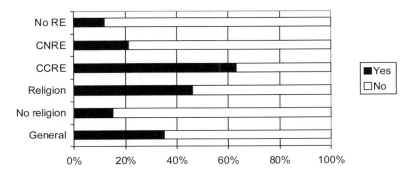

Figure 8.   'In my spare time, I prefer to go around with young people who have the same religious background as me', whole sample and by model of RE and religious background, % (Q. 77)

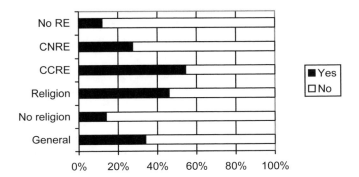

When comparing Figure 7 and 8, it becomes obvious that, in general, the preferences of Dutch pupils to go around with young people who have the same religious background as themselves was more or less independent of the occasion (school or spare time). About two third of the pupils did not prefer to go around with peers of their own religious background.

As Figures 7 and 8 show, there were significant differences between pupils who have experiences with different models of RE (no RE, CCRE and CNRE) with regard to the preferences of pupils to go around with young people who have the same/different religious backgrounds. It is interesting to see that more than half of the pupils who attend CCRE schools preferred to go around with young people who have the same religious background as themselves, both at school and after school. However, the percentage who preferred to do so in spare time, was smaller than the percentage with regard to school. For the pupils who attend CNRE schools there was also a (slight) difference between school and after school. However, to them, the difference was just the other way around: The percentage of pupils who preferred to go around with people who have the same religious background after school was a bit higher than the percentage of pupils who had this preference with regard to school time. To pupils who do not attend RE, there was no difference between school and spare time.

Figures 7 and 8 also make clear that there were significant differences between pupils who have a religion and pupils who do not have a religion with regard to preferences to go around with others, both in relation to school and spare time: Of the pupils who have no religion only 14.8% preferred to go around with young people of the same religious background, whereas this percentage was 45.8 for pupils who do have a religion. With regard to spare time, the percentages were more or less the same, namely 14.2% versus 44.6%.

Synopsis of data – religion in pupils' lives

It is difficult to say something about the importance of religion to the pupils in the Dutch sample in general, as there were big differences between pupils who assign themselves to a certain religion and pupils who do not, as well as between pupils who have experience with different kind of models of RE. Of the pupils who indicated having a religion and of the pupils who attend confessional religious education, half of the pupils stated that religion is very important to them. We find these differences between specific groups of pupils also with regard to their thoughts on the existence of God or life forces.

For all pupils family was a very important source to get information about religions. For religious pupils faith community and books were relatively important and for pupils without a religion internet and school were so. Pupils who attend CCRE schools attached significantly more importance to school as a source to get information about religion than did pupils who attend CNRE schools or No RE schools.

In general, pupils of the Dutch sample were quite positive about religion. Opinions differed most with regard to the statement 'religion is nonsense'. Pupils who have a religion and pupils who attend CCRE schools disagreed most with it.

Pupils who do not have a religion spoke significantly less often with others (family, friends, teachers etc.) about religion. Pupils who attend religious education spoke significantly more often about religion with classmates and teachers.

In general, two third of the pupils stated that most of their friends have the same views about religion as they themselves. This percentage was higher for pupils who have a religion. The general percentage of pupils who go around with young people from different religious backgrounds at school was higher than the percentage who do so after school. Pupils who attend CCRE had the least contacts with people of different religions and they had the strongest preference to go around with young people who have the same religious background as they themselves.

2.1.2   Data interpretation

When it comes to how pupils of different religions (learn to) live together, data findings about 'relations with others' are very interesting. We found that, in general, the percentage of pupils who go around with young people from different religious backgrounds at school was higher than the percentage who do so after school. This seems to be an indication that school is indeed a place where young people of different religions meet each other.

Pupils who attend CCRE schools had the least contacts with pupils from different religions backgrounds. Taking into account the selective criteria for admission of pupils to these (more or less) 'segregated schools' this is not so surprising. It is, however, surprising that pupils of these schools had relatively many contacts with peers of different religions after school: no significant differences were found with regard to 'After school, I go around with young people who have different religious backgrounds from me' for different models of RE (Figure 5). This means that although pupils who attend CCRE schools have less experience with religious diversity as such at school, they do have these contacts after school at (about) the same level as pupils who attend no RE schools and/or pupils who attend CNRE schools. However, it is true that these pupils prefer significantly more strongly to go around with young people who have the same religious background as they themselves both at school and after school. Pupils who indicated having a religion also had significantly stronger preferences to go around with people who have the same religious background than did pupils who do not have a religion. Unfortunately, we do not know what reasons the pupils had for these preferences. It might be possible that it has, at least, also something to do with 'simply' feeling more comfortable with people around you who are more or less like you yourself.

2.2   How do pupils see religion in school?

Now we have gone further into how pupils relate to religion and the role religion plays in their surroundings, we will, in this section, focus on how pupils look upon religion in school. The first part of the REDCo questionnaire dealt with this issue (Q. 1–36). First of all we will elaborate on pupils' experiences with religion in school.

2.2.1   Data description

Attending RE lessons

We asked the pupils how many years they have attended RE classes. We have to bear in mind here that we do not know exactly how pupils interpreted this question and what the RE-classes the pupils attended look like. Therefore we should be careful about drawing strong conclusions on the basis of this question, also because many pupils had problems remembering if and when they had attended RE classes. The answers of the pupils probably differ in some way from the school practice of the school they attended.

While we do not know exactly how pupils interpreted the question on attending RE-classes, and there is great diversity between RE classes, we must also be careful with regard to the question whether pupils attend RE-lessons this year or not. All in all, the pupils answered the question on whether they attend RE classes this year as follows: 443 pupils (77.6%) attend RE classes, 103 pupils (18%) do not (according to the pupils' own interpretations). From this finding we can conclude that a relative high proportion of Dutch pupils of secondary education do, in one way or the other, attend RE classes. In our introduction we already mentioned how the participating schools could be divided into models of RE. Officially 22.8% of the pupils do not attend RE; 38.9% attend compulsory confessional RE classes (CCRE, Christian or Muslim) and 37.8% of the pupils attend compulsory non-confessional RE classes (CNRE). It is important to mention that pupils who do not have a religion, have significantly less experiences with religious education in school. The mean value for the amount of years in which they attended RE is 3.78 in comparison to a mean value of 5.93 for those who have a religion. Having this in mind, we can go further into the experiences pupils have with religion in school.

Experiences with religion in school

As Figure 9 shows, pupils disagreed most with the statement 'learning about religions leads to conflicts in the classroom'. 67% of the pupils (strongly) disagreed with this statement. Next to that, the mean value for 'learning to have respect for everyone' is 2.0. This means that in general pupils agreed with this statement. Pupils also agreed, be it to a lesser extent, that learning about different religions at school helps them to live together. Pupils agreed less with the statement 'learning about religions at school helps me to learn about myself'. It seems that pupils were of the opinion that learning about religion at school has more impact on how they live together than on their personal development. With regard to the statement on what pupils think of the importance of religions as topic at school, the mean value (2.7) shows that pupils did not explicitly agree or disagree with this statement but that there was a very slight tendency towards a positive reaction. The distribution of frequencies is as follows: 17.3% strongly agreed, 30.3% agreed, 26.8% of the pupils neither agreed, nor disagreed, 14.5% disagreed and 10.0% strongly disagreed. All in all it seems that pupils from the Dutch sample were quite positive about attention to religions at school.

Figure 9:   **Experiences with religion in school by model of RE, religious background and gender, (means of estimates, scale from 1 – strongly agree to 5 – strongly disagree) (Q. 3–12)**

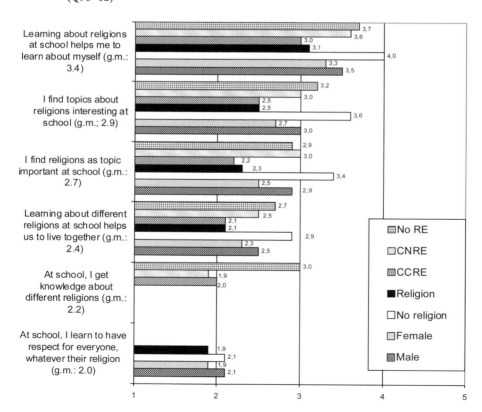

Figure 9 also shows differences with regard to gender, religious background and model of RE. Girls seemed to value religion in school higher than boys. Girls agreed significantly more strongly than boys with the statements 'I find religions as topic important at school' (f = 2.5 versus m = 2.9) and 'I find topics about religions interesting at school' (f = 2.7 versus m = 3.0). Next to that, girls were also more positive about what they learn at school with regard to religion. Girls agreed significantly more with 'At school, I learn to have respect for everyone, whatever their religion' (f = 1.9 versus m = 2.1), 'Learning about different religions at school helps us to live together' (f = 2.3 versus m = 2.5) and 'Learning about religions at school helps me to learn about myself' (f = 3.3 versus m = 3.5).

In general, pupils who attend CCRE schools attached greater importance to religion in school than other pupils do. They are more positive about the effects of learning about religions at school. One result, however, is that pupils who attend CNRE schools agreed significantly more strongly with the statement 'At school, I get knowledge about different religions' than the pupils who attend CCRE. There was also a significant difference between pupils who attend CCRE schools and pupils who do not attend RE at all: CNRE = 1.9, CCRE = 2.0, no RE = 3.0.

Pupils without a religious background were less positive about religious education. Pupils who do not have a religion agreed significantly less with statements as 'I find topics about religions interesting at school' (NR = 3.6 versus R = 2.5) and 'Learning about religions at school helps us to live together' (NR = 2.9 versus R = 2.1). Both groups, however, did not differ with regard to their thoughts about whether learning about religions leads to conflicts in the classroom. Both groups were inclined to disagree with this statement (NR = 4.0, R = 4.1).

Showing views about religion in school

In relation to the question on whether learning about different religions leads to conflicts in the classroom, two additional quotations of their European peers have been presented to the pupils in order to get an idea about whether pupils have the feeling that it is possible at school to show one's views about religion openly. Figure 10 shows the reactions of the pupils.

Figure 10:   Possible problems with showing ones views about religion openly at school by model of RE, religious background and gender, (means of estimates, scale from 1 – strongly agree to 5 – strongly disagree). (Q. 80, 81)

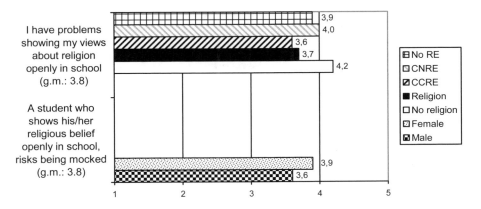

In general, pupils tended to disagree with both statements. It seems that pupils had the feeling that there is a possibility to show their view about religion openly in school and that they do not see much risk for being mocked. Pupils who attend CCRE schools had, interestingly enough, significantly more problems with showing their views about religion openly in school than pupils who attend CNRE schools. Pupils who have a religion also had more problems to showing their views then pupils who do not have a religion. Male pupils were significantly more strongly of the opinion that a student who shows his/her religious beliefs openly in school risks being mocked.

(Possible) position of religion in school

It is very interesting to have a closer look at the role religion should play if pupils were persons who could decide on school matters. Figure 11 shows the mean values of some statements which deal with this topic.

It becomes clear from Figure 11 that, in general, the pupils of the Dutch sample agreed that pupils should be able to wear discreet religious symbols. To a lesser degree they were also of the opinion that more visible religious symbols should be allowed. In general, the reactions of the pupils suggest that the pupils in the Dutch sample were quite open to religion in school and were of the opinion that pupils' religious needs should be, more or less, taken into account in school. However, pupils hesitated when it comes to allowing pupils to miss some classes for religious reasons: 32% of the pupils (strongly) agreed, 23% of the pupils had no clear opinion and 44% (strongly) disagreed on this issue. So, although pupils were willing to take into account religious backgrounds of (fellow) pupils, in general they were of the opinion that the school curriculum must be followed by all pupils, irrespective of their religion.

Figure 11: Position of religion in school, by model of RE, religious background and gender, (means of estimates, scale from 1 – strongly agree to 5 – strongly disagree) (Q. 13–19)

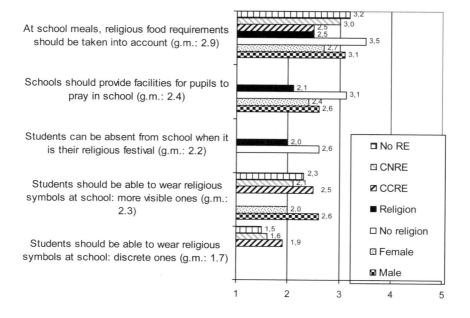

Female pupils were a bit more than boys of the opinion that the religious background of pupils should be taken into account in school life. Girls agreed significantly more with the statements 'School should provide facilities for pupils to pray in school' (f = 2.4 versus m = 2.6), 'Students should be able to wear religious symbols at school: more visible ones' (f = 2.0 versus m = 2.6) and 'At school meals, religious food requirements should be taken into account' (f = 2.7 versus m = 3.1).

Whereas pupils who attend CCRE schools agreed significantly more strongly with the statement that 'at school, religious food requirements should be taken into account' (CCRE = 2.5, CNRE = 3.0, No RE = 3.2), it is striking that these pupils agreed significantly less strongly with the statements that students should be able to wear religious symbols at school. (Discreet ones: CCRE = 1.9, CNRE = 1.6, no RE = 1.5; More visible ones: CCRE = 2.5, CNRE = 2.1, No RE = 2.3).

There were also differences between pupils with or without a religion in respect to the role they ascribe to religion in school. Pupils who have no religion disagreed significantly more strongly with the statement that 'At school meals, religious food requirements should be taken into account' (NR = 3.5 versus R = 2.5). They also disagreed significantly more strongly that 'Pupils should be allowed to miss lessons because of religious activities' (NR = 2.6 versus R = 2.0) and that 'Schools should provide facilities for pupils to pray' (NR = 3.1 versus R = 2.1). There were no significant differences between the two groups with regard to the wearing of religious symbols.

Positions towards different models of RE

Figure 12 shows the mean values of pupils' attitudes towards different models of religious education in school. From Figure 12 it becomes clear that the pupils from the Dutch sample were of the opinion that there should be a place for religion in school life. This does not come as a surprise, seeing the importance pupils attached to religion in general and the way they were willing to take into account religious diversity in school. Next to that, pupils tended to disagree with the statement that there is no need for the subject of religious education in school.

Figure 12 further makes clear that pupils were most in favour of a model of religious education where all students are taught RE together, irrespective of differences in their religious or denominational background. This finding is in accordance with the finding that, in general, pupils of the Dutch sample were of the opinion that students should not be excused from taking classes for religious reasons.

Figure 12 makes clear that pupils tended to agree with the statement that religious education should be optional: 55% (strongly) agreed, 16% had no explicit opinion and 29% disagreed. Figure 12 provides also information on differences with regard to gender, religious background and model of RE. There were different opinions, especially with regard to the statements 'There should be no place for religion in school life' and 'Pupils should study religious education separately in groups according to which religion they belong'. Girls agreed significantly less than boys with the statement that religious education should be optional (f = 2.7 versus m = 2.5) and with the statement that there should be no place for religion in school life (f = 4.3 versus m = 4.1).

Pupils who have experiences with different kinds of RE-models also had different thoughts about the possible models of RE. Pupils who attended CCRE schools did support less the statement that religious education should be optional and they agreed significantly more strongly with the statement that pupils should study religious education separately in groups according to which religion they belong.

With regard to the different models of religious education, it is apparent from the data analysis that pupils who do not have a religion were more in favour of optional religious education (NR = 2.3 versus R = 2.8), were more inclined to agree with the statement 'There should be no place for religion in school life' (NR = 3.8 versus R = 4.4) and agree(d) more often with the statement 'There is no need for the subject of religious education' (NR = 2.8 versus R = 3.9).

Figure 12: Positions towards different models of religious education in school, by model of RE, religious background and gender, (means of estimates, scale from 1 – strongly agree to 5 – strongly disagree). (Q. 26–31)

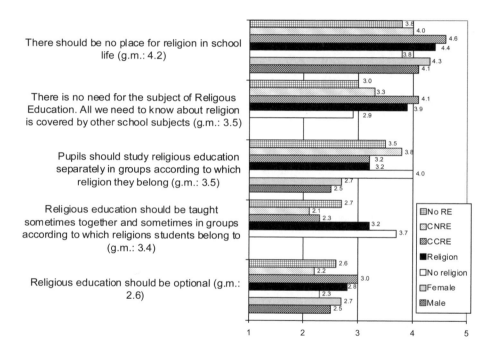

Aims of Religious Education

Figure 13 shows the reactions of the pupils to the block of questions related to 'How far do you agree that pupils at school should ...?' When taking a look at the results it immediately becomes clear that, in general, the pupils of the Dutch sample were negative about the (possible) aim of guiding pupils towards religious beliefs. Instead, they were much more in favour of learning to understand what religions teach and of learning to talk and communicate about religious issues.

When it comes to the aims of education, there were also some significant differences between boys and girls. Girls more strongly agreed than boys with statements that at school, students should '...learn to understand what religions teach' (f = 2.0 versus m = 2.3), '...Be able to talk and communicate about religious issues' (f = 2.1 versus m = 2.3) and '...Get an objective knowledge about different religions' (f = 2.3 versus m = 2.5).

Pupils who do not attend RE lessons agreed significantly less strongly with the statement that at schools pupils should get an objective knowledge about different religions. Pupils who attend non-confessional RE schools also agreed less with this statement than pupils who attend confessional schools. (No RE = 2.8, CCRE = 2.1, CNRE = 2.4) Whereas in general the pupils who attend confessional RE schools agreed most with the proposed learning goals and the pupils who attend no RE schools agreed less, the pupils who attend non-confessional RE schools disagreed more strongly with the statement that pupils should 'Be guided towards religious beliefs' than pupils who do not attend RE lessons. (No RE = 3.8, CCRE = 3.2, CNRE = 4.1).

Figure 13: **'At school, pupils should ...', by model of RE, religious background and gender, (means of estimates, scale from 1 – strongly agree to 5 – strongly disagree) (Q. 32–36)**

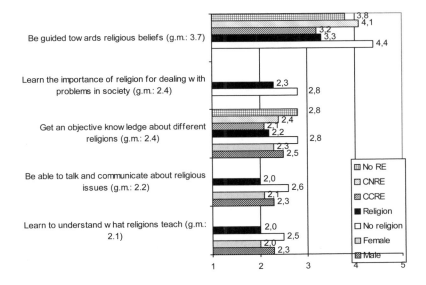

Pupils with and without religion had different ideas about the possible aims of learning in school. Pupils who do not have a religion attached less importance to getting objective knowledge about different religions (NR = 2.8 versus R = 2.2) and to learning to understand what religions teach (NR = 2.5 versus R = 2.0). They also attached less importance to the aim that at school pupils should learn to be able to talk and communicate about religion (NR = 2.6 versus R = 2.0) and that at school pupils should learn the importance of religion for dealing with problems in society (NR = 2.8 versus R = 2.3). The biggest difference between means is found, however, with regard to the aim of guiding pupils towards religious beliefs. Both groups were inclined to disagree with this aim, but the pupils who do not have a religion were more explicit in their position (NR = 4.4 versus R = 3.3).

Synopsis of data – religion in school
A relative high number of Dutch pupils of secondary education do, in one way or another, attend RE classes. 60% of the pupils attend denominational education, where RE classes are quite common, and also at some state schools pupils can attend a subject like 'World-

view' or 'History of Culture and Christianity'. Our findings indicate that in general pupils from the Dutch sample were quite positive about giving attention to religion at school. They did not have the feeling that learning about religions leads to conflicts in the classroom. Instead, in general pupils indicated that at school, they learn to have respect for everyone, whatever their religion might be. With regard to experiences with religion in school there are some significant differences with regard to gender, religious background and model of RE. Girls seemed to value religion in school more highly than boys. Next to that, pupils who attended CCRE schools attach greater importance to religion in school than pupils at CNRE and No RE schools. They were also more positive about the effects of learning about religions at school. One striking result, however, is that pupils who attend CNRE schools agreed significantly more strongly with the statement 'At school, I get knowledge about different religions' than pupils at CCRE schools. Pupils without a religious background were less positive about religious education.

On the basis of the collected data we have clues to indicate that, in general, pupils had the feeling that there is a possibility to show one's views about religion openly in school and that they did not see much risk for being mocked when doing so. However, pupils who attend CCRE schools and/or have a religion had more problems with showing their religion in school than pupils who attend CNRE and/or do not have a religious background.

In general, pupils of the Dutch sample seemed to be quite open to religion in school and subscribed to the view that pupils' religious needs should be, more or less, taken into account in school. However, pupils hesitated when it comes to allowing pupils to miss some classes for religious reasons. Next to that, pupils were in favour of a model of religious education where all students are taught RE together, irrespective of differences in their religious background. However, pupils who have experiences with different kind of RE-models also had different thoughts about the possible models of RE. Pupils who attend a CCRE school agreed less that religious education should be optional and they agreed significantly more strongly with the statement that pupils should study religious education separately in groups according to which religion they belong.

Pupils of the Dutch sample were, in general, negative about the (possible) aim of guiding pupils towards religious beliefs. Especially pupils who do not have a religion themselves were very negative about this aim. Instead, pupils were, in general, much more in favour of learning to understand what religions teach and of learning to talk and communicate about religious issues.

2.2.2   Data interpretation

We found that pupils who attend CNRE schools agreed significantly more strongly with the statement 'At school, I get knowledge about different religions' than pupils who attend CCRE schools or no RE schools. This can be explained when we bring into mind that two of the three schools which are classified as 'CCRE' are so called 'segregated schools' which focus more on 'teaching into religion' than on 'teaching about religion'. So pupils at CNRE schools learned most about different religions.

One striking finding is that pupils who attend CCRE schools had more problems with showing their views about religion openly in school than pupils who attend CNRE schools. At first sight, one would think that pupils who attend a school where religious diversity is relatively low would feel more at ease to talk about their own view. However, it is also possible that pupils who are more used to a (religiously) heterogeneous setting are more used to giving their own opinion and to communicate with others about different possible perspectives. Possibly, pupils who have the feeling that at their school one interpretation (of religion) is central, felt less secure about expressing their own thoughts as these thoughts might differ (to a certain extent) to what is expected to be the 'common faith'.

A general impression we have with regard to the way pupils look upon religion in school, is that they take their own actual situation and experiences as a background for interpretation and evaluation. We found apparent differences between pupils with and without a religion and between pupils who have experiences with different models of RE. We found, for instance, that pupils who do not attend RE lessons agreed significantly less strongly with the statement that at school pupils should get an objective knowledge about different religions. Also pupils who do not see themselves as adherents of a certain religion attached less importance to getting knowledge about religions at school. Our impression is that pupils' (religious) background and the role religion plays in their (family) life – including the choice for (non) confessional education or state schooling – really influences how pupils evaluate the role of religion in education.

2.3   How do pupils see the impact of religion?

2.3.1   Data description

Having dealt with how pupils look upon religion in school, now we will go further into how pupils assess the impact of religion in general (Q. 20–25, 87–112). We will especially focus on the question whether pupils are of the opinion that religions contribute to dialogue and/or to conflict.

Functions of learning about different religions

Pupils were asked how they look upon the impact of learning about different religions. They were offered several statements and were asked to indicate to what extent they agree with the statements. Figure 14 makes clear that in general the pupils of the Dutch sample tended to be positive about the impact of learning about different religions. Mean values of all items are between two and three, which stands for a mean point of view somewhere between 'agree' and 'neither agree nor disagree'. The item 'learning about different religions helps to understand others and live peacefully with them' received most positive reactions. This finding is compatible with the already described finding that learning about religion at school, has seemingly more impact on how pupils live together than on their personal development (see Figure 9).

There were some differences between boys and girls with regard to how they evaluate the effects of learning about different religions. Girls agreed more strongly than boys that learning about different religions helps to 'understand others and live peacefully with them' (f = 2.1 versus m = 2.3), 'learn about my own religion' (f = 2.4 versus m = 2.6) and 'gain a better understanding of current events' (f = 2.5 versus m = 2.7).

Pupils who attend confessional RE schools agreed significantly more often than other pupils that learning about different religions helps to understand others and to live peacefully with them. (CCRE = 1.8, CNRE = 2.4, No RE = 2.4). Pupils who attend confessional RE agreed also more strongly that learning about different religions helps to develop their own point of view, develop moral values and helps to learn about one's own religion.

Data analysis makes clear that also pupils with or without a religion differ significantly in their opinions on the possible functions of learning about different religions. Pupils who do not have a religion were less inclined to agree with the possible functions mentioned in the questionnaire.

Figure 14: **'Learning about different religions helps to …', by model of RE, religious background and gender, (means of estimates, scale from 1 – strongly agree to 5 –
strongly disagree). (Q. 20–25)**

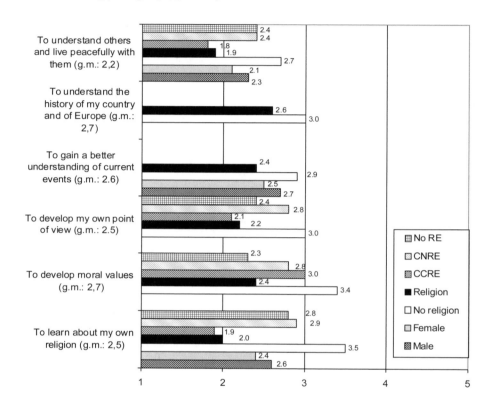

Reasons to talk or not to talk about religion

In section 2.1 we have already dealt with how often pupils talk with other persons in their surroundings about religion. We will now go further into reasons pupils might have to talk or not to talk with others (friends, but also other people) about religion. Figure 15 shows the mean values of pupils' reactions (on a five point scale) to several quotations of their European peers on this topic.

Figure 15 shows that the pupils of the Dutch sample tended to agree with statements which include a positive notion of talking about religion (the first group of items) and that they tended to disagree with statements which include more negative aspects of talking about religion. In general, pupils disagreed with the statement that talking about religion is embarrassing. They also disagreed with the possibility that they and their friends speak about how stupid religion is.

Figure 15: Reasons to talk or not to talk about religion, by model of RE, religious background and gender, (means of estimates, scale from 1 – strongly agree to 5 – strongly disagree). (Q. 87–97)

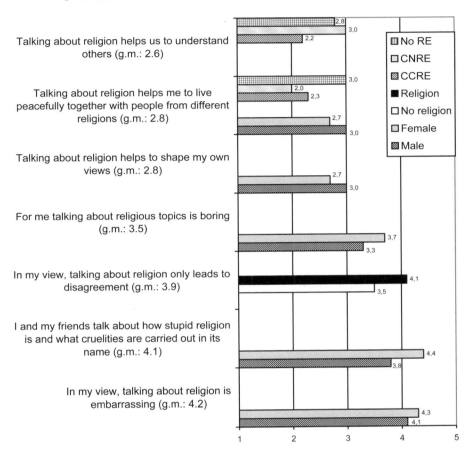

With regard to our focus on dialogue and conflict, it is interesting to elaborate a bit on the (possible) relation pupils saw between talking about religion and disagreement. The mean value of the item 'In my view, talking about religion only leads to disagreement' is 3.9. 68% of the pupils (strongly) disagreed with this statement. It seems that pupils have quite positive opinions on talking about religion. This is also evident in their reactions to the items 'Talking about religion helps us to understand others' and 'Talking about religion helps me to live peacefully together with people from different religions'. Pupils tended to agree with these statements. About 50% of the pupils (strongly) agreed with the first mentioned statement, and 43% did so with regard to the second mentioned statement. All in all the pupils of the Dutch sample tended to be quite positive about the functions of talking about religion.

With regard to reasons to talk or not to talk about religion (Figure 15) there are many significant differences between boys and girls. Again, girls were more positive about talking about religion than boys. For instance, they agreed less with statements as 'For me, talking about religious topics is boring' and 'In my view, talking about religion is embarrassing'.

Differences are also found between the pupils with different experiences related to model of RE with regard to the reasons they have to talk or not to talk about religion. Pupils at CCRE schools significantly agreed more often with the statements like 'Talking about religion helps to understand others' than pupils at CNRE and no RE schools. (CCRE = 2.2, CNRE = 3.0, No RE = 2.8), and with the statement 'Talking about religion helps me to live peacefully together with people from different religions' (CCRE = 2.3, CNRE = 3.0, No RE = 3.0). All in all, they were more positive about talking about different religions and were more convinced of its value.

Pupils who do not have a religion were significantly less positive about talking about religion as they agreed more strongly with statements like 'for me talking about religious topics is boring' (NR = 2.8 versus R = 3.9) and 'religion doesn't interest me – we have more important things to discuss' (NR = 2.6 versus R = 4.3). They were also significantly more inclined to agree with the statement 'In my view, talking about religion only leads to disagreement' (NR = 3.4 versus R = 4.1). However, the opinion of the two groups about whether talking about religion is embarrassing, did not differ significantly (NR = 4.3 versus R = 4.3).

Pupils' reactions in confrontation with another conviction

Pupils were asked what they would do when confronted with a pupil of a different religious faith who wants to convince the pupil that his/her religion is the best one. Figures 16 to 20 show the reactions of pupils to different alternatives. Pupils could choose between three options: 'That's exactly my reaction', 'That could be my reaction' or 'I would never react like that'. From Figure 16 to 20 it becomes clear that in general the possible reaction 'I listen but their views do not influence me' was the most approval from the pupils. The possible reaction 'I try to ignore him/her' is much less in line with the pupils' own reaction. In general pupils agreed the least with the statement 'I try to convince him/her that he/she is wrong'. 48% says this could be their own reaction. 24% stated they would exactly react like this and 28% stated that they would never react like this. 60% of the pupils, however, indicated that they would try to explain that their own opinions about religion are the best one and 87% (possibly) would try to discuss with the other about his/her opinion.

The different Figures also make clear that there are apparent differences between pupils with regard to gender, religious background and model of RE.

Figure 16: 'I listen but their views do not influence me', by gender, % (Q. 102)

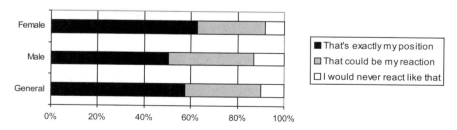

There are some significant patterns in how boys and girls would react (according to themselves) when confronted with someone who would try to convince them that his/her religion is the best one. Female pupils more often than males answered that 'I listen but their views do not influence me' is exactly their position (girls: 62%, boys: 50%). Male pupils tended to try to ignore the person who tries to convince him more often than female pupils. Finally, girls were also more eager to discuss with the other about his/her opinions than boys.

When confronted with religious differences, pupils who have experiences with different models of RE in their schools reacted, at some points, significantly differently. Pupils who attend CCRE schools were more inclined than pupils at CNRE schools to try to explain to the other that their own views about religion are the best ones. They were also more inclined to discuss with others about their opinion and to convince the other that he/she is wrong.

Figure 17: 'I try to ignore him/her', by gender, % (Q. 98)

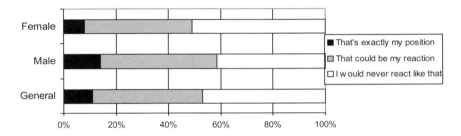

Figure 18: 'I try to discuss with him/her about his/her opinions', by model of RE, religious background and gender, % (Q. 99)

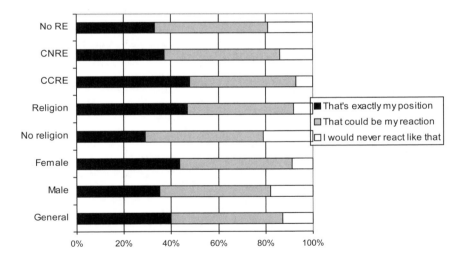

Figure 19: **'I try to convince him that he/she is wrong', by model of RE, religious background and gender, % (Q. 100)**

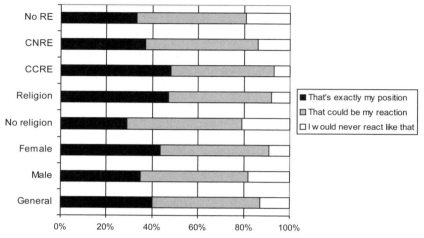

When confronted with religious differences, pupils with or without a religion reacted significantly differently: Pupils who have a religion were more inclined to discuss with the other about his/her ideas. They were also more inclined to try to convince the other that he/she is wrong and to try to explain that their own opinions about religion are the best ones.

Figure 20: **'I try to explain that my own opinions about religion are the best ones', by model of RE and religious background, % (Q. 101)**

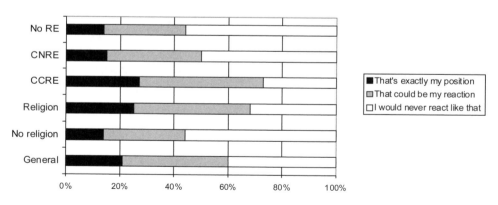

All in all, pupils' reactions on these statements seem to suggest that the pupils of the Dutch sample were ready to listen to the other person but had the impression that the views of the other will not influence them. Pupils tended to discuss with the other about his/her convictions, but not necessary by trying to explain to the other that their own opinions of religion are the best ones.

Opinions on people of different worldviews living together

In order to go further into pupils' thoughts whether or not and how people of different religions could live together, several quotations from European youngsters were added to the questionnaire. Figure 21 shows the mean values of the pupils of the Dutch sample on these statements.

Figure 21:   Opinions on people of different worldviews living together, by model of RE, reli-

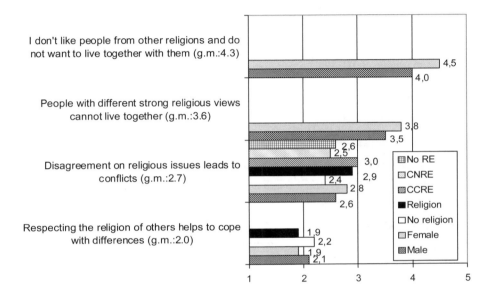

gious background and gender, %. (Q. 103–106)

From Figure 21 we learn that many pupils disagreed with the statement 'I don't like people from other religions and do not want to live together with them'. Related to the already described results on for instance the importance pupils attach to religion and their willingness to take religious backgrounds of pupils into account in school life, this finding does not come as a surprise. Girls disagreed significantly more strongly with this statement (f = 4.5 versus m = 4.0).

However, in general, pupils tended to agree with the statement that disagreement on religious issues leads to conflict (31% of the pupils agreed with this statement, 32% had no clear opinion). Apparently pupils are aware of the possibility that conflicts will arise when there is disagreement on religious issues. Again, boys agreed significantly more often than girls. Also pupils without a religion agreed significantly more often with this statement (NR = 2,4, R = 2,9) and there were also significant differences between pupils who attend CCRE schools and pupils who attend CNRE schools or no RE schools. Pupils who attend CCRE schools agreed least with this statement (CCRE = 3, CNRE = 2,5, no RE = 2,6). Nevertheless, many pupils were convinced that respecting the religion of others helps to cope with differences. It seems that they more strongly stressed the importance of respect as a way to help people of different religions to live in peace together than the idea that religion can be a matter of conflict in society. However, pupils with a religion agreed significantly more strongly with the statement on the role of respect than pupils without a religion. Girls also agreed significantly more strongly than boys.

In elaboration on these outcomes we will, finally, present the thoughts of pupils of the Dutch sample on what would help people of different religions to live together in peace. Figure 22 to 25 show the importance pupils attached to the different aspects. From Figure 22 it becomes clear that the pupils of the Dutch sample were quite well convinced that knowledge about each other's religion is a very important prerequisite for living in peace together. Pupils were less convinced that it is necessary that people share common interests (Figure 25).

Figure 22: **'If they know about each other's religions', by model of RE, religious background and gender, % (Q. 108)**

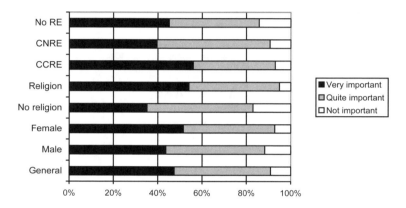

From Figure 22 it also becomes clear that there were significant differences with regard to gender, model of RE and religious versus no religious background.

Figure 23: **'If they personally know people from different religions', by model of RE and religious background, %. (Q. 109)**

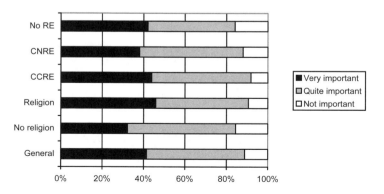

From comparing Figure 22, 23 and 24, 25 it becomes clear that in general pupils attached less importance to doing things together and sharing common interests than having (personal) knowledge about different religions. However, Figure 24 makes clear that pupils who do have a religion, attached greater importance to doing something together than pupils who do not have a religion.

Figure 24: 'If they do something together', by religious background, %. (Q. 110)

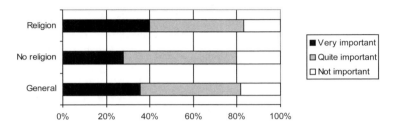

Figure 25 makes clear that pupils who have a religion also attached significantly more importance to sharing common interests than pupils who do not have a religion.

Figure 25: 'If people share common interests', by religious background, %. (Q. 107)

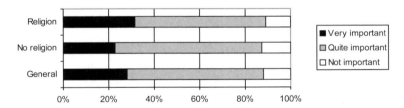

Finally, the data also show that only 8% of the pupils thought that, in order to live together in peace, it is very important that everyone keeps to their own religion in private. Apparently pupils saw no direct need to restrict religion to the private domain.

In general pupils also did attach not so much importance to state regulation: 18% of the pupils agreed that it would help for people of different worldviews to live together if the state has strong laws about the role of religion in society.

Synopsis of data – impact of religion

In general, pupils of the Dutch sample tended to be positive about the impact of learning about different religions. It was pupils' contention that especially learning about different religions does help to understand others and live peacefully with them. However, the thoughts of pupils with regard to the impact of learning about different religions were influenced by, among other things, their personal religious background. Pupils who do not adhere to a certain religion were less positive about it.

Data show that pupils had quite positive opinions on talking about religion. Pupils tended to agree that talking about religion helps to understand others and/or to live peacefully together with people from different religions. Again, we found that pupils who have a religion themselves or pupils who attend CCRE schools were more interested in talking about religion than pupils who do not have a religion or pupils who attend CNRE or No RE schools.

When confronted with people with another conviction, the most common reaction of the pupils of the Dutch sample was to listen but not to be influenced by the other. Some strikingly different reactions were found between pupils with or without a religion and between pupils who have experiences with different models of RE. Pupils who attend CCRE schools were, for instance, more inclined than others to try to explain to the other that their own views about religion are the best ones. Also pupils who have a religion themselves were more inclined to discuss with the other his/her ideas. The general impression is that pupils of the Dutch sample were ready to listen to the person holding on to an other conviction but they had the feeling this will not really influence their own opinions.

It was many pupils' contention that respecting the religion of others helps to cope with differences. It seems that pupils more strongly emphasized the importance of respect as a way to help people of different religions to live in peace than the fact that religion can be a matter of conflict in society (see Figure 21).

When it comes to pupils' thoughts on what would help people of different religions to live together in peace, it is remarkable that pupils of the Dutch sample saw knowledge about each others religions as a very important prerequisite. Pupils were less convinced that it is necessary that people share common interests. Least importance was attached to keeping religion to private life and/or strong state laws about the role of religion in society.

2.3.2   Data interpretation

The data show that pupils who attend confessional religious education were more willing to talk about religion, attach greater importance to religion, and were more inclined to stress the positive aspects of (talking about) religious differences. Next to that, they were most likely to defend their own position when confronted with differences. However, although we found several significant differences between pupils who have experiences with different RE models, we can not conclude from this analysis whether the model of religious education as such is a distinguishing factor here. It might also be possible that the religious backgrounds of pupils influenced their (and their parents') choice for a certain secondary school and thus the religious backgrounds of pupils is in fact more important.

One of the findings is that in general pupils seemed to be more inclined to stress the importance of respect as a way to help people of different religions to live in peace together than the fact that religion can be a matter of conflict in society. Pupils were also more inclined to stress the positive aspects of talking about religion and to reject the possible negative effects (for instance that talking about religion would only lead to disagreement). However, again, the personal background of pupils is at stake here. Pupils who have a religion and/or attend CCRE schools were much more positive about the impact of religion. It might be that they themselves have good experiences with religion and that by consequence they believed that the impact of religion in general is positive. It could also be, even at the same time, that pupils who have a religion were overestimating the positive effects of religion and/or underestimating the possible negative effects as a way to 'justify' their own position. At the same time, pupils who do not have a religion can have a certain bias which 'forced' them to express negative thoughts on religion, even if in everyday life they do not have so much experiences with negative effects of religion at all.

3.   Comparison with the results of the qualitative survey

Comparing the sample of this quantitative research with the qualitative study (see Ter Avest et al., 2008) the different degree of diversity is striking. Before going into the differences and communalities a short description of the school which participated in the qualitative research is helpful. The school is a Christian secondary school, in a medium-sized town in the western part of the Netherlands. There are only a few migrant students. Most of the students are from an average socio-economic background. The majority of teachers have a Christian background and are in different ways related to a church (some of them only attend church on Christmas Eve). Most of the students have a secularized Christian background. In the RE lessons teachers mainly teach according the 'teaching about'– combined with some elements of a 'teaching from religion'-approach. 71 pupils participated.

In the quantitative study eight schools participated, instead of one in the qualitative study. The schools include different educational levels and have different (religious) identities. Besides that, the schools differ in their location (rural, city) and in the (mean) social background of their pupils. With regard to the quantitative research we preferred to have a more diverse sample than the sample we used in the qualitative study as we were interested in knowing to what degree the fact that the qualitative research was carried out in a school which is officially a Christian school, but where in school practice and in the RE lessons there is no very clear focus on Christianity[17], has influenced our findings.

On the basis of the quantitative data we could go further into the relationships between the variables and gender, model of RE and religious background. Although the qualitative study did not allow us to focus on this in detail, we have clues that in both samples girls attached greater importance to religion than boys and that girls also talked more often about religion with others. As there was only one school included in the qualitative study, we could not make a distinction between models of religious education there. In the qualitative study we also did not go much further into differences with regard to religious background. Therefore it is hard to compare the two samples on this issue.

What role has religion in pupils' life and in their surroundings?

Pupils who participated in the qualitative study were less positive about religion and were less inclined to talk about it. In the present quantitative study pupils, in general, disagreed with the statement that talking about religious topics is boring and that 'religion doesn't interest me at all– we have more important things to talk about'. From the reactions of many pupils who participated in the qualitative research, we, however, concluded that pupils have more interesting topics to discuss and that they hardly talk about religion with their peers (see Ter Avest et al., 2008, pp. 94, 95). In the quantitative research the pupils attached greater importance to religion and they also talked more about it. One explanation for this finding might be the fact that in our sample we included two segregated schools with pupils with quite strong religious backgrounds, another denominational school with many Muslim pupils and another school with many teachers and pupils with a (more or less) Christian background. Seen the religious

---

17 In terms of 'model of RE' (see 1.2.2), it is not so obvious to code the school which participated in the qualitative research. In fact, with regard to religious identity the school has similarities with the *Christian lyceum* (quantitative study), but the focus on Christianity is less obvious. On the other hand, there is a stronger focus on Christianity than there is at for instance *Grotius College*.

backgrounds of these pupils, it is understandable that they attached greater importance to religion than the pupils of the school which was involved in the qualitative research.[18]

The finding that religion is more important to the pupils who participated in the quantitative research relates to some other differences we found between the results of the quantitative and qualitative study. One important result of the qualitative study was that family and school were the most important sources for pupils to get information about religion. In the present quantitative study we found that family was by far the most important source. School was important to quite some pupils as well, but it is striking that also great importance was attached to faith communities. We found that only few pupils stated that faith communities are 'a little bit important'. As we know that in the sample of the quantitative study more pupils have a specific religious background, it is not so much of a surprise that faith community was more often mentioned here as source to get information about religion.

How do pupils see religion in school?

With regard to the role of religion in school, there are quite some similarities between the quantitative and qualitative study. The most important commonality is that in both studies a majority of students agreed that religion should play a role in school and stressed that they favour a model of RE where all students are taught RE together, irrespective of their differences in religious or denominational background. In both studies quite some pupils favoured this model in combination with a model of optional RE in which pupils can decide for themselves whether they want to participate or not. There is also quite some overlap in what the pupils who participated in the two studies saw as the aims of (religious) education. From the qualitative study we concluded that pupils attach great importance to knowledge about different religions on the one hand and to learning how to live with others peacefully on the other hand. These two aspects, 'knowledge' and 'relationships', can also be detected in the quantitative material as well: Pupils attached importance to for instance 'learning to understand what religions teach' and agreed that pupils should be able to 'talk and communicate about religious issues' at school. Pupils' focus on the 'relational role' of religion also comes up in the quantitative study when pupils expressed their agreement with the statement that learning about different religions helps to understand others and live peacefully with them.

One striking difference between the two studies is that the pupils of the quantitative study have, in general, more experience with religious diversity (inside and/or outside the classroom). This is especially the case for pupils of state schools. This does, however, not result in clearly different experiences with religion in school. Both the pupils of the qualitative study and those of the quantitative study agreed that at school, they learn to have respect for everyone, whatever their religion. Pupils from both studies disagreed that learning about religions leads to conflicts in the classroom.

How do pupils see the impact of religion?

With regard to the impact of religion in society there are also communalities between the pupils of the two samples. One important communality is that pupils of both samples were inclined to state that people of different religions can live together peacefully and that 'respect

---

18 In an earlier study (Bertram-Troost, 2006) both the school which took part in the qualitative study (CCW) and one of the schools which took part in the quantitative study (GC) participated in an extensive research which was both quantitative and qualitative. Many differences with regard to the role religion plays in the life of pupils were found between the pupils of the two schools. 'Religious background' turned out to be one of the most important factors which influenced these differences.

for others' is very important. In the qualitative study 'respect for others' was mentioned as an important prerequisite for living together peacefully. Although we can not draw this conclusion directly from the quantitative study, we have clues that the pupils who participated in the quantitative study also attached great importance to this attitude of respect. Figure 21 for instance shows that pupils agreed quite strongly with the statement 'respecting the religion of others helps to cope with differences'. In both samples pupils showed a certain awareness of the fact that disagreement on religious issues can also be 'conflict potentials'. However, the idea that people of different religions can live peacefully together is more strongly present.

4.   Conclusions

In this part of the chapter we will concentrate on the main conclusions we can draw from the above described results. To structure the conclusions, we will respectively take the overall research questions (paragraph 4.1) and hypotheses (paragraph 4.2) as starting point. Although the sample is not representative and no additional data collection and/or data analysis has been carried out to further test the hypotheses, we can describe certain tendencies.

4.1   Answering research questions

What role has religion in pupils' life and in their surrounding?

From 2.1 we conclude that to the pupils of the Dutch sample, religion is rather important. This does, however, not mean that religion determines their whole life and that they are intensively involved in religious activities. Besides that, there are important differences between pupils who state they have a religion and pupils who do not. The majority of pupils disagreed with statements like 'Without religion, the world would be a better place' and 'Religion is a source of aggressiveness'. Family, school and faith community were important as sources to get information about different religions. Pupils were most likely to talk about religion within their family. 75% of the pupils talked to friends and/or classmates about religion at least sometimes. 65% of the pupils stated that most of their friends have the same views about religion as they themselves. About half of the pupils indicated tthey have contacts at school with people from different religious backgrounds and 44% said tthey have friends who belong to different religions. About one third of the pupils preferred both at school and in their spare time to go around with pupils who have the same religious background.

All in all, on the basis of the Dutch sample, one could answer the first research question by stating that to quite many Dutch pupils religion plays a (very) important role but that there is also a substantial group which personally does not attach much value to religion. There are big differences between, of course, pupils who adhere to a certain religion and pupils who do not and between pupils who have experience with different kind of models of RE. In general, two third of the pupils agreed that most of their friends have the same views about religion as they themselves. This percentage was higher for pupils who have a religion. The general percentage of pupils who go around with young people from different religious backgrounds at school was higher than the percentage who do so after school. Pupils who attend CCRE schools had the least contacts with people of different religions and they had the strongest preference to go around with young people who have their own religious background.

How do pupils see religion in school?

When it comes to religion in school, pupils of the Dutch sample were, in general, quite positive (see paragraph 2.2). A relatively great part of the pupils have experiences with religious education or with another subject in which religion is dealt with explicitly. Pupils disagreed quite strongly with the statement that learning about religions leads to conflicts in the classroom. In general, pupils tended to agree that religion is important as a topic in school and that learning about different religions at school helps to live peacefully together. Most pupils agreed with the statement that at school they learn to have respect for everyone, whatever their religion might be. The reactions of the pupils of the Dutch sample on statements on what role religion should play in school when they could decide upon that, also show that in general pupils were quite open to religion in school. Although most pupils were of the opinion that religious needs of pupils should be taken into account, they also had the view that school lessons should be attended by all pupils and that no exceptions should be made based on religious reasons. Next to that, pupils were in favour of a model of religious education where all students are taught religious education together. Besides, the majority (55%) were strongly in favour of optional RE. With regard to the content of religious education, it has become clear from the data that pupils of the Dutch sample were negative about the (possible) aim of guiding pupils towards religious beliefs. Instead, they were much more in favour of learning to understand what religions teach and of learning to talk and communicate about religious issues (knowledge and relationships).

How do pupils see the impact of religion?

The third sub-question (see paragraph 2.3) can be answered by focusing on for instance the functions pupils ascribed to learning about religions, their reasons to talk or not to talk about religion and their opinions on people of different worldviews living together. We have already shown that pupils of the Dutch sample were, in general, quite positive about the role of religion. Pupils agreed most with the statement that learning about different religions helps to understand others and live peacefully together with them. A majority of 68% of the pupils (strongly) disagreed with the statement 'In my view, talking about religion only leads to disagreement'. Instead, pupils tended to agree (strongly) with statements which mention positive values about (talking about) religion like 'Talking about religion helps us to understand others' and 'Talking about religion helps me to live peacefully together with people from different religions'. When personally confronted with religious diversity, a great deal of the pupils were willing to listen to the other person, but thought at the same time that his/her thoughts will not influence them. Next to that, quite many pupils indicate that they will try to discuss with the other about his/her opinions.

With regard to the 'conflict potential' of religion, data results show that pupils were aware of the possibility that conflicts will arise when there is disagreement on religious issues. Nevertheless, many pupils were of the opinion that respecting the religion of others helps to cope with differences. Besides that, pupils strongly disagreed with the statement 'I don't like people from other religions and do not want to live together with them'. It seems that pupils of the Dutch sample were more inclined to emphasize the possibilities for people of different religions to live together, than to stress possible conflicts due to religious diversity. Knowing about each other's religions was seen as an important aspect and as a prerequisite which could help people to live together in peace. Pupils did not attach much value to the role of the state in giving laws about the role of religion in society. Nor did they think that it helps if everyone keeps to their own religion in private. We can conclude that, in general, the pupils of the

Dutch sample were quite optimistic about the possibilities that people of different religions can live together peacefully. Besides, they were more inclined to focus on the positive functions of religions (for instance 'to understand others and live peacefully with them'). Nevertheless, they were aware of the conflict potentials of religion as they did not disagree with the statement 'Disagreement on religious issues leads to conflicts'.

4.2   Results in the light of research hypotheses

Religious background: tolerance and dialogue

Are religious students less tolerant than non-religious students? Our data point in the opposite direction: pupils who adhere to a religion indicated significantly more strongly they have respect for other people who believe (Figure 2). Besides, there was no significant difference between pupils who have a religion and pupils who do not with regard to their opinion on the statements 'Without religion the world would be a better place' and 'I don't like people from other religions and I do not want to live together with them'. The difference here is a matter of degree: pupils who have a religion preferred significantly more strongly than pupils who do not have a religion to go around with young people who have the same religious background as themselves (both at school and in their spare time). It is, however, the question whether this preference really has to do with tolerance. We found that there were no significant differences between pupils with and pupils without a religion with regard to the degree they go around with young people who have different religions from themselves after school. There were also no significant differences between the two groups with regard to the statement 'I have friends who belong to different religions'. Thus, we see some differences between the two groups with regard to their (preferred) contacts with people of different religions, but there are no direct clues that this has to do with tolerance.

Hypothesis 1b is that religious students are less open to dialogue on religious issues than non-religious students. As with hypothesis 1a, the data point in the opposite direction and again it is a matter of degree only. Pupils who do not have a religion agreed significantly less strongly with the statement that one of the aims of education should be to teach pupils to be able to talk and communicate about religious issues than pupils who have a religion. On the other hand, however, the two groups of respectively pupils with and without a religion did not differ so much on their reasons to talk or not to talk about religion. The only striking, and important, difference is that pupils who do not have a religion were less inclined to disagree with the statement 'In my view, talking about religion only leads to disagreement'. This indicates that pupils who do not have a religion might be less positive about talking about religion and might be less open to it.

Religious diversity in education: tolerance and dialogue

Are students who have encountered religious diversity in education are more tolerant? Seen our sample it is reasonable to state that both students who attend non-confessional religious education (CNRE schools) and pupils who do not attend RE (No RE schools) have (at least to a certain extent) experiences with religious diversity at school. The experience of encountering religious diversity is less in CCRE schools as, at least in the Netherlands, these schools are (more or less) segregated or pillarized (see Ter Avest et al., 2006).

We found that there were no significant differences between pupils who attend CNRE, CCRE or No RE schools with regard to their respect for other people who believe. Pupils who attend CCRE schools have of course, less contacts at school with young people who have a different religious background than pupils who attend CNRE or No RE schools. With regard to contacts after school no significant differences were found. On the other hand, it must be said that pupils who attend CCRE schools had less often friends who belong to different religions than pupils who attend CNRE or no RE schools. Pupils who attend CCRE schools also had a stronger preference for going around with young people who have the same religious background. As we already made clear, it is not obvious that this has really something to do with tolerance. It could also be a matter of 'habitual behaviour' or simply feeling more comfortable with people around you who are religiously and culturally more or less like you. Anyhow, there were no significant differences between the pupils who experienced different models of RE with regard to the statement 'I don't like people from other religions and I do not want to live together with them'. Next to that, pupils who attend CCRE schools, i.e. pupils who have relatively few experiences with religious diversity in the educational setting, significantly and remarkably disagreed more strongly with the statement 'Disagreement on religious issues leads to conflicts' than other pupils. This could be seen as an indication that pupils who do not have much experiences with religious diversity in education are less negative about the possible effects of disagreement on religious issues than pupils who do have experiences with religious diversity. All in all, we do not have clear indications that students who have encountered religious diversity in education are more tolerant than those who have not, as in CCRE schools. The impression is that pupils who do not have much experience with religious diversity, do not have so much an idea of what could possibly be difficult in contacts with people of different religions. Pupils who have these contacts themselves do have opinions on this and are more inclined to mention the conflict potential of disagreement on religious issues.

Hypothesis 2b states that students who have encountered religious diversity in education are more open to dialogue on religious issues. We found, however, no significant differences between the three groups (CNRE, CCRE, No RE schools) with regard to the degree to which they thought that learning to be able to talk and communicate about religious issues should be an aim of education. With regard to the reasons to talk or not to talk about religious issues too no significant differences between the three groups were found. When confronted with a person who has an other conviction, however, we see some differences: pupils who attend CCRE schools (that is pupils who have relatively few experiences with religious diversity at school), were more inclined than other pupils to discuss about the other persons opinions. They were also more inclined to try to convince the other that he/she is wrong. So, the conclusion seems unavoidable that in a way pupils who have relatively few experiences with religious diversity in education, as at CCRE schools, were in fact more open to dialogue on religious issues than other pupils who attend CNRE and No RE schools. One must, however, take into account here that these pupils were also more eager to convince others of their own rightness. So in a way this 'readiness for dialogue' was accompanied to a certain extent by a particular agenda on the side of these pupils of the CCRE schools, that is what they see as their missionary and apologiac duty. As already described above, this does, however, not necessarily mean that these pupils are also less tolerant than pupils who have encountered religious diversity in education.

We found that pupils who attend CCRE schools were relatively positive about for instance talking about religion with others and discussed with them about their ideas more than other pupils although they have less concrete contacts with people of different religions. It could be that the influence of their personal commitment to religion and the fact that they are raised in a surrounding in which religion is very important, stimulates them to develop a certain openness toward religion in general, including other religions than their own. Possibly, pupils who learned to see the value of religion for themselves and notice the importance at home, in their religious communities and in the school community or the school ethos, are also more willing to respect the religions of others. However, from the quantitative questionnaire many things with regard to these issues are not fully transparent yet, and are issues that need to be addressed in further research projects. For instance, we do not know what the everyday contacts pupils have with pupils of different religions really look like and what kind of discussions they have with each other.

All in all, the data show that, at least for the Dutch case, it is not so easy to state that religious diversity in education and/or a school with a heterogeneous religious population in itself stimulates dialogue and dealing with conflicts. But, as stated above, follow up research on these issues is really needed here.

Personal encountering of religious diversity: tolerance and dialogue

Hypothesis 3a is that students who have personally encountered religious diversity are more tolerant. Hypothesis 3b is that students who have personally encountered religious diversity are more open to dialogue on religious issues.

To explore our data from the perspective of this hypothesis we made use of the questions on 'people around you' (see also Figures 3 to 6). In our analysis we did not make a clear distinction between pupils who have personally encountered religious diversity and pupils who did not, as this was not necessary with regard to the main research questions. Therefore it is a bit more complicated to go into these two last hypotheses.

In general, pupils who have a religion themselves more often had friends who have the same views about religion than pupils who do not have a religion. Besides, we found that at school pupils who do not have a religion went around with young people who have different religious backgrounds significantly more often than pupils who have a religion.

Logically (at least in the Dutch case), pupils who attend CCRE schools had significantly less contacts at school with people of different religious backgrounds. They also had significantly fewer friends who belong to different religions than pupils who attend No RE or CNRE schools.

All in all there are clear indications that, in our sample, pupils who do not have a religion themselves and especially pupils who attend CNRE or No RE schools had more personal experience with religious diversity. As we already described in 2.1 these pupils also had, in comparison to pupils who have a religion and/or attend CCRE schools, a relatively low preference to go around with people who have the same religious background as they themselves. As we already made clear in 2.1.2 we do not really know what kind of reasons the pupils have for their preferences.

Above, we have already elaborated on the differences between pupils with and pupils without a religion (hypotheses 1a and 1b) and the differences with regard to religious diversity in education (hypotheses 2a and 2b). We did not find clear indications that religious students are less tolerant than non-religious students. On the contrary, it is even possible to postulate that religious students (who have, generally speaking, less personal experience with religious diversity) are more tolerant. Besides, we found that pupils who do not have a religion were less positive about talking about religion and are less open to it. We also found no clear indications that pupils who have encountered religious diversity in education (and these are also the pupils with relatively more personal experiences with religious diversity) were more tolerant. The only difference with regard to 'readiness for dialogue' we found is that pupils who attend CCRE schools were more inclined to try to convince the other of his/her own conviction. Further, strikingly enough it turns out that pupils who attend CCRE, CNRE or No RE schools had more or less the same ideas about the impact of and reasons to talk or not to talk about religion.

On the basis of our present data we cautiously conclude that there is no indication that students who have personally encountered religious diversity are more tolerant and/or more open to dialogue on religious issues. This result is a stimulus for further research in which these issues need to be carefully scrutinized and unravelled.

References

Bertram-Troost, G.D. (2006). *Geloven in bijzonder onderwijs. Levensbeschouwelijke identiteits-ontwikkeling van adolescenten in het voortgezet onderwijs.* [Belief in denominational education. Religious identity development of adolescents in secondary education.] Zoetermeer: Boekencentrum.

Ter Avest, I., Bakker, C., Bertram-Troost, G. & Miedema, S. (2007). Religion in Education in the Dutch Pillarized and Post-Pillarized Educational System: Historical Background and Current Debates. In R. Jackson, S. Miedema, W. Weisse & J.-P. Willaime (Eds.), *Religion and Education in Europe. Developments, Contexts and Debates.* Muenster: Waxmann, pp. 203–219.

Ter Avest, I., Bertram-Troost, G.D., Van Laar, A., Miedema, S. & Bakker, C. (2008). Religion in the Educational Lifeworld of Students: Results of a Dutch Qualitative Study. In T. Knauth, D.-P. Josza, G. Bertram-Troost & J. Ipgrave (Eds.), *Encountering Religious Pluralism in School and Society. A Qualitative Study of Teenage Perspectives in Europe.* Muenster: Waxmann, pp. 89–111.

Van de Donk, W.B.H.J., Jonkers, A.P., Kronjee, G.J. & Plum, R.J.J.M. (Eds.) (2006). *Geloven in het publieke domein* [Religion in the public domain]. Amsterdam: Amsterdam University Press.

Sean Neill

Commentary on 'Dutch Pupils' Views on Religion in School and Society – Report on a Quantitative Research'

From an English perspective perhaps the most surprising feature of the introduction, given the popular reputation of Holland as a progressive and liberal society, is the description of the school system as religiously polarised, or, as it is described, 'pillarised'. The descriptions of the schools demonstrate their individual character and marked divergence in religious values. However it is not clear how far this diverse tradition has been affected by developments such as Rotterdam's consultation of ethnic minorities about how they wanted the education system to operate in their parts of the city (Smit et al., 2001), though the description of 'El Habib' suggests that such initiatives may have increased the diversity and fragmentation of Dutch society. Events such as the '7/7' bombings in London have given rise to qualms about the potential causes of such fissiparity in England. As a result, there have been concerns about permitting English schools to diverge from the 'agreed syllabus' though a certain amount of local diversity is permissible. Paradoxically, the 'unconsidered' nature of English identity, conferred by the island geography of England, has led to a situation where religious identity is not a label of 'Englishness'; the ecumenical nature of the Anglican Church, though currently threatened by schismatic elements, has led to a situation where most people see religious enthusiasm as *'not British'*.

In contrast, countries such as the Netherlands, without defensible land frontiers as experience in many wars shows, have had to be much more thoughtful about differentiating themselves from their powerful neighbours: religious identity appears to have been one factor in this process of differentiation, and this is reflected in the diversity of the educational system. The importance of religious identity is also indicated by early two-thirds of Dutch students saying they had a religion or world-view, as opposed to half of the English students; relatively more English students gave esoteric or unclassifiable belief classifications. A striking difference between the two countries is the lesser emphasis on religious identity in England, despite a greater proportion of immigrant and non-Christian students, though, as the discussion of the Dutch sample indicates, this may be due to sampling artefacts.

It is therefore not surprising that there are marked differences (though it is not clear whether they are statistically significant) between students in their views on the importance of religion and its content, depending on their own religious background and educational experience. This also applies to sources of knowledge about religion; two striking differences from the English situation are the differences between students in the importance of their school (CCRE as opposed to others) and in the importance of the internet to non-religious pupils; this contrasts with the relative indifference of English pupils, whatever their belief status.

The general pattern of a more positive attitude to religion by girls and by those who have a religious belief themselves mirrors the English findings, but the difference in relation to confessional education found in Holland was not replicated in the English sample because confessional education is largely absent from the sample and from the English educational experience. A similar pattern of resemblances and differences occured in the results about talking with others about religion. The strong differentiation between Dutch students who have had different religious education experiences in relation to whom they wish to go around with is not replicated in the English sample because there is greater uniformity in religious educational experience, even in the one English school which is nominally denominational.

Similarly, because English students all experience the same duration of religious education, the English data also provides no evidence to correspond to the differences in amount of religious education experienced by the Dutch students. Attitudes towards the effects of religion in school, talking about religion and the effects of religious differences, the gender differences in these attitudes and the differences between those with or without a religion or world-view, are, however, fairly similar to those of English students. There is also general agreement between Dutch and English students about the aims of religious education (like English students, Dutch students generally favour education about religion rather than education *for* religion), but once more there are no differences in the English sample to correspond to the differences between Dutch students who attend different types of school. However there is a difference between the countries in that the English students who have a religion or worldview are more positive towards the 'enquiry-based approach' (education about religion) their Dutch peers who have a religion favour education for religion, though they do also show tolerance for other religions. Whereas in the Dutch sample students who have a religion tend to be more embarrassed by showing their religion than those who lack a religion, the converse is the situation in the English sample. The significance of this is discussed below.

The comparison between the qualitative and qualitative studies is hindered by the use of only a single school in the qualitative studies; given the marked differences between schools apparent from the quantitative study, the qualitative study would be expected to produce different results if it had been carried out in more than one school (as was done in England), as the authors point out.

So far as the actual conduct of the quantiative study is concerned, the Dutch pupils appear to have been more recalcitrant, especially in providing personal information, though their open comments about the questionnaire were similar to those of their English peers. However their overt recalcitrance may raise questions over the accuracy of their responses where subversion would be less detectable. It is possible to speculate about this as a result of the greater 'institutional salience' of religion in the more religiously differentiated Dutch system; this could also account for the greater reluctance of Dutch students who have a religion about displaying their allegiance than their English counterparts. This may also explain the more negative views expressed by the students in the qualitative study, who may have found the more personal qualitative research approach more embarrassing than the impersonal questionnaire used in the more quantitative study; they may have 'clammed up' as a result.

Given the teenage tendency to rebel against adult institutions, the more overt religious affiliation of many Dutch schools might be having the paradoxical effect of making students less overt about their religion than their English peers whose institutions are less denominational, or indeed organisationally secular. However this effect, if it exists, does not extend to intolerance to other religions, where type of school has little effect.

The overall general similarity in the attitudes of Dutch and English students are not surprising given the proximity, both geographically and in terms of political and religious similarity, of the two countries and their long historical interchange as maritime nations and frequent alliance against neighbouring powers; similarly, both have a similar system of values (Puurula et al., 2001).

References

Puurula, A., Neill, S., Vasileiou, L., Husbands, C., Lang, P., Katz, Y.J., Romi, S., Menezes, I. & Vriens, L. (2001). Teacher and student attitudes to affective education: a European collaborative research report. *Compare* 31/2, pp. 165–186.

Smit, F. Driessen, G & Sleegers, P. (2001). Relationships between parents of ethnic minority children, schools and supporting institutions in the local community – some ideas for the future, in: F. Smit, K. van der Wolf, & P. Sleegers (Eds.), *A Bridge to the Future: collaboration between parents, schools and communities.* Nijmegen: ITS.

Dan-Paul Jozsa, Thorsten Knauth & Wolfram Weisse

Views of Students on Religion in Education in the Netherlands – Perspectives from Hamburg and North Rhine-Westphalia

Remarkable findings

On the background of the findings in Germany where we compared Hamburg and NRW, two federal states with respectively a non-confessional and a confessional religious education model, it is conspicuous that in the Dutch sample there are remarkable differences between schools classified as CCRE, CNRE and 'no RE' schools.

In schools with CCRE 86.5% of the students indicated they have a religion, compared to 53.5% in schools with CNRE and 48.1% in schools with 'no RE'. Likewise 50% of the students in schools with CCRE, 24% in schools with CNRE and 24% in schools with 'no RE' state that religion is very important to them, while 3%, 25% and 25% state that religion is 'absolutely not important' to them. Likewise 89%, 41% and 49% respectively of the students in the three 'school types' think that 'there is God', while 6%, 26% and 31% state that they 'don't really think that there is any sort of God, spirit or life force'.

Compared with students who attend schools with a CNRE or a 'no RE' model, students who attend schools with a CCRE model tend to be more positive towards religion, tend to agree more that religion determines their whole life, to agree less that religion is nonsense and less that one can be a religious person without belonging to a particular faith community; they tend to speak more often about religion with family members, friends, classmates, other students at school, teachers and religious leaders. They tend to attach more importance to school and faith community as a source of information about religion, to be more positive about the effects of learning about religion in school; but they also tend to have more problems showing their religion openly in school. At the same time they tend to be more interested to talk about religion; they tend more often to agree that at school religious food requirements should be taken into account, while they more seldom agree that students should be able to wear discreet as well as more visible religious symbols at school. They tend to favour less an optional religious education, and more a religious education where students are taught separately according to their religious background. They tend to agree more that students should get in religious education an objective knowledge about different religions, but also that they should be guided towards religious belief. They tend more often to state they do not have students in their class or friends who belong to a different religion and that most of the students in their class as well as their friends have the same views about religion as themselves. They tend at school more seldom to go around with young people who have different religious backgrounds and at school as well as after school to prefer more to go around with young people who have the same religious background as themselves. They tend to like more to know what their best friend thinks about religion, and generally to care more what their friends think about religion; however they tend more often to state that learning about different religions helps to understand others and to live peacefully with them, to agree more that learning about different religions helps to develop their own point of view as well as moral values and helps more to learn about one's own religion. They tend to agree more that talking about religion helps to understand others and that it helps them to live peacefully together with people from different religions; when confronted with proselytism they tend more to convince the other that he is wrong and that their own views about religion are the best ones, however they also tend to agree less with the statement 'I don't like people from other religions and do not want to live together with them'.

Apart from that, it is remarkable that even among the students who attend a confessional religious education model in the Dutch sample, the majority favour a religious education model where all students are taught together irrespective of their religion, and only a small minority are in favour of a religious education model where students are guided towards religious belief.

Rather surprising is that the data seems to reveal the uncontested leading position of family as a hotspot for religious communication and the acquisition of knowledge about religion; and also that 'school' assumes only the fourth position behind 'faith community' and 'internet'. However, this does not necessarily restrict the role of school as important place for dealing with religion, but it sheds light on an additional educational arena outside school which should also be considered in further research.

The Dutch report is not an analysis about differences and commonalities between pupils of different religious backgrounds. It draws the distinction line rather between pupils who have religion and pupils who have none. It shows that there are for many items also differences between these two groups, such as the relevance of religion for their own life, the willingness to talk about religion and attitudes about the significance of religion in school. Nevertheless, it deserves to be mentioned that beside the stated differences between the groups, the overwhelming attitude towards others is respect and the guiding image of living together peacefully in society.

Next to that, it is astonishing that pupils who do not have a religion are apparently more experienced with religious diversity but tend to be more reluctant to talk about religion, whereas pupils who have a religion are less experienced with religious diversity and are more inclined to enter into dialogue with others. These results could be also interpreted as effects of the ongoing 'pillarized' Dutch school system.

Alternative interpretations

With regard to Hamburg and NRW, we found that the importance of religion is a factor that initiates a lot of differences with respect to the items of the questionnaire used. A lot of the differences between the worldview groups or on basis of the 'migration background' proved to be due to the 'importance of religion', when we took into consideration cross correlations between these two variables. When one takes into consideration the 'importance of religion' for the Dutch students, likewise some of the difference between students from CCRE schools and students from CNRE respectively and 'no RE' schools seem to only be caused by correlations between the 'importance of religion' and the 'type of school' attended. This finding could be regarded as a 'statistical argument', that the students or their parents choose which 'type of school' to attend according to the importance they accord to religion and that one of the reasons to explain the differences found with respect to the three considered 'school types' is that they attract groups of students, with regard to the 'importance' they accord to religion and the role religion plays in their life, and not that the school type itself 'initiates' (all, or maybe any of) these differences. It might be false to explain the differences found between the students in the three 'school types' by the impact of the model of religious education followed only; rather it is sensible to presuppose a complex interplay between the religious background, the selected school and the experienced RE. So far we do not know enough about this interplay.

Main commonalities and differences between the findings in the Dutch and the German context

Most students in the 'Dutch' as well as in the 'German' sample tend to accord religion a place in school; only a very small minority (6% in the Dutch and 11% in the German sample) agree that there should be no place for religion in school. For most of the students religion should have its place in religious education; only 17% of the students in the Dutch and 13% in the German sample think that there is no need for religious education in school because all they need to know about religion is covered by other school subjects.

Most students in the Dutch as well as in the German sample agree that at school they get knowledge about different religions; that they have opportunities to discuss religious issues from different perspectives and that they learn to respect everyone whatever their religion. Most of the students agree that learning about different religions helps them to live peacefully together and disagree that learning about religions at school leads to conflicts in the classroom.

Most of the students also consider that at school religious food requirements should be taken into account and that students should be able to wear discreet religious symbols and that they can be absent from school at the time of their religious festivals. In both contexts most of the students favour knowledge based religious education and advocate the communicative and societal dimension of religious education, where students get an objective knowledge about different religions, learn what the religions teach, learn the importance of religion for dealing with problems in society and also learn to talk and communicate about religious issues.

Only a minority (19% of the students in the Dutch sample and 24% in the German sample) agrees that students should be guided towards religious belief in religious education and that students should be excused from taking some classes for religious reasons. However it is the majority of the students in the Dutch sample but only a minority (29%) in the German sample who think that schools should provide facilities for pupils to pray in school. However, considerable minorities in both contexts (41% as opposed to 37%) agree that voluntary religious services could be part of school life.

A remarkable majority in both countries consider that sharing common interests, knowing about each other's religions, knowing personally people from different religions and doing something together, would help people from different religions to live together in peace. Likewise considerable majorities think that respecting the religion of others helps to cope with differences. In both countries only minorities think that it would help living together in peace if everyone keeps his own religion in private, however in the German sample students are more in favour of this 'strategy' – 46% agree, while only 26% do so in the Dutch sample. On the other side, although only minorities agree that it would help living together in peace, if the state has strong laws about the role of religion in society, the students in the Dutch sample are more positive about this 'strategy' – 44% agree, compared to 32% who do so in the German sample.

The main difference with regard to the positions of the students concerning religion in school seems at first sight to be that irrespective of the 'school type', i.e. schools with CCRE, CNRE and 'no RE', the majority of the students in the Dutch sample favour a religious education model where all students are taught together irrespective of their religious background, whereas in the German sample, the majority of students in NRW favour a religious education model where the students are taught separately, while the majority of students in Hamburg favour a model where all students are taught together. But this difference is overturned when one takes a closer look at another commonality, since the majority of the students in all three samples favour the model of RE they are used to. In NRW the students, used to a separated (confessional) model, favour a separated model. In Hamburg the students, used to a joint religious education (for all), favour a model of RE where all the students are taught together. In the Dutch context the students in all schools, irrespective of the particular approach to RE, confessional or not, etc., are used only to a model where all pupils are taught together, and that is the model they also favour.

A striking difference concerns the fact that only 60% of the students in the Dutch sample state they have students in their class who belong to a different religion, compared to 81% in the German sample. Likewise only 44% of the students in the Dutch sample state having friends who belong to different religions, compared to 81% in the German context. On the other side 65% compared to 59% of the students in the Dutch and German samples respectively state that most of their friends have the same views about religion as themselves, but when it comes to classmates 52% of the students in the Dutch but only 32% in the German sample state that most classmates have the same views about religion as themselves. 51% of the students in the Dutch sample compared to 79% in the German sample state that at school they go around with young people who have different religious backgrounds, while 45% compared to 56% do so after school, i.e. in both contexts contacts with students of a different religion are more often in school then after school. Somewhat on the same lines, 35% of the students in the Dutch sample state they prefer to go around with young people who have the same religious background as themselves at school, and 34% after school, while for the German sample the corresponding percentages are 21% and 23%. It is however not possible to say if these differences are an 'artefact' of the samples or if they are characteristic for the Dutch situation.

Generally it appears that the differences between the three 'types of school' in Holland with regard to the model of integrating religion in education are more distinctive and more prominent than the differences we found in the German sample with regard to the different models of RE employed in the two German federal states. However a closer look at 'different school types' in Hamburg and NRW with regard to dealing with religion in education, for example church schools versus state schools, might help to understand more the reasons for these differences.

Geir Skeie & Marie von der Lippe

Does Religion Matter to Young People in Norwegian Schools?

1.   Introduction

The somewhat casually put question in the title of this chapter is intended to point in two directions, both asking whether religion is an important part of young people's lives in Norway, and asking about the role of religion in schools, seen from the perspective of young people, aged 14–16 years.[1] In spite of its limitations we think this study offers an important insight into the world and views of our respondents and there is no direct parallel to this study in Norway.[2]

1.1   Setting the research scene

Before entering into the study itself, some contextual background information about Norway may be appropriate to an international readership. The country has a population of only 4,7 million people, it is long and narrow, and there are considerable regional differences. The demographical and socio-cultural differences are also related to issues of religion and worldview. The south-west of Norway is often called the "Bible-belt" by sociologists of religion as well as laypeople, while people living in the eastern and northern parts of the country are perceived as less religiously active. The Northern part of Norway has also a distinct Sami population with their own religious and cultural traditions.[3] In addition to the historical and regional differences, also immigration from the late 1960s has added to the pluralisation of Norway.

While some of the inner city schools in Oslo have up to 90% students with a 'minority' background, most schools in Norway are on the opposite end of the scale, with mainly students from an ethnic Norwegian background, and few with a minority background. Similar variations can be observed between schools in different parts of the cities, and in general between schools in urban and rural areas. The strong position of the *local* school for all children in each community has been combined with a rather centralised educational system in terms of policy, curricula and other regulations in order to secure the same quality of education for all irrespective of social and cultural background and where they live. There are however, at the moment visible changes in the system, like the establishment of 'free choice' of school in larger cities. In recent years there have also been attempts to introduce more private schools, but so far with only limited success. Often there is a higher concentration of

---

1   We would like to thank the Centre for Behavioural Research at University of Stavanger for assistance, especially Grete Sørensen Våland for coding the questionnaires and Edvin Bru for advice in analysing results.

2   The most recent research relevant is Erling Birkedal's investigation of faith in God and experiences with religious practice among 13 year old Norwegian pupils (Birkedal, 2001). Looking at the Nordic countries there are also relatively few studies of young people and religion, and they are difficult to compare. See the recent dissertation of Gunnar J. Gunnarsson (Gunnarsson, 2008, pp. 45–56) for a recent overview of relevant research.

3   Groups with a longstanding attachment to the country are defined as national minorities. In Norway these minorities are: Kvens (people of Finnish descent in Northern Norway), Jews, Forest Finns, Roma/Gypsies and Romani people/Travellers. See also Skeie, 2007.

children with a minority background in some schools. Introduction classes for children who recently have come to Norway are usually part of the local schools, while some cities have concentrated all these classes in particular schools with special competences.

Since 1997 a non-confessional, multi-faith religious education has been compulsory in the national public school curriculum. As a consequence of this all students have to attend religious education, independent of their religious and cultural background, and only have the right to limited exemption from the lessons (Skeie, 2007). Although private (religious) schools may follow the national core curriculum including religious education, they are allowed to have a special ethos influencing their own curriculum. The number of pupils attending private schools in Norway is still very low (less than 3%), and schools with confessional/faith based religious education are therefore very few.[4] It should be mentioned that the particular year of school the pupils of this study are in, is also the most common year for pupils to be confirmed in the Church of Norway, presently used by about 65% (43.000) of the age cohort, while approximately 10.000 of the same age group take part in a ritual called 'humanist' confirmation, arranged by The Norwegian Humanist Association.

1.2   Description of sampling and the schools

Based on our understanding of the Norwegian context discussed above, we decided, when selecting a sample for this research, to focus our attention on the following aspects: private/public schools, regional location, urban/rural community, socioeconomic and sociocultural background of pupils.

At an early stage it was decided not to include private (religious) schools in this quantitative study.[5] These schools are in themselves an interesting object for research, but in the present study, it would give a rather 'twisted' picture of the Norwegian situation to include them, bearing in mind how few schools there are of this kind. Also, these schools do not have a common 'model' of religious education, since some follow the national one, and others have separately acknowledged syllabuses. As a consequence, all schools participating in the quantitative research reported here are public schools, which means that all pupils in the sample are attending public schools and have had the non-confessional multi-faith religious education (KRL) throughout their school years.[6] Most of their teachers, however, would have had a more confessional experience of RE, both in their school years and in their teacher training before 1997.

Issues related to regional differences in Norway have been a main concern, and we have succeeded in getting a fair distribution in terms of local communities; covering both rural and differently sized urban areas, which can be seen as typical of Norway. An important addition

---

4   See Statistics Norway: http://www.ssb.no/english/subjects/04/02/20/utgrs_en/ accessed 10. October 2008. At the moment there are only religious private schools with a Christian ethos. For a shorter period there was an Islamic school in Oslo, but because of internal conflicts this school was closed in 2004.

5   In the qualitative study on young people's perceptions and experiences with religious diversity in Norway students from a Christian private school were included in the sample. Results from this research is elaborated in von der Lippe, 2008.

6   The school subject was at the time of this investigation officially named *Kristendoms-, religions- og livssynskunnskap* (Christian Knowledge and Religious and Ethical Education). In Norwegian the abbreviation 'KRL' is the common term, and will also be used in this report. It should be noted that the name of the subject has been changed in 2008, and it is now called *Religion, livssyn og etikk* (Religion, worldviews and ethics), 'RLE'.

Table 1:   Description of schools

School	Location	Characterisation	Classes	Number of pupils
Stavanger school (1)	The school is located in one of the suburbs of Stavanger. Stavanger is the fourth largest city in Norway, with approximately 120 000 inhabitants, located on the West Coast.	Secondary school with approximately 350 students from 8th – 10th grade. The students attending this school have mostly an ethnic Norwegian background, and come largely from a working class background. Most of the students have a Christian or non-religious background.	4	101
Sandnes school (2)	The school is located in Sandnes, a small city with approximately 62 000 inhabitants, close to Stavanger.	Secondary school with approximately 300 students from 8th – 10th grade. The majority of the students have an ethnic Norwegian background, however there are also students with religious and cultural minority backgrounds. Some of the students are very active in Christian organisations. The students mainly come from a middle-class background.	3	65
Oslo school (3)	The school is located in one of the multicultural suburbs in Oslo. Oslo is the capital of Norway, with approximately 560 485 inhabitants.	Secondary school with approximately 435 students from 8th – 10th grade. Almost 70% of the students in this school have a minority background, and the students come from working- and middle-class backgrounds. The suburb and school has a well-known reputation, working intensively with plurality, tolerance and minority issues.	6	125
Bergen east school (4)	The school is located in one of the suburbs in Bergen. Bergen is the second largest city in Norway with approximately 245 000 inhabitants.	Secondary school with approximately 510 students from 8th – 10th grade. Around 10% of the students in this school have a minority background. The students come from different socio-economic layers, and belong mostly to the working- and middle-class with a few with an upper-class background.	9	205
Bergen west school (5)	The school is located in one of the suburbs in Bergen.	Primary and secondary school with approximately 340 students altogether and 110 students at secondary level. The school is regarded as a multicultural school with ca 35% students with a minority background. The suburb is still one of Bergen's low status areas, and students have mainly lower working-class backgrounds.	4	102
Haugesund school (6)	Located in a rural area 10 km east of Haugesund city, on the West Coast.	Secondary school with approximately 300 students from 8th – 10th grade. The school is the only comprehensive school in the municipality which is not combined with a primary school. The students have mostly a majority background, and come largely from a working- and middle-class background. Most of the students have a Christian or non-religious background.	5	99
Total			31	707

to the variety is the choice of a school from Oslo situated within a multicultural part of the city. The following overview gives a general picture of the schools participating in the survey, but in order to get a clearer picture about the different local contexts it needs to be combined with a few characteristics we believe to be relevant as background information without going in too much detail. The total sample consists of 707 questionnaires and the mean age of respondents is 14,3 years.

1.2.1   Socio-cultural plurality in the sample

One of our interests behind composing the sample was to include the socio-cultural plurality of Norwegian society. When asked about their national background, the pupils' answers show that a large majority of them are born in Norway. About 10% are born in other countries, while this goes for 25–30% of the parents. The pupils that are not born in Norway come from a wide range of countries, but if we also include the background of parents the countries mentioned most often are Pakistan, Vietnam, Turkey, Iraq/Kurdistan, Somalia, England and Iran. In addition to these, 70 other countries are mentioned. These diverse backgrounds are not as present in all the sample schools, and one way of illustrating this is by showing the proportion of Norwegian born pupils and parents at each school.

Table 2:   Norwegian background of pupils at each school

School	Norwegian born pupils		Norwegian born mothers		Norwegian born fathers	
	N	%	N	%	N	%
1 Stavanger	99	99%	89	88%	91	90%
2 Sandnes	59	91%	52	80%	49	75%
3 Oslo	95	82%	51	45%	41	35%
4 Bergen east	198	99%	182	92%	182	92%
5 Bergen west	89	91%	74	76%	67	68%
6 Haugesund	92	96%	91	95%	86	90%
Total	632	92%	539	79%	516	75%

Norway, as well as other Scandinavian countries, is considered to have a quite secularised population.[7] This is also noticeable in our sample. When asked whether they 'have a certain religion or world-view' there is a small majority who answer 'yes'. This majority is clearer among the girls (60%/40%), while the boys are 50/50. The Stavanger, Bergen East and Bergen West schools all have around 50% answering 'yes', the percentage is close to 60% in the Sandnes and Haugesund schools. In the Oslo school 74% answer that they have a religion. So, the rural school as well as the urban ones with the strongest Muslim presence, are the schools where most pupils claim to have a religion, while the urban schools with dominance of Norwegian majority pupils are lowest on this scale.

---

7   See survey from 1998: http://www.nsd.uib.no/data/ny_individ/pdf-filer/rapport115.pdf accessed 20th October 2008.

In terms of concrete religious or world view affiliation, table 3 shows the total sample in frequency and valid percent as well as the pupils' religion- and worldview background in the various schools:

Table 3: **Declared religious and world view background of pupils in the sample**

Religion/ world view	Total numbers	Total valid %	School 1 valid %	School 2 valid %	School 3 valid %	School 4 valid %	School 5 valid %	School 6 valid %
Christian	265	75	96	80	44	84	62	94
Muslim	57	16	0	14	49	5	19	0
Humanist	8	2	2	3	0	4	0	4
Buddhist	8	2	2	0	3	1	9	0
Hindu	3	1	0	0	4	0	0	0
Others[8]	13	4	0	3	0	6	10	2
Total	354	100	100	100	100	100	100	100

1.2.2 Reflection on the sample

The limitations of this study in terms of how representative the sample is, is therefore not so much the lack of regional distribution, but rather the fact that it is based on the choice of whole classes in certain schools. There is nothing like a random selection of pupils, not even within the geographical area chosen for investigation. We used mainly contacts we already had to get schools with different profiles, and this also made it easier to get approval from the school administrators.

It is not easy to judge whether the distribution of national backgrounds in our sample is somewhere near representing the overall population. In the age-group 13–15, about 7% of the total Norwegian population has both parents born outside Norway. In the age group 0–17 the same figure is 20% for Norway as a whole. In Oslo 47% of children (0–17) had immigrant backgrounds in January 2008, while Rogaland county had 18% and Hordaland county 16%.[9] This means that the Oslo school (3) has more pupils with immigrant backgrounds than the average in Oslo, but is typical for its local area. The other schools have an average which is closer to the national statistics. Since the average amount of children with immigrant backgrounds tend to decrease by increasing age nationally, we expect that also the number of children with immigrant backgrounds from the west coast area is a little higher than the average in this region. This fits well with the fact that most of the schools chosen are located in larger urban areas. All in all it therefore seems that we have succeeded pretty well in getting a sample that reflects what we expected from the areas where we chose the schools. In terms of national representation we have a few more respondents with immigrant background(s) than the average. We also have slightly more girls than the average; 52% of the questionnaires are

---

8   The other religions and world-views mentioned are: Sikh, Jewish, Atheist, Jehovah's Witnesses, Pagan, Satanist, Agnostic, Old Norse Religion.

9   For this and the following, see Statistics Norway:
    http://www.ssb.no/emner/02/notat_200431/notat_200431.pdf accessed 10th September 2008 and
    http://www.ssb.no/emner/02/barn_og_unge/2008/tabeller/befolkning/bef0900.html accessed 10th September 2008

filled in by girls and 48% by boys, while the ratio nationally in this age group is about 51% boys and 49% girls.[10]

Compared with national statistics on faith communities, the sample is not reflecting the overall situation. Muslim and Humanist communities are usually considered to be about the same size, and neither of them much more than 2% of the total population.[11] If we break the sample down at a school level, we find that Islam is strongly represented in the Oslo school (3), with more than 25% Muslim pupils, and in this school this is slightly more than those who declare themselves to be Christians. This indicates that our intentions behind including this school were appropriate. The idea was to include one school from the Oslo area in order to ensure a stronger representation of non-Christian religions. The sample from one of the Bergen schools (5) as well shows a significant group of Muslim students (ca. 10%) and a few pupils from other non-Christian backgrounds. School 3 and school 5 have almost 30% Christians, school 4 about 35%, school 1 almost 40%, school 6 approximately 50% and school 2 about 60% Christian students. These differences in the sample show that adherence to the Christian religion is stronger in the least urbanised areas, which strengthens the representativeness of the sample.

In conclusion we find that broadly speaking our sample is an interesting and valuable one to analyse. Even if the religious backgrounds of pupils are not quite like the national averages, we have succeeded in getting a broad variety of socio-cultural background including a religious and world-view diversity which opens the possibility to investigate the increasing plurality of Norwegian society, keeping in mind the focus of the research questions on the role of religion in life and school.

1.3   Procedure

The practical and methodical issues related to distributing and collecting the questionnaires worked according to plan. Reports from the teachers administering the filling in of questionnaires were that some students found the research interesting and fun to answer, while others thought it was boring to fill out the questionnaire or did not like the way the questions were formulated. On the last page in the questionnaire, the pupils were invited to add personal comments, additions or remarks. In our sample two hundred students gave an answer to this open question. Some were commenting explicitly on the questions in the questionnaire, while others referred to religion in general, religion in school, religion and conflict, and peaceful coexistence in a plural society. Among those who were positive to the questionnaire, some expressed that the survey contributed to new understanding of peaceful coexistence between people with different backgrounds. But a few students found, on the contrary, some of the questions to be discriminating and even racist. Some thought the questions were too personal and a few did not like to answer questions about their parents or parents' occupation. Many students thought the questions were formulated in a very similar way, and would have appreciated a shorter questionnaire. Some found the questions odd or difficult to answer, and a couple of students would prefer the concept 'worldview' instead of 'religion' because they think world-view is a more inclusive term. A couple of comments in the questionnaires can illustrate the variety of reactions:

---

10 Statistics Norway: http://www.ssb.no/english/subjects/02/ accessed 10. September 2008.

11 In this particular case, however, it may be that some of the pupils who are Humanists answer 'no' to the question 'Do you have a certain religion or worldview'.

It seemed like you had 10 questions written 150 times in different ways! The questions seems irrelevant and stupid and too few and bad answer alternatives! (Especially if you think about that we are a secondary school and many don't believe in God)... Good luck! (2–3–12)

I think it is good with researches like this because it gives you insight in what we can possibly do to live together with people from other religions and you get the opportunity to learn something about your self and your own meanings. To know what to do together to solve conflicts with people with different religions is very important, I think (2–2–6)

2   General presentation of results

2.1   What role has religion in pupils' life?

2.1.1   Data description

Basic attitudes and practice

An important aim of this study is to get some indication about the role and position religion has in students' life; mentally, socially and in terms of practice. The question 'do you have a certain religion or worldview?' has given some indication of the affiliation and position of the pupils. To find out what role religion play in pupils' life they were additionally asked 'how important is religion to you?'

Figure 1:   Importance of religion, %

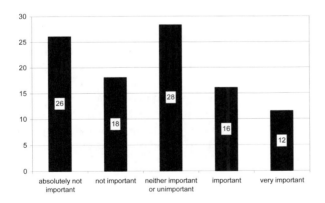

Almost one half of the pupils claim that religion is 'absolutely not' or 'not important' (44%). Another large group answers 'neither important nor unimportant' (28%), while a group of similar size (28%) say that religion is 'important' or 'very important' to them. A closer look at gender differences shows that more boys than girls find religion 'absolutely not important' (33% boys / 20% girls), while girls are relatively more strongly represented among those who answer 'neither important nor unimportant' (31% girls / 25% boys) and 'not important' (21% girls / 15% boys). Answering the question about belief in God shows a quite similar tendency among the pupils; also here the 'no'-group is the largest with 40%, while 20% think there is 'some sort of spirit or life force', and 33% believe 'there is a God'. More boys than girls state that they do *not* believe in God (46% / 35%), while more girls believe in God (36% / 29%) and in some 'sort of spirit or life force'.

By comparing the answers pupils give to the question 'do you have a certain religion or worldview' and the answers given on 'how important is religion to you?' we find that the 'yes'-group seems less homogenous in their answers than the 'no'-group. Twenty three percent of those who say they have a religion or world view at the same time say religion is 'absolutely not' or 'not important' to them, while in the 'no'-group only seven percent say that religion is 'very important' or 'important' to them. In Figure 5 the importance of religion has been cross-tabulated with the six sample schools and shows some significant differences:

Figure 2:   Importance of religion related to schools, %

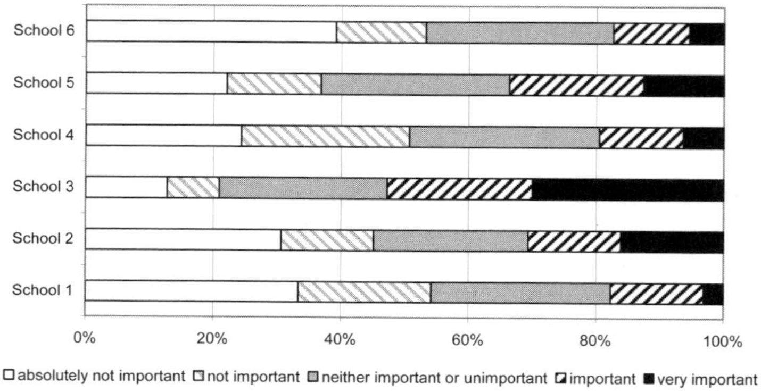

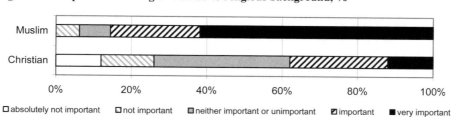

In all schools the group who find religion 'neither important or unimportant' is relatively high and quite similar in size, while the other groups differ more. More than 50% of the pupils in the Oslo school (3) answer that religion is 'very important' or 'important' to them, while the second highest score is found in the Bergen West school (5) with 34%. In the Stavanger (1), Sandnes (2) and Haugesund (6) schools the single largest group is the 'absolutely not important'. Similar patterns of differences can be traced in responses to the question about belief in God. In analysing the students' answers, we find that their answers about the importance of religion are the most relevant starting point for grouping them in terms of their positions. This has, however to be treated with caution since there are also differences within the groups.

Figure 3:   Importance of religion related to religious background, %

We have also looked for the importance of religion in relation to particular religions, but because religions other than Christianity and Islam only are represented by a few persons in the sample, it has only been meaningful to compare Christians and Muslims. Even if the number of Muslims (57) is much smaller than the number of Christians (265) the difference between the two groups may indicate a striking difference:

A significant larger group of Muslim pupils than Christian pupils finds religion to be very important, while the percentage for those who find religion to be important is almost equal in the two groups (23% / 26%). Another significant result is that 12% of the Christian pupils find religion to be of absolutely no importance, while none of the Muslims share this position. The largest group of Christians place themselves in the category 'neither important or unimportant', while only 8% of the Muslim pupils have chosen this alternative.

In addition to general attitudes towards religion and belief, the data also give information about religious practice. The Figure below shows the pupils' participation frequency in different religious activities across all religious affiliations:

Figure 4: Aspects of religious practice, %

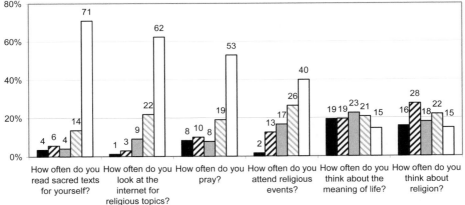

More than 50% of the pupils think about religion or the meaning of life about once a month or more often and 15–20% about every day, while about 15% never think about these issues. There are also about 30% who attend religious meetings once a month or more often, but the group 'never attending' is much higher (40%). More than half of the pupils never pray and even fewer look for religion at the internet or read religious texts on their own. The gender differences in these answers are quite minimal. Some more differences are visible in the material if we differentiate pupils according to whether they 'have a religion' or not. Those who say that they have a religion think about religion once a week, but even in this case the difference between these pupils and those who say they do not have a religion is smaller than the standard deviation within the two groups. The above mentioned differences between schools in terms of importance of religion can also to some extent be found in terms of religious practice. One example is the participation in religious events. But the patterns are not so clear. Even if the Oslo school (3) has the highest activity, also Stavanger (1), Sandnes (2) and Haugesund (6) schools have around 40% of pupils attending religious events once a month, while the Bergen schools (especially East (4)) have considerably lower activity.

There are several ways to approach young peoples' perceptions and attitudes towards religion. In this research the students were asked to react to statements made by European peers in another qualitative research study (Knauth, Jozsa, Bertram-Trost & Ipgrave, 2008).

Figure 5: **Positions regarding religion in general, (means of estimates, scale from 1 – strongly agree to 5 – strongly disagree)**

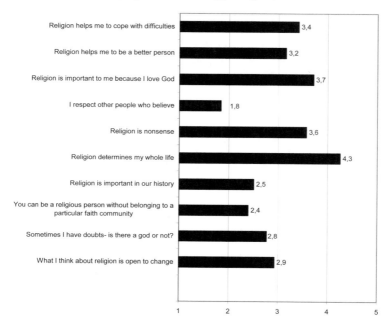

The pupils clearly support respect for others who believe, and acknowledge that religion is important for historical reasons. The means point in the direction of emphasis on values like respect/tolerance, and freedom to believe in your own way. Strong opinions about religion are not popular, whether they are positive or negative. 'I respect other people who believe' gets the strongest support, while statements like 'religion determines my whole life', 'religion is import to me because I love God' and 'religion is nonsense' were disagreed with the most. The background figures show that boys and girls are 'shadowing' each other closely in their answers, but girls are slightly more positive in all the positive formulations, and slightly less supportive towards the only negative one ('religion is nonsense'). Compared with each other the schools do not differ significantly, again with the exception of the Oslo school where the trend is more towards agreement apart from 'religion is nonsense'.

In order to find out more about the attitudes of different groups in our material towards tolerance and respect, we have related the attitudes of pupils towards respect for others to their own positions towards religion. Figure 6 shows that the most religiously committed pupils are the ones who are most united and come across strongest in their respect for 'other people who believe'.

Figure 6: Respect for other people who believe, %

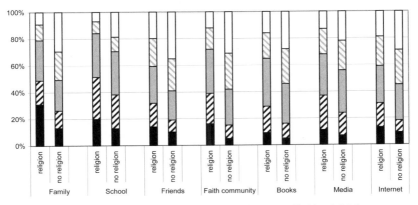

As Figure 6 shows, the value of respect is supported by a majority of all groups. Fifteen percent of the students who find religion to be of no importance strongly disagree with respecting religious persons, while none of the pupils who value religion to be very important disagree on this statement. It can be added that the two largest religious groups appearing in our material (Christians and Muslims) answer similarly on this issue.

Information and communication about religion

When we asked pupils about the sources of information they used for getting knowledge about religions these were all grouped closely around the alternative 'a little bit important' as a mean value (2,8–3,4) with a standard deviation between 1,2–1,4 indicating that individual differences are more striking than the middle of the road average might indicate. Listed in order of importance the channels of information are the following; school, family, media and faith community, and finally internet, friends and books. One indication of individual differences can be shown by cross-tabulating the questions about 'channels' of information with the question about the pupils' own religion or world-view.

Figure 7: Religious and non-religious pupils: Use of different information sources related to religion, %

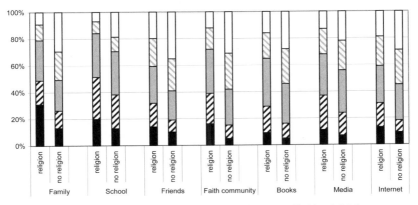

It is striking that all channels (including the internet) are important for the most committed group, with family at the top, while school is the most central information channel for the group who find religion 'not important'. Also in these tables the category 'a little bit important' is relatively high in both groups. For those who answered that they have a certain religion or worldview (the 'yes'-group), family, school and faith community are registered as important or very important by around 50% , and books, media and internet between 30–40%. Those who answered 'no' report considerably lower importance for all channels, but the differences are smaller in terms of school, friends, books, media and internet, than family and faith community. Family and faith community are for both groups the ones that get the highest percentage on (very) important, but the two groups differ in the sense that the 'yes'-group rank both school and family equally high, while school is rated as considerably more important than family by the 'no'-group. The answers of boys and girls are generally the same, but girls consequently report all sources of information to be a little more important than boys do. Looking at different schools, what stands out is the high percentage of pupils in the Oslo school (3) answering that family and faith community are 'very important' or 'important' sources of information.

Religion in the social context

To gain information about how religion is represented in the pupils' social life they were asked some questions related to friends and family. It seems clear that most of the students have friends and fellow students who belong to different religions, but this does not necessarily mean that these are the ones they are spending most time together with:

Figure 8:   People around you and religious diversity, %

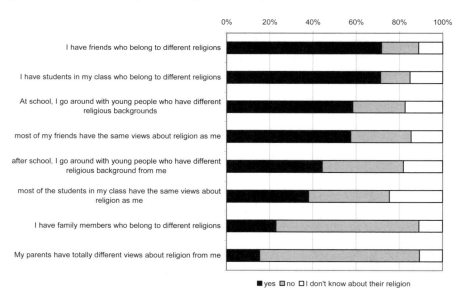

Many pupils (72%) have friends with another religion, but fewer spend time with these friends in school (58%), and even fewer mix with people of different background after school (44%). Part of the picture is also the quarter of the pupils who report that they do not know the religion of their classmates, and the 11% who do not even know the religion of their family members or parents. Families are more homogenous than the school classes, but most pupils have similar world-views to their parents (74%), and even other family members (66%). It should be noted though, that as many as 23% have family members with a different religious affiliation. In other words, many have experience with religious plurality in their closest surroundings, and a clear majority has this kind of experience in their wider social context, including school. There are also questions about social preferences, not only practice, and this seem to indicate that the pupils claim to be more open towards religious plurality in terms of attitudes, than their actual situation or practice seems to indicate. A clear majority (69%) has no preference to go about together with people of the same religious background in their own spare time, and this majority is even higher (74%) when asked about the school arena. In both cases the majority is higher among girls than boys. Generally the girls tend to perceive their social world as somewhat more plural than boys do. Several of these questions reveal that there are more boys (61%) than girls (39%) who 'do not know' about the religion of others.

A series of questions have tried to capture attitudes towards religion in the social and public space. Pupils are asked to respond to statements given by European peers and one in ten thinks that openly showing religious affiliation implies a risk of being mocked in school, but almost forty percent of the pupils 'disagree' or 'strongly disagree' with this statement; 14% have problems showing their views on religion in school, while almost 60% claim that they do not share this position. A majority of the students do not care about what their friends thinks about religion (60%), but at the same time more than one third (36%) of the pupils would like to know what their friends think about religion. The main trend is that the pupils tend to answer that they 'neither agree nor disagree' in these matters, even if individuals differ a lot as Figure 9 shows:

Figure 9:   Attitudes towards religion in the social and public space, %

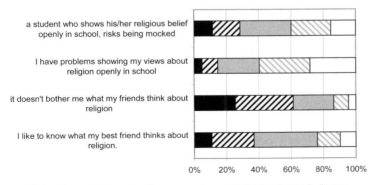

The statement that gets most answers leaning towards 'agree' is ' it doesn't bother me what my friends think about religion', and the one that leans towards 'disagree' is 'I have problems showing my views about religion openly in school'. There are not very clear differences between the sexes, with the possible exception of the statement 'I like to know what my best friend thinks about religion'. Earlier we have seen that girls already know more about this than boys, and the girls are those who want to know more. There seems to be a tendency to view religion as a private matter and at the same time students deny that there are problems with showing religious views openly in school. Differences between the schools are not particularly striking, so this seems not to be so much a question of local context.

Figure 10: Attitudes towards religion in the social and public space, %

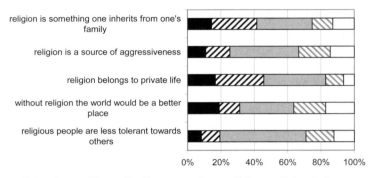

According to forty percent of the pupils, religion is inherited from family and an even larger group is of the opinion that religion belongs to the private sphere. One in four thinks that religion is a source of aggressiveness, while a larger group disagrees with this statement. Forty percent of the students have no opinion about this issue. An even larger group (50%) neither agrees nor disagrees on whether religious people are less tolerant than others. Almost 20% claim that religious people are less tolerant, while approximately 30% disagree on this position. The main tendency is that the pupils do not have strong opinions about these questions and therefore chose the category 'neither agree or disagree'.

A general impression of young people in Europe is that they seldom talk about religion. Another series of statements in this research therefore deals with the pupils' views on communication about religion, and the means are presented in Figure 11 below.

Also here the means are grouped around the 'indifferent' alternative ('neither agree or disagree'). Comparing reactions to the statements with each other, however, gives some indications. The statement with least support ('disagree' / 4) and with the lowest standard deviation (0,9) is 'in my view, talking about religion is embarrassing', and then 'I don't know much about religion and thus I can't have an opinion' (3,6). The most popular one (2,6) is 'talking about religion helps us to understand others'.

Figure 11: Communication about religion, (means of estimates, scale from 1 – strongly agree to 5 – strongly disagree)

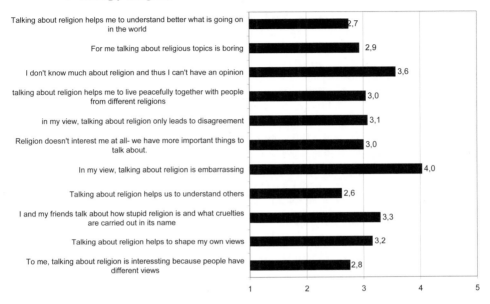

When confronted with the statement 'religion does not interest me at all' the majority place themselves in the middle – 'neither agree nor disagree'. This indicates their reluctance to have 'strong' opinions about religion, and at the same time the standard deviation is relatively high (1,4), which indicates that quite a few have differing opinions. This becomes particularly clear when the two issues are considered together. As in many other questions boys and girls tends to differ in the same ways regarding these issues. Within the standard deviations from the means, the girls agree more than the boys with the positive statements, and disagree more with the negative ones. A closer look at the schools shows that students in the Oslo school (3) give more support to the positive results of talking about religion, because it is interesting and helps understanding others, while the Haugesund school (6) and the Stavanger school (1) are more towards the other end of the spectrum on this issue.

Synopsis of data – religion in pupils' lives

Based on the answers of the questions about 'importance of religion' and 'belief in God or some sort of spirit or life force', we have differentiated three groups of pupils in terms of their generic attitude towards religion:

– Non-religious pupils – about 40%
– Indifferent pupils – about 30%
– Religiously orientated pupils – about 30%

These three groups are not evenly spread in the sample. In the Oslo school there are a higher proportion of pupils who find religion important, and more students who say they believe in God than in other schools. Another finding is that the only 'rural' school (Haugesund) we have included seems to be more secularised than the urban ones, which is contrary to popular opinion in Norway.

In terms of gender we do not find big differences in the material, but a general impression is that girls are being less categorical about issues of religion, than boys. Firstly, there are fewer girls in the group of 'absolutely not interested', and girls seem to value religion as a bit more important than boys. Secondly girls are more aware of their own position on these issues than boys are, and they think more often about the meaning of life than their male peers. Summing up; there are more boys being 'critical' and 'negative', while there are more girls being 'open' and 'distant'.

Among the young pupils it is quite common to think about religion or the meaning of life, but contrary to what some might think this does not lead towards searching for religion on the internet, reading religious texts or participating in religious events. These activities are clearly something for the very religiously interested. In terms of general attitudes, the majority accept that religion is an important part of history, but very few can imagine that religion should determine their whole life. The students share in general a tolerant attitude towards religion and religious belief, however the strongest respect for others who believe comes from those who value religion in their own life to be 'very important'. Those who find religion of absolutely no importance are the ones who are least united in their respect for others who believe.

When it comes to the importance of different channels of information and communication about religion, the most used ones are related to 'significant others', mainly family and friends. The majority seldom speak to anybody about religion, but when this happens the teacher is the one most often approached, followed by family, classmates, friends, faith community and other students at school.[12] There are no major differences between schools in these matters, apart from the Oslo school where pupils on average speak more with their parents about religion.

2.1.2 Interpretation of data on religion in pupils' lives

The other alternative for grouping pupils based on the attitudes towards religion is related to whether the pupil has 'a certain religion or worldview', which does not seem to give a better result because it has a yes/no answer, and the students might have understood the questions differently; some thinking of their own formal affiliation with institutionalised religion, others possibly thinking more of their religious background, while others again had more individual preferences. The figures do not fit easily with membership in religious organisations, and it is also difficult to relate it to the students' answers about how much religion means to them. One additional explanation may be that the answers to this question suffered from the ambiguities surrounding the term 'religion' in Norwegian. The three groups (non-religious, indifferent, and religious) are therefore used in the further analysis. There are however also important varieties within the three groups. This can be exemplified with the group who claim to find religion 'very important', where almost 20% say they 'never' attend a religious event, or the group finding religion 'absolutely not important' where still 14% attend religious events at least once a month and were 23% believe there is a God, spirit or life force. Another reason for caution is that the figures for religious belief and activity seem to be somewhat higher than expected compared with results from earlier surveys. One should also remember that the majority of the pupils in the sample are 9th graders and in their year of confirmation in The

---

12 The terms used in the Norwegian questionnaire is rather 'religious leaders' than 'faith community'.

Church of Norway, and therefore attend services in church more often than they normally would.

In terms of basic attitudes towards religion our results certainly show that the age group we have investigated is very heterogeneous. At the same time it should be underlined that many of the trends we are able to show are contradicted by smaller parts of the sample. This might suggest that many of the pupils are looking for individual or alternative conceptions of what to believe in, and there may be even some affiliation between young people and new religious movements such as 'new age'. But it might just as well be understood as reluctance towards institutional forms of Christianity and the traditional concept of God. According to Paul Otto Brunstad's research on Norwegian adolescents' attitudes towards religion (1998), the majority were positive to a spiritual universe, but this openness was not related to a traditional Christian belief. The adolescents' encounters with Christianity in school and church were mostly characterised in negative terms, and according to Brunstad they showed resistance against commitments to established traditions and institutions (Brunstad, 1998, p. 150). In another study Geir Winje found what he calls "a new map of worldviews" (Winje, 1998). This map is characterised of conceptions of belief, which do not fit into the traditional categories of religions and world-views. According to Winje late modern religiosity is rather highly syncretistic, individual, eclectic and tolerant (Winje, 1999). Related to these findings, the indifference towards religion of students in our compilation might well be resistance against institutionalised forms of religion, and not against religiosity or spirituality as such.

Another perspective would be to understand some of the pupils in the sample as 'cultural Christians' – which mean that they label themselves Christian, but that this does not necessarily imply a religious worldview or practice. Comparing Christian and Muslims students in our sample showed that none of the students who term themselves Muslims found religion to be of absolutely no importance. A parallel 'cultural Muslim' category is not easy to find in our material, and there seem to be significant differences between appearing as 'Muslim' and as 'Christian' in the social world of teenagers.

Studies related to religions on the internet have emphasised that online-religion is an alternative to the more traditional forms of religion, and therefore expected to have appeal especially among young people (Brasher, 2004; Højsgaard, 2004). Looking at our sample this seems nevertheless not to be the case. Most probably the pupils search the internet for information (related to home work or school projects) and not for religious purposes or religious activities.

On the basis of earlier surveys it is generally assumed that Norwegian women are more religiously interested or open than men (Botvar, 1993), and this is also reflected in this study. Our findings indicate that more boys than girls find religion uninteresting. The background for this seems to be that boys are more openly critical or negative towards religion, while the girls tend to be less categorical, they are more so-called 'politically correct'. Among the religiously committed both sexes are evenly represented.

Looking at the schools in the sample the Oslo school stands out in many aspects with a majority of students who believe in God and who consider religion to be important in their life. This may be related to the relatively high proportion of Muslim students in this school and the fact that more Muslim students in general (in this research) value religion to be of more importance than their Christian peers. This is an interesting result, related to a general impression that students in the urban areas are more secularized than students in more rural parts of the country. We expected to find differences related to the urban/rural dimension, but this is not clearly affirmed in this study. We believe that further investigation into this demands more contextual analysis. Differences in religious practice between the schools may for instance also have something to do with confirmation classes in the local community.

There is an impression that the students in general show a high tolerance towards religious people. These are interesting results, but it is out from this quantitative study still difficult to say what this tolerance is about and what it involves. It might first and foremost be some sort of *toleration* of the right of others to believe, more than *tolerance* towards what they actually believe in. The social life pictured in the pupils' answers seems to indicate that their attitudes are not necessary put into practice.

2.2   How do pupils see religion in school?

2.2.1   Data description

Being in the centralised Norwegian school system, all pupils in principle have the same education, and this also goes for religious education.[13] The responses on statements about religion in school however go in different directions.

Figure 12: Statements about religion in school, %

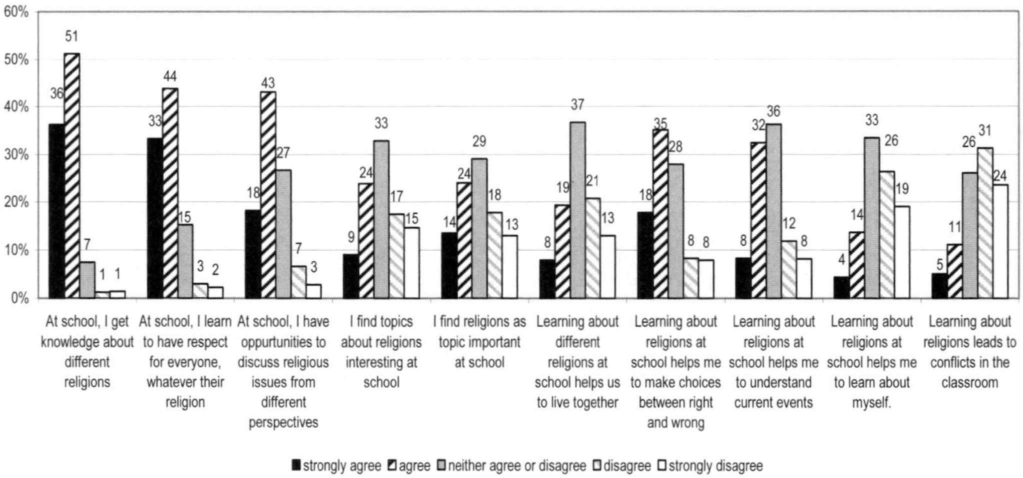

The statement 'at school I get knowledge about different religions' gets the strongest support of all, but also learning respect and getting a possibility to discuss religious issues is something the pupils seem to have experienced a lot of. There are quite a few who feel that religious education helps them to 'make choices between right and wrong'. In terms of how interesting the teaching is however, the answers are much more spread out, and a large group of students do not know what to answer. This goes even more for the question about whether

---

13   The fact that 98% of the students answer that they take part in religious education this year fits well with the subject being compulsory. When they are asked to tell how many years they have attended religious education (KRL) in school, this varies from seven to ten years depending on what grade they are in. The majority of the students in the research are 9th grade students and this fits well with 65% answering that they have attended KRL for 8–9 years.

religious topics are 'important' and the pupils are especially insecure about the effect of religious education on 'living together'. On the other hand the pupils are quite united in their rejection of 'learning about religion leads to conflict'. We do not find a distinct difference between girls and boys, or between the different groups of students based on how important religion is to them. There are some differences between the schools in the way these questions are answered, but this is mostly related to related to how many say they 'strongly agree' or only 'agree'.

A second set of statements on religion in school are concerned with practical aspects of religion in education, and in particular with attitudes towards the visibility of religion in school. In terms of the rules that should be in school regarding religion and religious artefacts, Chart 13 shows that there is a clear support for religious symbols being allowed in school and the pupils think there should be possibilities of taking care of religious needs in the 'passive' sense; allowing for absence in festivals, and dietary issues in school (ca. 60%).

Figure 13:   Statements about practical aspects of religion in school, %

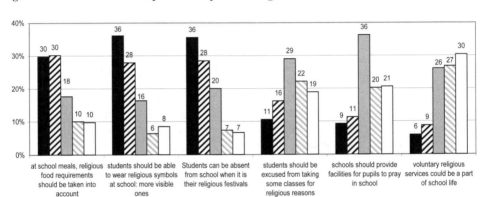

When it comes to arrangements that are more directly interfering with school life, like providing room for prayers or 'being excused from some classes for religious reasons' the pupils are more leaning towards the sceptical or not so sure about what they think. What is clear is that six out of ten do not want 'voluntary religious services to be part of school life'. Girls generally tend to be a little more 'liberal' than boys, but the differences are not distinctive. Looking at school differences the tendencies are the same for all , but with stronger support for allowing religious practice in the Oslo school. This pattern appears to follow religious commitment; the more religion is valued, the more the students tend to be supportive towards 'liberal' rules in school. This difference is particularly clear between those who find religion 'very important' and the rest, and most easy to see in the case of providing for facilities to pray:

Figure 14:   **Importance of religion and attitudes to providing facilities for praying in school, %**

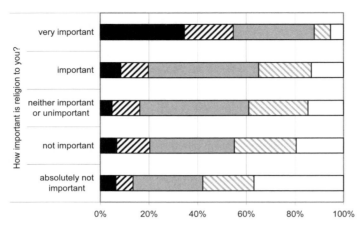

More than fifty percent of the religiously committed pupils think that school should provide facilities for praying in school, while almost forty percent among those who absolutely do not find religion to be of importance strongly disagree on this statement. When the pupils were asked about the wearing of visible religious symbols the answers were leaning more towards agree than disagree. Also here the same pattern appears and only a few percent in all categories strongly disagree, and the largest group (17%) who share this position is to be found among the pupils who think religion is absolutely not important.

Several questions were related to issues on religious education and religion in school, and one of the issues was related to models of religious education, and pupils' preferences. It seems that the pupils in our sample do not have very strong opinions about this. The only statement met with strong agreement is that 'religious education should be optional'. At the same time more than 50% support students being taught together in joint classes:

When asked about the possibility to combine joint classes and groups, more than 1/3 are not sure what they think. Rather more girls than boys think that religious education should be optional, that there should be no religion in education or that it is already covered in other subjects. Girls are also less sceptical towards partly or permanently separate religious education for different groups.

Figure 16: Statements on models for religion in school, %

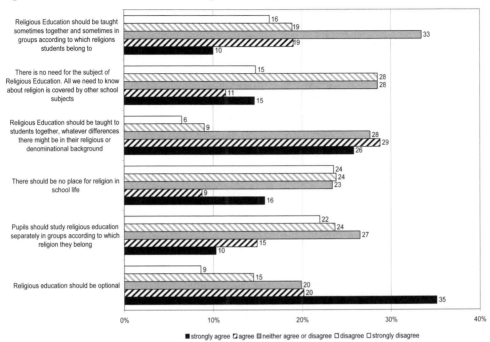

There are several models for religious education in Europe, and the aim of the subject varies in relation to the model. To see what the pupils think about aims and learning outcome in religious education they were asked to react to different statements, presented in Figure 17 below:

Figure 17: Statements about learning outcomes of religious education, %

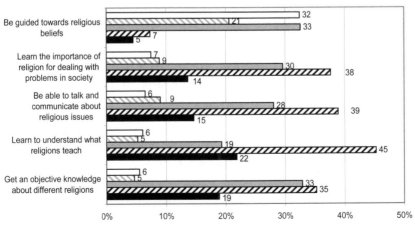

As with models, also opinions on the statements about learning outcomes related to religion in education are varied. The most pronounced majority is the one in favour of a religious education that provides 'objective knowledge' about religions and helps understanding their teachings. Also more than 50% like learning to communicate about religious issues or about the importance of religion for dealing with problems in society. But in both these cases, the group of 'neither agree or disagree' is quite large (30%). A clear majority of pupils are sure that they do not want to be 'guided towards religious belief', but there are also here 30% who are not sure what they think. In terms of being guided towards religious beliefs, the girls and boys are completely in agreement, but regarding the other learning outcomes for religious education the girls tend to agree more with all of them, while the boys pull in the direction of 'neither agree or disagree'. On the school level some more differences appear:

Figure 18:   Statement about the learning outcome 'being guided towards religious beliefs' related to schools, %

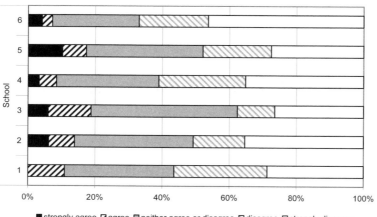

It is the Oslo school (3) which shows as most positive towards all the different aims ('agree'), and the one where the disagreement towards 'being guided towards religious beliefs' is at its lowest. But also here this type of learning outcome has very limited support, as shown below. The Oslo (3) and Sandnes schools (2) have most students who think religious education should guide them towards religious belief, but even in these schools this is less than one fifth. Except from the Oslo school (3) almost 50% of the students in all schools disagree with this statement. If we look at the pupils from the perspective of the 'importance/non-importance of religion', a comparison shows that all students tend to be negative towards 'being guided towards religious beliefs'. Those who find religion 'very important', 'important' or 'neither important or unimportant' are more positive towards the different aims in religious education, while those who find religion 'not important' or 'absolutely not important' are less sure about what they think of the different aims.

> **Synopsis of data – religion in school**
>
> According to the students school should be a place where they learn *about* religion (knowledge) and not *from* religion. At the same time school can be a forum where the students get the opportunity to discuss religion and to learn from each other, and were they learn to respect and live together irrespective of religious background. When asked about whether religious education is interesting or contributes to personal development, the students are not quite sure, but the more personal and social involvement that is mentioned the more the respondents disagree. Confirming that school contributes to knowledge and respect, they are not convinced that this will contribute to peaceful coexistence. At the same time they disagree that learning about religions may lead to conflicts between them.
>
> On issues related to more visible and practical aspects of religion in school the Norwegian students seem to be in favour of the right to wear religious symbols and that school should take account of religious food requirements. They also think school should allow for some days off during religious festivals. On the other hand they are more reluctant towards religious arrangements at school, such as prayer rooms and religious services. However, there seem to be a difference in their attitude related to the importance of religion in their personal life. The more important religion seems to be, the more liberal the students are towards religious arrangements.
>
> When asked about what kind of model of religious education the students would prefer, there is no clear tendency. More than half of the students favour religious education taught in joint classes, but at the same time 55% of the students think RE should be optional. Related to gender, girls seem to be somewhat less bound to the present Norwegian model for religious education than the boys. The students' opinion on the content of RE is also varied, but the majority want 'objective' knowledge. It seem also to be a tendency that the more important religion is to pupils, the more they are interested in dialogue and aspects of learning *from* religion.

2.2.3   Interpretation of data on pupils' views on religion in school

Many of the answers seem to reflect aspects of the Norwegian religious education curriculum and practice, with RE as a compulsory subject for all students in joint classes. They have no experience with other models of religious education. One of the reasons for introducing mandatory non-confessional religious education in Norway a decade ago was to prevent future conflicts over religious and cultural differences. Religious education was then thought of as a classroom forum where students could collectively learn about different religions to reject stereotypes and prejudices about 'the other'. There has been several changes and adjustments in the RE curriculum since then, and after being criticised first by the UN Human Rights Committee in 2004 and then by the European Court of Human Rights in 2007, there is now an emphasis in the new RE curriculum from 2008 on objective, critical and pluralistic teaching. This seems to be in line with the students' perceptions about religious education in school, and their generic reluctance being guided towards religious belief.

The fact that the pupils are liberal in terms of 'visible religion' in school is partly reflecting the liberal attitude prevailing in Norway in these matters. Even if there are discussions in the public sphere related to religion, there have been no attempts to change the legislation on the right to wear religious symbols in school. This may be related to the fact that less then 2% of the population in Norway belongs to Islam. There has however been more discussions related to questions about wearing the *hijab* or *nikab* in the Oslo schools were the Muslim population is more present. On issues related to religious practice in school the students are more reluctant. In the last couple of years there have been intense debates about religious services in school and the traditional church visit before Christmas. This has resulted in a more diverse practice between schools, and some have lately chosen a more secular end of term at school. There is obviously a connection between the students' opinion on these issues and the public and political debate. The more liberal position of the religiously committed pupils may also reflect some self-interest: since they are such a distinct group, they want to be more respected for their religious views.

2.3   How do pupils see the impact of religion?

2.3.1   Data description

This paragraph focuses on the views of pupils on a more general level and tries to capture whether they see religion contributing more towards dialogue or conflict. The strongest opinion coming through in the answers displayed in Chart 19 below is to have no opinion and the one that gets most positive support is 'religion belongs to the private life' with 44% in favour. The other statements are critical remarks about the impact of religion on people and their surroundings and here the pupils do not know whether the statements reflect the state of affairs or not. If we compare the attitudes of boys and girls, the different schools, pupils who say they have a religion and those who do not, the main trend is the same. If we differentiate the pupils according to importance of religion, those who say religion is 'absolutely not important' are the only ones who tend to support the statement: 'without religion the world would be a better place'.

Figure 19:   Religion as a subject in the communication among peers, %

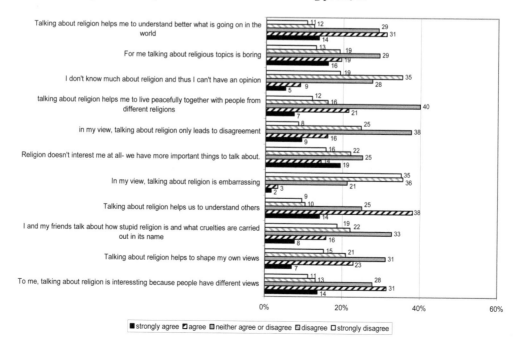

Most statements in Chart 19 are not explicit about which communication partners that may be referred to, but the use of 'we' and 'us' points in the direction of communication among peers. The general impression is that there is no clear indication that these statements are seen to capture the positions of the majority. But in two cases where quotations are indicating lack of knowledge about religion or embarrassment in talking about religion there is quite strong disagreement (71%).

The effects of talking about religion, in terms of whether it is leading towards disagreement or to peace, are not clear to the young people. On the other hand they find talking about religion to be interesting and a help to understand others. Girls and boys are following each other in terms of the main trends, but girls tend to be more optimistic than the boys in terms of the impact that talking about religion can make on their outlook on the world and other people.

Another aspect of communication is related to situations when religious believers try to convince others (see Chart 20 below). Here the respondents are asked to describe their reactions to peers proselytizing by answering whether a described reaction would be their own:

Figure 20: Reactions to proselytizing, %

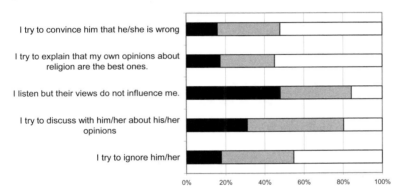

There is a strong perception among the students that they would listen, but not be influenced (84%). It is also very likely that they might go in to a discussion (81%), or try to ignore the person (37%). More than fifty percent would never try to convince them that they are wrong, or to say that their own position is the best. The general impression is a tendency to avoid being too involved in this kind of debate. Even though the reactions of boys and girls are more or less the same, there is a larger group of girls than boys who want to go into discussions. The majority of boys tend to try to convince the other, while the majority of girls answer that this would not be their position. There are also some differences among the schools but it is difficult to find a sustainable pattern. If we once more look into the groups of pupils based on 'importance of religion' we see that the extremes (the 'very important' and the 'absolutely not important') are mirroring each other. A clear majority of the religious pupils claim that they will not be influenced by the view of the other, 44% are sure they would discuss with the other, 1/3 would try to convince the other that they are mistaken and ¼ will explain that they are right themselves. The absolutely non-religious have parallel figures

(51%; 29%; 20% and 18%). On the statement that they would ignore the person 29% of the religious would do that, and 21% of the non-religious.

Another dimension of the impact of religion deals with the possibility of living together with people with different religious backgrounds. The pupils have been asked to react to statements about this coming from European peers and this is displayed in the Chart 21 below:

Figure 21: Reactions to statements about how to live together in peace, %

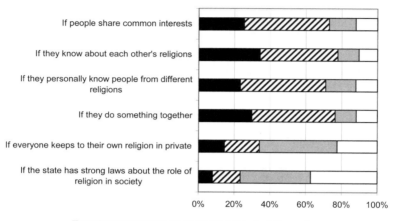

The answers show that the pupils tend to react against attitudes of scepticism towards religious plurality. They are not at all sure that disagreement on religious issues lead to conflict and they certainly think that people with different religions can live together. They think that respecting the religion of others helps in case of differences. When challenged to give reactions to reasons for peaceful coexistence between people with different religions and worldviews, the clear trend is that mutual knowledge, common action, personal knowledge of others and common interests are important factors. The respondents find much less reason to believe that peace is secured by everybody keeping their religion in private, and even less do they seem to believe that the state should enforce strong regulations of religion in society. But even this last strategy does get some degree of support from about 25% of the pupils. In both these cases the group who 'cannot say' is quite large; especially this is the case when answering about the role of the state.

Boys and girls tend to be of the same opinion, but girls are more confident than boys that respecting each other will be of help in dealing with diversity. They also reject very firmly the position of disliking others because of religion. The largest difference between girls and boys is observed in the reaction against the privatisation of religion where about 20% more of the girls than boys reject this position. But apart from that question, we see the 'shadowing' effect also here, with girls mainly being a little more positive towards the effect of good intentions.

Synopsis of data – impact of religion

When asked general questions about the impact of religion in society, a majority of the pupils do not come out with strong opinions. Categorical propositions about the impact of religion are there, but in smaller groups; the main group answer mostly that they 'neither agree or disagree'. Almost half of the students consider religion to belong to the private sphere, but at the same time they are not in favour of strong regulations from the state on religious issues. They seem to have no clear opinion whether conversations about religion may provide for peaceful coexistence in a religious diverse society, or if it leads to conflict. At the same time many students think that talking about religion might help them to better understand others' point of view. The statements related to communication about religion among peers show that it is difficult to draw clear conclusions on these issues, and that the pupils seem to be drawn in many directions.

Regarding proselytizing the students have clearer opinions. There is a strong perception among them that they would listen to the other, but try not to be influenced by the conversation. It is also very likely that they might go into discussions, and very few try to ignore the person, or convince them that they are wrong, or to say that their position is the best. The general impression is a tendency where the Norwegian students try to avoid being too involved in these kinds of discussions.

A general impression is that Norwegian students are positive towards a pluralistic society and think it is absolutely possible for people with different religious/cultural backgrounds to live together. Respect seems to be a keyword in this regard. In terms of what contributes to more peaceful coexistence they put strong emphasis on general knowledge about diversity combined with mutual interests or activities, while the more extreme solutions of privatisation and more direct state involvement are largely rejected.

2.3.2. Interpreting pupils' views on the impact of religion

In certain cases it is difficult to know if the pupils answering our questionnaires express their normative positions or their view on the state of affairs when they are reacting to some of the statements of European peers. Most likely they do not separate the two in their own minds either. When asked about the role of religion in society their answers go in many directions, and this may reflect contradictory information that young people get from the media and from personal experience. Media is an important source of information and often creates processes by which prejudices are reinforced rather than analysed (Gullestad 2002, p. 33), at the same time many of the students have friends belonging to other religions than themselves and this knowledge may deconstruct stereotypic religious images represented in the media. On the other hand, the spread of opinions seem to be a good starting point for discussions about these matters for instance in school. This is confirmed by many pupils agreeing that talking about religion is interesting and improves mutual understanding. Such discussions should take care to be open and respectful, and not be attempts to convert the other. Proselytising is not popular among the young, either in school or in conversation with peers. Still, they try to deal with attempts to convert them in ways that create as little controversy and conflict as possible. This confirms the general impression that the pupils are very aware of situations where conflicts may arise, and that they do their best to avoid such situations without ending with privatised isolation or authoritarian solutions. Their general attitude (or hope?) seems to be that knowledge and human contact is a possible way forward.

3.   Comparison with the qualitative survey

The chosen location for the qualitative research was based on the schools' willingness to participate in the study and their public/private, secular/religious character. To contrast the public schools a Christian private school (school B) was included in the study. A total of 154 students answered the qualitative questionnaires.[14]

Regarding *the role of religion in pupils' lives* both the qualitative and the quantitative survey present a majority who do not find religion important, while approximately one third of the students in both samples consider religion to be of personal importance. On the background of results from the qualitative survey we felt that if the pupils had been asked about a broader concept of belief in the questionnaire, this could have allowed for alternative perceptions of religiosity and spirituality. In the quantitative survey the category 'spirit and life force' seem to have captured those students who have alternative perceptions of religiosity and spirituality (27%).

In both samples the majority of students do not normally take part in religious activities or practice. In the qualitative survey a large amount of students did not answer the question on personal experience with religion, and during analysis this was interpreted as either lack of experience or difficulties writing them down. The results from the quantitative survey support the former interpretation, and on questions about religious practice the average student seems to attend religious events or pray more seldom than once a month.

In terms of getting information about the different religions, the quantitative and qualitative researches support each other. An interesting comparison might be done between the students from the Christian private school in the qualitative sample, and students from the Oslo school in the quantitative one. In both schools there is a distinct majority of students who believe in God and who are more likely to think religion is important, very important or determining for their way of life than their peers. Looking at religious practice the Oslo school had the most active students in the quantitative sample, and this was also the case with the students in the Christian private school in the qualitative study.

In choosing a model of *religion in school,* both samples prefer religious education in joint classes; the majority of students in both the qualitative and the quantitative research are in favour. However, there is a difference between the qualitative and quantitative sample regarding questions about models of RE. While the students in the quantitative sample have no strong opinions about whether 'religious education should be taught sometimes together and sometimes in confessional groups', or 'if there is a need for religious education at all' etc., the students in the qualitative research were quite clear about these issues – either they favoured religious education or they did not.

In both the qualitative and quantitative survey there is a strong support for learning *about* religion, in the sense 'to get knowledge about different religions', and scepticism towards learning *from* religion, understood as 'learning about religion to learn about myself'. In other words, objective teaching about religion in religious education is preferred, but there is also support for learning mutual respect for each other and to discuss religious issues. In the qualitative research there is a large group who think that knowledge about religion is important to understand diversity, and to develop tolerance and respect for different religions and believers. Many of the students who favour religious education in integrated classes think they will obtain this knowledge in dialogue about belief and religious practice with their fellow students. The quantitative survey indicates that the students are positive but not quite sure if

---

14 For more on the qualitative study see (Lippe, 2008)

knowledge about different religions necessarily leads to peaceful coexistence. The students do not consider religion to be a factor for conflict in the classroom (micro level), but are more likely to think that religion may be a source of conflict in the global society (macro level).

In both studies the views on *the impact of religion* are reflecting that religion is not a popular subject to discuss among the students themselves. In the quantitative research the only persons with whom the respondents speak less with about religion and religious issues compared with friends and classmates are religious leaders and other students in school. In the qualitative survey we asked only about friends and it is therefore not possible to compare other categories. The sample in the quantitative research is more diverse in terms of religious, cultural and ethnic background than the sample in the qualitative survey. More students in the quantitative study report that they have friends who belong to other religions than themselves, and more seem also to have experience with religious plurality in their surroundings. They emphasise the importance of tolerance and respect and the freedom to practise religion, but strong opinions about religion are perceived as being negative. In both studies the students tended to be very positive towards religious plurality and thought people with different religions could live peacefully together, but at the same time they reported quite limited contact with people from other cultural and/or religious backgrounds, and their tolerance was interpreted as rather unchallenged.

4.   Conclusions

Does religion matter to young people in Norwegian schools? Our answer is both 'no' and 'yes'. Certainly religion is not very important to many pupils, but to a minority it is very important. It depends on who you ask and on how you ask. In the following we will revisit our research questions and hypothesis and sum up our conclusion.

4.1   Reflections on the outcomes in the light of research questions

In drawing conclusions we would like to focus first on *the role of religion in pupils' lives*. The general impression of young people from our research in Norway is that religion is of little importance or little interest to a large group of the pupils. Based on our sample we suggest differentiating between three sub-groups in terms of attitudes towards religion:

a) Non-religious pupils (about 40%) where most do not find religion important and do not believe in a God, and where contact with religious practice is rare. If they have a relationship to organised religion it is usually Christianity.

b) Indifferent pupils (about 30%) are often reluctant to have distinct opinions on matters of religion and their relationship is distant towards religious practice. Many of them may be characterised as 'culturally Christians' but their indifference also can be seen as a distinct position. Some may even have an agnostic or ambivalent position towards religion.

c) Religiously orientated and committed pupils (about 30%) both find religion important, but there is a difference in the degree of religious activity, which justifies seeing a smaller group as religiously committed. Among Christian and Muslim pupils, there are more Muslims than Christians belonging to this last group.

Even if we find it justified to present these three groups, we need to stress that the age group we have investigated shows them to be very heterogeneous, and that many of the trends which we have been able to demonstrate, including this division in three groups, are contradicted if we go further into smaller groups within the sample. As an example of this, students' different answers on the question whether they belonged to a religion or not seemed to indicate that the question was understood differently among them. Some seemed to have interpreted the question on an institutional level (i.e. baptised or confirmed in Church of Norway), while others thought of family background or personal religious convictions. Therefore categories based on the importance of religion turned out to be more relevant to capture the students' attitude towards religion in their own life. Another reason for using the three groups is that the limitations of our sample in terms of representativeness speak in favour of operating with larger groups, not smaller. We still do not think it is possible systematically to deduce with certainty from the three groups the opinions that young people hold about issues related to religion that may be of direct use to discuss religion in education, because students who nominally belong to the same group may in fact have differing opinions.

Having established these three groups as our main reference, some further qualifications should be made. Since many of the 'indifferent' group nominally belong to the Church of Norway, it is possible that from the church point of view they will be perceived as 'Christians', and many of them participate in some religious practice from time to time. We still think that the group of 'indifferent' should be taken seriously as a position in its own right, rather than interpreting them as people who have not made up their mind yet. It may be better to label this group 'distant' than 'indifferent'. In this group there might also be students with an agnostic or ambivalent position towards religion, and in any case it would be interesting to do further analysis into this group. This goes also for the other groups. The non-religious group is interesting to investigate further in terms of their viewpoints on life-questions and existential issues in a broader sense. This group consists of students who do not have a religion and/or who do not find religion to be of any importance in their personal life. There is however no obvious connection between not having a religion and to have no interest in religion, and there are also students in the non-religious group who find interest in learning about religion in school. Another comment deals with the group of 'religious'. We have mentioned the possible distinction between those who find religion 'very important' and only 'important', and the fact that Muslim pupils belong to these two groups, and more than Christians among the 'committed'. The results from our research into frequency of religious practice show that this is quite low, whether the young perceive religion to be of importance or not. But those of the students who find religion to be 'very important' in their lives, tend to be distinctively more active than others and they also think more often about religious issues than their peers. A closer look into the last group shows that this may be a more common self-definition for young Muslims than young Christians. In other words it is more common between young Muslims to take part in collective and individual religious practice, than it is for young Christians. The other religions are represented by so few in our sample that it is not justifiable to draw any conclusions. Questions arise about the situation of religiously committed pupils, the character of their self-understanding, and their presentation of themselves in daily life inside and outside school. In what ways is it different to be a young Christian in comparison with being a young Muslim, and how does this vary between local communities?

It is important to note that most students have friends or fellow students who belong to different religions, but these are not necessarily those they spend most time with. At the same time as many as one quarter of the students do not know their classmates' religious affiliation, and some even do not know the religion of the members in their own family. This is significantly more common among boys than girls. This indicates that religion does not play a major role in students' life or in their social relations. In terms of attitudes they seem to be quite open towards religious diversity, but this is mainly on an abstract or ideological level, and less in daily practice.

The second research question asked about the *pupils' views on religion in school*. There is a general trend among the youngsters to prefer religious education in joint classes and to get objective knowledge. School is obviously not seen as a place for personal belief or religious practice, but a place to learn about different religions and also to discuss religious and ethical issues. Many students think of religious education as a subject where you learn mutual respect and tolerance towards people belonging to different religions. Even if they are positive to these effects of RE they are not sure that learning about religion will help towards peaceful coexistence. At the same time they do not believe that religion is a factor of conflict in the classroom.

In terms of the rules that should be in school regarding religion and religious artefacts, the tendency is one of great tolerance and a liberal attitude among the pupils. Most religious symbols should be allowed, and there should be possibilities for taking care of religious needs like absence at festivals or dietary issues in school. The limit seems to be in terms of special arrangements for prayers or religious services in school, even though students do not clearly disagree with these. This can be interpreted as reactions based on the practice in school which they know. It is allowed in Norwegian schools to wear religious symbols, and students are permitted to stay out of school during religious festivals. It also fits well with the fact that there are no general arrangements in Norwegian schools for religious services or special rooms for prayer. The heated hijab discussions which we know from e.g. France and Germany never reached Norway with the same temperature, and this might be one of the reasons why students are liberal towards wearing religious symbols in school. But it may also be that these debates do not have the same potential for controversy in the more liberal climate of Norway.

On the third research question focusing on the *impact of religion*, our results from the quantitative survey indicate that students to some extent are anxious that disagreement in matters of religion might lead to conflict. At the same time they think respect for others' religion can help to deal with religious and cultural diversity. They therefore reject the statements pointing towards religious diversity as a major problem or hindrance for dialogue. When challenged to give reasons for peaceful coexistence between people with different religions and worldviews, the clear trend is that knowledge about diversity, common action, personal knowledge of others and common interests are seen as important factors. They find little reason to believe that peace is secured if everybody keeps their religion private or if the state has strong regulation of religion in society.

4.2 Reflection on the results in light of the research hypothesises

At the beginning of this investigation we had some pre-defined hypothesises. The first had to do with the relationship between personal religion and tolerance: *Religious students are less tolerant than non-religious students*. Contrary to the hypothesis we have some indications that religious pupils are more tolerant than non-religious students towards having a religion. This is certainly only a matter of degree, not opposition. Also non-religious students are in the main very tolerant, but in terms of degree they are less tolerant than religious pupils. At the same time we find it important to emphasise that we do not fully know what this toleration actually contains. First and foremost it may be related to the right of having a religion and to be a believer. In this regard the issue is more pressing among the religious students than the non-religious students. This quantitative research does not give the opportunity to explore this more deeply. In other words this study can only say something about the students' *toleration* of the right to believe, and nothing about *tolerance* towards other religions or believers. This shows that we need further research on these issues to say something sustainable regarding the tested hypothesis.

The second hypothesis claims that *encountering religious diversity in education makes the students more tolerant and dialogue oriented.* This is difficult to answer from the Norwegian material because we only have one model of religious education in use in public schools, and this is a non-confessional/multi-faith religious education. Private schools with different syllabuses are very few and not included in the sample and even though this was included in the qualitative study, and even if they also are positive towards religious diversity and to dialogue, we have no evidence that this is thanks to religious education, – or not. At the same time the Norwegian students report that school is the main arena where they receive knowledge about religion. It is considered to be even more important than family. It might be that learning about different religions in joint classes in religious education makes the students more positive towards religious diversity. What we can say is that the school with most religious diversity among its students is also strong on tolerance and very much supports dialogue. This school has the most religiously active students of all in the sample and very many of them are Muslims. This might support the hypothesis.

Finally, *are pupils who have encountered religious diversity personally more tolerant and more dialogue oriented* than others? A majority of students have encountered religious diversity through classmates and friends, and some also come from mixed religious families. At the same time their tolerance towards religious diversity is perceived to be on a rather abstract level, and does not seem to be based on an understanding developed through personal relations. It is more a matter of principle. There are many students who do not know what to think about whether talking about religion contributes to positive results in terms of living together. This complicates answering about this hypothesis. Since personal experience with diversity does not automatically lead in one direction we need more in-depth analysis to answer this question. This hypothesis is therefore neither contradicted, nor affirmed.

References

Birkedal, E. (2001). Noen ganger tror jeg på Gud, men-? : en undersøkelse av gudstro og erfaring med religiøs praksis i tidlig ungdomsalder. KIFO Perspektiv 8. Trondheim: Tapir.

Botvar, P.K. (1993). Religion uten kirke: ikke-institusjonell religiøsitet i Norge, Storbritannia og Tyskland, (Rapport / Diakonhjemmets høgskolesenter, Forskningsavdelingen; 10/1993. Oslo: Diakonhjemmets høgskolesenter.

Brasher, B.E. (2004). *Give me that online religion.* New Brunswick: Rutgers University Press.

Brunstad, P. O. (1998). *Ungdom og livstolkning: En studie av unge menneskers tro og fremtidsforventninger.* Trondheim: Tapir.

Furseth, I. & Repstad, P. (2006). *An introduction to the sociology of religion: classical and contemporary perspectives.* Aldershot: Ashgate.

Gilhus, I.S. & Mikaelsson, L. (2001). *Nytt blikk på religion: studiet av religion i dag.* Oslo: Pax.

Gullestad, M. (2002). *Det norske sett med nye øyne.* Oslo: Universitetsforlaget.

(2007) Hva er religion (Oslo: Universitetsforlaget).

Gunnarsson, G.J. (2008). *"I Don't Believe the Meaning of Life is All That Profound" A study of Icelandic teenagers' life interpretation and values.* PhD thesis. Stockholm: Stockholms University.

Højsgaard, M. T. (2004). *Netværksreligion: religiøse strømninger i begyndelsen af det 21. århu ndrede belyst gennem analyser af organiseret, internetmedieret religionsdebat på dans.* København: Københavns Universitet.

Knauth, T., Jozsa, D.-P., Bertram-Troost, G. & Ipgrave, J. (Eds.). *Encountering Religious Pluralism in School and Society: A Qualitative Study of Teenage Perspectives in Europe.* Muenster: Waxmann.

Lippe, M. S. v. d. (2008). To believe or not to believe: Young people's perceptions and experiences with religion and religious education in Norway. In T. Knauth, D.-P. Jozsa, G. Bertram-Troost & J. Ipgrave (Eds.), *Encountering Religious Pluralism in School and Society: A Qualitative Study of Teenage Perspectives in Europe.* Muenster: Waxmann, pp. 149–171.

Repstad, P. & Henriksen, J.-O. (Eds.) (2005). *Mykere kristendom?: sørlandsreligion i endring Bergen*: Fagbokforlaget.

Skeie, G. (2007). Religion and Education in Norway, in R. Jackson, S. Miedema, W. Weisse & J.-P. Willaime (Eds.), *Religion and Education in Europe: Developments, Contexts and Debate.* Muenster: Waxmann, pp. 221–242.

Winje, G. (1998). Det religiøse mangfoldet blant unge i 90-åra, in: T. Bugge & L. Gjems (Eds.), *Time-Out! Bilder fra nye pedagogiske landskap.* Bergen: Fagbokforlaget.

Winje, G. (1999). *Fra bønn til magi: nye religioner og menneskesyn.* Kristiansand: Høyskoleforlaget.

Winsnes, O.G. (1988). E' du rel'giøs, eller – ? om konseptualisering og metodologi i empirisk religionsforskning. Trondheim: Den allmennvitenskapelige høgskolen, Universitetet i Trondheim.

Jean-Paul Willaime

French Views on the Results of the Norwegian Survey

To compare Norway with France, it is first necessary to outline the main features of the socio-religious landscape of each country (part 1) before scrutinizing several dimensions of the attitudes of the students towards religion (part 2). In part 3, we consider the preferences of the students in the matter of teaching of religions in school and in part 4 their views about the way of managing the place and visibility of religion in school. After that, we underline what this comparison between Norway and France teaches us beyond the differences between the two countries (part 5).

Norway and France: two different social contexts where the situation regarding religion in schools has recently changed

From a socio-religious perspective, France and Norway seem to have very little in common. The first is a majority Catholic country, while the second is mainly Lutheran. France maintains a strict separation between church and State, while Norway has a state religion. There is no school subject dedicated to the teaching of religious facts in France, whereas Norway has one (*Religion, worldviews and ethics*). Besides the substantial difference in population between the two countries (63 million in France vs. 4.7 million in Norway), one other difference should be mentioned. Both countries have a Muslim minority, but it is proportionally much more important in France (6%) than in Norway (2%). In addition, while 20% of French students go to private schools, less than 3% do so in Norway.

As we see, the socio-religious and educational environments of Norway and France are quite different. Nevertheless, we should immediately point out that they do have one thing in common. Although the humanist movement in Norway is not as extensive as the secular movement in France, this secular standpoint is not only present in both countries, but in Norway as in France, the people involved pay close attention to everything dealing with the place and role of religion in schools, and play an active part in this issue. The lawsuits that humanist families in Norway have brought before the European Court of Human Rights are proof of this.

Despite the major differences between the two countries, it is interesting to note that both of them have recently seen significant changes take place in how religion is handled in classrooms. In Norway, a non-confessional, multi-faith religious education has been compulsory in the national public school system since 1997. In France, after a reform of the school curriculum in 1996 increased the coverage of religious phenomena, the Debray report in 2002 on *teaching religious facts in secular schools* inspired many new initiatives for developing multidisciplinary, secular course material on religion, also allowing teachers to receive the training they needed on this topic. But since there is such a large difference between the socio-religious and educational environments of both countries, what is most remarkable is how similar Norwegian and French students' personal views on religion are, and how much they agree on the role religion should have in school instruction. This relatively unexpected observation was an important result of the REDCo surveys. Basically, it reveals two things: one, the consequences of secularisation in the two countries; two, the fact that young people can develop attitudes and reactions toward religion and its handling in schools which are fairly similar, even though they live in differing social contexts. However, especially with regard to the question on the visibility of religious symbols at school, pupils react differently (see below).

In Norway as in France, students are divided on how much importance to give to religion

In both countries, slightly more than half of students between 14 and 16 years old say they have a religion (or a *worldview* in the Norwegian survey) while almost all of the rest of the students (44% in Norway, 45% in France) say they do not have a religion. In Lutheran Norway as in Catholic France, we see a significant decline in young people's identification with religion. This is a phenomenon that the European and World Values Surveys (see Dogan, 2003; Halman et al., 2008) had already brought to light. We see a similar pattern in the answers that Norwegian and French students give when asked whether religion is important to them or not. For 45% of French students and 44% of Norwegian students, it is not important; only 32% of French students and 28% of Norwegian students say it is. 45% of Norwegian students and 40% of French students never attend religious services. On the other hand, the proportion of students who attend a religious service at least once a month is higher in Norway than France: 30% and 20% respectively. According to the data of European surveys showing that the level of religious practice is lower in Protestant countries than in Catholic countries, these findings may seem surprising. But among the Catholic countries, France is more secularized than others such as Italy or Ireland (see our study in Willaime 1998). Nevertheless, in Norway as in France, religion is not something young people discuss much with each other.

Norwegian and French students support instruction about religion

Norwegian and French students gave relatively similar answers to the various subsections of the question *What are your experiences with religion in school?*, but they did so in different proportions for each item. They agree that they *get knowledge about different religions* (89% in Norway and 68% in France), *learn to have respect for everyone, no matter what their religion* (77% and 89% respectively), and *have opportunities to discuss religious issues from different perspectives* in school (61% and 53%). However, Norwegian students are not at all as convinced as their French counterparts (27% vs. 70%) that *learning about different religions at school helps* [them] *to live together*. It is possible that they are less conscious than French students of how instruction on religious issues helps them become good citizens; the French public school system puts great emphasis on this aspect of the course material on religions. 53% of Norwegian students think that *learning about religions at school helps* [them] *to make choices between right and wrong*, while only 23% of French students agree with this statement. In this case, the traditional Norwegian association between ethics and instruction on religion, which was once given from a religious perspective but is now religiously neutral, is probably one reason explaining students' views on this topic, as the authors of the Norwegian report indicate. There is something paradoxical about the fact that French students, who are taught in the extremely secular context of French public schools, find *topics about religions at school* more *interesting* (50%) than their Norwegian counterparts (33%). Perhaps the French students are more curious about religions at school because they are not accustomed to regular teaching about religions (contrary to their Norwegian colleagues who have long since received regular teaching about this). A few Norwegian or French students (16% in both cases) feel that *learning about religions leads to conflicts in the classroom.*

Norwegian and French students agree that they must get an objective knowledge about different religions and be able to talk and communicate about religious issues. They also agree that they need to learn the importance of religion for dealing with problems in society. Both groups of students refuse to be guided towards religious beliefs at school. However, more Norwegian students than French students (67% vs. 56%) consider that they have to learn at school how to understand what religions teach. The way in which the authors of the Norwegian report summarise the students' position on religion in schools could be quoted word for word to describe the attitude of French students: "School is a place where students learn about religion (knowledge) as well as discuss religion and learn to respect and live together irrespective of religious background. [...] In school they learn about religion, but not from religion. Confirming that school contributes to respect and knowledge, they disagree that learning about religions may lead to conflicts".

Students are open-minded and are willing to give space to religion in school, but they respect the non-religious nature of school

As for the visibility of religion in school life or the need to take religious students' needs into account, Norwegian and French students both have a relatively open-minded point of view on the issue. An example of this is that the same percentage of Norwegian students as French ones believe that *religious food requirements should be taken into account at school meals.* But more Norwegian students than French students (64% vs. 52%) feel that *students should be allowed to be absent from school during their religious holidays.* More of them also feel that *students should be excused from taking some lessons for religious reasons* (27% vs. 17%). A much larger percentage of them, indeed the majority (64% vs. 17%) think that *students should be able to wear religious symbols at school: more visible ones.* In this area French students have internalised the 2004 law that only allows the wearing of *discreet* religious signs on school grounds. But it is important to note that despite these few differences, Norwegian and French students both express a clear desire for limits on the visible presence of religious practices at school: in both countries, only a small minority of students support places of worship within schools or optional religious services.

Conclusion

Ultimately, both in Norway and France, despite the occasional differences that we have mentioned, we can agree with the authors of the Norwegian report when they say: "There is a general trend among the youngsters to prefer religious education in joint classes and to get objective knowledge. School is obviously not seen as a place for personal belief or religious practice, but a place to learn about different religions and also to discuss religious and ethical issues". Both in Norway and in France we find large numbers of young people who do not identify with a particular religion. We also see in both countries the students' overall willingness to understand the specific status of schools, the specific role they play, and their substantial respect for that status and that role. Despite living in different socio-religious and educational environments, Norwegian and French students are nevertheless capable of grasping the main ideas of instruction dealing with religions and beliefs that is adapted to the secular and pluralist nature of the societies in which they live: *knowledge-oriented* instruction that scrupulously respects their personal choices in this matter.

References

Dogan, M. (2003). Religious Beliefs in Europe: Factors of Accelerated Decline, in: R.L. Piedmont & D.O. Moberg (Eds.), *Research in the Social Scientific Study of Religion*, Boston: Brill, pp. 161–188.

Halman, L. et al. (2008). *Changing Values and Beliefs in 85 countries. Trends from the Values Surveys 1981 to 2004*. Boston: Brill.

Willaime, J.-P. (1998). Religious and Secular France Between Northern and Southern Europe, *Social Compass, Revue Internationale de Sociologie de la Religion / International Review of Sociology of Religion*, 45, 1, pp. 155–174.

Dan-Paul Jozsa, Thorsten Knauth & Wolfram Weisse

Teenagers, Religions and Schools in Norway – Comments from a German Perspective

Norway and Germany have much in common when it comes to religion and education, but there are also considerable differences.[1] The following remarks do not represent an in-depth comparison of the findings in both countries, but intend to give impulses to the interpretation of the Norwegian data from a German perspective. They do not presume to set an end to a comparison of the quantitative findings of those two countries, but to open the forum on issues to be discussed further.

Main differences and commonalities between the two contexts

From a conceptual and structural point of view regarding religion and religious education in Germany and Norway, the main commonalties between the two countries are:

- Both countries have traditionally strong churches which are closely interrelated with the societal and political power-structures in their respective countries, but have declined in numbers and influence within the last decades.
- Mainly through migration, the picture of the religious landscape has changed towards a pluralisation of religions. This change has been gradually taking place over the past 30 years.
- The societal function of religion is discussed anew, with a focus directed to possibilities and limitations for peaceful coexistence.
- In both countries the subject of religious education is taught in public schools. Forms and aims of religious education are discussed academically and publicly in Germany as well as in Norway.

The differences lie mainly in the field of religion and education. They can be sketched as follows:

1. There are big differences in view of both the organisational forms and the aims of religious education seen in comparison between Norway-Germany, and within different regions of Germany itself.
2. In most of the German federal states ('Länder') – in Germany the 16 federal states are independent in their decisionmaking in the area of education, including the approaches to religious education used in their schools – there is a tendency to foster traditional structures, and that means to offer religious education separately along the lines of the adherence to the Protestant or Catholic confession. In some regions like in North Rhine-Westphalia 'Islam Study', Orthodox and Jewish religious education, etc. is also offered, basically in classes where students are separated along confessional lines. In Hamburg, religious education is offered as a religious education for all, where students are taught together in the same classes, irrespective of their religion, confession or world view.

---

1 See also: Skeie (2007); Knauth (2007, 2008); Jozsa (2007, 2008); von der Lippe (2008); Skeie & Weisse (2008); Weisse (2007).

3. In Norway, the change in the societal and religious situation over the past three decades has led to a different path. In cooperation between specialists in the pedagogical field, school authorities and the Lutheran Church, a new subject has been created with the name Kristendoms- religions- og livssynskunnskap (KRL). So there is no longer any Christian confessional religious education in public schools, but a new approach including all religions, which is compulsory for all students.

The comparison of the two contexts on a structural and conceptual level shows that there are many more commonalities than differences between Norway and Germany – one could even say that the commonalities in religious education are bigger between Norway and Hamburg (joint religious education) than between Hamburg and North Rhine-Westphalia (joint religious education vs separate religious education). So it might come as no surprise that many commonalities are also found between the results of the REDCo quantitative study in the two contexts as elaborated by Geir Skeie in his comments on the German results in this book.

Striking, interesting and unexpected points from a German perspective

Is it really astonishing to see that the data of our quantitative surveys in Norway and Germany show very similar structures of thinking? No and yes. No, as the contexts are so similar. Yes for two reasons: Similar contexts could equally well lead to different reactions and reflections by youngsters, and: The results in the two countries add up to a most impressive landscape of reflection of teenagers on religion, education and society. Taking both countries into consideration, we see both challenges from the Norwegian analysis which could stimulate further thinking in Germany, and stimuli for the Norwegian discussion on the background of our German perspective. The following points can illustrate this:

In Norway as well as in Germany it seems that encounter with religious diversity in education makes the students more tolerant and dialogue-oriented. In Norway, the quantitative survey has only been carried out in public schools, so that the data have been collected in schools where the students had no other experience than a multi-faith religious education. It is nonetheless impressive that our Norwegian colleagues underline, "that the school with the most religious diversity among its students is also very strong on tolerance and they very much support dialogue." Here, the situation and the data from Germany offer a differentiation of perspective. In Hamburg with its religious education for all, we see a very strong stream of thinking which favours religious and cultural plurality and where dialogue plays an important role. In NRW with its confessional and religious separation in religious education classes, we are nonetheless astonished by a strong pattern of support and high numbers (not as high as in Hamburg, but high nonetheless) in favour of religious plurality and dialogue. But maybe we have to go beyond the classification in terms of numbers and see what experiences are related to such statements. Here we see very limited opportunities for an interreligious encounter outside school in Norway as well as in HH and NRW. Thus the possibility of meeting students from other religions and cultures in school and entering into a dialogue on religious questions in the classroom appears as a major chance for an encounter holding the potential to make students more tolerant and dialogue-oriented.

Different ideas and interpretations

The Norwegian analysis considers it as an open question, maybe a contradiction, that students in Norway see religious education as a subject where they learn mutual respect with people of other religions, but at the same time are not sure that learning about religion will contribute to a peaceful coexistence in society. Maybe this tension could be interpreted as a very realistic attitude of students in Norway, being aware of both the possibilities and the limits of learning at school?

The Norwegian students underline the central importance of knowledge-based religious education more clearly than our data from Germany. Learning about religion is central to them. Such an approach understands the school subject 'religious education' as a 'normal' subject in the school curriculum like languages and mathematics. On the other hand: could the impetus of the experiences of German students with regard to the positional approach of "learning from religions" form an element to show students in Norway an internal perspective which can sometimes be more interesting for students and contribute to a special profile of religious education in comparison to the strictly knowledge-based subjects? Could it be that the French discussion on the question of religious facts (*faits religieux*) could stimulate a discussion in Norway as well as in Germany that goes beyond concentration on 'mere knowledge', but addresses the different layers of knowledge to which religious experiences could contribute?

This could also lead to a differentiation in the interpretation of the third hypothesis. Our Norwegian colleagues underline the encountering of religious diversity in school (and for some in the family as well). At the same time they conclude that the tolerance of the students "towards religious diversity is perceived on a rather abstract level". Although religious education must not be overestimated in its capabilities, the approach of religious education in Norway could be challenged by such an analysis. Could it be that religious education in Norway needs an additional element that integrates religious positions 'from inside', as outlined above? Would that possibly enhance elements which go beyond 'rather abstract' knowledge and lead into deeper dimensions of religious experiences? And if the students themselves do not have them, then this could lead to a demand to be made for material offering insights from religions or to invitations of persons who are willing and able to explain their view on religion 'from inside' into the classroom.

This does not mean that we propose a confessional type of religious education to our Norwegian colleagues. Rather, we arrive at a proposal to enter more readily into an exchange with more research in order to see whether and how there can be a combination of elements in religious education where knowledge and positions are more interrelated in order to develop and to foster interreligious learning and encounters in the (public) schools of our countries.

References

Jozsa, D.-P. (2008). Religious Education in North Rhine-Westphalia: Views and Experiences of Students, in: T. Knauth, D.-P. Jozsa, G. Bertram-Troost, & J. Ipgrave (Eds.), *Encountering Religious Pluralism in School and Society – A Qualitative Study of Teenage Perspectives in Europe.* Muenster: Waxmann, pp. 173–206.

Knauth, T. (2007). Religious education in Germany. A contribution to dialogue or Source of Conflict? Historical and contextual analysis of the development since the 1960s, in: R. Jackson, S. Miedema, S., W. Weisse & J.-P. Willlaime (Eds.), *Religion and Education in Europe: Developments, Contexts and Debates.* Muenster: Waxmann, pp. 243–265.

Knauth, T. (2008). "Better together than apart": Religion in School and Lifeworld of Students in Hamburg, in: T. Knauth, D.-P. Jozsa, G. Bertram-Troost, & J. Ipgrave (Eds.), *Encountering Religious Pluralism in School and Society – A Qualitative Study of Teenage Perspectives in Europe.* Muenster: Waxmann, pp. 207–245.

Lippe, M. von der (2008). To believe or not to believe: Young people's perceptions and experiences of religion and religious education in Norway, in: T. Knauth, D.-P. Jozsa, G. Bertram-Troost, & J. Ipgrave (Eds.), *Encountering Religious Pluralism in School and Society – A Qualitative Study of Teenage Perspectives in Europe.* Muenster: Waxmann, pp. 149–171.

Skeie, G. (2007). Religion and Education in Norway, in: R. Jackson, S. Miedema, S., W. Weisse & J.-P. Willlaime (Eds.), *Religion and Education in Europe: Developments, Contexts and Debates.* Muenster: Waxmann, pp. 221–241.

Skeie, G. & Weisse, W. (2008). Religion, Education, Dialogue and Conflict: Positions and Perspectives of students in Germany and Norway, in: T. Knauth, D.-P. Jozsa, G. Bertram-Troost, & J. Ipgrave (Eds.), *Encountering Religious Pluralism in School and Society – A Qualitative Study of Teenage Perspectives in Europe.* Muenster: Waxmann, pp. 327–338.

Weisse, W. (2007). The European Research project on Religion and education "REDCo". An introduction, in: R. Jackson, S. Miedema, S., W. Weisse & J.-P. Willlaime (Eds.), *Religion and Education in Europe: Developments, Contexts and Debates.* Muenster: Waxmann, pp. 9–25.

Fedor Kozyrev & Pille Valk

Saint-Petersburg Students' Views about Religion in Education – Results of the Quantitative Survey

1. Introduction

1.1 Remarks on national context

The most distinctive element of the Russian situation as regards religion in education is the long period of state atheism that had been a part of communist ideology officially promoted by the educational system. Now after 15 years of hot public debates, religion has begun to return on legitimate grounds far and wide to the curricula of Russian schools. A growing number of Russian schoolchildren study the basics of Orthodox culture or attend classes of spiritual and cultural formation based on Orthodox values. Islamic culture is an invariant part of the school curricula in 6 regions of the Russian Federation with a predominant Muslim population. The situation remains highly dynamic and heterogeneous. There are regions where Orthodox culture has been a compulsory subject in schools for several years (Kursk, Belgorod & Voronezh et al). There are other regions where religious education in any form is strictly avoided in public schools. St. Petersburg, the study area, belongs to the latter.

There are three main trends in Russian secondary education. *Comprehensive* (ordinary) state schools are the most widespread type of institution for secondary education. *Gymnasiums* and *lyceums* are other options offering an advanced level of education. They are believed to provide a sufficient platform for entering Universities. The borderline between the two options is vague, for there are a large number of comprehensive schools offering a relatively high level of education and also with different 'subject profiles', that is with an advanced level of education in one or several subjects (foreign language, biology etc.). The third trend is the vocational training system. Technical colleges and other institutions providing secondary general plus secondary professional education constitute this trend. Usually these institutions are affiliated to higher educational or scientific structures of the corresponding branch of the economy and are supported by them.

There is a small number of non-state schools in St. Petersburg, some of them with a religious affiliation or religious ethos. Even when accredited by the state these schools do not receive financial support from the state and that is the main reason why this sector of education remains undeveloped in Russia. Fees for education in this type of schools may reach the level of an average monthly salary of a middle class worker. As in big cities like St. Petersburg there is a variety of state *gymnasiums* that provide a good level of education for free, the non-state sector of education can not actually compete with the state one.

1.2 Description of the sample

All schools in the sample are from St. Petersburg and its surroundings. The total number of respondents questioned in St. Petersburg is 403. The sample is balanced as regards to gender (51% males and 49% females) and covers the target age range for 94% of the respondents, 45% of them being 15 and 42% 16 years old and 8% aged 14, 5,5% of the respondents are 17 years old. So the average age of the whole group is 15,5.

9 schools with 16 different class-groups in them were selected for the survey. Schools 1, 2 and 3 participated in the REDCo qualitative research a year ago. In schools 1 and 2 respondents were all new. In school 3 half of the respondents were the pupils who participated in the REDCo written questioning for the second time.

1.2.1 Introduction to the schools

School 1 (21 respondents): a non-state gymnasium, a heir of a pre-Revolutionary German-speaking gymnasium for foreigners. Beginning from the level of primary school, the gymnasium gives advanced education in humanities, especially in German language and culture. Tuition fees are as high as almost the average salary of civil servants. So this is a school for wealthy people. Almost all of the respondents in this school declared one or two of their parents run their own business.

This is the only school in the sample with compulsory RE. The Constitution of the school declares 'Christian nurture' among the aims of education. At grades 1–5 students participating in the research had regular religious classes on Christianity with a broad ecumenical setting. Now religious content still occupies a prominent place within several subjects, such as Philosophy, Ethics and History. Every year after Christmas vacations there is a Bible Week at school. During specially organized events students of all grades are offered presentations and discussions on Bible topics, take part in meetings with pastors and theologians and visit Christian communities.

Schools 2 (34 respondents) *and 9* (47 respondents) are high rating state gymnasiums located in prestigious districts of St. Petersburg. The graduates of the school usually easily win competitions to enter universities[1]. Students are mostly from middle class families. Business owners, representatives of intellectual professions and high ranked state service officers are parents of the majority of the group participating in the survey. School 2 provides several profiles of specialisation for senior students. Two class-groups participated in the research, related to humanities and economic sciences profiles. Students had an experience of informal initiation to religion some 3–4 years ago that produced mostly negative effects on their attitudes toward religion. School 9 has specialization in humanities

Schools 3 (23 respondents) *and 6* (75 respondents) are ordinary comprehensive state schools located in the central parts of St. Petersburg. The social position of the parents in these schools is notably lower than in the two gymnasiums presented above. A bigger percentage of parents are working class. In both schools the main form of introducing religious topics is through the literature classes. In school 3 five lessons on the Bible were given by a literature teacher for the class-group participating in the survey in the period between qualitative and quantitative surveys.

Schools 4 (54 respondents) *and 8* (18 respondents) are state gymnasiums with a medium position between high rating gymnasiums on one side and comprehensive schools on the other. This regards both the level of education offered by them and the social positions of the parents.

School 5 (62 respondents) is a comprehensive municipal school located in a suburban area near St. Petersburg and subordinated administratively to the regional government. In the Soviet time the main occupation of its inhabitants was connected with a fish farm and shipbuilding. Now the parents of schoolchildren work mostly in St. Petersburg, though a part of

---

1   Many universities in Russia according to the old tradition organize so called 'entering exams' for enrollees. Competition for entering universities is based mostly on the evaluation of the results of these exams.

them still are occupied in the shipbuilding industry. As to the level of education and the presence of migrants, this is comparable to that of schools 3 and 6.

School 7 (69 respondents) belongs to a special trend of education known as the vocational training system. It is a technical college attached to the St. Petersburg State Nautical University. It offers both general secondary and initial professional education in the field of nautical and shipbuilding engineering. The professional family background of the students in this college is no less diverse than in other schools and the connection with the sailing and shipbuilding professions is hardly stronger than in the school 5.

1.2.2   Religious background of students

Nearly half, 44% of students (178) in our survey declared they have a religion or worldview. There were 85% Christians (151) and 4% Muslims (7) among them. Other religions were mentioned occasionally, no more than 2 times each. These were Buddhism, Jehovah's Witness, Satanism, Paganism and some others.

The religious background of students in the sample may be regarded as rather typical for Russia. Official statistics constantly show believers to be 47–52% of the samples in all-Russian polls (Varzanova 1998, Roberson 1999, Russian Independent Institute 2000). Surveys conducted among youngsters in St. Petersburg previously (Kozyrev 2003, 2008; Klinetskaya 2005, 2006) showed the same proportion of believers. They also showed that Christians (mostly belonging to the Russian Orthodox Church) and persons without any certain religious affiliation make up the two biggest groups among believers (40–60%). The latter group may include those who believe in God's existence but do not participate in religious practice, those who go to Church from time to time but have a vague idea about their religious belonging, as well as those who do not want to disclose their religious identity. The third major group are Muslims (2–3%).

The latest statistics of the Russian Public Opinion Research Center (VCIOM) published on 16.10.2007 (Press-release No. 789) confirmed that "half of Russians are believers [...] One third of respondents (31%) consider the existence of God possible, but are only little interested in church life. Convinced atheists account for no more than 6% of respondents, whereas 8% do not give thought to the issue of religion". Orthodoxy presents the most wide-spread religion in Russia, practiced by 75% of believers: 8% are Muslims. No more than 1–2% respondents identify themselves as belonging to any other religion. The rest of believers do not practice any religion (8%) or have difficulties with defining their religious affiliation (6%). Compared to the data mentioned above, these Figures show a higher proportion of religiously affiliated people that may reflect the latest dynamics of religious life in Russia.

Statistics of religious situation in St. Petersburg do not differ considerably from the overall statistics for Russia (Klinetskaya, 2005). The same may be said about our sample. The characteristics of religious background are in good correspondence with the results of several researches conducted previously in some of the schools included in the sample. For instance in 2006 and 2007 surveys on the religiosity of students aged 13–14 years were conducted in school 5 by other researchers (not published). Their data support our findings in particular regarding the proportion of atheists (17% of students refused the existence of God in the previous research and 14% did so in our research).

1.2.3   National and social composition

The sample is very homogeneous regarding ethnic and national characteristics. About 10% of students may be regarded as having a migrant family background. The major part of these migrants, coming predominantly from Ukraine, Kazakhstan and Belarus may be supposed to have a Russian ethnic background. Only 2% of the students hold citizenship of another country and speak non-Russian languages at home.

The social backgrounds of the students in the sample are much more diverse. The fathers who can be identified as belonging to the working class make almost the same proportion as those belonging to white-collar professions, 26–27% each; 10% are declared to run their own business. The occupation of almost all others (30%) remained unknown. The position of the mothers differs much. First, they generally have higher social status than fathers according to the ESEC[2] index: 46% belong to the group covered by categories 1–3, and only 10% to the categories 8–9. It means they more often occupy positions requiring higher education. But in the Russian context it does not mean they earn more money. On the contrary, if a father is declared to be a worker or a driver it means he usually earns more money than his wife belonging to categories 2–3. About 11% of mothers do not have any occupation, and this situation is more common for wealthy families. Mothers' occupations were reported more frequently than fathers' (by 79% and 70% of respondents respectively).

1.2.4 Reflection on the sample

The sample represents the main trends, forms and levels of education provided within the modern Russian educational system. It includes one non-state school with a religious background and one suburban school. The ratio between the numbers of students presenting the main models of the educational system in the sample is the following:
– Comprehensive schools – 40%,
– Gymnasiums – 43%,
– Vocational training system (technical college) – 17%.

Compared to the real situation, the proportion of students who learn in ordinary comprehensive schools is underrepresented in the sample.

The sample quite adequately represents the confessional situation in St. Petersburg and in Russia. Ethnically St. Petersburg is one of for the most 'Russian' regions of Russia, and one should not forget that even in the European part of the Russian Federation there are many regions with a high proportion (more than a half) of other ethnicities (Tatars, Bashkirs, Kalmyks etc.) so the sample is not representative in this respect. In socio-economic terms, St. Petersburg as the 'cultural capital of Russia' may be characterized with a higher proportion of citizens working in the field of science, education and arts. Unfortunately it does not mean that the living standard in St. Petersburg is high. It is definitely lower than in Moscow and it is comparable to the majority of other Russian big cities. As to RE, St. Petersburg has been always among the regions where the local policy was strictly against inclusion of religious subjects into school curricula. This policy was typical for Russian regions some 5 years ago but now it cannot be regarded as representing the situation in Russia any more.

So, it is important to carry in mind that our sample is not representative. But it still allows us to look for some trends and patterns regarding the issues of Religion in education. Generalizations on the bases of our study have to be very careful.

---

2   European Socio-economic Classification home page: http://www.iser.essex.ac.uk/esec/guide/ (first accessed 12.11.2008)

1.3   Procedure

The questionnaire administration was organized during the school time and conducted either by the researcher or by teachers responsible for the classes in the period 5–29 February 2008. No serious incidents were registered except for one girl in school 1 who was offended by the laughter of her classmates when she showed she was born in Kazakhstan. Indicative of a certain ethnic intolerance in her peer group is her attempt to justify herself in the eyes of her peers: "I am from Kazakhstan, but it does not mean I am Kazakh". No signs of religious intolerance were shown during the research in any school.

The main problems were caused by questions 1–2 and 120–121. When students asked if they should classify lessons about the Bible or the history of religions as religious education, they were instructed to answer positively on questions 1 and 2 only if they had a special religious subject. This instruction seems not to be given properly in school 6, so somewhat higher number of those who claimed to participate in RE in this school should not be regarded as pointing to the peculiar characteristics of the curriculum there. Questions about the professions of the parents proved to be confusing, for the students could not decide if they should associate profession with the profile of education or with the present occupation of their parents. In many cases these two were quite different things.

Among the most revealing reactions were the repeated questions of students in schools 1, 3, 6 and 7 about the 'proper' answer to the last point of the questionnaire concerning their religious affiliation. It seems some students did not exercise personal religious freedom in their life and even did not comprehend the idea of it. Several students in school 3 asked their teacher: "What is the name of *our* religion, the one we have in Russia?" Some others seem to have more conscious problems with their religious affiliations. One student in school 1 asked if he should put his *official* religion or not.

A quarter (22%) of respondents used the opportunity to put down their comments and remarks at the end of the questionnaires. Students in schools 1, 2 and 5 were more active in producing comments.

The major proportion of comments (82%) may be ascribed to one or two of the 4 topics following, in decreasing order:
1)   ideas about RE (25%),
2)   ideas about religious identity (23%),
3)   affirmation or further explanation of the idea that religion belongs to private life (20%),
4)   comments on the questionnaire (14%).

To begin with the last, most problematic for respondents according to their comments was question 38 regarding the existence of God. "*At point 38 I don't agree with any of the statements*" (4–2–18, m)[3] – that is the commonest notion. One of the respondents confessed to be confused by the proposal to choose between the existence of God and the existence of spirit or life force, since she believed in both (1–2–2, f). For some others the range of options was too narrow.

Besides this particular point, criticism was targeted on the idea of such a research in general. A hidden agenda, to draw students into religion, was suspected by several respondents. One respondent accused the researchers of racism, not giving however explanations of his opinion.

---

3   First character in the respondent's code points on school number, f and m designate female and male respectively

Explicit xenophobia was exposed only occasionally, namely two respondents from school 5 put down the well-known slogan *"Russia for Russians!"* It is worth noticing that a year before in the suburb where the school was located a bloody ethnic conflict between Russians and Armenians (living in a diaspora) had taken place and these comments may be regarded as an echo of this conflict.

More than a half of the comments were of a critical nature, the others expressed appreciations and thanks. Mostly they were very short but some more extended.

Quite in agreement with the remarkably uniform position shown in students' reaction to point 84 of the questionnaire was the considerable proportion of their comments elaborating and passionately affirming the statement "religion belongs to private life".

Comments regarding the religious identity of the respondents came both from believers and unbelievers. The latter tried mostly to bring arguments against faith and these were hardly more than two: religion is invented for weak people and religion is a tool for gaining easy money and of oppression. The last argument was offered twice and in a rather aggressive form.

In some cases the comments were really helpful. For instance one respondent who claimed to be Christian and to have a Christian family background filled up only the last page of the questionnaire (V.113–127) but added the comment:

> *"I am a Jehovah's Witness and my views are in full correspondence with Bible, the Word of God."* (5–2–16, m)

The largest proportion of the comments concerning matters of religious identity belonged to those who identified themselves as religious persons but questioned their affiliation with a certain religion in different ways, for instance:

> *"I personally confess Christianity but only through going to Church and celebrating Christmas. I personally believe simply in God."* (4–1–18, m)

A number of students in our sample attempted to question the concept of religious belonging in a more general way. Though short enough, some of these comments are quite striking, for instance:

> *"For me, it does not matter what religion one has. I am not a racist!"* (4–2–13, m)

Faith in oneself was mentioned 2–3 times as the preferable type of religious commitment.

Among the 25 comments regarding religion in education, 6 were pro, 9 were contra religious subjects in school and 10 were more neutral and contained concrete advice or thoughts about the best way to deal with religious issues. The main anxiety about the presence of religion in school was associated with probable indoctrination and other negative impacts undermining personal freedoms.

Of special interest are two comments from school 5 in which students advocate separate religious education and base their arguments on the believers' interests and rights.

> *"I think that different religious schools should be established, because some people have bad attitudes to those who practice certain religions. So religious institutions are necessary to ensure all people's rights."* (5–1–1, f)

> *"Separate schools with religious education should be founded, so that those who don't need it would not suffer in vain. Because many of us don't find it [religion] necessary and those who believe would not feel comfortable with this kind of attitude."* (5–1–5, f)

Since both cited respondents identified themselves as persons without religion and without migration background, these comments may be qualified as remarkable examples of empathy and social responsibility exercised by teenagers.

Taken in general, the comments proved the ability of students to deal with difficult issues related to religion and education in a responsible and reflective way. Some comments covered several topics and connected logically different parts of the questionnaire, so that the inner coherence of the student's system of views could not be doubted. Here is a last quotation that looks like a quintessence of the overview of students' comments.

> *"In my view, tests like this are very important. I am not sure if religious education should be included into the curriculum, because I think religion is a personal matter. But at the same time it seems to me very important for people to have a certain idea about religion, because nowadays it becomes a sore problem. People of different religions should learn how to coexist, for the future of our society depends on that." (2–1–2)*

2. General presentation of the results

After setting the scene we can now turn to the presenting the research outcomes. The following sub-chapter is structured, on the bases of our research questions, into three major parts: religion in pupil's lives, religion in schools and the impact of religion in the society through the eyes of students. All three sections follow the same scheme – first the data presentation followed by the data interpretation. In-between these two parts one can find a compendium of the main analysis outcomes serving as a bridge from the heuristic to the hermeneutic parts of the chapter.

2.1 What role has Religion in pupils' lives?

This section is based on the description and interpretation of the respondents' reactions to the questions 37 – 79, 86, and 122–127 of the questionnaire. These are questions about respondents' religiosity, their perception of religion and the ways religion is present in their daily life and in their communication with people around.

2.1.1 Data description

The religiousness of students in St. Petersburg was evaluated in terms of importance of religion in their personal life (q. 37), having religious beliefs (q. 38) and affiliation with a certain religion or worldview (q. 126). Correlation analysis shows the three indicators of religiosity are interconnected rather loosely though not without a certain logic. Pair correlations for variables 37 /38 and 37 / 126 are negative (–0,47 and –0,45 respectively) and that for 38 / 126 is positive (+0,34) as might be expected. It might mean that all three approaches to the estimation of religiosity are important to use.

Nearly half (44%) of students declared having a certain religion or worldview (q. 126): Christians made 85% and Muslims 4% among the respondents who wished to declare their affiliation. The other confessions and beliefs were mentioned occasionally. As is seen from Figure 1, 46% of respondents said definitely "There is a God" (q. 38). The proportion of those who deny the existence of any sort of God, spirit or life force is 14%.

Figure 1:   **Responses of students to the question "Which of these statements comes closest to your position?" (%)**

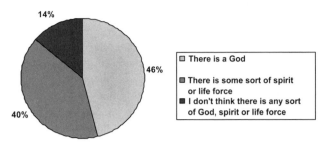

Regarding the personal importance of religion our students' positions were the following: slightly more that 1/3 of them (37%) chose the middle scores in between 'absolutely not important' and 'very important': 15% evaluated religion as absolutely not important for them, and the percentage of those to whom religion is very important was also 15%. The distribution of the positions is illustrated in Figure 2.

Figure 2:   **Positions of the students regarding the importance of religion in their life.**

How important is religion to you? Please choose a suitable position for yourself on the scale from 'not at all important' (0) to 'very important' (4)

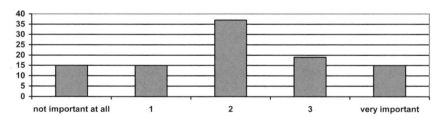

St. Petersburg students are not frequent church goers. Less than 10% of students attend religious events once a month or more. More than 60% claimed they never attend religious events. More than a half claimed to pray at least once a month. Only 10% disagreed with the assumption that one can be a religious person without belonging to a particular faith community and, remarkably, these are mostly not those 10% who attend regularly religious events ($r = 0.08$).

Reading of religious texts and looking for religious topics on the Internet is definitely not a popular habit among students in our sample. Less than 5% reported to do it each week. The frequency of thinking about the meaning of life is considerably higher. About a half of students do it almost every day according to their self evaluation. At the same time thoughts about religion occupy much less space in their life. One out of four students thinks about religion once a week.

A small minority agreed[4] with the extreme and contrasting ideas "Religion is nonsense" – "Religion determines my whole life" (10% each). These two appeared to be the least popular options regarding the role of religion in students' life. Notable is the high level of agreement with the idea that religion plays a role in our history. Only 8% disagreed with this. One out of three students has doubts about the existence of God, but only one out of six is ready to change religious views.

Family is the main agent of initiation into religion for St. Petersburg students. Only one student out of ten finds this source of information about religion not important. Friends and books are secondary sources. Religious communities are of the lowest rank, with half of the students denying their importance. Indicative and explicable is also the relatively low level of importance of school. It is not important for 30% of students, and 39% evaluated the role of the school as 'a little bit important'.

The majority of students are in harmony with their parents regarding religious views. Only 15% indicated their parents had totally different views about religion from themselves. The characteristics of the religious backgrounds of parents are similar to those of their children, and there is a relatively high level of knowledge about the religion of family members compared to the knowledge about the religion of classmates (q. 71, 72). Nevertheless only one third of respondents agreed that religion is something one inherits from one's family (q. 86)

There is a certain gender imbalance in the religious influence of parents. It can be definitely stated that mothers are more religious in the eyes of their children. The ratio of yes / no answers in questions about religious affiliation (q. 124, 122) was 4 / 3 for mothers and 3 / 4 for fathers. At the same time only 5% fewer children knew about the worldviews of their fathers compared to their mothers.

A special characteristic of the Russian sample is the unwillingness of respondents to talk about religion. More than a half the students state that they never speak about religion with their friends and classmates. Even the percentage of those who speak regularly about religion in their families is remarkably low: one third does this about once a month and one third never.

This "silent" style of religious life is echoed in many answers given to the blocks of questions mostly related to the topics of communication with others. Despite the highly homogeneous ethno-confessional situation in St. Petersburg schools mentioned above a half of the students stated that at school they went around with youngsters who have different religious backgrounds and more than a half stated they had friends who belong to different religions (q. 74, 70). At the same time, when asked if they share views about religion with their friends and classmates (q. 68, 69), the majority of respondents (52 and 62% respectively) did not give any definite answers and reported instead that they did not know about their religious views.

There are no statistical grounds to talk about xenophobic attitudes spread among students in our sample. Four out of five students claimed they had no preferences to go around with youngsters who have the same religious background either at school or in their spare time. This proportion was higher among students who stated that at school they go around with youngsters, or they have friends who belong to, different religions (85% and 86% correspondingly). Bivariate analysis (see table 1) showed significantly more disagreements with the statements

---

4   Here and henceforth – if it is not indicated, the responses 'strongly (dis)agree' and '(dis)agree' are
    summarized.

'At school, I prefer to go around with youngsters who have the same religious background as me' and 'In my spare time, I prefer to go around with youngsters who have the same religious background as me' (***)[5]

in the group of students who experienced both inter-religious communication or friendship (answers "yes" for q. 70, 74, 75) The distribution of the answers to the questions 70, 74, 75, 76, and 77, and cross-tabulation are summarized in the Table 1.

Table 1: **Distribution of the responses and cross-tabulation on the items related to communication and religion (%).**

		At school I prefer to go around with young people who have the same religious background as me		In my spare time I prefer to go around with youngsters who have the same religious background as me	
		Yes (20)	No (80)	Yes (21)	No (79)
I have friends who belong to different religions	Yes (59)	14	86	15	85
	No (21)	37	63	41	59
	? (20)	18	82	18	82
At school I go around with youngsters who have a different religious background	Yes (49)	12	88	15	85
	No (23)	37	63	36	64
	? (28)	18	82	19	81
After school I go around with youngsters who have a different religious background	Yes (35)	11	89	12	88
	No (36)	32	68	35	65
	? (29)	15	85	15	85

Similar patterns were also found in when looking at the answers to the questions 70, 74 and 75 in the relation to the statement *'I do not like people from other religions and do not want to live together with them'* (q. 105). The means of the positions regarding the statement are presented in Figure 3.

Figure 3. **Positions regarding xenophobia related to religion in relationships. (Means of estimates, scale from 1 – strongly agree to 5 – strongly disagree)**

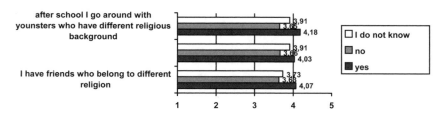

5   Here and henceforth statistical significance is meant by the term. If the value of significance (Sig.) is not indicated in the text, p< 0,05 level is considered. The significance of differences is marked as follows: p < 0.001 as ***, 0.001<p<0.01 as **, 0.01<p<0.05 as *.

So experience of personal contacts with people from other religions seems to produce a more positive attitude toward inter-religious communication.

Determinants of perceptions

Background variables such as religious affiliation, gender and school influenced in different ways and to different degrees the religious views of the students. The first factor identified, the self-affiliation of respondents with a certain religion (q. 126) proved to be most influential.[6]

Religious background. Religious students showed a more positive vision of religion and were more inclined to give religion more space in their private and social life. This trend was detected in almost all blocks of questions. They talk about religion in family, with teachers and with religious leaders much more often. They know more about the religion of their relatives and friends. To illustrate the significance of the difference, suffice it to say that the statement "it doesn't bother me what my friends think about religion" met strong agreement among one out of four religious and three out of four non-religious students. Religious students think more often not only about religion but also about the meaning of life. A general overview of the responses to the questions about the role of religion in students' life (q. 52–61) is presented in Figure 4.

Figure 4: **Rotle of religion in religious and nonreligious students' life (means of estimates, scale from 1 – strongly agree to 5 – strongly disagree)**

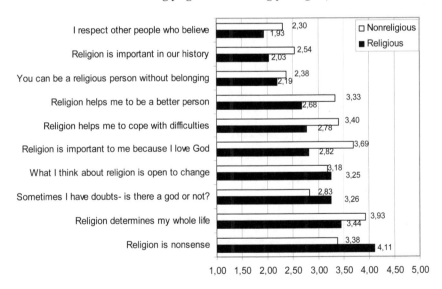

---

6   In the following text the students who answered to the 126 question (do you have a certain religion or worldview) positively, are marked as 'religious students' those, who replied negatively are named as 'non-religious' ones.

When evaluating statements of their European peers on what role religion may have in their life (q. 52–61), religious students showed more positive attitudes toward religion and more respect toward the other believers (***). In particular twice as many religious students strongly agreed with the statement "I respect other people who believe" (q. 55) than students without religious affiliation and correspondingly almost 4 times fewer strongly disagreed with the statement. As might be obvious, religious students had significantly less doubt about the existence of God (**). At the same time they agreed with unbelievers in the idea that one can be a religious person without religious belonging (p=0.06), and did not differ much from the non-religious students in openness to change their views on religion (p=0.6). The two sub-samples (i.e. religious and non) showed the same distribution of answers to questions about their preference to go around with young people of the same religious background.

Gender. Regarding the gender aspect, direct questions about the religiousness of the students (q. 37, 38, 126) did not give solid grounds to assert girls to be more religious than boys. Yet some important differences were found.

The proportion of those who did or did not claim their affiliation with a certain religion was 42% : 58% among boys and 50% : 50% among girls. The difference is not big enough to be considered as significant in statistical terms, but it is amplified by other findings. Though the number of those who declared that religion is not important in their lives was almost the same for girls and boys, the frequency of extreme negative answers (absolutely not important) was one and a half times higher among boys (18% : 12%). The same trend was found in the distribution of opinions about the existence of God (q. 38). The proportion of those who denied the existence of God was twice as high among boys (19% : 9%). Gender differences were found in the distribution of answers to this question, significant on a rather high level of probability (**). How gender differences were reflected in the answers about the role of religion in a person's life, is presented in Figure 5. In this block only the two first statements got significantly different answers from boys and girls (***and ** respectively).

Figure 5:   Gender differences of religions role in the students' life (means of estimates, scale from 1 – strongly agree to 5 – strongly disagree)

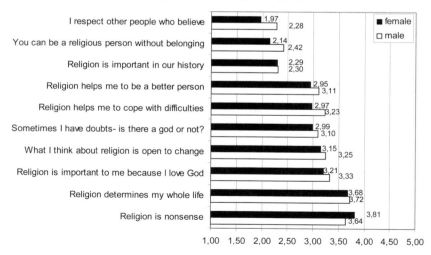

As to the sources of information about religion, girls prefer more than boys to read books (means 3.1 / 2.7, **)[7] and evaluate school more positively as a source of information (means 3.2 / 3.0, *), while boys are more positive about using the internet for this purpose (means 4.4 / 4.7, **). Notably, the last was the only point in this block of questions where gender differences were once more stronger than the differences between religious and non-religious students.

As is seen in Figure 6 girls are more open for communication with others. In all answers to the questions about pupils' interest in learning what other people think about religion the standard deviation of the boys' answers was higher and the means differed significantly (*** for q.78, 79, 87).

Figure 6:   Gender differences in the religious issues (means of estimates, scale from 1 – strongly agree to 5 – strongly disagree)

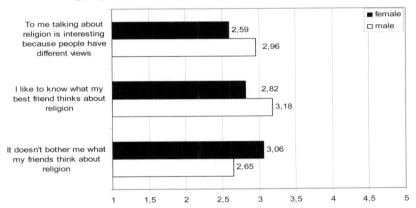

Significant gender differences were found also in the answers to questions about pupils' interest in learning what other people think about religion (*** for q. 78, 79, 87). Girls know better about the religious situation in their families and estimate the level of like-mindedness with their friends and classmates more optimistically (q. 68, 69, 71, Figure 7). Nevertheless the idea to socialize with young people of the same religious background is equally acceptable for girls and boys. 22% of boys and 21% of girls claimed they prefer to go around with youngsters of the same religious background (q. 77), though more girls declared they actually do so (29% / 41% for q. 75, Figure 7). Similarly not much difference can be found in the declarations made by girls and boys on how often they speak with others about religion.

---

7   Here and henceforth means are shown for boys / girls respectively.

Figure 7:   Religious diversity among boys and girls

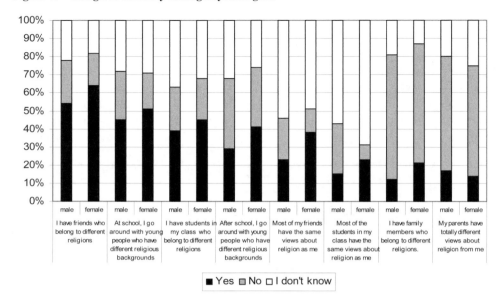

School. It is not easy to evaluate the influence of school education on the religious perceptions of students. The proportion of students from the Christian gymnasium (school 1) is too
small in the sample (21 against the total number of 403), so the analysis of the answers received in this particular school is hardly enough to make generalizations. The number of those
who stated that they had studied RE at school was higher (37), and a significantly more positive view of religion was registered in this group compared both to the rest of the students in
the sample and to the students from school 1. For instance, the statement "There should be no
place for religion in school" met the following reactions: mean 2.9 (St.d. 1.1) for the whole
sample, mean 3.3 for school 1; mean 3.5 for those who 'had studied RE at school'. Similar
distributions were found in many parts of the dataset. However, it is doubtful whether the
students' statements about their experience in RE reflect the real situation. They may rather
reflect their positive attitude to RE, so the analysis of religious perceptions in this group
hardly can provide information about school education as a factor shaping students' views.

As regards students from school 1, they were not found to be more religious than students
from other schools. On the contrary the percentage of those who denied the existence of God
(q. 38) was a little higher in this school (19% against 11–17% in other schools). They were in
the middle of the range regarding the importance of religion in their life (Mean = 1.90, for
other schools means are between 1.50 and 2.36 with quite high St.D. between 1.1–1.4)[8]. The
other differences found between this Christian gymnasium and other (state) gymnasiums and
schools were also not as predictable as they might be supposed to be. For instance students
from school 1 thought more than the others about religion, but they were not at the top of the
ranking in the question regarding school as a source of knowledge about religion (q. 46).
They claimed to read sacred texts less often than students of several secular schools; they did

---

8   St.deviation in school 1 was the highest and it means that the positions there were more diffused com-
     pared to the rest of the sample.

not speak about religion with others (except for teachers) more often than the rest of students, and they did not stand apart in the sample with the majority of other questions.

However comparisons between all schools participating in the research give grounds to regard school as a factor that may play an important role in shaping the religious perceptions of the students. In the main block of questions regarding the role of religion in students' life (q. 37–79) differences between schools significant at $p<.05$ were found for more than half the questions, and only in one out of ten cases did the school 1, providing formally religious education, occupy an extreme position in the range. Particularly students from school 3 and 6 evaluated the importance of almost all sources of information about religion more positively, compared to students from other schools including school 1.

While not so significant statistically, notable differences exist between schools in the reaction of their students to the assumption of preferable socialization with young people of the same religious background (q. 76, 77). Students from school 2 gave three to four times less positive answers to the assumption compared to schools 5 and 8 (9%, 27% and 33% respectively for q. 76 and 12%, 36% and 33% for q. 77). At the same time it was school 2 that proved to have the biggest number of students with negative attitudes toward religion and RE as estimated by their answers to the questions 37, 52, 57, 67 and some others (see table 2).

Synopsis of data – religion in students lives

Almost half of respondents in the sample believe in God's existence and affiliate themselves with a certain religion. Regarding the importance of religion in their lives, more than 1/3 of students chose the middle position in between 'important' and 'not important'.

Less than one in ten students attends religious events once a month or more, but more than a half claim to pray at least once a month. Family is the main agent of initiation into religion. A special characteristic of the sample is the unwillingness of respondents to talk about religion.

Religious students show a more positive vision of religion and of its role in private and social life. They talk more often about religion and know more about the religion of their relatives and friends. They show more respect toward other believers. At the same time they share with nonreligious students the idea that one can be a religious person without religious belonging.

The number of those who denied the existence of God is twice as great among boys. Girls are more open for communication with others. They are more respectful to the beliefs of other people and are more interested in learning what other people think about religion.

Comparisons between all schools participating in the research give grounds to regard school education as a factor that may play an important role in shaping the religious perceptions of the students.

2.1.2 Data interpretation

The figures designating religiosity of students in the sample are in good correspondence with official statistics (see 1.2.2). For instance, as regards the proportion of atheists, the students participating in the survey gave the same 14% proportion as the respondents in the VCIOM poll: and nearly half of respondents may be regarded as believers, which is again very close to the results of other surveys mentioned above. If the previous seven decades of state atheism in Russia are taken into account, the ratio of believers and atheists is impressive, and the Figures may be regarded as witness to the strong hidden resistance to the atheistic propaganda which existed among Soviet citizens. So much more that family is seen by students as a primary agent of initiation into religion. The parents of those 90% of 14–17 year old students who regarded family as an important source of information about religion were mostly brought up in Soviet schools in which the atheistic upbringing was one of the declared aims.

The religiosity of students may be described in general as rather loosely connected with religious communities. Young people very rarely attend religious worship, meet religious leaders and talk to them about religion. Some data obtained during the survey give ground to suggest that this loose connection is not only a consequence of certain historical circumstances but also a principle of the youth ethos linked with the values of pluralism and personal freedom of belief. Among these data is the fact that despite rather harmonious religious relations within families being usual for young people, two thirds of them do not consider religion as something one inherits from one's family. Indicative is also the remarkably high percentage of those who have no confessional preferences in socialization with their peers, and the fact that religious students did not differ from non-religious students in this respect.

Moreover the idea that one can be a religious person without belonging to a particular faith community was shared by the absolute majority of students, no matter whether religious or not. Religious students were even more decisive about that, and one may call this even a paradox, for the criterion of religiosity used in this comparison was the self-affiliation of students with a certain religious tradition.

Two reasons may be suggested to explain this phenomenon. First, it may be assigned to a high level of tolerance among religious students. They affiliate themselves consciously with a religious community, but do not want to impose this pattern of religiosity to others. This explanation is supported by some other findings discussed below (see 2.3) as well as by the written remarks of respondents mentioned above. The sentence "For me, it does not matter what religion one has. I am not a racist!" (see 1.3) may give a clue to understand what a proportion of students meant when denying the obligation to belong to a religion. The second explanation involves reference to the high level of religious illiteracy among the questioned students. A good percentage of the respondents who identified themselves as religiously affiliated people may be suspected to have a vague idea about religious identity and religious belonging. In our view both reasons contributed to the observed paradox. All these data, taken together, seem to portray religious students as open-minded persons accepting their religiousness with the same level of inner freedom as the rest of the students who refused to affiliate themselves with a certain religious tradition.

The silent type of religious life of students, with unwillingness to talk about religion, is another characteristic of the sample. It is really amazing that more than a half of respondents said they don't know about the religion of their friends! One may suppose that a part of those who said this actually did not want to share this knowledge. It is probable that the religiousness of students is *silent* because it is deliberately *hidden*. We find support for this idea in many segments of the data set, for instance in a quite special distribution of answers to questions about importance of religion in students' life (q. 37) with a high proportion of the 'indifferent' position. This may also be interpreted as an expression of a will not to answer the question. The other reason for this hidden and silent pattern of religious life may be connected with the low ability of students to talk and to think about religion, derived from a lack of religious education (see also below, 2.3).

Some of our findings related to gender prove, and some of them challenge, existing stereotypes about differences in the religious perceptions and attitudes of men and women, of boys and girls. The most challenging finding is the absence of significant difference in the general level of religiosity between male and female students. It is easy to see that this result produces a certain tension even within the set of data, namely when compared with the students' reports about the religiosity of their parents according to which their mothers are much more religious than fathers. Yet even here in these reports, one can find another challenging data issue: students claimed to know about the religion of their fathers almost as frequently as about the religion of their mothers. Taking into account a number of single parent families (where the parent is predominantly the mother) this statistic questions the widespread perception about the more active role of mothers in shaping the worldview of their children, and it is in good correspondence with the results of our qualitative survey.

At the same time new data proved that girls differ from boys in several respects. They try to avoid extreme negative judgments about religion and they identify themselves as atheists less frequently than boys. In the context of the other gender differences observed, this tendency may be considered as a consequence of a more general tendency of girls to avoid both conflict-generating situations and openly aggressive patterns of communication.

The religious attitudes of girls may be characterized as more open and respectful to the beliefs of other people. They are more communicative than boys in religious matters, being more interested in the religious perceptions of others. Maybe as a result of this interest, they know better about the religious situation in their families and recognize more diversity of opinions among their friends. There are also some minor differences between the religious perceptions of boys and girls that can be interpreted as implications of more general gender differences. For instance we are inclined to connect the better attitude of boys toward the internet as a source of religious knowledge with their generally more positive attitudes toward techniques.

Among the interesting and unexpected results of the survey is the low level of differences found in the religious perceptions of the students from the Christian gymnasium when compared to the rest of the sample. On one hand it may be regarded as a witness about the poor impact of religious education in this particular school into the religious development of its students. The higher level of atheists in this school may be even considered as a manifestation of a negative impact of religious education. On the other hand this lack of difference may indicate the high level of presence of elements of religious education in state schools. Especially revealing in this respect is the fact that students from the Christian gymnasium did not identify 'school' among the sources of knowledge about religion more often than did students from several state secular schools. The same occurred with the frequencies of reading sacred texts. The most probable explanation of this fact is that students in these state schools do study religious topics in their lessons on literature, history and some other subjects. Besides that, significant differences found between state schools with regard to these particular questions, as well as with many other points in the questionnaire, support the inference that state school education has a certain influence on students' religious perceptions and is a source of experience of dealing with religious issues, even without the formal inclusion of religion into school curricula.

It is difficult to come to any conclusion about the factors operating within the school environment that are responsible for the differences in the religious perceptions of students from different schools. Some sort of a correlation between openness to interfaith communication on one hand and negative attitude toward formal religious belonging on the other hand, that may be seen through comparison of views of the respondents from school 2 with views of students from other schools, is too weak and fragmentary evidence to base any generalizations on. An ethnic conflict that took place recently in the surroundings of school 5 (see 1.3) may explain why this particular school occupied the other pole in the range regarding interfaith communication. For school 8 the reason is not obvious at all and it might be the personal influence of teachers or groups of students which is responsible for the lower level of openness to interfaith relations there.

Anyhow the influence of school education and membership groups operating within school settings seems to be of a complex and multidimensional nature requiring more detailed description of the factor to analyze its effect.

2.2   How do students see religion in school?

Students' attitudes and ideas about religion in education were evaluated on the basis of several blocks of questions related to their experiences with religion at school (q. 1–12), their vision of the ways how Religious Education may be taught at school, (q. 13–19, 26–31), of the role religion can play in education (q. 20–25, 32–36) and of the problems it creates (q. 80, 81).

2.2.1   Data description

Answers to questions related to the models of religious education (q. 26–31) showed a generally positive attitude of students towards the subject. Optional RE was definitely at the top of the rating, with two thirds of students supporting this model, while other models of RE got the support of one fourth to a half of the respondents. Answers to the most radical statement, that there should be no religion in school, got the highest rate of responses 'neither agree neither disagree (47%). As to the choice between separated and joint studies, more students voted rather surprisingly for the former so that RE taught to students together occupied the lowest position in the rating. It is interesting to note that in most of their positions there were no significant differences in preferences between the religious and non-religious students. Figure 8 presents the frequencies of the answers given by the students when asked about their positions regarding different models of RE.

Figure 8:   Evaluation of different models of RE (%)

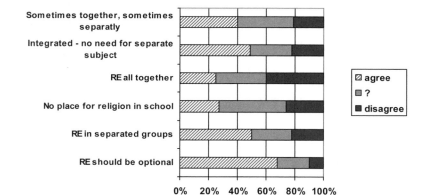

Reactions to the statements about the positive and negative roles of religion in education (q. 3–12) also revealed generally positive attitudes toward the presence of religion in school life. Students demonstrated firm disagreement with the idea that learning about religion may cause conflicts in the classroom. Only 12% of respondents agreed with this, and the statement gathered the highest disagreement rating among the ten (mean 3.82, St.d. 1.1). Their reaction to the idea that learning about different religions at school may help people to live together was much more neutral (mean 2.90, St.d. 1.1). The most positively evaluated statement was "At school I learn to have respect for everyone, whatever their religion" (mean 2.2, St.d. 1.0). Nevertheless the fact that almost all means (with exception for q. 4 and 8) lay on the negative side of the range (3.06–3.82) calls for interpretation.

This general observation is amplified by the answers to questions 20–25. The idea that learning about different religions may help one to understand others and live peacefully with them was evaluated positively by 62% of respondents, and only 13% disagreed with it. Still, a larger proportion of students (three out of four) connect the positive role of religious education with learning about their own religion (mean 2.05). The lowest rating in the range (mean 2.73) was for the idea that RE may be helpful in understanding current events.

The primary purpose of RE for St. Petersburg students is to give objective knowledge about different religions (mean 2.33 for q. 32). Guidance towards religious belief was on the contrary soundly rejected as an unacceptable aim for RE (mean 3.45 for q. 36). It is worthwhile to notice that the purpose of learning to understand what religions teach was accepted with a higher level of agreement than the purpose of developing communicative competences (means 2.43 / 2.92 for q. 33 / 34 respectively).

Questions concerning different forms of appearance of religion in school (q. 13–19) showed that students in our sample do not consider school as a proper place to organize voluntary religious services or prayers (means 3.50 and 3.47 for q. 19 and 18 respectively). Almost nine out of ten respondents agreed with the idea that students may wear discreet religious symbols (mean 1.68). At the same time only one out of five considered more visible religious symbols permissible at their school (mean 3.37). Religious and non-religious students had the same opinion that students cannot withdraw from classes and to be absent at school for religious reasons. In all other cases in regards to appearance of religion in school life, religious students advocated freedom of religious expression more intensively than the rest in the sample (** for q. 14, 15, 18, 19). They also indicated that they had more problems showing their views about religion openly in school (means 3.27 / 3.48; *).

Determinants of perceptions

Religious background. Regarding differences between religious and non-religious students (Figure 9), the former found religious topics important, interesting and helpful in distinguishing between right and wrong and learning about oneself more frequently than the latter (**). The two groups had similar positions regarding the conflict potential of religion in education (p=0.41).

Figure 9:   Experience with religion at school among religious and nonreligious students at school (means of estimates, scale from 1 – strongly agree to 5 – strongly disagree)

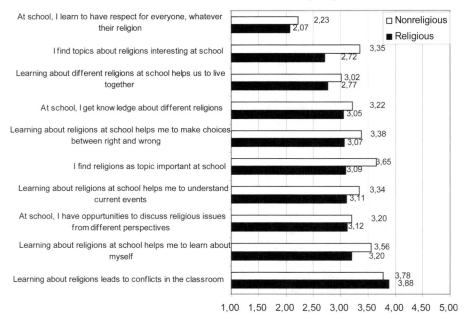

Evaluation of the aims of RE appeared to be interestingly different between religious and non-religious students. All differences were highly significant (***). Cross-tabulation results are presented in Figure 10.

Figure 10:   Aims for religious education among religious and nonreligious students (means of estimates, scale from 1 – strongly agree to 5 – strongly disagree).

To what extent do you agree that at school students should:

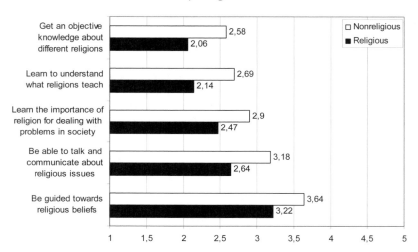

Gender. The factor of gender complemented factor of religious affiliation in a number of cases. In the first block of question about experiences with religion in education (q. 3–12) this complementarity was especially sound. Gender differences were found in the very points where differences between religious and non-religious students were minimal (q. 4, 5, 8). Girls claimed that at school they learn to have respect for everyone and have opportunities to discuss religious issues from different perspectives more intensively than boys. They also emphasized more strongly the positive peace-making role of learning about different religions.

The tendency shown by girls to evaluate more positively the role of religion in education, and to put emphasis on communicative aspects of this role, applied through the other sections of data. Girls were more motivated to study religions to be able to talk and communicate about religious issues and to gain a better understanding of current events (means 2.84 / 2.60, * for q. 22; means 3,01 / 2,82, * for q. 34), to understand others and to live peacefully with them (means 2.6 / 2.2, *** for q. 20). It is worthwhile to mention that the last option divided boys and girls more strongly than believers and unbelievers (means 2.26 / 2.52 correspondingly, q. 20). Girls showed more tendency to accept that talking about religion helps one to live peacefully together with people from different religions (means 3.16 / 2.97, p=.05 for q. 94). Girls also evaluated more positively the ability of RE to develop moral values (means 2,61 / 2,29, ** for q. 24), and they had less problems with showing their views about religion openly at school (means 3.26 / 3.51, * for .80).

The difference in attitudes towards different models of RE was surprising. The expectation that girls are more in favour of studying together was not supported by the quantitative research. Yet there were slight but statistically proved differences – girls were more in favor of optional studies (* for q. 26) and the mixed model (** for q. 31).

School. Experience with RE at school produced more visible effects, if compared to its effect on the perceptions of the role of religion in personal life discussed in the previous section. For instance students from school 1 were definitely more positive about the idea of providing facilities for students to pray at school (mean 2.71 against 3.03–3.97 in other schools, ***). Probably it was their own experiences of having a chapel inside their school that made this idea not as odd as it sounded for the others. They also denied in a firmer way the idea that school is not a proper place for religion (mean 3.29 against 3.13–2.49, ***), indicated that they more often speak about religion with teachers (mean 3.71 against 4.09–4.63, ***) and more positively evaluated all the proposed aims of RE besides guidance towards religious beliefs . In particular school 1 students showed the highest proportion of those who agreed that students should be able to communicate on religious issues (mean 2.38 against 2.75–3.36). And (together with the students from technical college) they insisted more firmly that learning about different religions may help to develop a personal point of view (mean 2.19 against 2.22 in school 7 and means 2.30–3.00 in other schools, *).

Yet, as regards many other questions about RE, school 1 did not occupy any special position in the range of schools. Differences between schools representing three other trends in Russian educational system were also significant and often more significant than the differences between school 1 and the rest of the sample (see table 2). For instance, significant differences between schools were found in the reactions to the statement "Learning about religions at school helps me to make decisions between right and wrong" (**). But school 1 occupied a middle position in the range (mean 3.48) while school 2 and 6 were at the extremes: means 3.88 and 2.87. The ideas that pupils may be absent from school because of religious festivals or should be excused from taking some classes for religious reasons also met significantly different reactions in different schools, and again school 1 was in the middle (means 3.05 and 3.19 for q. 16, 17) while students in school 2 took the most supportive position (means 2.06, 2.24 respectively) as opposed to the students from school 3 (mean 3.35 for q. 16) and 4 (mean 3.43 for q. 17). The students from school 2 showed the strongest resistance to the idea that school pupils should be guided towards religious belief, while the lowest level of protest was registered in school 3 (means 3.29 in school 1; 3.91 in school 2; 3.13 in school 3). However if all the data are taken together, school 1 showed in general the most positive attitude toward the presence of religion in education and it was not school 2 but school 5 that showed the most negative one. In the majority of cases these two schools occupied extreme positions in the range.

Synopsis of data– religion in school

The idea that there should be no place for religion in school life is supported by one out of four students. Optional RE is the most popular model, supported by two thirds of students. Respondents prefer to have RE separately in groups according to their religious affiliation rather than together.

The idea that learning about religion may cause conflicts in the classroom is the most unpopular, among the other ideas about roles of religion in education. Positive roles of religious education are associated by students with expectations to learn more about their own religion and to get a better understanding of others for peaceful coexistence with them. Guidance towards religious beliefs is the most unacceptable aim for RE.

School is not a proper place for organization of voluntary religious services or prayers, in students' view. Nine out of ten respondents agree that students may wear discreet religious symbols, but only one out of five consider more visible religious symbols permissible at their school.

Religious students advocate freedom of religious expression in education more intensively than the rest in the sample. They show more positive attitudes toward the presence of RE in school and are more in favour of all proposed educational aims, including both getting objective knowledge and being guided toward religious belief. However the same choice between separated, joint and optional study of religion is made by religious and non-religious students.

Girls are more motivated to study religions in order to be able to talk and communicate about religious issues, to gain a better understanding of current events and to understand others for peaceful coexistence with them.

Experiences with RE at school influence students' views regarding religion in education more strongly than their perceptions of the role of religion in personal life. Students from the Christian gymnasium are more positive about providing facilities for students to pray at school and more positively evaluate all proposed aims of RE besides except guidance towards religious beliefs. The most negative attitudes toward the presence of religion in education are demonstrated in schools 5 and 2.

2.2.2 Data interpretation

For the interpretation of data it is important not to forget that only 5% of students in the sample received formal RE at school. This is a sample representing students with the lowest level of experience with religion in school education compared not only to other European countries but also to many regions of Russia. Against this background the generally negative reaction to almost all statements in the first block of questions regarding experiences with religion at school hardly reflects a negative attitude toward religion, but rather diagnoses the state of affairs and may be interpreted as a witness to the fact of absence of religion in the school curriculum rather than to students' attitude toward this absence. It is difficult to find out actually what did a student who did not receive RE keep in mind when he did not agree with the sentence "I find religions as topics important at school". The most firm disagreement with the statement "Learning about religions leads to conflicts in the classroom" might be more indicative as regards evaluation of the negative role of religion.

Keeping in mind the mentioned important characteristic of students' educational background, it is remarkable that the statement "there should be no place for religion in school life", that actually reflects the state of affairs in St. Petersburg, was one among the least supported by the respondents. It seems that a good number of young Russians are not inclined to retain the status quo with religion in education in post-Soviet Russia, and look for the increasing presence of religious content in their curricula. While not in favour of having religion as a separate and compulsory school subject, students vote by two thirds for optional RE. It is their preferable model to deal with religion in education.

In other words it may be stated that our students showed generally positive attitudes towards the presence of religion in education. Moreover they evaluated religion as a tool for the encouragement of mutual understanding. The first support for this conclusion may be found in the fact that options "At school, I learn to have respect for everyone, irrespective of their religion" and "Learning about different religions at school helps us to live together" met the highest level of agreement compared to the other options in the block. The other support for this conclusion is that the task of getting objective knowledge about different religions appeared at the top of the list of educational priorities. At the same time it is notable that the tasks of getting knowledge and understanding of their own religion are among the students' priorities as well.

Taking into account the relative disregard of RE oriented toward the development of moral values and of abilities to develop students' own views, to communicate about religious issues and to understand current problems and events, one may also conclude that the concept of knowledge-oriented RE is more understandable for students than the concept of competences-oriented RE.

The most unfavorable attitude was shown by our respondents to the idea of education guiding toward religious belief. It means the concept of confessional RE is not attractive for students. At the same time it was surprisingly not the model of separated studies but the model in which RE is taught to students together that was rejected by students most intensively. The motives behind this reaction are not so clear. One explanation could be that the words "whatever differences there might be …" were regarded as something threatening to religious freedom and the option was refused. Some evidence for this interpretation can be found in the fact that the idea to study sometimes together and sometimes separately received an evaluation from students that was closer to their evaluation of the separated than joint studies model. On the other hand the preference given to the separated (and partly joint) studies quite probably may be a direct derivative of the interest shown by students in learning about their own religion.

It is worth noticing that students' opinions on the three discussed models of RE and on the statement "There should be no place for religion in school" lay in the neutral zone and did not actually differ much (means 2.6–3.2). The standard deviation was not high either (1.0–1.2). For comparison, more specific organizational questions regarding religious food requirements and religious services at school, wearing religious symbols etc., produced considerably more diverse reactions (means 1.7–3.5, St.d. 0.9–1.3). Of special interest is the contrast in opinions about wearing religious symbols of different kinds, discreet or more visible ones (means 1.7 / 3.4). It seems that the question about religious symbols is much more vital for students than the question about models of RE. This strange indifference to the choice between the very different ways of teaching religion at school indicates in our view that the problem of the choice was not properly realized and reflected by students. May be they had no stimulus for that reflection and not enough knowledge to define their point of view in the situation of their lack of experience with RE.

Differences between religious and non-religious respondents in their perceptions of problems connected with religion in education proved our previously made observation that religious students show as critical and open-minded an approach to the problems as their non-religious classmates. They are more in favour of the presence of religion in school life, but the positive vision of potential role of religion does not obstruct for them the view of religion having a conflict potential as well. Remarkably they did not show any more appreciation of the model of separated study of religion than non-religious respondents. However this does not mean that the concept of confessional RE does not meet a better reception among them. The fact that much more religious students voted in favour of education guiding toward religious belief shows that it does: but their understanding of organizational restrictions connected with the confessional approach may be rather vague. They also advocate freedom of religious expression in school more soundly than non-believers. Findings regarding gender are in perfect concordance with the observation made above (2.1.2) about the openness and better communicativeness of girls in religious matters. Girls evaluated more positively the role of religion in education and emphasized the communicative aspects of this role. Their intention to study religion was more strongly motivated by the perspective of discussing religious issues from different perspectives and thus getting better understanding of others. It seemed easier for them to show openly religious views in the classroom. In the context of these findings, the unexpected similarity of girls and boys in rejecting the model of studying religion together serves as an additional argument to interpret this rejection as resulting not from xenophobic attitudes but rather from the fears of compulsion and enforcement of shared religious views that had been provoked by the particular wording of the proposal.

It was found that one of the determinants of students' attitudes towards the presence of religion in education is their experience with it. For instance students from school 1, who had experience of having chapel at their school, diverged considerably from the rest of the students in their more positive view on the legitimacy of providing facilities for pupils to pray at school. Remarkable are the similar differences in the opinions of students who had or had no experience of religion in education about the aims and purposes of RE, and potential educational inputs of experiences with religion. These differences, taken together, give grounds to suggest that experienced students become more aware of the developmental functions of religion in education.

No evident reasons for the differences observed between secular schools were identified, but some regularities in the distribution of means may be seen, especially if compared to the data described in the previous section (2.1). It may be stated that schools 2 and 5 regularly showed a more negative attitude toward religion and its presence in education. School 2 was identified as the most 'atheistic' one during the qualitative research, and the reason for this was associated with the negative experience of informal and pedagogically inaccurate initiation into religion that took place in that school previously (Kozyrev, 2008). New data seem to support this image. As to school 5, the most obvious characteristic that put this school aside of the others is its suburban location. This geographical factor entails important socio-cultural derivatives that may be responsible for the regularities observed and mark the differences in religious perceptions of different strata of Russian society. It is important to mention however that students from schools 3 and 6, who differ strongly in their religious perceptions from the respondents in school 5, may be characterized as most similar to them regarding the social status of their parents.

2.3   How do pupils see the impact of religion?

Based on the answers to questions 82–112 these data are related more directly to the main REDCo question about religion as a contributor to dialogue or/and to conflict.

2.3.1 Data description

When answering questions about the role religion can play in the promotion of dialogue and of conflict, students once more demonstrated generally positive attitudes toward religion. Explicitly negative judgments about the social functions of religion were rejected with a high level of consensus. Only 7–8% of respondents agreed with the statements "Without religion the world would be a better place" and "Religion is a source of aggressiveness". In a striking contrast to these attitudes was an even more consensual disregard of social dimension in religious life, as the reaction to the statement "Religion belongs to private life" shows. Only 2% of respondents disagreed with it, while 92% agreed and among them, 62% agreed strongly. The idea that religious people are less tolerant towards others was supported by 20% of respondents; 35% disagreed and more than 40% took a neutral position.

Questions about reasons and motivations to talk or not to talk about religion (q. 87–97) add some more colours to the picture of religiosity of our young respondents. The perspectives of understanding others (q. 90) and of sharing different personal views on religion (q. 87) were put at the top of the motivation rating. Once again respondents did not support explicitly negative judgments about religion: 10% agreed with the statement "I and my friends talk about how stupid religion is and what cruelties are carried out in its name" while 60% disagreed. This statement stood aside in the range of motivations with mean 3.7 compared to means of 2.8–3.3 for other questions in the block.

When asked how they would behave if they meet religious proselytazion by another student, the majority of respondents chose non-conflicting ways of dealing with the situation. The option "I listen but their views do not influence me" was at the top of the scale: 53% reported that would be exactly their position, 39% said that could be their reaction and only 8% said they would never react like that. The idea to counteract by promoting one's own religious views gained the lowest support: 62% claimed they would never react like that. Not a big proportion of students would make attempts to convince the opponent that he or she was wrong (44% would never react like that) and the idea to ignore a person imposing his views was definitely more attractive for the sampled students (82% could react like that).

The statements "Disagreement on religious issues leads to conflicts" and "Respecting the religion of others helps to cope with differences" met very similar reactions. About a half of students agreed and one out of ten disagreed with both. Much less supported was the suggestion that people with different strong religious views cannot live together. One out of five agreed with that, and only 6% of respondents reported their dislike of people from other religions.

Answers to the last block of questions regarding methods of facilitating peaceful coexistence showed that the way to live together in peace was associated by our respondents much more with sharing common views and common activities (q. 107, 110) than with administrative measures (q. 112): 80–85% of respondents considered the former two approaches to peace important, while 44% considered the latter one important. Keeping religion in private was considered important for peaceful coexistence by half the respondents. Two thirds found it important for people of different religions to know each other in a personal way, and 76% of students agreed that it is important to know about religions of others. A general overview of the responses is given in the Figure 11.

Figure 11:   What helps people from different religions to live together in peace?

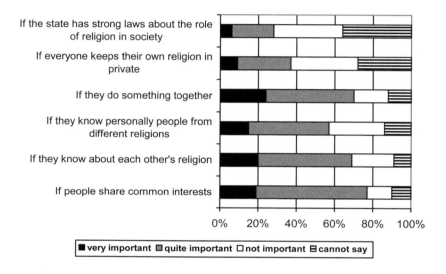

Determinants of perceptions

Religious background. Though the idea that religious people are less tolerant toward the others was supported by a prominent minority of respondents, it is not supported by the data themselves. First of all a strict equivalence was found in the reactions of respondents with and without religious affiliation to the idea that religion belongs to private life. Quite expectable were highly significant differences between the two subgroups in their reactions to the statement "Without religion the world would be a better place" or in their willingness to identify religion as a source of aggressiveness (*** for q. 83, 85). Religious students showed in both cases a more positive attitude toward religion. Less expected was to find the same statistically significant level of difference in students' answers to the whole set of questions regarding motivations to talk about religion (q. 87–97). In all answers religious students showed more positive motivation and more positive evaluation of religious dialogue (Figure 12). In particular, twice as many among them were sure that talking about religion helps them to live peacefully together with people from different religions and two times fewer of them accepted the idea that talking about religion only leads to disagreement.

Figure 12: Motivations to talk about religion for religious and nonreligious students (means of estimates, scale from 1 – strongly agree to 5 – strongly disagree)

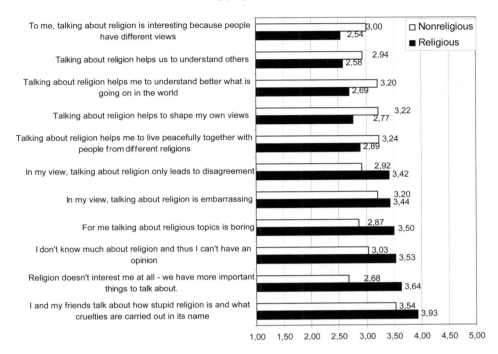

More significant differences between religious and non-religious students were found in their reactions to the statements "Disagreement on religious issues leads to conflict" (means 2.72 / 2.45, **) and "Respecting the religion of others helps to cope with differences", (means 2.34 / 2.68, ***) than in their views about dislike of people from other religions or in their evaluation of the assumption that people with different strong religious views cannot live together (** for V. 105, 106). And even for the first two variables frequencies were not so contrasting with each other (42% religious students and 52% non-religious agreed with V. 103 and 61% and 44% respectively with V. 104). However in all four cases religious students again consistently demonstrated a more optimistic vision of peaceful coexistence in a religiously plural society and a more positive attitude towards it.

When meeting religious proselyteision religious students are more inclined to initiate discussion. Significant differences were found in the reaction of the two subgroups to proposals either to ignore the proselyteision or to discuss the issue (means 1.95 / 1.80; means 1.74 / 2.00). Particularly religious students claimed two times less they would never try to enter discussion. Though not statistically significant (p=.015 for q. 100), a tendency was seen among non-religious students to rely more frequently on their ability to change their opponent's view compared to religious students. Differences in religious and non-religious students' preferences concerning the prerequisites of peaceful coexistence were not great. The only point in which views of the two subgroups significantly diverged was the option about knowing each other's religion. Many fewer religious students regarded this knowledge as not important (means 2.10 / 2.30).

Gender. Girls and boys did not differ in their common vision of religion as a totally private matter. They also shared almost the same vision of reasons to talk or not to talk about religion with two exceptions. Girls insisted more strongly that talking about religion is interesting because people have different views (***) and evaluated more positively the peace-making potential of talking about religion (*).

When faced with religious proselytism girls are much more open to discussion (means 2.00 / 1.76, ** for q. 99). Almost 3 times less frequently girls said "I would never react like this' to this option. Accordingly, they are much less inclined to ignore the challenge (means 1,79 / 1.95, * for q. 98). At the same time they are also slightly more reluctant to make attempts to convince their opponent.

The statement "I don't like people from other religions and do not want to live together with them" was less frequently supported by girls (means 3.80 / 4.02).

Schools. Significant differences between schools were found in questions 83, 84, 87, 88, 90, 92, 94, 104, 105, 108, 109, 110 (see table 2). Some regularities were found in the distribution of these differences again. School 5 consistently showed the most negative attitude toward talk about religion and towards almost all proposals related to the facilitation of peaceful coexistence. The only proposal it was less negative about compared to the others was one connected with state regulation (q. 112). Notably it was that very proposal that occupied the lowest position in the scale. Students from this school were also more critical than the others regarding the assumption that respecting the religion of others may help to cope with differences (mean 2.88 against 2.53 in the sample; **) and they claimed more frequently that they do not like people from other religions (mean 3.51 against 3.91 in the sample; **).

The opposite pole of the range was occupied most often by schools 3 and 6. School 1 was at the top of the range only when protesting against disinterest in religion (q. 92) and promoting respect for religions of others (q. 104): 70% agreed in this school that by the way of respecting different religions one may help to cope with difficulties, while only 30% shared this view in school 5. In all other cases students from this school did not evaluate the social role of religion and talk about religion higher than the students of secular schools. Students from school 2 who showed extreme negative attitudes concerning some issues of religion in education (see 2.2.1) confirmed these attitudes, showing the highest proportion of those who agreed that without religion the world would be a better place (mean 3.26 against 3.72 in the sample, **). They also demonstrated the highest agreement with the claim that religion belongs to private life (mean 1.21 against 1.48 in the sample; **).

Some less expected differences were registered too. For instance, when evaluating the statement "People with different strong religious views cannot live together" (q. 106) school 8 surprisingly gave extremely high support to it, while usually it occupied a medium position among other schools. A half of respondents in school 8 agreed with this statement, while in almost all other schools (except for school 2) the proportion of agreement was not higher than 25% and at school 3 it was less than 9%. Schools 2 and 5, which shared with each other many critical and negative points of view about religion, occupied opposite poles of the range when evaluating the assumption that religions can coexist if people share common interests (q. 107); 6% of students in school 2 and 34% in school 5 found this condition not important.

Table 2 helps to get a general impression of the differences between schools. It includes only variables that can be identified as suggesting either positive or negative statements about religion and in which significant differences with p<.05 were registered. Sub-samples that showed the most positive attitudes toward religion in the range are indicated in the table with "+". The opposite extreme position in the range indicated as "–".

Table 2: **Schools with the most positive and most negative perceptions of religion**

	Schools								
	1	**2**	**3**	**4**	**5**	**6**	**7**	**8**	**9**
Variables "+"	3, 18, 19, 23, 28, 32, 33, 34, 35, 39, 45, 58, 66, 92, 104, 110	109	35, 36, 40, 46, 48, 57, 87, 88, 89, 94, 105, 110	44		9, 37, 45, 46, 47, 48, 51, 52, 83, 87, 88, 94	23, 49, 58, 67, 92	38, 108	25, 83
Variables "–"	38	9, 23, 36, 37, 46, 47, 48, 51, 52, 57, 67, 83, 94	19		3, 18, 19, 25, 28, 32, 33, 34, 35, 39, 49, 58, 66, 88, 90, 92, 104, 105, 108, 109, 110			40, 45, 47, 87	44, 94
Total +	16	1	12	1	-	12	5	2	2
Total –	1	13	1	–	21	–	–	4	2

Encounters with religious diversity may be evaluated in general as a factor in developing a positive attitude toward a religiously plural society. Those students who reported they had contacts with students of different religious backgrounds at school and after school (q. 74, 75) produced a significantly more negative reaction to the statement "I don't like people from other religions and do not want to live together with them".

Synopsis of data – impact of religion

Respondents do not support explicit negative judgment about social functions of religion. At the same time they demonstrate consolidated disregard of social dimension of religious life: 92% agree with the statement "Religion belongs to private life".

Majority of respondents choose non-conflicting way of dealing with religious expansion on behalf of the other. The idea to counteract by promoting own religious views is not popular. About a half of students think that disagreement on religious issues leads to conflicts. Much less support is given to the idea that people with different strong religious views cannot live together. Only 6% of respondents report they don't like people from other religions.

The way to live together in peace is associated much more with sharing common views and common activities than with the administrative measures.

Respondents with and without religious affiliation react in the same way on the idea that religion belongs to private life

Religious students demonstrate more optimistic vision of peaceful coexistence in religiously plural society and more positive evaluation of inter-religious communication.

Girls and boys do not differ in their common vision of religion as a totally private matter and have similar reasons to talk or not to talk about religion, though girls evaluate more positively peace-making potential of religious dialogue. The statement "I don't like people from other religions and do not want to live together with them" is more frequently accepted by boys.

Most critical judgments about potential of religion and (inter-)religious dialogue in facilitation of peaceful coexistence come from school 5. The opposite pole of the range is occupied most often by schools 3 and 6.

2.3.2 Data interpretation

Data related to this section are in good conformity with the data presented in previous sections, especially as concerns the dominance of positive and neutral attitudes toward religion. The most important finding to focus on is the very high level of agreement with the statement "Religion belongs to private life". Nowhere else in the set of data was such an unanimity observed. The result is especially impressive if compared with a rather indifferent reaction of students to the other statements in the block. For instance, both opposite statements 'I like to know' and 'it does not bother me' what my friend thinks about religion (q. 78, 79) met with almost the same rather neutral reaction.

Basing on this finding, the picture of a hidden and silent pattern of religious life of our respondents described above (2.1) may be complemented by one more characteristic, namely by *asocial* type of religiosity. We are inclined to interpret this set of characteristics as interrelated and explainable in terms of a defence and a protest against potential and alas too probable politicization of religious life, and to associate this factor with fundamental socio-cultural and political reasons responsible for the low sociability of modern Russians.

Surely other factors may also lie behind such a consolidated denial of the social dimension in religious life. One may be connected with the low ability of our students to talk and to think about religion. This was one of the observations based on the results of the qualitative research; and this may be interpreted in our view as evidence about a lack of a competence to talk about religion derived from a lack of religious education.

It is important to notice further that despite this neglect of the social dimension of religious life, or may be due to it, our respondents proved to be quite open to inter-religious communication. The statement "*I don't like people from other religions*" was soundly refused. Accordingly they tend to choose non-conflicting behaviour patterns when meeting religious proselytism. The majority do not show a tendency to make attempts to change the opinions of their opponents.

With notable similarity, the two statements "Disagreement on religious issues leads to conflicts" and "Respecting the religion of others helps to cope with differences" divided respondents in half. A weak positive correlation between the reactions to these statements ($r = 0.15$, ** for q. 103, 104) shows that many students agreed or disagreed with both the statements; that could be a result of either a lack of serious reflection on the questions or a realistic view taking into account the probabilities of different scenarios. We consider the second interpretation more justifiable.

The most important prerequisites of peaceful coexistence for the majority of students are better knowledge about each other's religions and sharing common interests and common activities. Suspicion about the efficiency of political or juridical methods of encouraging religious tolerance may be interpreted as a sign of the 'legal nihilism' often attributed to Russian society. But it may be explained in another way. In one of the surveys carried out in the framework of the local REDCo project in St. Petersburg we have offered senior class students from the school 2 a very similar set of options to choose between. The question was what to do in order to avoid religious conflicts. One of the options which was absent in the main REDCo survey was "to begin with oneself and to manage to tolerate others around you". This was the very option that received the highest agreement. One may guess it would have got the same approval in this survey too and were this the case, it would mean that young people in St. Petersburg tend to see religious tolerance as a high and difficult moral value rather than a matter of political correctness.

Comparison of the perceptions of religious and non-religious students is of crucial importance for evaluation of the social functions of religion as regards dialogue and conflict. All the data prove that religiousness of students is a positive factor for their citizenship formation and for their ability to live in a plural society. In answers to 20 questions out of the 38 being presented in this section, religious students showed themselves more motivated for inter-religious communication and more optimistic about its perspectives. In particular they showed less dislike of people from other religions compared to non-religious students. And though statistically this difference is not significant, we interpret this result as an evidence of a higher level of tolerance among religious students, because it is quite more natural for them to distinguish between people belonging to different religions than for students who do not belong to any religion themselves.

Similarly one could expect a higher level of differences between religious and non-religious students in their reaction to the assumptions that people with different strong religious views cannot live together. The similarity between the two subgroups we have got instead allows us to suggest that for religiously affiliated young people the positive evaluation of religion in their lives does not produce an obstacle to seeing the conflict potential of religion and the negative sides of religious commitment. It means the presence of a good amount of critical reflection in the judgments of religious students about religion.

Differences found between girls and boys in their perceptions of social impacts of religion brought little to add to or to change previously made observations. They strengthened the general conclusion that girls emphasize more intensively the positive potential of religious and inter-religious dialogue and are more interested personally in knowing about religious views of others. Bi-variate analysis of the answers to the direct question about respondents' feelings toward people of other religious backgrounds (V. 105) allows us to characterize girls as appreciating more religious diversity than boys.

Interesting is the strict resemblance found in the reactions of boys and girls as well of religious and non-religious students to the idea that religion belongs to private life (V. 84). It seems that in this case the influence of gender and religious factors are exceeded by the more powerful socio-cultural or historical factors overcoming the group differences. In more practical terms it devalues attempts to explain this outstanding and stable characteristic of religiosity by reference to the extrication of Russian people from usual forms of religious practice .If this were so, religiously affiliated students would definitely be expected to give stronger voice for the importance of social dimension in religion. If this were not the case, the previously given explanation with reference to socio-political reasons seems more convincing and the finding seems to be an additional argument for the special type of a-social religiosity characteristic for Russians. It means also that it is hardly reasonable to hope that with religion entering more intensively into the public life of Russia the situation may be easily changed.

The differences found between schools completed the picture based on the previous observation and proved that some regularities in these differences really exist. The data give grounds to evaluate schools 2 and 5 as demonstrating the most negative attitudes and views about religion and its social role. Schools 1, 3 and 6 represent the opposite end of the range. Table 2 also shows that the influences of schools and membership groups are evidently complex and it is hardly possible to reduce this complexity to a couple of distinctive elements such as the model of religious education, general educational level or socio-cultural background of learners. Not all of the differences in the cross-tabulations can be ascribed to the influence of the systematic RE offered by school 1. Schools 3 and 6 are also relatively positive about religion as compared to the majority, though there is no formal affiliation with religion by these schools. The educational level in these two schools is not high. Most remarkably the characteristics of educational level and social background make these two schools closest to school 5, which presented on the contrary the most negative perceptions of religion in the sample.

Table 2 shows also that the influence of RE in school 1 affected mostly the views of students on the presence of religion in education but not the other aspects of their religiosity and religious perceptions.

In order to explain this distribution some more detailed (thick) description of the pedagogical situation at these schools may be of crucial importance.

Some information available about school 2 gives grounds to associate the negative religious attitudes of its students with misuses of religion in education that took place in this school several years before. In school 5 the inter-ethnic conflict mentioned above may be one explanation. The other may be relatively low social and educational background of the students. However the contrasting perceptions of students from schools 3 and 6 challenge the last explanation , for the social background is similar in the three schools when compared to the other six schools in the sample . Some differences in the reactions of students from schools 2 and 5 show that one may deal here with different types of negativism. Students from school 2 are definitely more focused on the idea of violation of personal freedoms as a probable negative outcome of socially active religion (perhaps resulting from their experience in this school) while students from school 5 seem to be simply more indifferent toward the issues connected with religion. The former negativism seems to be connected more with protest, the latter one – more with indifference and ignorance.

The influence of the general level of education may also produce different effects, and this ambiguity may be an explanation why gymnasiums occupied a middle position between the two extremes presented by comprehensive schools. One may guess that the relatively negative answers given by students of gymnasiums to the questions about the role of religion and RE are inspired not by their nihilism or lower knowledge about religion but rather by a more critical position and higher level of demand. The medium position occupied by state gymnasiums in our ranking may be caused consequently not by the indifference or lower sensitivity of their contingent to religious problems but by the interference of several factors. If it is true, the task to find an answer to the main REDCo question in the answers of students seems not as easily solvable as it might have seemed in the beginning.

3.   Comparison with the results of the qualitative survey

Criteria for sampling were similar in the two surveys, so the sample for quantitative research may be regarded as an extension of the sample we worked with during our qualitative study. Three types of education represented in the qualitative study were complemented by the fourth type of vocational training system (school 7). The type of non-state religious schools was represented by the same gymnasium in both cases (school 1). Schools 2 and 3, that had represented the other two types in the qualitative research, participated in the new research too. In schools 1 and 2 respondents were all new. In school 3 half of the respondents were the pupils who had participated in the REDCo qualitative questioning a year ago. Three more state gymnasiums and two more ordinary schools were included in the quantitative sample to represent the two main types of Russian educational system. Within the type of ordinary schools larger diversity was achieved by inclusion of a school located outside the city (school 5).

The samples were found to be very similar in confessional terms. Exactly the same percentage of students (44%) reported their religious affiliation and the proportion of Christians and Muslims among them as well as proportion of atheists in the whole sample did not differ much between the two samples.

Conclusions based on the results of qualitative survey were generally proved by the quantitative data. New data confirmed the dominant role of family in shaping youngsters' religious perceptions. Other sources of information about religion showed similar distributions of importance, with school occupying the second place on the ranking and with religious communities (places of worship) playing an insignificant role. The quantitative research showed a low frequency of confrontation on religious matters within families and thus amplified the previous findings.

The description of respondents' common perception of religion as something to do much more with personal faith and with the search for "protection, blessings and happiness" than with "commitments to a particular value system" (Kozyrev, 2008, 288) was strongly supported by the new data. Especially important in our view were findings revealing a special asocial type of religiosity peculiar to St. Petersburg students (see 2.3) as well as a hidden and silent pattern of religious life (see 2.1). Results of both surveys accentuate the commitment of our students to personal freedoms and their anxieties about violations of freedom of beliefs associated with the social dimension of religion.

Some comments left by respondents in the quantitative questionnaires were also revealing in this respect. One student who stated firmly that neither he nor his parents had a certain religion or worldview (q. 122–127), left the following comment: *"Religion is everybody's own matter. When we pray we come closer to God, we seek for help and for instruction. Religion helps to understand better one's own deeds"* (7–1–19, m). This comment draws attention to the already statistically registered phenomenon of the 'praying atheists' (Francis 2004) and gives grounds for us to consider it more seriously, probably by way of connecting it rather with conscious protection of the privacy of religious life than with simple inconsistency in youngsters' perceptions. It also challenges the routine approaches to the 'measurement of religiosity'.

To illustrate the latter remark one short comment from the quantitative survey may be helpful: *"Almost every day I think about religion, but I can't say for sure if I believe in God or not"* (8–1–2, f). The girl who left this comment was identified in our survey as non-religious according to the criteria used for V. 38 and V. 126. She chose the option "I don't know" to answer about the religion of her parents (V. 122, 124). Surely she would choose the same for herself if she was provided with this option. This comment, as only one among the many, highlights also the remarkable consistency of the new findings with one of the basic conclusions of the qualitative research: "One of the most impressive things we found in the students' answers was a strange combination of extreme openness on the one hand, and repeated warnings against intrusion into their religious lives on the other. The same students who shared with us the inmost feelings of love, hatred, hope and despair, were those that finished their questionnaires with dry and aloof reminders that religion is a private matter, and that they didn't like to talk about it" (Kozyrev, 2008, 308). Comments made by the respondents in the quantitative survey fit into this description and deepen the impression of this meaningful contradiction.

As regards religion in education, the clear preference of optional RE registered in the quantitative survey strongly supports the previous observation of an evident tension in youngsters' attitudes between a certain hunger for religious knowledge and religious self-expression on one hand, and fears of indoctrination and ideological pressure on the other hand. Still it is in the distribution of answers on questions about preferable models of RE where the main difference between the results of two surveys is found. In the quantitative sample definitely more students wanted to study religion separately in groups according to religious belonging than all together. The qualitative survey showed the two options to be equally evaluated by the respondents. The reason for that difference found is not clear and deserves special attention. One explanation may be the different wording of the options in two surveys as mentioned above (2.2).

Some minor differences were found in the answers to the questions about preferred topics and content of religious education (q. 20–25, 32–36). The interest about learning more about different religions clearly shown in the qualitative results was proved by the new data too. Accordingly students clearly rejected the vision of RE as an instrument for developing moral values or guidance toward religious beliefs. A new and a little bit surprising finding was the rather high level of interest in religious teaching (V. 33) and inclination to learn more about "my own religion" (q. 25) that had remained unnoticed during the previous research.

Despite the conviction of the overwhelming majority of the qualitative survey respondents that people from different religions can live together, the conclusion was made that "no consensus was found among youngsters on the role of religion in social life and particularly in school education" (Kozyrev, 2008, 307). Positive expectations connected with the potential social function of religion were obviously balanced by fears of religious fanaticism and aggressiveness experienced by a number of students personally. The quantitative survey added valuable material to reflect on this observation. The unique level of agreement with the statement "religion belongs to private life" characteristic of the Russian sample gave an important key to interpret the whole set of students' evaluations of the social potential of religion. Another source of information was opened by the bi-variate analysis of answers given by religious and nonreligious students. It showed how similar were the visions of conflict potential of religion in these two groups utterly contrasting in some other respects. That gave additional grounds to connect certain characteristics of religious perceptions shared by large groups of youngsters more with collective social experience and inherited presuppositions derived from these experiences, rather than with personal religious commitments. This quantitative analysis gave a much better opportunity to evaluate the role of religious affiliation in shaping views and attitudes toward religious diversity than the qualitative research.

Reflection on the results of the two surveys was especially fruitful in identification of factors shaping the religious perceptions of students. In a remarkably similar way the religiousness of respondents, gender and school were identified as the most influential factors in both surveys.

Concerning gender, the two surveys converge in the conclusion that girls generally try to avoid extreme negative judgments about religion and identify themselves as atheists much less frequently than boys. They are also more open for communication with others and more interested to know about them. At the same time the quantitative data demanded correction of two previous conclusions regarding gender. First, they disprove the idea that girls are more religious than boys. It is more accurate to talk only about differences concerning active denial of religion. Second, the tendency of girls to protest against studying religion separately, that was recognized as a gender characteristic in the qualitative survey, was not observed in the quantitative sample. This difference may be connected with the whole 'change of attitude' toward the two models of RE mentioned above.

The quantitative data provided grounds to correct conclusions regarding the influence of education on students' perceptions made after the qualitative survey. This influence was considered previously in terms of the co-effect of two factors: presence of religion in school curricula and the general level of education provided by school. The new data show this relation to be more complex.

Significant differences of the perceptions of students from different schools found in our sample strongly supported our previous assumption that learning communities should be regarded as a specific and highly influential factor shaping the perceptions of youngsters. School 2, that had shown the most critical views on the positive role of religion in education in the qualitative survey, confirmed its reputation. It shared the status of the 'most atheistic' school with school 5, utterly different to it according to formal criteria, such as the educational type, the general quality of education and qualification of personnel, and social status of parents. This result confirms our previous assumption that the reason for the negative attitudes of students from school 2 may be found in their negative experience with indoctrinarian teaching about religion that took place in a 'semi-official' way in their school (see: Kozyrev 2008, 306). It gives more solid ground for the assumption that particular school experiences can produce strong and long-term influences in students that should be taken into consideration when planning empirical surveys and interpreting their results.

The most intriguing result to support this view is the transformation of the image of school 3, as this was produced in the course of the two inter-school comparisons. A part of the respondents in this school participated in both surveys. During the qualitative survey some more nihilistic attitudes toward religion were registered among students of this school and were explained by a generally lower level of their education compared to the other two schools. Now, in the quantitative survey, this very school (together with the other relatively 'low level' school 6) occupied the opposite pole in the range and became one of the most "religiously educated" schools according to a good number of criteria (see for instance V. 40, 46, 88, 90).

Information available about school 3 gives some clues to explain the transformation. We suspect the situation really may change in a course of the year. First, students became one year older. In the previous survey, students of school 3 were the youngest, and that might play a role, more so as the literature syllabus for 10th grade is 'packed' with a Dostoevsky novel. This usually means that students pay more attention to religious issues during literature classes than before. In school 3 this was definitely the case. It is known that, besides focusing on the religious aspects of Dostoevsky's writings, the literature teacher gave a series of classes on the Bible between the two surveys. That can explain why so many students declared that they read sacred texts and listed school among the important sources of knowledge about religion. Second, a selection took place in this class-group because the transition to 10th grade means the transition to the high school level, and a good number of students usually leave school at that moment. Mostly these are the weakest learners, so, after the selection, the class-group appeared to be filled with more educated and talented students. The third reason may be the previous participation of a part of the respondents in the qualitative research, that made them feel in a way more 'familiar' with religion and thus stimulated more positive reactions.

Anyhow, whatever the explanation, comparison between the two surveys showed experiences with religion in school to have a potential for producing both negative and positive effects, these effects being not only long lasting but also rather rapid in their occurrence. From a methodological point of view it implies a transient nature of pedagogical situations in the school environment that should be taken into account when empirical studies are planned and their results are interpreted. It means also that 'thick' descriptions of these situations may be of an indispensable importance in some types of pedagogical research.

4.   Conclusions

4.1   Role of religion in personal life

The data obtained give grounds to claim that, despite decades of state atheism in Russia, St. Petersburg youngsters have generally positive attitudes toward religion. Nearly a half of the respondents are believers and the majority of the rest do not express explicitly negative attitudes toward religion. Openly negative attitudes are especially rare among girls.

Family is the main domain of religious life and the main source of information about religion. The disagreement of teenagers with parents on religious issues is not a so frequent phenomenon as could be expected. School plays a secondary role and is a much more active agent of religious initiation than media or religious communities.

Though the historical and cultural dimensions of religious life were found to be taken seriously by young people, they generally pay not much attention to formal expressions of religious belonging and do not appreciate the idea of strict links between personal religious commitments and formal religious belonging. They show a clear tendency to consider religion as an entirely private matter.

An absolute majority, including believers, think that it is possible to be a religious person without religious affiliation. Their participation in communal religious practice is not intensive, with average church attendance once in several months. Prayers and thoughts about religion and about the meaning of life seem to play a much more significant role in their spiritual life.

The religious life of students may be described as silent. They are motivated rather to hide their beliefs than to share them with others. More than a half of the students in the sample state they never speak about religion with their friends and classmates and even do not know about their religious views. Two thirds of students rarely or never speak about religious topics in their families. One may doubt whether this self-witness reflects the real situation, or if it resulted partly from a kind of protective strategy – a decision of respondents to withdraw from giving information about their families and friends 'just in case'. Anyhow this strategy itself, if it exists, is an expressive sign of the hidden pattern of religiosity shown by our respondents and rooted, in our view, in inherited forms of collective historical consciousness.

4.2   Students' views on religion in school

The idea that learning about religion causes conflicts is denied, and the interest in learning more about different religions is shared, by the large majority of respondent students. The presence of religion in education is widely recognized as a potential tool for the encouragement of mutual understanding, for getting objective knowledge about the religions of others and for helping students to understand better their own religion. Cross-national comparison of the results of the qualitative research shows that students are strongly determined by the state of affairs and prefer the model of RE they have. Against this general observation, the fact that the option "there should be no place for religion in school life" gathered a low level of support among St. Petersburg students who do not receive RE at school, emphasizing their positive expectations associated with religion in education.

At the same time, the inclusion of religion into school curricula in the form of a compulsory subject does not meet with common agreement. Studying religion together is less acceptable for the students than studying separately in groups according to the religion they belong to. More complex approaches (sometimes together, sometimes apart) are more welcomed. Optional study of religion is the most preferable model for dealing with religion in school. Two thirds of students supported this model, while the most preferred model of compulsory RE got the support of half of the respondents

4.3 Contribution of religion to dialogue or conflict

St. Petersburg students regard religion as belonging totally to private life. This consolidated opinion amplifies the image of a silent and hidden pattern of religious life and points to a more general characteristic of *asocial* religiosity that can be attributed to the respondents in our sample. Besides the fear of intrusion into personal religious life, some more positive motivations can be distinguished behind this asocial understanding of religion, including commitments to personal freedom of belief.

Surely this characteristic is not a factor that could facilitate dialogue on religious topics. Nevertheless, though not showing much enthusiasm about the presence of religion in the educational and public arena, St. Petersburg respondents show more agreement as concerns their attitudes toward religious plurality. They proved to be quite open to inter-religious communication: 80% of respondents did not claim preferences for communication with young people of the same religious background and the statement "I don't like people from other religions" was soundly refused.

When facing religious proselytism, St. Petersburg students prefer rather to ignore it than to debate on religious issues or to impose their own beliefs. This non-aggressive behavioral pattern corresponds to their vision of the ways toward peaceful coexistence of people with different religious backgrounds. The way to live together in peace was associated by our respondents much more with sharing common views and common activities than with administrative measures.

A number of 'feminine' features of religiosity more frequently shown by girls were found in the reactions to the questions regarding dialogue and conflict. They may be generalized in terms of higher communicativeness in religious matters and more positive expectations connected with religious diversity and inter-religious dialogue.

4.4 Empirical results in the light of research hypotheses

1. The first pair of hypotheses stating that religious students are less open to dialogue and less tolerant on religious issues than non-religious students may be rejected on the basis of our research. Comparison between students with and without religious affiliation showed religious students to be more open to dialogue and in some respects more tolerant than non-religious students. Religious students have more positive attitudes toward religion and more respect toward other believers. They are more informed about and more interested in the religious views of the others around. They do not show any more dislike of people from other religions than non-religious students and advocate freedom of religious expression more intensely.

At the same time, religious students seem to be quite aware of the conflict potential of religion and are far from taking an uncritical view of religious people and religious institutions. Based on the bi-variate analysis of the data, one may portray religious students in our sample as quite open-minded persons, accepting their religiousness with the same level of inner freedom as the students who refused to affiliate themselves with a religious tradition.

In more general terms, the data obtained give empirical grounds to consider the religiousness of students as a positive factor for their citizenship and their communicative competences to live in a plural society.

2. A more difficult task is to evaluate the influence of school education, and particularly of religion in education, on the perceptions and attitudes of students toward religious diversity. It is hardly possible to state that students who have encountered religious diversity in education are more tolerant or more open to dialogue on religious issues, as the second pair of hypotheses suggests. It may be more correct to speak about the ambiguity of the effects produced by experiences connected with religion in education and about the complex and multidimensional influence school may produce in students.

What may be proved by statistical analysis of variability within and between different schools is that encounters with religion at school can produce both positive and negative, both rapid and longstanding effects on students' views about religion and its social impacts.

Secondly, it may be stated that the overall effect of school is difficult to attribute to a specific element such as the level of education, its profile or the form of presence of religion in school curricula. Direct and indirect personal influences of teachers and other active agents of the educational process, producing negative and/or positive experiences with religion and religious diversity, may be the key force that affects students' religious perceptions and attitudes. The school 'membership groups' constituting learning communities may also influence their members through the collective micro-societal standards of values and norms functioning as criteria for judgments about different forms of behavior and religious expression. Formal RE may have some positive impact on the attitudes toward the presence of religion in education. For instance, in our sample, students who already have facilities to pray in school are definitely more positive about this arrangement. But these effects are comparable with the influence of other informal factors mentioned above.

3. Experience of personal encounters with young people from other religions seems to produce in general a more positive vision of religious diversity. So the third pair of hypotheses, stating that students who have personally encountered religious diversity are more tolerant and open to dialogue on religious issues, get some empirical support. Not only those students who reported they have friends of other religious backgrounds, but also those who just had inter-religious contacts at school, showed a more negative reaction to the assumptions and statements stating exclusivist or xenophobic ideas.

The influence of this factor was not simple too. Some data indicated the negative consequences of intercultural and interethnic encounters. It is difficult to evaluate the role of religious components in these intercultural encounters and conflicts. The reluctance of respondents to give information about the religious views of their friends and their family members makes things more complicated.

Anyhow, the religious perceptions of students proved to be dynamic, diverse and highly dependant on a complex of factors operating on macro- and micro-societal levels. In view of the previously made observation that schools may play a significant role in shaping youngsters' religious perceptions, this means that the presence of religion in school education has great potential to change students' views, in particular regarding their attitudes toward religious diversity.

References

Francis, L.J. (2004). Prayer, personality and purpose in life among churchgoing and non-churchgoing adolescents. In: L. Francis, M. Robbins & J. Astley (Eds.), *Religion, Education and Adolescence: international empirical perspectives*. Dublin: Lindisfarne Books.

Kozyrev, F. (2008). Religion and Education through the Eyes of Students from Saint-Petersburg, in: T. Knauth, D.-P. Jozsa, G. Bertram-Troost, & J. Ipgrave (Eds.), *Encountering Religious Pluralism in School and Society – A Qualitative Study of Teenage Perspectives in Europe*. Muenster: Waxmann, pp. 279–308.

Kozyrev, F.N. (2003). The Religious and Moral Beliefs of Adolescents in St. Petersburg, in *Journal of Education and Christian Belie*, 7 (1), pp. 69–91.

Варзанова Т. (1998). О религиозной ориентации молодых россиян, in: *Русская мысль,* 4205, 18 [Varzanova T. Religious orientation of young Russians, in: *Russian Thought* 4205, 18.

Клинецкая Н.В. (2005). Влияние религиозности на социальное здоровье молодежи // Актуальные проблемы исследования социального здоровья молодежи. Ч. 2. Информационно-аналитические материалы / Под. ред. Р.А. Зобова. – СПб.: Химиздат, 59–67 [Klinetskaya N. V. Influence of religion on the social health of youth, in: Zobov R. (Ed.) *Current problems in the study of the social health of youth.*] 2. St. Petersburg: Khimizdat.

Клинецкая Н.В. (2006). Социальное здоровье и религия // Молодежь и социальное здоровье / Под. ред. Р.А. Зобова. – СПб.: Химиздат, 140–154 [Klinetskaya N. V. Social health and religion, in: Zobov R. (Ed.) *Youth and social health.*] St. Petersburg: Khimizdat.

Роберсон Р. (1999). Восточно-христианские Церкви: Церковно-исторический справочник. – СПб: ВРФШ [Roberson R. *Eastern Christian Churches*] St. Petersburg: School of Religion and Philosophy.

Российский независимый институт социальных и национальных проблем (2000) Опрос – НГ–Религии 17 мая 2000 [Russian Independent Institute of Social and Nationalities Problems. A Poll – NG-Religions, May 17, 2000].

Olga Schihalejev

Comments on Russia from an Estonian Perspective

Introduction

The findings of our Russian colleagues have been of great interest to us and there are at least two special reasons for this. First, there is a big group of ethnic Russians living in Estonia which makes possible the comparison of two ethnic Russian groups, those living in Estonia and Russia, with each other. Second, Estonia and Russia share several decades of the common experience of the Soviet regime and its atheistic ideology, which, together with other influences, has changed the religious landscape in both countries. Even though the young people surveyed in the current study were born after the collapse of the Soviet Union, the influences and argumentations used in those decades are found among today's young generation.

Such a partly shared context makes it very interesting to compare the answers given in both countries.

In spite of the longer period of atheistic influence in Russia, we find more religiously affiliated students there than in Estonia. Also there were more religiously affiliated students among the Russian speaking students in Estonia than among Estonian speaking students, although the former are less affiliated than their peers in Russia. Some differences among the two Russian groups could be explained by the instructions given to teachers: in St Petersburg teachers were instructed to tell their students about their own Orthodox affiliation, if asked, while in Estonia such hints were not given and teachers rather answered students that they do not know their religious affiliation.

Religious education in both countries is rather an exception, to be found in a few schools, than the rule. Both countries share common struggles to introduce religious education; in Russia the proposed subject is seen in more confessional terms, introducing the Orthodox tradition whereas in Estonia RE is an optional subject, giving an introduction into world religions. Similar resistance to the subject could be found in both countries, and in spite of differing endeavours RE stays an enterprise of some exceptional schools. From a research perspective this gives wonderful possibilities to explore the impact of religious education, by comparing groups of students who have studied the subject or not, in different national contexts.

The role of religion in pupils' life and relationships

The loose interconnection of religious affiliation with beliefs and the importance of faith was similar in Russia and also in the Russian-speaking subsample of Estonia, while there was a much stronger correlation of these variables in the Estonian-speaking subsample. Despite the lower proportion of religiously affiliated students in the Russian-speaking subsample of Estonians, the distribution of different opinions among the Russian samples in both countries are almost exactly the same for the content of belief and the importance of religion to them. This finding adds value to the results. The same could be said about the frequencies of different religious activities: both Russian groups were significantly more active than Estonian speakers in all the activities, with the same distribution of answers except for attendance at religious events, which was rather exceptional for the great majority of students in both countries. Surprisingly the number of those who never attended religious events was the smallest among ethnic Estonians, while regular attendance was the highest among Estonian Russians, almost irrespective of their religious affiliation. These findings strengthen the conclusion made by our Russian colleague about the loose relationship between religious affiliation and religious beliefs and practices.

As to regard to the sources of information about religion, Russians valued all of them more highly than Estonians. The most highly valued sources of information about religion were family and friends for both Russian samples, while for Estonians family is valued almost equally to school. Estonians reported they spoke about religion more often at school, but this may be the 'tendency of the sample', as there were more students who studied RE in the Estonian sample. Surprisingly, if the answers on frequencies about sources of religious knowledge are compared, Russians do not speak remarkably more often about religion, neither with their family nor with their friends. This does not necessarily contradict the high importance of family, as Orthodox tradition is very much concerned with experience and mystical domains. Here may lie one of the reasons why, in both countries, Russian respondents had a 'silent' and private kind of religion. Many statements in the questionnaire presumed religion to be expressed verbally, as they asked about domains of speaking and knowing. From such a perspective the reason not to speak about religion for Russians in both samples can be explained, not strictly as an unwillingness to do so but rather as the fact that they do not see any need for speaking about personal matters.

In contrary to the rational approach to religion, Russian-speaking students tended to hold their notion of religion not so much as a matter of knowledge, but of experience and identity, which cannot be changed so easily. For example, the statement about the possibility to change ones' mind about religion ('What I think about religion is open to change') was really confusing for half of the Russian respondents in both samples, while not so much for the ethnic Estonians. Religion which is so integrally part of oneself, not only a matter of accepting some doctrines, cannot be changed so easily. The doubt, concerned with content of belief and not so much with experience ('Sometimes I have doubts – is there a god or not?'), was more possible to answer also for Russian respondents and it was valued more as a question to be revised, no matter whether they have religious affiliation or not.

Religion was classified as a personal matter for Russians in both samples more than for ethnic Estonians: (more agreement with 'Religion determines my whole life', 'Religion is important to me because I love God').

Their religion seems to be so much a personal choice that Russians in both samples disagree more than ethnic Estonians even with a statement that religion is inherited from family. Religion is seen here as a personal quest, not a blind obedience to the tradition of the family. Especially the fact that Russian religious students were more decisive about having no connection with religious community shows their understanding of religion as a personal exploration. Also, those Estonians, who have personally no attachment to any religion, agreed more that religion is determined by family tradition than their peers who have religious affiliation. Similarly, in the sample of St. Petersburg one finds that those for whom religions is not a personal matter, e.g. students who do not believe in any god, spirit or life force, supported more that religion is inherited from ones' family. The apparent paradox, about religiously affiliated students being more in favour of being a member of no faith community, can be also interpreted in the perspective of a personal quest in connection to an a-social understanding of religion – in spite of the fact that many of them were baptized in the Orthodox church, they do not see it as a prerequisite for their belief. For many Russian-speaking students religion is not a matter of a church or of a family, it is a personal enterprise, so there is no reason to choose friends by this variable either.

If the personal dimension was more important for ethnic Russians, then the opposite tendency was found when we looked for the social dimension – Estonians were more in favour of many of the sentences about the social dimension of religion. In spite of their lesser affiliation to religion ethnic Estonians were more likely to participate in religious events, agreed more that 'People with different strong religious views cannot live together', that 'a student who shows his/her religious belief openly in school, risks being mocked' and that strong laws could facilitate the peaceful co-existence of different religions. For other statements the sample of St. Petersburg remained between the two ethnic groups of Estonians and were more similar to ethnic Estonians than to their Russian fellows in Estonia. Ethnic Russians in Estonia showed remarkable detachment from society by believing least of all three groups in almost all means to change anything in society, either to improve relationships (by knowledge, personal contacts, shared interests, respect) or to cause conflicts (that people with strong beliefs cannot live together or that disagreement on religious issues leads to conflicts). Also Russian respondents in Estonia felt least of all groups that religion could be an influence in history, and valued least the importance of studying its influence on contemporary society.

Religion at school

Fascinating results reported by our colleagues in St Petersburg on the differences between schools draw our special attention. Here we can find three schools which are in different aspects more positive than others to religion and two schools which are more negative in many aspects.

From the table presented we find that all statements except one about the positive impact of school were scored highest in school 1. It shows clearly that students at this school appreciated the religious studies at their school.

Also many social impacts of religion were seen as most important at school 1 if compared to other schools – these students disagreed more that religion has no place at school, saw that religion is important in history and for dealing with problems in society, and valued respect as a means to cope with differences. Contrary to the social dimension of religion and good impacts of school, they agreed only with some personal statements about religion at the highest level – they valued religious studies in order to develop their own views and thought most frequently about religion.

Nevertheless, the statements of personal attachment to religion (importance of religion, frequency of religious activities, valuing friends or religious community as a source of information, valuing religion as a determinant of life or school as a place to be guided towards religious beliefs) were not agreed at the highest level by students at school 1. Probably it reflects the real situation in their school, namely that their RE was not designed to induct them into religion, but rather to have a more distanced perspective and learn about religion. Looking at the results we can assume that the school staff support the academic approach to religion; they take critical stances, have complex views on religious issues and do not try to make their students 'Orthodox'.

In spite of the fact that religious affiliation is the highest among the schools studied, students in school 1 held the most atheistic views ('I don't really think there is any sort of God, spirit or life force'), and rejected monotheistic views ('There is a God') more than the students from other schools. Here we can point out that students in Estonia who studied RE believed less in a monotheistic God. Probably a monotheistic notion of God has for them a too overloaded meaning and in order to not agree with some of its nuances (or even misinterpretations, as anthropomorphism), it is easier for them to use other options.

School 3 and 6 are surprising examples of schools with no RE. The students in school 3 were less religiously affiliated, nevertheless they valued more highly talking about religion; its impact on society; and religion as a determinant of their lives. Students from school 6 were the most positive regarding the personal importance of religion and personal gains from religion and studying religion ('Religion helps me to cope with difficulties', 'Learning about religions at school helps me to make choices between right and wrong', 'Learning about different religions helps me to develop my own point of view'); they also found differences to be interesting and enriching.

School 2 is an astonishing example of a long-lasting negative effect of initiation to religion, which probably did not concern the surveyed students directly, but has made all the school more cautious about such attempts. We see that students in this school were most critical about school as a source of information about religion and many personal statements about religion, while they did not have such striking differences for other statements.

Students in schools 3 and 5 seem to be similar in their socio-economic background, also having similar low religious affiliation among students and more students holding atheistic views, but the attitudes to religion are rather different. If students from school 3 held more positive attitudes regarding the societal impacts of religion and the good potential of school in promoting tolerance, then school 5 is an opposite of these views. Surprisingly the most negative students about religious studies provided at school and the possible gains of such studies were not at school 2, but rather at school 5. The students from school 2 opposed more than others the good effects of studying religion, saw fewer good effects of speaking about religion, and believed less in different ways to improve peaceful co-existence between religions.

Such findings show that promoting religious tolerance can be well enhanced not only by teachers of RE but also by those of other subjects, if the teacher is competent and willing to do so, as seen from the Russian chapter.

F. Javier Rosón Lorente

Schooling and Religion – some References to the Russian and Spanish Contexts

From a Spanish perspective, it is interesting to highlight that while Russia is going through a religious reconstruction in terms of civil society and state, Spain intends to de-construct these very same roots. This approach means both realities are comparable in the sense that they (both realities) share wide similarities in relation to religion and discourses about students' religiosity: while one is increasing the other is decreasing. Both seem to stand at intermediate positions. In this sense, while the Spanish trend is shifting towards ambiguity in religion, even though the majority define themselves as Christian Catholics, in the Russian case the feeling is the very opposite.

Having said that, it is noteworthy how the Russian conclusions reveal that, despite state and scientific atheism, according to the chapter in this book youngsters now generally have a positive attitude towards religion. Nearly half of the respondents are believers and the remaining majority does not express negative attitudes toward religion explicitly.

Another significant point is that in the Russian case families are the main source of information when talking about religion, although two thirds of respondents do not see it as a family legacy. Paradoxically, in most of cases religion develops within the private life, not publicly.

Moreover, it is striking how pupils from "school 1" (CCRE) were not considered to be more religious than students from other schools. On the contrary, the percentage of those who denied the existence of God was a little higher in this school. Similarly, students from this school thought more than the others about religion, but they were not at the top of the list when regarding school as a source of information on religion. In that matter it looks like CCRE is not the best approach in relation to RE. Regardless, it is at the top of the range only when we consider the responses of protesting against the lack of interest in religion and promoting respect for others' religions.

Similarly, it is interesting to note that religious practices do not seem to be related to belief or disbelief. In this respect the fact that 60% of the interviewees have never been to religious events is striking. Then again, regarding the importance of religion in their lives, most of their attitudes are rather ambiguous.

Family and school – two antagonistic realities?

There are five aspects to be aware of, from our national perspective. To start with, the relation that young people have with religious communities and/or religious leaders: in the Russian case the relationship is little or inexistent. As stated, historical circumstances may have something to do with this, but still it is considered to be a differential characteristic among youngsters, together with pluralistic values and freedom of beliefs. In the Spanish case, we should add the lack of interest in religion. That is, political and social debate is combined with a secularization and sceptical trend among pupils of certain ages.

In the second place, students think that religion is not something you inherit from your family. In this sense there are no differences between religious and non-religious students. From our point of view, this attitude would have been developed in relation to religious dogma, but even more in terms of daily practices. Religious praxis seems to have been limited for decades, since it was totally incompatible with people's jobs or education, for certain age groups. This principle could be extended to today, from what we know about the Russian case. Nevertheless, there are other references that suggest that family is the main agent of initiation into religion for St. Petersburg students. Does "undercover" religiosity related to dogmas exist, and then not be apparent in actual religious practice?

Thirdly, students believe that you can be religious without belonging to a particular religious community. According to "their explanations" this could be due to two reasons: on the one hand because of the high tolerance of students, who join a community but then do not want to impose their way of thinking on other people; or on the other hand, as a result of students' ignorance concerning religion.

The fourth point is related to the following statement: "It is really amazing that more than half of the respondents said they do not know about their friends' religion!" From our national point of view, this does not mean that students hide their religiosity in their respective settings, but that, to a great extent, religion is not a topical subject nor the main interest of the interviewed students, who focus their daily activities on other aspects that are not directly related to religious issues.

Finally, we have come to the conclusion that in the Russian case, there is a certain gender inequity with respect to parents' influence, i.e. mothers' influence is greater than that of fathers: "children see their mothers as being more religious". This claim should be considered in terms of the role women play in children care and socialisation. It is likely that they hold a greater presence and participation in all fields, not only in religious education.

Studemts' views – agreements and disagreements between Spain and Russia

One of the things that the Russian and Spanish cases have in common, regardless of the historical/religious backgrounds, is that the educational model chosen by students is the optional one and that which is separated by beliefs. In the Spanish context, it is a way of "counter-reacting" to the growing religious plurality, just as it is "in a way" how schools stand for the rights of religious minorities who claim the need to receive religion lessons that conform with their beliefs.

Another shared feature has to do with the freedom to wear religious symbols to school. In the Russian context 9 out of every ten pupils agree that students can wear discreet religious symbols. In the Spanish case, the interviewees agree with this assertion but are totally against more visible symbols.

The role school plays in relation to religion is minor in both cases, which is surprising, taking into account that they have contrary historical backgrounds to begin with. In this sense family is more appreciated than school or social groups. Yet there is one significant difference since in the Spanish case religion or religiosity is "inherited" from the family – which is more a question of socialisation than inheritance in this case.

Regarding gender in the survey, even though there are slight differences which we highlight in the Russian section, there is no gender difference in relation to the assertion "talking about religion is embarrassing". In the Spanish case, it was the only topic where most students expressed a flat rejection. This was the only question that showed differences between the sexes: females "disagreed" while males were less certain.

Last of all, we would like to talk about the statements: "disagreement on religious issues leads to conflicts" and "respecting the religion of others helps to handle differences". In the Russian case, both statements reveived similar reactions. About half of the students agreed and one out of every ten disagreed with both. In Spain, however, students totally agreed that regardless of the religion or worldview of others, they can live together. At this point we would like to add that students "agreed" that disagreement on religious topics creates conflicts, but "neither agreed nor disagreed" that if these differences and conflicts were strong, coexistence would become impossible. In this sense, in the Spanish national context students showed a certain ambiguity, which indicates another way of constructing the concept of "living together" as well as the perception of tolerance and respect for diverse opinions.

F. Javier Rosón Lorente & Aurora Alvarez Veinguer

Spanish Youth Facing Religious Diversity at School – Findings from a Quantitative Study

1. Introduction

1.1 The research setting

Religious education has persistently been a "controversial topic" in contemporary Spain. Astonishingly, however, the recipients and supposed beneficiaries of religious education, Spanish youth, have never been consulted on their views about religion, religious education at school, or the role of religion in society. The following analysis of the quantitative questionnaire data, collected within the framework of the comparative REDCO project[1], therefore, marks an explorative study on young people's attitudes, perceptions, beliefs and experiences with respect to religious education.

As illustrated below in more detail, the views reported in different regions by both religious and non-religious students, reflect the wider current debate taking place in Spanish society. Contending positions about religious education are disputed in the media and in political discourse nearly on a daily basis. Recently, the situation has become more complex, as two long-standing traditions are being challenged by the growing presence of Muslim (particularly Maghrebien) and Protestant (mostly Latin American) immigrants: firstly, Spanish society's self-perception as religiously homogeneous – Catholic, though scarcely practicing – and secondly, the close interrelation and frequent overlapping between the Catholic Church and the Spanish nation-state as institutions (Moreras, 2005). It is particularly the Muslim community (legally backed by the Spanish Constitution and the Concordat-like agreements signed in the nineties between the State and non-Catholic community representatives) that has been asserting its right to equal treatment and access to public schools (Tarrés Chamorro et al., 2007). The pluralisation of confessional religious education, currently being implemented in several pilot primary schools in districts with high percentages of Muslim pupils, has met strong resistance not only from the Catholic Church, but also from secular activists. Moreover, the current Socialist government's introduction of a non-confessional, compulsory subject, "citizenship education", (for one year in primary and two in secondary education) (Cortina, 2006), aimed at supplementing confessional Catholic religious education (RE) with "non-religious, universal values", has served only to fuel the fire.

Despite the ongoing political and media debates, certain features of the education system persist from previous decades; in particular, the existence of a mixed, three-fold school system that reflects the long tradition of transferring educational competences to the Catholic Church. From pre-primary to pre-university (*bachillerato*) levels, there are three school types: (1) public schools, owned and run by the central state, but now increasingly being transferred to the Autonomous Communities; (2) so-called *escuelas concertadas,* private schools mostly

---

1   A European project: Religion in Education. A contribution to Dialogue or a factor of Conflict in transforming societies of European Countries. We gratefully acknowledge the decisive collaboration of the other Granada and Melilla REDCO team members Francisca Ruiz, Iman Katarzyna Kluza and Latifa Abdelmalki, as well as the invaluable input and support obtained from the entire REDCO team, particularly from Gerdien Bertram-Troost.

owned and run by Church institutions, congregations, or religious orders, but almost completely subsidised by the state or regional government[2]; and (3) completely private schools owned by cooperatives or private enterprises, which do not receive any public resources[3].

1.2   Description of the sample

When implementing the questionnaire we decided, for practical reasons, to pay special attention to the heterogeneity of the sample[4] and the researchers' access to the schools. In selecting the schools to include in the study, we considered two criteria: (a) quality of contact with the school board and teachers, for example: previous contact, availability of the board and teachers (of both RE and other subjects) to take part in the project; (b) quality of the informants (as stakeholders); (c) having prerequisite permission from the school to conduct the research. Normally, permission was negotiated with the teacher and school administration, but in the case of Melilla we obtained permission of the relevant educational authorities, *Dirección Provincial de Educación* and *Órgano de Inspección Educativa,* to carry out the research in all secondary and *bachillerato* schools in the city. In this case, criteria 'a' and 'b' were combined, as the contact with boards and teachers from different schools had previously been facilitated. In every school, we held meetings with members of the board and the teachers, and selected the most receptive teachers to carry out the survey. The teachers collaborated intensively in the data collection process, and none raised any objections either to the questionnaires or to the aim of the study.

Consequently, the quantitative questionnaire was distributed in secondary schools in three regions or "Autonomous Communities": Andalusia, Murcia, and Melilla. The regions were chosen in order to diversify the sample internally with respect to the following bases of comparison: 1) urban vs. rural (Granada and Melilla vs. Murcia); 2) emerging vs. established region of immigration (Murcia v. Granada); and 3) strong tradition of mono-religious presence vs. long existing religious diversity (Granada and Murcia vs. Melilla).

From this population we selected six schools in Andalusia, one in Murcia (a total of 7 schools in the Peninsula), and seven in Melilla[5], and samples of 14–16 year old students in their 2nd or 3rd year of secondary education. Nevertheless, these groups may also include some older students (over 16 years old), such as those repeating years, or students with special education needs (ACNNE). For this study students not corresponding to the pre-established age group were eliminated from the final sample.

These schools follow different religious education models, have different gender balances, and present different levels of ethnic-religious diversity. We feel, therefore, that they reflect the religious and social plurality of Spain. The brief description of each of these points will justify this selection of the sample.

---

2   Both the public schools (71.4%) and the "concertados" (17.8%), which represent the majority of schools in Spain, have been accounted for in the present study (cf. INE curso 2005-2006).
3   To contextualize Spanish recent religious development see Dietz, et al. (2007) and Dietz (2007).
4   Non probability sampling methods were used, more specifically, judgmental sampling. For more details cf. the methodological section above.
5   With the aim of guaranteeing the anonymity of the schools, we eliminated names and explicit references to them from the discussion of the research findings.

1.2.1 Gender balance

The sample includes the opinions of 381 female (56.1%) and 298 male students (43.9%) from a total of 679 surveyed (1 no answer) in the 14 to 16 year old age group. In general terms no significant differences were noted between the responses of the two sexes. In this regard, a high level of consensus was evident both between populations of the different regions and the individual schools included in the study.

1.2.2 Students' religious background

It is important to make a distinction between those students who expressed that they practised a "certain religion or worldview" (64.6% of those surveyed) from those who do not (35.4 %)[6], although this study did not discriminate between different religious beliefs. In other words, all students who ascribed themselves to a certain religion were considered believing regardless of religious adherence.

In the case of Granada and Murcia[7], we observe that 76% of the students who practised a religion were Catholic, compared to 2% Muslim, 2% Protestant and 14% who did not specify, e.g., I believe in God, but not in the Church; I simply believe; I believe in something but I cannot define it; I believe in socialism, feminism, etc. We also observed that 1% considered themselves agnostics, 1% practised other religions (Mormon, Jehovah's Witnesses, Buddhists, Evangelists, or "mixed" Catholic and Muslim), while only 4% did not respond. In the case of Melilla, 52% of students who practised a "certain religion or worldview" chose Catholicism, while 38% chose Mohammedanism. In this region, 3% of students were Jewish and a further 3% practised other religions. It is also noteworthy that only 1% of students opted for another alternative and a mere 3% did not respond. This sample is representative although no official data was available: it is estimated that approximately 56% of the population is Catholic, 40% are Muslim, and the rest of the population comprise the Jewish and Hindu minorities (Ministerio de Educación y Ciencia 2006/2007). Mainly due to differential birth rates, the percentage of the native Muslim population is increasing in comparison to their Catholic, Jewish and Hindu neighbours.

1.2.3 Religious education model

In all schools optional Catholic RE classes were offered except in one case. In this school Catholic religious education was compulsory for all students and no alternative options existed. In the other education centres[8], students chose at enrolment from the subjects on offer. If they do not opt for Catholic Religious Education, the school offers an alternative subject. In the sample obtained, 56% of students surveyed received religious education, while 44% did not.

It is noteworthy to refer to the differences between the two schools, both of which are deemed prestigious, in the city of Granada. The disparity lies in the fact that school number three is a public school where only 30% of the students receive religious education, while number six is a subsidised private school where 100% of the students receive Catholic reli-

---

6   5.6% of the 680 students surveyed did not answer this question.
7   This sample corresponds to the national trend in so far as most are of Catholic background, but this tendency is beginning to reverse due to the increasing Muslim population born in Spain (second generation immigrants) or who have migrated to Spain in the last twenty years.
8   From here on the term "education centres" and "schools", referring to "Institutes of Secondary Education" (known as IESO in Spain) will be used interchangeably.

gious education. Similarly, in the case of Melilla we observed significant differences between the schools. There were schools where the majority received religious education while in others the opposite was true. In this case, one school provided religious education for only 11.8% of students even though 70% expressed that they practice a certain religion (approximately 80% of this student population were Muslim). Conversely, in another school, located in a neighbourhood in Melilla with the highest level of growth, and home to a high percentage of Spanish families (many Catholic), two thirds of the students received religious education.

1.3   Reflection on the sample

From the outset, the principal objective was to find a sufficiently heterogeneous sample to be representative of the entire country. In this regard, the description of the sample shows that it indeed met this goal in most respects: regarding the religious background of students, type of school, socio-economic background, RE model, urban versus rural, migration background. However, we must point out two possible deficiencies. First, with respect to "religious education model"[9] (cf. 1.2.3), 56% of the students surveyed receive religious education compared to 59.5% of those in Obligatory Secondary Education in Spain as a whole. Second, with respect to gender/sex division, the sample was 56.1% female and 43.9% male whereas the national average[10] was 49% female, 51% male[11]. In any case, strict mathematical representativeness of the sample was not the goal, nor do we consider these two aspects of the sample relevant to either our findings on the religiousness of students or on the role religion plays in their lives.

1.4   Description of the general procedure

1.4.1   Information on data collection

With regard to the survey process, implementation was negotiated with the teachers and school management, then carefully introduced/contextualised to the students in the study. Researchers from REDCO in Spain carried out the introduction. The data were analysed using SPSS.

During the process it was not difficult to motive students to answer the questionnaire; although, exceptionally, some did not particularly pay attention or were talking with their classmates as questions were being read. We always received extremely positive support from the teachers. While most students finished the questionnaire earlier than expected, we always suggested that they rethink and review their answers to avoid misunderstood or unanswered items. For that reason, we repeated that they should answer all questions, that they could take all the time they needed, and that they should not hesitate to ask for clarification of any doubts with respect to the items on the questionnaire.

In fact, some items on the questionnaire were often queried by students. This was the case with "how many years attended RE classes", where many had problems remembering the exact figure. It was therefore necessary to explain to them how to calculate the number of years (6 years in primary school, 3 or 4 in secondary school). Likewise, we had many cases of students who did not provide an answer or made a note beside the answer space such as "I

---

9   Source: Estadística de la Enseñanza en España niveles no universitarios. Oficina de Estadística del Ministerio de Educación y Ciencia (M.E.C). Curso 2005–2006.

10 National tendency. Instituto Nacional de Estadística 2007.

11 There are no official records about the sex of students who attended religion classes in Spain.

don't care." Thus, we clarified that the questions were asking about their preferences and we explained that a "no" answer did not necessarily imply the opposite, for example with respect to socialising with peers from a religious background different than their own. Finally, we note that the concept of "worldview" was unfamiliar to most students and provoked many queries. We noticed that in those classes where we defined the word in general terms without giving examples, practically no students provided answers; but when examples like socialism, feminism, humanism, etc. were given, substantially more students did so.

1.4.2   Additional student comments

With regard to the additional comments at the end of the survey, we received 188 from students out of a total sample of 680 questionnaires, i.e. 27.6% of those surveyed provided comments. Of these comments 119 came from students who expressed having a "certain religion or worldview", while only 65 came from students who expressed "not having any religion", and 2 came from students who did not specify. The majority of comments reflected on religion itself, on one or another religion in particular, or on the issue of religion in education. However, a notable but small number of students commented on the questionnaire itself and their opinion of it, as detailed below.

One of the most repeated comments (ten students) made reference to the length of the questionnaire: "*this is very long and tedious.*" (2–2–1) Similarly, four students (two of whom expressed having a certain religion) "*found it boring because [they were] not interested in this topic.*" (2–2–13)

Other comments referred to the level of students' interest in the questionnaire. On the one hand, eight students found it interesting for various reasons: "*to know more ... about the ideas on religion in education in my country ... because we can learn about the opinions of other young people like us ... it is interesting for other people to know our opinion on 'RELIGION'*" (2–2–2); "*actually this topic is interesting*" (2–1–21); and others because they "*like to study religion.*" Conversely, 11 students found it uninteresting because they were "*not interested in this topic.*" (7–1–9) This type of response can also be observed in students that consider the questionnaire as "*positive in order to become familiar with different opinions, but as for me I am not interested in this topic, since I don't find religion important*", (7–1–9) or "*fine to know different opinions.*" (6–2–1)

Some students commented on the degree of importance they assigned to the survey. One personally "*finds it of notable importance that such questionnaires are carried out, because they influence our opinion on religion. In short the opinions people, students, and citizens hold on this topic should be made known, more and more similar questionnaires should be carried out, even though there are many people that don't accept to comment on or express their opinions on their religion.*" (13–1–1)

Yet others focused on the "methodology" of the questionnaire or its validity: "*I think that all the answers are relative, depending on the degree of belief of the person or persons in question. It's impossible to establish a fixed rule on such topics.*" (3–3–16); "*I think that ... some questions are not specific enough and may be answered from varying points of view, and it may be possible that my answer varies in importance depending on who is reading it ... and as regards such a relevant test, the questions should be much clearer.*" (3–3–6)

2.   Presentation of the results

In analysing the results of the survey we focused on three dimensions: firstly, on the individual level with respect to the role of religion in students' lives and in their surroundings; secondly, on the organizational level with respect to how they perceive religion's role in school; thirdly, on the societal level with respect to the existing religious education model and its role in fostering dialogue and/or causing conflict.

2.1   The role of religion in students' lives and surroundings

This section is divided into four parts: firstly, students' opinions on religion and faith; secondly, students' practices in relation to religion; thirdly, students' sources of information about religion; and lastly, students' interest in their environment and the religion of their peers.

2.1.1   Data description

A variety of understandings: the importance of "Religion" and "God"

At the outset we examined the responses to "How important is religion to you?" A previous analysis of the data from all secondary education centres exhibited a global average (mean) of 2.1 on the 5-point Likert scale with a low standard deviation both within each centre and globally among them (1.3). This indicates a small degree of dispersion in the answers and a general average close to the central value (neither important or unimportant). Figure 1 presents information on the importance of religion for the group as a whole (general), for students self-described as having a religion, and for those self-described as having no religion. It reveals that two out of every five students surveyed (41%) found religion important or very important, in comparison to 29% who considered it unimportant or absolutely not important. The intermediate position of the remaining 30% of students reveals an ambivalence towards religion.

Figure 1:   Importance of religion in students' lives, by religion/no religion (%)

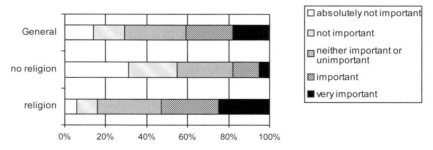

The importance of religion in students' lives was closely related to their belief, since analysis of both co-variables presented a high significance[12]. The typology elaborated for the survey

---

12 It is difficult to generalise, but on the whole p<0.01 would normally be considered significant and p<0.001 highly significant. In this case, f=142.255 p<0.001.

can be summarized in three positions: belief in God, belief in something, or belief in "noth-ing." Accordingly, 49% of those surveyed believed in God, while 39.9% considered them-selves atheists or agnostics. A mere 11.1% put themselves in an ambivalent position. The students' degree of belief was intimately related to their adscription to a particular religion or a specific world view. In this case, 64% of those with a certain religion or worldview affirmed believing in God, in contrast to 27% who believed in some sort of spirit, and only 9% who did not believe in God, or a spirit or life force. On the other hand, 22% of the students who did not follow a certain religion or a specific worldview believed that God does exist, 38% be-lieved in a spirit or life force, and 39.9% did not believe that any of these exists.

Another important set of items, summarized in Figure 2, concerns students' self-perception of the importance of religion in specific aspects of their daily lives. On this point, the most significant answer was "I respect other people who believe." Most students surveyed agreed with this statement (mean = 1.7). On the other hand, with respect to all other related items, variability was important (Sd. between 1.1–1.4). These could be divided into three groups: 1) statements of ambivalence (neither agree nor disagree), such as "it helps me to be a better person" (mean = 2.9), "it helps me to cope with difficult situations" (mean = 3.1); doubts about the existence of God or openness to change one's perception of religion, "religion is important to me because I love God" (mean = 3.2); 2) statements on the meaning of religion and its influence on one's life, "it determines my whole life" (mean = 3.6), or against it (they do not agree), meaning religion does affect their lives; 3) statements about religion in history (history as a subject, the historical past, religion in our history) (mean = 2.4), or the statement that one may be religious without belonging to a particular community of faith (mean = 2.3).

Figure 2: **Self-perception of the importance of religion in determined aspects of daily life, by RE model. (Means of estimates, scale from 1 – strongly agree to 5 – strongly disagree)**

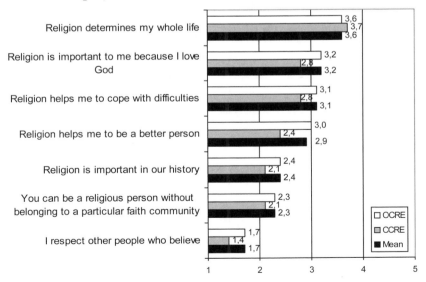

A facet of the survey that complements the items on perceptions and attitudes on religion concerns the very act of thinking about it (cf. Figure 3). On this point, we again distinguish between the students who have a certain religion or worldview and those who do not. While

60.4% of students with a certain religion or worldview thought about religion once a week or more, 36.3% of non-believers never thought about it. This tendency (belief > thinking, less belief or "no belief" < thinking), is further nuanced by those students who, apart from being believers, think about religion on a daily basis; 29.6%, as opposed to 30.8% who think about it only once a week.

Figure 3:   How often do students think about religion? (by religion, %)

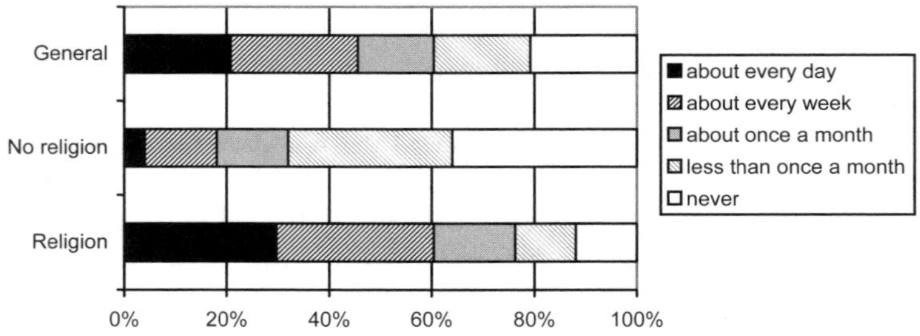

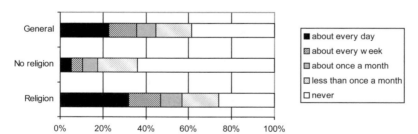

Students' daily praxis

We complete our analysis of the importance of religion for the students by examining their religious praxis. In this regard, (Figure 4), 32% of students claiming to be believers prayed "about every day", 15% "about every week", 10% "once a month", 17% "less than once a month", and 26% "never" prayed. With respect to non-believers, the data analysed demonstrate the contrary, notably 62% never prayed.

Figure 4:   How often do students pray? (by religion, %)

These items denote that the average student "thinks about religion and/or prays approximately once a month." Nevertheless, the average (approximately once a month) involved a high degree of dispersion (Sd. 1.4–1.6), especially in the case of prayer (Sd. = 1.6) where all possible answers were given. This is still the case with those having "a certain religion or worldview" (64.6%). For these students, practising and thinking about religion was more significant than for those who did not believe. Another variable related to a students' individual practice of religion, was, without a doubt, attendance at religious ceremonies. On this point, we can observe that students attended religious ceremonies approximately once a month (mean = 3.6), however those who attended denominational schools did so (mean = 3.1) more often than those who did not (mean = 4.0) and likewise more than students who had a certain religion or worldview (in OCRE's and CCRE's combined)[13] (mean = 3.4).

The students' personal connection with religion

An analysis of individual religious perceptions and praxis should involve students' sources of information on religion. On this point, the family was the most valued "source of religious information" for students (mean = 1.9). In comparison, school was not so highly valued, but considered "a little bit important" (mean = 2.8). However, in both cases an analysis of variance found significant differences between scores for this construct ($p = <0.001$), demonstrating that believing students deemed both family and school to be important sources of information, as opposed to the rest of the students. The other options (friends, religious community, books, media) are also considered important (mean = 2.8–3.2), but answers varied considerably (Sd. = 1.3). However, the religious community stood out as a valued source of information for non believing students (mean = 3.5). Finally, we point out that most of the students surveyed neither read the sacred text of their religion on their own initiative (mean = 4.4), nor did they search the Internet for related information (mean = 4.4).

The importance of religion in the life and surroundings of young Spaniards

Lastly, we examine how this praxis is carried out in the students' most immediate environment, based on the question "How often do you speak with others about religion?" In this case (Figure 5) the family was considered a preferred "source of information" (31% talked about religion with their families once a week or more), more important than teachers in the school (27%), their peers (17%), or other students at school (9%). The rest of the answers indicated that students talked about religion "less that once a month or never" with teachers (59%), classmates (66%), and friends (68%). At the opposite extreme were religious leaders and other students not friends, (79% seldom or never spoke to these groups).

Figure 5: **How often do you speak with others about religion?**

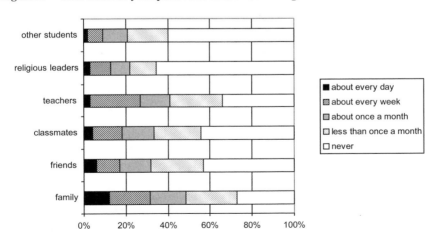

We can also see differences according to RE model regarding which groups of people were more important as sources of information about religion for students[14]. In this regard, students attending CCRE's attached significantly higher importance to teachers at school as a source of information (33%) than those attending OCRE (26%). In other words, 59% of those attending OCRE talked to their teachers about religion less than once a month, compared to 54% of those at CCRE's.

Considering that, on average, students talked about religion once a month, it would be worthwhile to ascertain their interest in the religion of those they spoke to and what religious diversity existed in their immediate surroundings. On this point, the data showed a notable trend: most students were ambivalent about or uninterested in the religion of others. Although the variability of the answers was not negligible, most of the students surveyed found the religion of others irrelevant (mean = 2.7) and vice versa, what knowledge others have of their own religion (mean 2.8).

Figure 6:   Contacts with the religions of the people around me, %

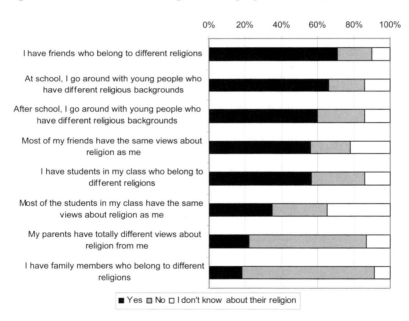

On the issue of the "religion of the people around me", we highlight the following: Firstly, most of the students (71%) had friends from different religious backgrounds, maintained relationships with them regardless of religion, and were aware of the religious diversity in their school and in their immediate environment. However, 56% admitted that most of their friends shared their point of view on religion. Secondly, whether believers (72%) or non-believers (75%), most recognised that no religious diversity existed in their immediate family. Likewise, the large majority of family members belonged to the same religion as the students

---

14 In this case, there were no significant differences between CCRE and OCRE with regard to religious
    leaders, other students at school, etc. The only differences were with regard to teachers and family.

(73%). Conversely, only 22% of parents and 18% of family members had another religion or worldview. Thirdly, paradoxically, although students recognised diversity in the classroom and in their immediate environment (56%), they did not acknowledge or did not know their classmates' points of view on religion. Only 35% are familiar with their classmates' opinions on religion. However the answers provided on this point were ambiguous, because students did not know (35%) the religion of their classmates, or whether their views were similar to their own (30%), indicating that over a third did not know what religion others belonged to.

Likewise, it may be noted that most classmates were considered friends outside of school regardless of religion. Approximately a third of students preferred to mix with "friends" of the same religion, and two thirds regardless of religion. Lastly, we note that we did not find differences with respect to RE model in the school or the religious background of the students.

Synopsis of data – religion in students' lives

As a starting point, the results indicate that a large percentage of students consider religion to be important or very important in their lives. However, a considerable number held ambivalent views on religion, seeing both its positive and negative aspects.

In regard to the importance of religion in the lives and surroundings of young Spaniards, we revisit the students' statements that revealed a certain scepticism. The questions carrying religious meaning comprised: "religion makes me a better person"; "it helps me with day to day problems"; and "God as the most important" element of belief. These were answered more ambivalently than questions carrying less religious significance, such as religion's importance in Spanish history, which were answered unambiguously in the affirmative. Nevertheless, most students seemed to agree that religion was a meaningful part of their lives, even though their ambivalence was quite significant. This "importance of religion" results in "thinking about it", and we noted that 60% of the students surveyed thought about religion at least once a week.

With regard to how the data relates to individual perception and daily praxis, we now turn to the sources of information students resorted to for knowledge on their own and others' religions. The role of religion in students' lives related mostly to family and the cultural traditions of their environment. On this question family was the most "important source of religious information." In comparison, other students at school were not so highly valued, and deemed "a little bit important." The other options (friends, religious community, books, media, Internet) were considered of some importance, but with a high degree of variability in the answers. Moreover, most students surveyed neither read the sacred texts of their religion on their own initiative, nor did they search the Internet for related information, suggesting a lack of interest in religious topics. The data exhibited a clear split by belief (in a certain religion or worldview). Students not defining themselves as believers did not indicate any interest in religious matters, meaning that they did not either search the Internet or read sacred texts. From these data we may conclude that the Internet is not a major source of information on religion for students.

Next, we address the role of religion vis-à-vis peer groups. The survey demonstrated that students considered talking about religion a private matter that normally does not occur in the public arena. In this regard, students revealed that religion does influence their lives and helps them relate to other students regardless of what religion they may practice: that is, although they confessed that they normally relate to people of their own religion (or worldview), when they interact with people of other religions they keep religious matters to themselves.

2.1.2 Data interpretation

As a starting point, we discuss the responses about the importance of religion in students' lives. The students' opinions denoted an affinity with the national culture with regard to religious education (religion traditionally introduced in schools). On the other hand, as is the case with the country as a whole, we confirmed "a certain decrease" (Elzo 2008:80) of those who define themselves as religious, and an increase of those who define themselves as agnostics or non-believers.[15] Moreover, students' views demonstrated mixed feelings and ambivalence (which we will try to describe over the course of this chapter). Perhaps this is natural given that a student's response presupposes describing one's own perception of religion, which entails a number of complex social and cultural ideological variables.

As noted earlier, students' perception of the importance of religion in their lives is intimately related to belief or lack of belief in God or a worldview. A closer look at these answers provides more insight into that role. This point may be ambiguous, since it is true that although one believes in God, religion itself may still mean little. Nevertheless, in some cases an "anti-religious" stance is clear, for example for those who neither believed in God nor in any kind of spirit/life force.

In the strict sense, a religious person is one who believes, is integrated into, and practises an institutional religion (Bericat, 2008, p. 49)[16]. About 41% of those surveyed believed that religion was "important or very important" while 49% believed in God. This suggests a dissatisfaction with religious institutions, palpable in the present debate in the political sphere, manifested by a belief in God or some kind of superior being, but a concurrent lack of interest in religious practice and religion itself. In this regard, opinions becomes polarized between the most anti-religious and the most religious (more numerous) due to the effect of (1) the recent debate in Spain and (2) the maximizing confessional character of the national RE curriculum that gives no other choice but to be in favour of or against it.

The importance of religion in the lives and surroundings of young Spaniards can be better assessed through the daily praxis of students. We clarify a priori that belief about the importance of religion in their lives does not necessarily have to relate to daily religious practice but may be a changeable cultural and social inclination. This can be confirmed by observing the practice of prayer and other practices considered of a private or an individual nature, such as attending religious ceremonies. In relation to the frequency of prayer, the majority of students prayed approximately once a month. Similarly, the "opposition dialectic" (Bericat, 2008, p. 48) can be demonstrated in the bipolarity of the respective cultural positions previously mentioned. Believing students on average reported praying much more frequently than non-believers. However, the tendencies were not "pure types", given that 31.5% of "believers" never or almost never pray and 37.8% of non-believers considered prayer something that they could on occasion or even on a daily basis practice.

With regard to religious ceremonies, we remarked that students on average attended once a month; but attendance can be cultural since it does not only mean going to a church or to a mosque for religious celebrations but includes traditional, cultural events like weddings, baptisms, festivals, etc. On the other hand, the very fact of attending confessional schools favours this kind of practice and reflection on religion.

---

15 For more details cf. (Dietz et al., 2007).
16 Which, from the point of view of the interviewees in the qualitative part, is directly associated with one's own religion.

Lastly, in relation to the view expressed by students about the role of religion with respect to their peers, we note that the present religious education model does not seem to help make knowledge of the religion of others inclusive. This tends to mean that religious diversity is recognized as such when one or various (even if not numerous) friends or acquaintances are perceived as "strangers" according to one's own religious criteria.

2.2 How do students see religion in school?

The present section is divided into three parts, concentrating firstly on student experiences with religion classes in school, secondly on how students would change them, and thirdly on what type of religious education model they consider appropriate.

2.2.1 Data description

The first question on the survey allows us to remark that a notable group of students received RE in primary school but did not opt for it upon reaching age 12 and entering secondary school, a group representing 10.6% of students (corresponding to reporting 6 years of RE). Second, the results indicate that many had been studying RE "their entire life" (45.6%), and doing so for 9–11 years, i.e., up to their third and fourth year of secondary education. Third, 13% of students received RE classes during years one through five of their primary education. Fourth, there were extreme cases, which were not significant, namely, 1% stated that they have been attending RE classes for 14–15 years. Fifth, in summary, many studied RE for 9 to 15 years (53.9% of students surveyed studied RE during "their entire life.")

Likewise, we noted that when carrying out the survey 56.1% of students were participating in RE classes, in comparison to 43.7% who were not. From the total number of students N = 680, 93.3% have received religious education for at least one year during their lifetime.

Religion classes in school

Given the above, the first noteworthy finding was that the majority of students "agreed" that at school they learn about different religions and this helps them to live together (mean = 2.3).[17] Likewise they agreed that they learn to respect others regardless of religion (for believing students mean = 1.7, for non-believers mean = 2).

Another significant aspect concerns whether students were given a chance to talk about religious topics from different points of view (mean = 2.5). If we relate this statement to: "at school, I receive knowledge about different religions", we note a certain ambivalence (mean = 2.9), since students "neither agreed nor disagreed" with this last statement.

Lastly, regarding student experiences in school, they significantly "neither agreed nor disagreed" with the following: "topics about religion are interesting at school", "religion as a topic is important at school", "learning about religions at school helps to make decisions between right and wrong", "learning about religions at school helps [them] learn about [them]selves", and "it helps to understand current events." In the case of all of these statements students took an intermediate and/or ambivalent position: "neither agree nor disagree" (means between 2.9–3.0).

Perhaps the most consequential question asked whether learning religion at school could "create conflict". It is important to note that while most denied this statement (3.7), the value was not very high and the variability of polarized answers was large. This variability corre-

---

17 Means from here on are calculated on the Likert scale: 1 = strongly agree, 2 = agree, 3 = neither agree nor disagree, 4 = disagree, 5 = strongly disagree.

sponded to the mean differences between believers (mean = 2.7), and non believers (mean = 3.2), i.e. the non believers were somewhat less convinced that RE does not cause conflict.[18]

This was likewise true among public school students and those in subsidised private schools (Figure 7). In this case, the differentiation between OCRE's and CCRE's confirms once again what we have described above: The students who go to denominational schools (CCRE's where RE is obligatory), affirmed more categorically that at school they obtain information on different religions (mean = 2.2 as opposed to OCRE centres where the mean = 2.6), a capacity to distinguish between right and wrong (CCRE mean = 2.6 vs. OCRE mean = 2.9),, and denied more expressly that RE leads to conflicts in the classroom (CCRE mean = 4.1 vs. OCRE mean = 3.7).

Figure 7:   **Evaluation of religious education by experience with RE ((Means of estimates, scale from 1 – strongly agree to 5 – strongly disagree)), by RE model**

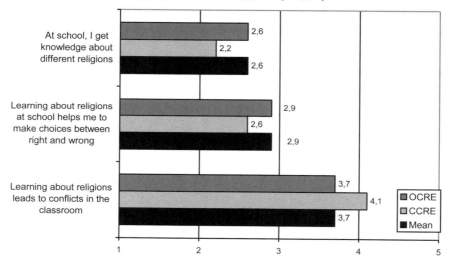

Experiences with religion in school

We ask what opinions students had on how RE classes should be conducted and what changes they would like to see. Figure 7 shows the mean values of some statements relevant to this topic. We note at the outset that students who filled in these items varied significantly in their responses (Sd. between 1.2–1.4). In the case of whether "students should be able to wear religious symbols at school", students would be in favour ("agree" mean = 2.3), but they "neither agree nor disagree" with a "more visible symbol" (p=0.057 mean = 3.0 Sd. = 1.2) (cf. Figure 8), especially CCRE students (mean = 3.8). Similarly, students thought that their mates should be excused from attending religious festivals organized by the school (mean = 2.3) if they do not celebrate these in their religion. On the other hand, they would not excuse them from classes for religious reasons (mean = 3.2). As for the possibility of religious food require-ments in school dining hall, students only slightly agreed, marking their ambivalence about the issue (mean = 2.6). The least valued statements were related to providing facilities for the

---

18   In this case, an Analysis of Variance (ANOVA) found no significant difference between scores for this construct (p=0.466).

students to pray and hosting voluntary religious services in schools. On this issue, students categorically disagreed (mean = 3.6). There were significant differences (p<0.01) between believers (mean = 3.4) and non-believers (mean = 3.9), as well as between OCRE and CCRE: CCRE students were ambivalent (mean = 2.3) as opposed to public school students (mean = 3.7). Students who do not ascribe to a religion had more "extreme" responses (mean = 3.9 "totally disagree").

Figure 8: **Position of religion in school, by religious affiliation and RE model. (Means of estimates, scale from 1 – strongly agree to 5 – strongly disagree)**

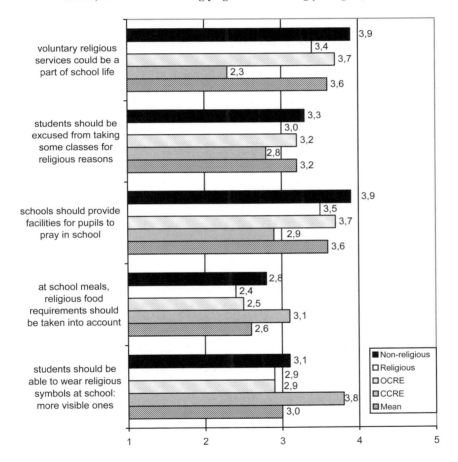

Preferred models of religious education: between integration and separation?

The above statements prompt us to consider which RE model students prefer.

First, students preferred a model where RE is optional (mean = 1.7), even though they considered the presence of religion in school positive (mean = 3.7). Moreover, they somewhat agreed that RE should be separated by religion (mean = 2.5), but the answers varied considerably (Sd. = 1.3). This would correspond with the current model. We stress, however, that most students deemed it necessary to obtain objective knowledge of world religions (mean = 2.3), as well as to learn about and understand their teachings (mean = 2.4), so that they can converse on religious topics (mean = 2.4).

On the other hand, they "neither agreed nor disagreed" that learning about religion is necessary to solve social problems (mean = 2.7). As for a model which would include both joint and separated education they "neither agreed nor disagreed" (mean = 2.8). Finally, the model where all religions are represented in one classroom was not considered positive (mean = 3.5), but the extreme variability of responses restricts the significance of this result (Sd. = 2.4). The variability was related to non-believers, who while rejecting this model more (mean = 3.7) than believers, varied extremely in their responses (Sd. = 3.7).

Synopsis of data – religion in school

At first sight, Spanish students seemed to view religion in schools as positive; a large majority agreed that learning about different religions helps them live with and respect others. The difficulty lies in distinguishing to what extent this is a result of their experience with RE classes and to what extent it issues from their education on values and respect towards "others" (intermulticulturality) transmitted in a transversal way in their other subjects. This can be clarified by observing their other responses: On the one hand, students affirmed that RE classes help them to talk about religious issues from varied points of view. Likewise, the majority believed that learning about other religions does not generate conflict in the classroom. On the other hand, students were ambivalent regarding the type of knowledge offered about other religions in their RE classes. In fact, an important number considered religion at school to be a factor of conflict.

The second point involves religious symbols in school. On this issue, students who filled out the questionnaire agreed with the presence of discreet religious symbols, but "neither agreed nor disagreed" with more visible displays. At play are the social norms of "respect and tolerance" towards diversity, which might be internalized and assimilated by students. However, students varied considerably in their responses. This lack of consensus reflects the heterogeneity of views on religion and the role it should play in society.

The differences between OCRE and CCRE were most significant on this point, polarized between the view of one's own religion and that of the "other." Bearing in mind that in these kinds of schools voluntary religious services and celebrations have a special meaning, students gave very positive answers to the questions related to making allowances for religious requirements (e.g. symbols, prayer). Nevertheless, CCRE students were ambivalent about "allowing" special religious facilities in their school; whereas OCRE students disagreed. This could mean that they have assimilated the presence of Catholic spaces of worship in their school, but would not consider it positive that other religions be accommodated in this space. It would be important to further analyse student attitudes when it comes to allowing visible religious symbols (like a headscarf), to which students from confessional schools totally disagreed while agreeing with wearing discreet symbols (like crosses).

In summary, while a majority of students considered the current model the most appropriate, the significance of this result should be further analysed by the religion of the pupils.

2.2.2 Data interpretation

In order to address the question "how many years have you studied RE at school?" we should keep in mind the following points about RE in Spain. Firstly, many students have not studied religion because their religion is not represented in primary or secondary schools. This is the case for Muslim students, who up to a few years ago had no opportunity to take Islamic RE classes, still not an option at any secondary school. These students correspond to the extreme (0 years of RE). Secondly, we should take into account the students who had RE in their countries of origin, but now their religion is not represented, or in the case that in their country of origin RE is optional. Thirdly, some students began RE classes only in secondary school. Fourthly, others opted out upon entering secondary education. Fifthly, the case of those who avowed having studied RE during their entire lives, needs to be clarified, since it would mean that they started attending classes at the age of 1. This contradicts a fact about the Spanish education system: kindergarten does not start until the age of 3 (earlier, the system was different (LOGSE – LOE) compulsory only between the ages of 6 and 16). Bearing in mind this differentiation, the maximum number of years during which students could have studied RE are: 13 in the case of 16 years olds; 12 in the case of 15 years olds; and 11 in the case of 14 year olds. In the case of students who repeated years, or who were over 16 at the time of the survey, this number could be one year more.

Taking this into consideration, we may deduce the following: there is a numerically important group of students who, having received RE classes during primary education, opted (or their parents have) for an alternative subject in secondary. This would correspond to the national average[19], where 78.8% receive RE in primary, 59.5% in secondary, and only 52.7% in pre-university education.

The current debate at the national level over religious education, a debate polarized between extremes, may be affecting student responses with respect to the item about RE as "a source of conflict." The bipolarity of the debate may carry over into students' ambivalence about the "continuity" of religious education in the Spanish system. That is, students may not have regarded RE as a factor of interreligious conflict per se but rather as a fiery and controversial social issue.

Lastly, in reference to religious symbols at school, we underscore that in Spain the controversy continues regarding whether Muslim girls should be allowed to wear headscarves at school. In that regard, we should consider what meanings students could associate with a "discreet" religious symbol and what type they imagine as a "visible" one–given that most surveyed were Catholic or culturally Catholic living in a culturally Catholic context with a growing Muslim minority. In a similar manner, students who are "non believers" may have assimilated religious symbolism because they are immersed in a society with overtly Catholic symbolism. Accordingly, this would help explain why students were for the use of discreet religious symbols but against the use of more visible ones.

2.3 How do students view the impact of religion?

2.3.1 Data description

This section is divided into four parts: first, the role religion plays in helping to understand others, living peacefully together, and contributing to inter-religious dialogue; second, stu-

---

19 Source: Estadística de la Enseñanza en España en niveles no universitarios. Oficina de Estadística del M.E.C. Cursos 2005-2006.

dents' interest in talking about religion and listening to "others"; third, analysis of values such as respect and coexistence; last, how these values can contribute to interaction between groups.

The role of religion in society

Students believed that learning about different religions helps them to learn about their own religion (mean = 2.2). On this point, "believers" (mean = 2.0) agreed, while "non-believers" were closer to ambivalence or disagreement (mean = 2.7). However, considering the mean obtained in the questions (between 2.3–2.4), the differences were not significant and the majority were situated closer to agreement, as seen in Figure 9. Students considered that learning about different religions helps them to understand others and to live peacefully together ("agree") and that it helps them to understand the history of their country and of Europe (mean = 2.3). As a result, they may adopt and modify the view they hold on their "own religion."

Figure 9:   **Outcomes of religious studies, by religious affiliation and RE model. (Means of estimates, scale from 1 – strongly agree to 5 – strongly disagree)**

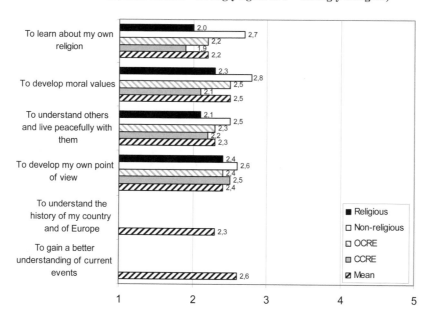

With regard to developing moral values through RE, students agreed (mean = 2.5), although their "agreement" and ambivalence should be clarified. In this case, students with a certain religion more convincingly agreed (mean = 2.3) than others (mean = 2.8). Likewise, the contribution of religion to understanding current events is considered ambiguous: students neither agreed nor disagreed (mean = 2.6).[20]

---

20 In this case, analysis of variance found no significant difference between scores (p>0.05).

However, with respect to religion's impact on and contribution to dialogue and conflict, students held ambivalent opinions towards both positive and negative aspects of religion. The only aspect where they showed agreement (cf. Figure 10)[21] referred to religion as a source of conflict or aggressiveness (mean = 3.8 Sd. = 1.1). Most students disagreed. ANOVA revealed a significant between-groups difference (p<0.001) for this statement, where non-believers were ambivalent (mean = 3.4) while believers (mean = 4.1) were clearly against it.

We address some questionnaire items related to the impact of religion in greater depth. First, students disagreed about whether "without religion the world would be a better place" (mean = 3.5),[22] students who had a religion or a worldview disagreed more strongly (mean = 3.9) than non-believing students (mean = 3.0); an analysis of variance found the difference significant (p<0.001). Second, with respect to "religion is a source of aggressiveness", ANOVA indicated that there was a between-group difference, although most of the respondents tended to disagree: Believing students largely rejected this statement (reaching a mean of 4.1 on the 5-point scale), while non-believers were less certain (mean = 3.4).

Figure 10: Religion in society, by religious affiliation and RE model. (Means of estimates, scale from 1 – about every day to 5 – never)

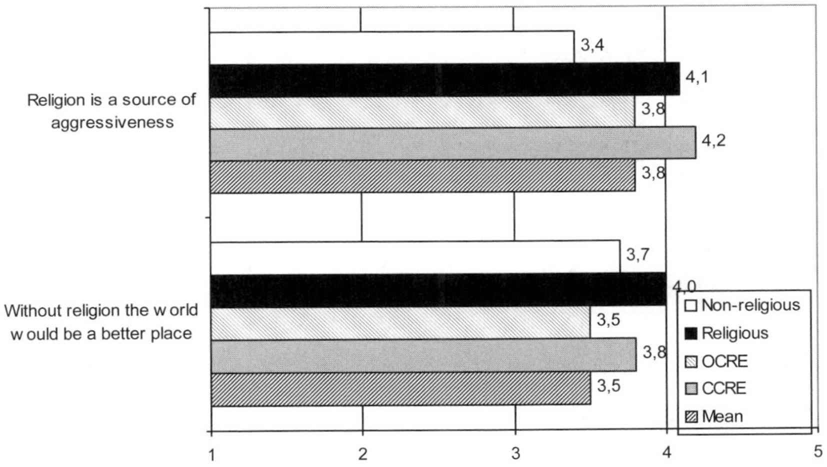

The importance of the peer group

So far we observed that students (more so students who believe) felt that learning about different religions helps them to understand others and live peacefully together. At the same time, however, students were ambivalent about the contribution religion makes to dialogue and conflict. But to what extent are students interested in talking about religion and listening to others? In that regard, the majority surveyed thought that talking about religion was interesting because people have different points of view. This question (mean = 2.4) complements the statement: "In my view, talking about religion is embarrassing", with which they "disagreed" (mean = 3.9 Sd. = 1), revealing that talking about religion was believed interesting rather than embarrassing.

---

21 Means from here on are calculated on a Likert scale: 1 = strongly agree, 2 = agree, 3 = neither agree nor disagree, 4 = disagree, 5 = strongly disagree.

22 An analysis of variance found significant difference between scores for this construct (P<0.001).

Nevertheless, from the remaining questions about the impact of religion we may conclude that some students had no motivation to talk about religion. These items addressed the positive aspects of religion: it helps to understand others (mean = 2.7), to understand the world (mean = 2.9), to live peacefully together (mean = 3.0), to shape [my] own views (mean = 2.7). In all cases, ANOVA showed between-group differences (p<0.001) and, as shown in Figure 11, demonstrated that those who had a certain religion or worldview stood more in agreement with these statements.

Figure 11: Reasons to talk or not to talk about religion, by religious affiliation and RE model. (Means of estimates, scale from 1 – strongly agree to 5 – strongly disagree)

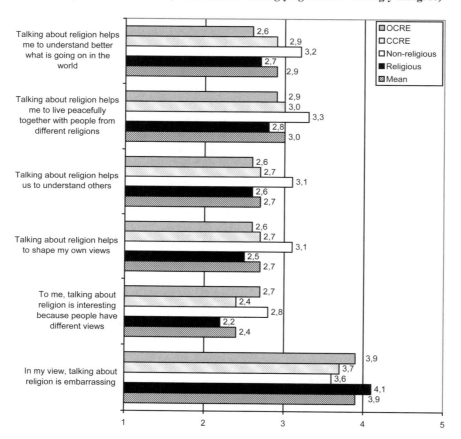

Regarding the possible negative opinions on religion, such as: talking about religion is boring (mean = 3.1), only leads to disagreements (mean = 3.2), or is not an important topic (mean = 3.3), students tended to be ambivalent. As discussed above, ambivalence does not mean that students overlooked the topic, seeing that they more clearly disagreed (mean = 3.5) with the most negative items about religion (religion is stupid, is associated with cruelties in the world).

The intermediate items referring to lack of interest in (mean = 3.1) or a lack of knowledge about (mean = 3.2) religion were answered equally ambivalently (deviation 1.1–1.2) slightly tending towards "I do not agree."

As for "talking about religion is embarrassing", (Figure 12) most students rejected this in a significant way. This was the only question that showed differences between the sexes (Figure 12): females (mean = 4.1) "disagreed" while males (mean = 3.6) were less certain.

**Figure 12:   Talking about religion, gender differences. (Means of estimates, scale from
1 – strongly agree to 5 – strongly disagree)**

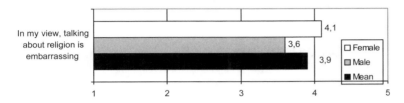

Respect and living together: the need to listen to one another

Integral to religious dialogue is regarding it as interesting, vital, and not embarrassing. This level of interaction would not mean that one's own beliefs are swayed, but would signal a mark of understanding between different religions or points of view. Most students confirmed this (56%), emphasising the need to listen to "others" although it would not necessarily influence their own vision of religion. Only 35% believed that they could discuss different view points and opinions, while 45% believed they could not. Similarly, 39% of students would "ignore" others if they try to proselytise them; however more would "listen" (33%) than would "totally ignore" (28%). Students showed a strong consensus against proselytism, 49% "would never" try to "convince him that he/she is wrong" and 54% "would never" try to "explain that my own opinions about religion are better." In other words, students would agree that everyone has their own religion and that they should practice it privately. Others' opinions are respected, even if ignored; but proselytism would scarcely be accepted as a way to "convert" or change those opinions, only 17% confessed that this would represent "their position exactly."

Living together: people of different worldviews and religions

Observing the openness towards listening to "others", though not towards changing one's perceptions of religion nor changing one's conduct due to persuasion, we investigate how viable students believed the possibility was of living together with those whose points of views differed from their own.

Regarding the possibility of living together with people of different worldviews and religions (cf. Figure 13), we see that students mostly agreed that this is possible if one respects the religions of others (mean = 2.3 Sd. = 1). On the other hand, ANOVA reveals a significant between-group difference (p<0.001), where students with a certain religion more strongly agreed (mean = 2.2) compared to the non-religious (mean = 2.5). At the same time they agreed that irrespective of the religion or worldview of others, they can live together with them (mean = 3.9 – the question assumed denial of the possibility). On this point we add that students "agreed" that disagreement on religious topics creates conflicts (mean = 2.5), but "neither agreed nor disagreed" that if these differences and conflicts were large coexistence would become impossible (mean = 3.3). In these two cases an analysis of variance found no significant difference between the scores of religious and non-religious students ($p>0.05$).

Figure 13: Views about people of different worldviews and religions, by belief and RE model.
(Means of estimates, scale from 1 – strongly agree to 5 – strongly disagree)

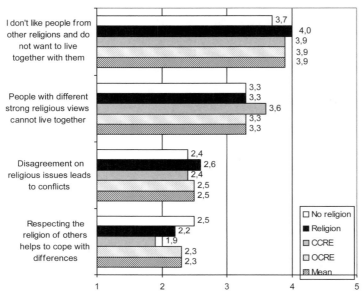

With regard to the possibility of living together with distinct groups or communities, the students thought that the most important value that encourages such interaction and coexistence is knowledge about and relationships with other people. In this case, 34% of students found it "very important" to mingle with "others" and their different view points, so that they may live peacefully together. About 50% considered it "quite important" and only 16% found that interaction and knowledge was not necessary for coexistence. If we combine the positive answers, "very" and "quite important", 84% of students shared this view.

Second, we can infer that sharing "common interests" also helps students to live together in peace, since 30% found it "very important." Although the number of answers at the extremes ("very important") was lower than with respect to "knowledge about others", the intermediate answer ("quite important") was the most valued one among all the available options in this unit, representing 58% of responses (Figure 14), while the negative response was the least popular (13%). If we combine the positive answers "very" and "quite important" 88% of the students would share this stance, showing that 4% of the students (84% vs. 88%) considered this statement to be more significant than "knowledge about others."

The statements: "if they do something together", and "if they know about each other's religions" (Figure 14) were uniformly valued, with a minimal variability to the answers. Specifically, 29% deem it "very important" to get to know the religion of "others" and to do activities together. To these same two statements respectively 52% and 53% found them "quite important" and only 18% and 19% deemed them "not important."

In addition, students believed that if everybody practices their religion only in private, the desirable interaction and coexistence would not be possible. Over 57% considered as negative practising one's own religion only in private, while 43% found the privacy of religion "very or quite important" to living together in peace.

Figure 14: Factors in living together with religious communities from other countries, %

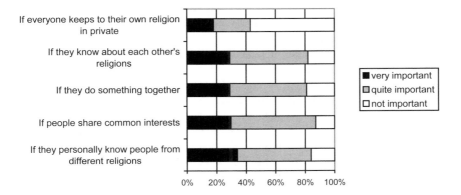

Synopsis of data – impact of religion

To begin, the results indicated that students with a religion or a certain worldview considered that learning about different religions helped them learn about their own religion, understand others, live peacefully together, and adapt their view of their "own religion."

Such a distinction indicates that religion, from the students' point of view, had an intrinsic value for their relationship with "others." This was confirmed by the items about religion "as a source of aggressiveness." While "believing" students strongly denied that religion was a source of aggressiveness, "non-believers" were ambivalent, "neither agreed nor disagreed."

This has to do with the relationships established between students in talking about religion and listening to one another. On this point we note that students who belong to a certain religion thought that talking about religion was interesting and not embarrassing, and in some ways helpful to understanding the world, living in peace, and facing up to their own opinions. Moreover, "believing" students were interested in religion and considered themselves valid spokespersons when expressing opinions of their own religion. However, "non believing" students tended to deny these aspects of religion. As regards listening to others, the majority of students agreed with this statement, but considered that talking to others would not modify their current points of view.

We should add, however, that with respect to conflicts and disagreements, most students, believers and non-believers, believed that disagreement on religious issues leads to conflict, and that where these differences are very large coexistence would be difficult or impossible.

Finally, for these students it was not deemed necessary to know exactly why "others" are different or diverse, because it was more important to have "common interests." Likewise, they considered it unnecessary to share or know about the religion of "others" or to carry out common activities in order to peacefully coexist.

2.3.2 Data interpretation

As a starting point, we address student opinions on the intrinsic value of religion and the role it plays in society. As noted above, believing students responded more decidedly in favour of the positive virtues of religion than against its negative aspects. From our point of view, the questions on the negative aspects of religion carry a negative, subjective connotation when experienced by a student who claims to be a "believer." In regard to the negative aspects of religion in a local, regional, national or international context (involving many cultural and ethno-religious problems), students may not have associated these with religion in-itself but with the religion (or lack of religion) of certain others. In the case of atheists and agnostics, the problems caused by religion would include those they associate with Catholics and (perhaps to a greater extent) with Muslims.

On this point we suggest a common component exists, that those who believe in religion itself incorporate other viewpoints but these viewpoints are denied by those from non-religious perspectives. In other words we would ask: Who would more firmly affirm that religion is positive, integrating, and not a source of aggressiveness? Without a doubt, it would be those students who recognised their own beliefs and were "tolerant" of others' beliefs.

This perspective on tolerance and respect for diverse opinions represents a starting point for a process of inclusion. However, even though both groups reveal this tendency, students who belong to a religion appear to be more tolerant in this regard.

Finally, in relation to the possibility of living together with diverse groups or communities, we point out that the process of constructing an identity requires the existence of "others"– different religions, perceptions of the world, even those who do not believe in anything – in order to construct "one's own" differentiated identity.

3   Comparison with the results of the qualitative survey

The qualitative (cf. Dietz et. al. 2007) and quantitative questionnaires, carried out within the framework of the REDCO project in secondary education centres, show many similarities in the samples: both were carried out in three regions (Granada, Murcia and Melilla). Likewise, different schools were selected with an eye to widening the diversity of the sample and its comparative significance. Both also kept in mind the regional and neighbourhood economic contexts. Lastly, the representation of one Catholic confessional school in Granada was retained.

With regard to data analysis, the qualitative and the quantitative reports complemented each other, given that we did not observe any deviation in the quantitative data sufficient enough to contradict our previous analysis of the qualitative study. However, for a deeper exploration of these similarities or differences, we address three topics: what role religion plays in students' lives and surroundings (cf. 3.1), how students view religion in school (cf. 3.2), and how students view the impact of religion (cf. 3.3).

3.1   What role does religion play in students' lives and surroundings?

A variety of understandings: the importance of "Religion" and "God"

As we observed in the quantitative analysis, a significant number of students consider the role religion plays in their lives as important or very important. Similarly, in the qualitative study, when asked about the relevance of religion in their lives, a majority of interviewees firmly believed in God and act accordingly. This group of "firm believers", analysed in both parts of the research, emphasise that God and religion were "always" or "nearly always" relevant to them, because "without them and divine creation 'the world' would not make any sense." Apart from a group that answered in "neutral" terms, a large majority automatically and immediately associated "religion" with their own confession.

Daily praxis

Likewise, in both cases, perceptions and attitudes towards religion were complemented by daily praxis: by the act of praying or thinking about religion. Even though the role of religion was considered important in their lives, for the majority their daily practice did not directly correlate to the type of belief they manifest. In both types of analysis we confirmed that for those who considered themselves believers practice was greater than for the two other groups: students that confess believing occasionally by following only certain religious rites (respondents mostly referred to specific and critical situations of illness, death and solitude), and the majority of non- believers, agnostics or atheists, who emphasised that believers act out of mere "despair."

The students' personal connection with religion

In the qualitative analysis, family was regarded by students as the main "source" of personal connection to religion and to their own faith. Schools, and more so religious communities, were considered secondary. Even though this point could not be quantified, we suggest that, in most cases, the faith of those students who identified themselves as "believers", and for whom religion or God were important, religion was originally passed on within their respective families. Likewise, the quantitative survey suggested that family was not only a source of personal connection with religion, but also considered a priority "source of information."

This discussion must not overlook the fact that students affirmed in the qualitative study that religion had been part of their lives since birth, like something innate or inherent to their family and the context in which they lived. There they learned how to pray, to attend religious services, and to participate in their religious community.

In the wake of such statements, we ascertain the role played by families for students who claimed to be non believers. We based this analysis on mothers because the qualitative analysis revealed that more reference was made to them by students when speaking about their religion. Paradoxically, observation of the data obtained in the quantitative analysis reveals that the majority of "believing" students, 86% of the total, knew what religion their mother belongs to, regardless of whether the mothers were believers or non believers. Conversely, 47% of "non believing" students did not know their mothers' religious preferences. To this point we add the percentage of "non believing" students who claimed that their mothers were also "non believers." Likewise, a notable 78% of "believing" students claimed that their mothers were also "believers", while only 11% of "non believing" students claim that their mothers are "believers."

In relation to other sources of information, in the qualitative analysis we observed how an important number of students made reference to Catechism or Koran classes, an idea further developed in the quantitative analysis. On the other hand, in both types of analyses, other sources of information, such as friends, religious community, books, and media, were deemed less important sources of information about religion.

3.2 How students view religion in school

Student experiences in RE classes

In the quantitative analysis of this point we observed that for the majority of students RE classes help them to understand others, live together, and learn about different religions. This forms part of what is desirable in RE classes, however it does not specifically correspond to the national model where RE classes, as we previously mentioned, mostly focus on the religion itself as the only alternative (Catholic religion). This was seen more clearly in the qualitative analysis in relation to the contents that should be provided in RE classes. While a large number of the interviewees demanded further information and deeper knowledge about their own and other religious traditions, many, consciously or not, still clung to a confessional, nearly catechism-like notion of religious education. We can therefore appreciate the different aims underlying this kind of RE: The qualitative study observed that some pupils, both Catholics and Muslims, asked for content about other religions in order to strengthen their own belief (cf. Dietz, 2007, p. 29) and to contrast those beliefs with those of others.

Preferred models of religious education: between integration and separation?

As observed throughout the quantitative analysis, on average students surveyed considered the present education system, optional RE classes, to be the most appropriate. This was confirmed in the qualitative analysis, where most interviewees were in favour of maintaining or reintroducing (at secondary level) religion as a subject at school, as opposed to a strong minority of students, who strictly opposed any religious education at school. Likewise, in both analyses students considered it necessary to obtain an objective knowledge of world religions. They felt a need for knowledge about "religions in general" and about "other people's religions and customs." Another RE option suggested by a minority in both analyses was: that religious knowledge should be shared by all students, independent of their beliefs. However, this broadly positive view of religious education was at odds with a strong minority who strictly opposed any religious education at school.

3.3 How students view the impact of religion

The role of religion throughout society

In both analyses we also observed that "living together", coexistence, and cross-confessional learning from each other were highly valued among the young people interviewed. However, the qualitative analysis showed that attitudes towards religion in society and religious education still reflect old, historical divisions, fears, and phobias originally formulated by the generation of the interviewees' grandparents. Today, this may still prevent young people from "daring" to engage in new experiments in inter-religious encounters. Both believers and non-believers shared an essentialist notion of religion, which they tended equate to culture, language and even nationality – an essentialism which avoids and abhors "mixing up" or "blurring" boundaries or hybridising religious practices or identities.

Likewise, in both analyses, students agreed that the possibility of living together with people of different worldviews and religions was possible. However, they did not agree on the reasons why coexistence and pluralism were possible or desirable. This question divided interviewees into two clear groups, cutting across confessional lines: on the one hand, a large majority agreed that coexistence is possible, that it exists, and that it is desirable; on the other hand, a still important minority, insisted on the impossibility of the peaceful coexistence of people from different religious backgrounds.

The importance of the peer group

We noted from the quantitative survey that talking about religion was interesting for the majority of students and that they did not find it embarrassing. This was confirmed by the qualitative analysis, where very few students admitted feeling *"ashamed"* or *"awkward"* when talking about *"such issues"* with their friends. However, it must be noted that in both parts of the research students expressed that they were not particularly motivated to talk about religion with peers. This aspect was also confirmed in the qualitative analysis, where most of the interviewed (61%) stated that they do not talk about religion in their respective peer groups at all.

4.   Conclusions

In this part of the report we address the main conclusions we can draw from the above results, taking the overall research questions (chapter 4.1) and hypotheses (chapter 4.2), respectively, as starting points[23].

4.1   Research questions

4.1.1   What is the role of religions in students' lives and surroundings?

From our point of view, approaching the daily practice of students with respect to dialogue (cf. 2.1), presupposes a state of equality (of rights, of responsibilities), at present qualified in Spain, seeing that not all students belonging to religious minorities (Muslims, Jews, Evangelicals, Protestants, etc.) can access their religion at school, regardless of the education model being implemented.[24] It likewise presupposes "the renouncement on the part of the interlocutors of any unilateral 'universalist'" temptation–not to say "imposing" posture (Muñoz, 2008, p. 40) – something that ought to be worked on, seeing that it still has not been effectively put into practice.

All this leads us to pose some questions: How do different religions, worldviews, and/or non-beliefs help us understand and dialogue with our neighbour within the context of religious education? It should be kept in mind that the ultimate purpose is not to eliminate difference, but rather to generate relations of mutual trust with respect to these "differences." Likewise we should consider: to what extent does the role of religion in students' lives help generate mutual interaction in contexts of socio-cultural diversity?

In response to "How important is religion to you?" the majority of students tended to hold ambivalent views. Intimately connected with this, they also deemed that family environment played a more important role in transmitting religious values than either school or their peer groups. Does this mean that religion is "neither important nor not important" in the daily lives of Spanish students? From our point of view, keeping in mind the socio-cultural context,

---

23 As the sample is not representative and no additional data collection or analysis has been carried out to further test the hypotheses, it is important to emphasize that we can only describe tendencies.

24 In this case, the process of approaching the "other", towards social and cultural diversity, does not occur in the religious education class, but rather in other classes, where students are not separated by faith (Cf. Dietz, 2007).

where religious diversity remains inchoate and minority religions still lack equal status, religion continues to be very important to students of faith, and may become an inclusive, or non-excluding, aspect of student life in the near future. To that end, schools should adopt a decisive role that could, independently of family tradition, present religious diversity in an objective way.

At this point, (universal) moral values, like tolerance, coexistence, listening to others, etc., can have an influence on the lives of students, and form part of their daily work. This means that although "religion/religiosity" initially develops in the private sphere of the family environment, once it enters the public realm it requires dialogue and interaction with the religious diversity of one's surroundings, even where, as we noted, this diversity remains inchoate.

4.1.2   How do students see religion in school?

Together the recent migratory process in Spain, which brought a clear trend towards religious diversity, and the incorporation of different religious education models (as is the case with incorporating classes of Islamic RE) opened a new range of possibilities and responses to how students view religious education in their schools. We emphasize that the majority of those between 14 and 16 years old, have not known or been able to opt for any religious instruction/education other than Catholicism. Likewise, they have not known until recently any educational model other than that traditionally implemented.[25] In this context, it stands to reason that most of these students associate religion and religious education classes with their own faith, and from this point of view, consider that the most appropriate model is the one currently being carried out: confessionally separated religious education activity.

Nonetheless, examining the responses obtained within the framework of the project, it is interesting to note that most students considered that learning about religion helps to understand others, live peacefully together, and better understand the history of their country. This suggests that the harmony and coexistence sought by multicultural societies (through dialogue, respect, and tolerance) contrasts with the values of the very religions whose disagreements these societies seek to overcome. In this case there is little real coexistence and interaction with the "other", seeing that religion class are segregated by faith.

On the one hand, students affirmed that religious education classes help them talk about religious issues and view them from different perspectives. Likewise, the majority of believing students consider it important to learn about other religions, which does not imply any type of conflict within the classroom. On the other hand, they were ambivalent regarding the type of knowledge about religions of the "other" presented in their RE classes.

4.1.3   How do students see the impact of religion?

We observed that students who reported having a certain religion, believed that religious education promotes dialogue between individuals (cf. 2.3). Those moral values help one comprehend what is happening in the world, to live peacefully, to understand the other, to modify one's point of view, as well as to get to know the "other" through his or her beliefs and practices. That being said, students' religiosity was significantly affected by the values transmitted from school, the family, and religion class, seeing that students who had a religion were closer to inclusivist rather than exclusivist towards the "other."

---

25 Ethics, "society culture, religion", education for citizenship, religious facts, etc., have been the only non-confessional alternatives.

Nevertheless, other "values", ones contrary to dialogue, also appeared in students' responses. In that respect, a great majority agreed that without dialogue between students of distinct religious points of view, religion would not be able to bridge their differences. This lead us to ask: to what point can groups coexist in a context of religious diversity without a recognition and understanding of that diversity throughout education?

In this regard, students' responses would qualify the need to get to know the "other" and the approach to religious dialogue, given that common interests, in themselves, already imply "coexistence." In particular, for a large number of students it was not necessary to know the religious adscription of the other in order to "coexist" with him or her. Consequently, the last resort, beyond religious affiliation, could lie in unifying common interests. However, in the absence of these unifying factors, ignorance of the other's religion would indeed become a factor of conflict rather than dialogue.

4.2   Research hypothesis

Religious students are less tolerant than non-religious students

Hypothesis 1a) Religious students are less tolerant than non-religious students. Looking at the questions on "tolerance" of students, we note a tendency to agree more with the positive aspects of religion (helps to cope with differences, respect others, living together, make the world a better place to live, etc.) than with its negative aspects (aggressiveness, conflict, intransigence, etc.) Nonetheless, that tendency is clearer in the case of students who ascribed to a religion.

Moreover, students who have a certain religion positioned themselves more against the negative aspects of religion and more "in favour" of its positive aspects than non-believers did. However, the degree of openness towards religion has to be qualified since students held ambivalent positions. This is the case with the statement "disagreement on religious issues leads to conflicts", towards which both groups expressed ambivalence.

Likewise, the degree of tolerance of the students did not show any extremes. In other words, the responses "totally agree" and "totally disagree" were avoided by the majority, independent of their religious belief or worldview. In this sense, the trend was towards ambiguous responses, especially in relation to negative aspects such as: "people with different strong religious views cannot live together", and "disagreement on religious issues leads to conflicts."

Religious students are less open to dialogue on religious issues than non-religious students

The 2a) hypothesis directly reflects upon dialogue, or rather, on what type of student is inclined towards interreligious, interethnic dialogue. Looking at the items over religious dialogue (or those that could be cause for conflict) we saw more of an inclination towards dialogue than towards conflict, even though the responses tended to be ambivalent. In other words, the negative aspects of dialogue between peer groups (stupid, embarrassing, cruel, unimportant, confusion, boring, etc.) were deemed doubtful, though closer to "neither agree nor disagree." Regarding the positive aspects of interreligious dialogue (helps to know the other, to know oneself, to communicate over different religious issues, to get to know friends, to comprehend what happens in the world, and to live in peace), students tended to be ambivalent, "neither agree nor disagree."

The opinions noted above vary greatly by faith. In this case, responses of believing students were closer to affirming the positive aspects of dialogue over religious issues, and further from acknowledging its negative aspects. Nevertheless, students who did not have a religion, tended to respond ambivalently to all the items regarding dialogue, whether positive or negative.

Students who have encountered religious diversity in education are more tolerant

Hypothesis 3a) purports to consider the necessity of the "other" when it comes to identity construction in contexts of religious diversity in the classroom and in school. It presupposes that students who have encountered religious diversity in the educational system are more tolerant than those who have not. Looking at the sample analysed above (cf. 1.2.3. Religious education model) we must focus our conclusions on the basis of a comparison between the OCRE and CCRE centres. We clarify *a priori*, that it would be difficult to deny or affirm any judgment about "tolerance", considering that religious diversity in the classroom is yet inchoate in Spain, and that there is little knowledge of the "other" offered by the education system. Likewise, we should not forget that the religious education offered in secondary education pertains only to the Catholic option.

In this vein, we assume from the outset that religious diversity in schools should help create interreligious relationships with students of different points of view, outside as well as within the school context. All the same, in both CCRE and in OCRE, the response to the question "I don't like people from other religions and do not want to live together with them" does not indicate any significant differences; all students, whether self-described believers or non-believers, tended to respond negatively.

However, respect and coexistence (adjacent aspects of the category "tolerance") do indeed substantially depend on valorisation of the religion of the other. That is to say, students "agreed" that disagreement on religious questions can create conflict, and that if these differences are very large coexistence may be impossible or improbable. This differentiation can be observed between the CCRE's and the OCRE's: The assertion "in respect we can coexist" was more conclusive for the confessional schools than for the OCRE's. Likewise, the OCRE's reaffirmed their stance against coexistence due to the negative aspects of the religion of the "other" (conflict, strong religious views).

This aspect of conflict, as earlier commented, is perceived through the lens of one's own religion. In other words, under this criterion students did not regard "their" religion as a source of conflict, rather that it respected other opinions and worldviews, and they did not see any "rigidness" in it that could create conflict or impede coexistence. Nevertheless, the non-religious (to a certain degree those sceptical of religion and, by especially, the non-believers, agnostics, and atheists), tended to deny the "goodness" of religion. They did so head-on, appearing exclusive in their thought, that is, shutting out the views of the believing "other."

Students who have encountered religious diversity in education are more open to dialogue on religious issues

As for Hypothesis 2b) we stress again that in the national context, encounters with religious diversity occur outside of religious education classes and that the option of dialogue or conflict is limited solely to the needs and choices of individuals in their external environment or during other classes.

In this regard, the differences between CCRE and OCRE, with respect to dialogue on religious issues, were not significant. However, CCRE's tended to deny the "negative" facets of religious dialogue: They denied more categorically that religion may be embarrassing, cruel, controversial, or uninteresting.

The positive aspects of dialogue on religious issues were affirmed more decisively by CCRE students than by those of OCRE's. On this point, however, we highlight that the intermediate questions, in reference to ignorance of and/or lack of interest in the religion of the "other", were answered with equal ambivalence by students of both types of schools, although they inclined towards "do not agree." This was more significant in the CCRE's, with a larger religious charge, than in the public schools. Similarly, the statement "religion is stupid and is related to the cruelties that occur in the world", was denied more resolutely in the CCRE's.

Another point on which we give pause bears on listening to the "other", seeing that "dialogue" implies a reciprocal process in which both parties participate. In this case, more than half the students (cf. 2.3.3) insisted on the necessity to listen to the "other", although this would not mean listening would affect their religious (or non-religious) points of view due to the influence of the "other." Moreover, only a third believed that they could discuss different points of view and opinions. And likewise, a third would ignore divergent points of view, although more would tend to listen to rather than "totally ignore" the "other." Does this mean that the value of "dialogue" is limited? As we commented, it remains difficult to determine to what extent students who have encountered religious diversity in education are more open to dialogue on religious issues.

Regarding the differences between CCRE's and OCRE's, we can note that CCRE students were scarcely aware of the religion of the other, but would indeed discuss with him or her, to reaffirm their own beliefs and without intent to proselytize, neither would they accept the religion of the "other" as a way of life.

Are students who have personally encountered religious diversity more tolerant or open to dialogue on religious issues?[26]

Hypotheses 3a) and 3b) are from the outset difficult to test because the questionnaire did not explicitly reference students' personal connection with the religious diversity of their environment. In any case, their preferences were analysed in relation to interacting with other students, both of their own and other religions and points of view. However, it would be equally inaccurate and unsound to assume that students of one or the other school have more or less contact with religious diversity in their surroundings. We focus, therefore, on student responses according to type of school attended, given that in the CCRE's there was no diversity of instruction since everyone attends the same Catholic religion classes, while in the other schools, students had other educational options (confessional or non-confessional).

In the case of the CCRE schools, a larger number of students did not know the religion of their classmates (21.1% vs. 13.9% in OCRE), an interesting detail, since it is supposed that the only religious option offered is Catholicism and the majority of the students would have to be Catholics. This is no longer certain, since the "concertado" schools now have a larger number of pupils who attend because they consider the education offered there better than in public schools, and because students who can pay for this type of education belong to social classes with better economic resources. Therefore, the variable of religion does not have to be associated directly with choice of school. In fact, 72% of the OCRE students do not have any classmates who belong to different religions, in comparison to only 66% of "concertado"

---

26 The two hypothesis cannot be analysed separately since they carry political and social connotations (discussed throughout the article) that intermingle the issues.

students. Nonetheless, it is very significant that OCRE students affirmed (69%) that they had friends of different religions, in contrast to only 25% of the CCRE students. From this point of view, we could deduce a larger tendency towards dialogue in OCRE's, based on friends outside of school, although, peculiarly, this does not mean that OCRE students are more "tolerant" towards their peers in school.

References

Bericat, E. (2008). El escepticismo religioso y secular en Europa, in: E. Bericat (Ed.), *El fenómeno religioso: Presencia de la religión y de la religiosidad en las sociedades avanzadas.* Sevilla: Centro de Estudios Andaluces – Consejería de la Presidencia – Junta de Andalucía, pp. 41–56.

Cortina, A. (2006). *Educar para una ciudadanía activa.* El País, December 30, 2006. Available online at: http://www.elpais.com/articulo/opinion/Educar/ciudadania/activa/elpepiopi/20061230elpepiopi _12/Tes (first accesed 25 November 2008).

CREM [Centro Regional de Estadística de Murcia] (2007). *Padrón Municipal de Habitantes.* Murcia: Consejería de Fomento y Trabajo.

Dietz, G. (2007). Invisibilizing or Ethnicizing Religious Diversity? The Transition of Religious Education Towards Pluralism in Contemporary Spain, in: R. Jackson, S. Miedema, W. Weisse & J.-P. Willaime (Eds.), *Religion and Education in Europe: developments, contents and debates.* Muenster: Waxmann, pp. 103–131.

Dietz, G., Rosón, J. & Ruiz, F. (2007). Religion and Education in the View of Spanish Youth: the legacy of mono-confessionalism in times of religious pluralisation, in: T. Knauth, G. Bertram-Troost, J. Ipgrave, D.P. Jozsa (Eds.). *Encountering Religious Pluralism in School and Society: a qualitative study of teenage perspectives in Europe.* Muenster:Waxmann, pp. 21–49.

Elzo, J. (2008). La evolución socio-religiosa en España en los últimos 30 años: una aproximación empírica, in: E. Bericat (Ed.), *El fenómeno religioso: Presencia de la religión y de la religiosidad en las sociedades avanzadas.* Sevilla: Centro de Estudios Andaluces – Consejería de la Presidencia – Junta de Andalucía, pp. 79–96.

NE [Instituto Nacional de Estadística] (2007). Madrid: INE.

Moreras, J. (2005). La situation de l'enseignement musulman en Espagne, in: J.-P. Willaime (Ed.). *Des Maîtres et des Dieux: écoles et religions en Europe,* pp. 165–179.

Muñoz, J. (2008) ¿Diálogo o conflicto entre civilizaciones? *Claves de razón práctica,* Vol. 179, 38–41.

Rosón, J. (2008) Etnificación de la diversidad religiosa en el barrio del Albayzín, in: M. Cantón, M. Cornejo & R. Llera (Eds.), *Teorías y prácticas emergentes en antropología de la religión,* Vol. 10. Donostia, XI Congreso de Antropologia, pp. 223–237.

Céline Béraud

The French Viewpoint on the Spanish Report

At the beginning of the REDCo project, Spain and France found themselves associated with each other. It is true that they are both countries that have traditionally had Catholic majorities. Moreover, in each country militant secular groups are increasingly contesting this Catholic hegemony (Proeschel, 2005), particularly in the area of education. These two characteristics unquestionably distinguish France and Spain from the other countries participating in the REDCo research programme. And yet, the comparison undertaken between the results of the qualitative surveys from each country puts this proximity into perspective, at least concerning adolescents, school and religion. We have therefore chosen to speak of "distant cousins" (Álvarez Veinguer & Béraud, 2008). The quantitative survey makes it possible to refine this comparison. But before presenting the main points the two contexts have in common, as well as their differences, I shall point out the most compelling results of the Spanish report; I shall then suggest some possible alternative interpretations of some of the data, not only from a French point of view but also from a sociological one.

Most striking, interesting or unexpected points

Among the many interesting analyses developed in the Spanish report, I would like to take a closer look at three points that seem to be the most noteworthy.

The survey carried out in the three *Autonomous Communities* of Andalusia, Murcia and Melilla confirms the overall Spanish trend toward a decline in religious affiliation, which is most clearly seen in younger generations. Slightly less than two out of three students surveyed say that they have a religion. By comparison, in 2002 more than 80% of Spanish adults in a nationwide survey identified with a religion. This figure, which is still high, is nevertheless indicative of a decline in religious affiliation, which has been observable since the 1970s (Pérez-Agote & Santiago, 2005). The results that our Spanish colleagues have obtained are all the more remarkable given that their research was carried out in quite possibly the most religious regions of the country (particularly if we compare them to other regions where religion is less important, most notably Catalonia). The Southern part of Spain "not only presents more Catholic attributes, but also has a high concentration of Muslim believers" (Olivera & Busser, 2005, p. 83).

Another reason the Spanish case is especially interesting is that it is an example of a country that has only recently had to deal with religious diversity, much later than in other European countries (France, but also Britain, the Netherlands or Germany). This diversity that Spain is experiencing is due to the arrival during the last two decades of immigrant populations, mainly North African Muslims and evangelical Protestants from Latin America. The presence of foreigners on Spanish territory has grown in a relatively short period of time, as census figures show There are six times as many of them as there were nine years ago; as of 2008 they officially make up slightly more than 11% of the total population. We should recall that until 1975 Spain was the opposite: a land of emigrants. From this perspective, the enclave of Melilla in North Africa is an exception. For the Spanish authorities, it has often appeared historically as a laboratory for handling religious diversity.

Unlike older generations, the adolescents surveyed have had to accept this diversity since they were children. In such a context, they seem to have developed an ambivalent attitude, as the report clearly shows. On the one hand, in the answers given by the students, we see a genuine acculturation to the values of respect, tolerance and living together in community. On the other hand, they still seem to be attached to an essentialist vision of religion, associating it with language and culture, and even with the nation as a whole.

The fact that Spain has a model of religious education which is confessional (mainly Catholic) does not keep those students surveyed from feeling that they learn things in school about all religions, and that this furthers the ideals of community life. The authors of the report insist upon the interconnected nature of this instruction, and therefore on the contributions that other school subjects make in this area.

2.   Different ideas and interpretations

Now, I will present two possible alternative ideas: the first one deals with a minor and technical point, the second one is more fundamental.

The term "worldview" does not seem to have any meaning to the Spanish adolescents surveyed (if the researchers did not give them an example, the adolescents could not say what it means; if they were given examples, they only repeated those given), any more than it has to French adolescents. In both countries, unlike some countries in Northern Europe, the network of associations promoting a non-religious vision of man and the world is limited, and does not benefit from a great deal of social recognition. To avoid any confusion, we chose not to translate this word in the French questionnaire. The Spanish team could have adopted a similar strategy.

In the Spanish report, the adolescents who acknowledged having some kind of religious affiliation are identified as "believers". Conversely, those that did not acknowledge such an affiliation were called "non-believers". Establishing a strict correspondence between acknowledging affiliation with a religion and belief proves itself to be problematic.

The British sociologist Grace Davie (1994) has highlighted the importance of the phenomenon of "believing without belonging" as a tendency that is characteristic of modern societies. The decline of religious institutions (with which people no longer acknowledge some kind of affiliation) does not mean the end of religious belief. This is one of the results of the research undertaken in sociology on the current status of religion (see in particular Léger, 1999; Lambert, 2003). For example, a large percentage of people who say they have no religion nevertheless say that they believe. Incidentally, the Spanish report reveals that among the adolescents surveyed who said they had no religion, 22% of them believe in God, and 38% of them believe in a spirit or a life force. Therefore, we cannot say that the majority of them are non-believers. We should add that more than a third of this same group says that they pray at least occasionally. And when asked about this phenomenon, many of the Spanish students surveyed agree with the following statement: "One may be a religious person without belonging to a particular community of faith."

Main differences and commonalities between the Spanish and French contexts

In this last part, I will focus on the main differences and commonalities between the two contexts, concerning religion in the students' life, how they see the role of religion in school and how they consider the social impact of religion.

Despite the tendency toward indifference to religion mentioned above, the percentage of young Spaniards surveyed who said they have a religion was higher than the percentage among the young French. Only half of French students said they have a religion, versus slightly less than two-thirds of the students in the three Spanish *Autonomous Communities* studied. If we categorise these students by their religion (for those who stated a religious affiliation), the importance of Catholicism remains higher among Spanish adolescents than among French ones: 75% say they are Catholic in the Spanish survey (excepting the North African enclave of Melilla), versus only 40% in the French survey (we should add that 25% say they are Christian without specifying which denomination).

The indicators of religious inclinations (belief in God; level of importance given to religion by young people; how often they think about religion, pray, attend a religious ceremony, etc.) are higher in general in the Spanish context than the French one.

The majority of adolescents surveyed have faith in their national model of education on religious matters. For French students, this means impartial instruction presented to all students through existing subjects (History in particular); for Spanish students, it means instruction where students are segregated along religious lines. Despite the great difference in character between the two models, some convergences between the two contexts become apparent.

In both countries, a minority of students declare themselves hostile toward giving religion any role in school.

In Spain, students lose interest in the course on religious education as their schooling progresses: the percentage still taking it in high school is much lower than it is in elementary school. A similar but more manifest tendency can be observed in the Alsace region of France and in the Moselle *département*, which have the same sort of system as Spain.

Spanish adolescents are in favour of letting students wear discreet religious signs on school grounds, but are against the wearing of more visible signs. They have thus adopted a point of view in accordance with the French law of March 2004, which incidentally most French students surveyed seem to endorse as well.

The acquisition of objective knowledge of different religions is an important priority for the adolescents surveyed in both countries. In both cases then, there is the same attachment to a knowledge-oriented type of approach.

Finally, in both countries, the overwhelming majority of the young people surveyed insist upon the importance of respect, and knowledge of other people's religions, so that everyone can learn to get along with each other. It is probably one of the most unexpected results in the REDCo research. Tolerance is a value shared by European youngsters, whatever their national model of education on religious matters.

References

Álvarez Veinguer A. & Béraud C. (2008). Religion and Education in the French and Spanish context: Distant cousins, in: T. Knauth, D.-P. Jozsa, G. Bertram-Troost, J. Ipgrave (Eds.), *Encountering Religious Pluralism in School and Society. A Quantitative Study of Teenage Perspectives in Europe* Münster: Waxmann, pp. 357–368.

Davie G. (1994). *Religion in Britain since 1945. Believing without belonging.* Oxford: Blackwell Publishing, "Institute of Contemporary British History".

Hervieu-Léger D. (1999). *Le pèlerin et le converti. La religion en mouvement.* Paris, Flammarion.

Lambert Y. (2003). Religion: développement du hors-piste et de la randonnée", in: P. Bréchon (Ed.), *Les valeurs des Français.* Paris, Armand Colin.

Olivera A. & Busser C. de (2005). Spain. Challenging centuries of Roman Catholic dominance, in: H. Knippenberg (Ed.), *The Changing Religious Landscape of Europe,* Amsterdam, Het Spinhuis, pp. 75-87.

Pérez-Agote, A. & Santiago, J.A. (2005). *La situación de la religión en España a principios del siglo XXI.* Madrid, Centro de Investigaciones Sociológicas.

Proeschel, C. (2005). *L'idée de laïcité en France et en Espagne.* Paris, L'Harmattan.

Vladimir Fedorov

The Findings of the REDCo Project in Spain as Read by a Russian Researcher

Reading data of research carried out in a country through the eyes of a foreign researcher engaged in the same problem contributes greatly to understanding of one's own data. It is still more interesting when the reader is Russian, and data of the REDCo project he deals with are Spanish: lying at the opposite poles of Europe, Spain in the south-west and the St Petersburg region of Russia in the north-east are geographically distant. Likewise different are the history and confessional cultures of the two countries. Still, there are some features that make their religious situations seem akin, viz. the coexistence of a prevailing confession (Catholicism in Spain and Orthodoxy in Russia) and, though limited in number, but a wide spectrum of, other Christian confessions, and also non-Christian religions, Islam in particular.

Owing to stereotypes from the world history and history of culture as taught at Russian schools, Russians tend to think of the confessional situation in Spain as strictly Catholic, so the findings of the Spanish survey are doubly valuable and instructive. Noteworthy is that the authors observe that religious education is a "controversial topic" in contemporary Spain. These same words can be said about contemporary Russia, which is in the latter case quite natural because of the seventy years gap in RE practice.

The main thesis of this brief review is that despite all the cultural, historical, political and confessional distinctions between the two countries, the conclusions from the quantitative and qualitative data analyses in the two countries engaged in the REDCo project are very much alike. At least, the tendencies are the same and at first sight, this impression may seem surprising.

The role of religion in pupils' life

A Russian did not expect to discover that there were only 64.6% of the students in Spain who ascribed themselves to a religion. In Russia, 44 % of the students declared having a certain religion or worldview; 46 % of respondents said definitely "There is a God". This is the first distinction between Russia and Spain. The proportion of Russians who deny the existence of any sort of God, spirit or life-force is 14 %. The Spanish data on the confessional spectrum of the respondents is close to the Russian picture. In the case of Granada and Murcia, we observe that 76% of the students who practised a religion were Catholic, compared to 2% Muslim, 2% Protestant and 14% who did not specify their confession. In Russia, Christians made up 85 % and Muslims 4 % among respondents who wished to declare their affiliation.

The Spanish results indicate that a large percentage of students consider religion to be important or very important in their lives. However, a considerable number held ambivalent views on religion, seeing both its positive and negative aspects. The same picture can be seen in Russia. Regarding the personal importance of religion, St Petersburg students' positions were as follows: slightly more that 1/3 of them (37%) chose the middle position in between 'absolutely not important' and 'very important'. 15% evaluated religion being absolutely not important for them, and the percentage of those to whom religion is very important was also 15%. As to students' practices in relation to religion, the situations in Spain and Russia are similar. In Spain 32% of students claiming to be believers prayed "about every day", 15%

"about every week", 10% "once a month", 17% "less than once a month", and 26% "never" prayed. In St Petersburg, less than 10% of the students attend religious events once a month or more often. More than a half claimed to pray at least once a month. In Spain 60% of the students surveyed thought about religion at least once a week. We see a somewhat larger degree of religiousness as manifested by the Spain sample, but this corresponds with a larger number of Spanish believers.

The role of religion in Spanish students' lives related mostly to family and cultural traditions in their environment. Their answers to the corresponding question showed that their family was the "most important source of religious information." Just the same, the family is the main agent of initiation into religion for St. Petersburg students. The Spanish survey demonstrated that students considered talking about religion as a private matter that normally does not occur in the public arena. Neither is talking about religion with peers characteristic of the Russian sample. More than a half of students state that they never speak about religion with their friends and classmates.

Role of religion at school

As to students' attitudes towards presence of religion in school, it is possible to affirm that both Spanish and Russian students seemed to view religious topics in schools as positive; a large majority agreed that learning about different religions helps them to live with and respect others. It should be kept in mind, however, that the experience of young Spaniards strongly differs from that of the Russians who can only have religious education in a very few confessional schools, and for the majority of Russian students, models of religious education are something too abstract to talk about. But as it turned out, the majority of Spanish respondents did not know or were unable to opt for any religious education other than Catholicism. In this context, it stands to reason that most of these students consider that the most appropriate model of religious education is the one currently being carried out: confessionally separated religious education. Noteworthy is that the qualitative study showed that there were pupils, both Catholics and Muslims, whose curiosity about other religions aimed at strengthening their own belief (Dietz, 2007) and helping them to advantageously contrast those beliefs with the belief of others.

How do students see the impact of religion? The contribution of religion to dialogue or conflict

The Spanish students who reported having a specific religion, believed that religious education promotes dialogue between individuals. The students who had a religion were closer to inclusivist rather than exclusivist attitudes towards the "other." These students' responses would qualify the need to get to know the "other" and the approach to religious dialogue, given that common interests, in themselves, already imply "coexistence." The Spanish survey showed that ignorance of the other's religion would indeed become a factor of conflict rather than dialogue.

When facing religious proselytism, St. Petersburg students would rather choose to ignore it than to debate about religious issues or to impose their own belief. This non-aggressive behavioural pattern corresponds to their vision of the ways toward the peaceful coexistence of people with different religious backgrounds. The way to live together in peace was associated by St Petersburg respondents much more with sharing common views and common activities than with administrative measures.

Research hypotheses

It is most interesting that the surveys conducted in the two different countries resulted in similar evaluations of the research hypotheses. The first pair of hypotheses, stating that religious students are expected to be less open to dialogue and less tolerant on religious issues than non-religious students, may be rejected on the basis of both of these surveys. Comparison between students with and without religious affiliation showed religious students to be more open to dialogue, and in some respects more tolerant, than non-religious students. Religious students have more positive attitudes towards religion and more respect towards other believers. They are more informed about and more interested in the religious views of the others in their environment. They do not show any more dislike of bearers of religious views different from their own than non-religious students do, and advocate freedom of religious expression more intensively. As to the second pair of hypotheses, it is hardly valid to conclude that students who have encountered religious diversity in education are more tolerant or more open to dialogue on religious issues, if only owing to the great number of complex and multidimensional, direct and indirect influences produced by any educational milieu. It may be more correct to speak about some ambiguity of the effects produced by experiences connected with religion in education. Looking at the items about religious dialogue (or at those that could be causes for conflict) we can see more of an inclination towards dialogue than towards conflict, even though the responses tended to be ambivalent. Noteworthy is that students who did not have a specific religion, tended to respond ambivalently to all the items regarding dialogue, whether positive or negative. Such vagueness of their responses, their inability to make a certain choice seen in both Spanish and Russian samples, is indicative of the religious situation in these countries as a whole. The third pair of hypotheses, stating that students who have experienced personal encounters with religiously different people are more tolerant and open to dialogue on religious issues, got some empirical support in Russia: not only those students who reported they had friends of other religious backgrounds but also those who just had inter-religious contacts at school tended to show more negative reactions to the assumptions and statements tinged with exclusivist or xenophobic ideas. However, the influence of this factor was not uni-dimensional. Some data witnessed to the negative consequences of intercultural and interethnic encounters. It was difficult to evaluate the role of the religious component in these intercultural encounters and conflicts.

Some remarks on the meaning of REDCo results for our countries

The most important thing that makes the Spanish students differ from their Russian peers is their experience of religious education: 56.1% of the students were participating in RE classes, in comparison to 43.7% who were not. From the total number of students N = 680, 93.3% have received religious education for at least one year during their lifetime"[1]. In the Russian sample, there was only one school with compulsory RE (5%).

Strictly speaking, the peculiarities of situations in religious education are adequately highlighted in the published research material. In volume 3 of the Religious Diversity and Education in Europe series (Jackson, Miedema, Weisse & Willlaime, 2007), in particular, the articles on the Spanish and Russian situations are adjacent. The first contains detailed analysis of the legacy of national Catholicism and assesses the movement of Religious Education towards pluralism in contemporary Spain (Dietz, 2007). The Russian article deals with historical roots

---

[1] See the article on the Spanish data in this book.

and cultural context. There are several other circumstantial analyses of the Russian situation (Lisovskaya & Vyacheslav, 2005; Kozyrev, 2001, 2003, 2007; Valk, 2008). It is worth saying some words about the topicality of the search for new modalities of religious education in the two countries. As to Spain, this issue is worked out by Gunther Dietz in the section 'Perspectives' of the above-mentioned article. For Russia, of the search for new modalities is first of all aimed at prevention of ethno-religious conflicts.

It looks quite probable that the distinctions found between the two countries in the samples' attitudes towards religion and religious education will tend increasingly to disappear, and fostering the same values, that is religious tolerance and pluralism, will be increasingly felt as a pressing need. It might be very interesting to see answers given to the same questions by the same samples three years later. It is not so much the social climate that may change, but the adolescents themselves are likely to personally grow, and one may hope, their responses, may become more definite. True, such a longitudinal survey is quite laborious, but it might well pay back. At least, our attempts to offer these same questions to 20–22 year old higher school Russian students have already disclosed this tendency.

Both of the surveys have shown generally positive attitudes towards the presence of religion in education. The main problem seems to be in the fact that most of the respondents are lacking in experience of good and up-to-date religious education, and under these circumstances, it is not only necessary to search for new models and approaches to teaching religion, but to provide better religious education to those persons engaged in teaching other subjects. Religious issues should be identified and highlighted in history, literature, arts, ethics, natural and social sciences, so that, guided by the teacher, the student might take religious education as the answer to his question, and not an ideological system imposed upon him or her from the outside. So the first and foremost task today seems to be adequate religious education of prospective teachers. This conclusion follows from analyzing the data of both Spanish and Russian researchers.

References

Dietz, G. (2007). Invisibilizing or Ethnicizing Religious Diversity?, in: R. Jackson, S. Miedema, W. Weisse, & J.-P. Willlaime (Eds.), *Religion and Education in Europe: Developments, Contexts and Debates*. Muenster: Waxmann, pp. 103–131.

Kozyrev, F.N. (2003). The Religious and Moral Beliefs of Adolescents in St. Petersburg, in *Journal of Education and Christian Belief*, 7 (1), pp. 69–91.

Kozyrev F.N. (2007). Die russische geistige und paedagogische Tradition als Ressource der Modernisierung des schulischen Religionsunterrichts in Europa, in: *Orthodoxes Christentum – ein unterschaetzter Faktor in Europa*: *EPD Documentation*, 4, pp. 40–55.

Kozyrev F.N. & Fedorov, V. (2007). Religion and Education in Russia/ Historical roots, Cultural Context and Recent Developments. In W. Weisse, & J.-P. Willlaime (Eds.), *Religion and Education in Europe: Developments, Contexts and Debates*. Muenster: Waxmann, pp. 133–158.

Kozyrev, F.N. (2008). Religion and Education through the Eyes of Students from St Petersburg, in T. Knauth, D.-P Jozsa, G. Bertram-Troost & J. Ipgrave (Eds.), *Encountering Religious Pluralism in School and Society – A Qualitative Study of Teenage Perspectives in Europe*. Muenster: Waxmann, pp. 279–308.

Kozyrev, F. & Valk, P. (2009). *St Petersburg students about religion in education: results of quantitative survey*, in: this volume.

Levy, J. (2007). *Welcome or Not, Orthodoxy Is Back in Russia's Public Schools,* in: New York Times, September 23th, 2007.

Lisovskaya, E & Vyacheslav, K. (2005). La religion dans les écoles russes, in: J.-P. Willaime & S. Mathieu (Eds.). *Des Maitres et des Dieux. Ecoles et religions en Europe*, pp. 181–192.

Céline Béraud

The Role of Religion in Students' Lives and their Surroundings

From Melilla to St. Petersburg, European teenagers filled out 6513 questionnaires in eight different national contexts (occasionally limited to regions as with the German and Spanish samples, or even to one city as with the Russian one)[1]. One part of the questionnaire was devoted to the role of religion in their daily lives and that of their peer groups. Unlike the two other aspects of the research[2] that were more innovative and exploratory, the data gathered here may be compared with what has been obtained in other international surveys that were much larger than ours (meaning: how large the samples were, how representative they are and how many countries were studied). For this reason a direct comparison between our research and these surveys is not applicable. However they will be used as reference points. Three such surveys[3] are: the European Values Survey (EVS), which contains thirty questions concerning religion (the "young" category in this survey comprises those participants from 18 to 29 years of age[4]); the International Social Survey Programme (ISSP), an annual survey that has focused in some years (1991 and 1998) on religion and ethics; and the quantitative research carried out by Hans-Georg Ziebertz and William K. Kay among 16–to 17–year-old teenagers, where a large part of their work is dedicated to the religiosity of these young people (Ziebertz & Kay (Eds.), 2005, 2006).

The contexts of the REDCo survey are nonetheless quite varied. Among the countries involved are many that have historically had a Protestant majority (England, The Netherlands, Norway and Estonia); two traditionally Catholic countries (Spain and France), one traditionally Orthodox (Russia); and one biconfessional (Catholic and Protestant) country (Germany). The diversity of the situations studied comes also from the presence of two countries marked by several decades of state atheism (Estonia and Russia) alongside others, from Western Europe, generally described as increasingly secular. We should point out that none of the countries studied by Ziebertz and Kay (2005, 2006) characterised by a very high level of religiosity among young people (Poland, Croatia, Ireland, Turkey and Israel) were included in the REDCo project.

After we discuss the principal results obtained on the religiosity of the teenagers surveyed, we will focus on the impact of this factor (being "religious" or "non-religious") on their tolerance and their openness to dialogue.

Summary of the data

To get a sense of the religiosity of the young people surveyed, we had different kinds of data at our disposal: religious self-affiliation, the importance religion had to them in their personal lives, their beliefs, their practices and activities involving religion, as well as the importance they gave to their peer group as a source of information on the matter and as people with

---

1   See in the first part of the book the chapter untitled "Who to survey? Considerations on sampling".
2   The two other research questions are: How do students see religion in school? How do they see the impact of religion in society?
3   I mention here the three surveys I will make some references in this text. Other quantitative research could be useful such as the Eurobarometer.
4   For results, see for example Campiche (1997) and Lambert (2005).

whom they could discuss these issues. We also gathered their points of view on "other people who believe" and on religion in general.

The nominal religious identity

The data relating to the definition that those surveyed gave of their religion or their worldview at the end of the questionnaire makes it possible to categorise the countries (or regions) through the declared level of religious affiliation.

The Estonian report reveals the most secularised national context among the countries participating in the REDCo project: only 15% of those surveyed said they have a religion. This was true for less than half of the teenagers surveyed in the English sample and in St. Petersburg, and for half of those in the French and Norwegian samples.

In the other samples, it seems as though the fact of having a religion is still the norm, even among young people. In the two German federal states studied, around 60% of those surveyed said they have a religious affiliation. This is true of slightly less than two thirds of those surveyed in the three Spanish *Autonomous Communities* involved in the project, which is the same proportion as that in the Dutch sample.

This classification of the countries involved corresponds to what is generally seen in the large-scale international surveys (Lambert, 2005, p. 67), with the exception of the role of the Netherlands, which is usually presented as one of the most secularised of the traditionally Protestant European countries. The fact that the young Dutch people surveyed in the REDCo project demonstrate one of the highest levels of religious affiliation can be explained by the over-representation of "segregated religious schools" in the sample.

We can also distinguish the countries by their level of religious diversity, as indicated by the responses of the young people surveyed.

Some countries have large non-Christian religious minorities. This is clearly the case in the French, English, German and Dutch samples. There are substantial percentages of young Muslims in these countries, more than 10% in all of them (13% of the French sample; 11% of the English; between 10 and 15% of the German sample depending on the federal state; and 23% of the Dutch sample). These statistics must be taken as a rough indicator of diversity. Given the special attention to certain criteria in the composition of the samples – the national origin of the students for example, or whether their schools are religious or not – there is often an overrepresentation of minority religions among those surveyed. In the Dutch sample for instance, the proportion of Muslim respondents is overrepresented, linked to the inclusion of a "segregated Islamic secondary school" in the project.

In the other national or regional configurations, the religious landscape seems to be more homogenous. This is true in St. Petersburg, in the Spanish regions of Granada and Murcia[5], and in Norway, as well as in Estonia where the religious diversity is internal to Christianity (with the presence of Russian-speaking Orthodox Christians in a country that was historically Lutheran).

Let us note that among the minorities represented, we were only able to draw solid conclusions on Muslim teenagers. The percentages of other religious groups or worldviews (Jews, Buddhists, Jehovah's Witnesses, Hindus, Sikhs, Satanists, humanists, agnostics, atheists, etc.) were too small in all of the countries to yield a satisfactory statistical analysis in the context of

---

5   Melilla, one of the Spanish enclaves in North Africa, is on the contrary marked by a long existing religious diversity.

this survey. We should, however, stress the diversity in religious and non-religious world-views.

The importance given to religion

The level of importance that the teenagers surveyed gave to religion also makes distinctions possible between national (or local) contexts that do not correspond exactly to the answers they gave regarding their religious affiliations.

One group corresponds to contexts where those surveyed tend to consider religion as relatively or completely unimportant. This is true for around half of the teenagers surveyed in the French, Norwegian and Estonian samples. There are sometimes differences in the answers given between sexes. For example, among the young Estonians surveyed, fewer girls than boys say that religion is unimportant to them. Conversely, they are overrepresented in the small group that considers religion as very important.

We may also note the presence of another group with the opposite tendency. Nearly half of the German teenagers surveyed feel that religion is important to them. Only 13% think that it is not important at all. The proportions in the Dutch sample are more or less comparable.

Compared with these two groups, the samples from St. Petersburg, England and Spain reveal an intermediate situation. In St. Petersburg, the teenagers surveyed are quite divided: a third of them think that religion is relatively or completely unimportant to them. The same percentage feels that religion is important or very important; the remaining third seems to have no opinion on the question. In the English survey, 40% of the respondents said it was absolutely not and not important and 39% said it was important or very important, with 20% having no opinion. In Spain, 41% of the sample sees religion as important or very important. As for the remainder, half say that it is not important and half have no opinion on the matter.

Beliefs

We note that in some of the samples a large percentage of those surveyed don't identify with a belief in God, or in a sort of spirit or life force. This is true of a third of Estonian teenagers. The percentage is the same in the French sample. It is slightly higher among the Norwegian teenagers surveyed. In other samples (Spain, Germany, the Netherlands), at least half of the teenagers say they believe in God. The percentage of those who say they believe in a kind of spirit or life force is greater than 25% in the Norwegian, French and English samples, and more than 40% in the Estonian and Russian samples.

Practices and activities relating to religion

We have adopted indicators that are not limited to attendance of religious services, but also cover more personal forms of activities related to religion: prayer of course, but also reading sacred texts or researching information on the Internet, as well as thinking about religion and the meaning of life.

The overall levels of religious practice are in general relatively low in all of the samples. Religious services are an area in which many of those surveyed have no personal experience. For example, in the French and Norwegian samples, four out of ten teenagers surveyed say that they have never attended a religious service. Half of those in the Estonian and English surveys say the same thing, as do six out of ten in St. Petersburg. Prayer is often more common, at least as an occasional activity. But in some cases, in particular among those surveyed in France and Estonia, it is conversely even less common than attendance of religious services.

Most of the teenagers surveyed do not regularly read sacred texts on their own initiative or surf the Internet for information regarding religion. Thinking about the meaning of life and, to a lesser extent, thinking about religion, seem to be more widespread among young people (in particular in the German, French and Estonian[6] samples). The Spanish teenagers surveyed think about religion more than they practice it on a daily basis.

Sources of information on religion

Nearly everywhere, the family is presented as the main source of information regarding religion, although its importance varies from one sample to the next. School is considered as somewhat more important than the family only in the Norwegian and English samples. It comes in second place in the Spanish, German and Estonian samples, excepting those Estonian teenagers who recently took a course in religious education and who therefore tend to give greater importance to school. In general, school has a lower ranking for the Dutch teenagers surveyed, but its importance is different depending on whether they have a religion or not. It only comes in third place for those surveyed in St. Petersburg and in fourth place for the young French people surveyed.

Who to talk to about religion?

We may also distinguish the national (or local) contexts in our analysis depending on whether or not religion figures as something young people discuss with their peer group. We should first point out that in most cases family members are the main people with whom teenagers discuss religion. The English and Estonian samples are the only exceptions: in the first case classmates are more important; in the second the teachers are. We should also note that religion is not an essential part of discussions that those surveyed have with their peers in any of the countries involved.

One group of countries is characterised by a lack of substantial discussions among the young people surveyed regarding religion. The sample from St. Petersburg reveals a "silent type of religious life among students". Half of those surveyed say they do not know their friends' religions. On the whole, they feel that this issue is something private. The Estonian data comes to a very similar conclusion. Since religion is considered an intimate subject that may lead to conflict, it is something that young people discuss rarely if at all. So it is not surprising that more than half of those surveyed say they know nothing about their classmates' beliefs. For the French teenagers surveyed, religion is not a regular topic of conversation. They mainly discuss it with their families and friends, in other words with those closest to them. This must be associated with the belief among half of those surveyed that religion is a private matter.

In another group of countries, discussions regarding religion are more common. This is most apparent in the Dutch[7] and English samples, but also to a lesser extent in the German, Norwegian and Spanish samples. Religion is discussed most often within the family; only a minority talk about these matters regularly with religious authorities. In the samples from England, Norway and Hamburg[8], the teenagers surveyed readily say that they talk about religion with their teachers, which is probably due to the kind of religious education they receive in their respective countries.

---

6 Actually, in Estonia they rather think about the meaning of life than about religion.
7 This might be influenced by the composition of the Dutch sample, including two "segregated religious schools".
8 The other German federal state studied in the survey is North Rhine-Westphalia.

Attitudes regarding religious people and religion in general

Some statements obtain divergent responses in the various countries involved. Most of the teenagers surveyed (the overwhelming majority in the German, French, Norwegian, Dutch and Spanish samples) say they respect other people who believe. Everywhere (but most noticeably in France), young people recognise the historical role of religions ("Religion is important in our history"). More than half of those surveyed in the various samples feel that "One can be a religious person without belonging to a certain religious community". There are two statements with which a majority of those surveyed disagree in comparable proportions: "Religion is nonsense" and "Religion determines my whole life". The statement "Religion is important to me because I love God" is equally unpopular.

But teenagers are more split in the responses they have to other statements. In some contexts they have a relatively positive attitude toward the statements, in others the views are more negative, and in all contexts a high percentage of those surveyed give no answer ("Neither agree, nor disagree"). This is true for two statements related to the personal impact that religion has on people ("Religion helps me to cope with difficulties" and "Religion helps me to be a better person")[9]. It is also true for two statements concerning the level of certainty people have regarding religion ("Sometimes I have doubts – is there a God or not?" and "What I think about religion is open to change")[10].

The REDCo survey's conclusions on the religiosity of the teenagers surveyed

What is a "religious student"? Measuring religious identity is undoubtedly a sociological challenge. The indicators are imprecise and insufficiently inclusive when considered separately (Campiche, 1997, p. 47–48). When the questionnaire was conceived, we used different indicators of religiosity. The first was based upon the assertion of a religious affiliation or a worldview, or the lack of such an assertion. As with the Norwegian report, we may wonder about how those surveyed understood the question: was it seen from an institutional point of view (having been baptised for example), from a familial and cultural point of view (having grown up in a Muslim family for example), or from an individual point of view of personal convictions? This indicator shows whether or not the people in question think of themselves as within an existing religious system, and whether or not they feel that they are part of a tradition. However, this relationship "is not necessarily a fundamental component of personality" (Campiche, 1997, p. 55). Moreover, it rules out other non-institutional forms of religiosity. To get a sense of personal commitment, the indicator associated with the importance given to religion in each person's life may be more significant. In some of the reports, it was clearly preferred as a way of measuring the level of teenagers' religiosity. The data gathered in the question dealing with belief also made distinctions possible. The frequency of religious activities appears as a less effective indicator for distinguishing religious students from non-religious ones. On the other hand, it was useful for highlighting the existence of very religious minorities.

Despite the limitations of our survey, involving either the indicators of religiosity or the samples chosen, we may draw several firmly established conclusions. We must first point out that some of these conclusions may seem to contradict each other; this is a result of the diver-

---

9   In this case, we observe a tendency in several samples for the teenagers surveyed to disagree with the statements.

10   In this second case, we see more of a tendency for the teenagers to agree with the statements.

sity of religious experience among the teenagers surveyed. This diversity is perceptible between national (or local) contexts, but even more so within them.

*1) The overall tendency toward a lack of interest in religious institutions is clearly perceptible
everywhere.* A good illustration of this is the relatively low percentages of the young people
surveyed who identify with a religion: in many cases they make up less than half of the sample. The influence of religious communities and their leaders appears everywhere as secondary. The young people surveyed have few opportunities to meet with religious authorities. It
is therefore not surprising that religious communities are not seen as important sources of
information regarding religion. In the case of St. Petersburg, this could be explained by historical circumstances, but also because here, as in all the other locations where the survey
took place, those surveyed tended to consider religiosity as the individual's business before
being something institutions need to deal with.

2) *This tendency does not stand in the way of the existence of active religious minorities with
an institutional presence among young people.* A small proportion of those surveyed consider
religion as something very important in their lives. These same people stand out by their high
level of belief and religious practice. On this point, young Muslims seem noteworthy. In the
Norwegian sample, five times more Muslim teenagers than Christian teenagers feel that religion is very important to their lives. The tendency is the same in the German and English
samples, although the difference between the groups is not as great. There is another remarkable distinction between young Muslims and young Christians concerning their level of belief
in God. Among young Muslims in the German and French samples this level is much higher
(94% and 97% respectively) than among young Christians in both samples (59% and 53%
respectively)[11]. The difference is not as large in the English sample: nearly all young Muslims
say they believe in God, vs. 75% of young Christians. The data from this same sample also
reveals a higher level of religious practice (particularly prayer and reading of sacred texts)
among young Muslims.

The insufficiently large size of the samples made it impossible to get an idea of distinctions
internal to Christianity: between denominations, but also between tendencies within these
denominations. The French report has some comments on young Protestants who belong to
charismatic, evangelical movements. In the national context, they seem to have many similarities with their Muslim peers. The impact of national origin on the internal diversity of the
various Christian and non-Christian denominations also deserves a more detailed analysis, but
here again a larger sample, and/or a qualitative methodology, would be required. The English
report seems to go in this direction when it draws a comparison between Muslim students of
South Asian origin and African Christians, who share strong theistic points of view.

3) We should add that *this lack of interest in religious institutions is not associated with a
large-scale acceptance of antireligious positions.* On the contrary, we find that only a very
small minority of teenagers declare themselves to be staunch atheists, including those in
Estonia and St. Petersburg where state atheism was promoted during the Soviet era, as well as
teenagers in France and Spain where anticlerical movements have historically had large fol-
lowings. In all of the regions involved, even the most secularised countries, those surveyed
strongly reject the most hostile statements regarding religions and religious people, such as
"Religion is nonsense." There are sometimes marked differences between sexes on this issue.

---

11 We should point out that in the French case, the comparison is with young people who consider themselves Catholic, not with all who identify with Christianity.

For example, in the samples from Estonia and St. Petersburg, girls are much less likely to give the most negative responses than boys are. This is another example of something already observed in the EVS surveys: "Vague beliefs and religious indifference are becoming much more prevalent among young Europeans than the well-reasoned rejection of religious systems" (Campiche, 1997, p. 53). In many national contexts, we may be able to establish a hypothesis of a break with previous generations on this matter: older generations seem to have a more negative image of religions and their most ardent followers. The French context seems to be a perfect example of this[12].

4) We find various signs of a tendency toward *"religion off the beaten track"*[13] (Lambert, 2005) among the young people surveyed, a phenomenon also described as a *mobile and flexible religiosity* modelled on the two ideal-typical figures of the "pilgrim" and the "convert"[14] (Hervieu-Léger, 1999). This phenomenon is part of a religious environment that is more complex than what was foreseen some years ago by the theory of a decreasing interest in religion (Berger, 1967).

The analysis of the answers given to the question dealing with belief in "God, a life force or a kind of spirit" reveals that *people without a religious affiliation are not necessarily non-believers or non-observant* (at least when it comes to prayer). Here we find another example of the phenomenon of "believing without belonging" that the British sociologist Grace Davie has observed (1994). The decline of religious institutions has not been accompanied by a decline in belief. Quite the reverse: some beliefs remain strong and are even growing, though with some wavering. The grand narratives of belief "function as stocks of symbolic resources that individuals appropriate freely" (Hervieu-Léger, 2005, p. 296). In addition, some teenagers who do not identify with any religion say they pray at least occasionally. This is true for more than a third of the young Spaniards surveyed who said they did not have a religion. A small minority of German teenagers who said they had no religion (between 4% and 8% depending on the federal state studied) even said they pray every day. In all cases, many of those surveyed agree with the following statement: "One may be a religious person without belonging to a particular community of faith." (The level of agreement is especially high in the Estonian, English, Spanish, Norwegian and St. Petersburg samples.) The young people surveyed thus seem to have taken note of the phenomenon of "the institutional deregulation of belief" (Hervieu-Léger, 1999).

There is only one question in the REDCo questionnaire – the one regarding "some sort of spirit or life force" – that allows us to evaluate *how much borrowing takes place from non-Christian belief systems*, which is another example of this mobile and flexible religiosity[15]. For example, 27% of the teenagers surveyed in the Norwegian sample feel that "some sort of spirit or life force" exists. In other words, these teenagers in a traditionally Lutheran country agree with an expression that has its roots in Oriental or New Age religions. A comparable proportion of teenagers in the French sample agree, in a country that has traditionally had a Catholic majority. The proportion is even higher in St. Petersburg (40%), in a context marked

---

12 See for example the data from the ISSP survey in 1998 as analysed by Yves Lambert (2001).

13 The French expression "religion hors-piste" (Lambert, 2005) has been translated in English in "religion off the beaten track".

14 The pilgrim travels alone and of his or her own free will. His or her practice revolves around "sacred places" and "profound experiences", not around day-to-day living. The convert chooses to commit himself or herself; as a result, this commitment acquires authenticity.

15 Sociologists use the metaphor of the "bricolage" to describe that kind of phenomenon. See Hervieu-Léger (2005).

by Orthodox Christianity followed by several decades of state atheism. Theses results are interesting but we lack other indicators often used in quantitative surveys on religiosity, such as belief in reincarnation or the practice of meditation, to go further on the question of "*brico-lage*" mixing Christian and non-Christian beliefs and practices.

Some doubts are often expressed. For example, more than 40% of French teenagers surveyed say they have doubts[16] about the existence or non-existence of God (the proportion is roughly the same in the Norwegian and German samples). In addition, some of those surveyed say they are *open to change*. This position ("What I think about religion is open to change") is clearly mentioned among the Spanish and Estonian teenagers surveyed, whether or not they identify with a particular religion. But some religious minorities resist this relativism, as shown by the young English Muslims surveyed who distinguish themselves from their classmates by disapproving strongly of doubts about the existence of God and by rejecting the possibility of future changes in their beliefs.

However, this tendency toward "religion off the beaten track" among the teenagers surveyed may be put into perspective through the importance they give to the family as a source of religious socialisation, as well as through the importance of the traditions inherited from their parents. This heritage can be seen in the relative correspondence between the religion or worldview of those surveyed and that of their mother or father, as well as in the divided opinions gathered on the statement "Religion is something one inherits from one's family", which did not make it possible to ascertain a clear tendency toward rejecting inherited religious affiliations.

5) *The role of religions in cultural heritage asserts itself at the very moment when religious institutions are becoming less socially relevant and are losing their hold on the faithful* (Boespflug, Dunand & Willaime, 1996). In all the samples, the statement "Religion is important in our history" obtains a majority of favourable opinions. The Norwegian report highlights the existence of a group of "cultural Christians", that is young people who identify with Christianity, but without necessarily sharing its beliefs or practices. We thus see here a form of "belonging without believing" in symmetry with the previously observed "believing without belonging". This category must necessarily exist in other samples, even though it is not explicitly mentioned.

Now I will reflect on these results in the light of two of our hypotheses.

Hypothesis 1a) Religious students are less tolerant than non-religious students.

The variables that were taken into account to measure the level of tolerance involve respect and, symmetrically, the rejection of positions hostile to religious people ("I respect other people who believe"), to people from other religions ("Respecting the religion of others helps to cope with differences"; "I don't like people from other religions and do not want to live together with them") and to religion in general ("Without religion the world would be a better place"; "Disagreement on religious issues leads to conflicts"; "People with different strong religious views cannot live together"). Attention was also paid to the degree of religious diversity in the social contexts of the teenagers surveyed, both in school and during their free time.

---

16 Note that 14–16 is the age when teenagers explore different value systems, which can be related to doubt with regard to their family's commitments.

1aa) Summary of the results obtained in the various national or local contexts

The *English respondents* with commitment to a religion/worldview appear as more tolerant in their outlook.

In the *Estonian sample*, the more those surveyed consider religion as important, the more they present themselves as tolerant and insist upon the importance of tolerance in improving relations between different religions or belief groups. As for fears about the risk of conflict, the differences are minimal between those considering religion as important and the others.

In the *French report*, we observe that the teenagers who are most critical of religion are those who do not claim any religious affiliation. This observation is qualified by the fact that the criticisms seem to be directed more toward religion in general (the social dimension of religious facts) than toward observant people.

The conclusions of the *German survey* are somewhat divergent. On the one hand, the more important religion is to the respondents, the more they show respect and consider respect related to religion important. On the other hand, they tend to prefer to socialise more with peers with the same views about religion and to have strong points of view about religion – "being ready to go so far as to try to convince others that their own views about religion are 'the best ones'".

Some of the answers given by the *Dutch teenagers* surveyed reveal a slightly higher level of tolerance among those who have some sort of religious affiliation than among those without any religion. Other answers did not enable the detection of significant differences between the two groups. On the contrary, one of the results could make it seem as though religious respondents were less tolerant: "A much larger percentage of pupils who have a religion than those who do not prefer to spend time with young people who have the same religious background as themselves".

In the *Norwegian report*, it is noted that "the most religiously committed pupils are the ones who are most united and come across strongest in their respect for 'other people who believe'", and that this is as true for young Muslims as it is for young Christians. But this is only a question of degree, not of position.

In the *St. Petersburg sample*, it appears as though religious students demonstrate more positive attitudes toward religion and seem to be more respectful of other observant people.

The *Spanish survey* indicates that all those surveyed tend to agree more with the positive aspects of religion (helps people cope with differences, respect others, live together, makes the world a better place to live, etc.) than with the negative ones (aggressiveness, conflict, intransigence, etc.). However, this phenomenon is more noticeable among those who say they have some sort of religious affiliation. Moreover, the Spanish teenagers surveyed generally avoided extreme positions ("totally agree" or "totally disagree"), demonstrating what may be interpreted as a certain level of caution in their answers.

1ab) Interpretations

In the light of these different results, we seem to be able to conclude that our survey does not confirm the hypothesis that "religious students are less tolerant than non-religious students" in the great majority of the contexts under study. Obtaining such a result from the research, however, means that we must examine it in greater depth when interpreting the data.

We must first stress that tolerance seems to be a value that is largely shared by all the teenagers surveyed from Melilla to St. Petersburg, whether or not they can be considered "religious". The marginal nature of antireligious positions is clearly apparent in all contexts.

We should also remind ourselves what is understood here by tolerance. The above mentioned indicators we used are very general statements for the most part, which do not go into the details either of religions or of precise aspects to which this tolerance applies (beliefs, practices, values). A more detailed investigation should be carried out to test the results of our first survey.

A more strategic analysis also leads us to put this result into perspective. Ultimately, how surprising is it that a greater percentage of religious students than other students say they are in favour of freedom of religion and respect for religious people, since they are the first to benefit from them?

Hypothesis 1b) Religious students are less open to dialogue on religious issues than non-religious students

The openness to dialogue of the teenagers surveyed was measured on the basis of the following variables: the importance given to the development of the students' capacities to discuss religion at school, the level of interest they had in the issue during discussions among peers and more specifically among friends, the kind of reactions they had toward proselytising behaviour from a classmate, their level of insistence upon the virtues of discussions on such a topic (they can make up their own minds; they understand others better; they can live with them in peace; they understand better what goes on in the world) or, on the contrary, the uselessness of the topic ("It's boring"; "I don't know enough so I have nothing to say") or even its dangers both on a personal and a societal level ("It's an embarrassing subject"; the risk of arguments).

1ba) Summary of the results obtained in the various national or local contexts

In the *English sample*, the teenagers demonstrating the greatest openness to dialogue are those who identify with a worldview regardless of whether this is religious or not.

In the *Estonian report*, it appears that those students who consider religion as important are more open to dialogue (in class but also as a discussion topic). They are more curious about other people's points of view on the issue and believe more in the social virtues of dialogue. Conversely, students who feel that religion is unimportant tend to agree more often with more intransigent positions. The less religion is presented as important by those surveyed, the more they tend to develop social relationships with people sharing this view.

In the *French sample*, religious students distinguish themselves by the greater interest they say they have in discussions dealing with religion. The Muslim students involved are given as a good example of this.

The *German report* comes to a similar conclusion: students to whom religion is more important tending to be more 'ready' or 'open' for dialogue.

In the *Dutch report*, it is noted that the teenagers surveyed who have a religion seem more open to dialogue than the others, but this is only a question of degree. In fact, the main difference is due to the fact that fewer of them support the statement "Talking about religion only leads to disagreement".

In the *Norwegian sample,* the attitudes that differ when it comes towards talking about religion, or what we may call dialogue on an everyday level, follow different patterns depending on the importance of religion to the respondents. The pupils who find religions important are generally much more optimistic about the different positive outcomes of talking about religion than those who find religion not to be important.

The report on *St. Petersburg* describes the religiosity of the teenagers surveyed "as a positive factor of their citizenship and their communicative competences to live in a plural society".

The data obtained in the *three Spanish regions* make it possible to discern two overall tendencies. On the whole, the answers students give tend more toward openness to dialogue than toward conflict. However, the students give neutral answers ("neither agree nor disagree") very often, which may indicate ambivalence or even embarrassment. If we then categorise the young people surveyed depending on whether or not they identify with a particular religion, we see that the first group is more open to dialogue than the second group. Students with a religious affiliation also distance themselves more from statements insisting upon the risk of conflict associated with religion than do those without such an affiliation.

1bb) Interpretations

Our second hypothesis, according to which "religious students are less open to dialogue than non-religious students", does not seem to be empirically valid either. But here again, we must avoid jumping to hasty conclusions.

As with the evaluation of the level of tolerance, we are essentially limited to generalisations here. The word "dialogue" is undeniably one of the more overused terms today. But the data gathered does not allow for a distinction to be made between "superficial and inconsequential contacts" (Lamine, 2004, p. 226) and other, more profound forms of exchange. Nor is it possible for us to decide if students discuss these issues out of a real interest in the beliefs, practices and values that religious traditions embody, or if their discussions are merely part of an overall interest they share in letting everyone speak their minds, which encompasses much more than just questions involving religion. This willingness to discuss issues openly can go hand-in-hand with a certain level of indifference toward other people's opinions (in the various samples, the majority of teenagers surveyed say that they are ready to have a discussion with a proselytising classmate, but that they will listen without letting his or her views influence them). It may even lead to a form of relativism[17].

Finally, we may wonder about the connections between tolerance and dialogue: does less openness to dialogue necessarily imply a lower level of tolerance? The lack of religious culture among teenagers without religion can explain by itself why they are so poorly prepared to have discussions on the topic. The lack of interest they have in religion is another explanation[18]. Topics involving the peer group's common interests, which are related to youth culture, are obviously more interesting for them. Conversely, religion seems to come up more easily as a matter of discussion among teenagers for whom religion has a great deal of importance in daily life.

Overall conclusion:

The data on the role of religion in the personal lives of teenagers highlights situations that contrast to a certain degree from one national (or local) context to another, but also within each context, as well as some tendencies that are partially contradictory. Our survey confirms

---

17 On the moral relativism that is quite widespread among teenagers, see Ziebertz & Kay (2005, p. 16–18).

18 The correlation between interest in other religions and personal involvement in religion has been highlighted in other quantitative surveys. See "Les Français et leurs croyances" CSA / La Vie / Le Monde poll carried out in March 2003: The Catholics surveyed who have a high level of belief and religious practice are those who say they are more interested in Islam, Judaism, Buddhism and Hinduism.

the tendency toward a lack of interest in religious institutions, excepting very religious minorities. This tendency does not mean either the end of forms of religiosity that willingly go "off the beaten track," or the end of the ability religions have to build identities, as demonstrated by the "cultural Christians" whose relationship to religious traditions is based on cultural heritage.

As for the issues of tolerance and dialogue, we may conclude by distinguishing diversity as a fact and as a value (pluralism). The first case concerns the presence of several distinct groups within a given society. The second corresponds to a "deliberate option [...] that intends to emphasise that diversity, to take it into account and even to promote it" (Lamine, 2004, p. 226). Whether or not we consider the teenagers surveyed to be "religious", they are clearly aware of how diverse the European societies to which they belong have become, even for those living in national contexts where this diversity remains quantitatively limited. Moreover, our survey underlines the support that most of the teenagers surveyed share toward diversity as a value (tolerance and openness to dialogue). Still, we must be very cautious about our conclusions in this area. With this quantitative survey, we have collected opinions. But to be able to assert that there is indeed tolerance and openness to dialogue, and thus that the values of diversity are experienced on a daily basis, these opinions must confront the facts. Stopping at the level of what is said means taking the risk of being caught in a form of "religious correctness" that teenagers have no trouble mastering. Moreover, we have to recognise the limits of our research regarding the forms of tolerance and dialogue that the questionnaire takes into account, and thus keep ourselves from being overly optimistic.

References

Berger, P. (1967). *The Sacred Canopy: Elements of Sociological Theory of Religion.* New-York: Doubleday.

Boepsflug, F., Dunand, F. & Willaime, J.-P. (1996). *Pour une mémoire des religions.* Paris: La Découverte.

Campiche, R.J. (Ed.) (1997). *Cultures jeunes et religions en Europe.* Paris: Cerf "Sciences humaines et religions".

Davie, G. (1994). *Religion in Britain since 1945. Believing without belonging.* Oxford: Blackwell Publishing "Institute of Contemporary British History".

Hervieu-Léger, D. (1999). *Le pèlerin et le converti. La religion en mouvement.* Paris: Flammarion.

Hervieu-Léger, D. (2005). Bricolage vaut-il dissémination? Quelques réflexions sur l'opérationnalité sociologique d'une métaphore problématique, in: *Social Compass,* 52 (3), pp. 295–308.

Lambert, Y. (2001). Attitudes sécularistes et fondamentalistes en France et dans divers pays occidentaux, in: *Social Compass,* 48 (1), pp. 37–49.

Lambert, Y. (2005). Un regain religieux chez les jeunes d'Europe de l'Ouest et de l'Est, in: O. Galland & B. Roudet (Eds.). *Les jeunes Européens et leurs valeurs.* Paris: La Découverte, "Recherches", pp. 65–91.

Lamine, A.-S. (2004). *La cohabitation des dieux. Pluralité religieuse et laïcité.* Paris: PUF, "Le Lien social".

Ziebertz, H.-G. & Kay, W.K. (Eds.) (2005). *Youth in Europe 1: an international empirical study about life perspectives.* Muenster: LIT Verlag.

Ziebertz, H.-G. & Kay, W.K. (Eds.) (2006). *Youth in Europe 2: an international empirical study about religiosity.* Muenster: LIT Verlag.

Gerdien Bertram-Troost

How do European Pupils See Religion in School?

1.   Introduction

On the basis of the national contributions it is possible to go further into the question how European pupils see religion in school. In this chapter I will try to give a more general overview and structure of the described results in the separate national sections on what pupils' experiences are with religion in school and what they think about it. In this chapter I will also deal with the two hypotheses related to the effect of religious diversity in education on the degree to which pupils are tolerant and/or open to dialogue. For the case of clarity I will describe important and/or striking findings in the different countries in the same order of countries for every section. In doing this, it is also easier to find patterns between (groups of) countries. The countries are grouped on the basis of the (formal) role of religion in education.

In the concluding section there will be a summing up of the main tendencies which appear when looking to the separate national findings. These tendencies are already touched upon in section two and three, but described more explicitly in the conclusions.

2.   Thoughts about and experiences with religious education of European youth

2.1   Attending religious education (RE) lessons

There are great differences in the possibilities European pupils in the different participating countries have to participate in RE lessons at school. Pupils in Estonia, France and Russia have the least experiences with a separate subject on religion. In *Estonia* only a few schools offer RE (about 10%) and, all in all, only about 1 to 2 % of the surveyed pupils have the possibility of attending RE classes. If RE is provided, it is offered as a voluntary subject. Just like in the French situation, most knowledge about religion is acquired by attending other school subjects like History, Civic Education and Literature. In *France*, only the students of the public school system in three departments in the east of the country, and some students in private schools, have confessional RE. History class seems to be the main subject where religion is discussed.

In *Saint-Petersburg*[1] only 5% of the students in the research sample received formal RE at school. However, in many other regions in Russia this percentage is rather higher.

In England most and in Norway all schools provide non-confessional religious education for all pupils. In *England* the majority of schools are non-denominational community schools which, by law, have to provide non-confessional religious education for all pupils. In *Norway*, all pupils in principle also have the same education, including religious education. All students attend the non-confessional subject KRL.

---

1   As in Russia the focus is only on pupils in Saint Petersburg, I will not refer to Russian pupils in general. Wherever I refer to the 'Russian sample', I have the pupils in Saint Petersburg in mind.

In *Spain* almost all students receive, during their years at school, at least one year religious education. This religious education is strongly influenced by the Catholic Church.

Mainly in Germany and the Netherlands the experiences with religious education and the kind of 'model of RE' pupils are confronted with, are dependent on what kind of school pupils attend and/or in which region of the country they live. In *Germany* there are different models of Religious Education in the different states. As a result, pupils in different parts of the country have different experiences with religious education at school. In NRW surveyed pupils have, in general, more experiences with religious education than pupils who live in Hamburg.

In *the Netherlands* about two-third of the pupils attend denominational education where they attend RE classes (either confessional or non-confessional). Although relatively rare, also at some state schools pupils can attend lessons on world view. There is a great variety between schools (both between and within different school systems) on how the actual lessons are given shape.

2.2   (Possible) role of religion in school life

Taken into account that the general school systems, the (formal) role of religion in education, the influence of the (State) Church, the relation between state and church (or other religious communities) and the way Religious Education is given shape are different in the different countries, it is understandable that European pupils have various experiences with and thoughts about religion in school.

The question on what role religion should play in school if pupils were persons who could decide on school matters revealed many interesting things. Questions 13 to 19 list several issues which deal with the question what the rights of pupils with regard to religion in school should be (according to pupils themselves). In *Estonia* only two of the mentioned rights were more accepted than rejected. Namely, the wearing of discrete religious symbols and the absence from school because of a religious festival. Other aspects, like a special room for praying or voluntary services were strongly rejected. Only for two aspects significant differences were found between pupils with and pupils without a religious affiliation: Pupils who have a religion agree significantly stronger that school should provide facilities for pupils to pray and that pupils should be able to wear discrete religious symbols.

In *France* pupils also make a clear distinction between discrete and more visible religious symbols. 78% agrees that pupils should be able to wear discrete symbols and only 17% agrees that pupils could wear more visible symbols. With regard to the issue on religious symbols there are no clear differences between pupils of public or private schools. Muslim pupils are slightly more in favour of allowing more visible religious symbols than other pupils.

In *Saint Petersburg,* for most mentioned issues significant differences were found between pupils with and pupils without a religious background. Pupils with a religion were more in favour of the right of religious people to express their belief, also in school life. Only with regard to the permission for students to withdraw from classes and to be absent for religious reasons, pupils with and pupils without a religion are on the same line. Another important finding in the Russian context is that one of the determinants of students' attitudes towards the presence of religion in education, is their (current) experience with it. For instance, pupils who have a chapel at their school (pupils at school 1) are more positive about the issue whether schools should provide facilities to pray.

From the findings in *England* it became clear that there are significant differences between pupils with and pupils without a worldview when it comes to their thoughts on the role of religion in school. Here, also a distinction between Muslim and Christian pupils could be made. In general, Muslim pupils are much more in favour of an explicit role for religion and the outward expressions of faith groups in school than Christian pupils.

In the *Norwegian* context there is a clear support for religious symbols being allowed in school (65% agrees that more visible symbols should be allowed in school) and, in general, about 60% also agrees that religious needs of pupils should also be taken into account in the sense that, for instance, absence for religious reasons and religious food requirements should be respected. However, especially with regard to whether schools should provide facilities to pray, Norwegian pupils are not so sure. An important finding is that the more importance pupils attach to religion, the more students tend to be supportive towards freedom of (showing ones) religion in school.

Spanish pupils most strongly agree that religious food requirements of pupils should be taken into account in school. Discrete religious symbols are more or less generally accepted, but with regard to more present religious symbols the Spanish pupils seem to be ambiguous. In general, pupils tend to disagree that voluntary religious services could be part of school life and that schools should provide facilities for pupils to pray in school. Pupils who attend compulsory religious education are especially much more of the opinion that voluntary religious services could be part of school life. And pupils who do not have a religion themselves are significantly stronger 'against' taking into account the religious needs of pupils in school. They especially disagree with the possibility that religious services would be part of school life and that schools should provide facilities for pupils to pray in school.

In the *German* sample pupils from both federal states agree that religious food requirements are taken into account, that students should be able to wear discrete religious symbols and that they can be absent from school for religious festivals. Pupils are however less positive about the possibility that students should be excused from taking some classes for religious reasons. As in (most of) the other countries, significant differences were found between pupils who have a religion and pupils who do not and between Muslims and Christians. In general, Muslim pupils are more in favour of freedom to express ones religion in school.

Pupils of the *Dutch* sample generally agree that the religious' needs of pupils should be, more or less, taken into account in school. However, pupils hesitate when it comes to allowing pupils to miss some classes for religious reasons. It seems that they are willing to take into account religious backgrounds of pupils, but that they, at the same time, think that the school curriculum must be followed by all pupils.

2.3 Learning about/from religion in school

Here I will go further into the reactions of the pupils on the question how much they agree that at school they learn certain things with regard to religion (Qst. 3–12). Questions on what learning about different religions helps to, according to pupils, are also included (Qst. 20–25). I relate these reactions, also on the basis of the national reports, to several background variables in order to structure the findings and to explore tendencies.

In the *Estonian context* a distinction has been made between pupils who have studied RE recently and students who had had RE long ago or had integrated RE. Pupils who have studied RE recently are significantly more positive about religious education. They state much more often that at school they learn to have respect for everyone, whatever their religion, that they have opportunities to discuss religious issues from different perspectives and that they get knowledge about different religions.

Of the listed aspects, *French pupils* agree most with the statements 'at school I learn to have respect for everyone, whatever their religion' (89% agrees), 'Learning about different religions at school helps me to live together' (70% agrees) and 'At school, I get knowledge about different religions' (68% agrees). Especially pupils who have a religion themselves see school as an important place to learn to live together and to have respect for everyone. In general, pupils put most emphasis on the social dimension of learning about religion in school. They indicate, for instance, much less that learning about religions at school helps to learn about themselves. However, one has to keep in mind that only 33% of the French pupils think that religion as a topic is important in school.

In *Saint Petersburg* the most positively evaluated statement was 'At school I learn to have respect for everyone, whatever their religion' (mean value 2.2). Pupils also agree that learning about different religions at school helps them to live together. However, they tend to disagree with items as 'At school I get knowledge about different religions', 'At school, I have opportunities to discuss religious issues from different perspectives' and 'I find religions as topic important at school'. These findings should of course been seen in the light of the fact that only 5% of the students in the Russian sample have experiences with RE. However, pupils do not agree with the idea that learning about religion may cause conflicts in the classroom (only 12% agrees with it). So although they don't have much experiences with it, they don't have the feeling that raising religious issues in school might cause conflicts.

The things *English pupils* agree with quite strongly in relation to learning at school, can be related to the inclusive approach in the English (religious) educational system: Learning to have respect for everyone, getting knowledge about different religions and having opportunities to discuss religious issues from different perspectives are highly valued. However, also the English pupils are inclined to disagree that learning about religions at school helps to learn about oneself.

In *Norway* pupils agree especially strong with the statements that at school they get knowledge about different religions, learn to have respect for everyone and get an opportunity to discuss religious issues. It is also interesting that Norwegian pupils also agree relatively strongly with the statement that at school they learn to make choices between right and wrong. This is probably a result of the fact that ethics are an important aspect of KRL.

In *Spain,* a majority of pupils agrees with the statements that at school they learn about different religions and that this helps them to live together. Pupils also have the feeling that at school they learn to respect everyone, regardless their religion. Pupils who have a religion agree with this stronger than pupils who do not have a religion themselves. However, Spanish pupils are rather ambiguous about how interesting and important religion as a topic is at school. They also do not have strong negative or positive thoughts about to what degree learning about religions at school help to learn about themselves, to learn to make decisions between right and wrong and/or to understand current events.

With regard to how far *German* pupils agree that certain things are learnt at school, there is not so much variation between pupils of the two participating federal states. A majority of pupils agree that at school they get knowledge about different religions, learn to have respect for everyone and have opportunities to discuss religious issues from different perspectives. It is striking that in both the NRW- and the Hamburg sample quite many pupils use the middle-option 'neither agree nor disagree' in relation to several questions on what they learn at school and what learning about religions at schools helps to.[2] It seems that also in the German

---

2   For instance with regard to the items 'Learning about religions at school helps me to understand current events', 'learning about religions at school helps me to learn about myself'.

context, pupils are mainly focused on the 'societal aspect' of Religious Education. They are not so much interested in the (possible) influence of Religious Education on their personal development.

Dutch pupils agree most strongly with the statement that at school they learn to have respect for everyone, whatever their religion. Pupils agree less with the statement that learning about different religions at school helps them to learn about themselves. It seems that pupils are of the opinion that learning about religion at school has more impact on how they live together than on their personal development. Besides that, pupils in general disagree with the statement that learning about religions leads to conflicts in the classroom. Pupils do not explicitly agree nor disagree with the statement that religions as topic are important at school. There is however a slight tendency towards a positive reaction.

2.4 Aims of religious education

A block of questions in the questionnaire (Q. 32–36) dealt with the issue what European pupils see as (possible) aims for religious education. In this section I will explore the main tendencies.

In the *Estonian* sample pupils agree most with the aim that pupils should get objective knowledge about different religions. However, the mean value is not very high (2.3). Pupils, irrespective whether they have experiences with RE at school or not, reject the idea that school should guide pupils towards religious beliefs. With regard to other possible aims, significant differences were found between pupils with and pupils without a religion. Pupils who have no experiences with RE in school agree, generally, less with the mentioned possible aims. Pupils who have a religion themselves, however, agree more with the mentioned aims. They are less negative about the aim of guiding pupils towards religious beliefs. However, also among the pupils who have a religion, this aim was the least favorite.

French pupils have a clear priority to get objective knowledge about different religions (63%) and to be able to talk and communicate about religious issues (63%). They also want to learn the importance of religion for dealing with problems in society (58%) and to learn to understand what religions teach (56%). So in fact they are quite positive about several possible aims. However, only 9% of the French pupils agrees that pupils should be guided towards religious beliefs. From these answers we get the impression that French pupils see school as an institute to get knowledge about different religions but definitely not as a place to practice religion and/or to discover one's own spirituality. Again, it seems that the French pupils have fully absorbed the French public thoughts on religion in public life (including education).

In *Saint Petersburg* pupils attach least importance to being guided towards religious beliefs. In comparison to the other countries it is striking that pupils of the Russian sample are also not so much interested in learning to be able to talk and communicate about religious issues. Instead, they see the acquiring of objective knowledge about different religions as the most important aim of religious education.

Unlike pupils of the Russian sample, *English* pupils generally agree with the aim that at school pupils should learn to be able to talk about religious issues. They value this aim (almost) as high as the mentioned aims of 'learning to understand what religions teach' and 'getting an objective knowledge about different religions'. Like pupils of all other countries, pupils of the English sample agree least with the possible aim of guiding pupils towards religious beliefs.

Norwegian pupils attach most importance to learning to understand what religions teach (67% agrees) and to getting objective knowledge about different religions (54% agrees). They also attach importance to learning about the importance of religion for dealing with problems in society and to being able to talk and communicate about religious issues. However, with regard to these last two possible aims there is also quite a big group (about 30%) who do not have a clear opinion (neither agree nor disagree). This is also the case in relation to the possible aim of being guided towards religious beliefs. However, here there is a group of at least 50% who is (strongly) against this aim. In general, it can be said that the more importance pupils attach to religion, the more positive they are towards the mentioned aims.

Spanish pupils generally indicate that they agree most with the aim of getting objective knowledge about different religions. Like the pupils in Saint Petersburg they attach relatively small importance to learning about the importance of religion for dealing with problems in society.

In *Germany* pupils from the two participating federal states are clearly in favour of the aim of getting objective knowledge about different religions and of learning to understand what religions teach. They also attach importance to learning to communicate about religious issues and to learning the importance of religion for dealing with problems in society. Only with regard to the possible aim of guiding pupils towards religious beliefs there is a significant difference between the pupils of Hamburg and NRW. Pupils of the NRW sample tend to agree more with this aim. However, still 38% disagrees with it. It is striking that the importance pupils attach to religion correlates strongest with all the possible aims: The more importance pupils attach to religion, the more they agree with the mentioned aims.

Pupils of the *Dutch* sample are most in favour of learning to understand what religions teach and of learning to be able to talk and communicate about religious issues. From the data material it becomes obvious that the pupils disagree with the aim of guiding pupils towards religious beliefs. Especially pupils who attend non-confessional RE schools and pupils who do not have a religion themselves disagree with this aim. Pupils who do not have a religion also attach less importance to several of the other mentioned aims.

2.5   Positions towards different models of RE

Questions 26 to 30 are added to the questionnaire to get an idea of how pupils look upon different models of religious education. Should it be optional? Is it needed at all? In this section I will summarize the findings of the different national samples.

In the *Estonian* sample more than 80% agrees that religious education should be optional. About 50% of the pupils agree that all they need to know about religion is covered by other subjects. However, Estonian pupils found it difficult to express their opinion on whether there should be a place for religion in school at all. Half of the pupils answered this question with 'neither agree nor disagree'. Pupils who have recently experienced religious education are significantly more in favour religious education as a separate subject and of religious education which is taught to students together. It is interesting that pupils who studied RE longer ago agree significantly less that RE should be taught to students together. (Possibly they are more skeptical because of the experiences they had with a Bible-oriented content of RE). However, the religious background of pupils plays the most important role in pupils' opinions about different models of religious education: Pupils who have a religion (quite a small group in the Estonian sample) are less in favour of optional religious education.

In *France* there is, among pupils, also a strong agreement that religious education must be optional (82%). Apart from that, it seemed also difficult for the French pupils to indicate what their position regarding different models of religious education in school is. About 60% does not agree with the statement that students should study Religious Education separately in groups according to which religion they belong. With regard to the other statements they are more divided and quite some pupils use the answer option 'neither agree nor disagree'. For French pupils, even religious ones, it is not obvious that there has to be a place for religion in school. In general, only 34% disagrees with the statement 'There should be no place for religion in school'. All in all, it seems that French pupils accept the decisions made in their country, namely that religious facts are taught within existing lessons. However, one must also take into account that they do not have other examples.

In *Saint Petersburg* pupils with a religion and pupils without a religion share the same opinions with regard to the preferred model of religious education. More differentiation with regard to preferences was found when the experiences pupils have with religion in school were taken into account. One of the statements which got least support from the pupils was: 'There should be no place for religion in school life'. This is interesting as the actual situation in St. Petersburg is exactly the absence of religion in school life. Pupils in the sample seem to be in favour of changing this. Two third of the pupils is in favour of optional Religious Education. Next to that, they prefer religious education in separate groups above education for all students together. One explanation given for this, is that pupils are eager to learn more about their own religion. However, with regard to pupils' thoughts about the preferred model of Religious Education, one must say that the opinions of Russian pupils are not very outspoken. One reason for this might be that it is difficult for pupils (like the Estonian and French pupils as well) to reflect on things they do not know any examples of (see conclusions).

A large majority of the *English* pupils, both pupils with and pupils without a religion, is in favour of integrated religious education. The fact that also pupils who have a religion favour religious education where all students are taught together, whatever differences there might be in their religious or denominational background, is a possible indication that these English religious pupils do not display intolerance towards other religions. All in all it seems that also in the English situation pupils seem to have absorbed the aspects of (religious) education as they usually experience them.

In the *Norwegian* context, there is only one statement which gets strong support: 'Religious education should be optional'. Next to that, more than 50% of the pupils is in favour of RE which is taught to all pupils together. Norwegian pupils are least sure about what to think of religious education which is taught sometimes together and sometimes in groups according to which religions students belong to. Girls are, however, a little bit more in favour of this last model than boys.

Spanish pupils are also most in favour of optional religious education. Next to that, they tend to prefer religious education which is separated according to which religion pupils belong. It is striking that this is exactly the model Spanish pupils have most experiences with in school. Religious education where all pupils are taught together gets the least support of the Spanish pupils. However, there is great variety in answers here. Pupils who do not have a religion are more against this model than pupils who have a religion. As in other countries, pupils have no strong opinions on whether religious education should be taught sometimes together and sometimes in groups according to which religions students belong to. Is seems that many pupils find it difficult to imagine how such a model would look like in practice.

In *Germany* there is agreement among the pupils, both in Hamburg and NRW, that religious education should be optional (61%, resp. 74%). The majority of pupils in both federal states also disagree that there should be no place for religion in school and/or that there is no need for the subject Religious Education. Data findings show that the importance pupils attach to religion and whether pupils attend Religious education this year or not have influence on how pupils look upon the different possible model of RE. Students to whom religion is important and students who currently attend RE agree less that RE should be optional and disagree more that religion should not have a place in school life. Differences are also found between pupils of different religions/worldviews: Christian pupils tend to agree less than pupils with 'no religion' that RE should be optional and both Christian and Muslim pupils agree less than others that there should be no religion in school life.

Although pupils in both federal states agree that RE should be optional and that there should be a place for a religion in school anyhow, they differ significantly in their thoughts on whether RE should be taught together or separately. Pupils in Hamburg favour the model of 'joint RE' and pupils of NRW prefer religious education separately in groups according to the religions of pupils. So also in the German context we see that pupils favour the RE model they are used to (see conclusions).

Pupils of the *Dutch* sample are convinced that there should be a place for religion in school. In general, they are most in favour of a model of religious education where all students are taught RE together. Next to that, there is a tendency among the Dutch pupils to prefer optional RE (55% agrees). Also from the Dutch data findings it becomes clear that the experiences pupils already have with a certain model of RE influence their thoughts on preferred models. Pupils who attend CCRE schools are less in favour of optional religious education and they agree significantly stronger with the statement that pupils should study religious education separately in groups according to which religion they belong. Also the personal religious background of pupils has an influence here: In comparison to pupils who have a religion, pupils who do not have a religion are more inclined to agree that there should be no place for religion in school life and that there is no need for the subject Religious education. They are also more in favour of optional religious education.

3.   European tendencies with regard to effects of religious diversity in education

In order to explore the data further and find tendencies which are worthwhile to investigate in further research, hypotheses have been formulated on, among others, the role of religious diversity in education. On the basis of the national contributions I will give an overview.

3.1   Students who have encountered religious diversity in education are more tolerant

In the *Estonian* context it is difficult to differentiate between schools where pupils meet religious diversity and schools where they don't. Therefore, in the Estonian chapter the authors pay more attention to the effect of the presence of Religious Education in school on the degree of tolerance of pupils. The authors rightly state that encountering religious diversity in education can take different forms and have different effects. However, there seems to be a tendency in the Estonian material that schools who have integrated religion in their everyday life have a positive influence on pupils' readiness for respect and tolerance. This can also be said for schools which provide separate RE lessons. Pupils without any experiences of RE expressed the most negative opinions towards religion in many questions of the questionnaire.

In *France* it was possible to compare the reactions of the pupils who attended private schools (relatively small religious diversity) and pupils who go to public schools (bigger religious diversity). Pupils of the private schools seem to be less open-minded. However, in the French contribution this has not been worked out further.

In the *Russian* chapter it is stressed that one needs to be cautious not to draw illegitimate conclusions on the effects of religious diversity on the basis of the data findings as we have them now. It is very difficult to separate the influence of school from the many other contextual influences pupils are confronted with. However, it seems to be the case that encountering religious diversity in school can have both positive and negative effects on pupils.

Also the *English* authors stress that on the basis of the current research there is only limited evidence to describe tendencies with regard to the hypothesis, as in most of the participating schools religious diversity is just a given. Only one school (school 14) is more or less 'mono cultural'. As throughout the questionnaire these pupils seemed to be less open-minded, there are some (however small) indications that, at least in the English context, it might be true that students who have encountered religious diversity in education are more tolerant.

With regard to the *Norwegian* sample it is also difficult to describe tendencies on the impact of religious diversity in education as all public schools have the same non-confessional religious education (KRL). Private schools were not included in the sample. However, pupils of the school with the highest degree of religious diversity are also the pupils who are very tolerant and who attach importance to dialogue. This might be a support for the mentioned hypothesis. However, at this school there are many pupils to whom religion (especially Islam) is important. This could also have an effect on the extent to which pupils are tolerant and/or open to dialogue. On the basis of the current data it is impossible to separate these effects.

In the *Spanish* context it was possible to compare pupils who attend optional confessional RE and pupils who attend compulsory confessional RE. One has to take into account, however, that religious education in the Spanish context basically deals with Catholicism as a consequence of historical Spanish context, and exceptionally with Islamic and Evangelic religion. No significant differences were found between pupils who have experiences with the two mentioned models with regard to their answer on the item 'I don't like people from other religions and I do not want to live together with them'. All students, even independent whether they have a religion themselves or not, responded negative. In the Spanish context no indications have been found that students who have encountered religious diversity are more tolerant.

In the *German* national chapter it is concluded that attitudes of 'intolerance towards other religions' are not related to encounters with religious diversity in education as such. However, there are correlations between (in)tolerance and both 'having friends who belong to different religions' and 'spending time with young people who have different religious background (both at school and after school). So, at least in the German context, it seems that the impact of personal encounters is much stronger than the issue whether religious diversity is met at school or not.

In the *Dutch* sample no significant differences were found with regard to the extent to which pupils respect other pupils who believe, between pupils who have more or less experiences with religious diversity in school. There are also no significant differences with regard to the item 'I don't like people from different religions and I do not want to live together with them'. Next to that, an indication was found that pupils who do not have much experiences with religious diversity in education (CCRE schools) are less negative about the possible effects of disagreement on religious issues than pupils who do have experiences with religious diversity. The impression is that pupils who do not have much experience with religious diversity, do not have so much an idea of what could possibly be difficult in contacts with people of different religions.

3.2   Students who have encountered religious diversity in education are more open to dialogue on religious issues

Also with regard to the relation between religious diversity in education and the openness to dialogue, the focus in the *Estonian* context has been on the impact of different models of RE. Significant differences were found between those who did not receive any RE and the other pupils. Students without any experience of religious education agree less that students should be able to talk and communicate about religious issues. They are also less eager to know what their best friends think about religion. There are also significant differences between pupils who received RE long time ago and pupils who received RE recently. Pupils who studied RE long time ago agree for instance more that talking about religion could lead to disagreement. They also feel less comfortable to talk about religion.

There is a slight tendency in the material that those who did not have any form of religious studies are less ready for dialogue and more likely to agree with hostile statements.

In the *French* national contribution it is made clear that it seems easier for students to engage in dialogue with each other if they meet religious diversity in school. However, pupils who meet religious diversity in school are not necessarily more open-minded than others. Just because they are more confronted with pupils of different religions they more strongly feel the need to discuss with others about religion.

As stated above, in the *Russian* context it was not possible to describe tendencies on the basis of the present data material.

The authors of the *Spanish* contribution stress that Spanish pupils can meet religious diversity both inside and outside classrooms. No significant differences were found between pupils who attend CCRE and pupils who attend OCRE with regard to the extent to which they are open to dialogue on religious issues. Nevertheless, there is a tendency for pupils who attend compulsory confessional religious education to (more strongly) deny the possible negative aspects of religion (for instance that religion is embarrassing, cruel etc.).

As made clear above, on the basis of the *English* material only few words have been spent on the hypotheses. The only tendency described is that pupils of the relatively 'mono cultural school' seem to be less open minded.

Also in the *Norwegian* case it is difficult, as described above, to describe tendencies on the impact of religious diversity in education.

In the *German* sample no significant correlations were found between the variable 'readiness for dialogue' and having or not having students in the class who have different religions. There are, however, significant correlations between pupils' readiness for dialogue and the degree to which they agree that at school they 'get knowledge about different religions', 'learn to respect everyone' and 'get opportunities to discuss religious issues from different perspectives'.

With regard to the *Dutch* sample one can say that there are hardly any differences between pupils who have experiences with different models of religious education. This e.g. applies for the question whether they think that learning to be able to talk about religious issues should be an aim of education. There are however differences between the three groups of pupils with regard to the way they react when confronted with a person who has another conviction. Pupils who have relatively few experiences with religious diversity at school (CCRE) are more inclined than other pupils to discuss about the other person's opinions. So it seems that they are more open to dialogue. However, these pupils are also more eager to convince others of their own right. All in all it is not so easy to state that religious diversity in education in itself stimulates dialogue. The religious background of pupils and the importance they attach to religion (in combination with the role religion plays in their family life) probably interfere with the impact of religious diversity in education.

4. Conclusions: main tendencies

In the final section of this chapter I will, as a summary of this chapter, describe general impressions and tendencies with regard to how European pupils look upon religion in education and what kind of experiences they have with it. I will also point out some directions for further research. It is, however, important to realize that the national samples are not representative. Therefore, cautiousness is needed and too strong conclusions need to be avoided. On the basis of our, very rich but not representative, material, we can however describe tendencies.

First of all it must be said that *the way Religious Education is given shape in the participating countries is very diverse. School systems, curricula, formal aims of RE, the role of the Church, role of religion in overall society are, among other things, different. Apart from that, the concrete experiences pupils have with religious education also vary from school to school, from teacher to teacher. Nevertheless, some general comments can be made on how European pupils look upon religious education.*

In none of the countries pupils give clearly positive answers on the statements how important and/or interesting they think it is to pay attention to religion in school. However, it was found that, for instance, attention to religion in school is more important for pupils who have a religious background, who attach importance to religion, who currently attend RE and who have experiences with confessional religious education than it is for other pupils.

The pupils' background is also very important when it comes to their opinions on the role religion should play in school and in how far (other) pupils' religious needs should be taken into account. It is striking that pupils who live in countries where religion first of all belongs to private life and not to public sphere, pupils are much more reluctant with regard to for instance the possibility of wearing religious symbols.

Pupils are, in general, of the opinion that is important to respect the religions of others and to take into account that pupils with different religions might have different festivals and food requirements. However, at the same time pupils attach great importance to 'equal treatment' and are reluctant to change too much in school (curriculum) for the sake of a particular group of students. Pupils seem to be very negative and reluctant about transforming the needs of some pupils into requirements for the whole group. In the French contribution this is well formulated: 'Students think that each of them has the right to do what he or she wants, on the one condition that whatever that is should not be required of other students' (quotation from the French chapter). Aspects like 'freedom', 'respect' and 'tolerance' seem to very important to the students. In all countries pupils have the least problems with other pupils wearing discrete religious symbols. They don't see much harm in this. However, as soon as symbols become more visible, more pupils express their negative feelings. This could possibly be seen in the line of the above mentioned impression: Pupils are willing to respect others and to give them freedom to have and express their own belief, but it should not be too obvious and other people should definitely not be bothered with it.

From many national contributions it becomes clear that pupils who have a religion them-selves are more willing to give space to religion in school than other pupils. It is striking that this is especially the case with regard to the issues whether schools should provide facilities to pray in school and whether voluntary religious services could be part of school life. Next to that, it seems that pupils who have (already) experiences with a certain issue (for instance with voluntary religious services) are more willing to agree that this certain issue should play a role in school. *So, in general, personal experiences of pupils with religion in school and their own religious background are of great importance when it comes to their views on the role of religion in school.* However, pupils of the Estonian sample take a quite exceptional perspective in this whole spectrum. They do value to learn to respect each other, but they– as being young people for whom religion seems not to be part of life – do not see 'any reason to guarantee rights for students with a religious background and so they rather refuse them' (except for wearing discrete religious symbols). *This brings me to the point that data findings make clear that the role religion plays in (the history of) the respective countries and the way religion is discussed in public discussions also have an influence on pupils' thoughts on reli-gion in education.* In countries where religion is more or less withdrawn from public life, pupils are more inclined to focus on RE as a way of getting information about religion. In countries where pupils are confronted with religious diversity in society as a given, where it is much more common that for instance religious issues are discussed in public debates and/or where religion is much more visible in public life, pupils are more inclined to stress the socie-tal function of religious education and to attach importance to religion in education at the first place.

The general impression is that European pupils have the feeling that learning about reli-gions at school has more impact on their knowledge on different religions, their respect for people of different religions and on how they (learn to) live together than on what they learn about themselves, current events and decisions between right and wrong. *The social dimen-sion of learning about religion in school (including getting knowledge about different reli-gions) is, so to say, much more accepted and appreciated by pupils than the personal dimen-sion.*

When it comes to what pupils see as the (possible) aims of religious education, we found that pupils take their own situation as an important background. *Especially the issues whether pupils have a religion or not and what their current experiences with religion in education are, have quite some impact on how they look upon the aims for religious education.* In gen-eral, pupils who have a religion are more positive about (almost) all the mentioned aims. Especially with regard to the aim of being guided towards religious beliefs, we see the influ-ence of the kind of religious education pupils are acquainted with. Pupils who have experi-ences with confessional religious education (for instance in the Netherlands and in NRW) are less negative about this aim. *However, the general tendency is that European pupils are not in favour of an approach of RE in education which guides pupils towards religious beliefs. Pupils are much more in favour of getting objective knowledge about different religions and also of learning to understand what religions teach.* To a lesser (but still quite strong) extent, pupils also want to learn how to communicate about religious issues and learn about the im-portance of religion for dealing with problems in society. Although pupils who do not have a religion generally attach less importance to the mentioned aims, they tend to agree that these issues should be dealt with at school.

The role of religion in society as a whole also seems to influence the way pupils look upon the different models of religious education. *It is striking that in (almost) all countries pupils are in favour of optional religious education.* However, although in all countries a majority of pupils prefers optional RE, there are differences between the countries with regard to the exact percentages of pupils who are in favour of this optional RE. Percentages run from 55% (The Netherlands) to more than 80% (in Estonia and France). This difference can possibly be explained when the actual experiences with religious education and their personal religious background are taken into account. For instance, unlike in France and Estonia, quite some pupils of the Dutch sample have experiences with compulsory confessional religious education. It is exactly these pupils who least support the ideas that RE should be optional and together, irrespective the religious backgrounds of pupils.

It is striking from the findings in different countries that the actual experiences pupils have (or not have) with religious education have a strong influence on how they look upon religious education in school and what they think about (possible) aims for it. Besides that, it turned out that pupils who don't have much (or any) experiences with religious education (as a separate school subject) find it difficult to imagine the mentioned options and to express their thoughts about it. Pupils take their own (national and local) situation as starting point and mostly they are in favour of the situation as they already know it. However, one interesting exemption of this 'rule' seems to be the pupils of the Russian sample. Although their background is a situation of relative absence of attention to religion in education, they disagree with the statement that there should be no place for religion in school life. However, one must be cautious to draw too big conclusions from this finding, as for the questions on model of religious education, the pupils of the Russian sample are very modest in their reactions. One explanation for this might be that just like the Estonian and French pupils, the Russian pupils find it difficult to express their opinion on something they (hardly) know any examples of.

I will end this conclusion with a few words on the hypotheses which deal with the impact of religious diversity in education. From the reactions of the national teams it has become clear, in the first place, that one must be very cautious drawing too quick conclusions on this. *From the present data findings it is very difficult, and in some countries even impossible, to know exactly the different levels and correlations of religious diversity, tolerance and dialogue.* It is obvious that more detailed research is needed here. This research should go further into questions as what 'meeting religious diversity in education' really means in school practice. Also more information is needed on how concrete schools in different countries deal with religious diversity (if present) in actual school life. A quantitative research as carried out in the frame of the REDCo project is not sufficient to deal with these complicated issues. Probably, a more thorough (qualitative) study would also give more tools to separate different background variables. This would give a better indication of the influence of religious diversity in education. For up till now it is impossible to state to what the degree a certain attitude ((in)tolerance) of a pupil is the effect of his of her personal background and the importance of religion in his or here life or of the fact that this pupil is (not) confronted with religious diversity in school. In the Estonian and French data some clear indications have been found that students who have encountered religious diversity in education are more tolerant. An interesting issue is raised by, among others, the German team. On the basis of their data they have the feeling that religious diversity in education as such is not so much a matter of influence. Personal encounters (in classroom) with people of different religions might have a much bigger influence on the degree to which pupils are tolerant towards others and/or open to dialogue on religious issues. It is very interesting to elaborate on this 'hypothesis' in relation to the question 'What does this mean for religious diversity in education?' One might conclude that it is not 'enough' that religious diversity in education is just there in the sense that pupils of different religious backgrounds go to the same school and attend the same lessons. It might be that this religious diversity in education only has an impact on pupils if they are confronted with religious diversity on a personal level and/or if religious diversity in education is not 'just there' at school, but actively dealt with as an important given pupils can learn from.

All in all it is clear that although we need to take into account the explorative character of the research and the fact that the samples are not representative, some very interesting tendencies can be described on the basis of the present research with regard to how European pupils look upon religion in education. Next to that it can been concluded that the present research serves as a very important step towards more elaborated and detailed research on the relative influence of, among other things, the religious background of pupils, the importance they attach to religion, the experiences they have with religion in education and their national context. With regard to the role of religious diversity in education, it would be especially interesting to investigate the possibilities and impact of personal encounters with pupils of different religions within the context of school education. As the impact of the mere presence of religious diversity in education on tolerance and dialogue is not so obvious, it would be insightful to have a better understanding on how religious diversity is actually dealt with in schools and how pupils perceive this.

Pille Valk

How do European Students See the Impact of Religion in Society?[1]

1.   Introduction

In the last pages of the book I will present the systematized overview of the European teenagers' perspectives regarding the third research question of the REDCo project quantitative survey. The guiding question is how pupils see the impact of Religion? To elaborate on this question, I have picked up mostly the items from the third part of the questionnaire: What role does religion play in the society according to the students' understandings? How far it is a topic for dialogue or does it contribute to conflict? How does religion occur as a topic in their conversations and what is talked about when talking about religion? How do the students see the possibilities for peaceful coexistence in the pluralistic society?

After looking at these questions I will turn to the third pair of the hypotheses we used to reflect upon the findings in our study:

H3a) Students who have personally encountered religious diversity are more tolerant, and

H3b) Students who have personally encountered religious diversity are more open to dialogue on religious issues.

The following synthetic presentation relies on the material presented in the national chapters of the book and will focus on the most evident patterns, tendencies, and striking findings across all the countries.

Before we can move to the search for these patterns and tendencies in the European religion and society landscape as seen through the eyes of European teenagers, one has to remember that the samples behind the data were not representative – thus, some calming caution is needed with regard to making generalisations. However, we will not underestimate the richness of our data.

2.   Evaluation of the role of religion in society by the European teenagers

In this section I will look upon the main tendencies in the responses given by the students to the items 82–85 and 103–106 in the questionnaire which is included in the end of this book. Students where asked to what extent they agree with the following statements made by their peers who participated in the qualitative survey of the REDCo project.

Regarding the statement that *religious people are less tolerant towards others* (q. 82) more students disagreed than agreed with the statement in all countries.[2] Among the others the Dutch students disagreed most soundly with this position – two out of three disagreed (strongly) with the statement, and only less than one out of ten agreed. It is interesting to note that the mode of answers to this statement in all other countries was 3 (in the Netherlands it

1   This article was supported by the European Union through the European Regional Development Fund (Centre of Excellence CECT).
2   Here and henceforth positive (agree and agree strongly) and negative (disagree and disagree strongly) responses are summarized if the individual categories are not mentioned specifically.

was 4). This 'neither nor' position was most popular in Norway and in Estonia, where almost every second student replied like this.

The next statement *"Without religion the world would be a better place"* (q. 83) gave more differing responses than the previous one. Dutch and German students disagreed with this statement most soundly – in both countries the most popular response was 'strongly disagree'. The rate of disagreement was also quite high in Russian sample. A different pattern of the positions occurred in Norway and France, both having quite a flat distribution (almost an equal groups for agree, neither agree or disagree, and disagree) of answers. In the Estonian sample half of the students chose a 'neither nor' position.

Do the students consider *religion as a private matter* or not was the item for the next question (q. 84). In the English and Spanish samples every third student disagreed with the statement. But the most striking results came form Russia. More than nine out of ten students in St. Petersburg agreed that religion belongs to private life. Only 2% of the students disagreed with the statement and some 6% chose the position 'neither agree nor disagree'. This was the sharpest profile of answers in all the study. As is emphasised also in the Russian chapter – there was a certain concept of a very private nature of religion among the students from St. Petersburg. This profile is one proof of these findings. A somewhat similar pattern of answers was found in the other post-soviet country – Estonia, where slightly more than two out of three agreed with the statement. Such pattern raises a question: is it possible to see behind these findings the shadow of the Soviet atheistic regime when everything connected to religion was ridiculed and banned from public life (Valk, 2007, pp. 161–162)?

It is interesting to mention that the most popular answer (mode) to this question not only in Estonia but also in France was 'agree'.

The next item described *religion as a source of aggressiveness* (q. 85). The connection between religion and aggressiveness was most soundly rejected by the students in the Dutch, English and Spanish samples. In all these countries the most popular answer to this statement was 'strongly disagree'. In Netherlands more than three out of four students disagreed with the statement. In all other countries the most popular answer was 'neither agree nor disagree' but all means lay on the disagreement side of the scale (from 3.12 for the Norwegian sample to 3.45 for the French and German ones). The rate of agreement with the statement was highest in Norway with 28% of respondents. There were three samples where the 'neither nor' position gained 40% or more supporters – Estonia, Norway and Russia. In the Netherlands, for example, this percentage was only 15%.

How far did our respondents agree that *disagreement on religious issues leads to conflicts* (q. 103)? Looking at the means of the responses in all countries one can see that students tend to position themselves on the 'agree-side' of the scale – between 2.14 (France) and 2.72 (Netherlands). The rate of those agreeing was significantly highest in France and England (72% and 62% of respondents respectively). In other countries the percentage of those who recognised the conflict potential of disagreement on religious issues lay between 44% (Netherlands) and 50% (Spain). Among Estonian, German, Norwegian and Russian respondents two out of five students preferred the 'neither nor' position. It is interesting to compare this pattern of responses with the answers given by the respondents to the questions about the possible reaction to proselytizing. In all samples the most supported position was '*I listen but their views do not influence me*'.

Respecting the religion of others as a way to cope with differences was the most unanimously agreed statement in the set of items in this section. In all countries more than half the respondents agreed with the statement. Agreement was most solid in France and Netherlands where 81% of students agreed with the statement, whereas the agreement in Russia and Estonia was slightly more moderate – 51% and 57% respectively. It is interesting to mention that in both countries more than one out of three respondents preferred the position 'neither agree nor disagree'.

While agreement with the statement about the importance of respect regarding the different religions in coping with differences was soundly supported by our respondents in all countries, the next statement – "*I don't like people from other religions and do not want to live together with them*" was disagreed with almost similarly soundly. Rejection was most strong in France (mean 4.47) and in The Netherlands (mean 4.31). Among the others, the two post-socialist countries, Estonia and Russia, share the salient pattern again. If in all other countries the most popular answer was 'strongly disagree', in these countries it was 'disagree'. Also the percentage of those, who preferred not to take a side regarding this statement, was highest in these countries – 29% in Estonia and 25% in Russia. The 'neither nor' position was also popular in Spain where 24% of respondents chose it.

The statement "*People with different strong religious views can not live together*" gave the following picture. The Estonian sample differed remarkably from others. First – almost every second student did not take a positive or negative position regarding this statement; and secondly the percentage of those who agreed with the statement was saliently higher (32%), than in all other countries. If in other countries the means of the answers lay in between 3.21 (for Russia) and 3.69 (for France) the mean for the Estonian sample was 2.83. And again – French and Dutch students are the most optimistic regarding the possibilities to overcome even strong differences in religious convictions.

General patterns

Looking at the findings regarding the role of religion in the society through the European teenagers' perspective, one can point out the following general patterns:

– Most of the teenagers surveyed see religion as a normal part of the societal life.
– The surveyed students mainly did not see religion as a source of aggressiveness nor an obstacle to tolerance.
– Students soundly disagreed with the xenophobic statement 'I don't like people from other religions and do not want to live together with them' in all our samples.
– The surveyed teenagers were quite aware of the conflict potential of religion. At the same time most of them were convinced that respecting the religion of others is a way to cope with differences.

After figureing the general picture, I will next turn to the national reports to look for some background variables shaping the positions of the respondents.

One of the common findings in the national chapters is the notion that the most influential factor in shaping the positions of students regarding the above mentioned statements is a student's religious affiliation. In several countries this appeared to be an even clearer divider than more detailed distinctions between particular religions or worldviews. In the countries where the proportion of the Muslim students was big enough for a statistical comparison, it appeared that they tend to be the ones with the most open attitudes toward others.

Here are some distinguishing outcomes from different national findings:

In England: Muslim students were more likely to strongly disagree with some of the negative statements than other religions; Christians mildly disagreed. Muslim students were significantly more likely to strongly disagree with views that 'Religious people were less tolerant towards others' and highly significantly more likely to disagree that 'religion should belong to private life'.

In Estonia: Religiously affiliated students disagreed significantly more with hostile statements that religion is a source of aggression and the world would be better without it or that religious people are less tolerant. The answers of students were compared also by how important they think religion is or what they believe in: the differences are quite remarkable, especially in regard to the importance of religion. 'Without religion the world would be a better place' was less agreed by those for whom religion was very important (mean 4.25), who had a religious affiliation (3.91) and who believed in God (3.87); most agreed by those for whom religion was not important at all (2.79) and who had no religious affiliation (2.82).

In France: Boys were slightly more critical about religion than girls, especially when considering the most definite answers possible (strongly agree / strongly disagree). The religious students had a more positive view of religion than those without religion, especially Muslim students who shared a much better image of religion than young Catholics, who were close to the average. Students without religion had a more critical attitude about religion than their religious classmates.

In Germany: Students with 'no religion' tended to agree significantly more than Christian and Muslim students that 'religious people are less tolerant towards others', while Muslim students tended to agree significantly less than Christians and students with 'no religion' that 'religion is a source of aggressiveness' and that 'without religion the world would be a better place'. It also occurred in the German study that students from schools with a 'lower educational level' as well as students with 'no religion' tended to agree more that they 'do not like the people from other religions'. Students to whom religion is more important and Muslim students tended to agree less with the statement that 'people with strong religious views cannot live together'.

In Norway: Those who say religion is 'absolutely not important' are the only ones who tend to support the statement 'without religion the world would be a better place'.

In Russia: Quite expectable were the highly significant differences between the two subgroups in their reactions to the statement 'Without religion the world would be a better place' or in their agreement with identifying religion as a source of aggressiveness. Religious students showed in both cases a more positive attitude toward religion.

In Spain: "...believing students responded more decidedly in favour of the positive virtues of religion than against its negative aspects [...] On this point we suggest a common component exists, that those who believe in religion itself incorporate other viewpoints but these viewpoints are denied by those from non-religious perspectives. In other words we could ask: Who would more firmly affirm that religion is positive, integrating, and not a source of aggressiveness? Without a doubt, it would be those students who recognised their own beliefs and were 'tolerant' of others' beliefs."

Thus, summing up – in all the national samples in REDCo survey an interesting and important similar pattern occurred:

Students with religious affiliation share much more positive positions regarding the impact of religion in society. They are more likely to disagree that religious people are less tolerant toward others, that the world would be a better place without religion and that religion is the source of aggressiveness. They also esteemed the role of respecting the religion of others in coping with differences significantly more highly.

On this point one could critically ask – are these findings really striking?

One possible explanation to this pattern was offered by the Dutch colleagues: "It might be that the students, who have themselves good experiences with religion, believe by consequence that the impact of religion in general is positive. It could also be, even at the same time, that pupils who have a religion are overestimating the positive effects of religion and/or underestimating the possible negative effects as a way to 'justify' their own position. At the same time, pupils who do not have a religion can have a certain bias which 'forces' them to express negative thoughts on religion, even if in everyday life they do not have so many experiences of the negative effects of religion at all."

Or another explanation: it might be that the students who themselves say that they have no religion are not acquainted with the possible influence of religion. We ask them something they just do not (yet) know about; and since it is unknown, they tend to be negative.

To give a definitive explanation of the complex impact of personal religious affiliation, more investigation is needed in the future.

To conclude this section, I would like to present some more thought-provoking findings. Cross-analysis of the above mentioned items pointed to the pedagogical background influences. The Estonian survey revealed the negative influence of missing continuity in RE studies. The students who had had RE only in primary school and who did not have religious studies in their upper grades in school tended to be more negative in their responses to religion, and to differences on religious grounds, than students who studied RE recently. These findings could be explained in the following way: It can be that students' understanding of religion has not become complex enough and consistent with their development, while the simplistic understandings they held in childhood are rejected. This is a strong argument for continuous age-appropriate RE through all the school career. It also points to the need of longitudinal research on the role and impact of RE in formation of the students views.

This train of thought could be complemented by the material from the Russian chapter where the point is made about the possible negative role of the misuse of, or unprofessional, teaching of RE in one of the schools several years ago. It is interesting to note that this influence is recognizable even long afterwards, even for the students who did not participate in those lessons and have therefore only received the influence second-hand. Thus, there is a need for more detailed (thick) description of the pedagogical situation in the school when researching the role of RE in the formation of students' views.

There is one more issue waiting for further investigation. What lies behind the undetermined positions 'neither agree nor disagree'? Is it an absence of any position or is it a signal that it is impossible to take a clear position regarding such ambivalent statements? Was it a problem of confusing wording or was it just reflection of the lack of motivation to take the survey more seriously? One possible interpretation is offered by the German colleges:

"This can be interpreted as an expression of realistic as well as balanced views on the issues discussed. Rather than an indication of indifference it could be concluded that students are quite aware of the ambivalent effects of religion on peoples' attitudes and social cohesion, which would be in line with findings of the qualitative studies regarding the societal dimension of religion." Anyway, it is one of the issues worth more attention when preparing forthcoming surveys.

3.   Religion as a contribution for dialogue

As is said in the first chapter of the book, we did not work with an elaborated specific theoretical concept of dialogue in our quantitative study. Instead, we decided to use the simple
wording 'talking about' as a flexible synonym for dialogue in our instrument.

The following section will look at the 'cross-country landscape' using the items 90, 91, 93,
94, and 97 from the questionnaire.

Three statements from this set explored the possible positive impact of dialogue on religious issues – *"Talking about religion helps to understand others", "Talking about religion
helps me to live peacefully together with people from different religions",* and *"Talking about
religion helps me to understand better what is going on in the world".*

When looking at the mean values of the responses to the first statement, it occurs that in all
samples they lay closely and firmly on the agreement side of the scale, between 2.44 (England) and 2.82 (Estonia). A similar pattern was found also in regarding to the third statement.
Here also all the means are below '3' from 2.49 (France) to 2.95 (Russia). Talking about religion as a prerequisite for the peaceful co-existence of people from different religions met a
slightly different response. Here the means lay between 2.75 (Dutch respondents) and 3.18
(French respondents). The means of the responses fell slightly into the disagreement side of
the scale in three samples – in France, St. Petersburg (3.07) and Norway (3.04).

The statement, that talking about religion only leads to disagreement was not agreed by the
'average respondent' in all countries – all the mean values lay on the disagreement side of the
scale from 3.07 (for Norway and Estonia) to 3.86 (for The Netherlands).

The statement reflecting the emotional reactions regarding religion as something to talk
about – "In my view talking about religion is embarrassing" was rejected by lot of respondents in all countries. The mildest disagreement was found among the St. Petersburg students
(3.31); the strongest disagreement was recorded among the Dutch students (4.25). There were
three samples where the mean value of the responses was higher than 4 (thus, in-between
'disagree' and 'strongly disagree') – in addition to The Netherlands this was the case also in
Germany and in Norway. The last detail is of particular interest because when looking at the
answers to *"For me talking about religious topics is boring",* Norwegian respondents together
with Estonians were the only ones whose mean response fell slightly to the agreement side of
the scale (2.96): is it the case that talking about religion is not embarrassing because it is just
not an issue to talk about?

These general findings regarding 'talking about religion' could be synthesized in the following way:

–   The surveyed students evaluate the dialogue on religious issues as an important mean of
      understanding others as well as the current events going on in the world.

–   The respondents were less optimistic about talking about religion as being a sufficient
      prerequisite for peaceful coexistence. Probably something more is needed.

–   Religion was not considered as an embarrassing topic to discuss about by our respon-
      dents. If they are not so eager to talk about religion in some countries it is because their
      main interests lay somewhere else.

Looking for the background variables regarding the 'talking about religion' issues I have
picked up several items from the national reports pointing out some background variables
shaping the positions of the respondents.

England: There were marked differences between students with different worldviews; contrary to what is often implied by some sections of the British media, Muslim students in this sample were both more committed to the value of religions and to the contribution of those with religious views to co-existence between those of different religions.

Estonia: All the positive attitudes towards the value of talking about religion are supported significantly more by the religiously affiliated students. It was also found that the statements were more agreed with, the more the person valued the importance of religion for him/herself.

Girls were significantly more optimistic about the positive effects of speaking about religious issues. They were especially positive about the impact of dialogue in understanding others.

France: Indifference to religious issues predominates among French students, more with boys than girls, and much more with those who have no religion than with religious students. The answers given by students without religion should not be interpreted as an unwillingness to talk about the matter as a school subject, but since religion has no meaning to them, their discussions with classmates must focus on other topics in everyday life. Muslims are the ones who talk about religion the most and are the most interested in it, probably because religion plays a more important role in their lives, and, probably, Muslim students who fight against the negative stereotypes that are propagated about Islam are interested in dialogue mostly to defend a positive image of their faith.

Germany: Religion is not a 'non-issue' in conversations among the German students.

The more significant correlations in 'dialogue' items occurred with students for whom religion is more important. They tend to agree more with all the positive statements and disagree with all the negative statements about the impact of talking about religion.

The Netherlands: The data show that pupils who attend confessional religious education are more willing to talk about religion, attach greater importance to religion, and are more inclined to stress the positive aspects of talking about religious differences. The Dutch team also stresses that these findings may be shaped also by the personal religious background of the students, as they (or their families) have chosen a school with a particular model of RE according to their personal affiliation.

Norway: There are some patterns of gender differences in the Norwegian study – the girls agree more than boys with the positive statements, and disagree more with the negative ones. There were also some important differences between the schools – the school from the capital was distinguished by its positive evaluation of talking about religion while the schools in smaller cities were more towards the other end of the spectrum on this issue.

Russia: Religious students demonstrate a more positive evaluation of inter-religious communication. Boys and girls have similar reasons to talk or not to talk about religion, though girls evaluate more positively the peace-making potential of religious dialogue. The finding that schools may play a significant role in shaping the views of students also finds confirmation regarding the issues of talking about religion.

Spain: A great majority of Spanish students agreed that without dialogue between the students of distinct religious points of view, religion would not be able to bridge their differences. This leads the Spanish researchers to ask: to what point can groups coexist in a context of religious diversity without a recognition and understanding of that diversity throughout education?

Summing up the main findings presented above, one can state that;
– Positive statements towards dialogue are evaluated more highly, and negative ones lower, by the students with religious affiliation.
– Girls in all countries tended to be more open for dialogue and more optimistic about the possible positive impact of such communication.
– Muslim students were distinguished by higher readiness for dialogue and communication in several countries. It is a challenging complex research question for future deeper investigation – how far their readiness to talk about religion is influenced by their reaction to the negative image propagated sometimes by the media, how far it is an apologetic position, how far there is deeper conscious readiness for dialogue. These questions can of course also be addressed to the readiness for dialogue of Christian pupils.

The Norwegian and St Petersburg material points to the need to investigate more deeply the impact of the particular schools upon the students' attitudes. This item for further research was complemented also by the findings by the Dutch team where the complex impact of the confessional schools was brought forward.

4.   Ways to peaceful coexistence

The last set of the items in the questionnaire dealt with the question: what would help people from different religions to live together in peace? The students were offered six options so as to evaluate their importance according to their own points of view.

In general, the most highly evaluated prerequisite for peaceful coexistence was, according to the students participating in our survey, '*if they know about each other's religions*'. This item was considered very important or important by more than 80% of respondents in The Netherlands (87%), England (85%), Estonia (83%) and Germany (81%). The most cautious estimation of the positive impact of knowledge for a harmonious society occurred among the St. Petersburg respondents, who also had the biggest group of those did not believe in the power of knowledge – 22% of Russian students considered knowledge about the other's religion not important for peaceful coexistence. A closely similar position appeared also in Spain, where more than a quarter of students did not see the importance of religion, or could not assess its importance.

The next condition for a peaceful state in the pluralistic society was '*if people share common interests*'. This item was most highly evaluated among the English (87%) and Estonian students (86%). French respondents evaluated the importance of this condition slightly lower than others – 68% agreed it was very or quite important. In the rest of the countries this evaluation was shared approximately by three out of four.

The next popular condition for peaceful coexistence was, according to the respondents of the survey, '*if they do something together*'. Common action was most highly estimated in France (83%) and Estonia (81%); Spanish and Russian respondents were more cautious, both with 69% of those who considered it very or quite important.

Personal contacts with the people from different religions were seen as important by 83% of Dutch respondents. The percentage of those who supported this item lay between 70% and 79% in other countries, with one exception. The pattern occurring in the St. Petersburg sample was significantly different – the importance of personal contacts was considered important by 59% of respondents and not important by 29% of them.

What lies behind a 'St. Petersburg pattern' is an interesting research question for the future. One of the possible ways ahead is outlined by the Russian colleague by stating that the special characteristic of the St. Petersburg sample is a hidden and silent pattern of religious life complemented by an *asocial* type of religiosity. The Russian colleagues incline to interpret this set of characteristics as interrelated and explainable in terms of a defence and a protest against potential, and alas too probable, politicisation of religious life, and to associate this factor with fundamental socio-cultural and political reasons responsible for the low sociability of modern Russians.

Two remaining statements regarding the preconditions for peaceful coexistence – 'If everyone keeps their own religion in private' and 'If the state has strong regulations about the role of religion in society' were rated in all countries participating in the REDCo project quite differently from the previous ones. The evaluation of both items includes a remarkably high percentage of those who chose the answer 'cannot say'. When the teenagers evaluated the importance of strong legislative regulations, 42% of the French sample and 38% of the Spanish one replied with 'cannot say'. The highest approval for the legislative means was given in The Netherlands where 45% of respondents considered it important. The most sceptical pattern of responses occurred in Norway and in Germany.

Our respondents were also not very optimistic about the option that keeping one's own religion in private will contribute to peaceful coexistence. More than half of the respondents rejected this option in the Dutch sample. A somewhat more positive evaluation of this item occurred in Germany and in France, where slightly less than half of students considered this option important. Anyway, the French respondents also had the biggest group of 'can not say' positions (29%).

Looking at the general tendencies in the surveyed students' views regarding the prerequisites for peaceful coexistence, one can point out the following issues:

– Students evaluate knowledge about the different religions and worldviews as one of the most important preconditions for peace in the pluralistic society.
– Common interests and joint action help to develop social cohesion. Personal contacts help to overcome separation and xenophobia.
– The relevance of the impact of legislative measures in attaining peaceful coexistence is less agreed upon, compared to the above-mentioned aspects such as knowledge, common interests and joint actions. Nevertheless legislative measures are also regarded as a useful instrument by a considerable proportion of pupils. Even less was the number of those who agreed that keeping religion as a private matter will solve the problems.

5.   Reflection on the hypotheses on the impact of personal encounters with religious diversity

What might be the impact of the encountering of religious diversity in one's life world upon opinions about the role and impact of religion in the society was one of the questions that lay behind the third set of research hypotheses of the REDCo project. We supposed that:

H3a) Students who have personally encountered religious diversity are more tolerant.
H3b) Students who have personally encountered religious diversity are more open to dialogue on religious issues.

What the reflection in the light of the research hypotheses brought forward in different countries, is the guiding question through the following section of the chapter[3]. Does the data tend to be 'in line' with the statements in the hypotheses or does it point in a different direction?

England

It was possible to point out on the basis of our data that the discussion of religious issues and personal belief was problematic for the indigenous white students in more rural areas and in mono-cultural schools in particular where they faced a climate of youth apathy and negativity towards religion. Religion was more often a topic of conversation in multi-cultural urban areas and among Muslims with South Asian and Christians with African backgrounds.

It is important to mention that the results in this section reflect the values propagated in the English inclusive approach to RE, where those who had a belief or worldview themselves were more oriented to inter-faith encounters. In the other words, those with a religion or worldview saw interpersonal encounters as the most productive way of ensuring harmony and of course school offers an arena for this. It is notable that Muslim students, despite their popular reputation to the contrary, were those most supportive of personal interfaith encounter.

Thus, in the English case it was possible to support the hypotheses from the data.

Estonia

The students who encountered religious diversity among their classmates as well as among friends believed significantly more in respect and claimed to respect people with different religious backgrounds, while those who were not aware of their friends' religious backgrounds were least in favour of respect. (At the same time one can ask – if a student has friends of different backgrounds and holds tolerant views, is he tolerant because he has such friends or does he have such friends because he is tolerant!). On the basis of the Estonian data it seems to be that, if the young people are put into the situation where religious diversity is visible and spoken about, they are forced to develop strategies supporting openness to otherness.

Regarding the second hypotheses it is possible to state on the basis of the Estonian data that the students who did not know the religion of their family or friends usually held the least dialogical views. Thus, in general both the hypotheses find some confirmation in the Estonian survey.

France

The school is the first place for many French students to experience diversity– almost three of four students declare that they go around with youngsters in school who have different religious backgrounds, and a similar proportion of students say that they have friends who belong to different religions. The students who declare they have personally encountered religious diversity give some answers that can be considered as a bit more tolerant, but the differences with the others were slight.

The students who declare they have personally encountered religious diversity respond in a way that can be considered as more open to dialogue. But the differences were also slight.

---

3   Before going to the findings it has to be remembered that we did not work with the hypotheses in the strict sense. Our aim was not to verify or falsify them. Instead we used them as working tools for reflection upon the findings. Thus, they have to be taken more as different perspectives or glasses to look at the field.

To conclude, one can surmise that tolerance and dialogue are shared values among French teenagers, not necessarily linked to personal experiences. But one can also add that, according to the responses of the students, to be in relationships with people coming from different religious backgrounds is something banal in their everyday life.

Germany

Students who have 'friends who belong to different religions' and who 'spend time with young people who have a different religions background' especially 'after school' tend to agree significantly more that they 'respect other people who believe', and less that they prefer at school as well as after school 'to go around with young people with the same religious background' as themselves, that 'they do not like people of other religions and do not want to live together with them' and that 'people with strong religious views can not live together'. Summing up it seems that students who have personally encountered religious diversity tend to be more 'tolerant' with respect to other religions.

There are also a lot of significant correlations between the items regarded as indicators for 'openness to dialogue' and having or not having 'friends who belong to different religions' and the items 'after school' and 'at school I spend time with young people who have a different religions background', with students who have friends of a different religion, and students who spend time with young people of a different religion in school as well as after school, tending to be more 'open' for dialogue on religious issues. So we conclude without going into detail that according to the outcomes from the German study – students who have encountered personally religious diversity are more open for dialogue on religious issues.

The Netherlands

The Dutch pattern regarding the above mentioned hypotheses was somewhat distinctive:

In general pupils who have a religion themselves more often have friends who have the same views about religion than pupils who do not have a religion. Besides, we found that at school pupils who do not have a religion go around with young people who have different religious backgrounds significantly more often than pupils who have a religion. It occurred in our analysis that the students with religious background and those who attend confessional schools, where the context is more homogeneous, are more tolerant and more open for dialogue on religious issues. At the same time we should keep in mind that these pupils also state that they will try to convince/convert the other into their own opinion. Thus, on the basis of our present data we cautiously conclude that there is no indication that students who have personally encountered religious diversity are more tolerant and/or more open to dialogue on religious issues. This result is a stimulus for further research in which these issues need to be carefully scrutinized and unravelled.

Norway

Norwegian colleges raised an interesting point when reflecting upon the students opinions regarding the religious diversity – could it be that the high estimation of tolerance and openness is just wishful thinking? They wrote:

A majority of students have encountered religious diversity through classmates and friends, and some from mixed families. In both studies (in qualitative as well in the quantitative one) the students tended to be very positive towards religious plurality and thought people with different religions could live peacefully together, but in the same time they reported quite limited contact with people from other cultural and/or religious backgrounds, and their tolerance was interpreted as rather unchallenged Thus, their tolerance towards religious diversity is perceived to be on a rather abstract level, and does not seem to be based on an understanding developed through personal relations. It is more a matter of principle. We need more in-depth analysis to answer this question. The hypothesis is therefore neither contradicted, nor affirmed.

Russia

On the bases of the data collected in the St. Petersburg region, one can say that encounters with religious diversity may be evaluated in general as a factor of developing positive attitude towards a religiously plural society. Those students who reported their contacts with students of different religious backgrounds at school and after school, disagreed significantly more with the statement *'I do not like people from other religions and do not want to live together with them'*. Experience of personal encounters with young people from other religions seems to produce in general a more positive vision of religious diversity. Not only those students who reported having friends of other religious backgrounds but also those who just had inter-religious contacts at school showed more negative reactions to the assumptions and statements charged with exclusivist or xenophobic ideas. But this complex issue needs deeper investigation to come up with firm statements.

Spain

The Spanish team reflected upon the hypotheses on the basis of the different school types. Thus, in the Spanish context it was possible to compare the students who attended the schools with compulsory confessional religious education (Catholic ones) and the schools where the option was offered between taking the confessional and non-confessional subjects. In fact, 72% of the pupils in the schools with the optional RE do not have any classmates who belong to different religions, in comparison to 66% of students in the confessional RE schools. Nonetheless, it is very significant that more than two out of three students in the schools with the optional RE affirmed that they have friends of different religions, in contrast to only 25% of the students in the schools with compulsory confessional RE. From this point of view, we could deduce a larger tendency towards more dialogue in the optional-RE schools, based on friends outside of school, although, peculiarly, this does not mean that the students from these schools are more tolerant. Thus, the relations between meeting religious diversity and tolerance, and openness to dialogue need more researching in the Spanish context also.

Summing up the outcomes of these reflections on the hypotheses one can say that three REDCo teams – English, Estonian and German – confirmed, more or less, the hypotheses. The French, Norwegian and Russian researches kept to a more modest position, pointing out the several interesting research questions for the future. The Spanish team took the most careful position and the Dutch one presented the challenging, somewhat striking, outcomes from their data.

Conclusion

Religious diversity and plurality of worldviews is the reality of the contexts European teenagers have to manage within. The REDCo project's quantitative survey is one of the researches painting the picture of teenagers' perspectives on the role of religion in their lives, schools and society. One of the firm conclusions we can draw from our research results is the certainty that religion could not be ignored neither in the European social arena nor in education. Knowledge about the different worldviews, skills of dialogue and constructive management of religious differences and conflicts are unavoidable preconditions for finding the way ahead in the pluralistic context toward a cohesive society.

References

Valk, P. (2007). Religious education in Estonia, in: R. Jackson, S. Miedema, W. Weisse & J.-P. Willaime (Eds.), *Religion and Education in Europe*. Developments, Contexts and Debates. Muenster: Waxmann, pp. 159–181.

Questionnaire on Religion and School

A survey of attitudes regarding religion among students of your age was conducted last year in Europe. This questionnaire has been designed on the basis of that survey. It aims to find out how students from eight European countries see the role of religion in school and in society in general. We would like your help in this research. We are interested in your personal views. Maybe some of the questions seem irrelevant to you and your context. Do not worry about this - the role of religion in different European countries is different. Choose the answer which fits you best.

If you have any problems understanding the questions, please ask for help. Please write your personal remarks, comments and additions on the last page of the questionnaire.

Thank you for your cooperation!
REDCo team

Filled by researchers:

MS	Country	Date	Model of RinE	Code

PART I: Religion in school

*When it comes to religion in school, European countries are different in several ways from each other. There are countries where religious education classes are compulsory for all students; and countries where such lessons are optional or not provided at school at all. There are countries in which religious education classes are taught from the point of view of a particular religion and others which mainly teach **about** religions.*
Topics about religion may come up in several subjects, e.g. literature or history, or may come up incidentally in general school life.

1. How many years have you studied Religious Education at school? ☐

2. Do you participate in Religious Education classes during this school year?   Yes   /   No

What are your experiences of religion in school? How much do you agree, that:

		Strongly agree	Agree	Neither agree or disagree	Dis-agree	Strongly disagree
3.	At school, I get knowledge about different religions.	1	2	3	4	5
4.	At school, I learn to have respect for everyone, whatever their religion.	1	2	3	4	5
5.	At school, I have opportunities to discuss religious issues from different perspectives.	1	2	3	4	5
6.	I find topics about religions interesting at school.	1	2	3	4	5
7.	I find religions as topic important at school.	1	2	3	4	5
8.	Learning about different religions at school helps us to live together.	1	2	3	4	5
9.	Learning about religions at school helps me to make choices between right and wrong.	1	2	3	4	5
10.	Learning about religions at school helps me to understand current events.	1	2	3	4	5
11.	Learning about religions at school helps me to learn about myself.	1	2	3	4	5
12.	Learning about religions leads to conflicts in the classroom	1	2	3	4	5

❖ **Religion could appear in the school in many different ways. Imagine you are a person in authority who can decide on school matters. How far would you agree with the following positions?**

		Strongly agree	Agree	Neither agree or disagree	Dis-agree	Strongly disagree
13.	At school meals, religious food requirements should be taken into account	1	2	3	4	5
14.	Students should be able to wear religious symbols at school …	... discreet ones (e.g. small crosses, etc on necklace)	1	2	3	4	5
15.		... more visible ones (e.g. headscarves)	1	2	3	4	5
16.	Students can be absent from school when it is their religious festivals.	1	2	3	4	5
17.	Students should be excused from taking some lessons for religious reasons.	1	2	3	4	5
18.	Schools should provide facilities for students to pray in school.	1	2	3	4	5
19.	Voluntary religious services (e.g. school worship, prayers) could be a part of school life	1	2	3	4	5

❖ **To what extent do you agree, that learning about different religions helps:**

		Strongly agree	Agree	Neither agree or disagree	Dis-agree	Strongly disagree
20.	To understand others and live peacefully with them.	1	2	3	4	5
21.	To understand the history of my country and of Europe.	1	2	3	4	5
22.	To gain a better understanding of current events.	1	2	3	4	5
23.	To develop my own point of view.	1	2	3	4	5
24.	To develop moral values.	1	2	3	4	5
25.	To learn about my own religion.	1	2	3	4	5

❖ **What is your position regarding different models of religious education in school?**

		Strongly agree	Agree	Neither agree or disagree	Dis-agree	Strongly disagree
26.	Religious Education should be optional.	1	2	3	4	5
27.	Students should study Religious Education separately in groups according to which religion they belong to.	1	2	3	4	5
28.	There should be no place for religion in school life.	1	2	3	4	5
29.	Religious Education should be taught to Students together, whatever differences there might be in their religious or denominational background.	1	2	3	4	5
30.	There is no need for the subject of Religious Education. All we need to know about religion is covered by other school subjects (e.g. literature, history etc).	1	2	3	4	5
31.	Religious Education should be taught sometimes together and sometimes in groups according to which religions students belong to.	1	2	3	4	5

❖ **To what extent do you agree that at school students should:**

		Strongly agree	Agree	Neither agree or disagree	Dis-agree	Strongly disagree
32.	Get an objective knowledge about different religions.	1	2	3	4	5
33.	Learn to understand what religions teach.	1	2	3	4	5
34.	Be able to talk and communicate about religious issues.	1	2	3	4	5
35.	Learn the importance of religion for dealing with problems in society.	1	2	3	4	5
36.	Be guided towards religious belief.	1	2	3	4	5

PART II. You and Religion

37. **How important is religion to you?** *Please, choose a suitable position for yourself on the following scale:*

Not at all important	0	1	2	3	4	very important

38. **Which of these statements comes closest to your position?**

1	There is a God
2	There is some sort of spirit or life force
3	I don't really think there is a God or any sort of spirit or life force.

❖ **How often do you:**

		About every day	About every week	About once a month	Less than once a month	Never
39.	think about religion	1	2	3	4	5
40.	read sacred texts (e.g. Bible, Qur'an) for yourself	1	2	3	4	5
41.	look on the internet for religious topics	1	2	3	4	5
42.	pray	1	2	3	4	5
43.	attend religious events (acts of worship, youth groups, etc)	1	2	3	4	5
44.	think about the meaning of life	1	2	3	4	5

❖ **How important are the following things to get information about different religions:**

		Very important	Important	Little bit important	Not important	Not important at all
45.	Family	1	2	3	4	5
46.	School	1	2	3	4	5
47.	Friends	1	2	3	4	5
48.	Faith community	1	2	3	4	5
49.	Books	1	2	3	4	5
50.	Media (e.g. newspapers, TV)	1	2	3	4	5
51.	Internet	1	2	3	4	5

❖ **Your peers in Europe have explained their positions regarding religion in different ways. To what extent do you agree with their statements?**

		Strongly agree	Agree	Neither agree or disagree	Dis-agree	Strongly dis-agree
52.	"Religion helps me to cope with difficulties."	1	2	3	4	5
53.	"Religion helps me to be a better person."	1	2	3	4	5
54.	"Religion is important to me because I love God."	1	2	3	4	5
55.	"I respect other people who believe."	1	2	3	4	5
56.	"Religion is nonsense."	1	2	3	4	5
57.	"Religion determines my whole life."	1	2	3	4	5
58.	"Religion is important in our history."	1	2	3	4	5
59.	"You can be a religious person without belonging to a particular faith community."	1	2	3	4	5
60.	"Sometimes I have doubts – is there a god or not?"	1	2	3	4	5
61.	"What I think about religion is open to change."	1	2	3	4	5

PART III. You and others

The following questions deal with your opinions regarding the role religions play in different relationships and contexts.

❖ **How often do you speak with others about religion?**

		About every day	About once a week	About once in a month	Less than once in a month	Never
62.	Family	1	2	3	4	5
63.	Friends	1	2	3	4	5
64.	Classmates	1	2	3	4	5
65.	Other students at school	1	2	3	4	5
66.	Teachers	1	2	3	4	5
67.	Religious leaders	1	2	3	4	5

❖   **People around you**

		Yes	No	I don't know about their views or religion
68.	Most of my friends have the same views about religion as me	1	2	3
69.	Most of the students in my class have the same views about religion as me	1	2	3
70.	I have friends who belong to different religions.	1	2	3
71.	I have family members who belong to different religions.	1	2	3
72.	I have students in my class who belong to different religions.	1	2	3
73.	My parents have totally different views about religion from me.	1	2	3
74.	At school, I go around with young people who have different religious backgrounds.	1	2	3
75.	After school, I go around with young people who have different religious backgrounds	1	2	3
76.	At school, I prefer to go around with young people who have the same religious background as me.	yes	no	
77.	In my spare time, I prefer to go around with young people who have the same religious background as me.	yes	no	

❖   **To what extent do you agree with the following statements your peers have made**?

		Strongly agree	Agree	Neither agree or disagree	Disagree	Strongly disagree
78.	"I like to know what my best friend thinks about religion "	1	2	3	4	5
79.	"It doesn't bother me what my friends think about religion."	1	2	3	4	5
80.	"I have problems showing my views about religion openly in school."	1	2	3	4	5
81.	"A student who shows his/her religious belief openly in school, risks being mocked."	1	2	3	4	5
82.	"Religious people are less tolerant towards others."	1	2	3	4	5
83.	"Without religion the world would be a better place."	1	2	3	4	5
84.	"Religion belongs to private life."	1	2	3	4	5
85.	"Religion is a source of aggressiveness."	1	2	3	4	5
86.	"Religion is something one inherits from one's family."	1	2	3	4	5

❖   **Students of your age have mentioned different reasons why religion is or is not a topic to discuss. To what extent do you agree with their views?**

		Strongly agree	Agree	Neither agree or disagree	Dis- agree	Strongly disagree
87.	"To me talking about religion is interesting because people have different views."	1	2	3	4	5
88.	"Talking about religion helps to shape my own views."	1	2	3	4	5
89.	"I and my friends talk about how stupid religion is and what cruelties are carried out in its name."	1	2	3	4	5
90.	"Talking about religion helps us to understand others."	1	2	3	4	5
91.	"In my view, talking about religion is embarrassing."	1	2	3	4	5
92.	"Religion doesn't interest me at all - we have more important things to talk about."	1	2	3	4	5
93.	"In my view, talking about religion only leads to disagreement."	1	2	3	4	5
94.	"Talking about religion helps me to live peacefully together with people from different religions."	1	2	3	4	5
95.	"I don't know much about religion and thus I can't have an opinion."	1	2	3	4	5
96.	"For me talking about religious topics is boring."	1	2	3	4	5
97.	"Talking about religion helps me to understand better what is going on in the world."	1	2	3	4	5

❖   **Imagine that a student of a different religious faith wants to convince you that his/her religion is the best one. How do you react?**

		That's exactly my reaction	That could be my reaction	I would never react like that
98.	I try to ignore him/her	1	2	3
99.	I try to discuss with him/her about his/her opinions	1	2	3
100.	I try to convince him that s/he is wrong	1	2	3
101.	I try to explain that my own opinions about religion are the best ones.	1	2	3
102.	I listen but their views do not influence me.	1	2	3

❖ **When discussing how people of different worldviews and religions can live together, other young people have made following statements. How far do you share the following views?**

		Strongly agree	Agree	Neither agree or disagree	Disagree	Strongly disagree
103.	"Disagreement on religious issues leads to conflicts."	1	2	3	4	5
104.	"Respecting the religion of others helps to cope with differences."	1	2	3	4	5
105.	"I don't like people from other religions and do not want to live together with them."	1	2	3	4	5
106.	"People with different strong religious views cannot live together."	1	2	3	4	5

❖ **There are people from different religions living in every country. What do you think would help them to live together in peace?**

		Very important	Quite important	Not important	Cannot say
107.	If people share common interests	1	2	3	4
108.	If they know about each other's religions	1	2	3	4
109.	If they personally know people from different religions	1	2	3	4
110.	If they do something together	1	2	3	4
111.	If everyone keeps to their own religion in private	1	2	3	4
112.	If the state has strong laws about the role of religion in society.	1	2	3	4

Finally we would like to ask some questions about you.

113. What is your age?   ☐

114. What is your gender?

male	1	female	2

115. In which country were you born?

....

116. In which country was your mother born?

....

117. In which country was your father born?

....

118. In which country do you hold citizenship?

....

119. What are the main languages spoken at your home?

....

120. What profession has your mother? ....

121. What profession has your father? ....

122.   Does your father have a certain religion or worldview? Yes / No / I do not know

123. If 'yes, which one? ....

124. Does your mother have a certain religion or worldview? Yes / No / I do not know

125. If 'yes', which one? ....

126. Do you have a certain religion or worldview? Yes / No

127. If 'yes', which one? ....

If you have personal comments, additions or remarks, please, write them here:

....
....
....
....
....
....
....
....
....
....

Thank you for your cooperation!

List of authors

Dr. Aurora Alvarez Veinguer is Senior Lecturer of Social Anthropology at *Universidad de Granada*, Spain. e-mail: auroraav@ugr.es

Dr. Ina ter Avest is Senior Researcher in Religious Education at the Faculty of Psychology and Education, *VU University Amsterdam* and Lecturer in Religious Education at *Utrecht University*, the Netherlands. e-mail: kh.ter.avest@psy.vu.nl.

Dr. Cok Bakker is Professor of Religious Education at the Faculty of Humanities (department of Theology) at *Utrecht University*, the Netherlands. e-mail: c.bakker@uu.nl.

Dr. Céline Béraud is Assistant Professor in the department of Sociology at the *University of Caen*, France. e-mail: celineberaud@club-internet.fr

Dr. Gerdien Bertram-Troost is post-doc Researcher at the Faculty of Psychology and Education, *VU University Amsterdam*, the Netherlands. e-mail: gd.bertram-troost@psy.vu.nl

Dr. Markus Friederici is Researcher and Interim Professor at the Institute of Physical Education at the *TU Chemnitz*, Germany. e-mail: m.friederici@gmx.de

Dr. Robert Jackson is Professor of Education at the *University of Warwick*, and Director of Warwick Religions and Education Research Unit, based in the Institute of Education at the University of Warwick, England. e-mail: r.jackson@warwick.ac.uk

Dr. Dan-Paul Jozsa is Researcher in Religious Education, Islamic Theology and Philosophy at the *University of Münster*, Centre for Religious Studies, Germany. e-mail: paul.jozsa@googlemail.com.

Thorsten Knauth is Professor for Religious Education with focus on interreligious learning, and Director of the Institute of Protestant Theology at the *University of Duisburg-Essen*, Germany. He was Director of Research Management and Co-Projectleader of the REDCo project. e-mail: thorsten.knauth@uni-due.de.

Dr. Fedor Kozyrev is a Professor and Director of Religious Pedagogy Institute at *Russian Christian Academy for Humanities* St. Petersburg, Russia. e-mail: fedorkozyrev@yandex.ru

Marie von der Lippe is Ph. D. student and Research Assistant in religious studies/religious education at the *University of Stavanger*, Norway. e-mail: marie.vonderlippe@uis.no

Dr. Bérengère Massignon is post-doc Researcher at the *'Groupe Sociétés, Religions, Laïcités'* (GSRL) and Lecturer at *the Institute for Political Studies of Paris*, France. e-mail: bmassignon@gmail.com.

Dr. Séverine Mathieu is Professeur agrégée de sciences sociales, *Ecole Pratique des Hautes Etudes*, GSRL (CNRS), Paris, France. e-mail: severine.mathieu@gsrl.cnrs.fr

Dr. Ursula McKenna, is a Research Fellow in Warwick Religions and Education Research Unit based in the Institute of Education at the *University of Warwick*, England. e-mail: u.mckenna@warwick.ac.uk

Dr. Siebren Miedema is Professor in Educational Foundations at the Faculty of Psychology and Education and Professor in Religious Education at the Faculty of Theology, *VU University Amsterdam*, the Netherlands. e-mail: s.miedema@psy.vu.nl.

Dr. Sean Neill is Associate Professor in Education at the Institute of Education, *University of Warwick*, England and a member of Warwick Religions and Education Research Unit. e-mail: sean.neill@warwick.ac.uk

Dr. Francisco Javier Rosón Lorente is Postdoctoral Researcher at *Universidad de Granada*, Laboratorio de Estudios Interculturales, in Granada, Spain. e-mail: fjroson@ugr.es.

Dr. Olga Schihalejev is Research Assistant in Religious Education at the Theological Faculty of *University of Tartu*. e-mail: olgasch@ut.ee

Dr. Geir Skeie is Associate Professor at the Faculty of Arts and Education, *University of Stavanger*, Norway, where he is researching and teaching in the field of religious studies and religious education. He is also guest professor at Stockholm University. e-mail: geir.skeie@uis.no .

Dr. Pille Valk is Associated Professor of Religious Education at the Faculty of Theology at the *University of Tartu*, Estonia. e-mail: pvalk@ut.ee

Dr. Wolfram Weisse is Professor of Religious Education at the *University of Hamburg*, Germany, Director of the interdisciplinary centre „World Religions in Dialogue" and coordinator of REDCo. e-mail: weisse@erzwiss.uni-hamburg.de

Dr. Jean-Paul Willaime is Research Director at l'*Ecole Pratique des Hautes Etudes*, Department of Religious Studies, Sorbonne, Paris, France; member of the *Groupe Sociétés, Religions, Laïcités* and Director of the *European Institute of Religious Studies*. e-mail:jean-paul.willaime@ephe.sorbonne.fr